WASHINGTON

MATTHEW LOMBARDI

Contents

DISCOVER
Washington

Tucked away in the upper left corner of the map, Washington exists on the fringes of the United States. That remoteness is key to the unique character of the place—you sense it in the landscape, the climate, and the people.

The fascination starts with the terrain. Consider the view from the observation deck of the Space Needle—Seattle's signature landmark, the city's sci-fi answer to the Eiffel Tower. Looking west you see Puget Sound, plied by massive cargo ships and ferries, and beyond it the peaks of the Olympic Mountains, glistening like a mirage on the horizon. To the north, skirting the sound, are hilly residential neighborhoods and little Lake Union, bustling with pleasure boats and seaplanes. To the east is larger Lake Washington, a cluster of satellite towns on its far shore, and, on a clear day, a glimpse of the Cascade mountain range. Pivot south to take in downtown's office towers, which seem diminutive against the backdrop of mighty, ominous Mount Rainier, arguably the most impressive peak in North America.

What you see in that 360-degree panorama is the essence of Washington: mountains and water. The state has other worthy allures—charming towns, exceptional food and wine, some world-class cultural institutions—but you

Clockwise from top left: Seattle's Space Needle; Olympic Peninsula coast; San Juan Island alpaca; Meerkerk Rhododendron Gardens on Whidbey Island; sculpture at Dick and Jane's Spot in Ellensburg; Skyline Trail at Mount Rainier.

haven't made the most of your visit until you've been up on a mountainside (whether by car, bike, or foot) and out on the water (whether by ferry, kayak, or whale-watching cruise).

Of course, the water is bound to find you whether you like it or not. Washington is notorious for its rain, and that reputation is well earned in the western part of the state. The Olympic Peninsula is truly the rainiest place in the United States: For three seasons out of four the Puget Sound area is frequently drizzly and overcast. (In contrast, large swaths of less-traveled eastern Washington are desert dry. The Cascades in between hold world records for snowfall.)

There are two ways to contend with western Washington's rain. Embrace it like a local—bring your waterproof shoes and hat and go about your business. It often sprinkles but rarely pours, and after all, it's the rain that makes the Olympic Peninsula a mossy, otherworldly wonder, with some of the tallest and oldest trees on the planet. Or come in the summer, when the clouds disappear, the temperatures remain mild, and the place feels a lot like Eden.

Caption from top left: Beach Haven Resort on Orcas Island; Pelindaba Lavender Farm on San Juan Island; Vista House on the Columbia River Gorge; North Cascades Lodge at Stehekin.

10 TOP EXPERIENCES

1 **Volcanic Peaks:** Washington's Cascade Range is studded with eye-catching peaks where outdoor recreation reigns, from **Mount Baker** (page 281) to iconic **Mount Rainier** (page 347) to **Mount St. Helens** (page 359).

2 **San Juan Islands:** Watch the whales, kayak, bike, hike, or just sit back and count your blessings in the San Juans (pages 230, 249, and 263), an old-school summer idyll.

>>>

3 **The Museum of Flight:** You don't have to be an aeronautics buff to be blown away by this giant collection of flying machines (page 62).

>>>

4 **Columbia River Gorge:** This **National Scenic Area** on the Washington-Oregon border offers access to natural beauty on a grand scale (page 372).

5 **Seattle's Dining Scene:** Chefs are the stars of Seattle culture today the way grunge rockers were in the 1990s (page 81).

6 **Lake Crescent:** It's hard not to feel serene while standing on the banks of this glacier-carved lake in **Olympic National Park** (page 151).

7 **Pike Place Market:** Seattle's old-timey market is home to quirky shops, the world's first Starbucks, and vendors selling beautiful fish, flowers, and produce (page 40).

8 **Coastal Olympic Peninsula:** Raw and wild, the Olympic Peninsula's coastline boasts the gorgeous bluffs of **Cape Flattery** (page 158), haunting mists of **Ruby Beach** (page 171), and miles of sea stacks, tide pools, and seals lounging on rocks.

^^^

9 **Hiking:** Washington's mountains and woods have more great trails than a dedicated hiker could cover in a lifetime (page 26). Good places to start include **Hurricane Ridge** (page 145) and **Heather Meadows** (page 285).

10 **Wine Tasting:** Experience Washington's wine country at its finest at laidback **Rattlesnake Hills** (page 397), prestigious **Red Mountain** (page 405), and charming **Walla Walla** (page 409).

<<<

Planning Your Trip

Where to Go

Seattle

Washington's major metropolis has a uniquely Pacific Northwest take on city life. In the booming, bustling urban core, historic **Pioneer Square** and **Pike Place Market** overlook Puget Sound, and the **Space Needle** offers panoramas of the city. Surrounding the city center is a cluster of laid-back residential neighborhoods studded with cultural attractions and an exceptional collection of **urban parks.** The city also boasts some of the country's **best restaurants,** from hip new ventures helmed by celebrity chefs to old-school seafood joints.

Olympic Peninsula and the Coast

Wet, lush, and wild, the Olympic Peninsula contains **rain forests** that are home to some of the largest trees on earth; a **rugged, misty coastline;** and, at its heart, a mountain range accessible only on foot. Much of that territory is preserved as giant **Olympic National Park,** circled by U.S. 101. Naturally, you'll find excellent **hiking** here. To the south the coast flattens out into long, sandy beaches dotted by fishing villages and **family-focused resort communities.** The water is too cold for all but the most intrepid swimmers; visitors content themselves with beachcombing, kite flying, and clam digging.

San Juan Islands and North Puget Sound

The San Juan Islands archipelago is an **idyllic summer getaway** that seems to exist in another time, where generations of vacationers

Gas Works Park in Seattle

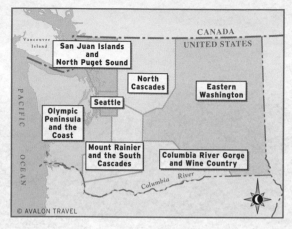

CANADA
UNITED STATES

© AVALON TRAVEL

Mount Rainier and the South Cascades

The highlights of the South Cascades are two iconic peaks. **Mount Rainier,** the king of the Cascades, is arguably the most impressive mountain in the contiguous United States, with a glacier-crowned peak that towers above the surrounding country and is visible over a 100-mile radius. **Mount St. Helens,** which experienced a massive eruption in 1980, is a testament to nature's wrath and resilience. I-90 stretches east from Seattle into the mountains, offering easy access to **hiking** trails and **ski slopes.**

have gone to unplug and relax. Each of the major islands has its own character. You can go **boating** in classic yacht-club style, **kayak** out of a hippie commune, **climb a mountain,** and **bike** through miles of rolling pasture. The most famous residents are the **orca pods** that inhabit the surrounding waters. **Whidbey Island** provides a similar experience closer to Seattle. In the North Puget Sound area, the **Skagit Valley** is blanketed with tulip fields, and the outdoorsy city of **Bellingham** is the gateway to the North Cascades.

North Cascades

For hard-core **mountaineers,** the North Cascades are Washington's destination of choice. The jagged peaks are one of the wildest places in the Lower 48. You can get a taste of the scenery on the beautiful **North Cascades Highway,** but spending more time here requires some effort—the best way to experience **North Cascades National Park** is on a multiday backcountry hike. More accessible destinations in the region include the resort area of **Lake Chelan** and the themed tourist towns of **Leavenworth** and **Winthrop.**

Columbia River Gorge and Wine Country

As it heads to the ocean along the Washington-Oregon border, the mighty Columbia cuts into the Cascades a deep, gorgeous gorge blanketed with lush greenery and dozens of **waterfalls** at its west end and desert-dry landscape 50 miles to the east. In the middle is **Hood River,** Oregon, a mecca for **kiteboarding** and **windsurfing.** Farther east and north are the visitor-friendly **wineries** and vineyards of **Walla Walla** and the **Yakima Valley,** epicenters of Washington's flourishing wine industry.

Eastern Washington

East of the Cascades, Washington flips stereotypes about the state on their head. The region is mainly desert, transformed by irrigation from the Columbia into farmland. Giant **Grand Coulee Dam** is the top tourist attraction, and farther downriver stunning **Gorge Amphitheatre** is the state's premier performance venue, drawing headline acts to play in the middle of nowhere. Near the Idaho border, **Spokane,** Washington's second-largest city, feels as much a part of the Rockies as the Pacific Northwest.

autumn in the San Juan Islands

When to Go

Summer is prime time for Washington. Mid-June-September the days are long and clear, with temperatures in the most popular destinations rarely climbing above the mid-80s. While much of the rest of the country swelters, the weather is spectacular here. Summer is also the time when all of nature seems to be open for business. Mountain passes and high-altitude **hiking** trails are clear of their last spring snow. The sunny, mild days are great for **kayaking.** Up in the San Juans the **orca pods** are out in full force.

Spring brings blooming flowers to the Skagit Valley, north of Seattle—especially notable during the **Skagit Valley Tulip Festival** in April. The mild weather of spring and **fall** is also well suited for visiting the Columbia River Gorge area on the Oregon border and the warmer regions that make up wine country, from the Yakima Valley to Walla Walla. **Wineries** in both areas have coordinated spring release and fall first-crush festivals.

Come **winter** the Cascades have numerous **downhill ski** runs. They won't be mistaken for the Rockies, but Snoqualmie Pass is an easy day trip from Seattle, Mount Baker is a **snowboarding** haven, and Crystal Mountain has the most developed facilities, as well as spectacular views of Mount Rainier. Washington's **cross-country skiing** is world-class, particularly around Mount Rainier and in the Methow Valley east of the Cascades.

The cultural attractions of **Seattle** make the city a destination for all seasons.

The Best of Washington

This itinerary takes you to Washington's best-known and most distinctive destinations: a towering peak, an ancient rain forest, a windswept coastline, a turquoise lake, a whale-friendly archipelago, and one of America's most appealing cities. Because so much of your time is spent outdoors, this trip is best suited for travel between June and September, during the long and glorious days of the Pacific Northwest summer. It's doable in May and October as well. In those months you get less sunshine and more rain, but you'll have fewer crowds to contend with.

You can pick any region of this itinerary for a shorter, more focused trip. There are suggestions here for lodging, but, with the exception of Seattle, you can also choose to camp on most nights. Washington boasts abundant campgrounds, some of them in spectacular locations.

Seattle

DAY 1

Depending on the logistics of your arrival, you may simply want to touch down in **Seattle,** have a good meal, and rest up. If you have time, head to the impressive **Museum of Flight** to the south of the central city on your way into town from Sea-Tac airport.

DAY 2

Seattle is a big, dynamic city with enough historical and cultural attractions to keep you busy for a month. Today, get the classic sightseeing experience by visiting **Pioneer Square, Pike Place Market,** and **Seattle Center,** home of the **Space Needle.**

DAY 3

Get off the tourist track to explore Seattle a little further. The city is a collection of colorful neighborhoods. If you only have time for one, make it **Capitol Hill,** which has fabulous restaurants, hopping nightlife, stately old mansions, and beautiful **Volunteer Park.** A little further afield, **Ballard** is also a great dining destination,

Pike Place Market

as well as the site of **Chittenden Locks,** a feat of ambitious early-20th-century engineering that remains the crucial link in Seattle's system of waterways.

Mount Rainier and the South Cascades

DAY 4

From Seattle a two-hour drive will get you to the White River entrance at the northeast corner of **Mount Rainier National Park.** A pretty, winding road climbs to the **Sunrise** area, a hub of park activity and the highest point on the mountain accessible by car. Get your bearings at the visitors center, have lunch at the cafeteria, and then head out for a couple of hours of alpine hiking.

In the late afternoon drive to the **Crystal Mountain** ski resort, where you'll be spending the night. Take the gondola up to **Summit House** for dinner. It's a pricey trip and the food is nothing special, but the spectacular view makes it all worthwhile: In one panorama, you take in Mounts Adams and St. Helens to the south and Baker to the north, with majestic Rainier front and center.

DAY 5

Head back into the park and make the drive around to the other side of the mountain, stopping along the way for a short hike on the **Grove of the Patriarchs Trail,** which is like a museum of old-growth trees. The road west from there is another gorgeous drive, eventually climbing to the **Paradise** area, where there's an impressive visitors center and a classic cedar lodge. After Sunrise and Crystal Mountain, this will be your third picture-book view of the mountaintop, each strikingly different from the others. It's also the starting point for numerous trails; spend the afternoon and early evening hiking. If you want to take it easy, sign up for a ranger-led nature walk.

Have dinner at the **Paradise Inn.** You can bed down there, or at the inn near the Nisqually entrance in the southwest corner of the park, or at one of the hotels just outside the entrance in the town of **Ashford.** No matter where you stay, you'll need a reservation.

WITH MORE TIME

Leaving Mount Rainier National Park from the Nisqually entrance, head west and then south

ranger talk at Paradise Inn at Mount Rainier National Park

Day Trips from Seattle

One of the appealing things about Seattle is what's outside of town. An impressive range of day trips will get you far beyond the city hubbub in less than two hours. Travel times given here are calculated from downtown Seattle.

ISLANDS

Some of the easiest getaways are the surrounding islands of the Puget Sound, which are only a ferry ride away.

- **Bainbridge Island (45 min.):** This attractive, affluent commuter and retiree community is just across Elliott Bay from downtown. A highlight is the Bloedel Reserve, which is reachable by bus from the ferry stop (page 106).

- **Vashon Island (1 hr.):** Vashon is Bainbridge's hipper, more agrarian, more remote neighbor to the south (page 108).

- **Whidbey Island (1:20):** On Whidbey you get some of the laid-back charm of the San Juans while spending half as much time in transit from Seattle (page 201).

outdoorsy Bellingham

HIKES

- **Tiger Mountain State Forest (1 hr.):** The 80 miles of trails near Issaquah are favorites of Eastside residents (page 111).

- **Mountain Loop Highway (1:15):** Hike through the part of the North Cascades most easily reached from the city (page 278).

- **Mount Si (45 min.):** This challenging ascent near Snoqualmie Falls is one of the most popular trails in the state (page 329).

- **Alpine Lakes Wilderness (1 hr.):** Explore a large region of high Cascades trails near Snoqualmie Pass (page 332).

TOWNS

- **Tacoma (40 min.):** The revitalized urban core includes first-class museums and a great park (page 112).

- **La Conner (1:20):** A riverside Skagit Valley artists' colony has grown old gracefully (page 218).

- **Edison (1:20):** This tiny town feels like a chunk of hipster Brooklyn plopped down in the middle of a field (page 220).

- **Bellingham (1:45):** Take beautiful Chuckanut Drive to this super-relaxed, outdoorsy college town (page 222).

AN AERONAUTICS MECCA

- **Future of Flight Aviation Center & Boeing Tour (30 min.):** In Mukilteo, take a firsthand look at how Boeing builds planes (page 203).

WINE AND WATERFALLS

- **Woodinville Wine Country (30 min.):** The Woodinville area is home to scores of Washington winemakers, from the biggest (Chateau Ste. Michelle) to the tiniest boutiques (page 111).

- **Snoqualmie Falls (45 min):** The biggest waterfall in the state is immortalized in the opening credits of *Twin Peaks* (page 328).

Quinault Rain Forest on the Olympic Peninsula

on I-5 to the turnoff for **Mount St. Helens**—a 2.5-hour drive in total. As you approach the **Johnston Ridge Observatory** at the base of the volcano it's hard not to be awed by the extent of the devastation caused by the eruption of St. Helens in 1980. The observatory is a first-class facility for viewing St. Helens and learning about the causes and consequences of the blast. Trails take you closer, and there are daily ranger-led walks.

Olympic Peninsula

DAY 6

Say goodbye to Rainier in your rearview mirror as you head west toward the **Olympic Peninsula.** Stop for lunch in the state capital, **Olympia,** at about the midpoint of a three-hour drive to **Lake Quinault,** located at the southern end of **Olympic National Park.** Here you'll experience the lush, primordial forest for which Washington is famous. The rain forest surrounding the lake is home to some of the tallest trees in the world, several of which are easily accessible on short roadside trails.

You're now in the rainiest region of the contiguous United States, averaging 150 inches a year, but the precipitation is seasonal—if you're here in summer you stand a good chance of getting a dry day. If it is showering, though, you can still get a great look around from the comfort of your car on the **Quinault Rain Forest Loop Drive.** For your overnight stay you have the option of a national park lodge on the lake or one of several modest hotels in the area.

DAY 7

Start the day by getting a taste of Washington's rugged Pacific coast. It's a 45-minute drive to **Ruby Beach,** a classic example of the misty, pebble-strewn coastline, studded with haystacks (giant rock formations). You won't need your swim trunks, but you'll want your camera to capture the ethereal beauty.

From here U.S. 101 heads back inland and turns north; after a 75-minute drive you reach glacier-carved **Lake Crescent,** the most beautiful lake in the state. You can stop along the way for lunch in **Forks,** the town made famous by the *Twilight* novels, but the sooner you get to the lake the more time you'll have for an afternoon spent

Lake Crescent Lodge

Whidbey Island's Coupeville wharf

floating on its tranquil, turquoise-green waters. (Kayaks and canoes are available for rent.) There's yet another national park lodge here where you can stay, or you can get a jump on the next day's driving by heading east another half hour to **Port Angeles,** where there are more lodging options.

DAY 8

In the morning, head up to the only part of the Olympic Mountains accessible by car: **Hurricane Ridge,** an hour's drive from Lake Crescent or 35 minutes from Port Angeles. The trails here offer a different kind of mountain experience from Mount Rainier. Fields filled with wildflowers give you vast vistas; you have a view to the north of the Strait of Juan de Fuca glimmering 5,000 feet below, and to the south of the neighboring Olympic peaks.

Come back down to sea level on the 90-minute drive to the charming town of **Port Townsend** at the northeast corner of the peninsula. You'll find lots of good dining options here, but for an earlier lunch you can stop at **Sequim** along the way. From Port Townsend take the 35-minute ferry ride to Keystone Landing on **Whidbey Island.**

(You can reserve a place on the ferry.) You'll be in **Ebey's Landing National Historical Reserve,** which includes, 10 minutes from the ferry dock, the old fishing town of **Coupeville,** where you'll overnight. Spend the evening strolling the quaint streets that make up the town, and if you're up for a short hike head to the bluffs above **Parego Lagoon,** where you get a gorgeous view of the Olympic Mountains and Strait of Juan de Fuca.

WITH MORE TIME

For a longer itinerary for the Olympic Peninsula, see page 27.

San Juan Islands
DAY 9

Drive north from Coupeville and over the picturesque bridge at **Deception Pass** to the town of **Anacortes,** a 45-minute trip, and catch the ferry to **Friday Harbor** on **San Juan Island.** The 75-minute cruise through the archipelago is a beautiful way to get into the San Juans state of mind. You can reserve a place on the ferry online, and in summer it's essential to do so. You also need to arrange lodging well ahead of time. There

Best Hikes

Whether you came to Washington to experience spruce-studded rain forests, take in sweeping mountaintop views, or spot a whale, hiking is the primary way of exploring the state's amazing variety of natural attractions. Washington is laced with hundreds of miles of trails; try to pick the best, and you're faced with an embarrassment of riches. Here are a few easy hikes that would qualify for any bucket list:

OLYMPIC PENINSULA

If you're going to get out of your car just three times on the Olympic Peninsula, do so for three fabulous trails: one in the mountains, one through the forest, and one overlooking the ocean. On Hurricane Ridge, the **Hurricane Hill Trail** (1.6 miles, page 145) through alpine meadows has views to set your spirits soaring. In the Hoh Rain Forest, the **Hall of Mosses Trail** (0.8 mile, page 169) takes you through stands of ancient, towering firs and moss-draped maples. And out on the far northwest corner, the **Cape Flattery Trail** (0.75 mile, page 158) emerges from deep woods to give you a spectacular view of the Pacific coast.

SAN JUAN ISLANDS

San Juan's **Lime Kiln Point State Park** (page 232) has 1.5 miles of coastal trails that lead you to a picturesque lighthouse and the best viewpoints on the islands for spotting the resident orcas. In Moran State Park on neighboring Orcas Island, the **Cascade Creek Trail** (3 miles, page 251) is a beautiful wooded jaunt between two lakes.

NORTH CASCADES

You could spend a lifetime exploring the trails of the Cascades and never run out of discoveries. To the north, the spectacular Mount Baker Highway leads to **Heather Meadows** (page 285), where multiple trailheads give you options ranging from easy loops to daylong treks, all with fabulous views.

Within the North Cascades National Park Service Complex hiking trails number in the hundreds. Pair the **Diablo Lake Trail** (3.8 miles, page 294) with a ferry ride on the lake. The short paved trail at **Washington Pass** (page 291) provides wonderful views of Liberty Bell and Early Winter Spires peaks.

Another great collection of trails is accessible

Hall of Mosses Trail in the Hoh Rain Forest

from the scenic Mountain Loop Highway. One of the highlights is the trail to **Lake 22** (2.7 miles, page 278), which goes through old-growth forest to mountain vistas and a beautiful alpine lake.

MOUNT RAINIER AND THE SOUTH CASCADES

Mount Rainier National Park has a summer's worth of wonderful day hikes and friendly, experienced rangers who can help you narrow down your choices. From the Paradise area, the **Skyline Trail** (5.5 miles, page 353) takes you up above the timberline. On the other side of the mountain, the trail to **Dege Peak** (1.7 miles, page 356) leads to a viewpoint where, on a clear day, you can see as far as Mount Baker to the north and Mount Adams to the south.

South of Mount St. Helens you can get a different sort of hiking experience in the **Ape Cave** (1.5-3 miles, page 364), a 12,810-foot-long lava tube. Headlamps are available for rent.

are lots of options—waterfront campsites, B&Bs, motels, fishing lodges, old-school resorts—but they all book up in summer.

Where you stay should dictate your touring strategy. You'll want to see **American Camp, Lime Kiln Point State Park, English Camp,** and **Roche Harbor;** begin with whichever is farthest from where you'll bed down for the evening, and work your way toward your lodging from there.

DAY 10

If you didn't have time for one of the main sights the previous day, you can make up for it in the morning, or get out on the water. You have two classic options: **rent a kayak** and go for a paddle—if this is your first time here you should take a guided tour—or go on a **whale-watching cruise** to meet the resident orcas.

Take an early-afternoon ferry back to Anacortes, then drive back to **Seattle.** If traffic is clear it's about a three-hour trip.

WITH MORE TIME

If your goal is to unwind and get away from it all, the best way to do that is to spend another night or two in the San Juans. You can ferry over to **Orcas Island,** or just stay put on San Juan, maybe paying a visit to one of the smaller sights such as the lavender farm or winery, or hanging at Lime Kiln Point State Park and watching for whales in Haro Strait.

To explore **Orcas Island,** catch a morning ferry from Friday Harbor. Orcas has an even more laid-back feel, with more than its share of artists and eccentrics. Head north from the ferry terminal to the main town of **Eastsound,** where you can have lunch and do some window-shopping, then continue on to **Moran State Park** and spend the afternoon taking in the view from the top of **Mount Constitution,** rowing a boat on **Mountain Lake,** and even having a lake swim. The restaurant at **Doe Bay Resort** is a great dinner choice on this part of the island. If you're into the hippie vibe there it can also be a good place to spend the night, but if you prefer something more mainstream choose one of the lodging options back in the direction of Eastsound.

The next morning, start your day with a **kayak trip.** Possible launching points include **Doe Bay, Smuggler's Villa Resort** at the north end of the island, and **Deer Harbor** on the west side. No matter where you start, kayaking around Orcas gives you the opportunity to paddle by smaller outlying islands, where the only inhabitants are wildlife. In the afternoon pay a visit to isolated **Orcas Island Pottery,** a one-of-a-kind studio and shop with a beautiful waterfront location on the western side of the island. In the evening have dinner at one of Eastsound's restaurants and take in the small-town nightlife.

Olympic Peninsula Road Trip

Jutting out on the western end of the state, the Olympic Peninsula is its own remote, lush world. At its center are the Olympic Mountains, largely accessible only on foot. The west side of the peninsula is the rainiest place in the Lower 48, with annual precipitation averaging as much as 150 inches. Trees love it; preserved within the Quinault and Hoh Rain Forests you'll find thousand-year-old giants rising to world-record heights. Fortunately the rains are seasonal. In summer dry spells can last for weeks, making that the time to take this tour. Come in winter only if you find a gloomy romance in short, dark days and perpetual showers. This road trip follows **U.S. 101** for most of the way as it loops around the peninsula.

Day 1

Starting from the Puget Sound area, head to **Edmonds,** half an hour north of Seattle, and make the 30-minute ferry ride to **Kingston.** From there it's an hour's drive north to **Port**

Ruby Beach

Townsend, the most charming town on the peninsula, with a historic, Victorian-style downtown. Stroll through town, make a visit to **Fort Worden State Park,** indulge in a good meal, and sack out at a quaint old waterfront hotel.

Day 2
From Port Townsend it's a 1.5-hour drive to **Hurricane Ridge,** the one location in the Olympic Mountains accessible by car. Spend the morning and early afternoon on the trails there, then head down to **Lake Crescent,** an hour away to the west. Unwind by taking a kayak or canoe out onto the gorgeous, turquoise-blue lake, and spend the night along the water at the **Lake Crescent Lodge.**

Day 3
Head west on the scenic **Strait of Juan de Fuca Highway** until, after 1.5 hours, you reach the end of the road at **Neah Bay,** part of the Makah Indian Reservation. There you'll find the fascinating **Makah Museum** and gorgeous **Cape Flattery,** where an easy hike takes you

to the northwesternmost point of the contiguous United States.

There's no coastal road along the wild stretch of Pacific shoreline to the south; you'll need to head back inland for a two-hour drive before returning to the coast at beautiful, mist-shrouded **Ruby Beach.** Take a late-afternoon stroll here, then head 10 minutes south to **Kalaloch,** where you can spend the night in waterfront lodging.

Day 4
The most famous destination on the peninsula is the **Hoh Rain Forest,** an hour's drive to the northeast of Kalaloch. It's a striking place with easily accessible, paved paths through moss-covered old-growth forest, and if you don't mind some extra driving it's a worthwhile detour. But you can save a couple of hours on the road by heading directly to your destination for the night, the national park lodge at **Lake Quinault,** 40 minutes southeast of Kalaloch. Quinault delivers a similar experience to Hoh—rain forest, even bigger ancient trees, and short, easy trails—along with a glacier-carved lake,

the lodge facilities, and other accommodations and dining options.

Day 5

Wrap up your trip by heading 2.5 hours south to Washington's most appealing coastal resort area, the **Long Beach Peninsula.** (Kurt Cobain fans can make a pilgrimage stop along the way at his hometown of **Aberdeen.**) Do some beachcombing, fly a kite, and take in the charming resort-town atmosphere. Long Beach has been a vacation destination for over a century, and part of its appeal is its selection of old-school resort lodgings, along with some contemporary choices. You have a good variety of places to choose from.

Day 6

Dedicate the morning to **Cape Disappointment State Park,** located at the point where the Columbia River dramatically crashes into the Pacific. Along with pleasant hiking trails leading to great views, the park has a top-quality museum dedicated to the Lewis and Clark expedition, which reached the Pacific at this location. After that, start working your way back to Seattle. For a leisurely trip, drive two hours to **Olympia,** the pretty state capital, where you can do some exploring and overnight in a chain hotel or B&B. If you're ready to wrap things up, get on I-5 in Olympia, and if the traffic is clear you'll be in Seattle in a little over an hour.

Wine and Waterfalls

This is a particularly good trip if you're coming from Portland, Oregon, or Vancouver, Washington, which are situated nearby, right along the Columbia River. It's a three-hour drive from Seattle to the itinerary's starting point at the west end of the Gorge. If you're coming from that direction, you might extend the trip a day and start off by making a visit to **Mount St. Helens.** Another viable strategy if you're starting in the Seattle area, especially if you're a wine lover, is to make **Mount Rainier** your first stop, and from there head to Yakima and pick up the Wine Country part of the itinerary.

Columbia River Gorge

DAY 1

Spend your morning on the Oregon side of the Columbia, where the scenic drive east takes you past the **West Gorge waterfalls** and you can tour the Depression-era **Bonneville Dam** and its adjacent fish hatchery. Cross over the river at Cascade Locks, work in lunch at **Skamania Lodge** or in the town of **Stevenson,** and then head 10 miles west and spend the afternoon on the switchback path up **Beacon Rock,** an 848-foot-tall monolith

that, after a surprisingly easy climb, provides unbeatable views of the Gorge. Cross back over to the Oregon side to spend the evening in **Hood River,** a fun, hip little resort town. Have dinner at one of Hood River's many **brewpubs.**

DAY 2

Traveling east from Hood River, over the course of 30 miles the Gorge makes a remarkable transformation from forestland to dry, barren bluffs. Back on the Washington side, about 45 minutes east of Hood River, is one of the state's most remarkable cultural institutions, the **Maryhill Museum of Art,** which contains a substantial, eclectic art collection. It's as impressive as it is incongruous.

Turn away from the river at this point, making the 1.5-hour drive on Route 97 to **Yakima,** your first stop in wine country. Along the way visit **Goldendale Observatory,** 13 miles past Maryhill. Its interpretive center has afternoon presentations, and the hilltop location provides good views of the surrounding region. In Yakima, the business hub for the surrounding farmland, your best lodging options are the plentiful chain hotels.

Wine Country

DAY 3

East of the town of Yakima, the **Yakima Valley** is a hotbed for Washington's thriving wine industry. The most satisfying winery-touring area is the **Rattlesnake Hills,** where country roads northeast of I-82 take you to eclectic, friendly wineries. **Owen Roe** arguably produces the finest wine here, and **Two Mountain Winery** has the most fun tasting room, but all of the producers in the region take an accessible, unpretentious approach to their craft. Also in the valley, it's worth stopping in the little town of **Toppenish,** which is decorated with more than 80 historical murals.

At the east end of the valley is the **Tri-Cities** area, a community of a quarter million with numerous chain hotels that are your best lodging choice. The main business is dismantling the Hanford nuclear site, a remnant of the atomic bombs dropped on Japan at the conclusion of World War II. It's an interesting, sobering place that you can visit on the **Hanford B Reactor Tour.**

DAY 4

You get a different kind of wine country experience an hour east of the Tri-Cities in **Walla Walla.** While the Tri-Cities and Yakima are home to a variety of other enterprises, in Walla Walla winemaking is the undisputed top priority. As a result there's a more hospitality-driven culture here, with appealing places to stay and a charming little downtown where tasting rooms share the retail blocks with cute shops and many good restaurants. Your best approach is to stop by a winery or two west of town on your way in, have lunch in town, and then head back out to visit more wineries at the old airport or in the vineyard area to the south. If that's too much wine for you, check out the historic **Whitman Mission** or **Fort Walla Walla Museum** instead. Wrap up the day with dinner back downtown at either **Brasserie Four** or **Saffron.**

DAY 5

If you're headed back to Seattle, buckle in the next morning for the 4.5-hour drive, which will take you back through Yakima and over Snoqualmie Pass. If you're driving a rental car, you can opt to drop it off at the airport and make one of the daily hour-long flights from Walla Walla to Seattle.

a vineyard on the Columbia River Gorge

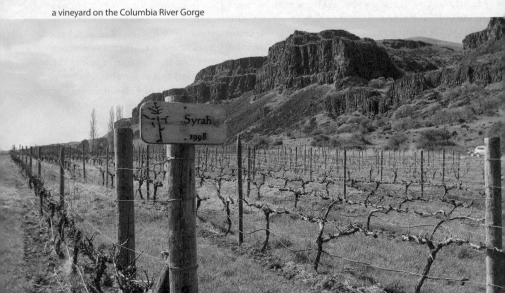

Best Skiing and Snowboarding

The Summit at Snoqualmie

Washingtonians' laid-back state of mind carries over into the skiing and snowboarding season. The slopes of the Cascades are mainly populated by families from in-state who are out for a day of fun. Most return home at the end of the day, so there isn't an emphasis placed on lodges and après-ski facilities. The main downhill-skiing resorts include:

- **Crystal Mountain:** Washington's top ski destination, located to the east of Mount Rainier, has more acreage and a higher elevation than any other slopes in the state (page 343).

- **The Summit at Snoqualmie:** The four ski areas at Snoqualmie Pass benefit from their location, just an hour east of Seattle along the biggest highway over the Cascades, but relatively low elevation means less reliable snow accumulation than at higher ski resorts (page 332).

- **White Pass Ski Area:** There are fewer slopes and facilities here than at Crystal Mountain just to the north, making for a quieter scene. It has the virtue of being more accessible for skiers coming from east of the Cascades (page 347).

- **Mt. Baker Ski Resort:** The main ski destination for Bellingham residents, Mount Baker historically has been known for its abundant snow—averaging 600 inches a year—and long season, November-April. Conditions are well suited for snowboarding (page 285).

- For **cross-country skiing,** the **Methow Valley** (page 302) is a major destination. The **Paradise** area (page 358) in Mount Rainier National Park and **Hurricane Ridge** (page 147) in Olympic National Park are also popular. In addition, Hurricane Ridge has a small downhill area with two rope tows and a Poma lift, and Paradise is open for **sledding.**

Seattle

Seattle is a city of compelling personalities. Its mix of idealism and ambition leads to intriguing contradictions.

How, for instance, can Seattle be home to both Amazon—the nemesis of the small bookseller—and the most thriving independent-bookstore culture in America? To solve that riddle, you need to come and see the city for yourself.

Wander the streets around Pioneer Square, where the city was born, and you can still feel the Old West frontier character from the days when this was the launching point for the Klondike gold rush. Walk a few blocks through downtown and you're at Pike Place Market, where vendors hawk their wares much the way they did a century ago. Looking from the market down onto Elliott Bay, you're knocked back into the present tense by the sight of massive cargo vessels that have arrived bearing goods from the other side of the world. Meanwhile, the unmistakable emblem of the city, the Space Needle, is a reminder that Seattle has been identified with innovation since long before the tech boom. One neighborhood away, in South Lake Union, the future is being built at the ever-expanding headquarters of Amazon.

Seattle is split through the middle by a combination of natural and manmade waterways known collectively as the ship canal, connecting Puget Sound to the west with Lake Washington to the east. North of Lake Union—one of the links in the canal—you see the tree-covered hills of Seattle's tightly knit old residential neighborhoods. Visit them and you feel like you've entered an overgrown college town, bustling with hipsters, liberal-leaning professionals, and aging hippies. It seems collegiate in large part because it is: The University of Washington, with over 50,000 students and 25,000 employees, is located here.

Even beyond the presence of UW, the college-town sensibility may be as close as you're going to get to summing up the character of Seattleites. There's a youthful energy to the city that transcends age. You can sense it in the enthusiasm for outdoor recreation, facilitated by beautiful parks, lakes, and waterways; the ubiquitous coffee shops, where serious-minded denizens stare into their laptops or engage in soul-searching conversations; the local music scene, still thriving long after the grunge heyday; the explosion

Previous: Seattle skyline; Pike Place Market and Elliott Bay. **Above:** *Hammering Man* sculpture by Jonathan Borofsky at the Seattle Art Museum.

Look for ★ to find recommended
sights, activities, dining, and lodging.

Highlights

★ **Pike Place Market:** Independent vendors sell a magnificent assortment of food, and a maze of halls and ramps leads to quirky, one-of-a-kind shops (page 40).

★ **Central Library:** This spaceship-like building set amid downtown's skyscrapers is Seattle's most interesting piece of architecture, both outside and in (page 45).

★ **Space Needle:** You get a better view from downtown's Columbia Tower, but it's hard to resist the allure of the Space Needle, Seattle's nerdy answer to the Eiffel Tower (page 49).

★ **Washington Park Arboretum and Japanese Garden:** Stroll through a peaceful urban park that serves as an open-air museum of plants (page 56).

★ **Chittenden Locks:** The locks separating the saltwater of Puget Sound from Seattle's lakes and canals are a monumental work of civil engineering where you can watch fish climb a ladder and boats rise and drop 20 feet as they pass through (page 58).

★ **Discovery Park:** Seattle's largest and wildest park contains woodland, meadows, and two miles of beach—and is teeming with animal life (page 60).

★ **The Museum of Flight:** View one of

the most impressive collections of aircraft in the world; you don't have to be an aeronautics buff to be struck by the beauty of these machines (page 62).

of hip, hyper-creative new restaurants that are the city's current mania; and the boundless ambition of the high-tech entrepreneurs who flock here with dreams of becoming the next Gates or Allen or Bezos.

PLANNING YOUR TIME

In just a couple of days, you can hit highlights of Seattle's city center: Pioneer Square, Pike Place Market, the Space Needle and surrounding Seattle Center, downtown's Central Library and Seattle Art Museum, and the aquarium and Olympic Sculpture Park along the waterfront. This can be managed entirely on foot or with minimal use of public transit or car services.

More time gives you the chance to experience a less touristed side of the city, including some of its best museums (such as The Museum of Flight). But you also have to give your lodging and transportation choices a little more thought. To see the surrounding city you need a car or to learn the public transit system. If you have a car, consider staying outside the main hotel district downtown, where parking is expensive and traffic in and out can get bad. If you don't have a car, the situation is reversed—downtown is the best place to stay, because it's the hub for public transit.

Some visitors worry about Seattle's reputation for rainy weather, but it's not as big a concern as you might think. Seattle averages about 38 inches of rain a year—less than many other U.S. cities, including New York, Atlanta, and Washington DC. In summer, Seattle is gorgeous, with mild temperatures, long days, and little precipitation. The rest of the year it seldom rains hard, but it often rains gently. (That's where the reputation comes from.) But, even for outdoor sightseeing, the occasional drizzle barely amounts to a nuisance.

A bigger factor in winter is the shortness of the days. Seattle is the northernmost large city in the United States. At winter solstice you get less than 8.5 hours of daylight. If you live for the nightlife that may not be a problem, but otherwise the lack of sun can weigh on you. There's no better explanation for why Seattleites drink so much coffee.

ORIENTATION
Downtown and the Waterfront

Seattle's city center is compact: Walking from Pioneer Square through downtown, Pike Place Market, and Belltown to Seattle Center takes less than an hour. **Downtown** falls in the middle of it all, on a grid bordered by 1st and 7th Avenues and Cherry and Stewart Streets. You can tell you're there by looking up—the business district is distinguished by its skyscrapers, which began sprouting en masse in the 1980s.

Because of its central location, downtown gets a lot of foot traffic. As you walk through you're keenly aware that you're in a hilly town. The avenues, which run parallel to the waterfront, are gradually sloped, but the streets, which run down toward the water, include some steep climbs.

Down a steep slope from **Pike Place Market** is the **waterfront** of Elliott Bay, which opens onto Puget Sound. At the south end of the bay massive cranes line the shore. On the waterfront directly below the market and downtown there's a carnival-like atmosphere, with a Ferris wheel, a merry-go-round, an aquarium, and ferries taking tourists and commuters to West Seattle, Bainbridge Island, and Bremerton.

Pioneer Square and the International District

The most historic part of Seattle is the **Pioneer Square** neighborhood, a 20-block district of handsome redbrick and stone buildings that borders the southern end of downtown. Pioneer Square is a sightseeing destination by day and a restaurant and nightlife draw by night. It's safe, but it's also a gathering place for Seattle's homeless at all hours.

Just to the southeast of Pioneer Square is another historic neighborhood, the **International District (ID).** Dating back to the 1860s, waves of immigrants from China, Japan, the Philippines, and Vietnam have

Seattle

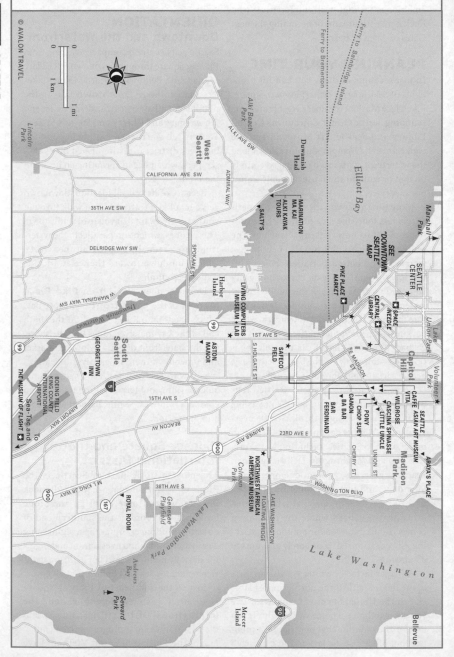

© AVALON TRAVEL

0
1 km
0
1 mi

Lincoln Park

West Seattle

Alki Beach Park

CALIFORNIA AVE SW

ALKI AVE SW

ADMIRAL WAY

35TH AVE SW

DELRIDGE WAY SW

SPOKANE ST

Duwamish Head

MARINATION MA KAI
ALKI KAYAK TOURS
SALTY'S

Elliott Bay

Ferry to Bainbridge Island

Ferry to Bremerton

Ferry to Bainbridge Island

Marshall Park

SEE "DOWNTOWN SEATTLE" MAP

SEATTLE CENTER

PIKE PLACE MARKET

SPACE NEEDLE

CENTRAL LIBRARY

Lake Union Park

W MARGINAL WAY SW

Harbor Island

Duwamish Waterway

LIVING COMPUTERS MUSEUM + LAB

99

99

South Seattle

GEORGETOWN INN

BOEING FIELD KING COUNTY INTERNATIONAL AIRPORT

To Sea-Tac and THE MUSEUM OF FLIGHT

AIRPORT WAY S

5

ASTON MANOR

1ST AVE S

S HOLGATE ST

SAFECO FIELD

15TH AVE S

BEACON AV

RAINIER AVE

23RD AVE E

900

900

167

M L KING JR WAY

38TH AVE S

ROYAL ROOM

Genesee Playfield

Colman Park

Genesee Park

NORTHWEST AFRICAN AMERICAN MUSEUM

FLOATING BRIDGE

WASHINGTON BLVD

NE MADISON ST

Capitol Hill

Volunteer Park

SEATTLE ASIAN ART MUSEUM
CAFFE VITA
WILDROSE
CASCINA SPINASSE
LITTLE UNCLE
CANON
PONY
CHOP SUEY
BAR FERDINAND
BA BAR

CHERRY ST

UNION ST

ARAYA'S PLACE

Madison Park

Andrews Bay

Seward Park

Lake Washington Park

LAKE WASHINGTON

90

Mercer Island

Bellevue

Lake Washington

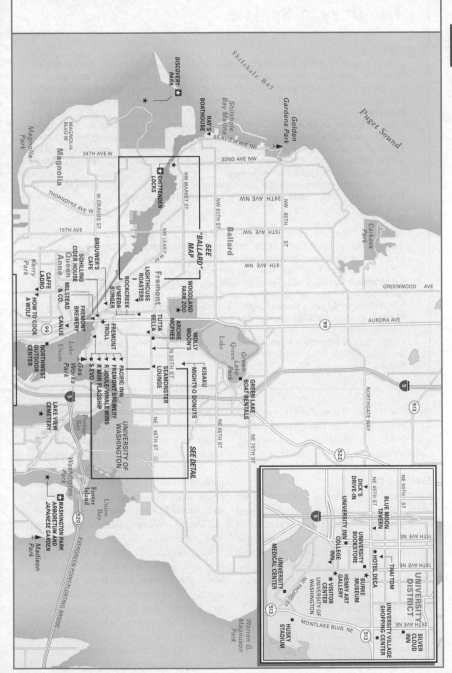

Two Days in Seattle

DAY 1

Start your day at **Pike Place Market,** the historic landmark where locals and tourists connect. Grab a bite of breakfast, browse the shops and food stalls, and enjoy the quirky street performers. You could easily spend a full morning here, but for a more varied experience—especially if you're traveling with kids—make the short walk down to the waterfront to visit the **Seattle Aquarium** and go up in the **Seattle Great Wheel.**

Start the afternoon by walking down 1st Avenue or hopping a convenient metro bus to Seattle's oldest neighborhood, **Pioneer Square.** Refuel at one of the appealing lunch spots— **Altstadt** for sausages, **Salumi** for sandwiches, or **Il Corvo** for pasta—then take one of the **underground tours** and visit the **Klondike Gold Rush National Historical Park** museum to get a sense of Seattle's early days.

Pike Place Market takes on another personality at night. Return there for dinner at **Matt's in the Market** (for the great food) or **The Pink Door** (for the fun experience).

DAY 2

Begin the day by heading a few minutes north of downtown to Queen Anne Hill, where a great diner breakfast awaits at **The 5 Spot,** after which you can stroll over to **Kerry Park** for a gorgeous view of the skyline, Elliott Bay, Bainbridge Island, and Mount Rainier.

If you have a car, head next to **Discovery Park** for hiking and beachcombing, or to **Chittenden Locks,** a beautiful engineering marvel. Both are convenient to the abundant lunch options in the hip Ballard neighborhood. If you don't have wheels, head by foot or public transit to nearby **Seattle Center,** where there's a concentration of attractions, including the **MoPOP** museum and **Chihuly Garden and Glass.**

No matter how you spend your afternoon, plan your evening around a trip to the top of Seattle Center's **Space Needle,** a wonderful place to take in a 360-degree view at sunset. Just down the street in the Belltown neighborhood, have dinner at boisterous **Tavolàta** or the classy **Dahlia Lounge.**

---

made the ID their home. The ID is a prime destination for Asian restaurants, shops, and markets. The Wing Luke Museum is the neighborhood's cultural showpiece.

Belltown

Belltown, located between downtown to the south, Pike Place Market and the waterfront to the west, and Seattle Center to the north, is a once-sketchy area that's been transformed into a hopping neighborhood filled with new high-rise apartment buildings. At street level there's a busy restaurant and nightlife scene.

Seattle Center and Queen Anne

Seattle Center, located north of downtown, was the site of the 1962 World's Fair. The 74-acre fairgrounds have evolved into a cluster

of museums, entertainment venues, playgrounds, and open-air stages. It's the most tourist-focused part of town (with Pike Place Market and the waterfront a close second). There's a lot to do here, including many kid-friendly activities, but the main attractions are pricey, and you can spend a day here and come away feeling like you haven't experienced the real Seattle—though you'll have gotten a great view of it from the Space Needle.

You don't have to go far from Seattle Center to get a taste of laid-back local life. The neighborhood of **Queen Anne** is just to the west and north. The streets directly adjacent to Seattle Center make up Lower Queen Anne, a mix of hotels, apartment buildings, restaurants, and bars. A steep ascent takes you to Upper Queen Anne, one of Seattle's most desirable residential neighborhoods, perched on the city's tallest hill. It's worth visiting to check out the restaurants and old Victorian mansions, but the highlights are the postcard-worthy views.

South Lake Union

As the name indicates, the South Lake Union area is located on the southern banks of Lake Union, between Route 99 and the Queen Anne neighborhood to the west and I-5 and Capitol Hill to the east. Throughout the 20th century it was an industrial and warehouse district. Today online retailing giant Amazon has transformed it into a bustling corporate campus with office towers holding 40,000 employees. Ongoing construction is projected to make room for 40,000 more by 2022.

Some of Seattle's leading restaurateurs have followed the Amazon throngs here, making the neighborhood an up-and-coming dining destination, filled mainly with spinoffs of restaurants that have been successful elsewhere in the city. South Lake Union's main sightseeing attraction is the **Museum of History and Industry.** Next door is the **Center for Wooden Boats,** a pleasant throwback where you can rent a vintage craft and take to the waters. In summer, the lake fills with kayaks, yachts, and floatplanes taking off or coming in for a landing.

Capitol Hill

I-5 divides Seattle's downtown neighborhoods to its west from Capitol Hill to its east. Capitol Hill, one of Seattle's liveliest, trendiest neighborhoods, shares some characteristics with New York's Greenwich Village. Its south end, along parallel **Pike Street** and **Pine Street,** is a busy nightlife district filled with restaurants, bars, live music venues, and fringe theaters. It once catered to a predominantly gay clientele, and gay culture still thrives, but now the nighttime scene along the Pike-Pine corridor consists primarily of straight twentysomething partiers.

Running north from Pike and Pine are Capitol Hill's main commercial thoroughfares, **Broadway** and **15th Avenue.** They run through a residential neighborhood that includes the handsome old mansions of "Millionaire's Row," a stretch of 14th Avenue to the south of **Volunteer Park**. The stately atmosphere carries over into the elegant, carefully manicured park, which sits at the high point of Capitol Hill.

The U District and Arboretum

The Lake Washington Ship Canal connects Lake Washington to Puget Sound and forms a dividing line through the central city. To the canal's north are mainly older residential neighborhoods—and the **University of Washington,** one of the largest urban universities in the United States. The neighborhood surrounding "U Dub" caters to the student body with bookstores, cafes, and inexpensive restaurants. The main drag is **University Way** south of 45th Street, commonly known as "the Ave." It can be scruffy, but it has college-town energy and spirit.

One part of the university that's definitely not scruffy is the **Washington Park Arboretum,** a 230-acre plot of parkland across the Montlake Bridge from the campus. It's home to more than 20,000 varieties of plants from around the world.

Fremont, Wallingford, and Green Lake

When people talk about Seattle being a city of neighborhoods, they're thinking of places like these three adjacent communities north of Lake Union. They're made up of block after block of modest—though no longer modestly priced—craftsman houses occupied by a population that ranges from young professionals to retirees.

Each neighborhood has its own landmarks and commercial centers, where local shops predominate and restaurants are often at the vanguard of Seattle's foodie culture. **Wallingford** is nearest to the university and has some off-campus student residents; its main attraction is the distinctive Gas Works Park along the northern banks of Lake Union. **Fremont** has long self-identified as Seattle's center for counterculture and free spirits, a reputation it vigorously asserts each summer at the spirited, clothing-optional Fremont Solstice Parade. More sedate **Green Lake,** north of Wallingford, is home to the city's zoo and a popular city park.

Ballard and Discovery Park

Ballard is northwest of Fremont, bordered to the south by the Lake Washington Ship Canal and to the west by Puget Sound. Historically, Ballard was populated largely by Scandinavian immigrants, and vestiges of Nordic culture remain, from pastry shops to festivals to a museum. To the surprise of many Seattleites, in the 2010s Ballard has become a hot neighborhood. Perhaps more than anywhere else in the city, it has felt the impact of young tech workers moving to town and looking for a hip and affordable place to live. **Ballard Avenue** is lined with stylish restaurants, and parking everywhere is a headache. Visitors are attracted to Ballard's burgeoning dining and nightlife scene as well as its long-established sights, particularly **Chittenden Locks,** a crucial feature of Seattle's waterways. Just to the south of the locks is **Discovery Park,** a former military base that's now Seattle's largest and wildest park.

South Seattle

On the way from Sea-Tac airport to the heart of town you'll pass through some seemingly unremarkable industrial and residential neighborhoods, but there's more here than first meets the eye. South Seattle, as the area is collectively called, includes the neighborhoods of Columbia City, Beacon Hill, Georgetown, and SoDo, all of which have pockets of ethnic diversity and bohemian cool. South Seattle is noteworthy for its up-and-coming restaurants and bar scene, and for one major attraction: **The Museum of Flight,** arguably Seattle's best and most distinctive museum.

West Seattle

Due west of South Seattle, a stretch of elevated highway leads over the Duwamish River to West Seattle, a neighborhood that includes the southern cusp of Elliott Bay and **Alki Point,** where the city's founders first settled before thinking better of it and crossing the bay to its east side. The area feels like a world apart from the rest of Seattle. There's a bit of a California vibe to it, enhanced by the longest stretch of beachfront in the city. Out-of-town visitors come here to get some beach time and to take in the view of the downtown skyline.

Sights

Most visitors dedicate their time to the sights of downtown, the waterfront, and Seattle Center. Those are worthwhile places, but Seattle's laid-back, liberal-minded culture comes through most clearly in the surrounding neighborhoods, where beautiful urban parks, stretches of waterfront, and appealing restaurants and shops are set amid snuggly packed blocks of craftsman houses. Some of the best and most popular tourist attractions also require you to stray from the city center—particularly The Museum of Flight in South Seattle and the Chittenden Locks in Ballard.

DOWNTOWN AND THE WATERFRONT

TOP EXPERIENCE

★ Pike Place Market

The Space Needle may be Seattle's most famous icon, but **Pike Place Market** (Pike Pl. between Pike St. and Virginia St., 206/682-7453, www.pikeplacemarket.org) is its most charming and enduring landmark. Over the course of a century what started as a produce market has evolved into a warren of shops and stands supplying the city not just with

Pike Place Market's Gum Wall

vegetables but also fresh fish, meat, and flowers—as well as specialty foods, snacks, and tchotchkes.

Entering the controlled chaos of Pike Place Market feels like stepping back into another time—namely the pre-World War II era, before supermarkets, fast food, and "big agra" came to dominate the American food supply. The vintage neon signs, the maze of arcades, and the vendors hawking their wares all contribute to the retro atmosphere. Though it can feel like a movie set, and tourists are the main clientele in the busy summer season, it's still the real deal: The produce, fish, meat, and flowers available are of high quality, the prepared foods are delicious and diverse, and quirky, one-of-a-kind shops are tucked away in the more remote corners.

The market is bigger than it appears at first glance. It consists of 22 buildings covering about 10 acres. All told there are some 250 stores, 100 fruit and vegetable stands, 200 craft vendors, and 30 restaurants. Though fish

is central to the market's identity, there are only four fresh-seafood retailers.

THE MAIN ARCADE, NORTH ARCADE, AND DOWN UNDER

The market's epicenter is beneath the big neon Public Market sign and clock in the **Main Arcade,** at the point where Pike Street meets Pike Place. Under the sign you'll find **Rachel the Pig,** the market's bronze mascot, and about 100 feet up Pike Street near the corner of 1st Avenue is the **market information booth,** where you can get a map and a list of merchants.

A few feet behind Rachel is **Pike Place Fish,** where the wisecracking crew is famous for throwing fish from the display case to the packaging area behind the counter. There's some question as to how and why the practice got started, but now it's strictly a piece of market theater. The same fish get tossed repeatedly until, the worse for wear, they're donated to the zoo for animal feed.

The Main Arcade stretches north along Pike Place and is packed with vendors selling produce, specialty foods, meat, and more fish. Two historic diner-style restaurants, **Lowell's** and the **Athenian Inn,** are situated side by side, both with knockout Elliott Bay views. As you work your way down the aisle the space narrows and becomes the **North Arcade,** lined with flower stalls offering some of the market's best bargains, followed by tables filled with handmade crafts, including jewelry, pottery, and toys.

The Main and North Arcades are some of the busiest places in the market. To find more elbow room, take the ramp to the floors below, known as the **Down Under,** where quirky retail shops sell, among other things, art, antiques, comic books, and model cars.

THE MARKETFRONT

In the summer of 2017, the market got even bigger when the ribbon was cut on its first expansion in nearly 40 years. The **MarketFront** area, facing the water to the west of the North

Downtown Seattle

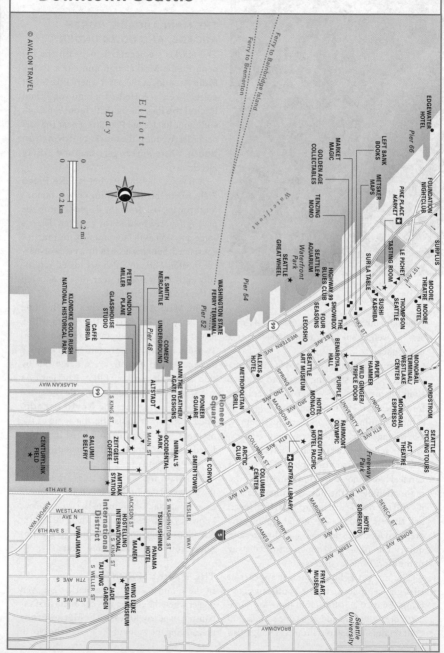

© AVALON TRAVEL

Elliott Bay

0   0.2 km
0   0.2 mi

Ferry to Bainbridge Island
Ferry to Bremerton

Waterfront

EDGEWATER
HOTEL

Pier 66

MARKET
MAGIC

LEFT BANK
BOOKS

GOLDEN AGE
COLLECTABLES

METSKER
MAPS

PIKE PLACE
MARKET

FOUNDATION
NIGHTCLUB

SURPLUS

TENZING
MOMO

LE PICHET

TASTING ROOM

MOORE
THEATRE

MOORE
HOTEL

SUR LA TABLE

SUSHI
KASHIBA

THOMPSON
SEATTLE

SEATTLE
GREAT WHEEL

HIGHWAY 99
BLUES CLUB

SEATTLE
AQUARIUM

Waterfront
Park

THE
SHOWBOX

FOUR
SEASONS

MONORAIL
TERMINAL/
WESTLAKE
CENTER

LECOSHO

PAPER
HAMMER

WILD GINGER/
TRIPLE DOOR

MONORAIL
ESPRESSO

WASHINGTON STATE
FERRY TERMINAL

Pier 54

BENAROYA
HALL

SEATTLE
ART MUSEUM

PURPLE

NORDSTROM

ALEXIS
HOTEL

HOTEL
MONACO

SEATTLE
CYCLING TOURS

PETER
MILLER

LONDON
PLANE

E. SMITH
MERCANTILE

Pier 52

Pier 48

COMEDY
UNDERGROUND

METROPOLITAN
GRILL

FAIRMONT
OLYMPIC

ACT
THEATRE

GLASSHOUSE
STUDIO

Pioneer
Square

EXECUTIVE
HOTEL PACIFIC

Freeway
Park

CAFFÈ
UMBRIA

DAMN THE WEATHER/
AGATE DESIGNS

PIONEER
SQUARE

COLUMBIA
CENTER

KLONDIKE GOLD RUSH
NATIONAL HISTORICAL PARK

ALTSTADT

OCCIDENTAL
PARK

NIRMAL'S

ARCTIC
CLUB

CENTRAL LIBRARY

ALASKAN WAY

99

ZEITGEIST
COFFEE

IL CORVO

SMITH TOWER

HOTEL
SORRENTO

CENTURYLINK
FIELD

SALUMI/
S BELFRY

S KING ST

S MAIN ST

AMTRAK
STATION

4TH AVE S

AIRPORT WAY
WESTLAKE
AVE N

6TH AVE S

JACKSON ST

HOSTELLING
INTERNATIONAL

TSUKUSHINBO

PANAMA
HOTEL

FRYE ART
MUSEUM

International
District

UWAJIMAYA

MANEKI

WING LUKE
ASIAN MUSEUM

JADE

TAI TUNG
GARDEN

7TH AVE S

8TH AVE S

S WASHINGTON ST

S KING ST

S WELLER ST

Seattle
University

BROADWAY

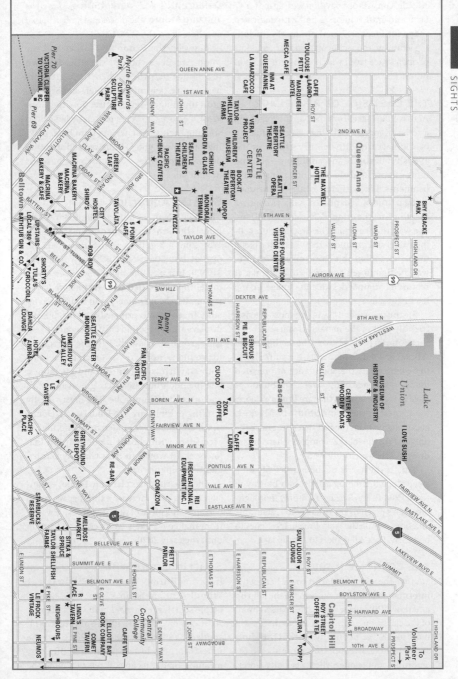

Arcade, consists of a pavilion with space for 47 farm and craft vendors, a hall with dedicated shops for local artisanal producers (including a brewer and a chocolate maker), and lots of open space from which to take in views of Elliott Bay.

THE EAST SIDE OF PIKE PLACE

Across Pike Place from the North Arcade are a series of market buildings—a combination of original early-20th-century structures and 1980s renovations and additions—housing more shops, food stands, and eating establishments. Likely there's a line out the door at the **original Starbucks.** Killjoys contend that this isn't the original Starbucks at all, and in a way, they're right: The first location, selling beans and ground coffee, was half a block to the north, but this store, opened in 1976, was the first to sell prepared coffee drinks. It retains its original design and signage, giving it a historic feel.

Starbucks aside, this is the most tourist-friendly part of the market. If you're here on vacation you probably won't be buying a fresh salmon or a bunch of carrots, but you're likely to be enticed by the abundance of prepared foods on this side of the street. The buildings have mazelike layouts that are fun to explore; the biggest of them, the **Sanitary Market,** gets its name from the fact that it was once the only part of the market complex where horse-drawn carts weren't allowed.

This eastern side of the market sits on a steep slope. Climbing a short half block you reach **Post Alley,** a pedestrian-only thoroughfare that's given over primarily to restaurants and bars. While the rest of the market goes to bed early, Post Alley likes to stay up late.

THE ECONOMY MARKET

South of the Sanitary Market you're back at the information booth. If you've made the loop up and down Pike Place you'll have passed by all of the classic open-air vendors, but there's still more to see. The **Economy Market Building** south of Pike Street houses more shops, including a couple of excellent specialty stores,

Delaurenti's and **MarketSpice,** as well as **Tenzing Momo,** the oldest and largest herbal apothecary on the West Coast.

Between the Economy Market and the Main Arcade, a cobbled street leads down to **Lower Post Alley,** where there are more bars and restaurants, a theater, and Seattle's most unsanitary tourist attraction, the **Gum Wall.** For over 20 years passersby have been sticking their used chewing gum here, making for a novel sight. (The newsstand at the top of Lower Post Alley does a thriving business in gum sales.)

Seattle Aquarium

The highlight of the touristy Elliott Bay waterfront is the **Seattle Aquarium** (1483 Alaskan Way, 206/386-4300, www.seattleaquarium. org, daily 9:30am-5pm, $29.95, youth 4-12 $19.95). Just past the ticket booth is a floor-to-ceiling tank filled with fish native to the region. It's the introduction to a midsized facility that's geared primarily to kids, but the displays are diverse and creative enough to engage grown-ups as well. Favorite attractions for young visitors are the touch tanks filled with starfish, sea urchins, and anemones, and the pools outside where gregarious seals and otters drift and frolic. The most visually striking exhibits are the Underwater Dome, in which you're surrounded by sealife, and an arch filled with ghostly moon jellyfish that looks like it would fit in at Chihuly Garden and Glass up the road.

The aquarium has plans for a major expansion that would increase exhibit space by 80 percent. This piece of the city's massive waterfront makeover likely won't come to fruition until the early 2020s.

Seattle Great Wheel

It's a small irony that the **Seattle Great Wheel** (1301 Alaskan Way, 206/623-8607, http://seattlegreatwheel.com, Sun.-Thurs. 10am-11pm, Fri.-Sat. 10am-midnight, $14, youth 4-11 $9) sits at the tip of Pier 57 on the waterfront, the lowest point in a hilly city, meaning that at its apex it reaches about the same elevation as street level in nearby downtown. That said, the views are still impressive as the 175-foot-tall Ferris wheel lifts you high above the water. The wheel has 42 enclosed glass gondolas, each with a capacity of eight people. Your ticket gets you three spins around, which take about 15 minutes total.

Columbia Center and Sky View Observatory

The king of Seattle skyscrapers is **Columbia Center** (701 5th Ave.). It rises 933 feet above the streets of downtown, making it the tallest building in Washington State and the second tallest on the West Coast (after the U.S. Bank Tower in Los Angeles). The sleek, smoked-glass tower was completed in 1985 and belongs to its era. If Gordon Gekko had lived in Seattle, his office would have been here.

You don't have to be a tycoon to take in the spectacular view. From 902 feet up at the 73rd-floor **Sky View Observatory** (206/386-5564, www.skyviewobservatory.com, daily 8am-11pm, $14.75, youth 6-12 $9.75) you look out over the city and Puget Sound, with Mount Baker to the north and Rainier to the south bookending a horizon of mountaintops. The downtown location gives you a bird's-eye view of the sports stadiums, the giant cranes of the seaport, the activity on Elliott Bay, historic Smith Tower, and the neighboring skyscrapers.

The view is fantastic, but the amenities are pretty bare-bones. You're on a floor in a 1980s-era office tower, minus the offices. There are wraparound windows, some seating, a snack counter, and signage describing the highlights of what you're looking at. To get the most out of the experience it helps to have some knowledge of Seattle, or to bring a companion who knows the city and can point things out.

★ Central Library

The most striking piece of downtown architecture is Seattle Public Library's **Central Library** (1000 4th Ave., 206/386-4636, www.spl.org, Mon.-Thurs. 10am-8pm, Fri.-Sat. 10am-6pm, Sun. noon-6pm, free), an 11-story structure that takes up an entire city block and looks like a giant steel-and-glass cube caught in the midst of transforming into a spaceship.

The 363,000-square-foot building has both an atrium-like openness and the out-of-the-way nooks and crannies you'd expect from a classic research library. It hosts worthwhile literary and cultural events for adults and kids virtually every day of the week, and has free, fast Wi-Fi. It's also just a fun place to spend an

Central Library

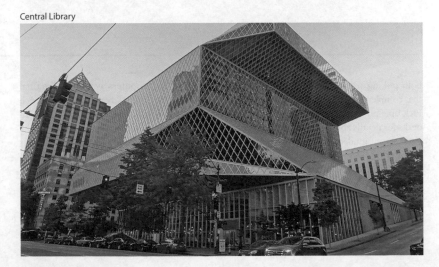

Seattle's Best Views

Seattle is a hilly city surrounded by bodies of water, with prominent mountain ranges to the east and west that include what's arguably the most visually striking peak in the United States. It's inevitable that you're going to get some fantastic views here—especially on a clear day. Here are some tips for where to find them:

THE SPACE NEEDLE VS. COLUMBIA CENTER

Two man-made observation points compete for primacy: the iconic Space Needle in Seattle Center and the less famous Columbia Center office tower downtown. They're the only two places in the city where you pay for the view, and neither is a bargain, so visitors usually choose one or the other.

Strictly in terms of the view, **Columbia Center** is more impressive. The observation area is significantly higher than the Space Needle (902 feet versus 520), delivering a broader vista, and the location is more interesting too, directly above the sports stadiums, the seaport, Elliott Bay, and downtown. The **Space Needle** makes up for its shortcomings with better bells and whistles. It's fun to go outside on the observation deck (Columbia Center has a standard office-tower window view), and creative interactive displays enhance the experience. If you're a view purist, Columbia Center is a better choice. If you (or your kids) want a more whiz-bang experience, opt for the Space Needle. The views there are still striking, just not as striking.

NATURAL HIGHS

Take advantage of Seattle's hills to get elevated views without going up in a tower. **Kerry Park** on Queen Anne Hill has the best from-the-ground view of the city, looking out over the Space Needle and downtown, with Mount Rainier visible on clear days. Capitol Hill's **Volunteer Park** has a good, though more distant, view of the city center as well. Climb the park's water tower for a glimpse of the Cascades.

THE SKYLINE

Enjoy a great view of the city skyline from across the water in **West Seattle** at Seacrest Dock, where the water taxi lands, or anywhere along the neighboring shore. **Gas Works Park,** on the north side of Lake Union, has another pleasing waterside view, made more entertaining in summer by the parade of boat and floatplane traffic on the lake.

---

hour poking around, decorated with artwork that complements the distinctive architecture. Pick up a brochure at any of the information desks for details about the highlights and how to take a self-guided tour using your cellphone.

Entering from the 4th Avenue side, a ride up the chartreuse escalator takes you to the "living room," which has the fiction section, a coffee stand, and space to sit and read beneath a 50-foot ceiling and a sloping wall of glass. Another trip on the escalator leads to the "mixing chamber," where you can consult with reference librarians or simply use one of

the 100-plus computers available. The final stop is the 10th-floor reading room, which has the building's most dramatic views. To get there the escalator ascends through the center of the book spiral: 30 miles of shelves containing over a million volumes, spread over four stories that spiral gently upward—so that those wandering the stacks don't have to climb a step.

Seattle Art Museum

The **Seattle Art Museum** (1300 1st Ave., 206/654-3100, www.seattleartmuseum.

view from Columbia Center's Sky View Observatory

SUNSETS

You get the best sunset views along the water, with the Olympic Mountains stretched out on the western horizon. Most summer evenings you'll find groups of sunset watchers at **Alki Beach** in West Seattle, **Olympic Sculpture Park** west of Seattle Center, the beach at **Discovery Park,** and **Golden Gardens Park** in Ballard. On a bluff just south of Golden Gardens, **Sunset Hill Park** (7531 34th Ave. NW) exists for one reason only.

VIEWS OF MOUNT RAINIER

When the weather is overcast you won't see Mount Rainier no matter where you are. When it's clear, though, the mammoth, looming peak is hard to miss—it's visible from anywhere that has an unobstructed southern outlook. The most beautifully composed Rainier view is on the **University of Washington campus,** where the Rainier Vista is laid out to frame the mountain. You also get a gorgeous view of Rainier as you're driving south on I-5 between downtown and the airport. For many visitors it's a memorable way to say farewell to Seattle and Washington.

org, Fri.-Sun. and Wed. 10am-5pm, Thurs. 10am-9pm, $19.95, youth 13-19 $12.95, 12 and under free) originated in 1933, and its expansion over the decades has reflected the growth and growing status of the city. Today it occupies half a block of downtown in a 312,000-square-foot facility spread over four floors and two seamlessly connected buildings.

The collection is suitably wide ranging, fulfilling SAM's role as Seattle's major art institution. There are galleries of work from Europe, Asia, Africa, Australia, the Middle East, and North America, including a wing of Native American art. Modern and contemporary pieces give SAM a chance to show off its whimsical and daring sides, both of which are conspicuous in John Grade's *Middle Fork,* a 105-foot-long sculpture of an old-growth Cascades cedar tree suspended from the ceiling of the main lobby. Within the museum the setting is more than equal to the art. Spaces range from intimate to expansive, and they're all gracefully lit.

Along with the downtown location, SAM has a sculpture park (with no admission fee) located along Elliott Bay north of Pike Place Market, and a museum dedicated to Asian art (where you can get in free with a ticket stub less than a week old from the downtown SAM) in Volunteer Park on Capitol Hill.

Frye Art Museum

Set among First Hill's hospitals and apartment buildings, the **Frye Art Museum** (704 Terry Ave., 206/622-9250, http://fryemuseum.org, Tues.-Wed. and Fri.-Sun. 11am-5pm, Thurs. 11am-7pm, free) is what you could classify as a boutique art-going experience. It was created and endowed by early Seattle business magnate Charles Frye and his wife, Emma, to display their collection of 230 19th- and early-20th-century German paintings. From that foundation the museum's collection has expanded to include American and European work of the same era.

Starting from that limited focus, the Frye's curators liven things up by presenting an interesting range of temporary exhibits, usually involving modern and contemporary art. The galleries are handsome and well maintained, and there's a pleasant cafe, all of which makes the Frye a good spot to spend a relaxed morning or afternoon in a location that's removed from the tourist fray.

PIONEER SQUARE AND THE INTERNATIONAL DISTRICT

Klondike Gold Rush National Historical Park

Klondike Gold Rush National Historical Park (319 2nd Ave. S, 206/220-4240, www. nps.gov/klse, June-Aug. daily 9am-5pm, Sept.-May daily 10am-5pm, free) is a museum devoted to the late-1890s gold rush. The event made a few prospectors rich and left many more of them poor, but its greatest lasting impact was on the development of Seattle.

The city was the launching point for the rush north to the remote Canadian Klondike Territory. It triggered a frenzy of development that proved crucial in establishing Seattle's role as the leading metropolis of the

Pacific Northwest. Re-creations of period structures (a miner's cabin, a supply shop), displays focusing on individual participants in the rush, and two 20-minute films combine to give you a good overview of this key period in the early life of the city. In summer, park volunteers conduct free tours of Pioneer Square on Friday, Saturday, and Sunday starting at 2pm.

Smith Tower

When it was built in 1914, 42-story **Smith Tower** (506 2nd Ave., 206/622-4004, http://smithtower.com, daily 10am-9pm, $19, youth 6-12 $15) was the tallest building in the United States west of the Mississippi, and it remained the tallest structure on the West Coast until the erection of the Space Needle in 1962. Today it's dwarfed by downtown's skyscrapers just to the north, but it remains a Seattle icon. Exhibits about the building's history are on the 1st and 2nd floors, and an observatory with an outside deck is on the 35th floor. Inside on the observatory level, a speakeasy-themed cocktail lounge occupies an ornately decorated meeting space formerly known as the Chinese Room.

Underground Tours

Early Seattleites in the Pioneer Square area had to contend with daily flooding at high tide. The city fathers' answer to the problem was audacious: They used landfill to raise the streets anywhere from 10 to 35 feet, thus turning the ground floor of every building into the basement.

Find out all of the details of the story on one of Seattle's underground tours, which take you beneath the streets to see the half-buried remnants of the early city. The experience is a bit like walking through a dingy basement, but it's fascinating nonetheless. The long-established **Bill Speidel's Underground Tour** (614 1st Ave., 206/682-4646, www. undergroundtour.com, $22, youth 7-12 $10) takes you on a lively exploration, mixing history with wisecracks. **Beneath the Streets** (102 Cherry St., 206/624-1237, www.

the Space Needle

beneath-the-streets.com, $19, youth 7-12 $10) is less playful and heavier on the facts.

The Wing Luke Museum
In the International District, **The Wing Luke Museum** (719 S. King St., 206/254-0811, www.wingluke.org, Tues.-Sun. 10am-5pm, $17, youth 5-12 $10) is devoted to the Asian Pacific immigrant experience in and around Seattle. It's housed in a handsomely repurposed hotel that for much of the 20th century served as a residence for waves of Asian immigrants. The 1st and 2nd floors have galleries with exhibits on the multiplicity of Asian Pacific cultures present in Seattle. On the 1st floor is a gallery room dedicated to martial arts superstar and Seattle native Bruce Lee.

Tours are a big part of the experience here. The price of admission includes a 45-minute tour of the upper floors of the hotel, where little has changed from when they were last occupied decades ago. Longer neighborhood tours, some including a meal, are also available for an additional charge.

BELLTOWN
Olympic Sculpture Park
The Seattle Art Museum's outdoor annex, the **Olympic Sculpture Park** (2901 Western Ave., 260/654-3100, www.seattleartmuseum. org, daily dawn-dusk, free), sits at the north end of the downtown waterfront, a couple of blocks southwest of Seattle Center. It occupies nine acres of former industrial space divided into three sections—Valley, Grove, and Shore—connected by a Z-shaped path that passes over a street and railroad tracks. The park's modern design feels both austere and peaceful. You're conscious of both the urban setting around you and the majestic Olympic Mountains floating on the horizon above Elliott Bay.

The sculpture is modern as well—pieces are elegant, jarring, and whimsical, occasionally all at the same time. Among the most conspicuous are Richard Serra's giant steel *Wake*, which takes up most of the Valley section; Alexander Calder's *Eagle,* ideally perched to take in the view; and Jaume Plensa's *Echo,* the 46-foot-tall head of a girl, rendered in white marble dust, facing the water and the mountains with eyes closed.

SEATTLE CENTER AND QUEEN ANNE
★ Space Needle
A lot has changed at Seattle Center since the 1962 World's Fair, but the biggest attraction remains the **Space Needle** (400 Broad St., 206/905-2100, www.spaceneedle.com, daily 8am-midnight, $29, youth 5-12 $18, discounts available before 10am or after 6pm). The 605-foot-tall tower was built for the fair and has become Seattle's definitive landmark. It's a piece of space-age kitsch that has grown respectable over time, symbolizing the guileless, innovation-minded ambition at the heart of some of Seattle's greatest successes, from software to grunge rock.

Experiencing the Space Needle means taking the 41-second elevator ride up to the 520-foot-high observation deck. As you walk around the outdoor deck you can see the towers of downtown; the docks of Elliott Bay and ships traversing Puget Sound; Lake Union, with glimpses of little Green Lake and big Lake Washington beyond it; and, along the horizon, the Olympic and Cascade mountain ranges, dominated by majestic Mount Rainier. Inside are interactive displays and food and drink concession, along with floor-to-ceiling windows.

During the summer tourist season there's usually a line to go up, especially in the afternoon. You can reduce the wait by buying your ticket in advance online. You benefit, of course, from visiting on a clear day. The deck is open until midnight, and the night-time view has the romantic allure of a landscape covered in twinkling lights. For the best of both worlds, come at sunset.

One floor down from the observation deck is the rotating restaurant **SkyCity** (206/905-2100, daily 10am-2:45pm and 5pm-9:45pm, $42-69), slated to reopen in May 2018 after renovations that include the addition of a glass floor. Prices are inflated, but diners don't pay the charge to take the elevator up. Every table has a view, and when you're finished you can go upstairs for a further look.

Chihuly Garden and Glass

Next door to the Space Needle is **Chihuly Garden and Glass** (305 Harrison St., 206/753-4940, www.chihulygardenandglass.com, Mon.-Thurs. 8:30am-8:30pm, Fri.-Sun. 8:30am-9:30pm, $29, youth 4-12 $18), an exhibition space dedicated to Seattle's most famous artist. For half a century Dale Chihuly has been making glass sculptures that share characteristics of Louis Comfort Tiffany, Jackson Pollock, and Andy Warhol. Like Tiffany, he works with brilliantly colored glass and often mimics the beauty found in nature. Like Pollock, he uses the force of gravity to shape his work, with many pieces capturing a sense of motion as glass cools and hardens while traveling through air. Like Warhol he's an impresario, overseeing a team of artisans who execute his pieces. Also like Warhol, he's a master self-promoter.

Most people have a visceral reaction to Chihuly's vibrant, intricate work. If you like it, you will love Chihuly Garden and Glass. If you're not so into it, this is your best chance of being won over—the displays here present the art in the most flattering setting imaginable. Eight themed rooms, each dramatically lit, touch on Chihuly's inspirations, including flowers, sealife, and the crafts of Pacific Northwest Indians. A glass conservatory is strategically located so that the Space Needle becomes a backdrop for the sculpture, and outside a garden is filled with real flowers and more luminous glass. Bring your camera; photography is encouraged.

There are two short films to give you some context, and a cafe decorated with items from Chihuly's wide-ranging collections—including dozens of accordions hanging from the ceiling as if in flight. In summer there are weekly evening concerts in the garden, and in the spring and fall there are sometimes glass-blowing demonstrations.

MoPOP

In 2000 the **MoPOP** (325 5th Ave. N, 206/770-2700, www.mopop.org, June-Aug. daily 10am-7pm, Sept.-May daily 10am-5pm, $33, youth 5-17 $22) opened as the Experience Music Project, dedicated to rock and pop music with an emphasis on the Pacific Northwest. In the ensuing years it has expanded its scope for broader appeal. There are still exhibits on Jimi Hendrix and Nirvana, but they now share space with elaborate galleries devoted to computer games and to movies and other works in the genres of science fiction, fantasy, and horror.

If there's a unifying theme, it's pop culture obsession. Kurt Cobain's handwritten lyrics, Captain Kirk's command chair from *Star Trek,* and Jack Nicholson's ax from *The Shining* are displayed like holy relics. Most fans will relish the experience, though because the topics covered are so broad, hardcore devotees may find some treatments don't delve as deeply as they'd like.

There are lots of interactive displays aimed

at kids—they can create their own fantasy worlds or rock out in a simulated live concert. And part of the experience is the building itself, an undulating metallic structure designed by famed architect Frank Gehry.

Gates Foundation Visitor Center

Kitty-corner from MoPOP, the **Gates Foundation Visitor Center** (440 5th Ave. N, 206/709-3100, ext. 7100, www.gatesfoundation.org/Visitor-Center, Tues.-Sat. 10am-6pm, free) sits on the ground floor of the Bill and Melinda Gates Foundation, a philanthropic organization with global ambitions and an endowment of over $40 billion. Using a short film and four rooms of interactive displays, the center strives to answer the question, "What is the richest person in the world doing to help humanity?" That turns out not to be such an easy task. The foundation's far-reaching goals prove difficult to encapsulate, and the displays feel by turns confusing, overly simplistic, and self-promotional. That said, you come away with a clear sense that the foundation is bringing the same innovative, entrepreneurial spirit to philanthropy that Bill Gates brought to the software business.

Pacific Science Center

After the Space Needle, the most distinctive structure remaining from the 1962 World's Fair is the **Pacific Science Center** (200 2nd Ave. N, 206/443-2001, www.pacificsciencecenter.org, June-Aug. daily 10am-6pm, Sept.-May Mon.-Fri. 10am-5pm, Sat.-Sun. 10am-6pm, $21.95, youth 6-15 $15.95, youth 3-5 $11.95). Tall, spindly white arches towering over the center's buildings and large courtyard create a retro space-age atmosphere—it feels like you're in *The Jetsons.* Inside there's a lot going on, including two Imax theaters (one for 3-D commercial releases, one for educational films), a laser dome, a butterfly house, and a small planetarium. (Imax screenings and the laser dome require additional fees.)

The center's exhibits are geared toward kids, with target audiences ranging from grade-schoolers to teens. Some of them feel dated, but for younger kids that's not a problem. They usually delight in the many buttons to push and levers to pull, as well as the mechanized dinosaurs and giant bugs, and the real-life mole rats and butterflies. For older kids and adults there are changing exhibits with a more topical, hard-science bent, usually put together in collaboration with one of the local universities or research centers.

Seattle Children's Museum

In the middle of Seattle Center is the multipurpose Armory building, and in the middle of the Armory is the **Seattle Children's Museum** (305 Harrison St., 206/441-1768, http://thechildrensmuseum.org, Mon.-Fri. 10am-5pm, Sat.-Sun. 10am-6pm, children and parents $10.50, grandparents $9.50). The name is a little misleading: It's not a museum with exhibits, but instead a 22,000-square-foot play area divided into different themed sections, including a stage where kids can put on improvised productions, a mountain they can climb on and camp out in, and a "global village" replicating settings from Ghana, Japan, and the Philippines.

The stated audience is children from 10 months to 10 years of age, but the museum is geared primarily to preschoolers. The goal is to give them a few prompts and let their imaginations take over. It's a low-tech environment—there are no touch screens or other computerized features—and kids seem to love it precisely because they aren't being overwhelmed with outside stimulation. All drop-in visitors must be accompanied by an adult, but in summer and during most periods when school isn't in session there are half- and full-day camps that don't require parental supervision.

Other Seattle Center Sights

For kids looking to blow off some steam (without putting a further dent in their parents' wallets), there's the free **Artists at Play,** a colorful and creative playground located between the Armory and MoPOP. Northwest of the Armory, the **International Fountain** functions as a public square, where kids and grown-ups alike can splash in the water or hang out on the edges of the fountain's massive basin.

Another Seattle Center novelty is the **monorail** (www.seattlemonorail.com, $2.25), which is little changed from when it first started running at the 1962 World's Fair. It departs every 10 minutes and has only one stop, downtown's Westlake Center. It starts running at 7:30am on weekdays and 8:30am on weekends and shuts down between 9pm and 11pm, depending on the season.

Kerry Park

Amid the handsome old houses on Queen Anne Hill are several small parks that provide gorgeous vistas. **Kerry Park** (211 W. Highland Dr., 24 hrs.) looks south over the Seattle Center, downtown, and Elliott Bay, with Mount Rainier visible on clear days. It's *the* classic place to take an all-encompassing photo of the city—you get the Space Needle, the skyscrapers, and the state's mightiest mountain all in one frame. The tiny park consists mainly of a viewing deck, with steps down to a playground.

A lesser-known Kerry Park alternative is **Bhy Kracke Park** (pronounced "by cracky," 1215 5th Ave. N, 4am-11:30pm). It's a steep plot of land sandwiched amid the houses about three-quarters of a mile to Kerry's east. It also has great downtown views, shifted a few degrees east to encompass Lake Union.

SOUTH LAKE UNION
Museum of History and Industry

The **Museum of History and Industry** (860 Terry Ave. N, 206/324-1126, www.mohai.org, daily 10am-5pm, Thurs. 10am-8pm, $19.95, youth 14 and under free), universally known by its acronym MOHAI, provides a comprehensive overview of Seattle's past, mixed with a dose of civic boosterism. It's situated in Lake Union Park on the southern banks of the lake in the Naval Reserve Armory.

The armory has been gracefully restored, with a central atrium encircled by three upper floors. It makes a striking first impression: Boeing's original commercial aircraft hangs from the ceiling, parked nearby is a pink "toe truck" that's a kitschy local icon, and at the other end of the hall there's a towering sculpture made from the remnants of an old schooner. Most of the ground floor consists of the Bezos Center for Innovation, a series of displays that celebrate Seattle's greatest business successes and promote creative thinking in visitors, especially younger ones. Upstairs, more conventional exhibits take you through the history of the city.

As you tour MOHAI you can sense that the museum has multiple, sometimes conflicting goals—to engage kids, educate the general public, and pay homage to the city's business leaders. For visitors who are unfamiliar with the history of Seattle, some of the displays may be difficult to appreciate, and it's easy to come away from the Bezos Center with the sense that it's a little too reverential. The greatest strength of the museum is its collection of artifacts, particularly as displayed in its changing themed exhibits, which are consistently entertaining and informative.

The Center for Wooden Boats

At the charming **Center for Wooden Boats** (1010 Valley St., 206/382-2628, http://cwb.org, Mar.-mid-Apr. Tues.-Sun. 10am-6pm, mid-Apr.-Aug. Tues.-Sun. 10am-8pm, Sept.-Oct. daily 10am-7pm, Nov.-Feb. Tues.-Sun. 10am-5pm, free) you can visit the exhibition space, chat with the laid-back staff, and walk the docks to check out the collection of small antique craft, including sailboats, steamboats, and longboats.

The center also rents rowboats, pedal boats, and sailboats ($30-40/hr.) and every Sunday conducts free group rides on its multi-passenger vessels—sign-up is first come, first served starting at 10am, and the hour-long trips are conducted between 11am and 3pm. Serious enthusiasts can take part in multi-session sailing and boatbuilding classes.

CAPITOL HILL
Volunteer Park

Among Seattle's diverse public parks, **Volunteer Park** (1247 15th Ave. E, 206/684-4075, www.seattle.gov/parks, 6am-10pm, free) feels the most refined. Its 48 acres are self-consciously beautiful, like an English garden, with flower beds, rolling lawns, and carefully composed vistas that make the most of the park's location at the highest point on Capitol Hill.

It's pleasant enough just to laze around here, go for a jog, or take the kids to the playground, but there are also several sights to explore. The centerpiece of the park is the **Seattle Asian Art Museum.** Nearby is the **Conservatory** (206/684-4743, www.volunteerparkconservatory.org, Tues.-Sun. 10am-4pm, $4, youth 13-17 $2), a Victorian-style hothouse built in 1912 that holds a collection of beautiful and exotic plants. (It's a great place to beat the doldrums on a dreary winter day.) For the loftiest view on Capitol Hill, you can climb to the observation deck of the 75-foot-tall brick **water tower** (10am-dusk, free), which dates from 1906. Windows on all sides provide panoramas of the downtown skyline, the Space Needle, and the Cascades.

In a city full of great views, this one ranks among the best.

Seattle Asian Art Museum

The **Seattle Asian Art Museum** (1400 E. Prospect St., 206/654-3100, www.seattleartmuseum.org), a branch of the Seattle Art Museum, occupies a monumental 1933 art deco building in Volunteer Park that was originally home to SAM's entire collection. Asian art is SAM's strong suit, and devoting this handsome building to it was an inspired idea.

In 2017 the museum began a major renovation—the first ever for the building. It will reopen in 2019 with much-needed improvements to its climate control system and art storage facilities, and, most conspicuously, a three-level addition at the back of the building that will include gallery space, a community meeting room, and staff offices.

Lake View Cemetery

Just north of Volunteer Park, **Lake View Cemetery** (1554 15th Ave. E, 206/322-1582, www.lakeviewcemeteryassociation.com, summer daily 9am-8pm, winter daily 9am-4:15pm, fall/spring daily 9am-6pm, free) is the resting place for some of Seattle's most

The Center for Wooden Boats

prominent early citizens, including names you'll recognize from touring Pioneer Square and downtown, such as Doc Maynard, Arthur Denny, Henry Yesler, John Nordstrom, and Princess Angeline, daughter of Chief Sealth, the man for whom the city was named. The most visited gravesites belong to more recent Seattleites: martial arts superstar Bruce Lee and his son Brandon, who are buried side by side. Visitors are welcome to stroll the cemetery's green slopes and explore the headstones.

Northwest African American Museum

The Central District, southeast of Capitol Hill, has long been the city's most ethnically diverse neighborhood. It had a concentration of Jewish and then Japanese residents in the first half of the 20th century, and in the second half was predominantly Black. Though the majority population is now White, the CD remains a stronghold of African-American culture.

The neighborhood's main cultural institution, the **Northwest African American Museum** (2300 S. Massachusetts St., 206/518-6000, www.naamnw.org, Wed. and Fri.-Sun. 11am-5pm, Thurs. 11am-7pm, $7), examines the Black experience in the Pacific Northwest and particularly Seattle. Its Journey Gallery displays historical artifacts and chronicles the accomplishments of leading figures in the Black community, and there are changing shows in two additional galleries, one exhibiting contemporary art, the other weaving together artistic, cultural, and historical themes.

The facility, which occupies the ground floor of a former school, is 17,000 square feet, and you may come away wishing it were larger. Frequent events, such as readings and discussions, enhance the experience of visiting; check the website's events calendar for a schedule.

THE U DISTRICT AND ARBORETUM
University of Washington

The **University of Washington** (www.washington.edu) is a hive of higher learning, with a campus that has some beautiful, strollworthy sections and a couple of cultural institutions to visit. The hub of campus is the Central Plaza, known to all by its nickname, **Red Square,** derived from its redbrick pavement. At the north end of the square in the Odegaard Library is the university's **visitors center** (206/543-9198, www.washington.edu/visit, Mon.-Fri. 8:30am-5pm), where you can pick up an annotated map of the campus.

Black Sun sculpture by Isamu Noguchi, Volunteer Park

Red Square's most notable building, **Suzzallo Library** (www.lib.washington.edu/suzzallo), is designed to resemble a Gothic cathedral. Inside, the impressive Reading Room feels like a church nave, with a vaulted ceiling, leaded glass windows, and study tables arranged like pews. It's open to the general public during library hours, which vary with the academic seasons. (Call the visitors center or check the library website for current hours.)

At the south end of Red Square a wide promenade leads down to **Drumheller Fountain** and beyond it **Rainier Vista.** The entire mall, over a third of a mile long, is laid out to frame a spectacular view of Mount Rainier. It's the most impressive feat of landscape architecture you'll find in the city.

To the east of Red Square is the **Quad,** a green space surrounded by seven academic buildings done in classic "collegiate Gothic" style—the setting could easily be mistaken for an Ivy League campus in New England. It's particularly striking in spring, when it's awash in pink as 30 Yoshino cherry trees blossom.

Burke Museum

The **Burke Museum** (17th Ave. NE at NE 45th St., 206/543-5990, www.burkemuseum.org, daily 10am-5pm, $10, youth 5 and over

and students $7.50), at the northwest corner of the UW campus, is the oldest museum in Washington, dating back to 1885, and has been the officially designated state museum since 1899. It's old, but in the process of becoming new again: In September 2018 it will close its existing facility, and in the summer of 2019 it will reopen in a new building next door, 66 percent larger, with five exhibition spaces. Burke's mission is to encompass Washington's past in broad terms. Exhibits capture the state's biological, geological, archaeological, and cultural development, with displays that include giant dinosaur replicas, an actual dinosaur bone, ancient fossils, and 11,000-year-old spear tips.

Henry Art Gallery

On the western edge of the UW campus, the 46,000-square-foot **Henry Art Gallery** (4100 15th Ave. NE, 206/543-2280, http://henryart.org, Wed. and Fri.-Sun. 11am-4pm, Thurs. 11am-9pm, $10, kids and students free) is the only museum in Seattle dedicated exclusively to contemporary art. Every year there are five or so temporary exhibits, which run the gamut from photography and painting to conceptual art and sight-specific multimedia installations. The museum's centerpiece

University of Washington's Quad during spring Cherry Blossom Festival

is James Turrell's *Light Reign,* a "sky space" sculpture that consists of an oval room with a large opening in the ceiling, through which you have an unobstructed view of the ever-changing sky. It's a quiet, meditative place that contrasts with the high energy often found in the Henry's other exhibits.

★ Washington Park Arboretum and Japanese Garden

South of the UW campus, across the Montlake Cut, **Washington Park Arboretum** (http://depts.washington.edu/uwbg, daily dawn-dusk, free) is one of the most tranquil places in the city. The 230 acres are managed jointly by the city and university and laid out in a roughly rectangular shape running north-south. Arboretum Creek and two roads, Lake Washington Boulevard and Arboretum Drive, span the park's length.

Get your bearings on the northeast side of the park at **Graham Visitors Center** (2300 Arboretum Dr. E, 260/543-8800, daily 9am-5pm), which has maps and volunteers to point you in the right direction. You've got some options for things to see, all accessible by walking paths. At the far north end are wetlands surrounding Foster and Marshall Islands, where you're likely to spot waterfowl and possibly turtles and beavers. At the south end the Pacific Connections Garden has plants from around the Pacific Rim. In spring the park comes into bloom, with Azalea Way, a 0.75-mile trail, and the rhododendron glen the star attractions. If you come on a warm summer day, cool off by the ponds of the Woodland Garden or under the canopy of giant sequoias along the park's northwest border.

At the southwest end of the park is the formal **Japanese Garden** (1075 Lake Washington Blvd. E, 206/684-4725, www.seattlejapanesegarden.org, Mar. Tues.-Sun. 10am-5pm; Apr. and Aug. Mon. noon-7pm, Tues.-Sun. 10am-7pm; May-July Mon. noon-8pm, Tues.-Sun. 10am-4pm; Sept. Mon. noon-6pm, Tues.-Sun. 10am-6pm; Oct. Mon. noon-5pm, Tues.-Sun. 10am-5pm; Nov. Mon. noon-4pm, Tues.-Sun. 10am-4pm, $6, youth 6-17 $4). It's the only part of the park that charges admission and has limited hours. Features include a pond, beds of camellias, azaleas, and rhododendrons, and over 500 boulders transported from the Cascades. A teahouse has a ceremonial service ($10) on most weekends April-October. Reservations are required.

Washington Park Arboretum

Fremont Troll

FREMONT, WALLINGFORD, AND GREEN LAKE

Gas Works Park

Among Seattle's many parks, **Gas Works Park** (2101 N. Northlake Way, 206/684-4075, www.seattle.gov/parks, daily 6am-10pm, free) is the most distinctive. It's set on the location of an old coal gasification plant at the south end of Wallingford, on a point of land poking out into Lake Union. The massive, rusting, vine-covered gasworks are still there, sitting like a piece of found art amid 19 acres of rolling lawn.

While the industrial relic gives the park its name, the real centerpiece is **Kite Hill** just to the west, a cleared grassy ridge that is indeed a great place for flying kites. It's also good for lounging around and watching the activity in front of you on Lake Union. The view beyond the lake is a panorama of central Seattle's neighborhoods: Capitol Hill to the east; South Lake Union, downtown, and the Space Needle dead ahead; and Queen Anne Hill to the west.

On the other side of the gasworks from the hill are the park's primary facilities, a picnic shelter and a play barn for kids full of modern play equipment set amid old (and child-safe) gasworks machinery. The park gets busy on summer weekends, and it's jam-packed on the June solstice, when it's the terminus for the Fremont Solstice Parade, and on the Fourth of July, when it's the best place in the city for watching fireworks.

Fremont Public Art

Fremont reinforces its reputation as Seattle's center for counterculture with a collection of novel public sculptures. They're within easy walking distance of one another, and checking them out is a good starting point for exploring the southern part of the neighborhood, which has lots of shops, restaurants, cafes, and bars.

Near the north end of the Fremont drawbridge is *Waiting for the Interurban* (N. 34th St. and Fremont Ave. N), a set of cast-aluminum figures awaiting a streetcar that's never going to arrive. The melancholy group regularly gets spruced up by neighborhood residents, who festoon the figures with gaudy clothes and other decorations.

From there you can head east a block (passing Schilling Cider House and Milstead Coffee, two good spots for refreshment) and up three short blocks on the street under the Aurora Bridge to visit the **Fremont Troll** (N. 36th St. and Troll Ave.), a playfully creepy creature made of steel and concrete, with an actual VW Beetle gripped in one hand. The troll is a favorite with kids, who love to climb on it, and parents, who love to take their picture doing so.

Walking down 36th Street and across Fremont Avenue brings you to an imposing 16-foot bronze **statue of Lenin** (N. 36th St. and Fremont Pl. N). It originally stood in a town square in the former Czechoslovakia and found its way here in 1995. Today it's viewed with varying degrees of irony by liberal-leaning Fremontsters. Like the *Interurban* figures, Lenin is frequently adorned with decorations.

A short block south of Lenin, the

53-foot-tall **Fremont Rocket** (N. 35th St. and Evanston Ave.) towers over a corner storefront. It's constructed from salvaged parts of a 1930s plane fuselage and looks like it would have fit right in on the set of a Cold War-era low-budget sci-fi flick. Emblazoned across it is Fremont's pseudo-Latin motto, *De Libertas Quirkas*—translated as "Freedom to Be Peculiar."

You can end your walk on a sweet note one block west at **Theo Chocolate** (3400 Phinney Ave. N, 206/632-5100, www.theochocolate. com), which conducts hour-long factory tours ($10) seven times a day. Theo is serious about its sophisticated, artisanal candies—tours include detailed background information about the chocolate-making process and aren't intended for younger kids.

Woodland Park Zoo

With over a million visitors a year, **Woodland Park Zoo** (5500 Phinney Ave. N, 206/548-2500, www.zoo.org, Apr.-Sept. daily 9:30am-6pm, Oct.-Mar. daily 9:30am-4pm, Apr.-Sept. $20.95, youth 3-12 $12.95, Oct.-Mar. $14.95, youth 3-12 $9.95) is one of Seattle's most popular attractions. It spans 92 acres on the western half of Woodland Park and is populated by over 1,000 animals from some 300 species, making it big enough for a 4-5-hour visit if you're a dedicated zoo-goer.

The zoo's origins date back to 1899. Starting in the 1970s it became a leader in the development of immersion exhibits, which mimic animals' native habitats, fostering better mental and physical health. The zoo is divided into areas representing different climates and terrain: Tropical Rain Forest (where animals include jaguars and toucans), Temperate Forest (flamingos, red pandas), Tropical Asia (orangutans, tigers), Northern Trail (gray wolves, grizzly bears), Australasia (wallabies, snow leopards), and African Savanna (giraffes, gorillas, hippopotamuses).

The amount of space afforded the animals means that they're not always easy to view. You'll generally get more sightings in the morning than the afternoon, particularly on summer days when many animals seek shade and seclusion during the warmest hours. You can avoid the $6 parking fee by skipping the lots and finding a place on a nearby street. (Street parking is easier to come by here than in many other neighborhoods.)

BALLARD AND DISCOVERY PARK
Fishermen's Terminal

At the south end of Ballard Bridge on Salmon Bay, the **Fishermen's Terminal** (3919 18th Ave. W, 206/787-3395, www.portseattle.org/ Commercial-Marine/Fishermens-Terminal, free) has been the base for the northern Pacific's fishing fleet for over a century. Today it's the home port for more than 500 vessels, making it the largest such facility in the United States. Nearly half of the caught (i.e., not farmed) fish sold in America comes through here.

You can spend a satisfying hour strolling the long docks and watching the fishermen (and women) engaged in their age-old trade. Onlookers are welcome; you might even get a friendly nod and a "hello" from the crew as they unload their catch or repair their nets. Things are liveliest in spring when the boats heading for Alaska prepare to launch, and in fall when they return home to dock for the winter. Look for the **Fishermen's Memorial,** which honors those who have lost their lives at sea. It's a revered monument for the people who work the terminal's fleet.

Several restaurants are in the terminal buildings: **Chinook's** specializes in seafood, **Highliner Public House** has pub grub, and the **Bay Cafe** serves diner fare. At **Wild Salmon Seafood Market** you can get fresh-off-the-boat fish to take home.

★ Chittenden Locks

The **Hiram Chittenden Locks** (3015 NW 54th St., 206/783-7059, www.nws.usace.army. mil, daily 7am-9pm, free), more commonly known to locals as the Ballard Locks, are one of the key human alterations to Seattle's waterways, making Lake Union and Lake

Ballard

Commodore Park

Burke-Gilman Tr.

W GOVERNMENT WAY

W COMMODORE WAY

W COMMODORE WAY

✦ CHITTENDEN LOCKS

★

32ND AVE NW

NW MARKET ST

NW 56TH ST

NW 57TH ST

NW 58TH ST

NW 59TH ST

NW 60TH ST

30TH AVE NW

28TH AVE NW

26TH AVE NW

★ NORDIC HERITAGE MUSEUM

24TH AVE NW

CAFE BESALU ■

Ballard Commons Park

22ND AVE NW

Salmon Bay

LA CARTA DE OAXACA ▼

SUNSET TAVERN ■

SONIC BOOM ▼

SHILSHOLE AVE NW

NW LEARY AVE

TRACTOR TAVERN ■

BALLARD INN ●

CAFFE FIORE

HOTEL BALLARD ●

STONEBURNER ▼

ASCENT OUTDOORS ▼

WALRUS & CARPENTER/ STAPLE & FANCY ▼

BALLARD AVE NW

RUSSELL AVE NW

TALLMAN AVE NW

BARNES AVE NW

NW DOCK PL

20TH AVE NW

17TH AVE NW

SHILSHOLE AVE NW

★ FISHERMEN'S TERMINAL

15TH AVE NW

14TH AVE NW

NW 45TH ST

NW 46TH ST

NW BALLARD WAY

NW LEARY WAY

NW 50TH ST

NW 51ST ST

NW 52ND ST

NW 53RD ST

NW 54TH ST

NW MARKET ST

STOUP ▼

11TH AVE NW

Gilman Playground

9TH AVE NW

HALE'S ALES ▼

POPULUXE ▼

NW 49TH ST

SLATE COFFEE BAR ▼

BRIMMER & HEELTAP ▼

6TH AVE NW

NW 6TH ST

0   0.20 km

0   0.20 mi

© AVALON TRAVEL

Washington accessible to boat traffic from Puget Sound. They were designed in large part by Hiram Chittenden, the Seattle district engineer for the Army Corps of Engineers, and opened on July 4, 1917, at the mouth of the Lake Washington Ship Canal.

It's fun to watch the system at work. The two locks and the adjacent spillway serve multiple purposes. First, they're a barrier between the saltwater of Puget Sound and the freshwater of the lakes. They're also used to maintain a consistent water level in the lakes, which is crucial for the floating bridges and houseboats. Most conspicuously, the locks raise and lower vessels between the two bodies of water—tens of thousands of them annually, from kayaks to yachts to commercial fishing boats. The change in water level can be as much as 26 feet at low tide. The locks fill and drain like gargantuan bathtubs while boats bob on the surface.

Other attractions here include a **fish ladder** that allows spawning salmon to circumvent the blockade and also attracts marine mammals and herons, who find the fish easy prey. There's an underwater viewing area (daily 7am-8:45pm) where you can watch the salmon fighting against the current; activity is greatest in late summer. Well-maintained **botanical gardens** are suitable for picnics and romping in the grass, and a **visitors center** (May-Sept. daily 10am-6pm, Oct.-Apr. Thurs.-Mon. 10am-4pm) has background information about the building and operation of the locks.

It's helpful to go on a free hour-long **guided tour,** which starts at the visitors center. Tours are conducted March-November on a variable schedule; call ahead for times.

★ Discovery Park

South of the Chittenden Locks, **Discovery Park** (3801 Discovery Park Blvd., 206/684-4075, www.seattle.gov/parks, daily 4am-11:30pm, free) juts out into Puget Sound at the western end of Magnolia, a quiet residential neighborhood bordering Queen Anne. Soon after entering, all signs of urban life disappear, and that's the park's fundamental appeal—you're five miles from downtown, yet feel like you're in wilderness.

Discovery Park is the largest park in Seattle, including 534 acres of woodland, meadows, sand dunes, and bluffs overlooking the sound, as well as 2 miles of beach and almost 12 miles of trails. Its history belies

Chittenden Locks

Rainy-Day Distractions

Seattle earns its rainy reputation October-May. If rain is in the forecast, how can you make the most of your visit?

PLANTS AND ANIMALS

It can be a pleasing experience to visit animals while the rain is coming down. Use your imagination and there's a sense of bonding with the fish when you go to the **Seattle Aquarium** or the fish ladder at **Chittenden Locks** on a wet day. Or visit one of Seattle's contained natural environments: Rain falling on the glass enclosures of the **Pacific Science Center's butterfly house** and **Volunteer Park Conservatory** adds to the venues' allure.

FOOD ADVENTURES

One of Seattle's main attractions, **Pike Place Market,** is better to visit on a rainy day: It's almost entirely covered, yet the rain keeps away some crowds, making for friendlier, more accessible vendors. In the International District, shopping at the giant Asian-focused supermarket **Uwajimaya** can be an adventure; along with rows of exotic noodles, sauces, and canned goods you'll find a food court, bookstore, and housewares department filled with potential souvenirs. In the Fremont neighborhood, tour the **Theo Chocolate factory.** In Capitol Hill, one short block on Melrose Avenue has an afternoon of foodie diversions, with the **Melrose Market,** a **Taylor Shellfish Farms** outlet, and the Willie Wonka-ish **Starbucks Reserve Roastery.**

BOOK TEMPLES

Seattle is a great bookstore town, with top billing going to Capitol Hill's **Elliott Bay Book Company,** where you can browse an extensive collection, get tips from the knowledgeable staff, and hang out in the cafe. Downtown, you could spend half a day exploring the **Central Library,** a glass-enclosed modern masterpiece. Or for a different experience check out the **Suzzallo Library** on the University of Washington campus: It's built in the style of a Gothic cathedral and has a reading room that feels like a church nave, with a vaulted ceiling, leaded glass windows, and study tables arranged like pews.

its untamed atmosphere—before becoming a park it was the home of Fort Lawton military base, a major installation during World War II that processed over a million troops on their way to the Pacific. Following the war the activity significantly declined, and the military ceded most of the property to the city in the 1970s.

One of the reasons the park feels so remote is that most of it isn't accessible by car. There are three main parking lots from which most visitors head out on foot. Pedestrians can circle the heart of the park on the 2.8-mile **Loop Trail,** which takes you through varied terrain and has access to side trails. Several of them make the steep descent to the beach, where a lighthouse at **West Point** marks the division

between Elliott Bay to the south and Shilshole Bay to the north; the name comes from the fact that this is the westernmost point in the city. **Wolf Tree Nature Trail,** near the north parking lot, is a half-mile loop that goes past two streams and through wooded wetlands with the greatest diversity of plant life in the park.

You're likely to encounter more wildlife here than anywhere else in the city. Seals and sea lions populate the waters offshore, and 270 species of birds have been identified in the park, making it Seattle's favorite destination for bird-watchers. You can pick up a bird brochure, as well as a park map and other information, at the **Environmental Learning Center** (206/386-4236, daily 8:30am-5pm), located next to the parking lot near the park's eastern entrance at West Government Way.

At the north end of the park (and accessible by car) is **Daybreak Star Indian Cultural Center** (5011 Bernie Whitebear Way, 206/285-4425, www.unitedindians.org, Mon.-Fri. 9am-5pm, free), run by the United Indians of All Nations Foundation. It has galleries with artistic and historical displays, and every July it hosts the Seafair Indian Days Powwow.

Nordic Heritage Museum

Ballard celebrates its Scandinavian roots at the **Nordic Heritage Museum** (2655 NW Market St., 206/789-5707, www.nordicmuseum.org, Tues.-Sat. 10am-4pm, Sun. noon-4pm, $8, youth 5 and over $6). After decades spent occupying an old schoolhouse in a residential area, in 2018 the museum opened a $45 million, built-from-the-ground-up facility on Northwest Market Street in the heart of Ballard's busy commercial district. The museum uses artifacts and dioramas to tell the story of Scandinavian immigration to the United States, and specifically to Ballard, in the late 19th century. There are temporary exhibits and galleries devoted to the five Scandinavian nationalities (Swedish, Norwegian, Finnish, Danish, and Icelandic).

SOUTH SEATTLE

TOP EXPERIENCE

★ The Museum of Flight

Seattle has a longtime reputation as a center for aeronautic innovation. The Boeing Company was founded here in the 1910s by William Boeing, a timber merchant who applied techniques for building wooden boats to the construction of airplanes. Boeing grew into a world leader in the development and manufacture of commercial and military aircraft, and though the corporate offices are now in Chicago, the company's production facilities continue to be the largest private employer in Washington State.

The Museum of Flight (9404 E. Marginal Way S, 206/764-5720, www.museumofflight.org, daily 10am-5pm, $23, youth 5-17 $14) is closely linked to Seattle's Boeing legacy but goes beyond it to present a broad overview of aviation history. There are six exhibition spaces, each of which could be a museum of its own. The most eye-catching is the glass-walled, light-filled Great Gallery, which has 39 historic planes on display—some hanging from the ceiling, others parked on the floor—that constitute a walk through the evolution of flight in the 20th

The Museum of Flight

century. It's hard not to be impressed by the show of technological innovation and sheer beauty of the aircraft, which have been restored to mint condition.

The red barn that served as the first Boeing factory contains artifacts from the early days of the company and a re-creation of the original workshop. There are two floors of dramatically displayed planes from World Wars I and II. In a separate building you can climb into the space shuttle training ship—it's not a shuttle that made it into outer space, but one that all of the astronauts used in simulation exercises to prepare for their journeys. The Aviation Pavilion houses bigger planes, some of which you can board, including the first jet-powered *Air Force One,* a Concorde, and Boeing's newest passenger plane, the 787 Dreamliner.

Note that the museum can be overwhelming; if you're a dedicated aviation enthusiast you could easily spend a day here. If you're not, it's a good idea before arriving to decide which exhibits sound the most appealing and prioritize accordingly.

Living Computers Museum + Labs

Microsoft cofounder Paul Allen is the financial engine driving some of Seattle's biggest cultural institutions, including the Seahawks football team and MoPOP, but you have to think he has a particular soft spot for the **Living Computers Museum + Labs** (2245 1st Ave. S, 206/342-2020, www.livingcomputers.org, Wed.-Sun. 10am-5pm, $12). Located on the upper floor of a nondescript warehouse in the SoDo area, the museum is a computer nerd's dream.

The museum is filled with relics from the pioneering days of computing, including massive mainframes, Teletype machines, punch-card sorters, minicomputers, and early microcomputers. All of the archaic machinery is "living" only because Allen, the museum's founder and funder, has put it on life support. A staff of engineers and technicians has restored everything to working order. They make it their business to maintain million-dollar, room-size computers that are less powerful than the smartphones in their pockets.

Visitors can use most of the machinery themselves, but unless you're versed in the technology you're better served by going on one of the free guided tours, conducted every hour starting at 15 minutes past the hour. It's also surprisingly engrossing to while away some time playing 1970s- and '80s-era games on the bank of vintage microcomputers. You'll sense a pro-Microsoft bent to the museum's portrayal of computer history, but it's easy to forgive the indulgence at what is, first and foremost, an uber-geek's labor of love.

WEST SEATTLE
Alki Beach

The waters are seldom warm enough for comfortable swimming, but otherwise **Alki Beach,** which runs along the western shore of West Seattle, has all the trappings of classic California-style beach culture. In summer residents from all over town come here to play volleyball, sunbathe, people-watch, and light bonfires after the sun goes down. **Alki Point Lighthouse,** built in 1913, stands at the beach's far western end, in the location where Seattle's founders first put down roots. They originally called their settlement New York-Alki—"Alki" meaning "eventually" in Chinook dialect. After a harsh winter here they decided to relocate to the eastern side of Elliott Bay.

Sightseeing on a Budget

FREE SIGHTS AND ACTIVITIES

In the heart of town, visit **Klondike Gold Rush National Historical Park** or **Frye Art Museum,** first-rate institutions that could easily get away with asking admission. Downtown's **Central Library** is also a fun, fascinating building to explore.

It doesn't cost a thing to stroll through **Pike Place Market,** though you may have a hard time keeping your wallet in your pocket when confronted with the abundance of food, flowers, and knickknacks. Head northwest along the water to arrive at the **Olympic Sculpture Park,** the impressive outdoor annex to the Seattle Art Museum.

Across the ship canal to the north, a short neighborhood stroll takes you past the whimsical **public art of Fremont.** Farther west along the water, watch the comings and goings at the **Fishermen's Terminal** and check out **Chittenden Locks.**

Discovery, Volunteer, Gas Works, and **Green Lake Parks,** as well as **Washington Park Arboretum** and the **beaches** of **Golden Gardens** and **Alki,** are some of the other free and beautiful outdoors options.

DISCOUNTS

Save money while taking in some of the more expensive sights by purchasing a **CityPass** (www. citypass.com/seattle, $79, youth 4-12 $59). It covers admission to five attractions: the Space Needle, the aquarium, a harbor cruise, Chihuly Garden & Glass *or* the Pacific Science Center, and MoPOP *or* Woodlawn Park Zoo. Visit all five and you'll save about 50 percent off standard admission. Purchase passes online or at participating sights. Passes are valid for nine days, starting from when you enter the first attraction.

You also get discounts by purchasing tickets to Chihuly Garden & Glass online in advance,

Entertainment and Events

After a day of sightseeing, you have a full range of ways to unwind and take in some culture. The number one evening recreational activity for Seattleites may now be dining out, but the music scene remains vibrant, with local and nationally known bands filling dozens of stages every night and a highly respected symphony performing at downtown's beautiful Benaroya Hall. Theatergoing options are also surprisingly impressive. And Seattle is a great place for knocking back a drink: Craft brews have taken over the taps at local bars, and you can get elegant cocktails at swanky lounges, or stiff ones at gritty dives.

NIGHTLIFE

Seattle's approach to alcohol has a lot in common with its approach to coffee: There's a premium put on carefully crafted, small-batch libations, ideally made by someone who's obsessed with the finished product, whether it's beer, wine, or a cocktail. You can sample the results all over town. There's hardly a bar or a restaurant that doesn't have local beer on tap and Washington wine by the glass. Come happy hour, you'll hear cocktail shakers jingling from Pioneer Square to Ballard.

Breweries and Brewpubs

The adjacent Fremont and Ballard neighborhoods are prime areas for craft beer production.

getting a combined Chihuly/Space Needle ticket, or visiting the Space Needle before 10am or after 6pm.

FIRST THURSDAYS

The first Thursday of every month is **free admission day** at many Seattle museums, including the Seattle Art Museum, Museum of History and Industry, Wing Luke Museum, Burke Museum, Henry Art Gallery, Northwest African American Museum, and Nordic Heritage Museum. You can get into The Museum of Flight for free 5pm-9pm. An evening gallery walk also takes place in Pioneer Square every first Thursday, allowing you to check out local art and sip free chardonnay.

THEATER TOURS

The Seattle Theatre Group (206/682-1414, www.stgpresents.org) conducts free tours once a month of **The Paramount** downtown, **The Moore** in Belltown, and **The Neptune Theatre** in the U District, at 10am on the first, second, and third Saturdays, respectively. Just show up at the theater entrance for a 90-minute walk-through of these early-20th-century movie houses, which are now some of Seattle's main live music venues. Call ahead to confirm the schedule.

You can also take free tours of Seattle's two most architecturally striking performance spaces. At downtown's **Benaroya Hall** (206/215-4856, www.seattlesymphony.org/benaroyahall/plan-visit/tours), where the Seattle Symphony plays, tours are conducted on roughly a monthly basis—usually on Monday afternoons, though dates vary. Tours of **McCaw Hall** (206/733-9725, www.mccawhall.com), home of the Seattle Opera and Pacific Northwest Ballet, take place the third Tuesday every month at noon. Sign up by the preceding Friday, either by calling or filling out a form online.

FREMONT, WALLINGFORD, AND GREEN LAKE

Fremont Brewery (1050 N. 34th St., 206/420-2407, www.fremontbrewing.com, daily 11am-9pm), one of Seattle's biggest small-brewery successes, produces a stellar IPA and more than a dozen other beers. Sample them in the tasting room and beer garden, located near the Lake Union waterfront a few blocks west of Gas Works Park.

Schilling Cider House (708 N. 34th St., 206/420-7088, www.schillingcider.com, daily noon-11pm) has the nation's largest selection of ciders on tap, with more than 30 to choose from. Ordering one of their tasting flights will broaden your concept of cider.

You'll find Seattle's largest selection of beer on tap—a staggering 64 choices—at **Brouwer's Cafe** (400 N. 35th St., 206/267-2437, www.brouwerscafe.com, Sun.-Thurs. 11am-midnight, Fri.-Sat. 11am-2am), which occupies an old warehouse that's been repurposed into a comfortable beer hall. They also have 300 bottled beers available, and beer-friendly Belgian cuisine.

BALLARD

An area straddling the Fremont and Ballard neighborhoods is home to **Hale's Ales** (4301 Leary Way NW, 206/782-0737, www.hales-brewery.com, Sun.-Thurs. 11am-10pm, Fri.-Sat. 11am-11pm). Hale's was a microbrewery before they were cool—it opened in 1983—and it's free of the hipster sensibility common to newer places. It has a bar and dining room serving a full menu of pub grub.

Microbreweries have sprung up like weeds in an old warehouse district of eastern Ballard. Two of the best are **Stoup** (108 NW 52nd St., 206/457-5524, www.stoupbrewing.com, Mon.-Thurs. 3pm-9pm, Fri. 3pm-10pm, Sat. noon-10pm, Sun. noon-9pm) and

Populuxe (826B NW 49th St., 206/706-3400, http://populuxebrewing.com, Thurs. 4:30pm-9pm, Fri. 4:30pm-10pm, Sat. noon-10pm, Sun. 1pm-8pm). Both have enthusiastic brewers, unusual beers, and fun tasting rooms that usually have food trucks parked outside.

Cocktail Lounges

Amid the bar scenes of Belltown and Capitol Hill are some distinctive cocktail lounges where mixing drinks is treated as a craft. For these places, atmosphere—usually a little or a lot old-fashioned—is everything.

BELLTOWN

Rob Roy (2332 2nd Ave., 206/956-8423, www.robroyseattle.com, daily 4pm-2am) is the kind of cocktail lounge you'd hope to find in Vegas, all softly lit corners and black-leather barstools. But the skilled, professional bartenders are what really make the place feel classy and cool.

For some Prohibition era ambience, head down the alley between 1st and 2nd Avenues off Blanchard Street and search out the entrance to **Bathtub Gin & Co.** (2205 2nd Ave., 206/728-6069, www.bathtubginseattle.com, daily 5pm-2am). This hideaway evokes a speakeasy with dim lights and lots of gin—there are more than two dozen varieties behind the bar.

CAPITOL HILL

On the west side of Capitol Hill, removed from the Pike-Pine hubbub, **Sun Liquor Lounge** (607 Summit Ave. E, 206/860-1130, www.sunliquor.com, daily 5pm-2am) mixes cocktails using its own gin, vodka, and rum in a pleasant, understated setting.

With a high-ceilinged, dark-paneled room, beautiful glassware, and a library of glowing liquor bottles behind the bar, **Canon** (928 12th Ave., 206/552-9755, www.canonseattle.com, daily 5pm-2am) fills you with nostalgia for a bygone era that in reality was probably never this stylish. The elaborate, award-winning cocktails match the setting, and there's good food too.

A soothing blond-wood interior, squeezed-to-order mixers, and friendly, fastidious bartenders give **Liberty Bar** (517 15th Ave. E, 206/323-9898, www.libertybars.com, 9am-2am) its unique aura: It's a cocktail lounge with the wholesome vibe of a juice bar. It serves coffee in the morning and sushi from noon.

Dive Bars

If you want cheap drinks and no pretensions, Seattle can meet your needs. Its dive bars are vestiges of a time when the city had more grit and a more working-class character, before Microsoft and Amazon and scores of other ambitious tech start-ups made their mark on the city's personality. The fact that many of these bars are stubbornly holding on is a sign that the old days aren't quite over.

BELLTOWN

In a block full of bars on 2nd Avenue, Coney Island-themed **Shorty's** (2222 2nd Ave., 206/441-5449, www.shortydog.com, daily noon-2am) is a lively place that keeps you fortified with hot dogs while you drink. A back room lit by neon beer signs holds more than a dozen pinball machines.

SEATTLE CENTER AND QUEEN ANNE

The Mecca Cafe and Bar (526 Queen Anne Ave. N, 206/285-9728, www.mecca-cafe.com, Sun.-Thurs. 7am-2am, Fri.-Sat. 7am-3am) has been a fixture in Lower Queen Anne since 1929. It's divided into two narrow rooms. One houses a good-quality, no-nonsense diner, and the other is a well-worn barroom where serious drinkers and part-timers cohabitate in peace. Having the diner right on site is a real bonus.

CAPITOL HILL

The dive bars have disappeared from trendy Capitol Hill, but you can pay tribute to the past at the **Comet Tavern** (922 E. Pike St., 206/323-5678, www.thecomettavern.com, daily noon-2am), which was once a filthy place where kids went to earn their punk-rock cred. After getting new ownership and

Blue Moon Tavern

Seattle's dive bar for writers and intellectuals. It was once the preferred watering hole of Theodore Roethke and Tom Robbins, and it's still a comfortable and welcoming place to get a drink. On most nights there's live music.

At the other end of Wallingford, on the cusp of Fremont, **The Pacific Inn** (3501 Stone Way N, 206/547-2967, daily 11am-2am) is a pleasant old bar with nautical decor that's famous for its fish-and-chips.

Wine Bars and Tasting Rooms

Along Post Alley in Pike Place Market you can sample a selection of wines from small Washington vintners at **The Tasting Room** (1924 Post Alley, 206/770-9463, www.winesofwashington.com, Sun.-Thurs. noon-8pm, Fri.-Sat. noon-11pm). They serve themed flights along with many wines by the glass.

No other wine bar pulls off casual sophistication quite like Capitol Hill's **Bar Ferdinand** (1424 11th Ave., 206/693-2434, www.barferdinandseattle.com, Tues.-Fri. 4pm-11pm, Sat.-Sun. 1pm-close). Set away from the street in the middle of Chophouse Row, a mixed-use development, it's an oasis from the Capitol Hill nightlife scene. Twenty wines from small producers the world over are available by the glass, and the creative food menu is a cut above other Seattle wine bars.

At **Le Caviste** (1919 7th Ave., 206/728-2657, www.lecavisteseattle.com, Mon.-Sat. 4pm-midnight), the goal is to transport you to France. It serves only French wine, along with French cheese and charcuterie, all listed in French on big chalkboards. It may feel a little affected, but the setting is casual and bustling, and gregarious servers are eager to translate and provide guidance on drinking and dining options.

Live Music
ROCK AND POP

The days of grunge rock may be over, but Seattle still has a lively music scene. Learn about upcoming shows from the two alternative weeklies, *The Stranger* (www.

---

a facelift in 2014, it's now nicer—with all the good and bad that that implies. Beer is still cheap, and as you sit on a barstool it's not hard to imagine the old divey days.

Linda's Tavern (707 E. Pine St., 206/325-1220, www.lindastavern.com, Mon.-Fri. 4pm-2am, Sat.-Sun. 10am-2am) doesn't quite have the requisite seediness to qualify as a dive bar, but it's a neighborhood institution and a comfortable, unpretentious place to drink, with Western-themed decor, a patio out back, and a kitchen serving burgers, bar food, and a good brunch on the weekend. It has the sad renown of being the last place Kurt Cobain was seen alive in public.

FREMONT, WALLINGFORD, AND GREEN LAKE

Just east of I-5—technically in the U District, but a mile from UW and a stone's throw from Wallingford—**Blue Moon Tavern** (712 NE 45th St., 206/675-9116, www.bluemoonseattle.wordpress.com, Mon.-Fri 2pm-2am, Sat.-Sun. noon-2am,) has a long history as thestranger.com) and *Seattle Weekly* (www.seattleweekly.com).

The greatest concentration of music venues is in downtown and a few blocks north in Belltown. The largest, the 2,800-seat **Paramount** (911 Pine St., 206/682-1414, www.stgpresents.org), is a beautifully restored old movie palace that hosts national acts as well as touring Broadway shows. In Belltown, **The Moore** (1932 2nd Ave., 206/467-5510, www.stgpresents.org), another old movie house, is the Paramount's lower-key cousin. It has a thousand fewer seats but still draws nationally known performers as well as a few headliner comedians.

The biggest downtown venue without theater seating is **The Showbox** (1426 1st Ave., 206/628-3151, www.showboxpresents.com) near Pike Place Market, which has standing-room capacity of about 1,000 and mixes up-and-coming performers with some reunion tours of old cult favorites. Full schedules of rock and other pop music acts are at **The Crocodile** (2200 2nd Ave., 206/441-4618, www.thecrocodile.com), a venerable Belltown rock club; **The Triple Door** (216 Union St., 206/838-4333, www.tripledoor.net), a classy supper club; and **El Corazon** (109 Eastlake Ave. E, 206/262-0482, www.elcorazonseattle.com), a rough-hewn venue between downtown and South Lake Union.

Neumos (925 E. Pike St., 206/709-9442, http://neumos.com), a club-style space with standing-room capacity of about 600, is the main music venue on Capitol Hill. It draws alternative rock and pop performers, and fills out its schedule with DJ nights. Lesser known, edgier rap and rock acts play at **Chop Suey** (1325 E. Madison St., 206/538-0556, http://chopsuey.com).

The Neptune Theatre (1303 NE 45th St., 206/682-1414, www.stgpresents.org), in the U District, is another old movie house—this one with nautical decor—that hosts touring rock and pop acts.

Brick-lined Ballard Avenue has two music clubs, the **Tractor Tavern** (5213 Ballard Ave. NW, 206/789-3599, www.tractortavern.com) and the smaller **Sunset Tavern** (5433 Ballard Ave. NW, 206/784-4880, www.sunsettavern.com, daily 5pm-2am), both of which have regular lineups of indie bands. The Tractor's schedule includes lots of rootsy country and folk performers.

JAZZ AND BLUES

Seattle's jazz and blues subculture congregates at a few clubs spread around the city. **Highway 99 Blues Club** (1414 Alaskan Way, 206/382-2171, www.highwayninetynine.com) is just south of Pike Place Market, and **Tula's Restaurant and Jazz Club** (2214 2nd Ave., 206/443-4221, www.tulas.com) and **Dimitriou's Jazz Alley** (2033 6th Ave., 206/441-9729, www.jazzalley.com) are in Belltown.

Farther off the beaten path, in South Seattle there's the Columbia City jazz club **The Royal Room** (5000 Rainier Ave. S, 206/906-9920, www.theroyalroomseattle.com). To the north in Wallingford, **The Seamonster Lounge** (2202 N. 45th St., 206/992-1120, www.seamonsterlounge.com) is Seattle's home of funk and electronic jazz.

ALL AGES

The **Vera Project** (305 Harrison St., 206/956-8372, www.theveraproject.org) in Seattle Center is an all-ages club that stages live rock acts and also has arts-related classes and activities for teens. They do a good job of booking interesting bands that don't pander to kids.

CLASSICAL AND OPERA

In downtown, sleekly modern **Benaroya Hall** (200 University St., 206/215-4700, www.seattlesymphony.org) is the home of the highly regarded Seattle Symphony and hosts mainstream pop performers looking to show off their classy side.

Gay and Lesbian Bars and Clubs

Capitol Hill has long been Seattle's hub of gay

life. There have been some culture clashes as the neighborhood's straight nightlife scene has grown, but this is still the place to go for gay bar- and club-hopping.

Neighbours (1509 Broadway, 206/324-5358, www.neighboursnightclub.com, Tues.-Thurs. 9pm-2am, Fri.-Sat. 9pm-4am, Sun. 10pm-2am), in operation since 1983, is the granddaddy of Seattle gay clubs. With two levels, an elaborately lit dance floor, and capacity of over 1,000, it's still going strong.

Other popular clubs are **R Place** (619 E. Pine St., 206/322-8828, www.rplaceseattle. com, Mon.-Fri. 4pm-2am, Sat.-Sun. 2pm-2am), which has three floors of dancing, and **Re-bar** (1114 Howell St., 206/233-9873, www. rebarseattle.com, Mon. 7pm-1am, Tues. 7pm-midnight, Thurs. 7pm-2am, Fri.-Sat. 7pm-4am, Sun. 10pm-2:30am), where there are live cabaret-style stage shows. If you're looking for something more along the lines of a gay dive bar, check out **Pony** (1221 E. Madison St., 206/324-2854, www.ponyseattle.com, Mon.-Thurs. 5pm-2am, Fri.-Sun. 3pm-2am).

Seattle's one and only full-time lesbian bar is **The Wildrose** (1021 E. Pike St., 206/324-9210, www.thewildrosebar.com, Mon. 5pm-midnight, Tues.-Thurs. 3pm-1am, Fri.-Sat. 3pm-2am, Sun. 3pm-midnight). Some kind of event is going on almost every night, including karaoke, open-mic poetry readings, and DJs on Friday and Saturday.

Dance Clubs

Seattle probably isn't going to wow you with its club scene, but there are plenty of places to go dancing. The gay clubs in town have busy dance floors, and some live venues such as Neumos and Chop Suey, as well as many bars around town, have DJ nights.

If you're looking for a club with throbbing beats, a large dance floor full of straight twentysomethings, and a VIP section with bottle service, there are two options within walking distance of downtown hotels: Pioneer Square's **Trinity Nightclub** (111 Yesler Way, 206/697-7702, www.trinitynightclub.com, Thurs.-Sat.

9pm-2am) and **Foundation Nightclub** (2218 Western Ave., 206/535-7285, www. foundation-nightclub.com, Wed. and Fri.-Sat. 10pm-2am) just north of Pike Place Market. The Georgetown section of South Seattle is home to the speakeasy-themed dance club **Aston Manor** (2946 1st Ave. S, 206/382-7866, www.astonmanorsea.com, Fri.-Sat. 10pm-2am).

Comedy Clubs

Nationally known performers complement the local talent at **Comedy Underground** (109 S. Washington St., 206/628-0303, http://comedyunderground.com); the downstairs venue in Pioneer Square looks nondescript, but it's Seattle's top comedy club. **Unexpected Productions** (1428 Post Alley, 206/587-2414, www.unexpectedproductions.org), next to the Gum Wall in Pike Place Market, specializes in improv, and in the U District **Jet City Improv** (5510 University Way NE, 206/352-8291, www.jetcityimprov.org) has been making it up as they go along for over two decades.

THE ARTS

There are about a dozen performance venues on the Seattle Center grounds, from a children's theater to an opera house to a football field. They host events throughout the year, but things kick into high gear during the annual **Folklife** and **Bumbershoot** music festivals, held on Memorial Day and Labor Day weekends, respectively.

Opera and Ballet

The Seattle Opera and Pacific Northwest Ballet perform at **McCaw Hall** (321 Mercer St., 206/733-9725, www.mccawhall.com), a beautifully renovated space in Seattle Center.

Live Theater

Seattle has two primary theater companies and several smaller ones that produce diverse and often excellent work. Though there are venues around the city, Seattle Center is the city's theater district, with four separate facilities dedicated to dramatic productions on its grounds and several more nearby.

In its fall-through-spring season the **Seattle Repertory Theatre** (155 Mercer St., 206/443-2222, www.seattlerep.org) stages consistently high-quality productions, mixing classics and new works, with most performances at the 800-seat Bagley Wright Theatre in Seattle Center. **ACT Theatre** (700 Union St., 206/292-7676, www.acttheatre.org), the second major company, has a beautiful multistage space downtown in the restored Eagles Auditorium, next door to the Washington State Convention Center. Its productions are generally more cutting-edge than Seattle Rep's.

Book-It Repertory (305 Harrison St., 206/216-0833, www.book-it.org) follows a novel premise—all of its productions are works of fiction turned into plays. Their performances are at the Center Theatre, in the Armory building in Seattle Center.

Seattle Children's Theatre (201 Thomas St., 206/441-3322, www.sct.org) is the country's second-largest theater for kids. It stages a full season of shows from fall through spring and has its own theater facility, located in Seattle Center north of the Pacific Science Center.

On the Boards (100 W. Roy St., 206/217-9886, www.ontheboards.org) stages contemporary, avant-garde dance, theater, and performance art, with productions that are usually either international in origin or the work of local artists.

FESTIVALS AND EVENTS

Seattle's biggest and best festivals play up an aspect of the local character, from fishing and boating to undressing and getting high.

- **Mid-May-early June:** The **Seattle International Film Festival** (www.siff.net), commonly known as SIFF, takes over local cinemas, showing hundreds of independent movies from around the world,

conducting lectures and discussions, and handing out awards.

- **Memorial Day Weekend:** The free **Northwest Folklife Festival** (www.nwfolklife.org) bills itself as the nation's largest community-powered arts festival. Thousands of musicians, dancers, and craftspeople do their thing at Seattle Center.

- **Saturday nearest summer solstice:** The Fremont neighborhood confirms its freaky status with the **Fremont Solstice Parade** (http://fremontartscouncil.org), which features zany floats, fantastic musicians, and over a thousand naked bicyclists (most adorned in body paint). Anyone with a bike can take part.

- **July: Seafair** (www.seafair.com) is the umbrella term for a month's worth of annual events that include Fourth of July fireworks over Lake Union, a campy pirates' landing on Alki Beach, a torchlight parade through downtown, boat races, daredevil airplane maneuvers by the Blue Angels, an Indian powwow in Discovery Park, and a marathon.

- **Late July:** Alternative/indie/hipster bands take over the Pike-Pine corridor for the weekend-long **Capitol Hill Block Party** (www.capitolhillblockparty.com).

- **Mid-August:** Pot smokers by the tens of thousands congregate at Myrtle Edwards Park along the shores of Elliott Bay for **Hempfest** (www.hempfest.org), a weekend-long pro-marijuana rally and festival that's come to feel almost mainstream since Washington State legalized marijuana in 2011.

- **Labor Day Weekend:** Seattle's biggest music festival, **Bumbershoot** (http://bumbershoot.com), fills Seattle Center with a lineup of (mostly) rock performers that spans generations.

- **Late September/early October:** The **Fishermen's Fall Festival** (www.fishermensfallfestival.org), at the Fishermen's

Terminal on the south end of Salmon Bay, celebrates the return of the fishing fleet from Alaska with lutefisk- and oyster-eating contests, singing of sea chanteys, and a giant salmon barbecue.

- **December: Winterfest** (www.seattle-center.com/winterfest) takes over Seattle Center. There's a skating rink, an elaborate model train and village, and kid-focused entertainment on the weekends. Things wrap up with New Year's Eve fireworks.

Shopping

Different neighborhoods in Seattle have different shopping strengths: Pioneer Square is good for art galleries and home decorating, downtown for department stores and clothing chains, Pike Place Market for food and quirky novelty shops, Capitol Hill for trend-conscious boutiques.

But there are two categories where Seattle shopping is a cut above what you'll find in other U.S. cities—and both of them say something about the nature of the town. The first is outdoor equipment. Given that Seattle is surrounded by so much natural beauty, it makes sense that retailers do a good business preparing people to go out and explore it. The number one stop is the flagship **REI** store in South Lake Union. It's so large and offers such a variety of merchandise that it qualifies as a tourist attraction. Other big-name outfitters include **Patagonia** (2100 1st Ave., 206/622-9700, www.patagonia.com) in Belltown and **North Face** (1023 1st Ave., 206/622-4111, www.thenorthface.com) downtown, and in neighborhoods throughout the city there are smaller independent stores that often specialize in specific types of gear.

The second category is bookstores—Seattle has more of them per capita than any other city in the country. You can attribute that to the short, gray winter days, or to the fact that, according to a study conducted by *Forbes*, Seattle is America's most educated large city. Whatever the reason, a booklover in Seattle is a happy soul. Elliott Bay Book Company on Capitol Hill is nationally renowned, and there are loads of neighborhood stores and specialty shops, including ones dedicated to architecture, cookbooks, children's books, and poetry. In the hometown of the independent bookseller's supposed nemesis, Amazon, bookstores are thriving.

DOWNTOWN AND THE WATERFRONT

There's sort of an old-fashioned feel to shopping downtown. Much like they did half a century ago, midrange to high-end shoppers stroll the streets, particularly in the vicinity of **5th and 6th Avenues** and **Pike and Pine Streets,** looking to fill out their wardrobes. Their choices now consist mainly of national chain stores, from Nike and H&M to Tiffany's and Barney's New York.

Books and Stationery

Paper Hammer (1400 2nd Ave., 206/682-3820, www.paper-hammer.com, Mon.-Sat. 10am-6pm) is a boutique shop that creates and sells hand-bound, letterpress-printed art books and cute, quirky cards and other paper products. It's a place that exemplifies the virtues of exacting traditional craftsmanship.

Malls and Department Stores

The center of the downtown-shopping world is the flagship location of the Seattle-based department store **Nordstrom** (500 Pine St., 206/628-2111, http://nordstrom.com, Mon.-Fri. 9:30am-9pm, Sat. 10am-9pm, Sun. 10:30am-7pm). It sells a large selection of clothing and accessories that fit a range of budgets—though the biggest bargains are next door in Westlake Center's **Nordstrom Rack** (400 Pine St., 206/448-8522, http://nordstrom. com, Mon.-Fri. 9:30am-9pm, Sat. 10am-9pm, Sun. 10am-7pm).

Downtown's two malls sit like bookends on either side of Nordstrom. To the northeast, **Pacific Place** (600 Pine St., 206/405-2655, www.pacificplaceseattle.com) skews toward the pricier chains and has a multiplex movie theater. To the southwest, **Westlake Center** (400 Pine St., 206/467-1600, www.westlake-center.com) struggles a bit to maintain tenants and define an identity. Its main features are the Nordstrom Rack and a food court.

PIKE PLACE MARKET

Amid Pike Place Market's iconic food vendors are some cool and quirky shops. Despite its high profile, the market is vigilant about keeping its tenants local and one of a kind.

Markets and Specialty Foods

There are loads of interesting, unique specialty shops throughout the market. Discovering your own favorites is one of the pleasures of visiting here, but these are a few places to keep an eye out for as you explore:

The market has several ethnic grocery stores selling uncommon imported products and regional specialties. The biggest and longest-established of them is Italian-themed **DeLaurenti Specialty Food & Wine** (145 1st Ave., 206/622-0141, www.delaurenti.com, Mon.-Sat. 9am-6pm, Sun. 10am-5pm), located at the corner of 1st Avenue and Pike Street. It has prosciutto and other cured meats at the deli counter, a great selection of cheese, and ready-to-eat soups and panini.

MarketSpice (85A Pike Pl., 206/622-6340, www.marketspice.com, Mon.-Sat. 9am-6pm, Sun. 9am-5pm) is known for its distinctive cinnamon-orange tea blend—they usually have free samples available. If you're enthusiastic about exotic seasonings, you should also head down the stairs and across Western Avenue to **World Spice Merchants** (1509 Western Ave., 206/682-7274, www.worldspice. com, Mon.-Sat. 10am-6pm, Sun. 11am-6pm),

which has an impressive selection from around the globe and also makes its own blends. The staff is helpful with suggestions for spicing up your barbecues and stews.

The market's fishmongers will freeze fresh fish and ship it home it for you, but an easier way to sample their bounty is to buy some smoked salmon, which you can take with you or eat on the spot. Arguably the best comes from **Pure Food Fish Market** (1511 Pike Pl., 206/622-5765, www.freshseafood.com, daily 7am-6pm), a century-old, family-run operation located in the middle of the Main Arcade.

Down the row from Pure Food, **Chukar Cherries** (1529 Pike Pl., 206/623-8043, www. chukar.com, daily 9am-6pm) sells over a dozen combinations of dried Yakima Valley fruit dipped in chocolate. They'll supply samples to help you settle on a favorite.

The row of buildings on the east side of Pike Place has the market's greatest concentration of food specialty shops. **Bavarian Meats** (1920 Pike Pl., 206/441-0942, http:// bavarianmeats.com, Mon.-Sat. 8am-5:45pm, Sun. 8am-4pm) has been making delicious traditional sausages for over half a century. Be nice to the ladies behind the counter and they might reward you with a hot dog.

Up the street, past the Starbucks, **Beecher's Cheese** (1600 Pike Pl., 206/956-1964, www.beechershandmadecheese.com, daily 9am-7pm) makes its well-balanced Flagship Cheddar and its addictive fresh cheese curds on-site. Kids get a kick out of watching the giant, churning, milk-filled vat in the window.

Farther up Pike Place, among the interior stalls of the Corner Market, **Britt's Pickles** (1500 Pike Pl., 253/666-6686, www.brittslive-culturefoods.com, daily 10am-5:45pm) sells pickles that are a class above what you find on supermarket shelves. There's no vinegar, heating, or pasteurization involved; instead, the cucumbers are fermented in oak barrels, resulting in a fresh, flavorful finished product that's rich in probiotics. Britt's also makes tasty kimchi and sauerkraut—which pairs nicely with a Bavarian Meats sausage.

Books and Maps

Along with a couple of used-book stores, the market is home to **Left Bank Books** (Economy Market, 92 Pike St., 206/622-0195, www.leftbankbooks.com, Mon.-Sat. 10am-7pm, Sun. 11am-6pm), a self-described specialist in radical, anarchist, and antiauthoritarian literature.

On the 1st Avenue side of the market, **Metsker Maps** (1511 1st Ave., 206/623-8747, www.metskers.com, Mon.-Fri. 9am-8pm, Sat. 10am-8pm, Sun. 10am-6pm) has a wonderful selection that includes everything from antiques to detailed road, trail, and topographical maps. They also sell travel-related books.

Kitchen Supplies

An exception to the rule about no chain stores in the market is **Sur La Table** (84 Pine St., 206/448-2244, www.surlatable.com, daily 9am-6:30pm), which, like Starbucks, gets a pass because this is its original location. The generally high-end kitchen-supply shop has lots of obscure cooking tools to go along with its sturdy pots and pans. If you nose around you're likely to discover a few bargains.

Apothecaries

You feel like you're entering another time and place when you cross the threshold of **Tenzing Momo** (Economy Market, 93 Pike St. No. 203, 206/623-9837, www.tenzing-momo.com, Mon.-Sat.10am-6pm, Sun. 10am-7pm), the largest and oldest herbal apothecary on the West Coast. Its old wooden shelves are laden with medicinal products, and the store also sells perfume, jewelry, and other gift items. On most afternoons you can get your cards read.

Novelties and Collectibles

The sometime overlooked **Down Under Arcade,** on the floors below the street-level vendors, is Pike Place Market's treasure chest of curiosities. There you'll find, among other things, **Market Magic** (206/624-4271, www.marketmagicshop.com, Mon.-Sat. 10am-5pm, Sun. 10:30am-5pm), a magicians' supply store; **Golden Age Collectables** (206/622-9799, www.goldenagecollectables.com, Sun.-Thurs. 9:30am-5:45pm, Fri. 9:30am-6:15pm, Sat. 9am-6:15pm), America's oldest comic book shop; and **The Miniature Car Dealer** (206/624-7799, daily 11am-6pm), a shop full of vintage toy cars.

PIONEER SQUARE AND THE INTERNATIONAL DISTRICT

The most interesting shopping in Pioneer Square plays off of the area's historic character. You'll find stores that would seem out of place anywhere other than in the neighborhood's vintage brick buildings.

Pioneer Square is home to about 50 art galleries. A good way to explore them is on the **art walk** (www.firstthursdayseattle.com) held the first Thursday of every month, when there's a party-like atmosphere as many of the galleries open new exhibits.

Books and Stationery

Peter Miller Architectural & Design Books and Supplies (Post Alley, 304 Alaska Way S, 206/441-4114, www.petermiller.com, Mon.-Sat. 10am-6pm) is a sophisticated, modish niche shop with beautiful books as well as stationery and other design-focused items that make stylish gifts.

Clothing and Miscellany

It's hard to categorize **E. Smith Mercantile** (208 1st Ave. S, 206/641-7250, www.esmithmercantile.com, Mon.-Sat. 10am-6pm, Sun. noon-5pm). The front of the shop has the varied selection of an old-fashioned mercantile store, with casual clothes, accessories, packaged food, cosmetics, and housewares. In the back there's a small bar (daily 3pm-10pm) serving craft cocktails. The uniting feature is a retro-hip style that fits in well with the historic neighborhood.

Jewelry and Home Decor

Agate Designs (120 1st Ave. S, 206/621-3063, www.agatedesigns.com, Mon.-Sat.

10am-6pm, Sun. 11am-4pm) sells a wide array of beautiful gems and fossils, some fashioned into jewelry or household bric-a-brac. Visiting the showroom is a little like stepping into a natural history museum.

You get more of that museum feeling at **The Belfry** (309A 3rd Ave. S, 206/682-2951, www.thebelfryoddities.com, Mon.-Fri. 10am-6pm, Sat. 11am-6pm), except here you've moved into the animal gallery. Skeletons sit under bell jars, and stuffed antelope heads hang on the walls alongside posters illustrating the anatomy of exotic animals. Almost all of the pieces are antique, which adds to the Addams Family-esque sense of macabre at one of Seattle's most novel stores.

Art Glass
See glassblowers in action at **Glasshouse Studio** (311 Occidental Ave. S, 206/682-9939, www.glasshouse-studio.com, Mon.-Sat. 10am-5pm, Sun. 11am-4pm), which has been in business since 1971. They sell hand-crafted objects ranging from paperweights to chandeliers.

BELLTOWN
There are some novel shops tucked in amid Belltown's busy restaurants and bars.

Music
Singles Going Steady (2219 2nd Ave., 206/441-7396, Sun.-Mon. noon-6pm, Tues.-Thurs. noon-7pm, Fri.-Sat. noon-8pm) is a gem for collectors of rock vinyl and CDs. They have a large selection of vintage records and memorabilia, primarily punk but also anything that qualifies as 1970s and '80s alternative—such as reggae, rockabilly, and ska.

Outdoor Equipment
When you're prepping for a trek into the wilderness you can pick up fancy gear at REI, Patagonia, or North Face … or you can go to **Federal Army & Navy Surplus** (2112 1st Ave., 206/276-9689, www.gr8gear.com, Mon.-Sat. 9:30am-6pm, Sun. 11am-5pm). It's a good alternative resource for well-priced outdoor

REI's climbing wall

equipment, as well as peacoats, duffel bags, and all kinds of other military miscellany.

SOUTH LAKE UNION
REI, a longtime fixture in South Lake Union, is reason enough for shoppers to visit the neighborhood.

Outdoor Equipment
The 80,000-square-foot flagship store of **REI** (222 Yale Ave. N, 206/223-1944, www.rei.com, Mon.-Sat. 9am-9pm, Sun. 10am-7pm) is the go-to equipment resource for Seattle's outdoor enthusiasts—and that constitutes most of the population. You can get everything you need (including things you didn't realize you needed) for venturing out into the wilds of Washington, from clothes and tents to kayaks and snow-shoes. In addition to the equipment for sale, there are bicycle and ski maintenance shops, gear rental, and even a ranger station where you can get trip-planning advice and purchase park passes. The store's most famous feature is its 65-foot climbing wall. Anyone can use it, but

there's a fee that varies from $15 to $50 depending on how long you climb and whether you have assistance from the staff. Reservations are recommended and can be made online (http://reiclimbingpinnacleseattle.wordpress.com).

CAPITOL HILL

Capitol Hill is Seattle's prime spot for clothing boutiques. Whether you're after something vintage or modern, it's the place to go for a new look and a hip attitude.

Books

Among Seattle's many bookstores, pride of place goes to **Elliott Bay Book Company** (1521 10th Ave., 206/624-6600, www.elliott-baybook.com, Mon.-Thurs. 10am-10pm, Fri.-Sat. 10am-11pm, Sun. 10am-9pm). It occupies an attractive old wood-beamed warehouse. Inside, sturdy cedar shelves are packed with over 150,000 titles covering a broad range of subjects and genres. The knowledgeable, gregarious staff is clearly devoted to the place; if you don't speak to one of them in person you can still get their recommendations through the annotated slips hung along the shelves. There's an upstairs space dedicated to kids' books, author readings are a nearly nightly occurrence, and a cafe with good food and coffee facilitates lingering.

If you need proof that Seattle is nerd heaven, pay a visit to **Ada's Technical Books and Cafe** (425 15th Ave. E, 206/322-1058, www.seattletechnicalbooks.com, Sun.-Thurs. 8am-9pm, Fri.-Sat. 8am-10pm). It's one of Seattle's most attractive bookshops, and it's dedicated to "technical" titles, covering science, computers, math, architecture, and engineering (with, naturally, a sci-fi section as well). The cafe, which occupies a significant part of the space, serves vegetarian meals and coffee. The shop is named for Ada Lovelace, a Victorian-era mathematician (and daughter of the Romantic poet Lord Byron) often considered to be the first computer programmer.

Clothing

Pretty Parlor Vintage Boutique (119 Summit Ave. E, 206/405-2883, http://prettyparlor.com, Mon.-Sat. 11am-7pm, Sun. noon-6pm) is a very pink, very spirited resource for clothing from the 1920s to the 1980s. The items may be used, but they've been carefully chosen and cared for. Though there's a feminine air to the place, it also has a selection of men's clothes.

Le Frock Vintage (613 E. Pike St., 206/623-5339, www.lefrockonline.com, Mon.-Sat 10am-7pm, Sun. noon-6pm) also sells high-quality, high-end used clothes, with a focus on contemporary designer wear.

For something brand new, visit **Veridis** (1205 E. Pike St., 206/402-3789, www.veridis-clothier.com, Tues.-Sun. 11am-7pm), which sells women's and men's casual wear from independent, often international designers that you won't find anywhere else in the city.

THE U DISTRICT

Shops along University Way (commonly known as **the Ave.**) in the heart of the U District are aimed mainly at students on a budget. Just northeast of campus, **University Village** is a completely different animal—it's a large, upscale mall.

Books

UW's **University Bookstore** (4326 University Way NE, 206/634-3400, http://ubookstore.com, Mon.-Fri. 9am-8pm, Sat. 10am-7pm, Sun. noon-5pm) is the place where students buy their textbooks, but it's also a large, full-service bookstore with a helpful staff and a good selection of travel and local-history titles. There are also lots of UW souvenirs.

Clothing

The Ave. has a couple of places where you can make used-clothing finds. **Red Light Vintage & Costume** (4560 University Way NE, 206/545-4044, www.redlight-vintage.com, Mon.-Sat. 11am-8pm, Sun. 11am-7pm) is choosy about its merchandise, which means you pay a little more and have to hunt a little less for good-quality pieces.

You can comparison shop down the street at **Buffalo Exchange** (4530 University Way NE, 206/545-0175, www.buffaloexchange.com, Mon.-Sat. 10am-9pm, Sun. 11am-8pm), a large outlet of the national used-clothing chain.

Malls

University Village (NE 45th St. and 25th Ave. NE, 206/523-0622, http://uvillage.com, Mon.-Sat. 9:30am-9pm, Sun. 11am-6pm) is a sprawling open-air mall filled primarily with high-end chain stores and some good restaurants. You feel like you're in the suburbs here—really ritzy suburbs. There are stands full of loaner umbrellas in case you encounter rain as you stroll from Eddie Bauer to Sephora.

FREMONT, WALLINGFORD, AND GREEN LAKE

The commercial areas in the residential neighborhoods north of the ship canal mainly serve the day-to-day needs of locals, but they also have some shopping treasures.

Books

Seattle's poetry bookshop, **Open Books** (2414 N. 45th St., 206/633-0811, www.openpoetrybooks.com, Tues.-Sat. 11am-6pm, Sun. noon-4pm) in Wallingford, is a great place to discover new poets and find obscure volumes.

Outdoor Equipment

Evo (3500 Stone Way N, 206/973-4470, www.evo.com, Sun.-Thurs. 11am-7pm, Fri.-Sat. 10am-8pm), located a few blocks to the northwest of Gas Works Park, started as a retailer of skiing and snowboarding equipment and has expanded to include other

adrenaline sports—surfing, skateboarding, mountain biking, and wakeboarding—as well as apparel. Skiing and snowboarding are still their main thing; the selection is great and the staff members know their stuff (though it helps to speak "bro" when interacting with some of them).

Novelties and Collectibles

Archie McPhee (1300 N. 45th St., 206/297-0240, http://archiemcpheeseattle.com, Mon.-Sat. 10am-8pm, Sun. 10am-7pm) in Wallingford is essentially a prankster's supply shop. It sells hundreds of gag gifts, toys, and random weird things you're unlikely to find anywhere else. A screaming pickle? Underpants candy? That's just some of the tamer stuff.

BALLARD
Music

Ballard's **Sonic Boom** (2209 NW Market St., 206/297-2666, www.sonicboomrecords.com, Mon.-Sat. 10am-10pm, Sun. 10am-7pm) is known primarily for its selection of indie rock, but it stocks a wide range of music on vinyl and CD. It was named one of America's great record stores by *Rolling Stone.*

Outdoor Equipment

Old Ballard's **Ascent Outdoors** (5209 Ballard Ave. NW, 206/545-8810, https://ascentoutdoors.com, Mon.-Wed. and Sat. 10am-7pm, Thurs.-Fri. 10am-8pm, Sun. 10am-6pm) rents mountaineering and snow-sports gear and sells good-quality secondhand equipment and apparel for many kinds of outdoor activities, including hiking, biking, camping, and skiing. It also stocks some new stuff. You can often find good deals on the clothing discount rack.

Sports and Recreation

Seattle residents are an active group. The city's extensive park system accommodates hiking, biking, and running, and the waters are good for kayaking, paddleboarding, and, when the conditions are right, swimming.

PARKS
Myrtle Edwards Park

Olympic Sculpture Park's shoreline path leads north into **Myrtle Edwards Park** (3130 Alaskan Way, 260/684-4075, www.seattle.gov/parks, 24 hrs.). The 1.25-mile section of path is popular with runners, walkers, and cyclists, who are drawn by the beautiful views and quiet setting. This is a good spot to get in a jog if you're staying nearby (you can work your way up the waterfront), and picnic tables and a rock-strewn beach make it also a good location for a relaxed picnic.

Green Lake and Woodland Parks

North Seattle's favorite destinations for outdoor recreation are adjacent **Green Lake Park** and **Woodland Park** (both 206/684-4075, www.seattle.gov/parks, Green Lake 24 hrs., Woodland 4am-11:30pm), which essentially make up one 415-acre park. The centerpiece is Green Lake, which comprises 259 acres and has 2.8 miles of shoreline. The wide path around the lake is hugely popular with walkers, joggers, cyclists, and skaters. If you want to see what the face of Seattle looks like, come here on a pleasant weekend afternoon—you'll encounter babies, senior citizens, and everyone in between, including a large cross-section of the city's dog population.

South of the lake there are playing fields, a track, a skate park, tennis courts, and a nine-hole pitch-and-putt golf course (206/632-2280, open March through October, first come first served, $8 greens fee). Aurora Avenue, one of Seattle's major north-south thoroughfares, divides the western half of Woodland Park from the rest of the parkland. This section holds Woodland Park Zoo.

Golden Gardens Park

Along with Alki Beach in West Seattle,

Golden Gardens Park

Golden Gardens Park (8498 Seaview Pl. NW, 206/684-4075, www.seattle.gov/parks, daily 4am-11:30pm, free) is the main spot Seattleites head to for a classic beachgoing experience (minus the swimming, unless you're willing to brave chilly waters). Located at the northwest corner of Ballard along Shilshole Bay, it has a long sand-and-pebble beachfront, as well as a wetland area at its north end with a short trail from which you're likely to see ducks, turtles, and an occasional heron. There are picnic sites, a playground, a playing field, and plenty of space for volleyball.

The biggest attraction, though, is the view over Puget Sound to the Olympic Mountains. In summer the beach fills every evening with an audience there to witness the spectacular sunset. Arrive early if you want to snag one of the dozen fire pits. Having supper on the sand and watching the sun go down is a classic Seattle experience.

BICYCLING

There's a large population of cyclists in Seattle. Follow their lead only if you're an experienced urban cyclist yourself. While riding is popular, it's also challenging and potentially dangerous. Seattle is hilly. As a pedestrian, you notice the steep ascent from Elliott Bay to downtown, but as a cyclist you also feel the longer climbs that are found almost everywhere you go. Seattle is also congested, and getting more so. There's a tense relationship between cars and cyclists, even when both have the best intentions.

For a more peaceful ride your best option is the **Burke-Gilman Trail,** which is long and in many places lovely. Other bike-friendly routes are **Elliott Bay Trail,** which has its southern end near Safeco Field and goes along the waterfront through the Olympic Sculpture Park and Myrtle Edwards Park, ending near the cruise ship terminal. It's only about 3.5 miles, but you can take Gilman Avenue up to the Chittenden Locks, cross over there into Ballard, and pick up the Burke-Gilman Trail to Golden Gardens. Further afield, the path along **Alki Beach** in West Seattle is a nice

six-mile ride. From the intersection of Harbor Avenue and Florida Street it runs along the shore to Alki Point Lighthouse.

Bike Tours and Rentals

Seattle Cycling Tours (714 Pike St., 206/356-5803, www.seattle-cycling-tours.com) leads daily tours of downtown ($55) and ventures farther afield to Fremont and Ballard ($89), South Seattle ($89), and Bainbridge Island ($140). It also rents bikes ($59/day); you need to arrange for rentals in advance and coordinate pick-up and drop-off times around the tour schedule.

The best-situated vendor for rentals if you want to ride the Burke-Gilman Trail is **Recycled Cycles** (1007 NE Boat St., 206/547-4491, www.recycledcycles.com, Mon.-Fri. 10am-7pm, Sat.-Sun. 10am-6pm), located in the U District along Lake Union, just south of the trail. It has a large selection of rental bikes, priced at $40-60 a day, $60-90 for two days.

RUNNING AND WALKING

The city's most popular place for runners and walkers is the pleasant 2.8-mile path around **Green Lake.** There are separate lanes for pedestrians and people on wheels (bikes, skateboards, etc.), but things can still get crowded—it's great for people-watching, but not as great if you want to get into a rhythm and zone out while you run. Runners looking for more peace can take the 4.5-mile unpaved path around the park's perimeter. There's also a track across the road to the south of the lake.

Another good running and strolling option is the **Burke-Gilman Trail.** You can pick it up at any point; starting at Gas Works Park, where there's a parking lot, and heading east is a good strategy. If you're staying downtown, the most convenient place to log a few miles is the **Elliott Bay Trail,** which is also popular with cyclists.

BOATING
Lake Union

Lake Union and the surrounding segments of the ship canal are great for kayaking and

The Burke-Gilman Trail

The Burke-Gilman Trail is a major pathway for nonmotorized traffic through the Seattle neighborhoods north of the ship canal. It was initiated in the 1970s along the route of an abandoned railway line, making it one of the nation's first "rail to trail" conversions. (Thomas Burke and Daniel Gilman led the group of investors who built the line in the late 19th century, hence the name.) It has expanded several times and now runs almost 19 miles—with one gap along the way—from Ballard to Bothell, a satellite town at the north end of Lake Washington.

The western end of the trail starts at Golden Gardens Park and runs down to the Chittenden Locks, where you hit the gap—frequently referred to as the missing link—of 1.4 miles. (Businesses in Ballard have blocked efforts to close the gap, but it may happen in the coming years.) The trail resumes at NW 45th Street and 11th Avenue NW (by the big Fred Meyer store) and continues unobstructed along the waters of the Fremont Cut, past Gas Works Park, through the University of Washington campus, and eventually up the western shore of Lake Washington, terminating at Bothell's Blyth Park. If you want to go farther, from there you can pick up the Sammamish River Trail, which follows the path of its namesake river to Marymoor Park in the town of Redmond.

The trail undergoes identity shifts as it runs its course, passing through waterfront areas, residential and business districts, and woodland. Traveling it by bike is an enjoyable way to experience several aspects of the city, with opportunities to stop along the way.

The trail is also a good practical alternative to driving, and thousands of Seattleites use it for that purpose every day. Bike traffic can get heavy during rush hours, so if you're planning a leisure ride it's best to do it at midday or on the weekend. Also keep in mind that cyclists share the path with runners, walkers, and skaters. If you're biking, give the pedestrians a wide berth. If you're a runner looking for a trail, the Burke-Gilman is a good option. The varied landscape makes things interesting, and the bikers who use it regularly are good about trail etiquette.

One final word of caution: The trail intersects with roads at a couple of points, and while cars are supposed to yield to the traffic on the trail, it doesn't always work that way. Approach with care.

all types of boating—there are places along the shore that rent canoes, rowboats, paddleboards, and sailboats as well as kayaks. Be aware, though, that the lake is a busy place. You'll be sharing the water with motorboats, cruise ships, industrial barges, crew teams, and floatplanes taking off and landing.

There's a variety of ways to get out onto Lake Union. The **Center for Wooden Boats** (1010 Valley St., 206/382-2628, cwb.org) at the south end of the lake rents vintage rowboats, pedal boats, and sailboats ($30-40/hr.). **Moss Bay Rowing & Kayak Center** (1001 Fairview Ave. N, 206/682-2031, http://mossbay.net) at the south of the lake, **Northwest Outdoor Center** (2100 Westlake Ave., 206/281-9694, www.nwoc.com) on the western shore, and **Agua Verde** (1307 NE Boat St., 206/545-8570, http://aguaverde.com) to the northeast on Portage Bay all rent paddleboards and kayaks for rates of around $20 an hour. All

of them also conduct guided tours. Moss Bay and Northwest Outdoor Center have boating lessons; Agua Verde is also home to a popular Mexican restaurant.

The best rental deal near Lake Union is at the **University of Washington Waterfront Activities Center** (3710 Montlake Blvd. NE, 206/543-9433, www.washington.edu/ima/ waterfront), located by the UW football stadium just east of the Montlake Cut. They rent rowboats and canoes for $12 an hour, with discounts for students, alumni, and school employees.

Union Bay
You can have a quieter experience if you head east of Lake Union to the southwest corner of Union Bay. There you can float among the turtles, ducks, herons, and beavers in the wetlands at the north end of **Washington Park Arboretum.**

Green Lake

You can take it easy on relatively small, placid Green Lake. On the eastern shore of the lake, **Green Lake Boat Rentals** (http://greenlake-boatrentals.net, 206/527-0171) rents rowboats, kayaks, canoes, and paddleboards, all for $22 an hour. Learn crew rowing by taking a class at the **Green Lake Small Craft Center** (206/684-4074, www.greenlakecrew.org).

Alki Beach

Another popular boating location with rental concessions is Alki Beach in West Seattle, from where you boat on Puget Sound. **Alki Kayak Tours** (1660 Harbor Ave. SW, 206/953-0237, www.kayakalki.com) gets you onto Puget Sound with kayak tours and rentals of kayaks ($15-38/hr. depending on day and size), paddleboards ($15-17/hr.), and motorized fishing boats ($80/2 hrs.).

SWIMMING

Swimming in Seattle's waters is a dicey proposition. From mid-June through August there are lifeguards at numerous public beaches managed by the city parks department (206/684-4075, www.seattle.gov/parks), but many of the beaches have one shortcoming or another. The Puget Sound waters at **Alki Beach** in West Seattle and **Golden Gardens** in Ballard are always frigid. There's a beach at the southwest corner of **Lake Union** that's all right for wading, but the lake is too busy with boat traffic to make for a relaxing swim. **Green Lake** is calm and has two designated swimming areas, but when the water warms up it's prone to algae infestations.

Your best options are on the east side of town in Lake Washington. It takes a while for the big lake to get warm, but toward the end of summer the water is fine. **Madison Park Beach** (4201 E. Madison St.), due east of Washington Park Arboretum, is the most convenient swimming area to the central city. **Matthews Beach Park** (5100 NE 93rd St.) to the north is the largest swimming beach in the city. It's located along the Burke-Gilman Trail, so you can coordinate a swim with a bike ride or a run. To the south at **Seward Park** (5900 Lake Washington Blvd. S) you can make a day of it with a hike in the woods, a picnic, and a swim.

SPECTATOR SPORTS

Seattle's two professional sports stadiums sit side by side in SoDo, just south of Pioneer Square and west of the ID.

The **Mariners** (www.mariners.com) baseball team plays at **Safeco Field** (1250 1st Ave. S, 206/346-4000, http://seattle.mariners.mlb.com/sea/ballpark). Tours of the field ($12) run 2-3 times a day during the season and twice every day except Monday the rest of the year. Note that the name Safeco Field officially changes at the end of the 2018 season, when Safeco Insurance gives up its naming rights.

Next door, the football **Seahawks** (www.seahawks.com) and soccer **Sounders** (www.soundersfc.com) play at **CenturyLink Field** (800 Occidental Ave. S, 206/381-7555, www.centurylinkfield.com). There are 90-minute tours ($12, youth 4-12 $5) of CenturyLink Field three times daily from June through August, and twice a day on Friday and Saturday for the rest of the year.

Seattle doesn't have a men's professional basketball team (the departure of the Sonics left a wound on the civic psyche that hasn't healed), but the women's team, the **Storm** (http://storm.wnba.com), competes at KeyArena in Seattle Center. The **University of Washington Huskies** (www.gohuskies.com) field the full assortment of college sports teams, including a major football program.

Food

TOP EXPERIENCE

According to Charles Cross, iconic Seattle journalist and biographer of Kurt Cobain, "Food has become the new rock and roll in Seattle. Our chefs are the current grunge stars."

In restaurant kitchens all over the city, tattooed twentysomethings prepare inventive, meticulously executed meals. They're learning from and competing with an older generation of ambitious chefs who for more than a decade have been raising the bar for Seattle dining. The most successful have built multi-restaurant mini-empires that boldly encompass a variety of cuisines. Go to a restaurant run by Tom Douglas, Ethan Stowell, Matt Dillon, Maria Hines, or Renee Erickson for food taken seriously.

That doesn't mean that Seattle restaurants are precious foodie temples. There's something for everyone, from pizzerias to Asian diners to old-school steak houses. Proximity to the water means fish is abundant; dozens of places compete for the titles of best clam chowder and best fish-and-chips.

Coffee

Seattle's coffee obsession deserves special mention. Maybe it's the cloudy weather, short winter days, or long hours put in by many tech workers; whatever the reason, there's more coffee consumption—and there are more coffee shops—here than in any other U.S. city. In between ubiquitous Starbucks are scores of independent cafes, most with skilled baristas pulling the espresso. Turn your morning caffeine fix into an adventure, getting to know Seattle's neighborhoods by visiting their coffee shops. A place exists to fit every mood, from homey to high-tech, laid-back to obsessively exacting.

Happy Hour

You may associate happy hour primarily with cheap early-evening drinks, but in Seattle it's a significant dining phenomenon. Virtually every restaurant with a bar has one, and while reduced-price drinks are part of it, the main attraction is the food, usually a selection of items from the dinner menu sold at a significant discount. If you don't mind eating early or late, this is a great way to experience some wonderful restaurants for a bargain price. Most happy hours run 4pm-6pm, though some start as early as 3pm and run as late as 7pm. A few places also have late-night happy hours, with discounts available starting at 9pm or 10pm.

DOWNTOWN

The restaurants set amid the office towers downtown tend to be showy, expense-account places. Every high-end hotel in the area has a restaurant where you're likely to get a good meal, but you can't help sensing a corporate committee vetted each item on the menu.

Coffee

Its modest walkup window gives **Monorail Espresso** (520 Pike St., 206/422-0736, Mon.-Fri. 6am-6pm, Sat. 8am-6pm, Sun. 9am-5pm) the charm of an underdog, but this place has been doing a thriving business since 1980 thanks to its smooth, rich espresso and friendly service. The burnt crème latte is a favorite among the specialty drinks. The shop also serves pastries from Macrina Bakery. There are a few seats on the sidewalk, so you can sit and watch the regulars grabbing their drinks on the way to work. Note that this is a cash-only establishment.

Eclectic

Purple Cafe and Wine Bar (1225 4th Ave., 206/829-2280, www.purplecafe.com, Mon.-Thurs. 11am-11pm, Fri. 11am-midnight, Sat. noon-midnight, Sun. noon-11pm, $13-39) has one of the most striking dining rooms

Best Breakfasts by Neighborhood

Like to start your day with eggs, bacon, and a stack of pancakes? Seattle does classic breakfast with the best of them, but it also gives you appealing alternatives. Here's a short list of great places to start your day.

- **Lowell's, Pike Place Market:** Lowell's is a market standby for good diner food with a view.

- **The London Plane, Pioneer Square:** This lovely, light-filled corner shop and restaurant is Seattle's most stylish place for breakfast.

- **Jade Garden, International District:** When the dim sum urge hits, Jade Garden is the place to get your fix.

- **Macrina Bakery, Belltown:** Along with tasty baked goods, this neighborhood gathering place serves egg sandwiches, quiche, and fruit-laced hot cereal.

- **The 5 Spot, Queen Anne:** Seattleites have an enduring love affair with The 5 Spot's red flannel hash, blueberry pancakes, and biscuits and gravy.

- **Serious Biscuit, South Lake Union:** The biscuits here come topped a dozen ways, from peanut butter and banana to ham hock and collards.

- **Ba Bar, Capitol Hill:** It doesn't open until 10am, so sleep late and then drop by Ba Bar for congee, the quintessential Asian breakfast porridge.

- **Portage Bay Café, U District:** The food here hits the Seattle trifecta: organic, sustainable, and delicious.

- **Cafe Besalu, Ballard:** Besalu is famous for its croissants, but it offers a full array of sweet and savory pastries.

in the city, with picture windows and a giant column of wine racks rising 20 feet to the ceiling, Wine is Purple's center of attention—there are more than 75 choices available by the glass, 25 three-glass flights, and a 60-page list of bottles, including unpretentious notes to help make the experience less overwhelming. The menu offers comfort-food classics, including sandwiches, steaks, and a popular lobster mac and cheese.

Located at the base of the luxe Harbor Steps apartment tower, **Lecosho** (89 University St., 206/623-2101, http://lecosho.com, $27-38) is a quiet oasis in the midst of the Pike Place/downtown hubbub. Locally sourced meats are the focus here, grilled or roasted in the open kitchen or transformed into house-made sausages and charcuterie. Lecosho also makes its own pasta and often pairs it with seafood or vegetables. If you're looking for Matt from Matt's in the Market, this is where you'll find him: Co-owner Matt Janke was the original chef at the lauded Pike Place restaurant that still bears his name.

Pan-Asian

Other places in town offer more authentic Asian cuisine, but **Wild Ginger** (1401 3rd Ave., 206/623-4450, www.wildginger.net, Mon.-Sat. 11:30am-11pm, Sun. 4pm-9pm, $15-34) earns its position as a Seattle institution by serving consistently good food in an attractive dining room for prices that are a bargain compared to many of downtown's high-end alternatives. The menu consists primarily of Chinese, Vietnamese, and Thai dishes. The fragrant duck, served with steamed buns, is a standout, and the noodle options are reliably satisfying.

Seattle's Kid-Friendly Chains

When it comes to kids' basic food groups, Seattle has things covered. These first-rate local chain establishments are as popular with adults as with children.

BURGERS

Dick's Drive-In (www.ddir.com, daily 10:30am-2am, $3-6) has been a Seattle favorite since 1954. It's classic fast food—hamburgers, fries, shakes, sodas, and ice cream—priced like McDonald's but fresher and tastier. The original location is in Wallingford (111 NE 45th St., 206/632-5125), and there are branches in Queen Anne (500 Queen Anne Ave. N, 206/285-5155) and Capitol Hill (115 Broadway Ave. E, 206/323-1300) as well as in the outer suburbs. There's limited outdoor seating, but this is the kind of meal that's okay to eat in the car, and all of the locations have retro drive-in charm.

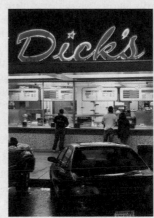

Dick's Drive-In

PIZZA

For a sit-down meal, **Tutta Bella Neapolitan Pizzeria** (http://tuttabella.com, Sun.-Thurs. 11am-10pm, Fri.-Sat. 11am-11pm, $10-18) satisfies both kids and adults. The full bar and the wood-fired pizzas, made to conform to strict Italian regulations, appeal to grown-up tastes, but on any given evening half the tables may have diners under the age of 10 (who also, clearly, appreciate authentic Neapolitan pizza). There are Seattle locations in Wallingford (4411 Stone Way N, 206/633-3800), South Lake Union (2200 Westlake Ave., 206/624-4422), and Columbia City (4918 Rainier Ave. S, 206/721-3501), as well as two east of Lake Washington in Bellevue and Issaquah.

ICE CREAM

The ice cream shop most likely to have lines out the door is **Molly Moon's** (www.mollymoonicecream.com, daily noon-11pm), which, like Tutta Bella, manages to add some sophistication to a kid favorite while still satisfying the kids. The crowds come here for salted caramel, balsamic strawberry, and a dozen other creative flavor combinations. There are eight locations, including in Queen Anne (321 W. Galer St., 206/457-8854), Capitol Hill (917 E. Pine St., 206/708-7947), and Wallingford (conveniently halfway between Dick's and Tutta Bella, 1622 N. 45th St., 206/547-5105).

Steak

The Metropolitan Grill (820 2nd Ave., 206/624-3287, www.themetropolitangrill.com, Mon.-Thurs. 11am-10pm, Fri. 11am-10:30pm, Sat. 4pm-11pm, Sun. 4pm-10pm, $29-89) fills the role of Seattle's old-school palace of beef. It plays the part well, with a brass- and mahogany-filled dining room, chummy but polished waiters, and steaks so well prepared they almost seem worth the steep price tag. You can economize by coming here for lunch or, better yet, the weekday 3pm-6pm happy hour.

PIKE PLACE MARKET

While there are other things to buy at Pike Place Market, food has always been the main attraction. There are French, Russian, and Chinese bakeries, Turkish, Mexican, and Filipino lunch counters, and a first-rate, no-nonsense oyster bar, among many other shops and stalls. When it comes to sit-down meals, the market has 30 places to choose from—everything from greasy-spoon diners to a high-end farm-to-table restaurant. Diners are primarily tourists, which may explain why the restaurants here tend to be more conservative than elsewhere in town. Most have been around for a while, have mastered their specialties, and aren't going to stray from their script. That's not a bad thing—you're going to eat well almost anywhere you go. But if you want to find Seattle's most innovative restaurants, look to other neighborhoods.

Coffee

In the heart of the market you can join the line at the **original Starbucks** (1912 Pike Place, 206/448-8762, daily 6am-9pm), but there are also some less famous local places nearby that take their coffee seriously. It's worth a detour half a block up Pike Street to visit **Seattle Coffee Works** (107 Pike St., 206/340-8867, www.seattlecoffeeworks.com, Mon.-Fri. 6:30am-7pm, Sat. 7:30am-7pm, Sun. 8am-6pm), which makes some of the city's most esteemed coffee from single-source beans it roasts itself. Along with the standard coffee bar there's also a "slow bar" where you can taste and compare coffees from around the world, made using six different brewing methods.

Seafood

Despite the name, **Steelhead Diner** (95 Pine St., 206/625-0129, www.steelheaddiner.com, daily 11am-10pm, $15-52) serves something more ambitious than diner fare. The fish-focused menu has some pricier entrées that seem too fancy for their own good, but the simpler Southern-influenced options, like the oyster po'boy and the fried chicken, are winners. (It's no surprise the executive chef cut his teeth in New Orleans.) Crab and shrimp tater tots are a highlight of the appetizer list.

Creative Contemporary

An accomplished kitchen and a great location make ★ **Matt's in the Market** (94 Pike St. No. 32, 206/467-7909, www.mattsin-themarket.com, Mon.-Sat. 11:30am-2:30pm and 5:30pm-10pm, $32-48) a star among Pike Place restaurants. The casual but romantic dining room is on the top floor of the Corner Market building, with large arched windows facing the neon Public Market sign across the street. The changing menu is rooted in a farm-to-table sensibility—count on several perfectly cooked fish entrées along with meat options (there's not much for vegetarians), all prepared with sure-handed creative touches—such as arctic char with fermented

Matt's in the Market

chilies, mushroom broth, and scallop bottarga. Dinner at Matt's is pricey. Lunch ($14-18), which consists mainly of sandwiches, is a more affordable option.

Bakeries

Many market visitors like to start the morning with a baked good, and they have several good choices. For coffee and a croissant there's **Le Panier** (1902 Pike Pl., 206/441-3669, www.lepanier.com, Mon.-Sat. 7am-6pm, Sun. 7am-5pm), which lends some Parisian sophistication to the market and has more seating than the other bakeries. Things are a little homier at **The Crumpet Shop** (1503 1st Ave., 206/682-1598, www.thecrumpetshop.com, Mon. and Wed.-Thurs. 7am-3pm, Fri.-Sun. 7am-4pm), where the namesake griddle cake gets dressed up with sweet and savory toppings. And it's takeaway only at the tiny but very popular **Piroshky Piroshky** (1908 Pike Pl., 206/441-6068, http://piroshkybakery.com, daily 8am-7pm), which sells Russian pastries filled with everything from smoked salmon to rhubarb.

Diners

Sitting side by side in the Main Arcade are two Pike Place landmarks, **Lowell's** (1519 Pike Pl., 206/622-2036, www.eatatlowells.com, Mon.-Sat. 7am-9pm, Sun. 7am-8pm, $16-31) and the **Athenian Inn** (1517 Pike Pl., 206/624-7166, www.athenianseattle.com, Mon.-Sat. 8am-9pm, Sun. 8am-4:30pm, $10-29). Lowell's is more expensive and more polished, but they're both salty old diners with decent food—including classic seafood dishes and ample breakfasts—and fabulous views of Elliott Bay. Prices are marked up to reflect the prime location, but you can get better deals at happy hour. If you go then, you'll be joined at the bar by market vendors sharing an after-work beer.

Filipino

For an only-in-the-market experience, find your way to **Oriental Mart Grocery and Kitchenette** (1506 Pike Pl., 206/622-8488, Mon.-Sat. 9am-6pm, Sun. 10am-5pm, $7-14) in the Corner Market area. You don't have to have been to the Philippines to sense that the little lunch counter here is serving up authentic Filipino home cooking; the playfully imperious women in the kitchen and their happy expat customers don't seem like they'd settle for imitations. Salmon-tip soup, chicken wings, and pork adobo are menu favorites. Just remember: wait for eye contact before ordering.

French

Cafe Campagne (1600 Post Alley, 206/728-2233, www.cafecampagne.com, Mon.-Thurs. 11am-10pm, Fri. 11am-11pm, Sat. 8am-11pm, Sun. 8am-10pm, $17-26) provides a timeless bistro experience in the midst of the market. The menu consists of French classics (steak frites, roast chicken, cassoulet). The waitstaff bustles about in traditional garcon garb of black vests and white aprons, and the dining room gives off a warm glow. This is a good spot for weekend brunch.

Italian

There's the air of a speakeasy at **The Pink Door** (1919 Post Alley, 206/443-3241, www.thepinkdoor.net, Mon.-Thurs. 11:30am-10pm, Fri.-Sat. 11:30am-11pm, Sun. 4pm-11pm, $18-39). It doesn't have a sign, though between the door (painted pink) and the large dining room along Post Alley, finding it isn't difficult. Most nights there's entertainment, which could come in the form of a jazz band or a trapeze artist dangling from the 20-foot ceiling. Amid the burlesque style, the menu is a short collection of refined but unpretentious Italian dishes, including fish fresh from the market and pasta with sauces that change according to the season.

Japanese

After selling his Belltown restaurant in 2014, Shiro Kashiba, Seattle's venerable sushi master, opened a new place in Pike Place Market. Not surprisingly, the experience at **Sushi Kashiba** (86 Pine St., 206/441-8844, http://sushikashiba.com, daily 5pm-10pm, $40-95) has a lot in common with that at Shiro's—exceptional fish, including some exotic options, is meticulously prepared in traditional style. If you score a place at the sushi bar you'll be served by the affable Kashiba himself (on nights when he's working), and if you sit at a table you'll have a view overlooking the market. Tables can be reserved; bar seats cannot.

PIONEER SQUARE AND THE INTERNATIONAL DISTRICT

There's good Asian cuisine to be found all over Seattle, but the ID is still the place to go for an unpretentious, inexpensive East Asian meal. You get more bang for your buck here than anywhere else in the city (with the possible exception of the U District). Pioneer Square, meanwhile, is one of the hottest restaurant neighborhoods in the city.

Coffee

Across the street from the Klondike gold rush museum, long-established **Zeitgeist Coffee** (171 S. Jackson St., 206/583-0497, http://zeitgeistcoffee.com, Mon.-Fri. 6am-7pm, Sat. 7am-7pm, Sun. 8am-6pm) is a roomy, attractively paneled cafe that doubles as an art gallery.

On the Occidental Mall, **Caffè Umbria** (320 Occidental Ave. S, 206/624-5847, www.caffeumbria.com, Mon.-Fri. 6am-7pm, Sat. 7am-6pm, Sun. 8am-5pm) is an elegant Italian-style coffeehouse run by a third-generation roaster with roots in the old country. Along with coffee they serve pastries, panini, gelato, beer, and wine.

Creative Contemporary

Half of the relatively small space at **Damn the Weather** (116 1st Ave. S, 206/946-1283, www.damntheweather.com, Mon.-Thurs. 11am-midnight, Fri. 11am-2am, Sat. 4pm-2am, Sun. 4pm-11pm, $14-22) is given over to the bar, where creative cocktails are mixed, and the menu ostensibly consists of bar food—but it's bar food of the highest level, whether you're in for a snack, such as fried fava beans or lingcod

gravlax, or something substantial, like roast chicken or spaghetti Bolognese.

It's hard to sum up **The London Plane** (300 and 322 Occidental Ave. S, 206/624-1374, www.thelondonplaneseattle.com, Mon. 8am-5pm, Tues.-Fri. 8am-9pm, Sat. 9am-9pm, Sun. 9am-3pm, $11-22). The creation of local star chef Matt Dillon is a market by day where you can buy pastries, coffee, groceries, and flowers, or sit down to breakfast or lunch offerings that are simple preparations of high-quality, rigorously local ingredients. In the evening Tuesday-Saturday, it serves dinner following the same philosophy, with a short but slightly more sophisticated menu.

Markets

Giant ★ **Uwajimaya** (600 5th Ave. S, 206/624-6248, www.uwajimaya.com, Mon.-Sat. 8am-10pm, Sun. 9am-9pm) has such an extensive selection of items from all over Asia that it's not just a supermarket—it's a foodie sightseeing destination. Along with row after row of noodles, sauces, and sake, there's a fish counter to rival the vendors at Pike Place, a food court, housewares department, and bookstore with shelves full of manga.

Chinese

Tai Tung (655 S. King St. 206/622-7372, www.taitungrestaurant.com, Mon.-Thurs. 11am-10:30pm, Fri.-Sat. 11am-midnight, Sun. 11am-10pm, $8-14) is a local institution where Seattleites come to relive meals from their childhood. Stepping through the door feels like making a trip back to the 1970s, and the long menu includes Americanized preparations that were common to that era. Soups are consistently good, the almond chicken is a standout, and you can get more authentic dishes by ordering from the specials posted on the wall.

For first-rate dim sum in the ID, check out **Jade Garden** (424 7th Ave. S, 206/622-8181, daily 9am-2:30am, $7-12). It's a little grungy, but the food is cheap and good, with a large selection that includes classics like shrimp dumplings and steamed pork buns.

The Starbucks Experience

Seattle is the birthplace of Starbucks, and fans of the world's biggest coffee chain have some fun places to explore here. In Pike Place Market the original Starbucks (1912 Pike Place, 206/448-8762, daily 6am-9pm) is a hugely popular nostalgia trip—when the market gets busy you can wait 30 minutes under the cafe's original, R-rated sign for a cup of coffee. There's no seating or food, but you can buy a souvenir mug.

Serious devotees head up to Capitol Hill, where the Starbucks Reserve Roastery and Tasting Room (1124 Pike St., 206/624-0173, http://roastery.starbucks.com, daily 7am-11pm) is the world's largest and most refined Starbucks location. You're greeted at the door by friendly maître d's who explain the workings of the sophisticated bar, where they serve small-batch coffee that's been roasted using the giant, Rube Goldberg-like contraption at the back of the store. This place is Willy Wonka's factory for coffee lovers.

Farther north in Capitol Hill is Roy Street Coffee and Tea (700 Broadway, 206/325-2211, www.roystreetcoffee.com, daily 6:30am-10:30pm), which says in small print on its drink menu, "Inspired by Starbucks." More significantly, it's owned by Starbucks—this "undercover" store is where the company tests new concepts, including the Clover brewing system and the addition of tea, wine, and beer service. It's classy and comfortable.

If you're thirsting for a Starbucks like the one back home, you won't have to look far. There are over 400 locations in the greater Seattle area.

German

Cavernous Altstadt (209 1st Ave. S, 206/602-6442, www.altstadtseattle.com, Sun.-Mon. 11am-10pm, Tues.-Thurs. 11am-midnight, Fri.-Sat. 11am-2am, $10-18) manages to be both a traditional German beer hall and a hipster hangout. The rough-ground, house-made sausage and exceptional fries satisfy diners across the sociological spectrum, especially when washed down with one of the dozen German beers on tap.

Indian

Seattle doesn't have a lot of Indian food options, but it has a standout in Nirmal's (106 Occidental Ave. S, 206/683-970, www.nirmalseattle.com, Mon.-Sat. 11am-2pm and 5:30pm-10pm, $16-38). Nirmal Monteiro, who earned acclaim as a chef in Mumbai, draws on traditionally Indian as well as local Pacific Northwest ingredients to create his menu, which is served in an exposed-brick dining room that's classic Pioneer Square.

Italian

The restaurant with the biggest cult following in Seattle barely qualifies as a restaurant at all. From its modest storefront Salumi (309 3rd Ave. S, 206/621-8772, www.salumicuredmeats.com, Mon. takeout only 11am-1:30pm, Tues.-Fri. 11am-3:30pm, $10-17) sells Italian-style cured meats and sandwiches, along with an occasional soup or pasta. It's open only for weekday lunch; rain or shine, devotees line up, waiting as much as 45 minutes for porchetta, meatball, sausage, and finocchiona sandwiches—to name a few of the favorites. There's limited seating in the back, but most customers take their orders to go.

Another delicious Italian-style lunchtime option is Il Corvo (217 James St., 206/538-0999, www.ilcorvopasta.com, Mon.-Fri. 11am-3pm, $11-17), where the only thing served is fresh, handmade pasta, topped with seasonal sauces that change daily. The emphasis on high-quality ingredients and simple preparations captures the spirit of authentic Italian cooking.

Japanese

For over a century ★ Maneki (304 6th Ave. S, 206/622-2631, www.manekirestaurant.com, Tues.-Sun. 5:30pm-10:30pm, $13-25) has been serving up traditional Japanese home cooking. You can get good sushi here, but what distinguishes this spot is the cooked dishes: The miso-glazed black cod collar and deep-fried agedashi tofu are stellar, and adventurous eaters will find only-in-Japan novelties among the daily specials. Maneki's prices are moderate and its reputation big, meaning most nights the place is packed; reservations are essential.

If you can't get a table at Maneki, try around the corner at **Tsukushinbo** (515 S. Main St., 206/467-4004, daily 5:30pm-10pm and Tues.-Fri. 11:45am-2pm, $7-20), a tiny, unpretentious, bargain-priced sushi bar that's also adept at cooked dishes. Ramen, served only on Friday at lunch, is worth a special trip, but get there early—they always sell out.

Vietnamese

Green Leaf (2800 1st Ave., 206/448-3318, www.greenleaftaste.com, daily 11am-10pm, $9-15) is the humble star of Vietnamese cuisine in Seattle. The prices are low, the service is friendly, and the bamboo-accented dining room is attractive. Foremost, of course, are the classic Vietnamese dishes—spring rolls, salads, noodles—which are consistently fresh and delicious. A second location is in Belltown (2800 1st Ave., 206/448-3318, daily 11am-2am).

BELLTOWN
Pacific Northwest

The name for **Local 360** (2234 1st Ave., 206/441-9360, www.local360.org, Mon.-Thurs. 11am-10pm, Fri. 11am-11pm, Sat. 9am-11pm, Sun. 9am-10pm, $14-42) comes from the restaurant's commitment to sourcing ingredients from within a 360-mile radius whenever possible. The result is hearty, homey food, including deviled eggs, pork roast, and fried chicken. (There are fish specials, but most of the sourcing is from the land.) It's a satisfying, unpretentious menu served in a two-level dining room done up in farmhouse style.

Local star chef Tom Douglas, who presides over more than a dozen Seattle restaurants, started his empire two decades ago with the

Dahlia Lounge (2001 4th Ave., 206/682-4142, www.dahlialounge.com, Mon.-Fri 11am-2pm and 5pm-10pm, Sat. 9am-2pm and 5pm-10pm, Sun. 9am-2pm and 5pm-9pm, $21-52). It's still going strong, serving something to please everyone while keeping the focus on foods of the Pacific Northwest. There's plenty of seafood, including crab cakes and an Asia-influenced raw bar, lots of fresh vegetables, and pork, duck, and steak all cooked over an open flame. The busy but softly lit dining room works for both business dinners and romantic meals.

Bakeries

Macrina Bakery (2408 1st Ave., 206/448-4032, www.macrinabakery.com, daily 7am-6pm, $5-12), one of the leading bread suppliers for Seattle restaurants, operates this popular retail outlet and cafe where you can get sophisticated pastries and sandwiches. It functions as a local gathering place the way that neighborhood coffee shops do in other parts of town.

French

Le Pichet (1933 1st Ave., 206/256-1499, www.lepichetseattle.com, daily 8am-midnight, $22-25) has the feel of a casual Parisian bistro. It serves traditional French fare, but features dishes that don't typically make it to American French restaurants. If you're up for something unusual—say, roasted salmon with lovage broth and semolina dumplings—check out this avant-garde restaurant. You can also get lunch and breakfast here seven days a week.

Italian

Pasta is the draw at casually hip **Tavolàta** (2323 2nd Ave., 206/838-8008, www.ethanstowellrestaurants.com, daily 5pm-11pm, $17-30). Ten varieties are made fresh daily and matched with traditional Italian ingredients, such as rigatoni with sausage and tomatoes or ricotta-filled ravioli with sage, walnuts, and brown butter. The menu also includes grilled meats and a long list of appetizers. It's a boisterous place, with most seating at a long communal table.

Japanese

Shiro Kashiba, Seattle's most esteemed sushi chef, left the restaurant that bears his name in 2014 after two decades at the helm, but **Shiro's** (2401 2nd Ave., 206/443-9844, www.shiros.com, daily 5:30pm-10:30pm, $30-75) continues to practice his exacting, traditional ways. Expect a pleasant but minimally decorated dining room, premium-quality fish, soy sauce and wasabi applied by the chef, and a selection straight out of Tokyo—some exotic fish choices, but no zany combination rolls. There are also cooked dishes, among which the geoduck sautéed in butter and broiled black cod get especially high marks. You can reserve a table, but seats at the sushi bar are first come, first served.

SEATTLE CENTER AND QUEEN ANNE

In the middle of everything at the Seattle Center is the refurbished **Armory** (305 Harrison St., 206/684-7200), which, along with housing the Children's Museum, serves as a food court featuring local vendors. There are over a dozen dining options, including pizza, tacos, bagels, burgers, and, of course, coffee.

At the top of Queen Anne Hill the main commercial street has an array of good neighborhood restaurants where locals outnumber tourists. At the bottom of the hill the demographic is reversed, thanks to the proximity of Seattle Center.

Coffee

Seattle Center is home to one of the city's most distinctive coffee shops, **La Marzocco Cafe & Showroom** (472 1st Ave. N, 206/388-3500, www.lamarzoccousa.com, Mon.-Thurs. 7am-6pm, Fri. 7am-7pm, Sat. 8am-7pm, Sun. 8am-6pm). The Italian company La Marzocco is a leading manufacturer of espresso makers, and the cafe doubles as a showroom for its sleek machines. The cafe's greatest claim to fame,

though, is its location: It's in the performance space of KEXP, Seattle's iconic indie radio station, and the station's offices and broadcast booth next door help give the cafe an added buzz. To top it off, there's a new featured coffee roaster every month.

Caffè Ladro (www.caffeladro.com), a local favorite with eight locations, originated in Upper Queen Anne (2205 Queen Anne Ave. N, 206/282-5313, Mon.-Fri. 5:30am-8pm, Sat.-Sun. 6am-8pm) and has a branch down the hill in Lower Queen Anne (600 Queen Anne Ave. N, 206/282-1549, Sun.-Thurs. 5:30am-8pm, Fri.-Sat. 5:30am-9pm). These comfortable, paneled cafes aren't flashy, but Ladro roasts its own coffee and makes its own baked goods, and both locations have a dedicated following. The signature drink is the Medici—a mocha with a twist of orange.

Seafood

Taylor Shellfish Farms (124 Republican St., 206/501-4442, http://tayloroysterbars.com, daily 11:30am-10pm, $12-24), one of the largest seafood producers in the Pacific Northwest, runs a bright, modern oyster bar across the street from KeyArena and Seattle Center. Along with half a dozen or so varieties of raw oysters on the half shell, the menu includes oysters cooked four ways, prawn cocktail, steamed clams, and raw geoduck. If you love shellfish you'll be happy here, or at their two other Seattle locations, in Pioneer Square (410 Occidental Ave.) and on Capitol Hill (1521 Melrose Ave.).

Creative Contemporary

For half a century Seattleites have been celebrating special occasions at ★ **Canlis** (2576 Aurora Ave. N, 206/283-3313, www.canlis.com, Mon.-Sat. 5:30pm-10pm, Fri.-Sat. 5pm-10pm, $105-150 prix fixe), on the edge of Queen Anne just south of the Aurora Avenue bridge. This is the one place in town with a dress code—jackets are requested for men, and you'd feel out of place without one in the elegant, mid-century-modern dining room overlooking Lake Union. It's a setting where Frank Sinatra and the Rat Pack would feel at home, but what keeps it from seeming dated is the innovative and exceptionally good food. The menu sounds simple—conventional seafood, beef, and poultry options—but the execution is of the highest order. And the service is legendary; the staff manages to be highly polished and genuinely caring at the same time.

Cajun

New Orleans-inspired **Toulouse Petit** (601 Queen Anne Ave. N, 206/432-9069, www.toulousepetit.com, daily 8am-2am, $16-48) is Lower Queen Anne's most hopping place for a high-end meal. The long menu includes numerous seafood and steak options, with some dishes getting a Cajun/creole treatment. Late hours and a fantastic happy hour menu keep the bar busy, and you can come back in the morning for beignets at breakfast.

Diners

The 5 Spot (1502 Queen Anne Ave. N, 206/285-7768, www.chowfoods.com, Mon.-Fri. 8am-11pm, Sat.-Sun. 8am-3pm and 5pm-midnight, $13-23) is a handsome old diner with a cute theme: its ongoing "American Food Festival Series," in which part of the menu changes regularly to highlight the cuisine of a particular state. This is one of Seattle's most popular breakfast spots. On weekends, there's usually a line out the door waiting for biscuits and gravy, red flannel hash, and blueberry pancakes. Don't confuse The 5 Spot, in Upper Queen Anne, with Belltown's **5 Point Cafe** (415 Cedar St., 206/448-9991, http://the-5pointcafe.com, $10-15), a 24-hour diner and dive bar with the motto "Alcoholics serving alcoholics since 1929."

Italian

How to Cook a Wolf (2208 Queen Anne Ave. N, 206/838-8090, www.ethanstowellrestaurants.com, daily 5pm-11pm, $17-31) takes its name from a book by legendary food writer M. F. K. Fisher that was meant to help Europeans in the midst of World War II make the most of their meager provisions. Chef-owner Ethan Stowell adapts that sensibility here by creating sophisticated, Italian-inspired dishes that have only a few ingredients. The emphasis is on fresh pasta, and the atmosphere is subdued and refined. Stowell also owns **Tavolàta** in Belltown (as well as a dozen other local restaurants).

SOUTH LAKE UNION

The growing complex of Amazon offices in South Lake Union has spawned a restaurant scene. Many are the creations of restaurateurs capitalizing on earlier success elsewhere in the city.

Coffee

For a caffeine fix with South Lake Union's Amazonians, head to **Zoka Coffee** (351 Boren Ave., 206/624-1927, www.zokacoffee.com, Mon.-Fri. 7am-6pm), run by one of Seattle's premium roasters. About a block away is another local favorite, **Caffè Ladro** (400 Fairview Ave. N, 206/ 906-9334, www.caffeladro.com, Mon.-Fri. 6am-6pm).

Italian and Pizza

One of local dining mogul Tom Douglas's most successful concepts is **Serious Pie** (401 Westlake Ave., 206/436-0050, www.seriouspieseattle.com, Sun.-Thurs. 11am-10pm, Fri.-Sat. 11am-11pm, $17-19), which serves char-crusted personal pizzas with regional and artisanal toppings (fennel sausage, Penn Cove mussels, mushrooms with truffle cheese). There are also locations in Belltown (316 Virginia St.) and Capitol Hill (401 Westlake Ave. N), but this one is the most appealing. The dining room is on the 2nd floor, overlooking Douglas's baking facility. On the ground floor there's a bar with 22 beers on tap and pizza service, and **Serious Biscuit** (Mon.-Fri. 7am-3pm, Sat.-Sun. 9am-3pm), where for breakfast or lunch you can get biscuits topped a dozen ways.

Douglas's Italian restaurant, **Cuoco** (10 Terry Ave. N, 206/971-0710, http://cuoco-seattle.com, Mon.-Thurs. 11:30am-9pm, Fri.

11:30am-10pm, Sat. 4:30pm-10pm, $19-34), has a big, paneled, candlelit dining room and a menu of creative appetizers, simply prepared meats, and handmade pasta.

Mediterranean

Mbar (400 Fairview Ave. N, 206/457-8287, www.mbarseattle.com, Mon.-Tues. 4pm-9pm, Wed.-Thurs. 4pm-10pm, Fri. 4pm-11pm, Sat. 5pm-11pm, Sun. 5pm-9pm, $21-34) makes the most of its office-rooftop location with a deck and a dining room that both have views of the Space Needle and Lake Union. It's a beautiful setting for dining on Mediterranean- and Middle Eastern-influenced cuisine that, in classic Seattle style, touts its use of local and regional ingredients.

CAPITOL HILL

Though it's rivaled by Belltown and increasingly Ballard and Pioneer Square, Capitol Hill is Seattle's number one neighborhood for hip dining and nightlife. On weekend evenings the streets can be crowded with revelers. Even if that's not your scene, you can duck inside one of the inventive restaurants and have a pleasurable experience.

Coffee

Capitol Hill is home to the roastery and flagship coffeehouse of **Caffè Vita** (1005 E. Pike St., 206/709-4440, www.caffevita.com, Mon.-Fri. 6am-11pm, Sat.-Sun. 7am-11pm), one of Seattle's most successful independent coffee chains, with six locations in town and branches as far away as Los Angeles and New York. (They also sell beans to many local restaurants.) Drinks are expertly made, and the sizable seating area has a classy feel, with wood walls and floor stained a matching blond. At the back you can peer into the roasting room.

Toward the north end of Capitol Hill, **Victrola Coffee** (411 15th Ave. E, 206/325-6520, www.victrolacoffee.com, Mon.-Sat. 6am-10pm, Sun. 6am-9pm) roasts its own beans and feels like the neighborhood's living room. It has comfortable seating, local art

for sale on the walls, and weekly free cuppings (comparative coffee tastings).

Creative Contemporary

Poppy (622 Broadway E, 206/324-1108, http://poppyseattle.com, Sun.-Thurs. 5pm-10:30pm, Fri.-Sat. 5pm-11:30pm, $28-32) applies the Indian concept of the *thali* (a single entrée consisting of multiple small dishes) to seasonal Northwest cuisine. There are several *thalis* to choose from, and they reflect culinary influences from all over the map; you might end up with osso bucco, pineapple soup, grilled endive, black-eyed peas, tamarind green beans, and pickled carrots all on one plate. It's handled with impressive finesse, resulting in bright, delicious meals. The dining room is filled with blond wood and clean, Scandinavian-style design. Poppy also has one of the city's most creative happy hour menus.

No place epitomizes Seattle's hipster dining culture better than ★ **Sitka & Spruce** (1531 Melrose Ave., 206/324-0662, www.sitkaandspruce.com, Mon.-Fri. 11:30am-2pm and 5pm-10pm, Sat.-Sun. 10am-2pm and 5pm-10pm, $20-35), which occupies a former auto repair shop at the back of Melrose Market. It's zealous about using locally sourced ingredients produced in traditional, sometimes archaic ways. It employs the stove as a last resort, preferring other cooking methods—smoking, curing, pickling, and especially, roasting in its wood-burning oven. And it creates dishes that go out of their way to defy convention. It's managed to become one of Seattle's most lauded restaurants because what ends up on your plate is, more often than not, as delicious as it is unusual. The ever-changing menu isn't easily summarized, but expect lots of local produce, meats that are flavorful but seldom dominate the meal, and at least one ingredient you've never heard of.

Markets

Melrose Market (1501-1535 Melrose Ave., 206/661-7979, http://melrosemarketseattle.com, various hours) is a magnet for hip foodies. Under one roof at the western edge of

Capitol Hill you get a butcher, a cheese vendor, a wine shop, a produce and flower stand, and, at the back, one of the neighborhood's best restaurants, **Sitka & Spruce**—all places firmly dedicated to high-quality, local, sustainable, handcrafted products. Step outside, and next door there's a **Taylor Shellfish Farms** outlet (1521 Melrose Ave., 206/501-4321, Sun.-Thurs. 11am-9pm, Fri.-Sat. 11am-10pm) where you can buy seafood to take home or sit down and slurp back a few oysters. Two doors down, at the corner of Melrose and Pike, is the impressive if not particularly hip **Starbucks Reserve Roastery** (1124 Pike St., 206/624-0173, daily 6:30am-11pm).

Italian

This decade has seen a proliferation of sophisticated Italian restaurants in Seattle. For these places, Italian is, more than anything, an attitude about cooking: using high-quality local ingredients and preparing them in an exacting but unostentatious style.

The fanciest of them all is **Altura** (617 Broadway E, 206/402-6749, www.alturarestaurant.com, Tues.-Thurs. 5:30pm-10pm, Fri.-Sat. 5pm-10pm, $137 prix fixe), whose menu favors the bold. Various pasta sauces use anchovy, oxtail, bone marrow, and porcini mushrooms; other dishes feature duck liver and pork cheek. The tasting menu consists of 10-15 courses, and a meal here typically lasts 2-3 hours.

You get a similar sensibility, without the tasting-menu investment, at **Cascina Spinasse** (1531 14th Ave., 206/251-7673, www.spinasse.com, Sun.-Thurs. 5pm-10pm, Fri.-Sat. 5pm-11pm, $26-45). The seasonal menu focuses on the cuisine of the northern Italy's Piedmont region, and care is taken to stick to culinary traditions. Pasta sauces could include beef ragu or gorgonzola cream, and for meat you might have braised rabbit and grilled rib eye to choose from.

Thai

In the spirit of doing just a few things but doing them well, **Little Uncle** (1523 E. Madison St., 206/549-6507, www.littleuncle-seattle.com, Tues.-Sat. 11am-3pm and 5pm-9pm, $12-15) has a menu of only 10 items, including steamed pork buns, pad thai, *khao soi gai* (chicken curry with egg noodles), and a dessert special. Seating is limited to a counter and a few small tables; many customers take their orders to go. With this kind of approach, the food needs to be good. Legions of fans can attest that it is.

Sitka & Spruce

Vietnamese

Vietnamese street food meets industrial chic at ★ **Ba Bar** (550 12th Ave., 206/328-2030, www.babarseattle.com, Sun.-Thurs. 10am-2am, Fri.-Sat. 10am-4am, $12-19), located south of the Pike-Pine corridor at a point where Capitol Hill segues into the Central District. The menu is a mix of noodles, rotisserie meats, and a long list of appetizers that constitute a Vietnamese answer to dim sum. It's all addictively delicious, with a striking variety and complexity of flavors. You can start the day here with coffee and congee and end it with a late-night bowl of delectable, fortifying pho. There's also a location in South Lake Union (500 Terry Ave. N, 206/623-2711, Tues.-Sat. 11am-11pm, Sun.-Mon. 11am-9pm).

THE U DISTRICT

University Way—aka the Ave.—in the heart of the U District is lined with bargain ethnic restaurants catering to students. Diners looking for something tasty on the cheap will find more choices here than anywhere else in the city.

Coffee

For a classic bohemian cafe vibe, as well as some Seattle coffee history, turn down the alley off of 42nd Street between University Way and 15th Avenue to **Cafe Allegro** (4214 University Way NE, 206/633-3030, http://seattleallegro.com, Mon.-Fri. 6:30am-10pm, Sat. 7:30am-10pm, Sun. 8am-10pm). In operation since 1975, this is Seattle's oldest espresso bar. The original owner, Dave Olsen, was a collaborator with Howard Schultz of Starbucks. Olsen developed the espresso roast that Starbucks still uses, and Allegro's laid-back atmosphere was the inspiration for the megachain's decor scheme. Today it's scruffy by Starbucks standards, with exposed brick walls and simple wood furnishings. This is the type of place where poets and philosophy students meet to debate the meaning of life.

Diners

Portage Bay Café (4130 Roosevelt Way NE, 206/547-8230, www.portagebaycafe.com, daily 7:30am-2:30pm, $14-18), at the west end of the U District, is an ideal place for students to take visiting parents. The mid-priced menu is high-quality diner food with a conscience—organic, sustainable eggs, pancakes, sandwiches, and salads—served in a bustling but attractive dining room, with patio seating in fair weather. Locations are also in South Lake Union (391 Terry Ave. N, 206/462-6400) and Ballard (2821 NW Market St., 206/783-1547), with the same hours as the U District outpost.

Middle Eastern

If you're looking for a classic student fill-up joint, you won't do better than **Aladdin Gyro-cery** (4139 University Way NE, 206/632-5253, daily 10am-2:30am, $6-10). The gyro and vegetarian platters are delicious, substantial, and cheap, the service is friendly, and there's a cute (though not very well ventilated) dining room in the back.

Thai

The open kitchen takes up half the space in tiny, intense **Thai Tom** (4543 University Way NE, 206/548-9548, Mon.-Fri. 11:30am-9pm, Sat. 11:30am-10pm, Sun. noon-9pm, $10-16); if you sit at the counter you feel like your eyebrows could be singed by the flaming woks. For decades the seared noodles coming from those woks have made this place the most popular Thai spot on the Ave.

FREMONT, WALLINGFORD, AND GREEN LAKE

The area in the Green Lake neighborhood known as **Tangletown,** on 55th and 56th Streets between Meridian Avenue and Kirkwood Place, has a cluster of good restaurants. It's convenient to Green Lake Park and Woodland Park Zoo, as well as being a pleasant area to visit if you want to see how locals go about their daily lives.

Stone Way, the unofficial border between Wallingford and Fremont, has an impressive range of dining options, from the hip to the homey. There are also good neighborhood restaurants, including half a dozen Japanese places, on **45th Street,** Wallingford's main commercial thoroughfare.

The Fremont neighborhood's commercial activity follows two paths, starting at the Fremont Bridge: north up **Fremont Avenue** and west along **36th Street,** which turns into Leary Way. Most of the restaurants along these two roads are neighborhood joints, but among them there are some places worth seeking out.

Coffee

Among the hundreds of Seattle coffeehouses, **MiiR Flagship** (3400 Stone Way N, 206/566-7207, www.miir.com, Mon.-Fri. 7am-9pm, Sat. 8am-9pm, Sun. 8am-7pm) stands apart for its unique store, where you can buy a bicycle, a water bottle, a beer, or a cup of coffee. It's all tied together by a socially conscious business model: you purchase a bike, MiiR gives a bike to a person in need in a developing country; you get a cup of coffee, a person in need gets clean drinking water for a day. Philanthropic virtues aside, MiiR provides well-balanced espresso and a mod, clean-lined space to drink it in, with an outdoor seating area.

Connoisseurs consider **Milstead and Co.** (770 N. 34th St., 206/659-4814, http://milsteadandco.com, Mon.-Fri. 6am-6pm, Sat.-Sun. 7am-6pm) one of America's finest coffeehouses. The reason is that it's a rare multi-roaster cafe, sourcing beans from several suppliers and carefully selecting which ones it uses to make its drinks. Coffees are switched out daily, giving each visit the potential for a new experience. Friendly baristas will talk you through your options.

A former Winchell's doughnut stop on upper Fremont Avenue is the unlikely setting for Seattle's most authentic European-style neighborhood bar. Stop in at **Vif** (4401 Fremont Ave. N, 206/557-7357, www.vifseattle.com, Mon. 7am-4pm, Tues.-Fri. 7am-7pm, Sat. 8am-6pm, Sun. 8am-5pm) for well-made espresso drinks, tasty snacks, and a vigorously vetted list of all-natural, mostly European wines.

Seafood

Ivar's is one of Seattle's longest-standing culinary institutions, with over a dozen restaurants in the area serving clam chowder, grilled salmon, and baskets of deep-fried seafood. Its showpiece is **Ivar's Salmon House** (401 NE Northlake Way, 206/632-0767, www.ivars.com, Sun.-Thurs. 11am-9pm, Sat. 11am-10pm, $20-36). It's located in a replica Indian cedar longhouse, complete with canoes hanging from the ceiling, set along the northern shore of Lake Union. The food here is more varied and elaborate than at other Ivar's locations, but it's still old-school seafood fare, highlighted by alder-smoked salmon and tasty chowder. The large happy hour menu is available all night. When the weather is nice, sitting out on the deck is a quintessential Seattle pleasure.

Most restaurants in Seattle dedicated to seafood are either traditional fish houses or oyster bars. An exception is ★ **RockCreek** (4300 Fremont Ave. N, 206/557-7532, www.rockcreekseattle.com, Mon.-Fri. 4pm-midnight, Sat.-Sun. 9am-midnight, $27-38). You'll get the same inventiveness found in other ambitious kitchens around town, but without the dedication to local sources. RockCreek's fish comes from all over the map; the result is a selection unlike anything you'll find elsewhere in the city, including Mexican grouper (with caramelized onions and sherry), Maine monkfish (with mushrooms and red wine), and Hawaiian mackerel (with dates and almonds). RockCreek's mastery of the delicate art of cooking fish comes through in every dish.

Creative Contemporary

The Whale Wins (3506 Stone Way N, 206/632-9425, www.thewhalewins.com, Mon.-Sat. 5pm-10pm, Sun. 5pm-9pm, $25-45) is a rustic-chic restaurant from local star chef Renee Erickson. The short menu features meats and vegetables, in most cases cooked in a wood-fired oven, along with bar-food-style nibbles—nuts, olives, pickles, and toasts.

Burgers

For a hamburger joint with more substance and variety than Dick's Drive-In (or one that, unlike Dick's, has a liquor license), your best bet is **Uneeda Burger** (4302 Fremont Ave. N, 206/547-2600, www.uneedaburger. com, daily 11am-9pm, $8-14). Things are still plenty straightforward. Pick your burger from among 10 options, and stake out a seat in the pleasant dining area or outside at the picnic tables. Most of the burgers are heavily laden with toppings. Take, for instance, the Madame (as in croque madame): a beef patty topped with Black Forest ham, gruyere, mayo, shoe-string potatoes, and a fried egg. It's decadent, delicious, and impossible to wrap your mouth around. Silverware and napkins are essential.

Donuts

Organic, vegan donuts? Fried in oil sourced from an ecofriendly producer? Welcome to Seattle! **Mighty-O Donuts** (2110 N. 55th St., 206/547-0335, www.mightyo.com, Mon.-Fri. 6am-5pm, Sat.-Sun. 7am-5pm) are good in every sense of the word. Kids (and adults) scarf them down with delight. Along with this

Tangletown location there are also Mighty-O shops in Ballard (1555 NW Market S.) and Capitol Hill (1400 12th Ave.).

Japanese

Kisaku (2101 N. 55th St., 206/545-9050, www. kisaku.com, Mon. and Wed.-Sat. 11:30am-2pm and 5pm-10pm, Sun. 5pm-10pm, $19-26) sits inconspicuously in the midst of Tangletown and has the decor of a generic mid-priced Asian restaurant; it almost dares you to underestimate it. But this is one of Seattle's best sushi restaurants, and the packed dining room proves that it doesn't need bells and whistles to attract a crowd. Esteemed chef Ryu Nakano leads an adept team that delivers delicious fish as well as an appealing array of appetizers.

Korean

Joule (3506 Stone Way N, 206/632-5685, www.joulerestaurant.com, Mon.-Fri. 5pm-10pm, Sat.-Sun. 10am-2pm, 5pm-10pm, $16-35) uses Korean cuisine as the starting point for creating food that highlights the bounty of the Pacific Northwest. The menu is divided into basic categories: "rice and noodle," "vegetable," "steak," "other than steak." Dishes like rice cakes with chorizo and mustard greens

RockCreek

achieve an impressive balance between inventive cooking and comfort food. You're meant to share. One of the six-ounce steaks, for instance, isn't really enough to make a meal, but order three or four dishes for two people and you'll be in good shape.

BALLARD

In the past decade, the old low-rise brick buildings that line Ballard Avenue have been transformed from industrial supply stores and dive bars into trendy restaurants and boutiques, with a few holdovers hanging in there from the former days. Walk down the street on any evening and you'll have a couple of dozen restaurants to choose from, all vying for hipster cred—which means creative food and decor at best, and imitations of both at worst. This strip is the most concentrated example of the changes that are going on throughout Ballard. What once was a modest middle-class neighborhood has become a destination.

Coffee

In the heart of the Old Ballard business district, **Caffè Fiore** (5405 Leary Ave. NW, 206/706-0421, www.caffefiore.com, Mon.-Fri. 6am-6pm, Sat.-Sun. 7am-6pm) is a top-quality, organic-only espresso bar with stylishly rustic furniture and dramatic chandeliers.

Just off Market Street in a largely residential part of East Ballard, little **Slate Coffee Bar** (5413 6th Ave. NW, 206/701-4238, www.slatecoffee.com, Mon.-Thurs 7am-5pm, Fri. 7am-6pm, Sat. 8am-6pm, Sun. 8am-5pm) has distinguished itself as one of Seattle's most earnest and exacting cafes. They roast their own coffee, and along with standard espresso drinks they offer "deconstructed" espresso and milk, tasting flights, and nontraditional brewing methods.

Seafood

Renee Erickson, one of Seattle's trendsetting chefs, is the driving force behind **The Walrus and the Carpenter** (4739 Ballard Ave. NW,

206/395-9227, www.thewalrusbar.com, daily 4pm-10pm, small plates $11-16), a French-inflected seafood restaurant that was a sensation when it opened in 2010 and continues to pack in diners. The main attraction is a choice selection of raw oysters, complemented by small plates primarily of fish (scallop crudo, grilled sardines) with a few meaty options (lamb carpaccio, steak tartare). As those examples indicate, this isn't your traditional fish house. Reservations aren't accepted; if you can't get a table, you might try **Staple and Fancy** (206/789-1200, www.ethanstowellrestaurants.com, daily 5pm-11pm, $17-33), a trattoria located in the same building and run by another local star chef, Ethan Stowell.

If you're after a more old-school fish meal, one of your best options is **Ray's Boathouse** (6049 Seaview Ave. NW, 206/789-3770, www.rays.com, daily 11:30am-10pm), set on Shilshole Bay half a mile north of Chittenden Locks. Downstairs is a classy, high-end restaurant ($38-62) where tables by the window feel like they're practically floating on the water. Upstairs the cafe ($15-59) is more casual but has the same fantastic bay views, best seen from the outdoor deck.

Creative Contemporary

To experience what makes the current Seattle restaurant scene distinctive and satisfying, you can't do much better than ★ **Brimmer and Heeltap** (425 NW Market St., 206/420-2534, www.brimmerandheeltap.com, Sun.-Mon. and Wed.-Thurs. 5pm-11pm, Fri-Sat. 5pm-midnight, $28-34), a neighborhood restaurant in a primarily residential area of East Ballard (across the street from Slate Coffee Bar). The short, seasonal menu consists of quirky comfort food. Familiar dishes are done with creative twists, like grilled pork shoulder with apple kimchi, and coriander-crusted tuna with a pungent North African herb sauce. You get the feeling the chef has license to take chances that wouldn't fly in a restaurant downtown, and the results are usually delicious. The setting is casual and warm, with a few playful touches. It's a comfortable place to hang out, especially on the partly covered back patio, which has a fire pit and twinkles with candlelight after dark.

Bakeries
A few blocks north of Market Street is Seattle's king of croissants, **Cafe Besalu** (5909 24th Ave. NW, 206/789-1463, http://cafebesalu. com, Wed.-Sun. 7am-3pm). This small French bakery produces an array of delicious sweet and savory pastries. You can get a coffee drink and, if you're lucky, snag one of the few tables. Weekend lines stretch out onto the sidewalk.

Italian and Pizza
Stoneburner (5214 Ballard Ave. NW, 206/695-2051, www.stoneburnerseattle.com, Mon.-Fri. 3pm-10pm, Sat. 10am-11pm, Sun. 10am-10pm, $18-29), on the ground floor of Hotel Ballard, is one of Seattle's casually cool Italian restaurants that breaks decisively from the stereotype of the old-fashioned red-sauce joint. Its pizzas, pastas, and grilled fish and meats emphasize fresh regional ingredients and creative flavor combinations. The pizza topped with potatoes, onions, and morels is fantastic.

Mexican
In the midst of style-conscious downtown Ballard, **La Carta de Oaxaca** (5431 Ballard Ave. NW, 206/782-8722, www.lacartadeoaxaca.com, Mon. 5pm-11pm, Tues.-Thurs. 11:30am-3pm and 5pm-11pm, Fri.-Sat. 11:30am-3pm and 5pm-midnight, $8-15) flourishes by keeping things traditional and fresh. Watch in the open kitchen as chefs make tortillas by hand and preside over the skillets and stewpots. The menu's Oaxacan dishes include tamales, posole, and beef or chicken in mole sauce, the house specialty. The bargain prices might make you think this is a hole-in-the-wall, but the dining room is

attractive, with track lighting and scores of black-and-white photos.

WEST SEATTLE
Most visitors to West Seattle come here for Alki Beach and the view of downtown across Elliott Bay. Two very different restaurants give you a chance to incorporate a meal into those experiences.

Seafood
Salty's (1936 Harbor Ave. SW, 206/937-1600, www.saltys.com/seattle, Mon.-Fri. 11am-3pm and 4:30pm-9pm, Sat.-Sun. 9:30am-1:30pm and 4:30pm-9pm, $19-75) is a venerable high-end seafood restaurant that serves lots of good-quality grilled fish, has a couple of steak options for the fish-averse, and makes the most of its prime waterfront location. If you want the view without the hefty bill you can order from the bar menu, which is discounted at happy hour.

Pan-Asian
A popular Korean/Hawaiian food truck spawned brick-and-mortar ★ **Marination Ma Kai** (1660 Harbor Ave. SW, 206/328-8226, www.marinationmobile.com, Mon.-Thurs. 11am-9pm, Fri.-Sat. 9am-10pm, Sun. 9am-9pm, $9-13), along the water by Seacrest Dock where the water taxi lands. It's a casual spot: Order and pick up your food at a counter, then find a seat on a deck looking out at the city. Or get takeout if you're headed for the beach. The food is an explosion of flavors. From the miso ginger chicken tacos to the Hawaiian mac and cheese, everything is creative and delicious. You can also get the Marination experience at storefronts in Capitol Hill (1412 Harvard Ave., 206/325-8226, Mon.-Sat. 11am-8pm, Sun. noon-8pm) and South Lake Union (2000 6th Ave., 206/327-9860, Mon.-Sat. 11am-8pm) or at the original food truck, which changes locations daily.

Accommodations

If you're prepared to splurge, you have lots of appealing hotels to choose from in Seattle. On the other end of the spectrum, if you're traveling on a shoestring and happy to share a room with strangers, you can stay at one of several first-rate, low-cost hostels. If you fall in between those two categories, things are more challenging. One symptom of Seattle's growth in the past few years is major inflation in the cost of lodging.

Prices listed are standard high-season rates. In the off-season, October-April, rooms are usually less expensive, sometimes significantly so. Note that you will be taxed 15.6 percent at establishments with 60 or more rooms. Places smaller than that, including B&Bs, are taxed at 9.5 percent.

DOWNTOWN AND THE WATERFRONT

There are lots of hotels downtown, most in older, restored high-rise buildings. They're pricey as a rule; because they cater primarily to business travelers, rates tend to be lower on the weekends, especially in non-summer months. Downtown hotels that have parking charge a premium for it, with rates typically running $40 a night or more. On the flip side, if you're planning to spend most of your time in the city center, you can stay downtown and manage without a car by walking and using public transportation.

Under $100

Green Tortoise Hostel (105 Pike St., 206/340-1222, www.greentortoise.net) is a busy place with a friendly, hippie vibe and a location directly across from Pike Place Market that fancier hotels would die for. There are four-, six-, and eight-bed hostel rooms ($33-40 per bed), some coed and some all-female, as well as a couple of private rooms ($84). Perks include a full kitchen and free breakfast.

$150-200

You feel hidden away in the middle of everything at **Pensione Nichols** (1923 1st Ave., 206/441-7125, www.pensionenichols.com, $180-220), a B&B perched above Pike Place Market. Ten small rooms, half without windows, share four bathrooms and a common area, and there are also two suites ($340) with private baths, kitchens, and water views. It's not fancy, but it's comfortable, with a great location and simple but good-quality breakfast.

Over $250

You get a good location, next door to the Central Library, for a comparatively reasonable price at **Executive Hotel Pacific** (400 Spring St., 206/623-3900, www.executivehotels.net, $229-355 d). The downside is that rooms are cramped; renovations have made things pleasantly snug, but this isn't your place if you want something more than a comfortable bed for the night.

The name says it all at **Inn at the Market** (86 Pine St., 206/443-3600, www.innatthemarket.com, $450-600 d). The 70-room, seven-story inn is set along Post Alley in Pike Place Market. It's a modern construction with contemporary design that's a little generic, but everything is well maintained and meticulously run, and when you look out over the market and the bay and the Olympic Mountains on the horizon, you sense that you're in a special place.

The eye-catching glass box across 1st Avenue from Pike Place Market is **Thompson Seattle** (110 Stewart St., 206/623-4600, www.thompsonhotels.com, $429-659). Inside, the floor-to-ceiling windows look out over Elliott Bay from guest rooms outfitted in midcentury-modern style. Views are even better from the rooftop bar.

The Kimpton chain has four hotels downtown, the best of which are the **Alexis** (1007

1st Ave., 206/624-4844, www.alexishotel. com, $375-495 d) and **Hotel Monaco** (1101 4th Ave., 206/621-1770, www.monaco-seattle.com, $225-415 d), located within a few blocks of one another. Both offer attractive, comfortable guest rooms and lively lobbies and restaurants. In keeping with Kimpton's trademark features, each has touches of hip design, a free wine hour every evening, and a pets-welcome policy.

The Arctic Club (700 3rd Ave., 206/340-0340, http://thearcticclubseattle.com, $260-540 d) was built in 1917 as a private club for the fortunate few who had struck it rich in the Klondike gold rush. It's a beautiful building, with distinctive terra-cotta walrus heads adorning the exterior and a giant glass-domed ceiling in the main meeting room. Dark paneling and overstuffed armchairs give guest rooms a clubby atmosphere.

Four Seasons (99 Union St., 206/749-7000, www.fourseasons.com/seattle, $560-940 d) is the alpha dog of Seattle hotels. It's sleek and modern, with an Elliott Bay view and a few rustic design touches to remind the corporate execs who stay here that they're in the Pacific Northwest. Amenities include a heated infinity pool overlooking the bay and a full-service spa.

When you think "grand hotel" you probably picture a place like the **Fairmont Olympic** (411 University St., 206/621-1700, www.fairmont.com/seattle, $269-639 d). It's a big, high-end facility that, unlike most of its competitors, has no ambitions toward hipness. The stately building, dating from 1924, occupies an entire downtown block, and houses a large, bustling lobby with an adjacent bar and magnificent banquet room. The 450 renovated guest rooms are spacious and tastefully appointed.

Set between Capitol Hill and downtown on First Hill, ★ **Hotel Sorrento** (900 Madison St., 206/622-6400, www.hotelsorrento.com, $439-579 d) is one of Seattle's most historic lodgings, in operation since 1909. It's been remodeled to emphasize its old-fashioned charm, which comes through clearly in the handsome paneled lobby lounge. The 76 guest rooms—half standard, half junior suites—are decorated with classic, understated elegance. Stay here and you'll feel like William Powell and Myrna Loy might be in the room next door.

PIONEER SQUARE AND THE INTERNATIONAL DISTRICT

This area just south of downtown is historic by day and sketchy by night. You can get some bargains here on lodging that's within walking distance of the central city sights, but if you don't want urban grit to be part of your Seattle experience you'll be happier staying elsewhere. A bonus for budget travelers is that you're close to **Uwajimaya** (600 5th Ave. S), a fantastic Asian-oriented supermarket where you can stock up on supplies.

Under $100

One of the largest hostels on the West Coast, **Hostelling International at the American Hotel** (520 S. King St., 206/622-5443, www. americanhotelseattle.com) has clean but Spartan facilities. A bunk in a four- or six-person room runs $37; a two-bed room is $97, four-bed $140, both with private bath. A light breakfast is included in the price.

$100-150

The International District was once filled with hotels that served as first homes for immigrants arriving from East Asia. **Panama Hotel** (605 1/2 S. Main St., 206/223-9242, www.panamahotel.net, $109-135 d) is one such establishment. It continues to provide modest accommodations with a few touches of character, including attractive period furniture and a teahouse on the ground floor. It's not for everyone—bathrooms are shared, and you have to climb two flights of stairs to reach the reception area—but it gives you the atmosphere of another era at a relatively bargain price. It's also a footnote in rock-and-roll history: Jimi Hendrix lived here for a time.

BELLTOWN

Just north of downtown the skyscrapers disappear, but you're still in an urban setting: the formerly sketchy, now trendy neighborhood of Belltown. Amid the restaurants, nightspots, and new apartment buildings there's a more varied selection of lodging than downtown has to offer.

Under $100

In the heart of Belltown, **City Hostel** (2327 2nd Ave., 206/706-3255, www.hostelseattle. com) adds creative touches to a hostel stay. Murals by local artists decorate every room, and a basement theater hosts frequent live performances. Room options include four-bed ($38) and six-bed ($34) dorms, both coed and all-female, and private rooms with shared bath ($100) or private bath ($119). Guests get free breakfast and use of a full kitchen and garden with a grill.

$100-150

Moore Hotel (1926 2nd Ave., 206/448-4851, www.moorehotel.com, $99-147) is an old-school urban budget lodging. It's been in operation since 1907, and a few design features hark back to the early days, but the 125 guest rooms have been remodeled in simple, dorm-room style. Options include singles and doubles with private or shared bath. Nineteen suites in various configurations feature more stylish decor.

The Belltown branch of ★ **Ace Hotel** (2423 1st Ave., 206/448-4721, www.ace-hotel.com/seattle) was the first location of this international cheap/hip chain. Of the 28 rooms, 14 have private baths ($239) and 14 share seven bathrooms on the hall ($129). The decor mixes minimalist, industrial, and thrift-store style with enough finesse to look like something from the pages of a design magazine. A do-it-yourself breakfast of juice, coffee, and waffles comes with the room. Note that you have to climb a flight of stairs to get to the hotel.

Over $250

Hotel Andra (2000 4th Ave., 206/448-8600, www.hotelandra.com, $359-379 d) gives a touch of Scandinavian cool to an old Seattle hotel (a Claremont in its previous incarnation) on the edge of Belltown. Guest rooms are good-sized, and the greatest virtue of the place is its attention to detail, from the plush towels to the ergonomic desk chairs.

★ **The Edgewater** (2411 Alaskan Way,

The Edgewater hotel

206/728-7000, www.edgewaterhotel.com, $369-550 d) is the luxury hotel that most distinctly captures the character of Seattle. That's primarily due to its location; true to its name, it sits right on the edge of Elliott Bay, about halfway between the aquarium and Olympic Sculpture Park. A night here feels a little like staying on a giant, fancy houseboat. Just over half of the 223 rooms have water views, and all rooms are equipped with gas fireplaces and well-appointed bathrooms. The hotel has an upscale lodge feel to it, with lots of exposed wood.

SEATTLE CENTER AND QUEEN ANNE
$200-250
In Seattle's expensive lodging market, **The Inn at Queen Anne** (505 1st Ave N, 206/282-7357, www.innatqueenanne.com, $206-249 d) qualifies as a budget option. It's a former apartment building that's been remodeled in functional, late-20th-century style. Rooms are large and come with kitchenettes, and the inn is right next to Seattle Center.

Over $250
Playful modern/retro design and attentive customer service make **The Maxwell Hotel** (300 Roy St., 206/286-0629, www.themaxwellhotel.com, $319-359 d) an appealing option a few blocks from Seattle Center. Perks include an indoor pool, shuttle service to Pike Place Market and the zoo, loaner bikes, and coffee and cupcakes in the afternoon, all at no additional charge.

MarQueen Hotel (600 Queen Anne Ave. N, 206/282-7407, www.marqueen.com, $309-409 d) is located in a former apartment building near Seattle Center, and it gets a lot of mileage out of its old-fashioned apartment atmosphere. The spacious rooms have high ceilings, hardwood floors, solid dark-stained furnishings, and bright breakfast nooks. The three-story building doesn't have an elevator; you climb the stairs just like the former residents did.

SOUTH LAKE UNION
Over $250
Lodging options in South Lake Union are expanding to keep pace with the growing Amazon corporate headquarters. For a modern, fully equipped, efficiently run place to stay, it's hard to beat the sleek ★ **Pan Pacific Hotel Seattle** (2125 Terry Ave., 206/264-8111, www.panpacific.com/seattle, $425-475). It's part of a condo complex at the south end of the Amazon headquarters development in South Lake Union, and while the area lacks the character of downtown, you have views of the lake and the Space Needle, easy access to Seattle Center, and a Whole Foods supermarket directly below you. Complimentary shuttle service runs within a two-mile radius, and the South Lake Union streetcar heading downtown stops right outside.

CAPITOL HILL
Capitol Hill's most abundant lodging options are B&Bs, taking advantage of the neighborhood's large, attractive old houses.

$150-200
You get a taste of Capitol Hill's stately homes at ★ **Gaslight Inn B&B** (1727 15th Ave., 206/325-3654, www.gaslight-inn.com). The interior has heavy oak paneling and a mix of contemporary and period decorations, including mounted game heads and a collection of Pacific Northwest glass. In the backyard is a heated pool surrounded by a lush garden. Six guest rooms have private baths ($168-208) and two share a bath ($148-168). The simple continental breakfast includes fruit, cheese, yogurt, and croissants.

$200-250
11th Avenue Inn Bed and Breakfast (121 11th Ave. E, 206/720-7161, www.11thavenueinn.com, $189-249 d) is an early-20th-century boardinghouse that's been renovated with restraint. The 11 rooms (two in separate outbuildings) aren't frilly or packed with tchotchkes, but instead are furnished

with handsome, mostly Victorian-style armoires, desks, and headboards. Breakfasts are substantial (but aren't included for guests in the outbuildings). There are minimum-stay requirements that vary throughout the year; rates drop significantly in the off-season.

THE U DISTRICT
$100-150

Dating from 1909, **The College Inn** (4000 University Way NE, 206/633-4441, www.collegeinnseattle.com, $110-140 d) in the U District is the granddaddy of Seattle's bargain hotels. The four-story, Tudor-style building is bare-bones, with no elevator, well-worn furnishings, and shared bathrooms. But it's a safe, clean place to spend the night, with friendly staff and a decent complimentary continental breakfast.

Over $250

The high-rise **Hotel Deca** (4507 Brooklyn Ave. NE, 206/634-2000, www.hoteldeca.com, $319-354 d) dates from the 1930s and has some art deco touches to go with comfortable midrange guest rooms. It primarily serves visitors to the U District—you're a block from University Way and two blocks from campus—but it's a marginally better value than most downtown hotels, making it worth considering even if you're planning to spend most of your time elsewhere in the city.

University Inn (4140 Roosevelt Way NE, 206/632-5055, www.universityinnseattle.com, $269-329 d) has many of the same virtues as the Deca—it's a decent value for a comfortable room close to the university—and it adds some nice perks, including free continental breakfast, free use of bicycles, and free shuttle service to downtown, the university, and the zoo.

FREMONT, WALLINGFORD, AND GREEN LAKE
Under $100

Seattle's chicest hostel is Fremont's ★ **Hotel Hotel Hostel** (3515 Fremont Ave. N,

206/257-4543, www.hotelhotel.co). It has the feel of a hip boutique hotel, with track lighting, hardwood floors, and exposed brick walls. There are coed and female-only dorm rooms ($31-34 per bed) and private rooms with shared bath ($110) and private bath ($128). Guests have use of a fully equipped kitchen and a lounge, and the restaurants and nightlife of Fremont are just out the front door. You're a block from a bus stop that will get you downtown in 10-20 minutes.

BALLARD

Trendy but quaint Ballard has a couple of boutique accommodations along its historic main drag.

$150-200

Ballard Inn (5300 Ballard Ave. NW, 206/789-5011, www.ballardinnseattle.com) does the best it can given the limits of its physical structure, a small former bank building. The location on Ballard Avenue is great, set in the middle of the neighborhood's shops and restaurants, and the inn has polished and professional management, but the 16 rooms are small and amenities are limited. Four rooms have private baths ($229) and 12 share facilities down the hall ($149-179). Street noise and the lack of air-conditioning can make things uncomfortable when Seattle has a spate of hot weather.

Over $250

The Ballard Inn's sister property down the street, **Hotel Ballard** (5216 Ballard Ave. NW, 206/789-5012, www.hotelballardseattle.com), offers something fancier. It has 29 rooms, 12 of them suites ($359-399) and the remainder standard doubles ($299). All are tripped out with designer appointments and high-end linens; most have balconies or rooftop decks. The suites can sleep four and have soaking tubs and fireplaces.

SOUTH SEATTLE
$150-200

Get a good deal and discover an off-the-beaten-path neighborhood at **Georgetown**

Inn (6100 Corson Ave. S, 206/762-2233, www. georgetowninnseattle.com, $159-189 d). It's an unflashy but well-maintained motel a couple of blocks from a cluster of hip, casual restaurants and bars in the Georgetown neighborhood. You're about four miles south of downtown; a city bus will get you there in around 20 minutes.

Information and Services

TOURIST INFORMATION

Seattle's official resource for tourist information is **Visit Seattle** (701 Pike St., Ste. 800, 206/461-5840, www.visitseattle.org, year-round Mon.-Fri. 9am-5pm, June-Aug. also Sat.-Sun. 9am-5pm). At its visitors center, in the lobby of the Washington State Convention Center at Pike Street and 7th Avenue, you can get maps, brochures, and trip-planning advice. Call ahead or contact them through their website and they'll send you a packet of maps and information in advance.

MEDIA

Seattle's daily print newspaper, the *Times* (www.seattletimes.com), delivers local news and mainstream cultural information; its online edition has limited access for nonsubscribers. The *Post-Intelligencer* (www.seattlepi.com), formerly a print daily, now lives only online in a somewhat diminished form. A more thorough and more opinionated online-only news source is *Crosscut* (http://crosscut.com). Devote some time to the coverage here and you'll know more about local political and cultural issues than many residents do.

Seattle has two free alternative weeklies available from newspaper boxes around town as well as online: *The Stranger* (www.thestranger.com) and *Seattle Weekly* (www.seattleweekly.com). Look to them for events listings and recommendations, restaurant reviews, and other cultural insights. Two monthly lifestyle magazines, *Seattle Met* (www.seattlemet.com) and *Seattle Magazine* (www.seattlemag.com), both cover the goings-on in and around the city.

You can also get a feel for the city by listening to the radio. The NPR station **KUOW** (94.9 FM, kuow.org) will fill you in on local news, while on **KEXP** (90.3 FM, www.kexp. org), a longtime leader in the indie and alternative music scene, you'll hear interesting bands and learn when they're playing in town.

Transportation

GETTING THERE
Air
Sea-Tac International Airport (17801 International Blvd., 206/787-5388, www. portseattle.org/sea-tac) is about 14 miles south of downtown via I-5, halfway between Seattle and Tacoma (hence the name). All commercial passenger flights come and go from here. The two airlines with the largest presence are Alaska and Delta.

PUBLIC TRANSIT TO AND FROM SEA-TAC
Sound Transit's **Link Light Rail** (888/889-6368, www.soundtransit.org) connects the airport to downtown, Capitol Hill, and the University of Washington campus, with 14 stops along the way. The light rail is in service Monday through Saturday from 5am to 1am and Sunday from 5am to midnight. Trains run every 8-15-minutes, depending on the time of

day. The one-way fare ranges from $2.25-3.25, depending on how far you travel. (Trips from Sea-Tac into the heart of the city require the highest fare.) You reach the Sea-Tac Link station from the airport via a walkway on the 4th floor of the parking garage directly adjacent to the terminal.

TAXIS, CAR SERVICES, AND SHUTTLES

The Sea-Tac taxi stand is located on the 3rd floor of the parking garage adjacent to the terminal. Fares between the airport and downtown usually run $50-60. On the 3rd floor of the garage there are also car services that will get you to your destination for a flat fee, normally about the same as the taxi fare, and a designated rideshare pickup area.

You can get a shared shuttle van to or from Sea-Tac with **Shuttle Express** (425/981-7000, http://shuttleexpress.com). It has door-to-door service all over the Puget Sound area with variable rates. Reservations are required. A trip to a major downtown hotel costs about $20 per person.

RENTAL CAR PICKUP

All rental car agencies operate from an off-site facility reached from the airport by shuttle bus. Two curbside bus pickup points are by the exits near baggage claim carousels 1 and 15.

Train

Seattle's train traffic comes through **King Street Station** (3rd Ave. S and King St. S), a restored redbrick terminal opened in 1906 at the south end of the Pioneer Square neighborhood. You can identify it at a distance by its sturdy clock tower, modeled after the campanile on Piazza San Marco in Venice.

Amtrak (800/872-7245, www.amtrak.com) has daily arrivals and departures at the station on the Cascades (Vancouver, BC-Portland), Empire Builder (Chicago-Seattle), and Coast Starlight (Los Angeles-Seattle) lines.

On weekdays multiple Sound Transit **Sounder** (888/889-6368, www.soundtransit. org) commuter trains run between Tacoma

and Everett, making stops at King Street Station.

Bus

There's intercity bus service to destinations throughout the United States on **Greyhound** (206/624-0618, www.greyhound.com) from the carrier's station in SoDo (503 S. Royal Brougham Way) a block east of Safeco Field. **Northwestern Trailways** (800/366-3830, www.northwesterntrailways.com) has a route between Spokane and Tacoma that stops in Seattle at both the Greyhound station and Amtrak's King Street Station (3rd Ave. S and King St. S).

GETTING AROUND
Bus

Bus service run by **King County Metro Transit** (206/553-3000, http://metro.king-county.gov) is Seattle's main means of public transportation. It's a big system, with nearly 200 routes. Fares are $2.75-3.25 at peak hours (weekdays 6am-9am and 3pm-6pm) and $2.50 at other times. You have to pay with exact change. Transfers can be used for any additional rides within a two-hour window.

You can also use an **Orca Card** to pay your fare; cards are available online or from vending machines at King Street Station and at Link light rail stations. The upside of getting a card is that you don't have to carry the exact fare, but the downside is that you have to pay an initial $5 fee, and if you don't use up all of the value you load on the card you can get a refund only if you pay a $10 fee. Unless you're going to be in Seattle for an extended period of time and you're planning to use the bus regularly, you're better off paying in cash.

The best way to figure out how to get where you want to go is by using the Metro trip planner, available as a mobile app or on the Metro website. Every place mentioned in this chapter is accessible by bus, though trips can be significantly longer than travel by car, especially if you have to transfer, which is often the case when you're going between downtown and a neighborhood north of the ship canal. Buses run every 15 to 30 minutes.

When touring downtown, the bus system can be used as a shuttle to cut down on your walking. Many lines run up and down the avenues (particularly 3rd Avenue); as long as you're going a short distance it doesn't matter which bus line you take (they're all covering the same path), so you seldom have to wait. After you pay your initial fare you can use your transfer for any additional rides over the next two hours.

Light Rail and Streetcar

Link Light Rail (888/889-6368, www. soundtransit.org) runs between Sea-Tac Airport and the University of Washington with 14 stops along the way, including SoDo, the sports stadiums, downtown, and Capitol Hill. For those areas, light rail can be a good alternative to navigating the congested streets by car or bus. Fares are $2.25-3.25, depending on the length of your ride. Major expansion plans are in store for the Link system and will gradually come to fruition over the coming 20 years. The next addition, scheduled to open in 2021, will connect the UW station with the Northgate area at the north end of the city.

The city also has a growing streetcar system (www.seattlestreetcar.org). The **South Lake Union Streetcar** runs from Westlake Center north to Lake Union, making 11 stops throughout the South Lake Union area. Cars run every 10 to 15 minutes, with service starting at 6am and stopping at 9pm Monday through Thursday and 11pm Friday and Saturday. Hours on Sundays and holidays are 10am-7pm. The **First Hill Streetcar** goes from Pioneer Square up First Hill, then makes a looping turn and heads up Broadway into Capitol Hill. It runs Monday through Saturday 5am-1am, with the same Sunday and holiday hours as South Lake Union. Fares on both lines are $2.25 and can be paid using cash or an Orca Card.

Plans are in the works for a line downtown that will run between the South Lake Union

line terminus at Westlake Center and the First Hill line terminus in Pioneer Square, thus connecting them. The project is scheduled for completion in 2020.

Water Taxi

West Seattle, home to Alki Beach, is a roundabout trip by car. A more direct, scenic means of getting there is on the **West Seattle Water Taxi** (www.kingcounty.gov/depts/transportation.aspx), a publicly run passenger ferry. It docks downtown at Pier 50 at the foot of Yesler Way, and in West Seattle at Seacrest Dock (1660 Harbor Ave. SW). The trip lasts 15 minutes and costs $5.25, making it one of the cheapest ways to get out onto the waters of Elliott Bay.

On weekdays ferries run every 30 minutes 6am-6pm, and on weekends once an hour 8:30am-8pm, with later trips on Friday and Saturday nights. From the dock in West Seattle you can ride the 775 bus along the water to Alki Point or the 773 bus to West Seattle's central commercial area for free.

Car

Seattle makes every list of U.S. cities with the worst traffic congestion. There are only two north-south highways to handle commuter traffic, **I-5** and **Route 99.** During rush hours traffic crawls on these roads, and especially on I-5 backups can occur at other times for no discernible reason.

Those commuting from the Eastside to Seattle have it just as bad. Two floating bridges span Lake Washington, for **I-90** and **Route 520,** and both have heavy congestion every rush hour. (Note that 520 is a toll bridge without toll booths. Locals equip their cars with electronic passes that sensors read and then bill the driver. If you don't have a pass the sensor will record your license plate number and bill you by mail, at a higher rate.)

Off the highways, traffic is notoriously bad along **Denny Way** north of downtown. There can also be congestion on the bridges crossing the ship canal—there are only six of them, including the ones for I-5 and Route 99. Beyond that, things aren't so awful. Downtown doesn't usually experience gridlock, and the arterial streets of the surrounding neighborhoods tend to have only short tie-ups.

PARKING

Most of the street parking in the most congested neighborhoods—downtown, Capitol Hill, Ballard—is metered. You pay by credit card or coins at a street-side pay station and get a sticker you put on your window showing when your time expires. Parking places are hard to come by in these areas. In downtown, if you can't find a space on the street you can pony up for one of the many pay lots and garages. In Capitol Hill and Ballard you don't have that option; you have to circle around until you find a space on the street. In the other neighborhoods, if there isn't a place on the main drag you can turn down a residential street and you'll usually discover one pretty quickly.

Vicinity of Seattle

If you want a change of scenery with a quick trip outside the city, you have options in all directions. Bainbridge and Vashon, the two main islands directly west of Seattle, have a lot in common. They're both an easy and charming ferry ride away from the city, making them ideal for day trips, and they're both known for easygoing lifestyles and arts communities that are much more robust than you might expect from such small populations. The simplest way to differentiate between the two is to think of Bainbridge as mainstream and Vashon as alternative. If you like the idea of visiting meticulously maintained gardens on the former estate of a timber baron and dining at an upscale farm-to-market restaurant, head to Bainbridge. If you're more attracted to roadside honor-system produce stands, waterfront parks, and quirky art galleries, all easily accessible by bike, pay a visit to Vashon.

To the east across Lake Washington is the area collectively known as the Eastside, a cluster of former farming towns that have boomed into wealthy suburbs surrounding the offices of Microsoft and other tech businesses. The region doesn't have a lot of sights, but it's a prime hiking destination and booming winemaking district.

It's a 45-minute drive south (in clear traffic) to Tacoma. Washington's third-largest city still carries the shadow of its reputation as a drab paper-mill town, but today it has a youthful energy, brought on in part by new residents who have been priced out of the Seattle market.

BAINBRIDGE ISLAND

As you stand along the Elliott Bay waterfront in Seattle and gaze out over Puget Sound, the landmass you see across the water is Bainbridge Island (pop. 23,000). The island is a quaint, well-to-do community, made up primarily of commuters and retirees.

Once you've disembarked the ferry you can

Vicinity of Seattle

Woodinville
CHATEAU STE. MICHELLE
Duvall
BLOEDEL RESERVE
Bainbridge Island
BAINBRIDGE ISLAND ART MUSEUM
Redmond
Carnation
BAINBRIDGE ISLAND HISTORICAL MUSEUM
SEATTLE
Bellevue
Fall City
Blake Island
TILLICUM VILLAGE
Issaquah
Tiger Mountain State Forest
Vashon Island
KVI BEACH
POINT ROBINSON PARK
BURTON ACRES PARK
Auburn
Tacoma
Enumclaw
© AVALON TRAVEL

get a good dose of the small-town atmosphere on foot. A half-mile stroll takes you past the shops, galleries, and cafes of the main street, Winslow Way, as well as the Bainbridge Island Art Museum. If you want to go farther afield, bring a car on the ferry or rent a bike from the stand near the ferry landing. Bainbridge has more than a dozen parks and reserves, including the island's most noteworthy attraction, Bloedel Reserve, which is reachable by bus.

Sights

The **Bainbridge Island Art Museum** (550 Winslow Way E, 206/842-4451, www.biart-museum.org, daily 10am-6pm, free), located a quarter mile from the ferry dock, is a handsome modern structure with a curving, two-story wall of windows. The museum showcases art from the island and the surrounding region. The quality and sophistication of the work on display—including paintings, sculpture, book illustrations, and various crafts—is a testimony to the talent that resides in this laid-back corner of the world.

The **Bainbridge Island Historical Museum** (215 Ericksen Ave. NE, 206/842-2773, bainbridgehistory.org, daily 10am-4pm, $4), about half a mile from the ferry, is a small-town, volunteer-run cultural institution, with a cobbled-together collection of artifacts supplemented by narrative videos. The most powerful story the museum tells is of the World War II internment of Bainbridge residents of Japanese descent, who had been the backbone of the island's farming community.

The island's main attraction, up at its northern tip, is the 150-acre **Bloedel Reserve** (7571 NE Dolphin Dr., 206/842-7631, www.bloedelreserve.org, mid-May-early Sept. Tues.-Wed. 10am-4pm, Thurs.-Sun. 10am-6pm, early Sept.-mid-May Tues.-Sun. 10am-4pm, adults $17, students $10, kids under 12 $6). A loop trail takes you through forests, bogs, expansive lawns, and carefully manicured gardens. There are beautiful views of Puget Sound, and in spring the rhododendrons are magnificent. The reserve is 7.5 miles from the ferry landing. There's bus service six times a day run by **Kitsap Transit** (800/501-7433, www.kitsaptransit.com/service/routed-buses/bi-ride), with the last bus of the day leaving the reserve at 2:20pm on weekdays and 3:15pm on weekends; call or check the website to confirm the current schedule.

Food

Bainbridge has several good places to eat within walking distance of the ferry, including

Bloedel Reserve

a couple of restaurants so highly lauded that Seattleites make the trip across Elliott Bay to eat at them. One such place is **Hitchcock** (133 Winslow Way E, 206/201-3789, http://hitchcockrestaurant.com, Tues.-Sun. 5pm-9pm, $23-96). Chef Brendan McGill applies sophisticated techniques learned in kitchens throughout the world to the fish, meat, and produce of the island.

You get upscale bistro fare with lots of seafood options at **Restaurant Marché** (150 Madrone Ln. N, 206/842-1633, www.restaurantmarchebainbridge.com, Tues.-Sat. 11:30am-2:30pm and 5pm-9pm, $18-50), run by a former chef of Seattle's esteemed Canlis.

For something more casual, there's the **Nola Cafe** (101 Winslow Way E, 206/842-3822, www.cafenola.com, Mon.-Fri. 11am-3pm and 5pm-9pm, Sat.-Sun. 9:30am-3pm and 5pm-9pm, $14-34), which has an eclectic menu offering everything from fish tacos to asparagus risotto to bacon-wrapped filet mignon.

The **Madison Diner** (305 Madison Ave. N, 206/842-5786, www.themadisondiner.com, Sun.-Tues. 7am-3pm, Wed.-Sat. 7am-8pm, $11-15) serves healthy portions of classic diner food (burgers, salads, sandwiches, dozens of breakfast options) in a retro, 1950s-era setting.

Blackbird Bakery (210 Winslow Way E, 206/780-1322, http://blackbirdbakery.com, Mon.-Fri. 6am-6pm, Sat. 6:30am-6pm, Sun. 7am-6pm) is a community gathering place where you can pick up a pastry and a coffee for breakfast, and soup or a savory tart for lunch. There's both indoor and patio seating.

Information

You can get nuts-and-bolts visitors information online or by phone from the **Bainbridge Island Chamber of Commerce** (206/842-3700, http://visitbainbridge.com).

Transportation

The **Washington State Ferry** (206/464-6400, www.wsdot.wa.gov/Ferries) runs between Seattle and Bainbridge every 45 minutes to an hour, starting before 6am and continuing until after midnight. On the Seattle side it docks at Pier 52 along Elliott Bay; on Bainbridge the dock is at around the midpoint of the eastern side of the island. The trip takes about 35 minutes each way. The fare from Seattle to Bainbridge is $8.35 for walk-ons and car passengers, $18.70 for cars and drivers. Trips in the other direction cost the same for cars, but passengers ride for free. You can't make reservations—all vehicles and passengers ride on a first-come, first-served basis.

In summer you can pick up a bike near the ferry landing at **Bike Barn Rentals** (260 Olympic Way SE, 206/842-3434, www.bikebarnrentals.com, June-Sept. daily 10am-4pm). Hybrids start at $25 for two hours, and road bikes are available by the day for $75. It's a good idea to reserve a bike in advance.

The limited island bus service, including the route from the ferry landing to Bloedel Reserve, is run by **Kitsap Transit** (800/501-7433, www.kitsaptransit.com).

VASHON ISLAND

Vashon Island is a 20-minute ferry ride from the Fauntleroy terminal, located at the southwest corner of West Seattle. The ferry takes cars and bicycles as well as people, and your mode of transportation is your most crucial trip-planning decision.

The island is small—about 13 miles long and 4-8 miles wide—but it's big enough that you can't really do it justice on foot. The easiest option is to take a car if you have one, but on a long, sunny summer day Vashon is an ideal cycling destination, crisscrossed by peaceful country roads, with just enough hills to get your heart pumping. You'll pass farms, orchards, and horse stables, as well as numerous parks encompassing coastline and second-growth forest. If you don't have a bike of your own, once you reach the Vashon ferry dock you can take the local bus five miles into town (or try to bum a ride from someone on the ferry with a car), and rent a bike from the shop there. Or take your car with you, drive to the rental shop, and bike it from there.

The little town of Vashon has a friendly, hippie vibe and a concentration of art galleries. Most shops and other public buildings are situated along Vashon Highway, more commonly known to the locals as Main Street. Off to the southeast is **Maury Island,** a piece of land connected to Vashon by a natural sandbar supplemented with man-made fill (and thus not really an island at all).

Parks and Beaches

Vashon is studded with parkland. One of the most pleasant places is **Burton Acres Park** (8900 SW Harbor Dr., 206/463-9602, vashonparks.org), located on a little peninsula that juts into Quartermaster Harbor facing Maury Island. It's covered with second-growth forest that's laced with hiking and horseback-riding trails.

Along the water at the east end of the park is **Jensen Point,** where in summer you can rent kayaks, canoes, and paddleboards from **Vashon Watersports** (206/463-9257, www.vashonwatersports.com), with rates ranging from $15 to $30 an hour. Contact them in advance to reserve and schedule a rental.

At the eastern tip of Maury Island, **Point Robinson Park** (3705 SW Pt. Robinson Rd., 206/463-9602, vashonparks.org) has a sand-and-pebble beach from which on clear days you get nice views of the sound, Tacoma, and Mount Rainier. There are picnic tables and hiking trails through the inland woods and marshland. **Point Robinson Lighthouse** is a local landmark that's still functioning under automated controls.

The finest sand is on the eastern side of the island halfway down at **KVI Beach** (off SW Ellisport Rd.), so named because the local radio station, KVI, owns the property and has its tower there.

Galleries and Performance Spaces

The island's arts hub is **Vashon Center for the Arts** (19704 Vashon Hwy. SW, 206/463-5131, http://vashoncenterforthearts.org). It has a 300-seat theater, education facilities, and a gallery space for shows by local and regional artists.

The first Friday of every month 6pm-9pm is Vashon's gallery-walk night, when the island's many galleries open new shows. In the best tradition of gallery walks, it's an open-air party where the people are often as interesting as the art. While you're making the rounds stop in at **VALISE** (17633 Vashon Hwy. SW, 206/463-4006, www.valisegallery.com, Thurs-Sat. 11am-5pm), a first-rate gallery run by a collective of local artists.

Food

Vashon's small farmers bring the fruits of their labor to town for an acclaimed **farmers market** (17519 Vashon Hwy. SW, http://viga-vashon.org). It's in operation April-December on Saturdays 10am-2pm and June-August on Wednesdays 3pm-6pm.

In the town of Vashon, **Vashon Island Baking Co.** (17506 Vashon Hwy. SW, 206/463-1441, www.vashonislandbakingco.com, Tues.-Sat. 6am-6pm, Sun. 7am-5pm) sells sweet and savory handmade pastries, including vegan and gluten-free items.

The **Burton Coffee Stand** (23919 Vashon Hwy. SW, Mon.-Fri. 7am-3pm, Sat.-Sun. 8am-3pm) is where the friendly locals like to hang out, sip good coffee, snack, and shoot the breeze.

The island's most popular restaurant is **The Hardware Store** (17601 Vashon Hwy. SW, 206/463-1800, http://thsrestaurant.com, daily 8am-9pm, $12-22), a predictably laid-back place located in the oldest standing building on the island. It serves three meals a day of high-quality comfort food, including burgers, fish-and-chips, and particularly good fried chicken.

Information

You can get some basic visitors information on the website of the **Bainbridge Island Chamber of Commerce** (www.vashon-chamber.com). Another potentially useful site is **Sustainable Tourism on Vashon** (www.stov.us).

Transportation

The **Washington State Ferry** (206/464-6400, www.wsdot.wa.gov/Ferries) runs between the Fauntleroy terminal in West Seattle and Vashon at intervals of 20-40 minutes, starting before 6am continuing until after midnight. The trip takes about 20 minutes each way. The fare from Fauntleroy to Vashon is $5.45 for walk-ons and car passengers, $23.90 for cars and drivers. There's no charge for the trip going back to Fauntleroy. You can't make reservations—all vehicles and passengers ride on a first-come, first-served basis. There's also a ferry between Point Defiance in Tacoma and Tahlequah at the south end of Vashon Island. Fares for trips originating at Point Defiance are $5.45 for walk-ons and car passengers, $23.90 for cars and drivers. There's no charge going the other direction.

King County Metro Transit (206/553-3000, http://metro.kingcounty.gov) bus routes 118 and 119 run on an intermittent schedule through Vashon, with the most service in the early morning and evening for Seattle commuters. The routes have some connecting buses running to and from downtown Seattle.

Bikes are for rent at **Spider's Ski and Sports** (17626 Vashon Hwy. SW, 206/408-7474, www.spidersportsvashon.com, Tues.-Fri. 10am-6pm, Sat. 10am-5pm, Sun. noon-5pm) in the town of Vashon. Rates run $45-55 a day.

BLAKE ISLAND

Between Bainbridge and Vashon is little **Blake Island** (360/731-8330, http://parks.state.wa.us), a 475-acre state park not serviced by the ferry system. On the island is **Tillicum Village,** where visitors on a tourist cruise (206/623-1445, www.argosycruises.com, adults $84, youth under 12 $32) have a salmon meal in a reproduction Indian longhouse and watch a stage show reenacting traditional Indian dances.

THE EASTSIDE

Lake Washington forms the eastern border of Seattle. The Eastside was once primarily agricultural, until two floating bridges—which remain the longest in the world—were built across the lake, in 1940 and 1963, transforming the towns into bedroom communities for Seattle commuters. Then, in the 1980s, Microsoft established its headquarters here, launching the area as one of the world's tech hubs. Today the Eastside—including the towns of Issaquah, Bellevue, and Woodinville—has a population of half a million. Although now associated with the tech industry, many of the Eastside's sights are linked to its past: vestiges of small-town charm, natural beauty, and agriculture-related industry.

Bellevue

The Eastside's leading cultural institution is the **Bellevue Arts Museum** (510 Bellevue Way NE, Bellevue, 425/519-0770, www.bellevuearts.org, Tues.-Sun. 11am-6pm, $12), a 36,000-square-foot facility designed by acclaimed architect Steven Holl. All of its exhibits are temporary and feature the work of contemporary artists, with an emphasis on crafts and design. The museum has an artist-in-residence studio and an art school, and puts on a wide range of talks, performances, kids programs, workshops, and classes.

Bellevue Botanical Garden (12001 Main St., Bellevue, 425/462-2750, www.bellevuebotanical.org, daily dawn-dusk, free) has 53 acres dedicated to plant life of the Pacific Northwest, including cultivated gardens, woodlands, and wetlands. The blooming of the dahlias in midsummer is an annual highlight.

The Issaquah Alps

At the south end of the Eastside, Issaquah takes pride in a chain of nearby mountains—the Issaquah Alps—that are older than the Cascades (but not nearly as large). The Tiger Mountain area is one of Washington's most popular places to hike, attracting hundreds of hikers and mountain bikers on sunny summer days. Also here are many shallow talus caves that are fun to explore.

The **Issaquah Alps Trails Club** (www.issaquahalps.org) organizes hikes every Saturday and Sunday, plus some days during the week, throughout the year to points of interest along 200 miles of trails in these mountains. No membership or previous registration is necessary.

Tiger Mountain State Forest covers 13,500 acres of forested lands and has a network of 80 miles of trails, all less than a 30-minute drive from Seattle. To get here take I-90 to Exit 20 (High Point Road). Take the next two rights and look for the sign for Tradition Lake Trailhead. You can pick your hike from the posted signage, but it's a good idea to get a map of your own (which is a good excuse for going to Seattle's REI store). West Tiger 3 is the most popular trail.

Woodinville Wine Country

Winemaking is a large and growing industry in Washington. It has a major presence in Woodinville, one of the least urbanized areas of the Eastside. Only a few token grapevines are grown here, but there are over a hundred wineries using grapes brought across the Cascades from eastern Washington. The area as a whole is called **Woodinville Wine Country** (http://woodinvillewinecountry.com), but there's not a lot that's country about it. It has two sections: the **Warehouse District,** which is exactly what the name says, and **Hollywood District,** which consists of two facing strip malls. Tasting here isn't glamorous, but it's fun—and very popular. There's everything from the state's biggest producer, Chateau Ste. Michelle, to tiny operations run by ambitious hobbyists. You'll sample varietals and blends that you'd never find in your neighborhood wine shop, and get to meet winemakers who are often passionate and sometimes eccentric. Note that many places are open only on weekends, and most charge a nominal tasting fee.

Chateau Ste. Michelle (14111 NE 145th St., 425/488-1133, www.ste-michelle.com, daily 10am-5pm) in the Hollywood District produces most of its wine in eastern Washington, but its Woodinville winery is its showpiece, located at the former residence of lumber baron Fred Stimson and surrounded by 87 acres of manicured grounds that include experimental vineyards, an arboretum, trout ponds, and an amphitheater that's the site of summer concerts. You're given several options for sampling wine, from a free tour and tasting to a $10 themed flight to a $100 "ultimate tour" that requires a reservation one week in advance (425/415-3633).

Chateau Ste. Michelle is pretty but has a corporate feel. Tasting at most of the other Woodinville wineries is the opposite experience. Often the person filling your glass also made the wine, and though some tasting rooms are attractively decorated, many are bare-bones facilities with tanks, barrels, and bottling machines on full display.

DeLille Cellars (14421 Woodinville-Redmond Rd. NE, 425/489-0544, www.delillecellars.com, Sun.-Thurs. noon-5pm, Fri. noon-7pm, Sat. 11am-5pm) wins "Best in Washington" awards for its high-end bordeaux blends, which come at prices to match their accolades. The winery's Carriage House tasting room is one of the Hollywood District's most pleasant spots.

In the Warehouse District, seek out **Two Vintners** (18572 142nd Ave. NE, 425/205-8680, www.twovintners.com, Sat. noon-5pm), which likes doing things out of the ordinary, such as a white grenache, and **The Bunnell Family Cellar** (19501 144th Ave. NE, 425/286-2964, www.bunnellfamilycellar.com, Thurs.-Fri. 4pm-7pm, Sat.-Sun. 1pm-6pm), known for high-quality syrahs and uncommon varietals such as aligoté. They're busy enough that they take tasting reservations.

Food

Din Tai Fung (700 Bellevue Way NE, 425/698-1095, http://dintaifungusa.com, Mon.-Fri. 11am-10pm, Sat.-Sun. 10am-10pm, $10-14) in Bellevue is the best and busiest place in the Seattle area for dim sum. Other locations are in Seattle's Pacific Place and University Village malls.

In Issaquah, **Noodle Boat Thai Cuisine** (700 NW Gilman Blvd., 425/391-8096, http://noodleboat.com, lunch Mon.-Fri. 11am-2:30pm, dinner daily 5pm-8:30pm, $12-16) is a modest-looking place with a big reputation for both delicious Thai standards and unusual dishes you won't find elsewhere.

Cafe Juanita (9702 NE 120th Pl., 425/823-1505, http://cafejuanita.com, Tues.-Thurs. 5pm-9pm, Fri.-Sat. 5pm-10pm, $25-95) in Kirkland, about five miles southwest of Woodinville's Hollywood District, has long worn the mantle of the Eastside's best restaurant, thanks to its sophisticated northern Italian food and its simple but elegant setting.

For a nice meal to go with all that wine in Woodinville, head to the Hollywood District's **Purple Cafe** (14459 Woodinville-Redmond Rd. NE, 425/483-7129, Sun.-Thurs. 11am-9pm, Fri.-Sat. 11am-10pm, $14-39), a branch of the downtown Seattle restaurant with the same menu of high-quality comfort food.

The Seattle area's most over-the-top extravagant meal is served in Woodinville at **The Herbfarm** (14590 NE 145th St., 425/485-5300, www.theherbfarm.com, Thurs.-Sun. seating at 7pm, $205-295 prix fixe). You begin with a tour of the wine cellar and the herb garden before settling in for a set menu of nine courses paired with six wines. Dinners usually have a theme and always emphasize fresh, seasonal ingredients. French-influenced preparations are likely to include a few ingredients and methods you've never before encountered.

Transportation

From downtown Seattle it's about 10 miles across Lake Washington, a 15-minute drive, to Bellevue on I-90 East and north on Bellevue Way. It's about 18 miles to Issaquah on I-90 East, and about 22 miles to Woodinville on I-90 East and I-405 North; the drive is about 30 minutes to either.

TACOMA

Thirty miles south of Seattle, Tacoma (pop. 200,000) has long had a reputation as a drab paper-mill town, but it's reinvented itself as an appealing midsize city. Today, most of the smelly mills have closed, and Tacoma is known for its impressive collection of museums and revitalized downtown, where a grand old train station has been renovated, warehouses have become artists' lofts, and a theater district has come to life.

You aren't going to mistake Tacoma for Seattle, which is probably fine with everyone involved. The pace of life here is slower, and locals stake their pride on a handful of beloved civic institutions. Two of the biggest points of pride are beautiful 700-acre Point Defiance Park and renowned glass artist Dale Chihuly, a native son whose work is prominently displayed throughout Tacoma and who has helped turn the city into a center for glassmaking.

Museums

Tacoma's Museum Row along the waterfront south of Commencement Bay gives you at least a full day's worth of things to look at, with museums dedicated to state history, regional art, and glass lined up side by side, along with a children's museum and the restored train station. Car aficionados have to go a few blocks farther south, next to the Tacoma Dome, to visit the impressive LeMay automobile museum.

The 100,000-square-foot **Washington State History Museum** (1911 Pacific Ave., 253/272-9747, www.washingtonhistory.org, Tues.-Sun. 10am-5pm, $12) sits next to historic Union Station and echoes the station's design in a series of three vaulted arches. Inside, visitors walk through a maze of exhibits, many of them interactive. They include a Salish plank house, a collection of Indian baskets, dioramas of mining and logging towns, and a theater with a video about the Columbia River.

The **Tacoma Art Museum** (1701 Pacific Ave., 253/272-4258, www.tacomaartmuseum.org, Tues.-Sun. 10am-5pm, $15), housed in a striking modern building, emphasizes art of the Pacific Northwest. Works by regional

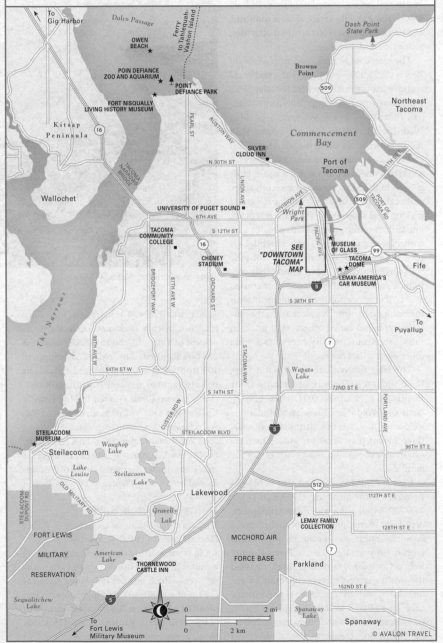

Tacoma

To
Gig Harbor

Dalco Passage

OWEN
BEACH ★

Ferry
to Tahlequah-
Vashton Island

Dash Point
State Park

POIN DEFIANCE
ZOO AND AQUARIUM ★

POINT
DEFIANCE PARK

FORT NISQUALLY
LIVING HISTORY MUSEUM ★

Browns
Point

509

Northeast
Tacoma

*Kitsap
Peninsula*

16

PEARL ST

RUSTON WAY

*Commencement
Bay*

Port of
Tacoma

11TH ST

PORT OF TACOMA RD

509

99

Wallochet

TACOMA
NARROWS
BRIDGE

SILVER
CLOUD INN

N 30TH ST

UNION AVE

DIVISION AVE

Wright
Park

PACIFIC AVE

MUSEUM
OF GLASS ★

TACOMA
DOME ★

Fife

UNIVERSITY OF PUGET SOUND

6TH AVE

S 12TH ST

SEE
"DOWNTOWN
TACOMA"
MAP

★★ LEMAY-AMERICA'S
CAR MUSEUM

TACOMA
COMMUNITY
COLLEGE

16

CHENEY
STADIUM

5

The Narrows

BRIDGEPORT WAY

67TH AVE W

ORCHARD ST

S 38TH ST

To
Puyallup

99TH AVE W

54TH ST W

S TACOMA WAY

*Wapato
Lake*

7

72ND ST E

PORTLAND AVE

CUSTER RD W

S 74TH ST

STEILACOOM
MUSEUM ★

Steilacoom

*Waughop
Lake*

STEILACOOM BLVD

5

96TH ST E

*Lake
Louise*

*Steilacoom
Lake*

Lakewood

512

112TH ST E

OLD MILITARY RD

*Gravelly
Lake*

MCCHORD AIR

★ LEMAY FAMILY
COLLECTION

128TH ST E

STEILACOOM-DUPONT RD

FORT LEWIS

MILITARY

*American
Lake*

THORNEWOOD
CASTLE INN ●

FORCE BASE

Parkland

7

152ND ST E

RESERVATION

5

*Sequalitchew
Lake*

To
Fort Lewis
Military Museum

0   2 mi

0   2 km

*Spanaway
Lake*

Spanaway

© AVALON TRAVEL

artists make up two-thirds of its collection, which consists primarily of 19th- and 20th-century pieces, including lots of Dale Chihuly glass. New exhibits arrive almost monthly, and there are frequent lectures and activities, plus a fine museum shop.

The most conspicuous resident of Museum Row is the 75,000-square-foot **International Glass Museum** (1801 Dock St., 866/468-7386, www.museumofglass.org, June-Aug. Mon.-Sat. 10am-5pm, Sun. noon-5pm, Sept.-May Wed.-Sat. 10am-5pm, Sun. noon-5pm, $15). It covers two acres along the waterfront and encompasses galleries and exhibition spaces, a workshop where you can watch artisans blow glass, a multimedia theater, a museum shop, and a cafe. The structure containing the glass-making workshop juts up above the rest of the museum, forming a giant tilted cone. It's a favorite Tacoma photo op. Another highlight is the Chihuly Bridge of Glass, a 500-foot-long walkway created by Dale Chihuly that surrounds you with brilliant colors as it crosses over I-705, connecting the glass museum with the history museum. This piece aside, the museum exhibits a varied collection of work. In this Chihuly-obsessed city, here you see what other glass artists can do.

The least flashy place on Museum Row, the **Children's Museum of Tacoma** (1501 Pacific Ave., 253/627-6031, www.playtacoma.org, Wed.-Sun. 10am-5pm, donations welcome) has five fun, stimulating, well-thought-out play areas for kids. The pay-what-you-choose admission is a blessing for families.

Classic-car lovers shouldn't miss **LeMay—America's Car Museum** (2702 East D St., 253/779-8490, www.americascarmuseum.org, daily 10am-5pm, $18), located south of downtown next door to the Tacoma Dome. Over many years the owner of Pierce County Refuse Company, Harold E. LeMay, amassed the world's largest private collection of automobiles, with over 2,500 rare and vintage cars. In addition to the Chevrolets, Fords, Cadillacs, Packards, and Hudsons, the collection includes Duesenbergs, Cords, and even a

Tacoma's International Glass Museum

1920 Pierce Arrow. The handsome four-story museum, with a sleek metal exterior reminiscent of a streamlined auto body, shows off 250 cars acquired from LeMay's collection and 100 from other sources. Diehard enthusiasts will also want to make the trip nine miles farther south on Route 7 to the **LeMay Family Collection** (325 152nd St. E, 253/272-2336, www.lemaymarymount.org, Tues.-Sat. 9am-5pm, Sun. noon-5pm, $15). This less flashy facility is where the majority of LeMay's cars reside, still under the management of the family and on rotating display.

Point Defiance Park

Tacoma's most famous attraction is **Point Defiance Park** (5400 N. Pearl St., 253/305-1000, www.metroparkstacoma.org, daily 30 minutes before sunrise-30 minutes after sunset, free), which juts out into Puget Sound at the tip of a peninsula capping the north end of the city. Its almost 700 acres includes cliffs, old-growth forest, gardens, footpaths, shady picnic areas, and a substantial zoo.

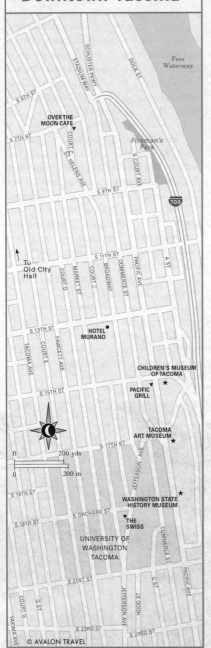

Downtown Tacoma

NATURAL AREAS

Most of Port Defiance Park's undeveloped areas are visible from numerous hiking paths (no bikes on unpaved trails) and a loop road, **Five-Mile Drive,** that's shared by cyclists, cars, and foot traffic, with viewpoints and picnic stops along the way. The outer loop (the part that runs deepest into the park) is closed to motorized vehicles weekday mornings until 10am and weekends until 1pm, giving the road over to walkers, joggers, and cyclists.

WATERFRONT

Owen Beach on Commencement Bay is a popular place for sunbathing in the summer and shoreline strolling any time of year, with views across the water to Vashon Island. You can rent a boat with a small motor at Point Defiance's **Boathouse Marina** (253/591-5325, May-Sept. $75/3 hr., Oct.-Apr. $60/3 hr.). A state ferry running to the south end of Vashon docks here as well.

GARDENS

Point Defiance Park has several beautifully maintained gardens. The **Japanese Garden** features a pagoda built in 1914, plus pools, a waterfall, and immaculate landscaping. The **Rhododendron Garden** covers almost five acres and is striking in the spring when 115 varieties of rhododendrons are in bloom. The **Rose Garden** contains a rustic gazebo and some 1,500 rosebushes that flower June through September. Other featured gardens at Point Defiance are the **Iris Garden**, the **Dahlia Trial Garden** (best viewed in August), and the **Northwest Native Garden** with plants from all six biotic zones in the Northwest.

ZOO AND AQUARIUM

Point Defiance Zoo and Aquarium (5400 N. Pearl St., 253/591-5337, www.pdza.org, June-Aug. daily 9:30am-6pm, May and Sept. daily 9:30am-5pm, Nov.-Feb. Thurs.-Mon. 9:30am-4pm, Mar.-Apr. daily 9:30am-4pm, adults $17.95, youth 5-12 $13.95, youth 3-4

$9.95) is home to polar bears, sharks, tigers, red wolves, and many more animals. The biggest draws are the ocean exhibits, including a tropical reef filled with brilliantly colored fish, a huge cold-water aquarium with life from the Puget Sound area, and a large tank where you can come face to face with five species of sharks, some reaching up to 10 feet long.

FORT NISQUALLY
Fort Nisqually Living History Museum (253/591-5339, www.fortnisqually.org, May-Sept. daily 11am-5pm, Oct.-Apr. Wed.-Sun. 11am-4pm, adults $8, youth 5-17 $5), on the southwest side of Point Defiance Park, has a half-dozen historic and reconstructed buildings inside log bastions. Fort Nisqually was a Hudson's Bay Company trading post in the mid-1800s and was originally located 17 miles to the south on the Nisqually Delta near present-day Fort Lewis. Structures include a working blacksmith shop, a factor's house, a trade store, and a storehouse built in 1851, which is believed to be the oldest standing building in Washington. The staff is clad in period garb from the 1850s and offers living-history demonstrations on everything from spinning to black powder shooting.

Food
The Swiss (1904 S. Jefferson, 253/572-2821, www.theswisspub.com, daily 11am-midnight, $12-16), a slightly divey old pub near Museum Row, serves good sandwiches, salads, and fried oysters to go with dozens of beers on tap. There's lots of barroom entertainment—pool and darts, trivia nights, and live music on weekends. A display of Chihuly glass above the bar classes up the joint.

Tacoma's most charming area for dining, boutique shopping, and nightlife is Opera Alley, and one of its best places to eat is **Over the Moon Cafe** (709 Opera Alley, 253/284-3722, http://overthemooncafe.net, Tues.-Thurs. 11:30am-2:30pm and 4pm-9pm, Fri.-Sat. 11:30am-2:30pm and 4pm-10pm, $19-36). It's a bohemian little bistro with soft lights and mismatched furniture, and a French-influenced menu of stews, pasta, and pan-seared meats.

A warm, brick-walled dining room, friendly service, and a satisfying but sophisticated surf-and-turf menu contribute to the popularity of downtown's **Pacific Grill** (1502 Pacific Ave., 253/627-3535, www.pacificgrilltacoma.com, Mon.-Thurs. 11am-10pm, Fri. 11am-11pm, Sat. 10am-11pm, Sun.

Opera Alley, a Tacoma hub of shopping, dining, and nightlife

10pm-10pm, $15-45). You'll eat well at this comfortable place—and if you take advantage of their great happy hour deals, you'll get a bargain, too.

Accommodations

Tacoma may have the biggest selection of chain hotels in the state. If you want to stay somewhere straightforward and familiar, you have lots of choices.

For something more distinctive, look into downtown's **Hotel Murano** (1320 Broadway, 253/238-8000, www.hotelmuranotacoma. com, $219-259 d). It's a modern high-rise that takes glassmaking as its theme. The lobby and other public spaces are decorated with art-glass pieces from around the world. Each floor is dedicated to a particular glassmaker, with works and background information on display in the hall. Rooms have contemporary decor and elaborate amenities.

The **Silver Cloud Inn** (2317 Ruston Way, 253/272-1300, www.silvercloud.com/Tacoma, $249-349 d) sits on a pier between downtown and Point Defiance Park. The location is great and the rooms are serviceable—furnishings are run-of-the-mill, but some have Jacuzzi tubs looking out onto the south end of Puget Sound.

Southwest of town you can have a uniquely indulgent bed-and-breakfast experience at **Thornewood Castle B&B** (8601 N. Thorne Lane SW, 253/584-4393, www.thornewood-castle.com, $300-500 d), a magnificent 1910 Tudor-style mansion with a half-acre sunken English garden set along American Lake. The 27,000-square-foot home has 16th-century stained glass and other ornate furnishings. There's nothing else quite like it in Washington.

Information

The **Tacoma Visitor Information Center**
(1516 Commerce St., 253/284-3254, www. traveltacoma.com, Tues.-Fri. 10am-4pm, Sat. 10am-3pm), located in the lobby of the Greater Tacoma Convention and Trade Center, has information on Tacoma and the surrounding area. On weekends from Memorial Day through Labor Day there's also a visitors center open just inside **Point Defiance Park** (5715 Roberts Garden Rd., 253/305-1000, Sat.-Sun. 10am-5pm), located across from the tennis courts as you enter the park from Pearl Street.

Transportation

Pierce Transit (253/581-8000, www.pierce-transit.org) runs daily bus service between downtown Seattle (there's a stop at 2nd Ave. and Stewart St.) and the Tacoma Dome, with some buses stopping at Union Station. It also has more than 30 other local and regional routes.

Amtrak (800/872-7245, www.amtrak. com) serves Tacoma from its passenger station at 1001 Puyallup Avenue. The Coast Starlight (between Seattle and Los Angeles) and Cascades (between Vancouver, BC, and Portland) lines make stops there.

A **Washington State Ferry** (206/464-6400, www.wsdot.wa.gov/Ferries) runs between Point Defiance and Tahlequah at the south end of Vashon Island. Fares from Point Defiance to Tahlequah are $5.45 for walk-ons and car passengers, $23.90 for cars and drivers. There's no charge for trips going the other direction.

Tacoma's **Link Light Rail** (888/889-6368, www.soundtransit.org/tacomalink) is a free service with six stops: the Tacoma Dome, South 25th Street, Union Station, the Convention Center, South 11th Street, and the Theater District. Trains run weekdays 5am-10pm, Saturdays 8am-10pm, Sundays and holidays 10am-6pm.

Olympic Peninsula and the Coast

The Olympic Peninsula feels like God's terrarium: perpetually damp and mind-blowingly fertile, with trees as tall as skyscrapers and a pervading lushness that overwhelms your senses.

Here, Washington earns its nickname, the Evergreen State, and its reputation for rain. The Olympic Mountains trap moisture coming in off the Pacific, which is released as rain—more than 150 inches annually—onto the forest floor.

You can visit Olympic National Park the easy way or the hard way. The easy way is by car: U.S. 101 takes a meandering loop around the park, and by following access roads off it you'll reach some striking locales, including Lake Crescent to the north and the Hoh Rain Forest to the south. But most of the park can be reached only on foot (the hard way). Six hundred miles of hiking trails take you deep into the woods and up into the mountains. It requires a tolerance for moisture and a fair degree of fitness, but a backcountry trip here is an experience you'll never forget.

The northern half of the state's Pacific coastline is also part of the park. A couple of points are accessible by car, but for stretches of 20 miles or more there's no way in except on foot. The result is truly wild and rugged beaches, spiked with sea stacks (giant rock formations) and populated by marine mammals and seabirds in numbers matched nowhere else on the U.S. Pacific coast, and equaled by few other places in the world.

As you head south on the coast the shoreline flattens into long stretches of fine sand, and commercial development increases. Beach resorts draw thousands of visitors each year, but you won't find them frolicking in the surf or working on their tans—the water is too cool and the winds too strong. Instead, favorite activities are beachcombing, deep-sea fishing, kite-flying, and whale-watching.

PLANNING YOUR TIME

To see some highlights of the peninsula, devote two nights to it at a minimum. If the unique character of the place sounds appealing you'll find a week spent here well worth it. Tack on

Previous: swimmers at Shi Shi Beach; Hall of Mosses Trail in the Hoh Rain Forest. **Above:** Kurt Cobain Riverfront Park in Aberdeen.

Look for ★ to find recommended sights, activities, dining, and lodging.

Highlights

★ **Port Townsend:** The peninsula's most appealing town combines Victorian architecture and a laid-back attitude (page 122).

★ **Hurricane Ridge:** The visitors center here offers majestic alpine views—which get even more impressive if you hike one of the area's trails (page 145).

★ **Lake Crescent:** Paddling a canoe or kayak on this glacier-carved, turquoise-green lake is about as tranquil an experience as you're likely to find anywhere (page 151).

★ **Cape Flattery:** The trail out to the north-westernmost point in the Lower 48 is one of Washington's best short hikes (page 158).

★ **Ruby Beach:** Among the rugged, scenic beaches of the peninsula, Ruby Beach has a winning combination of beauty and accessibility (page 171).

★ **Lake Quinault and Quinault Rain Forest:** The southwest corner of Olympic National Park gives you two pleasures in one: glacier-fed Lake Quinault and the surrounding rain forest, home to some of the tallest trees in the world (page 172).

★ **Cape Disappointment State Park:** Near the mouth of the Columbia, where Lewis

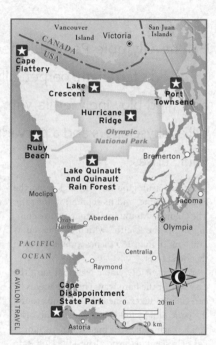

and Clark finally reached the Pacific, this multi-faceted state park has a museum dedicated to the explorers' expedition, hiking trails, beaches, and two old lighthouses (page 183).

Olympic Peninsula and the Coast

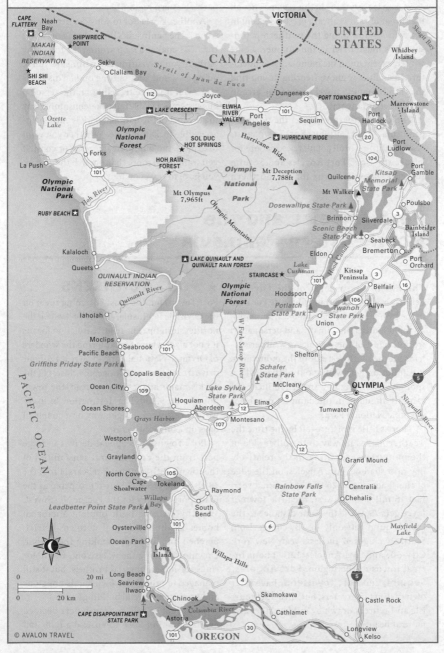

an additional night or two if you want to venture down to the southern Washington coast.

Season is everything in this region. Though the threat of rain is always present (except in the rain shadow along the northern peninsula), it's much drier in the summer. Come winter, except for in the mountains, temperatures usually stay above freezing. If you find the rain romantic, travel around the area in December or January.

The three largest towns on the northern peninsula—**Port Angeles, Port Townsend,** and **Sequim**—are all popular destinations for leisure travelers. Port Angeles and Sequim serve as gateway towns for the northern portion of Olympic National Park, while tiny **Forks** is the primary base for exploring the park's western region.

Another key factor to consider in planning a trip is the peninsula's limited road network. **U.S. 101** makes a loop around the top of the park; if you're visiting the peninsula you're going to spend a lot of time on it. This holds true even if you're traveling on the regional bus system—a viable but time-consuming way to go. Most of the national park is entirely inaccessible by automobile. Whether you want to explore the mountains, forests, or coast, if you want to do more than scratch the surface you have to travel on foot.

Port Angeles and the Northeastern Peninsula

The northeastern coast of the Olympic Peninsula along the Strait of Juan de Fuca sits in the rain shadow of the Olympic Mountains, giving it a different climate, and personality, from the rest of the region. As weather systems hit the southwest side of the mountains, precipitation gets wrung out of them like a sponge, depositing upward of 150 inches of rainfall annually in the dampest depths of Olympic National Park.

There's little moisture left by the time the weather makes its way to the other side of the mountains, resulting in the relatively dry rain shadow. Port Angeles, on the edge of the shadow, gets 26 inches of rain a year. Just 16 miles to the west, the little town of Joyce gets 75, while the same distance to the east, Sequim gets only 16. (By comparison, Seattle averages 37 inches a year, New York City 50, and Los Angeles 12.). The principal towns of the region, **Port Angeles, Sequim,** and **Port Townsend,** have their own distinct characters, but all attract tourists and retirees drawn by mild weather and natural beauty.

★ PORT TOWNSEND

Port Townsend, the most charming town on the Olympic Peninsula, sits off by itself on the northeastern tip. The relative isolation means it's not a good base for exploring the wonders of Olympic National Park—you're a 1.5-hour drive from Hurricane Ridge, the closest of the park's major attractions. Instead, the town, population 9,200, is a destination in itself, worthy of a weekend getaway or a couple of days on a longer itinerary.

Port Townsend's appeal derives in large part from the architectural sensibilities of the town's 19th-century forebears. From the 1860s to the 1880s the town prospered as the main port of entry for the Pacific Northwest. Wealthy citizens built opulent Victorian homes in the residential uptown district, perched on a bluff overlooking the harbor. Downtown, along the waterfront, was notorious for its saloons and brothels, but it still managed to produce its own handsome stone and brick commercial buildings.

In the 1890s railway developers decided against making Port Townsend a hub, and

Port Townsend

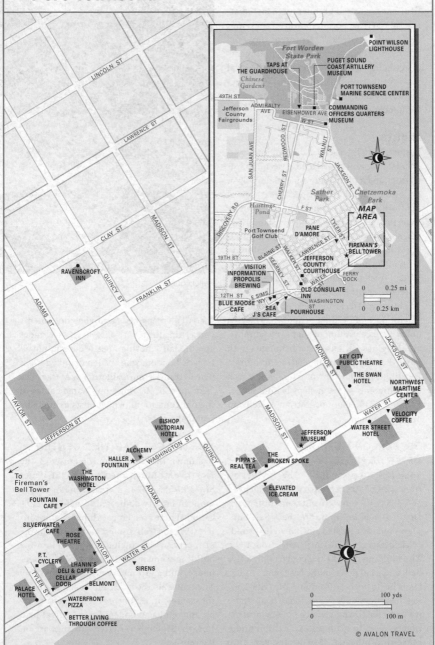

Fort Worden State Park

- POINT WILSON LIGHTHOUSE
- TAPS AT THE GUARDHOUSE
- PUGET SOUND COAST ARTILLERY MUSEUM
- PORT TOWNSEND MARINE SCIENCE CENTER
- COMMANDING OFFICERS QUARTERS MUSEUM

Chinese Gardens

49TH ST

ADMIRALTY AVE

Jefferson County Fairgrounds

EISENHOWER AVE
W ST

SAN JUAN AVE

REDWOOD ST

CHERRY ST

WALNUT

JACKSON ST

Sather Park

Chetzemoka Park

DISCOVERY RD

F ST

MAP AREA

TYLER ST

Hastings Pond

Port Townsend Golf Club

BLAINE ST

WALKER ST

- PANE D'AMORE
- FIREMAN'S BELL TOWER

19TH ST

LAWRENCE ST

KEARNEY ST

JEFFERSON COUNTY COURTHOUSE

FERRY DOCK

VISITOR INFORMATION
PROPOLIS BREWING

0   0.25 mi

12TH ST
E SIMS WY

WATER

0   0.25 km

BLUE MOOSE CAFE

SEA J'S CAFE

- OLD CONSULATE INN

WASHINGTON ST

- POURHOUSE

LINCOLN ST

LAWRENCE ST

CLAY ST

MADISON ST

FRANKLIN ST

- RAVENSCROFT INN

QUINCY ST

ADAMS ST

JACKSON ST

MONROE ST

- KEY CITY PUBLIC THEATRE
- THE SWAN HOTEL

NORTHWEST MARITIME CENTER ★

WATER ST

- VELOCITY COFFEE

TAYLOR ST

JEFFERSON ST

WASHINGTON ST

MADISON ST

- BISHOP VICTORIAN HOTEL

- JEFFERSON MUSEUM

WATER STREET HOTEL

QUINCY ST

- ALCHEMY
- HALLER FOUNTAIN

- PIPPA'S REAL TEA
- THE BROKEN SPOKE

→ To Fireman's Bell Tower

THE WASHINGTON HOTEL

ADAMS ST

- ELEVATED ICE CREAM

- FOUNTAIN CAFE

- SILVERWATER CAFE

ROSE THEATRE

TAYLOR ST

WATER ST

- P.T. CYCLERY
- LHANIN'S DELI & CAFFEE
- CELLAR DOOR
- BELMONT

- SIRENS

TYLER ST

- PALACE HOTEL

- WATERFRONT PIZZA
- BETTER LIVING THROUGH COFFEE

0   100 yds

0   100 m

© AVALON TRAVEL

the town fell into a decline from which it never fully recovered. In the 1970s the beautiful but neglected architecture started attracting artists, counterculture types, and eventually, retirees. The present-day Port Townsend population has large contingents of aging hippies and workers from the local paper mill, as well as shipbuilders and recreational sailors drawn by the prime waterfront location.

Sights

Historic Port Townsend is divided into commercial downtown, wedged between the waterfront and a bluff, and residential uptown, sitting atop the bluff. (You get a great view of the town's two layers when you approach by water on the ferry from Whidbey Island.) The neighborhoods are easily walkable, and strolling around town is a major recreational activity. Old downtown is only seven blocks long. Water Street, the main thoroughfare, is aptly located along the waterfront, and behind it Washington Street runs parallel; beyond that you hit the bluff leading to uptown. The area holds a concentration of shops, restaurants, and lodgings, all local establishments with more than their share of charm and quirks. Heading from downtown to uptown takes a little climbing—a set of steps behind Haller Fountain is the main pedestrian route from one to the other.

Haller Fountain

the jail's creepy cells and view documents concerning the town's once-lively vice trades and the jail's most famous occupant, novelist Jack London, who spent a drunken night here in transit from California to Alaska. The "Art" part of the museum's name comes in the old courtroom, which hosts exhibits by regional artists.

JEFFERSON MUSEUM OF ART & HISTORY

Your first stop should be the **Jefferson Museum of Art & History** (540 Water St., 360/385-1003, www.jchsmuseum.org, Mar.-Dec. daily 11am-4pm, Jan.-Feb. Sat.-Sun. 11am-4pm, $6), located downtown in the redbrick former city hall, which dates from 1892. The building once held a courtroom, a fire hall, and a jail down in the basement. Today, visits begin with a 10-minute film illustrating the history of Port Townsend. From there it's on to the fire hall, which houses local artifacts, including a maritime exhibit and a horse-drawn hearse. Downstairs, gaze into

NORTHWEST MARITIME CENTER

Just down the street from the museum, the **Northwest Maritime Center** (431 Water St., 360/385-3628, nwmaritime.org) is a modern facility dedicated to nautical education. There aren't any exhibits, but it's interesting to stroll around and check out the property, which includes a workshop for building wooden boats, a waterside coffeehouse, and a gift and boating-supply shop. The center also hosts lectures, conducts boating classes, and sponsors events, most notably the annual Wooden Boats Festival held in early September. Activity listings are on its website.

HISTORIC BUILDINGS

Two noteworthy public buildings a few blocks south of downtown are the **post office** (1322 Washington St.), built in 1893 as the town's customs house, and the hulking **Jefferson County Courthouse** (1820 Jefferson St.), which dates from 1892 and is topped by an impressive clock tower.

HALLER FOUNTAIN

Downtown's most conspicuous piece of public art is **Haller Fountain,** located where Taylor Street meets Washington Street. The fountain's centerpiece is a nude bronze, thought to represent either Venus or Galatea (a sea nymph from Greek mythology). The original was first exhibited in Chicago at the 1893 World's Columbian Exposition and was donated to Port Townsend in 1906. After a century of wear and tear, on its hundredth birthday in 1993 it was replaced by the replica that stands in the fountain today.

Stairs behind Haller Fountain leads to uptown Port Townsend. The first landmark you encounter, a block south of the steps, is the **Fireman's Bell Tower** (intersection of Tyler St. and Jefferson St.), erected in 1890 and used for 50 years to call volunteer firefighters to duty. From the base of the tower there's a view of downtown's beautiful old buildings and the bay beyond them.

ROTHSCHILD HOUSE

Uptown is known for its grand Victorian mansions, but the only home that's open for the public to tour, the **Rothschild House** (418 Taylor St., 360/385-1003, www.jchs-museum.org, May-Sept. daily 11am-4pm, $6), dates from an earlier era. It was built in 1868 by local merchant D. C. H. Rothschild, and remained in the family for 90 years until it was donated to the state in 1959. The exterior looks modest compared to its Victorian neighbors, but inside it's a fascinating time capsule. The family was meticulous about maintaining the original furnishings; there are even antique clothes hanging in the closets.

Most of the rest of the uptown houses are private residences, so you have to be content with strolling by and admiring the exteriors. To learn more, and even create your own walking tour, check out the website **www.PTguide.com.** Click on "History & Attractions" for detailed descriptions of three dozen historic homes.

FORT WORDEN STATE PARK

At the northern edge of town, 1.5 miles from the downtown waterfront, **Fort Worden State Park** (200 Battery Way, 360/344-4434, fortworden.org, http://parks.state.wa.us/511) is a thriving park and cultural center. The fort, situated on Point Wilson at the mouth of Puget Sound, was opened in 1902 as part of the "triangle of fire," along with nearby Fort Flagler and Fort Casey on Whidbey Island. Together they were meant to protect Puget Sound from foreign attacks that never materialized. The fort was closed in 1953 and converted into a juvenile detention facility. In 1973 it became part of the state parks system.

The main entrance to the park leads directly to the fort's parade ground, which is the site of two museums. On the south side of the ground are the officers' quarters, a row of comfortable houses that includes, on the far end, the **Commanding Officer's Quarters Museum** (360/385-1003, Apr.-Sept. daily noon-5pm, $6). It re-creates the furnishings and atmosphere of the home in its early years and has military-themed exhibits.

Across the parade ground, in the middle of the row of old barracks, is the **Coast Artillery Museum** (360/385-0373, http://coastartillery.org, daily 11am-4pm, $4), which has displays about the history of the fort and the other harbor defenses of Puget Sound. In summer museum volunteers conduct tours on Saturdays of **Artillery Hill** behind the barracks, where trails lead through old gun emplacements and bunkers; call to confirm tour times. You can also get a brochure at the museum for a self-guided tour.

At the end of the parade ground a road leads down to the shore along Admiralty Inlet, site of the **Port Townsend Marine**

Science Center (532 Battery Way, 360/385-5582, www.ptmsc.org, June-Aug. Wed.-Mon. 11am-5pm, Sept.-May Fri.-Sun. noon-5pm, $5). It has two exhibit spaces, one with touch pools and aquariums, and another focusing on natural history. Farther down the road along the inlet there are campsites and, at the tip of the point, **Point Wilson Lighthouse.** It's closed to the public and not maintained, but it's a scenic spot, particularly at sunrise and sunset.

There's much more to see in the park—it has hiking trails, a rhododendron garden, a spa, and an impressive indoor/outdoor theater, the McCurdy Pavilion, that was converted from an old military balloon hangar. The park is the home of the **Centrum Foundation** (223 Battery Way, 360/385-3102, centrum.org), which stages musical performance and conducts writing workshops and youth programs.

You need a Discover Pass to park along the waterfront, but not up in the area around the parade ground. Along with camping, you can overnight here in the old officers' quarters.

PORT TOWNSEND AERO MUSEUM

Five miles south of town, near the local airport, the **Port Townsend Aero Museum** (105 Airport Rd., 360/379-5244, www.ptaeromuseum.com, Wed.-Sun. 9am-4pm, $10) displays an impressive collection of 1920s-1940s aircraft.

PORT LUDLOW

Twenty miles south of Port Townsend and seven miles north of the Hood Canal Bridge, **Port Ludlow** consists primarily of a resort surrounded by an upmarket retirement community. The resort has the swankest lodging in the region at The Inn at Port Ludlow, along with a 300-slip marina and 27 holes of golf. There's a country club-like ambience to the place. Stop for lunch and a stroll around the waterfront property, or take advantage of the surrounding trails that are maintained by the community, including the half-mile loop to pretty **Ludlow Falls.** The trailhead is at a parking lot along Breaker Lane, about a mile west of the resort. Maps for all of the area trails are available in the resort lobby.

Entertainment and Events

Port Townsend keeps things lively with a long list of annual festivals and a vigorous local arts community. Events take place both in town and at Fort Worden.

NIGHTLIFE

Port Townsend's nightlife takes place mainly in downtown restaurants that have busy bar scenes and live music. A prime example is **Sirens Pub** (823 Water St., 360/379-1100, www.sirenspub.com, daily noon-2am), a multiroom restaurant on the 2nd story of a classic old Water Street building. During the week it hosts fiddle jams, karaoke, and an open mic, and on weekends there's a DJ spinning dance music, along with occasional live performers earlier in the evening. But the biggest draw here is the deck, which has great views of the bay.

The **Cellar Door** (940 Water St., 360/385-6959, www.cellardoorpt.com, Sun.-Tues. 5pm-midnight, Wed.-Sat. 5pm-2am) is an atmospheric basement restaurant and bar that prides itself on its craft cocktails. On most nights it has some kind of live entertainment, from jazz and blues to karaoke and open mic. Note that while the address says Water Street, the entrance is on Tyler.

BARS

Beer drinkers have a couple of appealing destinations in the boatyard area few blocks south of downtown. **The Pourhouse** (2231 Washington St., 360/379-5586, www.ptpourhouse.com, daily noon-midnight) is a comfortable, unpretentious spot to sample regional beers—12 on tap, 200 more in can or bottle—and occasionally hear live music. Port Townsend's contribution to the craft beer scene, **Propolis Brewing** (2457 Jefferson St., https://propolisbrewing.com, Wed.-Fri. 2pm-8pm, Sat. noon-8pm, Sun. noon-6pm), specializes in herbal ales made in the traditional Belgian farmhouse style.

At Fort Worden, the old jail has been converted into **Taps at the Guardhouse** (300 Eisenhower Ave., 360/344-4400 ext. 105, fortworden.org, daily noon-10pm), an atmospheric bar specializing in cocktails, microbrews, and a menu of small plates.

FILM AND THEATER

One of Port Townsend's architectural gems is the **Rose Theatre** (235 Taylor St., 360/385-1089, http://rosetheatre.com), which opened in 1907 as a vaudeville house and began showing movies in the early days of Hollywood. It still shows first-run features, in an old-timey setting that's a whole different experience from your standard multiplex. Upstairs an additional theater, the Starlight Room, screens films in a cushy setting, with couches and armchairs for seats, a full bar, and a menu of snacks. (You have to be of drinking age to watch a movie here.)

Key City Public Theatre (419 Washington St., 360/385-5278, www.keycitypublictheatre. org) stages half a dozen plays each year, including a summer Shakespeare-in-the-park production, and also hosts concerts.

FESTIVALS AND EVENTS

Port Townsend knows how to do festivals. There are over 30 every year, ranging from playfully irreverent to loftily artistic. The biggest generator of activity is the **Centrum Foundation** (9223 Battery Way, 360/385-3102, centrum.org), a nonprofit based at Fort Worden with the overarching mission of fostering creativity. It sponsors more than a dozen annual events, most involving music that ranges from classical to jazz to blues. There's even a popular ukulele festival in the fall. For a list of Centrum events, which also include creative workshops and kids' activities, check out the foundation's website. For a full calendar of Port Townsend festivals go to http://enjoypt.com.

Things kick into gear the third weekend in May with the **Rhody Festival** (360/301-0783, www.rhodyfestival.org), which since 1936 has been celebrating the flowers with a parade and the crowning of a Rhody Queen. July has three major music festivals: the **Festival of American Fiddle Tunes** early in the month, and **Jazz Port Townsend** and the **Acoustic Blues Festival** toward the end. All three are overseen by Centrum. The highlight of August is the **Jefferson County Fair** (360/385-1013, www.jeffcofairgrounds.com), an old-school celebration of local farming and industry.

In September there's the **Wooden Boat Festival** (360/385-3628, http://nwmaritime. org), the biggest celebration of its kind in the world, with over 300 boats filling the bay. Later in the month the **Port Townsend Film Festival** (360/379-1333, www.ptfilmfest.com) takes over town with some 90 screenings as well as talks with directors, producers, and actors. October brings the **Kinetic Sculpture Race** (360/379-4972, www.ptkineticrace.org), an over-the-top, tongue-in-cheek competition where glory goes not to the swift, but to the weird.

Port Townsend also has many galleries along its downtown shopping corridor. A great way to take them in is on the **gallery walk** that happens on the first Saturday of every month 5:30pm-8pm. The event is essentially a big party where you can mingle with gallery owners and artists. Stalwarts of the gallery scene include **Northwind Arts Center** (701 Water St., 360/379-1086, http://northwindarts.org, Wed.-Mon. 11:30am-5:30pm), **Port Townsend Gallery** (715 Water St., 360/379-8110, http://porttownsendgallery.com, daily 10am-6pm), and **Gallery Nine** (1012 Water St., 360/379-8881, www.gallery-9.com, daily 10am-6pm).

Shopping

Downtown Port Townsend is filled with quirky and colorful shops. A walk up Water Street and back down Washington can make for an afternoon of happy browsing for enthusiastic shoppers. You'll find clothing boutiques, bookshops, and home furnishing stores, all unique, independently run operations.

It's fitting that in a town so tied to its past there are all kinds of stores selling used merchandise. **Fancy Feathers** (910 Water St., 360/385-1414) is a consignment shop with a good selection of both women's and men's clothes. **William James Bookseller** (829 Water St., 360/385-7313) is one of the region's leading used bookstores, with a particular emphasis on nautical titles. Arguably the showiest storefront in town, and indisputably the priciest store, belongs to **Bergstrom Antique Auto** (809 Washington St., 360/385-5061); the shop refurbishes and sells classic cars.

Sports and Recreation
CHETZEMOKA PARK
At the northeast end of uptown, **Chetzemoka Park** (intersection Jackson St. and Blaine St.), named for an Indian chief who befriended early settlers, overlooks Admiralty Inlet. It's a classic little urban park with eight flower gardens, a playground, picnic tables, a bandstand, and beach access.

FORT FLAGLER STATE PARK
Across the bay from Port Townsend, **Fort Flagler State Park** (10541 Flagler Rd., 360/385-1259, www.fortflagler.net, http://parks.state.wa.us/508, Discovery Pass required) is a rough mirror image of Fort Worden. Both were corners of the "triangle of fire," equipped with heavy artillery, barracks, and officers' quarters, and they both have picturesque lighthouses. Due to its more remote location on Marrowstone Island, Flagler has been less developed than Worden in its second life as a park. Though it has its own museum and gun-emplacement tours, the main attraction is the beach that surrounds the park on three sides. It's a good spot for crabbing, clam digging, picnicking, and camping.

HIKING AND BICYCLING
Port Townsend has good spots to get some fresh air and stretch your legs. **Fort Worden State Park** (200 Battery Way, 360/344-4434, fortworden.org, http://parks.state.wa.us/511)

has 12 miles of hiking and biking trails, mainly along the beach and around the old emplacements on Artillery Hill. **Fort Flagler State Park** (10541 Flagler Rd., 360/385-1259, www.fortflagler.net, http://parks.state.wa.us/508) has five miles of wooded trails.

Closer to the heart of town, the **Larry Scott Trail** begins at the far end of the boatyard, a few blocks south of downtown. It starts on the waterfront and then cuts inland along an old railway line for seven miles. This is a popular paved route for local joggers, strollers, and cyclists, and it also is the eastern terminus of the Olympic Discovery Trail, an ongoing project that, once completed, will stretch all the way to La Push.

Port Townsend has a busy enough cycling scene to keep two full-service bike shops in business a block apart in downtown. **P. T. Cyclery** (252 Tyler St., 360/385-6470, www.ptcyclery.com, Mon.-Sat. 10am-6pm) and **The Broken Spoke** (230 Taylor St., 360/379-1295, http://thebrokenspokept.blogspot.com, Mon.-Sat. 9am-6pm, Sun. 11am-4pm) both rent bikes along with doing sales and repairs.

KAYAKING AND PADDLEBOARDING
Memorial Day-Labor Day, **Port Townsend Paddlesports** (360/316-9253, www.ptpaddlesports.com, daily 10am-4pm weather permitting) rents kayaks and stand-up paddleboards (rates for either $35/2 hrs., $10 each additional hr.) from waterfront stands downtown by the Northwest Maritime Center and in Fort Worden State Park by the Marine Science Center. It only takes reservations for groups of five or more.

Food
Taking advantage of bountiful farms in the rain shadow and abundant seafood just offshore, Port Townsend has more good places to eat than anywhere else on the Olympic Peninsula. The one across-the-board shortcoming is inconsistency, both in the kitchen and the dining room. It's tough to find enough reliable line cooks and servers to keep the town's many eateries hitting on all cylinders.

COFFEE AND TEA

Within a few blocks downtown there are three appealing places to get a cup of coffee and a bite to eat. **Better Living through Coffee** (100 Tyler St., 360/385-3388, www. bltcoffee.com, daily 7am-7pm) sits right on the water and cultivates a bit of a hipster vibe. **Velocity Coffee** (431 Water St., 360/379-5383, daily 6:30am-5pm) occupies a handsome paneled space at the Maritime Center. Along with coffee, **Lehani's Eat Local Cafe** (221 Taylor St., 360/385-3961, Mon.-Thurs. 8am-4pm, Fri.-Sat. 8am-5pm, Sun. 9am-4pm), next door to the Rose Theatre, has frittatas for breakfast, creative soups and sandwiches for lunch, and a case full of locally made chocolates.

Pippa's Real Tea (636 Water St., 360/385-6060, http://pippasrealtea.com, Wed.-Sun. 10am-5pm) has a large selection of tea, snacks (including scones and clotted cream), and contemporary decor without a stitch of lace.

BREAKFAST

Uptown's **Pane d'Amore** (617 Tyler St., 360/385-1199, http://panedamore.com, Mon.-Fri. 7am-5pm, Sat. 7am-4pm, Sun. 8am-4pm) is Port Townsend's bakery of choice for fresh breads and pastries, with a selection ranging from baguettes and ficelle to muffins and cinnamon rolls.

Unpretentious **Blue Moose Cafe** (311 Haines Pl., 360/385-7339, Mon.-Fri. 6:30am-2pm, Sat.-Sun. 7:30am-2pm, $8-14), located by the boatyard south of downtown, is the place to go for substantial breakfasts, including corned beef hash, French toast, and biscuits and gravy. At lunchtime the cafe has a couple of Mexican items along with sandwiches, soups, and salads.

AMERICAN

Bustling **Doc's Marina Grill** (141 Hudson St., 360/344-3627, www.docsgrill.com, daily 11am-11pm, $12-32) is Port Townsend's most family-friendly restaurant, with a straightforward menu that includes burgers and fish-and-chips along with steaks and half a dozen seafood entrées. The location, on Point Hudson at the north end of downtown, has wraparound water views.

Sea J's Cafe (2501 Washington St., 360/385-6312, daily 6am-8pm, $6-11), located near the water about a mile southwest of downtown, is a genuine hole-in-the-wall that's locally famous for two things: fish-and-chips and milk shakes. The burgers are pretty good, too.

ECLECTIC

Set in a prime corner location next to the Haller Fountain, **Alchemy Bistro and Wine Bar** (842 Washington St., 360/385-5225, http://alchemybistroandwinebar.com, Mon.-Sat. 11am-10pm, Sun. 9am-10pm, $22-31) serves mainly French-influenced dishes—cassoulet, braised rabbit, croque monsieur at lunch—in an attractive setting with a touch of bohemian flair. The food doesn't always live up to the extravagant descriptions on the menu, but if you temper your expectations you're likely to leave satisfied.

The Belmont (925 Water St., 360/385-3007, www.thebelmontpt.com, Thurs.-Tues. 11:30am-8pm, $13-35) is officially Port Townsend's oldest operating saloon, but it doesn't feel at all like a relic. The upscale casual setting mixes exposed brick with picture windows looking out on the bay, and the menu includes classics like poached Dover sole, seafood linguine, and filet mignon.

★ **Fountain Cafe** (920 Washington St., 360/385-1364, www.fountaincafept.com, daily 11am-3pm and 5pm-9pm, $16-26), two doors up from Haller Fountain, is an intimate little bistro that's arguably Port Townsend's most charming restaurant. The eclectic menu ranges from cioppino to Moroccan chicken to Mexican black bean cakes, and the cafe manages to do everything well, including vegetarian options.

Silverwater Cafe (237 Taylor St., 360/385-6448, www.silverwatercafe.com, daily 11:30am-9pm, $12-29) started as a fish-and-chips shack, and though it's gone upscale, it retains an unpretentious vibe. The long menu lets you keep it simple with a burger or fish tacos, or go for something fancier like braised lamb shank or wine-poached salmon.

PIZZA

For a filling, reasonably priced meal, there's **Waterfront Pizza** (951 Water St., 360/385-6629, Sun.-Thurs. 11am-8pm, Fri.-Sat. 11am-9pm, $8-16), which serves pies laden with a wide variety of toppings. Take it to go or head upstairs to the dining room, where you have a bird's-eye view of the comings and goings on Water Street.

ICE CREAM

Port Townsend's best culinary experience is found at an old-timey ice cream parlor. ★ **Elevated Ice Cream Co.** (631 Water St., 360/385-1156, www.elevatedicecream.com, Fri.-Sat. 10am-10pm, Sun.-Thurs. 10am-9pm) makes an artisanal product in the best sense—ingredients are of high quality, batches are small and made in-house, and flavors range from traditional (vanilla, chocolate, strawberry) to unusual (cardamom, ginger). Seasonal specials include fresh fruit in summer and peppermint around Christmas. It's all delicious. The ice cream parlor also runs a candy shop next door.

FARM STANDS AND TASTING ROOMS

Ten miles south of Port Townsend at the intersection of Route 19 and Center Road are a couple of local foodie landmarks. **Chimacum Corner Farmstand** (9122 Rhody Dr., 360/732-0107, http://chimacumcorner.com, daily 8am-8pm) is a great place to pick up organic, locally grown produce and meats. Two hundred yards away, **Finnriver Cidery** (124 Center Rd., 360/732-4337, www.finnriver.com, daily noon-5pm), one of Washington's most successful and sophisticated cider makers, has its tasting room. You can sample and buy a remarkable range of hard ciders. On weekends there's often a food truck and live music.

Elevated Ice Cream Co.

Accommodations

The old-fashioned character of Port Townsend comes through in its lodging choices, which fall roughly into two categories: restored 19th-century hotels downtown and B&Bs uptown. "Quaint" could be used to describe virtually every option. There are no truly luxury properties and no chains.

There are also no places with elevators. Ask for a room on the ground floor, when that option is available, if you don't want to climb stairs. Also note that room rates fluctuate significantly here. Most lodgings have varying rates for winter and summer and for weekends and weekdays, and prices can double during Port Townsend's biggest festivals.

$100-150

Downtown along Water Street are several quirky old hotels with similar characteristics: high ceilings and lots of exposed brick, but also worn furnishings and the potential for some street noise.

The classic example is **The Waterstreet**

Hotel (635 Water St., 360/385-5467, www. watersthotel.com, $70-120 d). It's full of character—as you climb the stairs it's easy to imagine it as both a bustling 19th-century office building and a 1970s hippie den. No two rooms are alike. The five cheapest share two bathrooms. Suites ($145-225) can sleep 4-6 and have full kitchens. Rooms facing the water have great views.

The Palace Hotel (1004 Water St, 360/385-0773, www.palacehotelpt.com, $109-219 d) has plenty of Victorian atmosphere, including rooms named after ladies of the night who once plied their trade here. Generally speaking the Palace has a higher level of maintenance and customer service than the Waterstreet Hotel, but it doesn't have water views.

$150-200

The biggest plusses of **The Bishop Victorian Hotel** (714 Washington St., 360/385-6122, www.bishopvictorian.com, $160-220 d) are a downtown location that's central without being on busy Water Street, and spacious quarters—all rooms are suites, some with kitchenettes and almost all with gas fireplaces. The furnishings have Victorian touches but are more comfortable than stylish.

Another place with a prime location at the north end of downtown is **The Swan Hotel** (222 Monroe St., 360/385-1718, www. theswanhotel.com, $125-185 d). You get more character outside than in: the main building has a three-story, New Orleans-style veranda, and there are four small cottages fronted by a white picket fence. Rooms are bright and basic, with good views from the upper stories.

★ **The Washington Hotel** (825 Washington St., 360/774-0213, http://washingtonhotelporttownsend.com), located downtown above a row of shops, is an anomaly: a Port Townsend lodging not done up in Victorian style. Instead you get fully restored accommodations with comfortable, clean-lined modern decor—three two-bedroom suites ($160-200) and one standard double ($130). Thanks to keyless passcode

entry you may not see a staff member during your stay, but behind the scenes management keeps the place in good shape, and if you seek it out you'll get helpful advice for planning your visit.

Uptown's **Old Consulate Inn** (313 Walker St., 360/385-6753, www.oldconsulate.com, $140-245 d) has all the earmarks of a historic house successfully converted into a B&B. Each room is unique, but they're all well maintained and decorated with period furniture. Bathrooms facilities are a later addition and in some cases are cramped, and light sleepers may be bothered by the courthouse bell tower, which rings on the hour throughout the night. A three-course breakfast is served in the handsome old dining room.

Ravenscroft Inn (533 Quincy St., 360/205-2147, www.ravenscroftinn.com, $140-250 d) provides the B&B experience without the quirks of staying in a converted 19th-century house. It's located in a newer uptown structure that was built to be a bed-and-breakfast, with a colonial design inspired by the architecture of Charleston, South Carolina. It's well appointed from top to bottom and has good views, and the owners are friendly and professional.

OVER $250

The former military residences at **Fort Worden State Park** (200 Battery Way, 360/344-4400, http://fortworden.org, $230-490 houses) have been turned into guest lodging that can be a good option if you're traveling in a group and an old-time resort atmosphere sounds more appealing than staying in town. The sturdy and attractive officers' houses range from two to five bedrooms and have full kitchens. There are also a few more unusual options, including the Castle (really more like a turret), the oldest structure on the park grounds.

The Inn at Port Ludlow (1 Heron Rd., 360/437-7000, www.portludlowresort. com, $251-350 d), part of the Resort at Port Ludlow, is 20 miles south of Port Townsend. It's far removed from town, but it's the only full-service, upscale lodging in the region. It has a country club atmosphere, with a spa, golf course, and marina where you can park your boat or rent a kayak.

CAMPING

Fort Worden State Park (200 Battery Way, 360/344-4431, http://fortworden.org) has 50 year-round beachside campsites and another 30 near the conference center ($49-54 full hookup, $39-44 partial). Both campgrounds have bathrooms and showers. Reservations can be made through the Fort Worden website.

Four miles south of town, **Fort Townsend State Park** (1370 Old Fort Townsend Rd., 360/385-3595, http://parks.state.wa.us/510) has 40 shaded standard campsites ($25-35). The park has two restrooms and one shower. Reservations can be made by phone (888/226-7688) or online (http://washington.goingto-camp.com).

On the water at the north end of downtown, **Point Hudson Marina and RV Park** (103 Hudson St., 360/385-2828, http://por-tofPT.com, $40-56) has 46 sites with full hookups and two without hookups.

Information

Get planning tips and pick up maps, brochures, and event schedules at the **Port Townsend Visitor Information Center** (2409 Jefferson St., 360/385-2722, http://en-joypt.com, Mon.-Fri. 9am-5pm, Sat. 10am-4pm, Sun. 11am-4pm).

If you're coming from Seattle via the Kingston or Bainbridge ferries you'll cross the Hood Canal Bridge on Route 104. After the bridge, at the turnoff for Route 19, is the **Olympic Peninsula Gateway Visitor Center** (93 Beaver Valley Rd., 360/437-0120, www.olympicpeninsula.org, May-Aug. daily 9am-5pm, Sept.-Apr. daily 10am-4pm), another resource for tips and printed material.

Transportation

Port Townsend is at the north end of Route 20 on Quimper Peninsula, at the northeast corner of the Olympic Peninsula. To get to here by car from the greater Seattle area you have three options: Take the **Edmonds-Kingston Ferry** north of the city; take the **Seattle-Bainbridge Ferry** from central Seattle to Bainbridge Island; or bypass the ferry system by looping south on I-5 to Tacoma and heading back north on Route 16. The best option depends on where you're starting from, traffic, and ferry schedules (206/464-6400, www.wsdot.wa.gov/ferries). From central Seattle any of the three routes can take 2.5-3.5 hours depending on traffic. The Edmonds-Kingston and Seattle-Bainbridge Ferries both sail every 45-60 minutes 6am-midnight, charge $18.70 per car, and don't take reservations.

By car from Bellingham and other points to the east-northeast, head to central Whidbey Island and take the **Coupeville-Port Townsend Ferry,** which drops you right in town. You can reserve a place on this ferry. Check schedules, get fare updates, and reserve a place on the Coupeville-Port Townsend Ferry through the state department of transportation (206/464-6400, www.wsdot.wa.gov/Ferries). The ferry runs 10-15 times a day depending on the season, and the trip takes 35 minutes. Fares are $14.45 per car and driver, $3.35 for each additional passenger and for walk-ons. An additional charge ($0.50) applies for a walk-on with a bicycle.

There's bus service to Port Townsend on the Dungeness Line operated by **Olympic Bus Lines** (800/457-4492, http://olympic-buslines.com). The route runs between Sea-Tac airport and Port Angeles, with three stops in Seattle. The trip between Sea-Tac and Port Townsend takes 3.5 hours. Between Port Townsend and Port Angeles it's 30 minutes. For most of the year there are two eastbound trips and two westbound trips per day.

SEQUIM AND DUNGENESS VALLEY

The little town of Sequim (pronounced *Skwim*), population 7,000, sits front and center in the Olympic rain shadow, making

Sequim and Dungeness Valley

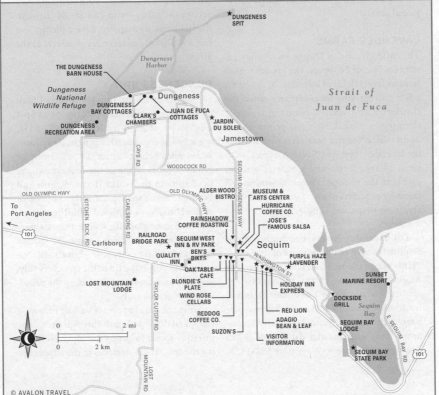

it the driest, sunniest town on the Olympic Peninsula. It used to be a hub for the local dairy industry, but cows are mostly gone. Lavender is now the area's signature crop, resulting in colorful, aromatic farms that double as tourist attractions.

For visitors the main draws are the lavender fields, wildlife-friendly Dungeness Spit, and relatively close access to Olympic National Park—Hurricane Ridge and Lake Crescent are just under an hour away. The town itself is both literally and figuratively middle ground between Port Townsend and Port Angeles. It's not as remote or as charming as the former, not as central or rough-and-tumble as the latter.

Sights

MUSEUM AND ARTS CENTER

One block north of U.S. 101, the **Museum and Arts Center** (175 W. Cedar St., 360/683-8110, http://sequimmuseum.com, Mon.-Sat. 11am-3pm, donation requested) displays 13,800-year-old bones from the Manis Mastodon, discovered in 1977 by local farmer Emmanuel Manis while he was digging a pit for a pond. The site also yielded evidence that humans inhabited the area at the time—4,000 years earlier than previously believed—and that they hunted the elephant-like mastodons. There's a video about the archeological digs narrated by Manis himself. The museum also houses a more typical small-town collection of late-19th and early 20th-century artifacts such as cars and farming implements, and there's a changing exhibit of works by regional artists.

LAVENDER FARMS

The mild climate of Dungeness Valley resembles that of Provence, the French region famous for its fields of lavender. In the 1990s a few enterprising local farmers noted the similarity and started planting lavender themselves. Cultivation has grown to the point where Sequim now identifies itself as the lavender capital of North America, with some 30 area farms and a quarter-million plants in the ground. Shops in Sequim sell lavender products of every imaginable variety, from soaps and candles to cookies and ice cream.

For lavender lovers the highlight of Sequim is a visit to one or more of the farms. Plants are in bloom from late June through August, and some of the producers, including **Purple Haze Lavender** (180 Bell Bottom Rd., 360/683-1714, https://purple-hazelavender.com, June-Aug. daily 10am-5pm, free) and **Jardin du Soleil** (3932 Sequim Dungeness Way, 360/582-1185, http://jardindusoleil.com, June-Aug. daily 10am-5pm, free), welcome visitors throughout the summer months. Both farms are very accommodating—you can stroll through the fields, pick bouquets, have a picnic, and buy a multitude of lavender products at the gift shops.

DUNGENESS SPIT

Slicing 4.5 miles out into the Strait of Juan de Fuca like a giant sickle, **Dungeness Spit** (554 Voice of America Rd., 360/457-8451, www.fws.gov/refuge/Dungeness, daily 7am-30 minutes before sunset, $3 per family or group of four) is one of the longest natural sand spits in the world. The U.S. Fish and Wildlife Service manages it as the centerpiece of the Dungeness National Wildlife Refuge, and it's a great place for seeing animals, particularly migratory birds—some 250 species come and go here every year—but also harbor seals, who pup at the tip of the spit every July, and many sea creatures, including the namesake Dungeness crab.

From the parking area it's a half mile on a flat, partially paved path through pretty coniferous forest to get to the bluff overlooking the spit, which stretches to the edge of the

Dungeness Spit

horizon. From there you can descend to the sand and walk out as far as your stamina will take you (though some of the farthest reaches are submerged at high tide). The most striking thing about the spit is the abundance of driftwood, in all shapes and sizes—it's like a long natural sculpture park. On clear days you can see both the Olympic Mountains and Mount Baker.

It's a beautiful, peaceful place for a stroll on the beach, with the added novelty of water on both sides. Pets, bicycles, kites, Frisbees, ball-playing, Jet-Skiing, windsurfing, camping, and fires are all prohibited, which makes for a tranquil experience. You are allowed to fish, in season and with a license.

If you have the fortitude and patience to make it all the way to the tip of the spit, pay a visit to the **New Dungeness Lighthouse** (open for tours daily 9am-5pm). It was erected in 1857, making it the oldest lighthouse in the Puget Sound area.

Entertainment and Events
NIGHTLIFE
Things are quiet in Sequim at night, but you can find some life at the **Wind Rose Cellars** (143 W. Washington St., 360/681-0690, www.windrosecellars.com, Tues.-Thurs. 1pm-6pm, Fri. 1pm-10pm, Sat. noon-10pm). It plays multiple roles: wine-tasting room, art gallery, snack bar (serving mainly charcuterie and cheese to go with the wine), and, on Friday and Saturday evenings, live-music venue.

FESTIVALS AND EVENTS
First held in 1896, the **Sequim Irrigation Festival** (www.irrigationfestival.com) celebrates the original trench dug to bring water to the farms of Dungeness Valley. It's the longest continuously running festival in the state, taking place each year in the first week of May, and it's a catchall event with a parade, a logging show, a strongman competition, a carnival, fireworks, and at least a dozen more activities. All told, it's a timeless celebration of small-town life.

The **Sequim Lavender Weekend,** held on the third weekend in July, typically draws upward of 20,000 attendees. The **Sequim Lavender Growers Association** (www.lavenderfestival.com) conducts a festival in town with live music and food stands, and opens several member farms to the public free of charge. A dozen or so independent farms

lavender farm in Sequim

also welcome visitors, with some charging admission. The Sequim visitors center produces the event map, which you can download at the center's website, www.visitsunnysequim.com.

Sports and Recreation
RAILROAD BRIDGE PARK

One of the most picturesque spots in Sequim is **Railroad Bridge Park,** which is home to the **Dungeness River Audubon Center** (2151 W. Hendrickson Rd., 360/681-4076, http://dungenessrivercenter.org, Tues.-Sat. 10am-4pm, Sun. noon-4pm, free). The park's namesake, a handsome century-old bridge west of town, is now a link in the Olympic Discovery Trail. You'll find locals here taking a stroll or a jog, eating a picnic lunch, or having a dip in the Dungeness River. The Audubon Center is essentially a one-room natural history museum with information about the surrounding terrain and wildlife, including many mounted animals. On Wednesday mornings 8:30am-10:30am the center conducts free guided birding walks.

SEQUIM BAY STATE PARK

To the east of town **Sequim Bay State Park** (269035 U.S. 101, 360/683-4235, http://parks.state.wa.us/582, Discovery Pass required for parking) has 5,000 feet of waterfront that makes for pleasant strolls and is a popular spot for crabbing and clamming. (Information about required fishing licenses is available at http://wdfw.wa.gov/fishing/washington.)

KAYAKING

GoXpeditions (2577 W. Sequim Bay Rd., 360/300-7544) rents kayaks from the John Wayne Marina on Sequim Bay, just east of town.

BICYCLING

Ben's Bikes (1251 W. Washington St., 360/683-2666, www.bensbikessequim.com, daily 9am-7pm) rents comfort bicycles for $30 a day and full-suspension mountain bikes for $65 a day.

For an easygoing, paved bike path, check out the Sequim portion of the **Olympic Discovery Trail** (https://olympicdiscovery-trail.org), an ambitious ongoing project that starts in Port Townsend and, when completed, will reach the ocean at La Push. The trail runs through Sequim alongside Washington Street in the middle of town. To the west it takes you through Railroad Bridge State Park and continues on to Port Angeles. To the east it loops through Sequim Bay State Park and around the bay.

Experienced off-road cyclists looking for a thrill should check out the **Lower Dungeness-Gold Creek Loop** (www.fs.usda.gov/recmain/olympic/recreation, click on "Bicycling"), which takes you along the Dungeness River valley in Olympic National Forest. You get there on Forest Service Road 2860, reached via Palo Alto Road, a turnoff from U.S. 101 three miles east of Sequim. Getting there can be an adventure in itself; it's best to get detailed directions from Ben's Bikes.

Food
COFFEE

Coffee lovers will be happy to find several good, independently run cafes in Sequim. A two-block radius in the heart of town contains **Hurricane Coffee Co.** (104 W. Washington St., 360/681-6008, Mon.-Sat. 7am-6pm, Sun. 8am-6pm), **Suzon's** (145 E. Washington St., 260/683-8442, Mon.-Fri. 7am-5pm, Sat. 8am-4pm), and **RainShadow Coffee Roasting** (157 W. Cedar St., 360/681-0650, www.rainshadowcoffee.com, Mon.-Sat. 8am-4pm), which all serve espresso drinks and pastries in comfortable settings. Get your latte to go from the drive-through windows at **Adagio Bean and Leaf** (981 E. Washington St., 360/582-0024, http://adagiobeanandleaf.com, daily 6am-5pm) and **Reddog Coffee Co.** (521 S. Sequim Ave., 360/681-0304, daily 6am-6:30pm), the latter of which is just off U.S. 101.

BREAKFAST

For a substantial breakfast made with care and served with a smile, head to **The Oak**

Table Cafe (292 W. Bell St., 360/683-2179, www.oaktablecafe.com, daily 7am-3pm, $10-14). You can get omelets or eggs Benedict, but the claim to fame here is pancakes, made from scratch and served in interesting varieties, including puffy German and wafer-thin Swedish. At lunchtime they serve burgers, sandwiches, and salads.

ECLECTIC
★ Alder Wood Bistro (139 W. Alder St., 360/683-4321, www.alderwoodbistro.com, Thurs.-Sat. 11:30am-2:30pm and 4:30pm-8:30pm, $19-27) does the best job in Sequim of producing consistently satisfying food with creative flair. The seasonal menu has grilled meat, fish, pasta, and wood-fired pizzas that mix traditional and unconventional toppings in novel, delicious combinations. The dining room is usually crowded, so reserve a table and expect some noise. There's also patio seating.

Style-conscious Blondie's Plate (134 S. 2nd Ave., 360/683-2233, www.blondiesplate. com, Sun.-Thurs. 4pm-9pm, Fri.-Sat. 4pm-10pm, $15-39) takes a former church, fills it with sleek modern furniture, and serves up a menu of small plates divided into categories that include "surf," "pasture," and "starch." The food is tasty and often heartier than the setting might lead you to expect—roasted chicken, mac and cheese, and seared salmon are among the 30 or so choices.

Set on a long-established herb farm south of town, Nourish (101 Provence View Ln., 360/797-1480, www.nourishsequim.com, Wed.-Sat. 11:30am-8pm, Sun. 11am-8pm, $16-28) feels at once timeless and trendy. It fully embraces the contemporary farm-to-table ethos and serves organic, gluten-free foods that include numerous vegan options. The creative menu includes a halibut with roasted tomatoes, herb-rubbed lamb chops, and veggie lasagna.

MEXICAN
Jose's Famous Salsa (126 E. Washington St., 360/681-8598, www.josesfamoussalsa. com, Sun.-Thurs. 11am-9pm, Fri.-Sat. 11am-10pm, $7-13) is a good spot for a reasonably priced meal with some bold flavors. The menu is simple, well-made Mexican street food—burritos, tacos, and tamales—spiced up with an extensive salsa bar.

FINE DINING
The Dockside Grill (2577 West Sequim Bay Rd., 360/683-7510, www.docksidegrill-sequim.com, Wed.-Sun. 11:30am-3pm and 4pm-9pm, $20-40) is located at the John Wayne Marina on Sequim Bay, and it's reasonable to suspect this is a place the Duke would have liked. It's casually upscale, with nice water views (ask for a table in the front room) and a menu of tried-and-true classics like oysters Rockefeller, grilled salmon salad, and rib eye steak. The only thing that can be hard to swallow is the prices, which seem like they belong to a fancier joint.

Accommodations
Unlike in Port Townsend and Port Angeles, in Sequim the majority of lodgings are chain hotels, including Econo Lodge (801 E. Washington St., 360/683-7113, www. econolodge.com), Holiday Inn Express (1441 E. Washington St., 360/681-8756, www.ihg.com/holidayinnexpress), Red Lion (1095 E. Washington St., 360/683-1775, www. redlion.com/sequim), and Quality Inn & Suites (134 River Rd., 360/683-2800, www. qualityinn.com).

It's feasible to make Sequim your base for visiting the sights of northern Olympic National Park—you're just under an hour from Hurricane Ridge and Lake Crescent—but you'll save about half an hour if you stay in Port Angeles.

$100-150
Sequim West Inn and RV Park (740 W. Washington St., 360/683-4144, http://sequimwestinn.com, $125-142 d) provides basic, somewhat worn lodging in a central location. It also has one- to three-bedroom cottages—actually trailer homes—that have more room and fully equipped kitchens for $125-199.

Lighthouse Keeper for a Week

The New Dungeness Lighthouse provides a unique opportunity to live the life of a lighthouse keeper. Throughout the year, in weeklong stints, guests take up residence in the keeper's quarters, a quaint four-bedroom house that sleeps up to eight. Guests perform basic tasks—raising and lowering the flag, mowing the lawn, polishing the brass, and showing around visitors who have made the five-mile walk to the end of Dungeness Spit. Most of your time, though, is your own—to relax, watch the abundant wildlife and the passing ships, and gaze at the stars.

The cost for the stay is $395 per adult and $195 per child ages 6 to 17. (Younger kids aren't allowed, and every week there have to be at least four adults in residence.). Groups can have the whole place to themselves for $2,370. The fees are a primary source of finances for maintaining the lighthouse, which receives no government funding. You have to bring your own food, but the house has a fully equipped kitchen, as well as laundry facilities, cable TV, Wi-Fi, and pool and Ping-Pong in the basement.

The experience isn't for everyone, and there's a certain amount of luck involved—unless you rent the entire house, you'll be sharing it for a week with strangers. In most cases, though, housemates are kindred spirits who end the week as friends. To learn all the details, check availability, and initiate the process of arranging a stay, go to http://newdungenesslighthouse.com.

Five miles east of the town center, **Sequim Bay Lodge** (268522 U.S. 101, 360/683-0691, www.sequimbaylodge.com, $89-149 d) has bare-bones, motel-style accommodations for lower rates than chain hotels.

Clark's Chambers Bed & Breakfast Inn (322 Clark Rd., 360/683-4431, http://olypen.com/clacha, $125 d), north of town near Dungeness Spit, consists of four guest rooms in an old farmhouse that's been in the same family for over 150 years. Rooms are simple and homey, with floral wallpaper and water views.

$200-250

★ **Dungeness Barn House B&B** (42 Marine Dr., 360/582-1663, http://dungeness-barnhouse.com) is an old dairy barn overlooking Dungeness Bay that's been beautifully converted into two king suites ($210-230), two small single-occupancy rooms that share a bathroom ($155-165), and a large communal living room. Great views and attractive, unfussy antique decor make this one of Sequim's most pleasant places to stay.

The Sequim area has several old-school rustic resorts with cabins that are good for families or groups who want laid-back lodgings on the water with full kitchen facilities. On Sequim Bay there's the **Sunset Marine Resort** (40 Buzzard Ridge Rd., 360/591-4303, www.sunsetmarineresort.com, $205-275). And overlooking Dungeness Bay are **Dungeness Bay Cottages** (140 Marine Dr., 360/683-3013, http://dungenessbaycottages.com, $160-220) and the pricier **Juan de Fuca Cottages** (182 Marine Dr., 360/683-4433, www.juandefuca.com, $242-352), where accommodations come with jetted tubs and some have fireplaces. At all three places, most of the cabins sleep four or more, and a two-night minimum stay is required in summer.

OVER $250

Sequim's most indulgent accommodations are found at **Lost Mountain Lodge** (303 Sunny View Dr., 360/683-2431, www.lostmountainlodge.com, $200-320), which identifies itself as a B&B but doesn't have the typical quaint B&B atmosphere. It's a newer construction that feels like a cross between a luxurious private house and a miniature high-end resort. This is the type of place where you're told the thread count of your sheets and the name of the farm that supplied your organic eggs for breakfast.

CAMPING

Waterfront **Sequim Bay State Park** (269035 U.S. 101, 360/683-4235, http://parks.state.wa.us/582, $25-45, Discovery Pass required for parking) has two loops of camping sites with 48 tent spaces, 15 utility spaces, three restrooms, and three showers. Note that the herbs planted near the check-in building are for your use when preparing meals. Reservations can be by phone (888/226-7688) or online (http://washington.goingtocamp.com).

There are 66 campsites at the county-run **Dungeness Recreation Area** (554 Voice of America Rd. W., 360/683-5847, www.clallam.net/Parks/Dungeness.html, $23), which sits on a bluff overlooking the Strait of Juan de Fuca and Dungeness Spit, making it a great place for bird-watching. Sites are arranged in two wooded loops, with three restrooms and two coin-operated showers. Reserve sites on the county website for an additional $10 fee.

Information

The **Sequim Visitor Information Center** (1192 E. Washington St., 360/683-6197, www.visitsunnysequim.com, June-Aug. Mon.-Sat. 9am-5pm and Sun. 10am-4pm, Sept.-May Mon.-Sat. 10am-4pm and Sun. 10am-1pm) has maps and brochures for local attractions and events.

Transportation

Sequim is on U.S. 101, 30 miles west of Port Townsend (0.75 hr.), 18 miles (0.5 hr.) east of Port Angeles via Route 20, and 36 miles (1 hr.) northeast of the Hurricane Ridge Visitor Center in Olympic National Park.

Bus service to Sequim on the Dungeness Line is operated by **Olympic Bus Lines** (800/457-4492, http://olympicbuslines.com). The route runs between Sea-Tac airport and Port Angeles, with three stops in Seattle. The trip between Sea-Tac and Sequim takes 3.5 hours. Between Sequim and Port Angeles it's half an hour. For most of the year there are two eastbound trips and two westbound trips per day.

Clallam Transit (360/452-4511, www.clallamtransit.com) provides daily regional bus service for Clallam County, which covers most of the northern Olympic Peninsula, including Sequim, Port Angeles, Neah Bay, Forks, and La Push. Service between Port Townsend and Sequim, a trip that takes about an hour, is handled by **Jefferson Transit** (360/385-4777, http://jeffersontransit.com).

PORT ANGELES

Port Angeles (pop. 19,000) is the biggest town on the Olympic Peninsula. Its deep harbor, protected by the long Ediz Hook sand spit, is visited daily by commercial ships and the ferry from Victoria on British Columbia's Vancouver Island, which on a clear day you can spy across the Strait of Juan de Fuca. The view from the Port Angeles city pier is striking: To the south, rocky Klahhane Ridge, made more ominous by wispy cloud cover, seems to rise directly out of the strait's turbulent waters, barely leaving room for the town to wedge itself in between.

Port Angeles is perfectly situated to be the gateway to the northern end of Olympic National Park, and it serves that purpose, but it also holds onto its personality as a gritty commercial harbor and lumber-milling town. It's got a lot of character and some hipster cool, but don't expect to have a luxurious stay here.

Sights

The most conspicuous attraction is the **City Pier,** which has an observation tower with 360-degree views and a sandy beach with a picnic area. On the pier near the ferry dock, the **Feiro Marine Life Center** (315 N. Lincoln St., 360/417-6254, http://feiromarinelifecenter.org, June-Sept. daily 10am-5pm, Oct.-May daily noon-4pm, $5) has hands-on exhibits of more than 80 species of local marinelife.

In the Landing Mall across from the ferry terminal, the **Olympic Coast Discovery Center** (115 E. Railroad Ave., 360/452-3255,

Port Angeles

© AVALON TRAVEL

Strait of Juan de Fuca

To Airport

To Forks

Clallam County Fairgrounds

Lincoln Park

LAURIDSEN BLVD

W 16TH ST

I ST

D ST
C ST
B ST
A ST

Shane Park

TUMWATER TRUCK RT

BLACK DIAMOND RD

101

MARINE DR

HILLS ST

EDIZ HOOK RD

W 12TH ST
W 11TH ST
W 9TH ST
W 8TH ST
W 7TH ST

SABAI THAI

PINE ST

LAUREL ST

TOGA'S SOUP HOUSE

FIVE SEASONS

CHERRY ST
OAK ST

LITTLE DEVILS LUNCH BOX

PARK AVE

HEART O' THE HILLS PKWY

Olympic National Park

CHASE ST
E 12TH ST
E 11TH ST
E 10TH ST
E 9TH ST
E 8TH ST
E 7TH ST
E 6TH ST
E 5TH ST
E 4TH ST

LAUREL ST
LINCOLN ST
E 2ND ST
E 1ST ST
FRONT ST

SEE DETAIL

Port Angeles Harbor

EDIZ HOOK

LAURIDSEN BLVD

To Hurricane Ridge

EUNICE ST
FRANCIS ST
RACE ST

ALBERT ST

WASHINGTON ST
CHAMBERS ST
JONES ST

PORT ANGELES FINE ART CENTER

CHESTNUT COTTAGE

ENNIS ST

101

FRUGALS

Ferry to Victoria, BC

OLYMPIC LODGE

To Domaine Madeleine and Sequim

101

0   0.5 mi
0   0.5 km

Detail inset:

LAUREL ST
4TH ST
9TH ST
LINCOLN ST
CHASE ST
PEABODY ST
VINE ST

101

3RD

CONRAD DYAR MEMORIAL FOUNTAIN

NEXT DOOR GASTROPUB

DOWNTOWN HOTEL

PORT ANGELES INN

ELWHA KLALLAM HERITAGE CENTER

BELLA ITALIA

KOKOPELLI GRILL

RED LION HOTEL

FLAGSTONE MOTEL

ROYAL VICTORIAN

WINE ON THE WATERFRONT

RAILROAD AVE

SOUND BIKES & KAYAKS

OLYMPIC COAST DISCOVERY CENTER

VISITOR CENTER

FEIRO MARINE LIFE CENTER

CITY PIER

FRONT ST

Waterfront Trail

olympiccoast.noaa.gov/visitor, June-Aug. daily 10am-5pm, Sept.-Oct. Sat.-Sun. 10am-5pm, free) is the information center for the Olympic Coast National Marine Sanctuary, which encompasses much of the peninsula's coastline. Come here to get travel tips for touring along the coast, and to experience a few exhibits.

Get some background on the area's Indian culture at the **Elwha Klallam Heritage Center** (401 E. 1st. St., 360/417-8545, www.elwha.org, Mon.-Fri. 8am-5pm, free). In its great hall there are displays of Klallam artifacts found near Ediz Hook as well as rotating art shows.

Port Angeles is a more colorful place thanks to the public art downtown. There are numerous murals—look for the nice trompe l'oeil in the **Kalakala Ferry mural** on Laurel Street between First and Front, and half a block away is the impressive **Conrad Dyar Memorial Fountain**, surrounded by murals. The **Art on the Town** project funds and promotes a collection of sculptures found throughout downtown. Pick up an art map at the Port Angeles visitors center (121 E. Railroad Ave., 360/452-2363, www.visitportangeles.com, June-Aug. daily 8am-9pm, Sept.-May daily 10am-4pm).

Port Angeles Fine Arts Center (1203 E. Lauridsen Blvd., 360/457-3532, www.pafac.org, Mar.-Oct. Thurs.-Sun. 11am-5pm, Nov.-Feb. Thurs.-Sun. 10am-4pm, free), perched on a hill above town, displays work by regional artists in a small gallery with picture windows overlooking the bay. The biggest attraction here, though, is the wooded sculpture park with trails that meander around the gallery. It's open daily from dawn until dusk.

The Olympic Peninsula makes a modest contribution to Washington's wine industry. The original producer in the region is **Olympic Cellars Winery** (255410 U.S. 101, 360/452-0160, www.olympiccellars.com, Apr.-Oct. daily 11am-6pm, Nov.-Mar. daily 11am-5pm), located between Sequim and Port Angeles on U.S. 101. It's operated by three women and uses classic French varietals, including cabernet sauvignon, syrah, and petit verdot, mostly grown in eastern Washington. The tasting room is an attractively repurposed red barn.

Entertainment and Events
NIGHTLIFE
Head upstairs at the Landing Mall across from the ferry terminal to find **Wine on the Waterfront** (115 E. Railroad Ave., 360/565-8466, Tues.-Thurs. noon-10pm, Fri.-Sat. noon-11pm, Sun. noon-5:30pm). It's a bright, high-ceilinged wine bar with a casual atmosphere where you can spend an evening sampling from the wide selection and nibbling from a cheese plate. They also sell wine to go.

FESTIVALS AND EVENTS
Memorial Day weekend is marked in Port Angeles by the **Juan de Fuca Festival** (360/457-5411, jffa.org), which takes over town with performances by some 30 to 40 bands playing all varieties of pop music, from blues to folk to rock and roll. There are also kids' activities and a street fair. Be prepared to stay up late—the after-hours jams can be the highlight of the weekend.

The **Dungeness Crab & Seafood Festival** (360/452-6300, www.crabfestival.org), held in early October, celebrates the bounty of the sea with cooking demonstrations, a chowder contest, streets full of food stands, and whimsical events like the Marine Debris Art Show and the Grab-a-Crab Derby.

At the mid-October **Forest Storytelling Festival** (360/452-8092, www.clallamstorypeople.org) professional storytellers from around the country gather to practice their craft. Spend the weekend listening to yarns or take part in a workshop and let your own story be heard in a friendly, supportive setting. The event takes place at Peninsula College (1502 E. Lauridsen Blvd.), two miles southeast of downtown.

Sports and Recreation
Adventures through Kayaking (2358 U.S. 101, 360/417-3015, www.atkayaking.com) is a

first-rate, all-purpose outfitter offering tours and instruction not only for kayaking, but also stand-up paddleboarding, white-water rafting, and off-road biking. There are trips tailored to the full range of skill levels, and they also rent equipment for those who want to go it on their own—rates for mountain bikes, kayaks, and paddleboards are $15/hour, $57/day.

Sound Bikes & Kayaks (120 E. Front St, 360/457-1240, www.soundbikeskayaks.com, Mon.-Sat. 10am-6pm) rents kayaks ($15/hour, $50/day) and bikes ($10/hour, $45/day). It's located downtown just off the harbor.

The **Waterfront Trail,** part of the peninsula-long Olympic Discovery Trail, is a pleasant six-mile paved path that follows the downtown shoreline and continues out to the Coast Guard base on Ediz Hook—a 3.5-mile natural sand spit protecting the Northwest's deepest harbor. Along the way you get prime views of Vancouver Island to the north and the snowcapped Olympics to the south. The spit is a good place to picnic, do some beachcombing, and watch the freighters come and go.

Food
BREAKFAST
You get breakfasts hearty enough to fuel a day of hiking at **First Street Haven** (107 E. 1st St., 360/457-0352, Mon.-Sat. 7am-4pm, Sun. 8am-2pm, $10-14), a narrow, wood-paneled downtown diner that's a local favorite. Menu highlights include omelets, French toast, and cinnamon rolls. They serve good sandwiches and salads at lunch, but breakfast is their claim to fame.

About a mile east of downtown on U.S. 101, **Chestnut Cottage** (929 E. Front St., 360/452-8344, http://chestnutcottagerestaurant.com, daily 7am-3pm, $10-16) is another solid choice for substantial breakfasts, from scrambles to biscuits and gravy to crème brulee French toast. The lunch menu is eclectic, with enchiladas, stir-fries, quiche, and half a dozen kinds of sandwiches.

AMERICAN
Conveniently located along U.S. 101, **Frugals** (1520 E. Front St., 360/452-4320, www.frugalburger.com, Sun.-Thurs. 10:30am-10pm, Fri.-Sat. 10:30am-11pm, $6-8) is a drive-through fast-food joint locally famous for juicy burgers, huckleberry shakes, and seasoned fries. If you're considering a stop at the nearby McDonald's, upgrade your experience by going here instead.

Toga's Soup House Deli & Gourmet (122 W. Lauridsen Blvd., 360/452-1952, www.togassouphouse.com, Mon.-Fri. 7am-4pm, $5-14) fills an old Victorian house with the aroma of five soups prepared fresh daily from a rotating menu of some 30 varieties. They also make substantial salads and sandwiches, which are good options for a picnic—the location just off the highway south of downtown is an easy stop on the way to the national park. Seating is limited; much of their business is takeout, and they have a drive-through window.

ECLECTIC
A young, lively scene can be found at **Next Door GastroPub** (13 W. 1st St., 360/504-2613, www.nextdoorgastropub.com, Mon.-Thurs. 11am-11pm, Fri.-Sat. 11am-midnight, Sun. 10am-11pm, $9-26), where the bar specializes in microbrews and craft cocktails and the kitchen turns out first-rate pub food, from tacos and sliders to shepherd's pie and fish-and-chips.

The owners of **Kokopelli Grill** (203 E. Front St., 360/457-6040, www.kokopelli-grill.com, Mon.-Thurs. 11am-9pm, Fri.-Sat. 11am-10pm, Sun. 2pm-8pm, $12-32) are a pair of Texans who have brought Southwestern cuisine to downtown Port Angeles. They serve grilled meats and fish, chicken-fried steak, and lots of chili pepper-infused dishes.

ITALIAN
Any *Twilight* fan will tell you that Bella and Edward went on their first date to ★ **Bella Italia** (118 E. 1st St., 360/457-5442, www.bellaitaliapa.com, daily 5pm-10pm, $10-34).

It shows they had good taste—this is Port Angeles's best Italian restaurant, serving creative pizzas, pastas, and entrées that make good use of local seafood and produce. The setting is cheery and intimate. It's still a good place for a date, despite the fact that it draws lots of teenagers with parents in tow.

MEXICAN
Little Devil's Lunchbox (324 W. 1st St., 360/504-2959, https://devilslunch.com, Mon.-Fri. 10am-6pm, Sat. 11am-3pm, $8-11) serves Mexican street-food standards—burritos, tacos—and throws in a few curveballs, like a Cubano sandwich and a sandwich with Cajun prawns and Tillamook cheese. The vibe is part hipster, part hole-in-the-wall.

THAI
One of the most reliable places for dinner in Port Angeles is **Sabai Thai** (903 W. 8th St., 360/452-4505, www.sabaithaipa.com, Mon.-Sat. 4pm-9pm, $13-18). It serves consistently good Thai cuisine, including numerous vegetarian options, in a pleasant setting with attentive, professional service.

FINE DINING
Dining at **C'est Si Bon** (23 Cedar Park Rd., 360/452-8888, www.cestsibon-frenchcuisine.com, Tues.-Sun. 5pm-11pm, $30-35), five miles east of downtown along U.S. 101, is like entering an alternate universe. It's a bastion of French haute cuisine, served in an opulent setting of white tablecloths, crystal chandeliers, and deep-red walls hung with Rococo paintings. The food—escargot, crab soufflé, steak au poivre—is executed with the confident hand of chef who's been making these dishes for over 30 years. There's no other place like it on the Olympic Peninsula.

For fine dining with small-town flair, check out **Dupuis** (256861 U.S. 101, 360/457-8033, Wed.-Sat. 4pm-8pm, $15-30). Since the 1920s it's been serving seafood and steaks out of a cabin with antique-mall decor on U.S. 101 halfway between Port Angeles and Sequim—look for the neon sign. The menu sticks to classics like oyster stew, cioppino, and bacon-wrapped filet mignon.

Accommodations
Lodging options are primarily motels that have seen better days. Because of the prime location, both for park visitors and passengers on the morning ferry to Victoria, those motels charge eyepoppingly high rates.

UNDER $100
The Downtown Hotel (101 E. Front St., 360/565-1125, http://portangelesdowntown-hotel.com, $60-80 d) is the rare Port Angeles lodging that offers rooms in the busy summer season for under $100 a night. Furnishings are basic, and 12 guest rooms share four bathrooms, which explains the lower price. The location is in the heart of downtown, one block from the ferry terminal.

$100-150
The Royal Victorian (521 E. 1st St., 360/452-8400, www.royalvictorian.net, $114-149 d) and **The Flagstone Motel** (415 E. 1st St., www.flagstonemotel.com, 360/457-9434, $110-160 d) are old budget motels located within a block of one another along U.S. 101, half a mile east of the ferry terminal. At either one you can save a few bucks if you're okay with dated rooms and a somewhat run-down neighborhood. Ask for a room away from the road.

$150-200
Port Angeles Inn (111 E. 2nd St., 360/452-9285, www.portangelesinn.com, $110-175) and **Quality Inn Uptown** (101 E. 2nd St., 360/849-1513, www.choicehotels.com, $150-200) sit side by side on a bluff overlooking the harbor, and both offer functional, somewhat dated accommodations. Rooms facing the water have nice harbor views, and a set of stairs on the bluff gives easy access to downtown and the ferry.

Red Lion Hotel (221 North Lincoln St., 360/452-9215, www.redlion.com/port-angeles,

$179-214 d) isn't fancy, but it has renovated rooms in a prime waterfront location two blocks from the ferry terminal. Premium rooms, which cost $20 more than standard, have striking views directly out onto the water.

Calling it a lodge isn't quite accurate, but **Olympic Lodge** (140 Del Guzzi Dr., 360/452-2993, www.olympiclodge.com, $169-209 d), located along U.S. 101 two miles east of the ferry terminal, has an attractive lobby and the large, comfortable rooms you'd expect from a well-run mid-priced business hotel. Ask for a room in the back, away from the road with a view of the neighboring golf course.

Five SeaSuns (1006 S. Lincoln St., 360/452-8248, www.seasuns.com, $159-195), off U.S. 101 just south of town, is a classic B&B experience: an attractive older house filled with antiques and cozy little rooms, and an elaborate breakfast to start the day.

OVER $250

About midway between Sequim and Port Angeles, along the bluffs overlooking the water, a cluster of high-end B&Bs constitute the area's luxury lodging options. **George Washington Inn** (939 Finn Hall Rd., www.georgewashingtoninn.com, $260-300) is a modern replica of Washington's iconic home, Mount Vernon, set on a lavender farm. **Domaine Madeleine** (146 Wildflower Ln., 360/457-4174, http://domainemadeleine.com, $285-361) is distinguished by clean-lined, Asian-inspired design. **Colette's Bed & Breakfast** (339 Finn Hall Rd., 360/457-9197, www.colettes.com, $295-375) emphasizes the views with suites that all have picture windows looking out over the water. **Sea Cliff Gardens** (397 Monterra Dr., 360/452-2322, www.seacliffgardens.com, $235-270) has ornately furnished rooms and a large, well-tended garden above the bluffs.

Information and Services

Pick up maps, brochures, and travel tips at the **Port Angeles Visitor Center** (121 E. Railroad Ave., 360/452-2363, www.visitportangeles.com, Mon.-Fri. 8am-5pm, Sat.

10am-4pm, Sun. noon-4pm). If you're taking the ferry to Victoria, you might want to stop in at the **Port Angeles-Victoria Tourist Bureau** (115 E. Railroad Ave., 360/452-7084, daily 7am-5pm), which shares the same location as the visitors center. It has information about sights and activities on Vancouver Island and can help with booking lodging.

Transportation

Port Angeles is on U.S. 101, 18 miles (0.5 hr.) west of Sequim, 47 miles (1 hr.) west of Port Townsend via Route 20, and 19 miles (0.75 hr.) north of the Hurricane Ridge Visitor Center in Olympic National Park.

There's bus service to Port Angeles on the Dungeness Line operated by **Olympic Bus Lines** (800/457-4492, http://olympicbuslines.com). The route runs between Sea-Tac airport and Port Angeles, with three stops in Seattle. Some buses also stop in Sequim and some in Port Townsend, though never both on the same trip. The ride between Sea-Tac and Port Angeles takes about four hours. There are two eastbound trips and two westbound trips per day.

Clallam Transit (360/452-4511, www.clallamtransit.com) provides daily regional bus service for Clallam County, which covers most of the northern Olympic Peninsula, including Sequim, Port Angeles, Neah Bay, Forks, and La Push. For service between Port Townsend and Port Angeles, transfer in Sequim for **Jefferson Transit** (360/385-4777, http://jeffersontransit.com).

The privately owned **Black Ball Ferry Line** (360/457-4491, www.cohoferry.com) runs the *MV Coho* between Port Angeles and Victoria, British Columbia. There are four trips a day mid-June-early September, with the number tapering off to one in January and February. The trip takes 90 minutes. One-way fares are $18.50 for adult passengers, $9.25 for children, $64 for vehicles under 18 feet and driver, $37 for motorcycle and rider, and $6.50 to bring on a bicycle. There's also a reservation fee for vehicles—one-way is $11 online or $16 by phone, round-trip $16 online or $26 by phone.

Northern Olympic National Park

Four of the most popular destinations within massive Olympic National Park are along its northern border, within driving distance of Port Angeles: Hurricane Ridge, Lake Crescent, the Elwha Valley, and Sol Duc Valley. You can get a taste of all four over the course of a few days, but these are places that reward you for dedicating more time to them. Whether your goal is outdoor adventure or just lying back and watching the world go by, you can do it here.

Any trip to the park benefits from a stop first at the **Olympic National Park Visitor Center** (3002 Mount Angeles Rd., 360/565-3130, www.nps.gov/olym), located on the outskirts of Port Angeles along the road leading to Hurricane Ridge. There you can watch a 25-minute orientation video, look at displays about flora and fauna, pick up maps and literature, and get guidance from one of the rangers on staff. Housed in the center is the **Wilderness Information Center** (360/565-3100), where hikers planning on venturing into the backcountry can get up-to-date weather and trail reports and purchase overnight permits ($8 pp per night). Both centers are open daily throughout the year, but hours vary seasonally depending on funding. It's smart to call ahead and make sure they're open, especially in winter.

★ HURRICANE RIDGE

One of the Olympic National Park's most scenic and visited areas, Hurricane Ridge towers 5,200 feet over the Strait of Juan de Fuca. By car it's a straight shot along Port Angeles's Race Street, which becomes Mount Angeles Road and then Hurricane Ridge Road as it snakes up the mountainside for 17 picturesque miles at an easy 7 percent grade.

As the road nears its end you reach the **Hurricane Ridge Visitor Center**, which serves as an invaluable base for exploration. The center has exhibits, a snack bar, and a gift shop, but its greatest asset is its team of rangers, who are there to advise you about the best way to spend your time on the ridge—which usually means suggesting a hiking trail that suits you. In summer rangers also lead daily guided nature walks.

Even if you' never set foot on a trail, it's worth the trip up just for the views of the snowcapped peaks from the observation deck. This is also an easy place to have wildlife encounters. Black-tailed deer frequently meander down to the parking lot, and you might spot a marmot along the quarter-mile meadow path adjacent to the visitors center.

If you're up for a scenic, white-knuckle drive, turn off onto **Obstruction Pass Road** just before the visitors center parking lot. It's eight miles of gravel road with spectacular views but no guardrails. RVs and trailers aren't allowed.

Hurricane Ridge Road and the visitors center are open daily mid-May-mid-October and Friday-Sunday the rest of the year, so long as the road up is passable. The visitors center's information desk, snack bar, and gift shop are operational mid-May-late September and late December-March. Daily hours for the center vary depending on the season and on funding. Confirm hours, and also find out when ranger-led walks are scheduled, by calling the park's general-information line, 360/565-3130. In winter to find out if the road is open call 360/565-3131.

TOP EXPERIENCE

Hiking

A relatively simple hike along the **Hurricane Hill Trail** (1.6 miles one-way, 700-foot elevation gain) takes you through fields of wildflowers and up to a ridge where you can see the Olympics to one side and the Strait of Juan de Fuca, far below you, to the other. On a clear day it can be absolutely uplifting. You may

Olympic National Park

© AVALON TRAVEL

0   10 km
0   10 mi

PACIFIC OCEAN

MAKAH INDIAN RESERVATION

Cape Alava
Shi Shi Beach
Point of Arches
Ozette
Lake Ozette
Ozette

RIALTO BEACH
La Push
MORA CAMPGROUND
MORA RANGER STATION
Forks

Olympic National Park
HOH INDIAN RESERVATION
Destruction Island

Sol Duc River
Beaver
Sappho
Sekiu
Clallam Bay

Strait of Juan de Fuca

112

KALALOCH LODGE
BROWNS POINT
RUBY BEACH
KALALOCH CAMPGROUND
KALALOCH RANGER STATION
SOUTH BEACH CAMPGROUND
Queets

HOH OXBOW CAMPGROUND
WILLOUGHBY CREEK CAMPGROUND
MINNIE PETERSON CAMPGROUND
HOH RAIN FOREST/HOH RAIN FOREST CAMPGROUND

Clearwater River
Hoh River

101

Olympic National Forest

FAIRHOLME CAMPGROUND
LAKE CRESCENT
SALMON CASCADES
SOL DUC RANGER STATION
EAGLE LODGE
HOT SPRINGS RESORT/SOL DUC CAMPGROUND
SOL DUC FALLS
HOT SPRINGS
LAKE CRESCENT LODGE
OLYMPIC VIEWPOINT
GLINES CANYON VIEWPOINT

LOG CABIN RESORT
DEVIL'S PUNCHBOWL
Joyce

Olympic National Forest

QUINAULT INDIAN RESERVATION

LAKE QUINAULT AND QUINAULT RAIN FOREST
QUINAULT WILDERNESS INFORMATION OFFICE

Olympic National Forest

QUINAULT RAIN FOREST RANGER STATION
COLONEL BOB MOUNTAIN

Queets River
Quinault River

Mt Olympus 7,965 ft
Glacier Meadows
Bogachiel Peak 5,474 ft

Olympic Mountains

Olympic National Park

Elwha River

ELWHA RANGER STATION
MADISON FALLS
HURRICANE HILL TRAIL
Hurricane Ridge
Mt Deception 7,788 ft

Port Angeles

CANADA
USA
Ferry to Victoria, BC

HURRICANE RIDGE
HEART O'THE HILLS CAMPGROUND
DEER PARK CAMPGROUND

Sequim

101

Enchanted Valley
Anderson Pass
Duckabush River

STAIRCASE CAMPGROUND
STAIRCASE RANGER STATION

Lake Cushman

119

Lilliwaup
Eldon

101

Quinault River
Dosewallips River

DOSEWALLIPS CAMPGROUND
Dosewallips State Park

Mt Walker
Quilcene

Olympic National Forest

Hood Canal
Brinnon
Kitsap Peninsula

Hurricane Hill Trail

playground—you can downhill ski, cross-country ski, snowboard, tube, and snowshoe. The road and the visitors center are open Friday through Sunday (and also Monday holidays), weather permitting—call 360/565-3131 to check the current status. All vehicles are required to carry tire chains, regardless of the weather conditions.

For downhill skiing there are two rope tows and one Poma lift, managed by the **Hurricane Ridge Winter Sports Club** (360/452-5144, www.hurricaneridge.com). Passes range $13-34 for a full day; you also have to pay standard park admission. The visitors center gift shop rents downhill skis ($37/day), cross-country skis ($32/day), and snowshoes ($17/day).

You can take part in a ranger-led, easy-to-moderate **snowshoe walk** at 2pm on most winter days when the park is open. Walks cost $7, including loaner snowshoes, and groups are limited to 25. Sign up 30 minutes before the start time at the visitors center information desk.

have to struggle with the impulse to throw your arms wide and belt out the opening bars of "The Sound of Music."

Eight day hikes begin from the visitors center, ranging from short, paved paths to eight-mile descents into the neighboring valleys. For dedicated hikers a great option is the 13-mile loop that combines the **Klahhane Ridge** and **Mount Angeles** trails, a rigorous climb taking you past mountain vistas and picturesque Lake Angeles. The hike starts and ends at the Heart O' the Hills campground near the park's Hurricane Ridge entrance.

One of the park's best multiday backcountry experiences is the 32-mile **Cameron Creek Trail,** which goes deep into the wilderness. Access to the trailhead is from unpaved Deer Park Road, which connects with U.S. 101 five miles east of Port Angeles.

Winter Activities

From late December through March Hurricane Ridge turns into a winter

Camping

Heart o' the Hills Campground is near the park entrance along Hurricane Ridge Road, 12 miles from the Hurricane Ridge Visitor Center. It has 105 sites suitable for RVs up to 21 feet, with some sites that can accommodate rigs up to 35 feet. It's open year-round and has running water. Sites are $20 and are available on a first-come, first-served basis.

To the east of Hurricane Ridge, the **Deer Park Campground** is the only alpine camping location in Olympic National Park. It's accessible by unpaved Deer Park Road, off of U.S. 101 five miles east of Port Angeles, and is open seasonally depending on the snowmelt. There are 14 tent-only sites, available for $15 on a first-come, first-served basis, with pit toilets and no running water. Your compensation for the primitive conditions is a gorgeous setting, with both mountain and water views, spectacular sunsets, and unobstructed stargazing.

Olympic National Park at a Glance

Visitors to different parts of Olympic National Park have distinctly different experiences. The 1,400-square-mile park covers the entire center of the peninsula, as well as a long, separate stretch of the western coastline. The territory surrounding the park includes 980 square miles of national forest. All told, it's a giant chunk of rugged, mostly wild terrain.

BASIC INFORMATION

Seasons: The park welcomes visitors year-round, though some roads, campgrounds, and other facilities are open only in summer.

Admission and Fees: A one-week pass costs $25 per vehicle, $10 if you enter on foot or bicycle, and $15-20 per motorcycle. You can get a one-year pass for $50. There's no charge for entry to the two parts of the park that are crossed by U.S. 101, at Lake Crescent and along the coastline south from Ruby Beach. To camp in the backcountry you need a permit ($8 pp per night) available at the Wilderness Information Center (360/565-3100) within the main visitors center near Port Angeles, and also at some ranger stations. Campgrounds charge $15-22 per night for a site. They're all first come, first served except for at Sol Duc and Kalaloch.

Visitor Information: The park's main **visitors center** (3002 Mount Angeles Rd.) is at the south end of Port Angeles. There are also visitors centers on Hurricane Ridge and in the Hoh Rain Forest, and a recreation information office at Lake Quinault. Get visitor information online at www.nps.gov/olym and by phone at 360/565-3130. The road and weather hotline is 360/565-3131.

TRANSPORTATION AND ACCESS POINTS

U.S. 101, which circles three sides of the large central portion of the park, is the major thoroughfare on the peninsula. Branching from it are several paved roads that enter the central park.

Transportation

Hurricane Ridge is 19 miles, about 45 minutes, south of downtown Port Angeles, starting on Race Street, which becomes Mount Angeles Road and then Hurricane Ridge Road. There's no public transit to the visitors center, but you can get there as part of a tour with **All Points Charters and Tours** (360/460-7131, www.goallpoints. com), which will give you a few hours to take a walk with a naturalist or explore on your own.

ELWHA RIVER VALLEY

The biggest change in Olympic National Park's recent history is the restoration of the peninsula's largest river, the Elwha. Early in the 20th century the Glines Canyon and Elwha Dams were built to harness the river's power for paper milling in Port Angeles, with significant environmental repercussions, including decimation of a major salmon run. After decades of wrangling, the dams were

removed between 2011 and 2014 in the world's largest undamming project.

The dams are now gone, but the process of restoration will unfold over the course of many years. It's a joint enterprise between man and nature, with water being coaxed back to its old channels, salmon swimming upstream to places where they haven't been seen in a century, and a former reservoir bed getting reseeded to hasten its return to forest. From the **Glines Canyon Viewpoint** along Whiskey Bend Road you can look down on the remnants of the dam and witness the transformation of the old reservoir.

Stories abound of fishermen reeling in 100-pound salmon from the Elwha in the days before the dams, and with five salmon species in the river (Chinook, coho, chum, sockeye, and pink) as well as abundant trout, fishing is likely to be one of the main draws for this area of the park. Until at least 2019, though, there's a fishing moratorium in place as part of the river restoration project. Until

Northern Access Points: You can work the four northern access points into a single visit, requiring two days at a minimum. In a nutshell, **Hurricane Ridge** gives you gorgeous alpine trails—it's by far the most accessible mountainous region of the park. **Lake Crescent** has a classic old national park resort on the banks of a striking, turquoise-blue lake. The **Elwha River** is notable for its restoration after a huge undamming project. **Sol Duc River Valley** is best known for its hot springs, but it also has some of the park's most beautiful short wooded hikes.

Western Access Points: As the eagle flies it's less than 10 miles between Sol Duc Hot Springs and the visitors center at the **Hoh Rain Forest,** the park's west-central entrance. To get from one point to the other by car, though, you have to take a 70-mile, two-hour loop around the mountains. It's viable to do this drive, visit the rain forest, and spend the night at one of the campsites or lodgings on or near the coast. About two hours south of the Hoh visitors center is **Lake Quinault,** the park's southwestern entry point, which combines several features found elsewhere in the park, including a historic lodge like Lake Crescent and rain forest like the Hoh area.

Eastern Access Point: You can reach the remote east side at Staircase, nine miles west of U.S. 101 at Hoodsport.

One thing all of the access points have in common is that they just scratch the surface. The interior of the park is accessible only on foot, or in some places on horseback. Climbing Mount Olympus, the highest peak, is a major expedition, and most of the interior trails are suitable only for experienced hikers. That goes for the long sliver of coast that's part of the park as well. U.S. 101 runs along the bottom quarter of this coastal area; in the middle there are roads to **La Push** and **Rialto Beach;** at the top you can drive to **Lake Ozette.** Beyond that the 73 miles of beach are reachable only on foot.

it's lifted, visitors will be coming here to hike the pleasant wooded trails and watch the river's transformation. One thing they won't be doing is camping; the area's two campgrounds have been wiped out by the river as it has changed course.

Madison Falls

Just as you cross into the park, before reaching the Elwha entrance station, you encounter Madison Falls. It isn't the most spectacular falls in the park. (For the region's more impressive offerings, check out Marymere Falls near Lake Crescent and Sol Duc Falls in the Sol Duc Valley.) It's still worth a look though, and it's easily reached by a paved, wheelchair-accessible 200-foot path from the parking area.

Olympic Hot Springs

While Sol Duc Hot Springs a few miles to the west is better known and more developed, remote Olympic Hot Springs has something of

a cult status among thermal-water enthusiasts. The seven natural pools are primitive, with mud and rocks at the bottom, and shallow, reaching about waist height when sitting. Temperatures range 85-105 degrees Fahrenheit.

There was once a large resort here, but now the experience has a back-to-nature feel to it, which may explain why bathers frequently choose to skinny-dip. Park officials have established a bathe-at-your-own-risk policy, warning of potentially high bacteria levels while also stating that they don't maintain or monitor the water quality. Bathers are undeterred. On weekends you may have to wait for space in a pool. To reach Olympic Hot Springs, drive to the end of Olympic Hot Springs Road and then follow the Boulder Lake Trail 2.5 miles, making a gentle, steady climb on the way there.

Hiking

There are half a dozen day hikes through

the wooded valley ranging from a mile to 12 miles, as well as several longer trails that connect to adjacent Hurricane Ridge and the Sol Duc River valley. They can also be used to reach paths deeper into the park for multiday backcountry trips.

One of the most popular hikes is the **Humes Ranch Loop.** Get to it by taking the narrow, gravel Whiskey Bend Road, which forks off from Olympic Hot Springs Road just past the ranger station. After about four miles the road comes to an end as you reach the trailhead for the loop (and also for the Elwha River Trail, which goes all the way across the park). It's a shady, wooded walk that takes you past two long-abandoned early-20th-century homesteads, Michael's Cabin and Humes Ranch, with the loop back (if you're going clockwise) skirting along the eastern bank of the Elwha. (If you choose to go counterclockwise, passing the river first, you avoid a steep climb at the end of your hike.) There's a short turnoff to reach Goblin Gates, a picturesque spot where the river rushes between two rocky outcroppings. The loop is 6.5 miles, but you can shorten it by taking the turn to Krause Bottom before reaching Michael's Cabin.

For a view of the changing Elwha between the two former dam sites, take the **West Elwha Trail,** which goes north from a trailhead near the former Altair Campground. There's an initial climb that takes you away from the river, but you quickly descend again to the banks, where you get views of rapids, as well as the opportunity to see eagles, harlequin ducks, and other wildlife. The trail runs for 3 miles, crossing over the park's border into private property, but Freeman Creek, at about the 2.5-mile point, is a good spot to turn around.

Farther into the park, and away from the river, **Boulder Lake Trail** is used primarily for its access to Olympic Hot Springs, but it's a rewarding hike on its own merits. The trailhead is at the end of Olympic Hot Springs Road, the main road through the valley. The

Glines Canyon Viewpoint

trail makes a gentle climb through old-growth forest, initially along a former roadbed. At 2.5 miles it reaches the hot springs, just after crossing Boulder Creek. At this point you can check out the pools and hop in or save them for a dip on the way back. Continuing for another 2.5 miles or so, passing a turnoff for Appleton Pass along the way, you reach the beautiful green-tinted lake, with Boulder Peak looming above it. (There's a primitive campsite here; you can spend the night, but to do so you need a backcountry pass, available at the Wilderness Information Center and some ranger stations and visitors centers.) Head back the way you came, or pick up **Happy Lake Ridge Trail,** an eight-mile hike with beautiful mountain views that deposits you back on Olympic Hot Springs Road two miles down from the Boulder Lake trailhead where you started.

For a major multiday hike, cross the entire expanse of the park from north to south starting on the **Elwha River Trail,** which shares a trailhead with the Humes Ranch Loop at the end of Whiskey Bend Road. It follows the path of the Elwha for 28 miles and then turns into the North Fork Quinault River Trail, ending after another 16 miles at Lake Quinault. Consult with the Wilderness Information Center (360/565-3100) before taking this on.

Accommodations

Overlooking the river from a secluded spot bordering the park, **Elwha Ranch Bed & Bath** (905 Herrick Rd., 360/457-6540, www.elwharanch.com, $130-150 d) has a lot going for it in terms of location—you're at the edge of the wilderness but just 10 miles from civilization in Port Angeles. The rooms—two suites and a cabin—are spare and dated, and note that this "B&B" doesn't include breakfast, so you should bring your own food. A two-night minimum is required, and cash or a check is necessary; credit cards are not accepted.

Information and Services

The **Elwha Ranger Station,** located along Olympic Hot Springs Road, has posted information and is staffed intermittently in summer. When no one is around, direct questions to the information desk at the park's main visitors center, 360/565-3130.

Transportation

The Elwha entrance to the park is about 11 miles, a drive of 15-20 minutes, southwest of downtown Port Angeles, reached from U.S. 101 via Olympic Hot Springs Road. The road continues into the park for 10 miles, first following the course of the Elwha and then doglegging right and ending at the Boulder Creek trailhead.

You can reach the intersection of U.S. 101 and Olympic Hot Springs Road by bus on **Clallam Transit** (360/452-4511, www.clallamtransit.com) Route 14, which runs between Port Angeles and Forks about every two hours 6am-7pm. That puts you about two miles from the park entrance.

★ LAKE CRESCENT

Lake Crescent is the place to go if you're looking for beauty and tranquility in Olympic National Park without having to rough it. The glacier-carved lake is gorgeous, 12 miles long and over 600 feet deep, surrounded by old-growth forest that ascends steep ridges to the horizon. The water is translucent turquoise green, made clear by a lack of nitrogen, which inhibits the growth of microalgae. At points along the lake's surface you can see down to a depth of 60 feet.

The view from the water's edge is reason enough to pay Lake Crescent a visit. If you spend some time here you can get out on the water in kayaks, rowboats, and paddleboards; you can fish; and though the water is cold, you can swim in summer. If you're traveling as a family, or have a teenager who's enthusiastic about science and the great outdoors, you may want to look into **NatureBridge** (415/992-4700, www.naturebridge.org), an environmental education organization with a facility near the lake. It has weekend family programs in the spring and summer and two-week science summer camps for teens.

This is one of two locations within the northern part of the park that has lodging—the other being Sol Duc Hot Springs—and the only one with a classic, rustic national park lodge. It also has the park's swankiest, most expensive restaurant. U.S. 101 cuts into the park here to the south of the lake. Because the entrance is also a main thoroughfare there's no fee charged for going into this part of the park.

Hiking

Hikes around the lake up on the neighboring slopes are a beautiful mix of woods as well as lake and mountain views. Get maps and information about day hikes in the lodge lobby or at the Storm King Ranger Station, just east of the lodge, which is staffed daily in summer and intermittently other times of year. The station is the starting point for the **Marymere Falls Trail,** a gentle 0.8-mile walk in the woods culminating with a view of the 90-foot falls, which is arguably the most picturesque in the entire park.

After half a mile on the path to the falls there's a turnoff for the **Mount Storm King Trail.** It's a rigorous hike, steeply ascending 1,700 feet over 1.9 miles of switchback trail. At 1.4 miles, a stunning viewpoint overlooks the lake and out to Mount Pyramid. If you climb the remaining half mile you'll reach another outlook that faces away from the lake but has a good view of Barnes Valley on the other side. Note that the trail has steep and narrow points with no guardrail, and in three places there are ropes to help you pull your way up (and steady your descent). This isn't a good hike for young children.

The four-mile-long **Spruce Railroad Trail** is the best place for a lakeside hike. It follows along the northern shore, accessed via East Shore Road, a turnoff from U.S. 101 just to the east of the lake. As the name indicates, much of the trail is a repurposed railroad track that was once used for hauling Sitka spruce—you even go through a tunnel. It's now a segment of the Olympic Discovery Trail, which means walkers and cyclists share the path. The plan is for the entire trail to be paved by 2019, and there's already a paved 6.5-mile extension that connects on its west end with U.S. 101.

About one mile from its eastern starting point you reach the Spruce Railroad Trail's highlight: **Devil's Punchbowl,** a calm cove surrounded by tall bluffs and crossed by a picturesque bridge, at the end of which you get a postcard-worthy view of Mount Storm King. This spot is a popular swimming hole.

Boating and Fishing

There's a distinctive kind of bliss that comes from getting out on the lake in a boat. At Lake Crescent Lodge and the Log Cabin Resort you can rent kayaks, rowboats, canoes, and paddleboards, all for the same rates: $20 for one hour, $30 for two hours, $45 for up to five hours, and $60 for up to eight hours. You can also bring your own motorboat—the lake has three boat launches—but personal watercraft, such as Jet Skis, are forbidden.

There are two subspecies of trout swimming in the lake, Beardslee rainbow and Crescenti cutthroat, that aren't found anywhere else in the world. You can fish for them, as well as more abundant kokanee, from May through October. Fishing is strictly catch-and-release, and you can use only an artificial

kayaking on Lake Crescent

lure weighing two ounces or less with a barb-less single-point hook.

Food

Granny's Cafe (235471 U.S. 101, 360/928-3266, http://grannyscafe.net, Thurs.-Tues. 9am-7:30pm, $9-18), on U.S. 101 east of the lake, is a charming down-home diner where they make eggs and pancakes for breakfast and sandwiches, soups, and salads for lunch and dinner. It's not fancy, but everything is well prepared and served with a smile. This place and the Indian Valley Motel next door are nice alternatives to the pricey, sometimes disappointing options inside the park.

The restaurant at **Lake Crescent Lodge** (416 Lake Crescent Rd., 360/928-3211, www. olympicnationalparks.com, May-Dec. daily 7am-2:30pm and 5pm-9pm, $14-46) is fancier and more expensive than it probably should be, but bear in mind that you're paying for the view (so ask for a window table), and the food is usually good. Lunch ($14-19) and breakfast ($8-19) won't take as big a bite out of your wallet.

A modest restaurant at the **Log Cabin Resort** (3183 E. Beach Rd., 360/928-3325, www.olympicnationalparks.com, late May-Sept. daily 8am-11am, noon-4pm, and 5pm-9pm, $9-13) serves a breakfast buffet ($14) and sandwiches, salads, and pizza for lunch and dinner. It's straightforward, institutional fare. If you're staying at the resort you can save money and probably eat better by bringing your own food. On the grounds there are picnic tables and fire rings where you can grill. Some cabins have kitchens; you have to bring your own plates and utensils.

Accommodations

Indian Valley Motel (235471 U.S. 101, 360/928-3266, http://grannyscafe.net, $85 d), on U.S. 101 about halfway between Lake Crescent and the Elwha park entrance, has small, simple, well-maintained rooms at reasonable rates. It's about everything you could hope to find in an out-of-the-way, family-run budget motel. There's a good restaurant, Granny's Cafe, on-site, as well as a small farm with kid-friendly animals.

The oldest parts of the **Lake Crescent Lodge** (416 Lake Crescent Rd., 360/928-3211, www.olympicnationalparks.com, May-Dec., $185-285 d) date from 1915, but the complex has grown over time, and there are now six types of lodging available, from paneled cabins with fireplaces to conventional motel-style rooms. The main lodge building has only five simple guest rooms upstairs with shared bath, but it's the hub for lake activity, with a restaurant, bar, and gift shop. It's worth taking a look inside for the ambience even if you're just passing through.

Log Cabin Resort (3183 E. Beach Rd., 360/928-3325, www.olympicnationalparks. com, late May-Sept., $108-175 d) at the north end of Lake Crescent has a gorgeous waterfront location, but the lodgings—primarily cabins and a few larger chalets—are decades old and the worse for wear. If you stay here, expect beautiful views and conditions of disrepair that go beyond "no frills." There's also an RV campground.

CAMPING

Fairholme Campground at the west end of the lake has 88 sites for tent camping or RVs up to 21 feet. Some sites have water views. On the downside, you're near U.S. 101, so there can be road noise. It's open late May-early October and has running water. Sites are $20 and are available on a first-come, first-served basis.

Information and Services

The **Storm King Ranger Station** is just east of the lodge. It's staffed daily in summer and intermittently other times of year. When no one is around, take your questions to the front desk in the lobby of the lodge, or call the information desk at the park's main visitors center, 360/565-3130.

Transportation

U.S. 101 runs along the southern side of Lake Crescent. The lodge, located near the middle of the southern shore, is about 21 miles away, a 30-minute drive west of downtown Port Angeles.

Reach Lake Crescent Lodge and other points along the lake by bus on **Clallam Transit** (360/452-4511, www.clallamtransit.com) Route 14, which runs between Port Angeles and Forks.

SOL DUC RIVER VALLEY

Much like the Elwha entrance, Sol Duc (pronounced "Saul Duck," like a long-lost cousin of Donald) takes you into the park on a paved road running beside a river. It's the westernmost entry point on the north side of the inland park, 9 miles from Lake Crescent Lodge and 30 from Port Angeles. With old-growth forest looming on either side, Sol Duc Road is a beautiful 12-mile drive, and the hiking here feels like something out of a fairy tale, with beams of sunlight breaking through the high tree branches and dappling the forest floor.

This is a great place to witness the spawning habits of salmon and trout. The Sol Duc is a rare river where salmonids run throughout the year. About five miles in on Sol Duc Road there's a viewing platform overlooking **Salmon Cascades,** where you can watch steelhead trout in the spring and coho salmon

in the fall as they fly through the air, struggling to climb a small waterfall on their way upstream. Farther upriver, the Lover's Lane Trail takes you past side channels where the fish spawn.

Sol Duc Hot Springs

A mile from the end of Sol Duc Road you come to the area's most famous feature, Sol Duc Hot Springs. The region's Indian tribes had known of the spring's thermal waters for centuries before a giant recreational facility was built here in 1912, trumpeted by its owners as the most elaborate spa on the Pacific coast. It had an elegant hotel, a sanatorium, theater, bowling alley, and golf links, and it drew tens of thousands of guests. In 1916 it was ravaged by fire, and over the following decades it lived a checkered existence, never returning to its original grandeur.

If you come to the springs expecting something either luxurious or backwoodsy, you'll be in for a surprise. The facility that stands here now, **Sol Duc Hot Springs Resort** (12076 Sol Duc Rd., 360/327-3583, www.olympicnationalparks.com, Apr.-mid-Oct.), was built in the 1980s and feels like a suburban rec center plopped down in the middle of the woods. There are three cement soaking

Sol Duc Hot Springs Resort

pools with temperatures ranging 98-104 degrees Fahrenheit, and one large, nonthermal swimming pool. It's a busy place in summer, as soakers share the space with sunbathers, lap swimmers, and playing kids. Day passes are $15 for adults, $10 for children 4 to 12, and free for 3 and under. There's no towel service; either bring your own towel or purchase one there.

Hiking

Starting and ending at the resort, the **Lover's Lane Trail** is an easy, scenic six-mile loop that takes you through lush terrain along the banks of the river. Halfway through, at the point where you cross the river to head back downstream, you reach Sol Duc Falls, which roars vigorously while making a two-level, 50-foot drop. The best viewing is from the bridge, where you're close enough to get spritzed with a gentle mist. Reach the falls with less of a walk by driving to Sol Duc Road's end point, one mile beyond the resort, and taking the **Sol Duc Falls Trail** (a segment of Lover's Lane) for a little less than a mile.

From Sol Duc Falls a rocky, uphill, three-mile trek on the **Deer Lake Trail** leads to a lake surrounded by woods that are in fact thick with deer. This a demanding day hike and also the first leg on one of the park's best multiday backcountry trips, the 22-mile **Seven Lakes Loop.** It takes you along the High Divide, which has spectacular views of Mount Olympus, and into the idyllic Seven Lakes Basin. The park limits the number of backcountry camping permits it issues for this area, and it takes reservations for them through an antiquated system where you have to fax or mail in a reservation form. To learn how it's done, call the Wilderness Information Center at 360/565-3100 or go to www.nps.gov/olym and do a search for "wilderness reservations."

Rafting

In late winter and spring when water levels are high, **Adventures through Kayaking** (2358 U.S. 101, 360/417-3015, www.atkayaking.com) leads half-day Class II and III trips on the Sol Duc. Rates are $79 including gear.

Fishing

You can fish the Sol Duc from June through October. You have to use an artificial lure with a barbless single-point hook, and all fishing is catch-and-release with the exception of clipped hatchery steelhead, of which you can keep two. For full fishing regulations, pick up a brochure at the main visitors center or download a copy from the park's website, www.nps.gov/olym. From the homepage click on "Fishing Regulations."

Food

You don't have a lot of choices for food in the Sol Duc area. You're too far from Port Angeles to eat there, and it's almost an hour each way to the limited dining options at Lake Crescent. The resort's **Springs Restaurant** (360/327-3583, www.olympicnationalparks.com, Apr.-mid-Oct. daily 7am-10:30am, 11am-4pm, and 5pm-9pm) and **Poolside Deli** (Apr.-mid-Oct. daily 11:30am-4:30pm) serve cafeteria-quality breakfast ($7-14), lunch ($13-21), and dinner ($14-34) at steep prices. The only alternative is to bring your own food. Note that some cabins have kitchens.

Accommodations

The lodging at **Sol Duc Hot Springs Resort** (12076 Sol Duc Rd., 360/327-3583, www.olympicnationalparks.com, Apr.-mid-Oct., $176-217) consists of 32 no-frills cabins in a cleared field next to the hot springs complex. Most have two double beds, and the more expensive ones have kitchens. Note that some cabins are duplexes, meaning there's a thin wall between you and your neighbor. There are also reservable RV sites ($35) with water and electrical hookups, picnic tables, and fire rings.

CAMPING

Sol Duc Campground, just south of the hot springs on the other side of the river, has 82 sites for tent camping or RVs up to 21 feet. It's open year-round, with running water May-September and pit toilets the rest of the year. Sites can be reserved at www.recreation. gov; they cost $24 with a reservation and $21 without one. Some are along the riverbank, and all are in the forest. The ones farthest from the resort have the highest chance of animal sightings.

Information and Services

The **Eagle Ranger Station,** located just north of the hot springs, is staffed intermittently in summer and closed at other times of year. When no one is around, call questions to the information desk at the park's main visitors center, 360/565-3130.

Transportation

The Sol Duc entrance to the park is about 30 miles (0.75 hr.) west of downtown Port Angeles, reached from U.S. 101 via Sol Duc Road.

Reach the Sol Duc entrance at the intersection of U.S. 101 and Sol Duc Road by bus on **Clallam Transit** (360/452-4511, www.clallamtransit.com) Route 14, which runs between Port Angeles and Forks. From the entrance it's about 5 miles to the Salmon Cascades and 11 miles to the hot springs.

The Northwestern Peninsula

If you're looking to get away from it all, you're likely to enjoy the northwest corner of the Olympic Peninsula. There are two main destinations here: the town of Neah Bay on the Makah Indian Reservation, from which you can make a beautiful hike out to Cape Flattery, the northwesternmost point in the lower 48 states, and Lake Ozette, from which you can hike to Cape Alava, and the westernmost point in the lower 48. Despite their remoteness, it's easy to find these two places—they're the end of the line for the two main roads in the region. Just keep driving and you'll get there. Luckily, the drive is a pleasure, winding through woods and, at the western end, hugging bluffs above the coast.

STRAIT OF JUAN DE FUCA HIGHWAY

Port Angeles may feel like a small town, but as you travel west on **Route 112,** the Strait of Juan de Fuca Highway, you get a new perspective on what "small" can mean. The highway parallels the coast, passing a couple of tiny fishing villages but mainly threading through forest and skirting the shoreline. Along the highway there's no town with a population over 1,000. More seals live in this part of the strait than people. The beautiful drive includes lots of curves, especially on its western reaches; speed limits set between 40 and 50 miles an hour help make negotiating them easier. Be sure to give any logging trucks you encounter a wide berth.

Salt Creek and Freshwater Bay Parks

A few miles west of the Elwha you pass turnoffs for two neighboring county parks, **Salt Creek** and **Freshwater Bay** (www.clallam. net/Parks). This is the main recreational area along the central portion of the strait. From the small Salt Creek parking area a short path leads to a sandy beach with a picturesque sea stack. It's a favorite spot for picnicking families.

KAYAKING

Freshwater Bay is a calm location for launching kayaks, and the surrounding area is a great place to explore from the water, with many opportunities to sight marine mammals. **Adventures through Kayaking** (2358 U.S. 101, 360/417-3015, www.atkayaking.com) launches half-day guided tours ($79 adults, $59 kids 8-12) April-September.

CAMPING

There are water views from most of the 92 sites at **Salt Creek Campground** (3506 Camp Hayden Rd., 360/928-3441, www.clallam.net/Parks, $25-30). Reserve sites on the county parks website.

Joyce to Clallam Bay and Sekiu

Past the park turnoffs you go through the town of **Joyce,** which has a general store, a couple of restaurants, and a local **museum** (50883 Rt. 112, 360/928-3568, summer Thurs.-Mon. 10am-4pm, off-season Fri.-Sun. 10am-4pm, free) in its old railroad depot. From there it's 21 miles on or near the coast to **Pillar Point County Park** (www.clallam.net/Parks), a scenic spot with beach access where you can stop to stretch your legs or have a picnic.

The road cuts into the woods for 13 miles and then returns to the water at the neighboring towns of **Clallam Bay** and **Sekiu** (pronounced SEE-kyoo). Logging and commercial fishing were once the main occupations in these tiny towns, but now seasonal sportfishing is the primary activity, populating the bay with boats in summer. In Clallam Bay there's a footbridge to a beachfront park where you can stroll out onto sandy Clallam Spit.

FISHING AND DIVING

This is a great stretch of water for diving and fishing, and **Curley's Resort & Dive Center** (291 Front St., Sekiu, 360/963-2281, www.curleysresort.com) leads expeditions for both. It also rents and sells equipment, including kayak rentals.

FOOD

You can stock up on supplies at the century-old **General Store** (50883 Rt. 112, Joyce, 360/928-3568, https://joycegeneral.com, daily 8am-8pm) or have a meal at the **Blackberry Cafe** (50530 Rt. 112, 360/928-0141, daily 7am-8pm, $6-18), a classic roadside diner with a few berry specialties, including blackberry barbecue sauce and homemade pies.

Sekiu's town diner, **By the Bay Cafe** (343 Front St., Sekiu, 360/963-2998, daily 7am-10pm, $8-22), does a serviceable job with standards like eggs, pizza, burgers, and fish-and-chips.

ACCOMMODATIONS

Despite its tiny size, Sekiu has several lodging options, all catering primarily to sportfishing clientele looking for a no-frills place to bunk for the night. **Curley's Resort & Dive Center** (291 Front St., Sekiu, 360/963-2281, www.curleysresort.com, $55-110 d) fills the bill with simple motel rooms and cabins.

Chito Beach Resort (7639 Rt. 112, Sekiu, 360/963-2581, www.chitobeach.com, Apr.-Sept., $160-220), five miles west of Sekiu's town center, is a little more upscale without losing any of the straightforward, unpretentious vibe that prevails in the region. Six comfortable cabins, most sleeping three or four, are all located on the beach and have full kitchens, grills, and picnic tables.

Shipwreck Point

The 20 miles of highway between Sekiu and Neah Bay make for one of the most dramatic shoreline drives in Washington, as the road winds along bluffs with beautiful views. About halfway between the two towns is **Shipwreck Point,** a 472-acre conservation area encompassing easily accessible beach and second-growth Douglas fir, cedar, spruce, and hemlock. It's a good place to pull over for beachcombing, with tide pools, views across the strait to Vancouver Island, and the possibility of spotting migrating whales offshore.

Farther along the highway, just outside the border of the Makah Indian Reservation, keep a lookout for **Salt and Sail Rocks,** two sea stacks jutting out from the water. They're a favorite place for gray whales to feed.

NEAH BAY

Neah Bay sits tucked away in the far northwest corner of the contiguous United States on the 44-square-mile Makah Indian Reservation. Anyone who has spent time in a remote Alaskan village will sense a similarity. Unpaved streets pass through blocks of ramshackle houses and derelict cars, and signs nailed to telephone poles remind the 865 residents that "Meth Equals Death."

The town wears the hardships of reservation life on its sleeve, but there are excellent reasons for visiting here, and the three primary ones involve successful initiatives from the Makah tribe. One is the exceptional Makah Museum, part of the Makah Cultural and Research Center. The other two are Cape Flattery and Shi Shi Beach, two gorgeous pieces of rugged coastline made accessible thanks to road and trail enhancements undertaken by the Makah.

Makah Museum

In 1970 a winter storm caused ground to shift at Ozette, an old Makah coastal village near Lake Ozette, revealing a cache of wooden artifacts. The discovery prompted an 11-year archeological dig that would uncover six longhouses buried in a mudslide dating to around 1560. It made for a smaller, Pacific Northwest version of Pompeii: 55,000 artifacts—implements of daily life, from weapons and tools to beadwork and ceremonial masks—were discovered in remarkably well-preserved condition. The main mission of the **Makah Museum** (1880 Bayview Ave., 360/645-2711, http://makahmuseum.com, daily 10am-5pm, $5) is to exhibit the Ozette finds and put them in the context of tribal culture. Eighteen showcases display artifacts along with photos and descriptive text, and there are dioramas and replicas of canoes and a longhouse. It's an engrossing display, dynamic enough to engage kids and in-depth enough to hold the interest of adults.

Cape Flattery

TOP EXPERIENCE

★ Cape Flattery

Visiting the northwesternmost point of the contiguous United States on Cape Flattery is more than a novelty—it's also an opportunity to hike one of the most scenic short trails in the state. In the course of three quarters of a mile the trail out to the end of the cape delivers much of what you probably envision when you think about hiking the Olympic Peninsula.

An undulating path, made easier to navigate by cedar boardwalks, goes through old-growth Sitka spruce, with vibrant green ferns carpeting the sun-dappled forest floor, and takes you out onto the cape, where there are coves to either side. From observation platforms, you can look down on the waters of the Pacific crashing around sea stacks and into caves. Listen for a chorus of birdcalls. The woods and surrounding waters teem with life, from swifts, loons, puffins, and cormorants to seals, otters, sea lions, and, in spring, gray whales. Picnic tables along the way allow you to have lunch as you take it all in.

At the end of the trail an observation deck gives you a view half a mile out to Tatoosh Island, where a lighthouse, built in 1857 and now unmanned, still stands. To your left is the Pacific, to your right the entrance of the

Strait of Juan de Fuca, and behind you all of America.

To get here, take Bayview Avenue, the main road through Neah Bay, west, and then zigzag onto Cape Flattery Road, following the yellow directional indicators on the pavement. After 3 miles the road doglegs right and becomes Cape Loop Road, which after another 4.5 miles gets you to the parking lot for the **Cape Flattery Trail.** To park, you need a **Makah Recreation Pass** ($10 per car, valid for the calendar year in which it's purchased). Passes are available at the Makah Marina, Makah Museum, Washburn's General Store, and other Neah Bay shops.

Shi Shi Beach

For a stretch of coastal beauty more isolated than Cape Flattery, head to Shi Shi (pronounced "shy shy") Beach, which you reach by hiking a two-mile trail through damp woods. Boardwalks cover much of the early part of the way, but farther on you're still likely to encounter muddy patches, so wear water-resistant boots and bring an extra pair of socks. The trail is flat until the end, where there's a steep, rope-assisted descent to the beach.

As you reach the beach you cross from the Makah Reservation into the northernmost point of Olympic National Park's coastal area. (No entrance fee is required.) You don't come here to swim or sunbathe, but rather to take in the awesome, sometimes ferocious beauty. Ancient woods loom over a sandy 2.5-mile crescent flecked with driftwood. It's best to be here at low tide, when tide pools inhabited by starfish and sea urchins are exposed. Out in the water there's abundant marine mammal life throughout the year. In spring this is one of the best places along the coast for spotting gray whales.

At the end of the beach is the feature that makes Shi Shi Beach special: **Point of Arches,** a group of giant rock formations that are arguably the most impressive sea stacks on the Washington coast. When the tide is out, this is also the best place on the beach for exploring tide pools. You can scramble over

rocks to two more coves to the south, but keep an eye on the tides. If they come in while you're out there, you can end up stranded.

To get to Shi Shi Beach, take Cape Flattery Road west of Neah Bay for 2.5 miles and turn south onto Hobuck Beach Road. After crossing the Sooes River the road changes names to Sooes Beach Road, which takes you to the trailhead. The parking area is for day use only and requires a **Makah Recreation Pass** ($10 per car, valid for the calendar year in which it's purchased), available at the Makah Marina, Makah Museum, Washburn's General Store, and other Neah Bay shops.

Festivals and Events

Makah Days is Neah Bay's big annual event, celebrating the day in 1913 when the reservation first raised the American flag. Held over the weekend that falls closest to August 26, the three-day festival is highlighted by a parade, dances, fireworks, a salmon bake, canoe races, and bone games (traditional gambling).

Food

You don't have a lot of dining options in Neah Bay, but your choices are surprisingly good.

★ **Take Home Fish Company** (881 Woodland Ave., 360/640-0262, hours vary) is a foodie fantasy: a genuine hole-in-the-wall in an out-of-the-way town with a quirky owner who makes one thing exceptionally well—in this case, smoked salmon. As the name indicates, it's strictly takeaway. You can get your fish still hot from the smoker or vacuum packed. The location is a block off Bayview Avenue, near the marina, and hours are irregular. Call ahead, or just drop by and take your chances.

Thin-crust pizza is the main thing that comes out of the oven at **Linda's Wood Fired Kitchen** (1110 Bayview Ave., 360/640-2192, Wed.-Mon. noon-8pm, $8-18), but there's also delicious locally caught fish, a frequent special that's worth paying extra for.

Across the street from Linda's, **Pat's Place** (1111 Bayview Ave., Tues.-Sat. noon-6pm, $9-10) specializes in Indian fry bread, a simple but delectable piece of fried dough that's crispy on the outside, fluffy on the inside. Friendly owners Pat and Julio serve it savory—topped with taco fillings—and sweet—with peach jam or cinnamon sugar. Pat also bakes tasty pies. This place is the ultimate in casual dining: Hours are flexible, there are only three tables (with more seating outdoors), there's no phone, and payment is cash-only.

Warmhouse Restaurant (1431 Bayview Ave., 360/645-2077, Sun.-Thurs. 7am-7pm, Fri.-Sat. 7am-8pm, $8-20) serves big portions of decent diner food—breakfasts, burgers, sandwiches, and fried seafood. The dining room is short on character but has nice views of the water.

Washburn's General Store (1450 Bayview Ave., 360/645-2211, Mon.-Sat. 9am-7pm, Sun. 9am-6pm) is one-stop shopping for groceries and general supplies, from over-the-counter medicine to fishing equipment.

Accommodations

The best lodging option in town is the **Cape Resort** (1510 Bayview Ave., 360/645-2250, http://cape-resort.com, $115), run by the Makah tribe. Along the main road across from the marina it has 10 modern cabins with kitchenettes, along with RV hookups ($40) and tent sites ($25).

Off of Hobuck Beach Road on the way to Shi Shi Beach, **Hobuck Beach Resort** (2726 Makah Passage, 360/645-2339, www.hobuckbeachresort.com, $150-200) has four types of cabins that can sleep 4-6. They're basic but in good shape, and they all have kitchens. (Given the isolated location, you'll want to bring your own food.) Despite the isolation, the location is the highlight here—you're right by Hobuck Beach, with nice ocean views. There are also RV hookups ($40) and tent sites ($20).

CAMPING

Shi Shi Beach is a popular spot for primitive camping—on summer weekends there can be upward of 200 campers on the beach. There are no facilities beyond pit toilets, and

Lodging of Last Resort

If you hear the term *resort* and think of luxurious all-inclusives with beach cabanas and pampering spas, picture the opposite of that and you'll be close to understanding what *resort* means on the Olympic Peninsula. Traditionally resorts in this part of the world have been bare-bones places where fishermen and hunters can get out of the rain while they sleep. In the most primitive versions running water isn't a given, and if there's heat it comes from a fireplace or wood-burning stove.

As tourism on the peninsula has increased, most resorts have added a few amenities, like bathrooms, and some are downright comfortable. But they still serve the same basic purpose: getting a roof over your head for the night, with the assumption that you're going to spend your waking hours outdoors.

it's treated as a backcountry site by the park administration, which means you need to purchase a permit, available at the Wilderness Information Center in Port Angeles (360/565-3100) and at some ranger stations and other park facilities. Note that for overnight parking you can't use the lot at the trailhead. Secure spaces are available for a charge on private property half a mile back up the road.

Information and Services

The **Neah Bay Chamber of Commerce** (www.neahbaywa.com) doesn't operate a walk-in visitors office, but its website is worth checking out for travel information and background about the Makah tribe.

Transportation

Heading west out of Port Angeles on U.S. 101, take the turnoff for Route 112 just before reaching the Elwha River, and from there it's a straight 65-mile shot west to Neah Bay. The drive from Port Angeles takes about 1.75 hours. From Forks to the south the trip takes a little over an hour via U.S. 101, Route 113, and Route 112.

LAKE OZETTE

At eight miles long and three miles wide, Lake Ozette is the third-largest natural lake in Washington. It's only three miles from the Pacific coast, and the area from its eastern shore to the coastline is part of the national park, with a park pass required for admission. The main reason for coming here isn't the lake but the coastline and its impressive wildlife, best experienced via a gorgeous hike to Cape Alava.

Hiking

At the end of Hoko-Ozette Road there's a **ranger station** (360/963-2725, June-Sept. daily, intermittent openings off-season) that serves as a trailhead for two routes to the beach: **Cape Alava Trail** to the north and **Sand Point Trail** to the south. They both go through three miles of prairie and forest, mostly over boardwalk, and reach the coast at points three miles apart. Take one in and the other out, connecting the two with a walk on the beach, and you have a nine-mile loop—the **Ozette Triangle,** one of the park's most popular coastal hikes. If you do this as a long day hike, it's a good strategy to go out on the Sand Point Trail and back on Cape Alava; walking north on the beach means you're more likely to have the wind at your back. It's also vital that you plan your trip for when the tide is out. At high tide parts of the beach are impassible, and you'll be required to detour on a primitive inland trail.

The coastline's biggest draw is the wildlife. Bald eagles fly overhead, deer wander down to the beach, sea lions and seals lounge out on the rocks, gray whales pass by in the spring, and abundant tide pools are like little aquariums at your feet. More than anything, though, this is the domain of sea otters—there's a greater concentration of them here than anywhere else in the Lower 48. Particularly large numbers congregate in the kelp beds off Sand Point.

Other highlights of the hike include **Cape Alava,** the westernmost point of the contiguous United States. (At high tide it's just five longitudinal seconds—about 360 feet—farther west than Cape Flattery.) Near the point where the Cape Alava Trail reaches the beach is the site, now grown over, of the Makah village that's the source of the archeological treasures found in the Makah Museum in Neah Bay. The beach is strewn with rocks and driftwood, along with an anchor from a ship that ran aground here. About a mile south of Cape Alava you reach the **Wedding Rocks,** a series of Indian petroglyphs depicting, among other things, whales, fertility figures, and a European ship. They get their name from the fact that Makah wedding ceremonies were held here.

Accommodations

The privately run **Lost Resort** (20860 Hoko Ozette Rd., 360/963-2899, www.lostresort.net) is located just outside the park entrance. It offers Ozette's only alternative to camping: primitive cabins ($85) with no running water. It also has 30 campsites ($20). The Lost Resort also operates a general store where from mid-May to mid-September you can get breakfast, sandwiches, espresso, and beer. Campers and cabin-dwellers use the store's bathroom facilities, which include a shower.

CAMPING

The most popular camping option is to **camp on the beach.** It's so popular that the park limits the number of overnight permits it issues in order to avoid overcrowding. You can reserve a permit through an antiquated system that requires you to fax or mail in a reservation form. To learn how it's done, call the Wilderness Information Center at 360/565-3130 or go to www.nps.gov/olym and search for "wilderness reservations." The beach has pit toilets and no other facilities. You have to store all food and garbage in park-approved bear canisters (to protect against raccoons, not bears); get them at the Wilderness Information Center in Port Angeles.

The **Ozette Campground,** located on the lake near the ranger station, has 15 sites for tent camping or RVs up to 21 feet. It's open year-round and has no running water, only pit toilets. Sites cost $20 and are available on a first-come, first-served basis.

Information and Services
The **Ozette Ranger Station** (360/963-2725), located at the end of Hoko-Ozette Road, is open daily from June through September, with intermittent openings during the rest of the year.

Transportation
To reach Lake Ozette, turn off Route 112 just west of Sekiu onto Hoko-Ozette Road and drive 21 miles south to the road's end. The drive to Lake Ozette's Cape Alava trailhead is about 30 miles (1 hr.) from Sekiu, 40 miles (1.5 hrs.) from Forks, and 80 miles (2 hrs.) from Port Angeles.

Forks and La Push

The upper segment of the U.S. 101 loop makes a turn to the south at Lake Pleasant and enters the West End, the remote part of the peninsula to the west of the Olympic Mountains. This incredibly wet region makes for a fertile environment for timber, the main crop. As you drive along 101 you pass miles of second- and third-growth forest, interspersed with patches of clear-cut, and you share the road with trucks hauling out the felled trees. The town of Forks is the main commercial and tourism hub for the western portion of Olympic National Park, but it's a small, backwoods place with rudimentary facilities for travelers. Despite the rain, there are more campsites than hotel rooms on the West End.

FORKS
For an unassuming town of 3,500 that you can drive through in three minutes, Forks has a lot of backstory. It's the westernmost incorporated township in the contiguous United States, and also the wettest, averaging 120 inches and 212 days of precipitation annually. Forks has the region's largest supply of lodging and restaurants for visitors making day trips to the national park and other natural attractions. That doesn't mean there's a lot, just more than anywhere else.

Forks earned the nickname Logging Capital of the World at the height of its prosperity in the 1970s. Today the lumber industry is a smaller but still crucial part of the local economy, and the town's identity remains closely tied to logging.

And then there's *Twilight,* the hugely popular series of vampire romance novels and movies set in and around Forks. The Forks of *Twilight* is the product of author Stephenie Meyer's imagination—at the time she was writing the first book she'd never been to the actual town—but locals have done their best to accommodate fans with *Twilight* tours, gift shops, and an annual birthday party for the saga's heroine, Bella. The final book in the series came out in 2008 and the final movie in 2012, but devotees continue to flock here.

Sights
To get a tangible sense for the local logging culture, check out the **Forks Timber Museum** (1421 S. Forks Ave., 360/374-9663, http://forkstimbermuseum.org, Mon.-Sat. 10am-5pm, Sun. 11am-4pm, $3), a 3,000-square-foot facility constructed in 1990 by a Forks High carpentry class. Among the historical displays are a steam donkey (a steam-powered winch used to move logs), chainsaws from different eras, and a replica of a logging camp bunkhouse. Outside are a memorial to loggers killed on the job and a replica of a fire lookout tower.

Twilight fans will get a thrill out of the **Forever Twilight in Forks Collection** (11 N. Forks Ave., 360/374-2531, www.

forevertwilightinforks.com, June-mid-Sept. Thurs.-Mon. noon-4pm, mid-Sept.-May Fri.-Sat. noon-4pm, free). There's a display of costumes and props from the movies, including Jacob's motorcycle and the trellis from Bella and Edward's wedding, as well as book memorabilia.

Another Forks novelty is **John's Beachcombing Museum** (143 Andersonville Ave., 360/640-0320, June-Aug. daily 10am-5pm, $5), a warehouse filled floor to ceiling with one man's finds from four decades of scouring the local shoreline. Amid the glass floats and fishing nets there are such oddities as a mammoth tooth and a Boeing 727 engine spinner cone.

Tours

From late May through early September the Forks Chamber of Commerce conducts a **Logging & Mill Tour** every Wednesday morning starting at nine. For three hours retired timber-industry workers guide you through active logging sites and mills, providing an insider's perspective on the business. Tours are free but donations are encouraged. Call the chamber of commerce (360/374-2531) to reserve a place on a tour.

Sports and Recreation
BOGACHIEL STATE PARK

Six miles south of Forks on U.S. 101, **Bogachiel State Park** (185983 U.S. 101, 360/374-6356, http://parks.state.wa.us/478, Discover Pass required for parking) covers 123 acres along the Bogachiel River. The appeal of the park is that it gives you a taste of lush rain forest greenery without having to detour from the highway. There's a one-mile nature trail along with picnic and camping facilities.

FISHING

The Hoh, Bogachiel, Sol Duc, Quillayute, and Calawah Rivers of the West End are legendary for their fishing, with giant king salmon running in the fall and steelhead trout in the winter and spring. You can get master guidance from Forks-based **Bob's Piscatorial Pursuits** (360/374-2091 or 866/347-4232, www.piscatorialpursuits.com), though it doesn't come cheap. A full day of fishing costs $340 for an individual and $225 per person for two people sharing a boat. Clicking through Bob's website is a crash course on fishing in the region.

Forks Timber Museum

Food

Forks restaurants are unpretentious spots to go for refueling, not fine dining. There isn't a place in town where a logger coming straight from work would feel out of place.

The stuffed elk head staring down at the booths gives a dash of local character to **Forks Coffee Shop** (241 S. Forks Ave., 360/374-6769, daily 5:30am-8pm, $8-18), where large portions of classic diner food—eggs a dozen ways, burgers, fried fish—will fill you up without any surprises.

Pacific Pizza (870 S. Forks Ave., 360/374-2626, Sun.-Thurs. 11am-9pm, Fri.-Sat. 11am-10pm, $8-12) serves cheese-laden specialty pizzas as well as pasta and sandwiches. It's pretty basic, and service is erratic, but if you want a sit-down meal in Forks that's not diner food, this is probably your best option.

There aren't any fast-food chains in town, but there is a classic burger joint, **Sully's Drive-In** (220 N. Forks Ave., 360/374-5075, Mon.-Sat. 11am-9pm, $5-8). Along with the standard burgers and fries, there are blackberry shakes to remind you that you're in the PNW.

You have to be of drinking age to eat at **BBG Blakeslee's Bar and Grill** (1222 S. Forks Ave., 360/374-5003, Mon.-Thurs. 11am-11pm, Fri.-Sat. 11am-2am, Sun. noon-9pm, $10-26), the local watering hole. The burgers and sandwiches are its strong suit, the salads hit-and-miss. The dining room is nondescript, but there's a handsome bar where you can drink microbrews and get the logger's perspective on the world from your neighbor on the next barstool.

Forks Outfitters (950 S. Forks Ave., 360/374-6161, www.forksoutfitters.com, daily 8am-9pm) is the local supermarket and general store, good for picking up groceries as well as outdoor gear and basic clothing and hardware.

Accommodations

Lodging in Forks consists mainly of independently run, no-frills motels on or near U.S. 101. In summer they fill up with national park visitors paying premium rates; prices drop in the off-season. Away from the main road are a few smaller places with a bit more character.

Forks motels all deliver a comparable no-frills experience, but the **Dew Drop Inn** (100 Fern Hill Rd., 360/374-4055, www.dewdropinnmotel.com, $114) and **Olympic Suites** (800 Olympic Dr., 360/374-5400, www.olympicsuitesinn.com, $109-129) tend to do the best with upkeep. **The Forks Motel** (351 S. Forks Ave., 360/374-6243, www.forksmotel.com, $95-119 d) and **Pacific Inn Motel** (352 S. Forks Ave., 360/374-9400, http://pacificinnmotel.com, $104-114 d) score points for laundry facilities on-site, and the Forks Motel has a pool.

Miller Tree Inn B&B (654 E. Division St., 360/374-6806, http://millertreeinn.com, $170-275), located in town half a mile from U.S. 101, is a rambling house from 1916 with a warm atmosphere and friendly host. There are eight guest rooms, each with a different design, some with gas fireplaces and jetted tubs. It's the general consensus that this is the house in Forks that most closely resembles the Cullen family home in the *Twilight* novels, and the owners play up the connection.

You're just a mile north of town but already out in the woods at **Huckleberry Lodge** (1171 Big Pine Way, 360/374-4090, www.huckleberryforks.com, $94-145), four cabins that mix a rustic sensibility with solid, modern construction. There's not much in the way of service—you pick up your key in your room and may not meet anyone who works there—but if you're looking for something more outdoorsy than a motel, this is a good option. Note that the cheapest cabin has an outdoor bathroom.

If you like B&Bs decorated with frilled linens and knickknacks, you'll be happy at **Misty Valley Inn** (194894 U.S. 101, 877/374-9389, http://mistyvalleyinn.com, $135-175), three miles north of Forks. The house is surrounded by gardens, and the hosts lay out a spread of desserts in the evening as well as ample breakfasts. The less expensive rooms are tight quarters, with bathroom facilities added on where space allowed.

CAMPING
Bogachiel State Park (185983 U.S. 101, 360/374-6356, http://parks.state.wa.us/478) is near U.S. 101, but its campground feels deep in the woods, with thick tree cover. There are 26 standard campsites ($25-35), 6 sites with power and water ($30-40), and restrooms and showers. The campground is open year-round and can accommodate RVs up to 40 feet. All sites are first come, first served.

Information and Services
The **Forks Chamber of Commerce Visitor Center** (1411 S. Forks Ave., 360/374-2531, http://forkswa.com, June-Sept. Mon.-Sat. 10am-5pm, Sun. 11am-4pm, Oct.-May Mon.-Sat. 10am-4pm, Sun. 11am-4pm) has volunteers to help you plan your visit to the town and the surrounding area. It provides a *Twilight* brochure with a self-guided tour. The **Forest Service Ranger District Office** (437 Tillicum Ln., 360/374-6522, Mon.-Fri. 8am-4:30pm, closed for lunch) has area maps and can supply permits for gathering firewood and mushrooms.

Transportation
Forks is on U.S. 101. Approaching from the north it's about 50 miles (1.25 hrs.) from both Neah Bay and Port Angeles. To the south Forks is 35 miles (0.75 hr.) from Kalaloch, 65 miles (1.25 hrs.) from Lake Quinault, 105 miles (2 hrs.) from Aberdeen, and 150 miles (3 hrs.) from Olympia.

Forks is the bus terminus for **Clallam Transit** (360/452-4511, www.clallamtransit.com) Route 14, which comes from Port Angeles, and Route 16 from Neah Bay. Route 15 runs twice a day between Forks and La Push; the trip takes 25 minutes. The Olympic Connection operated by **Jefferson Transit** (360/385-4777, http://jeffersontransit.com) goes between Forks and Lake Quinault, with multiple stops, including Kalaloch.

LA PUSH AREA
A 15-mile drive west from Forks takes you through logged forest, into the coastal section of the national park, and finally to the 640-acre Quileute Indian Reservation and the town of La Push (pop. 371). This area is the only part of the coast accessible by car for 20 miles in either direction. It's a magnet for travelers, including intrepid surfers and kayakers, who want to experience Washington's rugged shores.

The most famous member of the Quileute tribe is a fictional one: Jacob Black, the romantic foil from the *Twilight* series. Attention from *Twilight* has been a mixed blessing for the Quileute, bringing income from tourism but forging an identity for the tribe that has little to do with reality. Seattle's Burke Museum teamed with tribe members to create the website **Truth versus Twilight** (www.burkemuseum.org/static/truth_vs_twilight) in order to correct some misconceptions and introduce readers to the actual tribal culture. It's a good starting point for learning about the Quileute.

Beaches
The area has four separate but roughly similar beaches, three that are part of the national park and one on tribal land. The Quillayute River meets the ocean at the north end of La Push. First, Second, and Third Beaches (those are their names) are on the La Push side of the river's mouth, and the fourth, Rialto Beach, is across the water. You can see Rialto from La Push, but to get to it you have to drive back inland six miles in order to cross the river.

Which beach you choose to visit may depend on how much you value accessibility. There's a parking lot within 200 feet of Rialto Beach, and First Beach is right by La Push. Both are good options if you're traveling with young children or don't want to hike to get to the water; however, because they're easily reached, they're busier than the two more remote options. It's a 0.7-mile hike through woods from the parking area to Second Beach, and it's 1.4 miles to Third. Both trails end with steep descents to the sand. As a result the crowds are smaller and skew more toward seasoned outdoor types, including campers who don't mind the lack of facilities.

Regardless of which beach you visit, be prepared for harsh weather. Even in summer it can be chilly, blustery, and damp. From fall through spring those conditions are the norm.

RIALTO BEACH

Reach Rialto Beach by taking the right fork from Route 110 onto Mora Road. After about three miles you cross into the national park (there's no charge for entry here) and pass Mora Campground and the Mora Ranger Station, where you can pick up literature about the area. The road ends at the parking lot 200 feet from the beach; to get to the waterfront you may have to maneuver around some driftwood at the end of the short trail. You can walk the beach for about 1.5 miles to the north from the access point, passing picturesque piles of driftwood along the way, while out in the water waves crash against dramatic sea stacks, the bigger ones topped with trees that seem rooted in the stone. At the far end of the beach you come to the **Hole in the Wall,** a large natural stone arch that's passable only at low tide.

FIRST BEACH

First Beach, on reservation land south of the mouth of the Quillayute River, is even easier to get to than Rialto. From the parking lot adjacent to the Quileute Oceanside Resort you can stroll onto the sand. The beach is a one-mile crescent bookended by a sand spit to the north and an impassable head to the south. It's a popular spot for **surfers,** who put up with 50-60-degree waters and floating driftwood in order to ride the waves. The most conspicuous sight from the beach is **James Island,** a broad, 160-foot-tall sea stack that was once connected to the mainland, before the Army Corps of Engineers rerouted the river. The Quileute call the island Akalat, meaning "top of the rock," and have used it

as a burial site for chiefs. Only tribe members are allowed on it.

SECOND BEACH

The parking area for Second Beach is two miles south of La Push on Route 110 (aka La Push Rd.). You park on reservation property but cross into the national park in the course of the 0.7-mile hike to the beach. It's a well-maintained trail through Sitka spruce with a dramatic ending, where you hear the crashing of the waves before emerging out of the woods and seeing the starkly beautiful coastline before you. Once you're there a short walk to the north takes you to a natural arch that's worth checking out, but most of the beach is to your south, where you can walk for over a mile before coming to an impassable head that also has a natural arch in it. Just offshore are the **Quillayute Needles,** a cluster of sea stacks that serve as breeding ground for thousands of seabirds.

THIRD BEACH

Third Beach isn't as scenic as Second, and it's harder to get to. The parking area is located off Route 110 half a mile east of the Second Beach lot. The hike is 1.4 miles, starting on an old road and then veering left through the woods. While Third may not be quite as picturesque as Second, it's still striking, with a wide, sandy beach, towering bluffs, and lots of driftwood (which sometimes can obstruct passage). Also, it benefits from greater isolation; the kind of rough beauty found along the coast just seems to resonate more when there are fewer people around. If you hike south for a little over half a mile you'll come to **Strawberry Bay Falls,** which at low tide plummet directly onto the beach. Third Beach is also noteworthy as the northern end of a 17-mile multiday hike with a southern terminus at **Oil City** (which isn't a city, but got the name when speculators contemplated drilling in the 1930s). Consult with the Wilderness Information Center in Port Angeles (360/565-3100) before taking this hike on.

Boating and Kayaking

The Quileute Tribe operates a **marina** (360/374-5392 for harbormaster) that can accommodate up to 60 boats. From February through September **Rainforest Paddlers** (4883 Upper Hoh Rd., 360/374-5254, www.rainforestpaddlers.com) runs morning and evening guided kayak trips down the Quillayute River, finishing at the ocean. Prices are $59 in the morning and $69 in the evening, with a $10 discount for kids 5-10.

Surfing

Surfers on First Beach can rent gear from **North by Northwest Surf Co.** (360/452-5144, http://nxnwsurf.com), which is based in Port Angeles but, May-September, operates a rental trailer on the property of the Oceanside Resort. It's usually there Friday-Sunday 10am-5pm; call to reserve gear and double-check hours. Boards and wetsuits are both $25 a day. You can also make arrangements in advance for surfing lessons.

Festivals and Events

The big event of the year is **Quileute Days** (www.quileutenation.org), held over a mid-July weekend. It features canoe races, a tug-of-war, a fish bake, bone games (traditional Indian gambling), and fireworks.

Food

Most visitors spending more than a night or two make at least some of their meals themselves, and most lodging options include cooking facilities. (Campfires are permitted on the beaches; you need a $2 permit, available at the Oceanside Resort office, to build a fire on First Beach.)

In La Push, **River's Edge Restaurant** (41 Main St., 360/374-0777, daily 8am-9pm, $8-20) has great views of the Quillayute estuary and First Beach. The food includes basic breakfast fare and fish-and-chips and fresh fish entrées. Service is usually friendly but can be slow and unpolished.

The grill and fryer stay busy at casual **Three Rivers Resort** (7765 La Push Rd., 360/374-5300, www.threeriversresortandguideservice.com, daily 9am-9pm, $7-14), where burgers and fried fish are the specialties. Blackberry milk shakes are another favorite, and a small breakfast menu is available in the morning.

Lonesome Creek Grocery Store (490 Ocean Dr., 360/374-4333, Mon.-Fri. 6am-10pm, Sat.-Sun. 7am-10pm), next to the Oceanside Resort, has some pricey provisions. You're wise to stock up in a more developed area, but it's good to have this place as a fallback resource.

Accommodations

On the reservation property in La Push there's only one lodging option, **Quileute Oceanside Resort** (330 Ocean Dr., 360/374-5267, www.quileuteoceanside.com), but it offers lots of choices: motel rooms ($134-189); a wide range of cabins ($99-299), from rudimentary A-frames with no hot water to deluxe duplexes with fireplaces and jetted tubs; RV sites (full hookup $40); and tent sites in the RV park or on the beach ($20). True to its name, the resort faces First Beach, and most of the lodging choices have water views.

Three Rivers Resort (7765 La Push Rd., 360/374-5300, www.threeriversresortandguideservice.com), six miles east of La Push and nine miles west of Forks, is a multipurpose base for visits to the area. It has six basic but well-equipped cabins that can sleep two ($103), four ($113), or six ($123), as well as a campground with RV hookups (full $30, partial $27) and tent sites ($22). It also runs guided fishing trips and operates a restaurant and a convenience store where you can gas up the car.

Manitou Lodge Bed and Breakfast (813 Kilmer Rd., 360/374-6295, http://manitoulodge.com) is tucked into the woods a mile off of Mora Road, five miles from Rialto Beach and eight from La Push. It offers two ways to spend the night: in a handsome lodge with seven tasteful guest rooms ($159-199), or in a quirky campsite where all of the gear is already set up for you, in the form of either a tent ($59-69), an RV ($59-189), or a primitive cabin ($89-99).

The five suites at **Quillayute River Resort** (473 Mora Rd., 360/374-7447, http://qriverresort.com, $195-225) are tripped out by West End standards. They all look out onto the river and have TVs, phones, fully equipped kitchens, living rooms with fireplaces and pullout couches, and bathrooms with heated tile floors.

Olson's Cabins (2423 Mora Rd., 360/374-3142, www.olsonscabin.com), five minutes by car from Rialto Beach, comprise two pleasant contemporary cabins with separate living rooms and full kitchens. Cabin 1 ($99) can sleep up to five if you use the pullout sofa, while the newer, more stylish Cabin 2 ($135) can sleep three, with one on the sofa.

CAMPING

Along with the sites at Quileute Oceanside Resort and Three Rivers Resort, there's camping in the area at the **Mora Campground** within the national park, with 94 sites for tents or RVs up to 21 feet. You're in the woods here along the Quillayute River, two miles from Rialto Beach. Sites cost $20 and are first come, first served. They're available year-round, with running water throughout the year.

There's also primitive camping allowed on **Second** and **Third Beaches.** You need to get a backcountry permit from the Wilderness Information Center in Port Angeles (360/565-3100), and you're required to keep all food in a bear canister, which you can pick up at the Wilderness Information Center. There's no running water and there are no toilets of any kind.

Information and Services

Find background information about La Push on the website of the **Quileute Tribe** (www.quileutenation.org). Next to the Mora Campground is **Mora Ranger Station** (360/374-5460), where you can get information about the area and backcountry permits. It is open intermittently in the summer.

Transportation

The only way to get to the La Push area by car is by taking Route 110, also called La Push Road, from Forks 15 miles to the east, about a 20-minute drive. From Route 110 there are turnoffs for Quillayute Road and Mora Road, both of which take you to Mora Campground and Rialto Beach.

Twice a day a bus runs Route 15 of **Clallam Transit** (360/452-4511, www.clallamtransit.com) between Forks and La Push.

Western Olympic National Park

The Olympic Peninsula's defining characteristics are massive rain and massive trees, so it makes sense that the most famous part of the national park is its rain forest, which stretches across the Hoh, Queets, and Quinault river valleys to the west of the Olympic Range. National park status has helped preserve trees over 200 feet tall and more than a thousand years old. The park's original mission statement expressed the goal of preserving "the finest example of primeval forests," and as you walk among the giant spruce and hemlocks it

feels like things haven't changed much in the past millennium.

The region has an otherworldly aura. The forest is so lush it feels like, if you took a nap by the side of the trail, you'd wake up covered in moss. On the coast, U.S. 101 cuts into a narrow strip of national park land, providing easy access to mist-shrouded beaches where winter storm-watching is considered a recreational activity.

This is the wettest area in the continental United States, averaging over 100 inches of precipitation on the storm-battered coast and upward of 150 inland, but that doesn't mean showers are nonstop. The amount of rainfall varies drastically from season to season. The Hoh Rain Forest, for example, averages 18 inches a month in winter and only 3 in summer. In July and August it's possible to see several weeks in a row without a raindrop.

HOH RAIN FOREST

The Hoh Rain Forest is the most popular and visitor-friendly place to explore the western peninsula's lush environment. Facilities accommodate a wide range of visitors, but it's worth noting that the closest lodging options other than camping are 45 minutes away in Forks. If you want to visit and sleep with a roof over your head, you're going to do some driving. Restaurants are similarly scarce. There's nowhere to eat in the park and only one tiny place on the drive in.

Hoh Rain Forest Visitor Center

The **Hoh Rain Forest Visitor Center** (360/374-6925, mid-June-Aug. daily 9am-5pm, Sept.-Dec. and Mar.-mid-June Fri.-Sun. variable hours) has exhibits about the wonders of the forest and an information desk where rangers answer questions and suggest strategies for exploring. Outside the center is the starting point for several short trails that are the busiest in the park, as well as longer hikes that lead deep into the forest. In summer there are daily ranger-led interpretive walks, and on most Friday and Saturday evenings there's a ranger presentation in the campground amphitheater.

Hiking

Starting from the visitors center you can take a five-minute stroll through old-growth forest, climb to the summit of Mount Olympus, or do something in between. The shortest walk, the **Mini-Rain Forest Trail**, is a quarter-mile, accessible-with-assistance loop with interpretive signage. The evocatively named **Hall of**

Mosses Trail is an easy 0.8-mile loop past 200-foot firs, big-leaf maples festooned with moss, and licorice ferns carpeting the forest floor. A third loop, the **Spruce Nature Trail,** takes you through the forest to the banks of the Hoh River. On all of these trails you can observe some of the defining characteristics of a temperate rain forest, including abundant moss and lichen; nurse logs (fallen trees from which seedlings grow); and trees "standing" on their exposed, gnarled roots, a result of having sprouted from nurse logs or stumps that later rotted out beneath them.

If you're up for more of a hike you have a good option in the **Hoh River Trail,** which follows the river valley for 17.5 miles. It works as an adaptable out-and-back day trip—it's a satisfying hike however far you choose to go—and also as an overnight backpacking excursion. The first 12 miles are a flat walk in the woods, with opportunities for sighting bald eagles in the trees, elk in the meadows, and otters in the water. The trail then starts to climb, passing a 100-foot canyon on the way up to Glacier Meadows, where wildflowers are interspersed among glacial moraine and Mount Olympus looms above you.

Climbing

The end of the Hoh River Trail is the most popular launching point for those scaling 7,965-foot **Mount Olympus,** the tallest peak in the park. It's a technically demanding scramble over glaciers, requiring pickaxes, ropes, and crampons, and the over the years it's claimed some casualties. For a guide-led climb try **Mountain Madness** (3018 SW Charlestown St., Seattle, 206/937-8389, www.mountainmadness.com), a decades-old organization with experience on peaks all over the world.

Kayaking and Rafting

Downriver from the national park you can take guided trips, either by raft or kayak, on Class I and II stretches of the Hoh with **Rainforest Paddlers** (360/374-5254, www.

rainforestpaddlers.com, $44 half day or $79 full day).

Food

There's no food available in the Hoh Rain Forest area. If you want to eat during your visit the two options are to bring your own food or to stop at the **Hard Rain Cafe and RV Park** (5763 Upper Hoh Rd., 360/374-9288, www.hardraincafe.com, daily 9am-7pm, $6-14). It's a quirky, middle-of-nowhere sort of place offering burgers, sandwiches, and bacon and eggs for breakfast. Service tends to be friendly but slow.

Camping

If you want to overnight in or around the Hoh Rain Forest your only option is to camp. Within the park, **Hoh Rain Forest Campground,** occupying three circles near the river and the visitors center, has 88 sites for tent camping or RVs up to 21 feet. It's open year-round, with running water, accessible bathrooms, and animal-proof food lockers. Sites cost $20 and are available on a first-come, first-served basis.

Along the **Hoh River Trail** there are eight small preexisting camping areas that require backcountry permits. They're available on a first-come, first-served basis. Check with the Wilderness Information Center in Port Angeles (360/565-3100) for help with choosing a site and putting together a backcountry camping plan.

Outside of the park, the **Hard Rain Cafe and RV Park** (5763 Upper Hoh Rd., 360/374-9288, www.hardraincafe.com), 12 miles west of the visitors center, has both RV sites ($25 electric and water, $30 full hookup) and tent sites ($20-25).

The Washington State Department of Natural Resources manages three small, primitive campgrounds along the Hoh River: **Willoughby Creek** and **Minnie Peterson,** both along Upper Hoh Road on the way to the rain forest, and **Hoh Oxbow,** along U.S. 101 between mile markers 176 and 177. There's no charge for camping here, but you need a state

the Hoh Rain Forest

Discover Pass for your vehicle. For more information contact the department's Olympic Region office in Forks (111 Tillicum Ln., 360/374-6131).

Transportation

Regardless of where you're starting from, to get to the Hoh Rain Forest area by car you need to take U.S. 101 to Upper Hoh Road and drive the road's 18-mile length to the visitors center. It's about 30 miles (0.75 hr.) from Forks to the north, 40 miles (1 hr.) from Kalaloch and 70 miles (1.5 hrs.) from Lake Quinault to the south, and 90 miles (2 hrs.) from Port Angeles to the northeast.

KALALOCH

The stretch between the small Hoh Indian Reservation to the north and the large Quinault Reservation to the south comprises the southern coastal portion of Olympic National Park, known as the Kalaloch (CLAY-lock) area. The name derives from a Quinault term meaning "sheltered landing," and it ties with Sequim for having the most confusing pronunciation on the peninsula.

For many travelers Kalaloch hits a sweet spot: unlike the northern coast it's easily accessed from the highway, but thanks to its protected status it maintains a wild feel. In terms of geography, it's a middle ground—sandier and less jagged than the beaches farther north, but more rugged than those in the southern reaches of the Washington coast. And there are two good (and popular) options for spending the night—a comfortable national park lodge and a beautiful beach campground— that are close enough to the Hoh Rain Forest and Lake Quinault to serve as a base for day trips to either. Note that the Kalaloch area is one of the places in the national park where you don't need to purchase an access pass to enter. There are seven points where you can get down to the water from U.S. 101. The one farthest north, Ruby Beach, is the most striking and most popular.

TOP EXPERIENCE

★ Ruby Beach

Sea stacks and driftwood decorate Ruby Beach, which transitions from smooth rocks to sand as it gets closer to the water. From the parking area, which has an overlook, a paved quarter-mile switchback trail takes you through woods and tall undergrowth down to the shore. Even at the height of summer a romantic mist can linger in the air, shrouding the tall bluffs and Abbey Island, a giant sea stack anchored offshore. It's best to come at low tide, when you have clear passage up and down the beach, and tide pools are on full display. Barring that, it's good to wear waterproof shoes. If you're up for a hike you can go as far as 4.5 miles north, into the Hoh Indian Reservation and to the mouth of the Hoh River.

Other Beaches

Other beaches in the area are **South Beach,** the southernmost beach in Olympic National Park; **Kalaloch Beach,** site of the lodge and campgrounds, 7.5 miles south of Ruby; and six more, numbered One through Six from south to north, not all of them accessible. **Beach Four** is especially good for tide pool viewing. In summer park rangers conduct guided tours of the pools. Contact the **Kalaloch Ranger Station** (360/962-2283) to find out the current tour schedule.

A good way to put some distance between you and the crowds is to hike from Kalaloch north for 1.5 miles over wide, sandy beach

Ruby Beach

to **Browns Point,** a rocky protuberance with caves and a sandstone arch to explore at low tide.

Food

Kalaloch Lodge's **Creekside Restaurant** (157151 U.S. 101, 360/962-2271, ext. 4007, www.thekalalochlodge.com, daily 8am-8pm) fills several roles, serving pancakes and eggs for breakfast ($8-20), sandwiches and burgers for lunch and dinner ($13-20), and adding a few higher-end entrées, including steaks and fish, at dinnertime ($13-38). The food is consistently good and the dining room has nice water views. In summer reservations are essential.

Your other option is to cook for yourself. Groceries and supplies are available at the lodge's general store, **Kalaloch Mercantile** (360/962-2271, ext. 1016), open daily 7am-9pm in summer and 8am-7pm the rest of the year.

Accommodations

Sitting on a bluff overlooking the ocean, **Kalaloch Lodge** (157151 U.S. 101, 360/962-2271, www.thekalalochlodge.com) delivers easy beach access and, in some of its accommodations, spectacular views. There are several ways to stay here. The larger Bluff Cabins ($254-350) deliver the views; most have kitchens, most can sleep four, and some have fireplaces or wood-burning stoves. Kalaloch Cabins ($246) are smaller and don't have views; they all have two queen beds, kitchens or kitchenettes, and wood-burning stoves. The main lodge has several guest rooms ($195-215) and two suites ($311). Things are well maintained, but don't expect luxury; you're paying primarily for location. Significant discounts can be had in winter, when rugged souls come here to watch the storms crashing along the coastline.

CAMPING

You get great views for a fraction of the cost at the neighboring **Kalaloch Campground,** which has 170 sites ($22) for tents or RVs up to 21 feet, with some spaces that can

accommodate rigs up to 35 feet. There's running water year-round, and rangers conduct campfire programs in the summer. There's also the convenience of a general store at the lodge nearby. This is the most popular campground in the park, and it and Sol Duc are the only ones (except for a few remote backcountry locations) where you can reserve sites. Reservations are available from mid-June to mid-September; they can be made up to six months in advance at www.recreation.gov ($9 fee) or by calling 877/444-6777 ($10 fee).

South Beach Campground is open from Memorial Day to late September and has 55 sites ($15) for tents or RVs up to 21 feet, with some spaces that can accommodate RVs up to 35 feet. Availability is first come, first served. There are fire pits, picnic tables, and flush toilets, but otherwise no running water. The conveniences of the lodge are three miles away.

Information and Services

The **Kalaloch Ranger Station** (360/962-2283) is open daily in summer. Through the rest of the year your best resource for information on the area is the Kalaloch Lodge reception area.

Transportation

Kalaloch's location on U.S. 101 makes getting to and from here straightforward. To the north it's 35 miles (0.75 hr.) to Forks and 90 miles (1.75 hrs.) to Port Angeles. Heading south and east it's 35 miles (0.75 hr.) to Lake Quinault, 75 miles (1.5 hrs.) to Aberdeen, and 120 miles (2.25 hrs.) to Olympia.

The Olympic Connection bus line operated by **Jefferson Transit** (360/385-4777, http://jeffersontransit.com) goes between Forks and Lake Quinault four times a day on weekdays and twice on weekends, with a stop at Kalaloch.

★ LAKE QUINAULT AND QUINAULT RAIN FOREST

Lake Quinault and the surrounding rain forest offer a couple of classic Olympic Peninsula

world's largest Sitka spruce

the Quinault Nation's fishing and boating regulations, which are more changeable and sometimes stricter than those in the park. No facility here is as impressive as the Hoh Rain Forest Visitor Center, but you have more short trails to choose from for easy rain forest hikes, with fewer hikers on them.

Quinault Rain Forest Loop Drive

One of the pluses of visiting the Quinault region is that you can experience the territory from the seat of your car. The **Quinault Rain Forest Loop Drive** is a 31-mile trip that goes around the lake and then up one side of the Quinault River and back down the other. In about two hours you get a highlight tour of the region, including views of the lake, the rain forest, and waterfalls, with the potential for sighting elk and bald eagles. Along the way, stop for a picnic or stretch your legs on short hikes. The parts of North Shore and South Shore Roads farthest upriver are dirt; the park service advises against taking trailers or RVs on them, but they're passable for cars.

Hiking

There are trails near the lake providing opportunities for short-to-medium-length, family-friendly day hikes. On the south side the half-mile **Rain Forest Nature Trail** loop has interpretive signs and is partly wheelchair accessible. The 1.5-mile **Falls Creek Loop** takes you to several cascades, and hiking 2.5 miles around the **Trail of the Giants** presents you with stands of towering Douglas firs. A short hop down the road at the eastern corner of the lake is a 0.2-mile path to the **world's largest Sitka spruce.** On the north side, the **Kestner Homestead Trail** loops 1.3 miles through a maple glade and past an old pioneer farm.

Experienced hikers looking for a challenge can make the 14.5-mile, 4,000-foot climb to the top of **Colonel Bob Mountain** from a trailhead on South Shore Road east of the lake. The **Enchanted Valley Trail,** another backcountry experience, heads east from the

experiences in a single location. The 3.8-mile-long, 2-mile-wide, 240-foot-deep **Lake Quinault** is a glacier-fed natural reservoir of the Quinault River. It doesn't quite match the unique dazzle of Lake Crescent, but it's still placid and beautiful, and like Lake Crescent it has a lodge that's in the National Register of Historic Places. You can boat, fish, and swim in summer, and hang out watching the rain fall the rest of the year. The surrounding **Quinault Rain Forest** is just as rainy, and just as impressive, as the more famous Hoh. Within the forest are some huge trees, including the world's largest spruce, which is readily accessible by trail.

The lake itself is administered by the Quinault Indian Nation, whose reservation stretches from the lake's southwest shore all the way to the ocean and south to the town of Moclips. The southeastern shore is part of Olympic National Forest, and the northern shore is part of Olympic National Park. You may hardly notice the distinction when you visit, but it's evident in a few ways, such

Graves Creek Campground for 13 miles into a glaciated valley that's one of the national park's most gorgeous settings.

Fishing and Boating

The Quinault Nation regulates activities on the lake and has vacillated some on its rules over the years. More often than not trout fishing is allowed in summer months, but double-check before casting a line; the **Quinault Wilderness Information Office** (360/288-0232), the **ranger station** (360/288-2444), and lodgings around the lake will have current information.

Kayaks, paddleboards, canoes, and rowboats are all available for rent from the Lake Quinault Lodge from May through September, with rates ranging from $15 to $25 for an hour and $50 to $55 for a day. Privately owned boats, including motorboats, are subject to changing regulations. You may be required to have your boat declared free of invasive species before putting it in the water. Check with the **Quinault Wilderness Information Office** (360/288-0232).

Food

The lodge's **Roosevelt Dining Room** (345 South Shore Rd., 360/288-2900, www.olympicnationalparks.com, daily 7:30am-3pm and 5pm-9pm) serves three meals a day with lake views. Breakfasts ($10-18) come in big portions and include lots of egg options. Lunch ($14-18) is mainly sandwiches. Dinner ($20-45) is more turf than surf—there are beef, chicken, and duck entrées, along with salmon and fish-and-chips.

The same way that the Rain Forest Resort Village is a less expensive, less atmospheric alternative to the Lake Quinault Lodge, the resort's **Salmon House Restaurant** (516 South Shore Rd., 360/288-2535, www.rainforestresort.com, daily 4pm-9pm, $15-29) is your first option for a less expensive meal than at the Roosevelt Dining Room. Salmon is the specialty, and they do it well, prepared four ways. You can also get chicken, steaks, and pasta. The atmosphere doesn't match that of the lodge, but there are nice lake views.

Across the road from the lodge, **Quinault Mercantile** (352 South Shore Rd., 360/288-2277, Apr.-Sept. daily 7am-8pm, $11-15) is a mom-and-pop general store with a small restaurant serving breakfasts, sandwiches, milk shakes, and pizzas. It's also a good spot for groceries and camping supplies.

Accommodations

The iconic place to stay here is **Lake Quinault Lodge** (345 South Shore Rd., 360/288-2900, www.olympicnationalparks.com, $239-339), built in 1926. It's a classic national park hotel designed by the architect of the Old Faithful Lodge in Yellowstone National Park. There are three options for guest rooms: the original lodge, a newer building with larger rooms, and a small annex that actually predates the lodge by three years. In typical national park lodge fashion, you get more character than comfort here, and prices are high for the quaint but plain accommodations. The highlight is the lobby, with a massive fireplace surrounded by leather sofas. It's worth checking out regardless of whether you're staying here.

You get a little more bang for your buck a mile up the shoreline at **Rain Forest Resort Village** (516 South Shore Rd., 360/288-2535, www.rainforestresort.com), which has motel rooms ($135-195) and fireplace cabins ($179-259), some of which sleep four, as well as 31 RV sites ($35). Facilities are dated but functional. Some accommodations have kitchens, which can be invaluable given the area's limited dining options.

In the postage-stamp town of Amanda Park, along the Quinault River at the southwest end of the lake, **Quinault River Inn** (8 River Dr., 360/288-2237, www.quinaultriverinn.com $159 d) is popular with anglers looking for a place to stay while fishing the river. It has basic, clean, comfortable rooms for reasonable rates. There are five RV sites ($40).

CAMPING

The U.S. Forest Service maintains three campgrounds on the south shore of the lake: **Willaby** is open year-round and has both tent and RV sites for $25. **Falls Creek** is open from May through September and has 25 tent and RV sites ($25) and 10 walk-in sites ($20). **Gatton Creek** is open from May through September and has five walk-in sites ($20). Willaby and Falls Creek sites can be reserved online at www.recreation.gov. Gatton Creek sites are first come, first served.

Farther into the forest there are two National Park Service campgrounds. **Graves Creek** has 30 primitive sites ($20) at the end of Graves Creek Road along the Quinault River. **North Fork** has nine primitive sites ($15) at the end of North Shore Road along the North Fork Quinault River. Both campgrounds are open year-round, available first come, first served, and have pit toilets.

Information and Services

The **Quinault Wilderness Information Office** (353 South Shore Rd., 360/288-0232, Mon.-Fri. 8am-4:30pm) and the **Quinault Rain Forest Ranger Station** (902 North Shore Rd., 360/288-2444, late June-mid-Sept. Thurs.-Mon.) are both resources for information about the area. The Lake Quinault Lodge also has literature and maps.

Transportation

U.S. 101 skirts the western edge of Lake Quinault. To the north it's 65 miles (1.25 hrs.) to Forks and 120 miles (2.5 hrs.) to Port Angeles. Heading south it's a little under 45 miles (1 hr.) to Aberdeen, from where it's about another 50 miles (1 hr.) east to Olympia.

The Olympic Connection bus line operated by **Jefferson Transit** (360/385-4777, http://jeffersontransit.com) goes between Forks and Lake Quinault, with a stop at Kalaloch.

Grays Harbor and Vicinity

The southern half of the Washington coastline is a different world from the coast of the Olympic Peninsula above it or Oregon below. Around Grays Harbor, one of the biggest inlets on the U.S. Pacific coast, you get long, flat expanses of sand. With average annual rainfall of over 70 inches, summer high temperatures typically in the 60s, and vigorous winds that kick up throughout year, this isn't a place where vacationers work on their tans and splash in the waves.

It's still beach, though, and without the constraints of national park status the southern coast has the development you'd expect from a family-friendly getaway, particularly in Ocean Shores. There are tourist-focused hotels and restaurants, almost all better bargains than what you find farther north, as well as gift shops, go-karts, and miniature golf. Many communities allow automobiles on the beaches, which are fun to drive over—the sand is like a wide, smooth road with no lanes or curbs. Serious (and not-so-serious) kite-flying aficionados take advantage of the open spaces and strong winds to let their kites soar, and digging for razor clams is a mania fall-spring.

ABERDEEN AND HOQUIAM

If you're heading for the shore on either side of Grays Harbor you're likely approaching from the north or south on U.S. 101, or from the east on Route 12. Either way, you'll pass through Aberdeen, the town on the east end of the bay at the mouth of the Chehalis River, which together with the neighboring town of Hoquiam makes up a community of about 25,000. The local economy is closely tied to the lumber industry, and as that business has slowed in the region the area has experienced hard times. For leisure travelers there are a couple of points of interest worth checking on the way through.

Sights

Aberdeen is famous for being the town Kurt Cobain escaped from on the way to becoming the icon of the 1990s grunge rock movement with his band Nirvana. **Kurt Cobain Riverfront Park,** at the end of East 2nd Street where the Young Street Bridge crosses the Wishkah River, is a pilgrimage site for Cobain fans. A sculpture of a guitar stands alongside the bridge, which Cobain would sit under as a disaffected teenager, writing lyrics that would one day be known the world over. You can sit in the same spot; despite being covered in graffiti, it's a peaceful place to linger and contemplate Cobain's life. His childhood home is a few blocks away, at 1st Street and Chicago Avenue.

Grays Harbor Historical Seaport (500 N. Custer St., 360/532-8611, http://historical-seaport.org), located along the Chehalis River in Aberdeen, is home to two replicas of 18th-century tall ships, the *Hawaiian Chieftain* and *Lady Washington,* the latter of which appeared in the *Pirates of the Caribbean* movie series. For most of the year the ships are traveling up and down the West Coast, but when they're home they're open for tours (free, with $5 suggested donation) and for a variety of sailing expeditions, usually two or three hours long and manned by a crew in period costume, with tickets ranging $42-79. Call or check the schedule on the website to see when the ships are in Aberdeen.

Food

Billy's Bar & Grill (322 E. Heron St., 360/533-7144, www.billysaberdeen.com, Mon.-Sat. 8am-11pm, Sun. 8am-9pm, $8-23) is a reliable pit stop when passing through Aberdeen. You can get three meals a day with a dose of hometown character—the cozy establishment is a local institution in a building dating from the 19th century. Burgers and sandwiches are the staples for lunch and dinner, with steaks and seafood if you're craving something more substantial.

Both the fanciest and the hippest place to eat in Aberdeen is **Rediviva** (118 E. Wishkah St., 360/637-9259, http://redivivarestaurant. com, Tues.-Sat. 4pm-11pm, $15-35). The dining room is casual but sleekly modern, and the menu, featuring fish, meat, and produce sourced from around the region, looks like something you'd find in Seattle.

Accommodations

The Aberdeen/Hoquiam area doesn't draw a lot of overnight leisure travelers—most stay along the nearby coast—and the hotels are pretty run-down. There is, however, one of the best B&Bs in the region: **A Harbor View Inn** (111 W. 11th St., 360/533-0433, www.aharbor-view.com, $139-169). The bright guest rooms have an old-timey ambience without feeling stuffy, and from the hillside location you get a view of the harbor in the distance.

Information and Services

In Aberdeen the **Greater Grays Harbor Visitor Center** (506 Duffy St., 800/321-1924, www.graysharbor.org, June-Aug. daily 8am-5pm, Sept.-May Mon.-Fri. 8am-5pm) has information about the town and the surrounding area.

Transportation

Aberdeen is at the west end of Route 12, 110 miles (2 hrs.) from Seattle. North on U.S. 101 it's 45 miles (1 hr.) to Lake Quinault and 105 miles (2 hrs.) to Forks. Along the north side of Grays Harbor on Route 109 it's 25 miles (0.75 hr.) to Ocean Shores, and along the south side of the harbor it's 20 miles (0.5 hr.) on Route 105 to Westport.

Grays Harbor Transit (360/532-2770, www.ghtransit.com) provides bus service in and around Aberdeen and Hoquiam as well as between the area and Lake Quinault and the North Beach area north of Grays Harbor.

OCEAN SHORES

The busiest coastal destination in the Grays Harbor area is Ocean Shores, a vacation and retirement community developed in the 1960s

Ocean Shores storefront

can be reached from six turnoffs along Ocean Shores Boulevard. The beach is considered part of the state highway system—it's legal to drive on it. The same basic driving regulations that apply on the road apply here. Vehicles and drivers have to be licensed. The speed limit is 25 miles an hour, and pedestrians have the right of way at all times.

KITE FLYING

Steady breezes and flat, open beach make Ocean Shores, like the rest of the southern Washington coastline, a great place for flying kites. Choose from a large selection of kites, get tips on flying, and pick up other beach toys and paraphernalia at **Ocean Shores Kites** (www.oceanshoreskites.com), which has locations in the Shores Mall (172 W. Chance la Mer, 360/289-4103) and at the Boardwalk Shops (759 Pt. Brown Ave., 360/289-3229). Both are open year-round; hours vary with the weather.

HORSEBACK RIDING

The conditions that make Ocean Shores good for driving and flying kites make it well suited to horseback riding. Go on guided rides with **Chenois Creek Horse Rentals** (on the beach at Damon Rd., 360/533-5591, www.chenoiscreekhorserentals.com, $20/hr.) and **Honey Pearl Ranch** (on the beach at W. Chance la Mer, 360/589-0230, www.honey-pearlranch.com, $25/hr.).

BIKES AND MOPEDS

Bikes and mopeds are another popular way to get around Ocean Shores, both on the road and the beach. **Apollo Mopeds** (172 W. Chance la Mer NW, 360/290-0919, www.apollomopeds.com, Mon.-Fri. 10:30am-6pm, Sat.-Sun. 10am-7pm) rents mopeds ($25/hr., $45/2 hrs.), beach-cruiser bikes ($11/hr., $18/2 hrs.), and other pedal-powered vehicles.

BEACHCOMBING AND BIRD-WATCHING

The most rugged, scenic parts of the peninsula are at its far southern reaches. This is also

on the six-mile-long peninsula at the north side of the harbor entrance. It's not hard to imagine a cartoon of developers sitting in a boardroom, looking at a map and photos of the beach, thinking they'd discovered a gold mine—while somehow overlooking weather reports disclosing the peninsula's damp, windy conditions. Half a century later the residential neighborhoods are filled with "For Sale" signs. Deer wander the back streets, staring at humans as if to say, "Are you still here?"

It may not have lived up to the developers' expectations, but Ocean Shores is a popular destination in July and August, with vacationers filling the hotels, flying kites on the beach, playing miniature golf, and scooting up and down the peninsula on mopeds and bikes. **Ocean Shores Boulevard,** the main drag running through the commercial district, is lined with hotels, restaurants, and shops.

Sports and Recreation

The main attraction of Ocean Shores, the beach, runs the length of the peninsula and

OLYMPIC PENINSULA AND THE COAST

GRAYS HARBOR AND VICINITY

Razor Clam Mania

Outside of summer, the busiest times on the beaches of the southern Washington coast are days when digging is permitted in the bountiful razor clam beds. The season runs October-April. Within that period the state Department of Fish and Wildlife designates specific dates and times when clamming is allowed. There can be anywhere from 15-35 days per season, depending on the clam population. To find the schedule go to http://wdfw.wa.gov and click on "shellfish" from the fishing dropdown menu. Note that dates vary from beach to beach.

To dig you need a license, which you can purchase at local shops or online at http://fishhunt. dfw.wa.gov. You're limited to 15 clams a day, and you can't be picky—you have to take the first 15 you find. Harvesting has the feel of a community event. Hundreds of people, often in families, don their rain gear and head for the beach, armed with "clamming guns" (boring tools) and shovels. Everyone comes away a winner—on most days it's easy to reach your limit in under an hour.

prime bird-watching territory, with over 200 species having been recorded.

At the end of Ocean Shores Road, **North Jetty** juts into the ocean, making a good, quiet spot for picnicking and watching sunsets and ocean storms. Just to its east, **Oyhut Wildlife Recreation Area** has trails through the marshy landscape populated with a variety of birds. The biggest draw for birders, though, is isolated **Damon Point State Park** at the southeastern tip of the peninsula, one of the last remaining nesting sites of the snowy plover. Walk out onto the point to look for plovers, as well as eagles, ospreys, and many other birds. While you're there you'll get views of Grays Harbor, the port of Westport, and the Olympic Mountains to the north.

Learn more about what you're seeing in the area at the **Coastal Interpretive Center** (1033 Catala Ave. SE, 360/289-4617, Apr.-Sept. daily 11am-4pm, Oct.-Mar. Sat.-Sun. 11am-4pm, free), across small Armstrong Bay from Damon Point. It's a volunteer-run museum packed with natural and historical artifacts.

Entertainment and Events

For classic vacation amusements, head to **Pacific Paradise Family Fun Center** (767 Minard Ave. NW, 360/289-9537, www.pacificparadisefun.com, daily 10am-9pm), which has bumper boats (the aquatic version of bumper cars), 36 holes of miniature golf, and an

arcade with video games, pinball machines, and air hockey.

You get grown-up diversions along the water north of town at the **Quinault Beach Resort and Casino** (Rte. 115, 360/289-9466, www.quinaultbeachresort.com), which has the usual assortment of slot machines, video poker, blackjack tables, and other gambling. It also has reasonably priced restaurants and nice hotel rooms.

Food

Restaurants in Ocean Shores tend to stick to the basics—steaks and burgers, fried food, and pizza. Though there's lots of fish-and-chips, it isn't easy to find fresh, local seafood. If creative cooking is a priority, you'll be happier staying down the coast in the Long Beach area, or making the drive up to Moclips for a meal at the Ocean Crest Resort.

For breakfast, **Our Place** (676 Ocean Shores Blvd. NW, 360/940-7314, Wed.-Mon. 7am-2pm, $6-11) is a longtime favorite, a busy little joint where you can get your day started with eggs, pancakes, or waffles.

For fast food with the flavor of the ocean try **Bennett's Fish Shack** (105 W. Chance la Mer NW, 360/289-2847, Sun.-Thurs. 10am-9pm, Fri.-Sat. 10am-10pm, $9-12), where fish-and-chips and other fried seafood make up most of the menu.

Your best choice for pizza is **Red Genie** (766 Ocean Shores Blvd. NW, 360/289-8144,

Tues.-Thurs. 3pm-9pm, Fri.-Sat. 11am-10pm, Sun. 11am-8pm, $9-13), a mom-and-pop operation serving handmade pies loaded with toppings in a paneled dining room filled with local bric-a-brac.

Galway Bay (880 Point Brown Ave. NE, 360/289-2300, www.galwaybayirishpub.com, daily 11am-10pm, $11-30) is a big, cheerful pub and restaurant serving a wide selection of food, most of it with an Irish theme. Though it's a pub, it's family friendly, with a kids' menu. Friday and Saturday nights there's often live music.

Mariah's (615 Ocean Shores Blvd. NW, 360/289-3361, www.thepolynesian.com, daily 4pm-8:30pm, Sun. also 8:30am-1pm, $10-28) is the restaurant at the Polynesian, and it keeps with the hotel's family-friendly atmosphere. Get a burger or chicken sandwich, or choose from entrées that include steaks, grilled salmon, and fish-and-chips. A buffet brunch is available on Sundays.

Celebrate a good day at the slot machines with a steak dinner at **Emily's** (78 Rte. 115, 855/637-3114, www.quinaultbeachresort.com, daily 8am-2pm and 4pm-9pm, $22-37), the main restaurant at the Quinault Beach Resort and Casino. The dinner menu is the most expensive in the Ocean Shores area, but breakfast and lunch are less pricey. A prime rib buffet is offered on Wednesdays ($16.95) and surf-and-turf buffet on Fridays ($29.95).

Accommodations

There are lots of beds here, with about 30 hotels on the peninsula, more than half of them on the commercial strip of Ocean Shores Boulevard. Choose between locally run places and national chains, including Days Inn, Comfort Inn, and Ramada. Hotels on the ocean side of the road have easier beach access, but none are actually on the beach—there's a dune in between.

$100-150
The Polynesian (615 Ocean Shores Blvd. NW, 360/289-3361, www.thepolynesian.com, $139-229 d) is a good family option, with rooms in a variety of configurations, free continental breakfast, a game room, an indoor pool, and picnic facilities with barbecue grills.

Many of the clean, basic guest rooms at **MorningGlory Inn & Suites** (685 Ocean Shores Blvd. NW, 360/289-4900, www.guesthouseintl.com, $99-129 d) have beach views. Rooms come with a continental breakfast and some have jetted tubs and kitchenettes.

$150-200
The Grey Gull (651 Ocean Shores Blvd. NW, 360/289-3381, www.thegreygull.com, $145-195 d) rents 37 condominiums, ranging from studios to two-bedrooms, each decorated differently, but most with kitchens and gas fireplaces. You can sort through pictures of them online.

Quinault Beach Resort and Casino (78 Rte. 115, 855/637-3114, www.quinaultbeachresort.com, $149-199) to the north of town feels a little isolated, but it has comfortable rooms, some with ocean views. If you enjoy gambling and the amenities of a casino—reasonably priced buffet dinners, live entertainment—you're likely to be happy here.

$200-250
The swankiest place to stay along the strip is **Judith Ann Inn** (855 Ocean Shores Blvd., 360/289-0222, www.judithanninn.com, $199-239). It consists of 10 suites done in Victorian style, with jetted tubs, full kitchens, and decks looking out on the water.

Information and Services
The **Ocean Shores Visitor Information Center** (20 W. Chance la Mer NW, 360/289-9586, www.tourismoceanshores.com, Mon.-Fri. 10am-4pm, Sat.-Sun. 11am-2pm), located at the west end of the convention center, has lots of information and volunteers to help you with your plans.

Transportation
Ocean Shores is about 25 miles (0.75 hr.) west of Aberdeen on Route 109, and 135 miles (2.5 hrs.) southwest of Seattle via I-5 and U.S. 12.

Grays Harbor Transit (360/532-2770, www.ghtransit.com) provides bus services in and around Ocean Shores, along the North Beach area north of Grays Harbor as well as to Aberdeen.

SEABROOK

The area up the coast from Grays Harbor consists of a series of beaches and tiny towns. Notable among them is Seabrook, a development of vacation homes started in 2004 on a bluff above the ocean. It looks like a movie-set version of a 1950s New England town, the kind of place where neighbors wave to one another across picket fences and parents let their kids play in the street. Seabrook pointedly defines itself by its differences from Ocean Shores. It's smaller, more exclusive, and designed to encourage pedestrian traffic instead of automotive. Travelers passing through can have a meal at the town's restaurant, get supplies at the town store, walk down a wooden staircase on the bluff to reach the beach, and spend a night in one of the cottages.

Food

Mill 109 (5 W. Myrtle Ln., 360/276-4884, www.mill109.com, Sun.-Thurs. 9am-9pm, Fri.-Sat. 9am-10pm, $13-38) serves many of the same staples you'll find at other eateries on the coast—burgers, pasta, fish-and-chips—and adds some fancier choices, like crab-stuffed mushrooms and filet mignon.

Since the 1950s ★ **Ocean Crest Resort** (4651 Rte. 109, 360/276-4465, www.oceancrestresort.com, daily 8:30am-3pm and 4:30pm-9pm, $29-48), a few miles north in the oceanside town of Moclips, has been a prime example of old-school Pacific Northwest sophistication. The menu features lots of local seafood as well as duck, chicken, beef, and venison, all prepared in a refined, but not fussy, style. The dining room has beautiful ocean views. The restaurant also does a good job with breakfast ($9-19) and lunch ($9-29), which don't require as much of an investment.

Accommodations

You can rent houses at **Seabrook** (24 Front St., 877/779-9990, www.seabrookwa.com, $274-538), usually for a minimum of two days in summer. There's a large and varied selection, all sleeping at least four, and you get access to the community swimming pool and other recreational facilities. Base rental prices get bumped up by cleaning and processing fees.

North of town in nearby Moclips, you get a genuine old-timey experience at **Ocean Crest Resort** (4651 Rte. 109, 360/558-3763, www.oceancrestresort.com, $87-237). It feels dated but not neglected, and the age gives its simple rooms some added charm. The beach is accessible via a staircase down the bluff on which the resort sits.

CAMPING

The campgrounds at **Pacific Beach State Park** (49 2nd St., 360/276-4297, http://parks.state.wa.us/557) are best suited to RVs, while those at **Ocean City State Park** (148 Rte. 115, 360/289-3553, http://parks.state.wa.us/554) work well for either RVs or tents. Sites at both run $35-45 and can be reserved by phone (888/226-7688) and online (http://washington.goingtocamp.com). Pacific Beach also has two yurts ($64-74) that can accommodate up to five.

Transportation

Seabrook is located on Route 109, 18 miles up the coast from Ocean Shores and about a 30-minute drive.

WESTPORT

On the southern side of the mouth of Grays Harbor is Westport (pop. 2,000), which once called itself the Salmon Fishing Capital of the World. The catch has declined, but fishing is still the main business and the marina is the center of activity.

For leisure travelers, Westport fills a couple of roles. If you want to go on a deep-sea fishing charter, this is the place to do it. In spring the fishing boats double as whale-watching cruisers, taking tourists out to catch a glimpse of migrating gray whales. And the waters off Westhaven State Park are among the state's most popular places to surf.

Sights

The town's main cultural attraction is the **Westport Maritime Museum** (2201 Westhaven Dr., 360/268-0078, www.westportmaritimemuseum.com, Apr.-Sept. Thurs.-Mon. 10am-4pm, Oct.-Mar. Thurs.-Mon. noon-4pm, $5), housed in an impressive old Coast Guard station built in 1939. Inside are Coast Guard memorabilia, exhibits about the local logging and cranberry-growing industries, and photographs of the early Aberdeen-Westport plank road. Out front in glass cases are gray whale, minke whale, sea lion, and porpoise skeletons. Also on the display is the massive Destruction Island Lighthouse lens, built in France in 1888 and in service 1891-1995.

The museum also manages the **Grays Harbor Lighthouse** (1020 W. Ocean Ave., 360/268-0078, www.westportmaritimemuseum.com, June-Aug. Thurs.-Mon. 10am-4pm, Feb.-May and Sept.-Nov. Fri.-Sun. noon-4pm, $5). Built in 1897-1898, it stands 107 feet tall, making it the tallest lighthouse in Washington. Originally it was 300 feet from the ocean, but now it's set amid trees some 3,000 feet away, the result of land shifts brought on in part by the development of a jetty system in the early 20th century. Climb the tower to the lantern room and check out the original lens.

Sports and Recreation

WESTHAVEN STATE PARK AND WESTPORT LIGHT STATE PARK

Westhaven State Park (2700 Jetty Haul Rd., 360/268-9717, http://parks.state.wa.us/285) and **Westport Light State Park** (1595 Ocean Ave., 360/268-9717, http://parks.state.wa.us/284) are both small day-use coastal parks protected by dunes and connected to one another by a 1.3-mile boardwalk. Westhaven's location, just south of a long jetty, makes it well suited to surfing. Westport Light is the site of Grays Harbor Lighthouse. Like all state parks, they require a Discover Pass for parking.

FISHING

Westport's harbor is packed with fishing vessels, and charter operators line the marina. Most charters leave early—around 6am—and get you back on land by midafternoon.

Westport waterfront

A couple that earn high marks are **Westport Charters** (2411 Westhaven Dr., 360/268-0900, http://westportcharters.com) and **Deep Sea Charters** (across from Float 6, 360/268-9300, www.deepseacharters.biz). Costs vary depending on what you're fishing for: salmon and bottom-fish trips typically run around $150 per person, halibut $250-300, and tuna $400 for one day, $600 for two. Halibut and tuna expeditions travel farther out to sea and can start as early as 3am.

There's also lots of fishing done from the shore. The jetty near Westhaven State Park is a good spot for catching salmon, lingcod, and rockfish. The Westport Fishing Pier, off the end of Float 20 at the marina, is another popular location.

SURFING
If you want to brave the cold water and join the surfers at Westhaven State Park, rent gear at **The Surf Shop** (207 N. Montesano St., 360/268-0992, http://westportsurfshop.com). Boards go for $15 a day, and wetsuits are also $15.

WHALE-WATCHING
Ocean Sportfishing Charters (2549 Westhaven Dr., 360/268-1000, www.oceansportfishing.com) conducts twice-daily expeditions in March and April to view migrating gray whales. The trip costs $45 ($35 for kids under 14) and lasts around two hours.

Food
Blue Buoy Restaurant (2323 Westhaven Dr., 360/268-7065, daily 8am-2pm, $8-20) is an old-school dockside diner serving steak and eggs, crab omelets, and massive sides of hash browns for breakfast and primarily seafood specialties, such as smoked albacore sandwiches and oyster po'boys, at lunch.

Bennett's Fish Shack (2581 Westhaven Dr., 360/268-7380, www.bennettsdining.com, daily 11am-9pm, $9-12) is a popular fried-fish joint where meals are a greasy indulgence.

There's a higher-end Bennett's seven miles to the south in Grayland, but the shack is a better bargain.

Just down the road from Grays Harbor Lighthouse, family-run **Odysseus** (1155 W. Ocean Ave., 360/268-0039, Tues.-Sat. 10am-5pm, $10-18) has a menu that's part Greek (gyros, dolmas), part diner (burgers, fried fish, baked pasta). Expect large portions and a busy dining room.

Accommodations
For a place to bunk before an early-morning fishing expedition, **Mariners Cove Inn** (303 W. Ocean Ave., 360/268-6000, www.marinerscoveinn.com, $99-109) does the trick with clean, quiet rooms near the docks. There's even a fish-cleaning station.

Glenacres Historic Inn (222 N. Montesano St., 360/268-0958, www.glenacresinn.com, $100-115 d) occupies a handsome old house and has low-key, country-style furnishings—it's essentially a B&B without the breakfast. In addition to the eight guest rooms there are four cottages ($136-220), the largest of which is well suited for families.

The Westport Inn (2501 N. Nyhus St., 360/268-0111, www.westportwamotel.com, $125-179) is a comfortable three-story motel with a great location near the pier and Westhaven State Park.

Information and Services
Get information and guidance from the **Westport/Grayland Chamber of Commerce** (2985 S. Montesano St., 360/268-9422, http://westportgrayland-chamber.org, daily 10am-3pm).

Transportation
It's 46 miles (1 hr.) from Ocean Shores to Westport, a clockwise drive to the south around Grays Harbor on Routes 109 and 105. It's 80 miles (1.75 hrs.) south to Long Beach on Routes 105 and 101, and 65 miles (1.5 hrs.) north to Lake Quinault on Routes 105 and 101.

Long Beach Peninsula

The southernmost part of the Washington coast ends with a bang at Cape Disappointment, where the mighty Columbia River crashes into the Pacific. North from there the Long Beach Peninsula pokes up like a giant fishhook, 28 miles long and two miles wide, attached to the mainland at its south end. The west side faces the Pacific and has what is indeed a very long beach (though not the longest in the world, as a prominent arch in town claims). To the east is Willapa Bay, where the marshy waters are prime oyster-farming territory.

Vacationers have been drawn here for over a century, building sand castles and bonfires on the beach and sticking their toes in the water when the sun comes out in July and August. At the south end of the peninsula the small towns of **Ilwaco, Seaview,** and **Long Beach** have a laid-back, lived-in charm. As you head farther north things start to feel very remote. The northern tip of the peninsula is Leadbetter Point State Park, a wildlife preserve that's an appealing, underutilized site for bird-watching and beachcombing.

★ CAPE DISAPPOINTMENT STATE PARK

The 1,882-acre **Cape Disappointment State Park** (44 Robert Gray Dr., Ilwaco, 360/642-3078, http://parks.state.wa.us/486, Discover Pass required for parking) is one of the jewels of the Washington State Park System. In it you'll find wooded trails, sandy coves, dramatic vistas of the Pacific and the mouth of the Columbia, a museum dedicated to Lewis and Clark, two historic lighthouses, good fishing, and campsites, yurts, and cabins for overnight stays.

The name Cape Disappointment was coined by British fur trader John Meares in 1788. He had heard there was an enormous river here, which he hoped would lead to the fabled Northwest Passage, but when he approached the cape he couldn't locate the river's mouth—hence the disappointment. The Columbia is surprisingly easy to miss from sea; George Vancouver also failed to spot it when he sailed by. It was finally "discovered" in 1792 by American captain Robert Gray, who sailed his ship *Columbia Rediviva* into the treacherous river mouth. More than 230 ships were wrecked or sunk on the Columbia bar before jetties were constructed, and even with them the passage remains perilous. The North Jetty, reaching a half-mile out from the end of the cape, is a popular place to fish for salmon and perch.

Lewis and Clark Interpretive Center

It was on Cape Disappointment in November of 1805 that Meriwether Lewis and William Clark finally reached "the ocean, this great Pacific Ocean which we been so long anxious to see." The park now contains the **Lewis and Clark Interpretive Center** (360/642-3029, http://parks.state.wa.us/187, Apr.-Oct. daily 10am-5pm, Nov.-Mar. Wed.-Sun. 10am-5pm, $5), a museum with a film about the expedition and exhibits tracking its journey up the Missouri River, over the Rockies, and down the Columbia.

There's also a room with a wall of picture windows looking out on Cape Disappointment Lighthouse, the Columbia, and the Pacific. Within the room displays tell tales of the "Graveyard of the Pacific," the bar at the mouth of the Columbia that's been the final resting place for more than 200 ships and countless smaller boats, with over 700 lives lost. You'll also learn about the evolution of rescue methods. The Coast Guard continues to maintain a rescue station at Point Disappointment, as well as the only school in the United States specifically for training

Long Beach

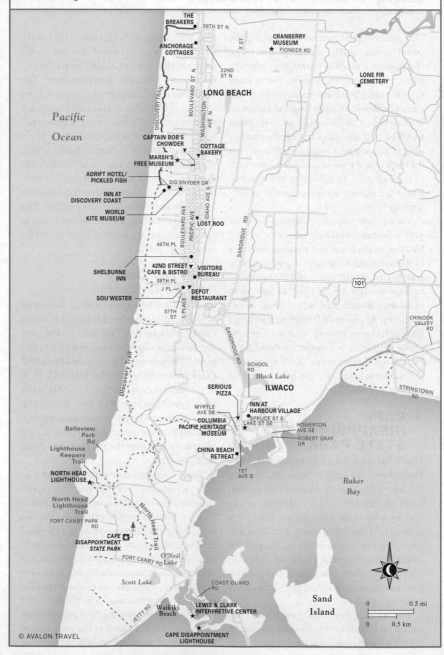

THE BREAKERS

26TH ST N

ANCHORAGE COTTAGES

X ST

CRANBERRY MUSEUM
PIONEER RD

LONE FIR CEMETERY

22ND ST N

BOULEVARD ST N

WASHINGTON AVE N

LONG BEACH

Pacific

Ocean

CAPTAIN BOB'S CHOWDER

COTTAGE BAKERY

MARSH'S FREE MUSEUM

ADRIFT HOTEL/ PICKLED FISH

SID SNYDER DR

INN AT DISCOVERY COAST

WORLD KITE MUSEUM

BOULEVARD AVE

PACIFIC AVE

IDAHO AVE S

SANDRIDGE RD

LOST ROO

45TH PL

SHELBURNE INN

42ND STREET CAFE & BISTRO

VISITORS BUREAU

101

38TH PL

J PL

DEPOT RESTAURANT

SOU'WESTER

37TH ST

L PLACE

SANDRIDGE RD

CHINOOK VALLEY RD

DISCOVERY TRAIL

SCHOOL RD

Black Lake

STRINGTOWN RD

SERIOUS PIZZA

ILWACO

MYRTLE AVE SE

INN AT HARBOUR VILLAGE

Belleview Park Rd

COLUMBIA PACIFIC HERITAGE MUSEUM

SPRUCE ST E

LAKE ST SE

HOWERTON AVE SE

Lighthouse Keepers Trail

CHINA BEACH RETREAT

ROBERT GRAY DR

NORTH HEAD LIGHTHOUSE

1ST AVE S

Baker Bay

North Head Lighthouse Trail

FORT CANBY PARK RD

North Head Trail

CAPE DISAPPOINTMENT STATE PARK

O'Neil Lake

FORT CANBY RD

Scott Lake

COAST GUARD RD

JETTY RD

Waikiki Beach

LEWIS & CLARK INTERPRETIVE CENTER

Sand Island

Baker Bay

0   0.5 mi

0   0.5 km

CAPE DISAPPOINTMENT LIGHTHOUSE

© AVALON TRAVEL

Cape Disappointment Lighthouse

Westwind Trail one mile through more old growth to Beards Hollow, where you can pick up the **Discovery Trail,** which takes you out of the park and to the town of Long Beach, four miles to the north.

To the south of North Head Lighthouse, walk among the dunes and driftwood of **Benson Beach,** which is accessible from the campground. Tiny **Waikiki Beach,** reached by a trail from the interpretive center, is a scenic spot for a picnic. The beach gets its name from a Hawaiian sailor who washed ashore here in 1811 after his ship wrecked while attempting to cross the Columbia bar.

While hiking around, be on the lookout for **The Confluence Project** (www.confluenceproject.org), an ambitious environmental artwork by Maya Lin, the creator of the Vietnam Veterans Memorial in Washington DC. Parts of the project are found along the Columbia River as far east as the Tri-Cities. Within the park, project elements include a boardwalk to Waikiki Beach decorated with inscriptions from Lewis and Clark's journals and, overlooking Baker Bay, a fish-cleaning table with text from a Chinook legend carved into it.

sailors to handle boats in extreme weather and dangerous seas.

Lighthouses

From the interpretive center, a quarter-mile trail leads to **Cape Disappointment Lighthouse,** the oldest lighthouse in Washington, built in 1856. There are good views from here of the mouth of the Columbia and Jetty A. **North Head Lighthouse,** built in 1898, stands on the ocean side of the cape above Dead Man's Hollow. It's reached by a short walk through the woods from a parking area at the end of North Head Road. The North Head Lighthouse is open for tours ($3) May-September. Call the interpretive center (360/642-3029) for tour schedules.

Hiking

The park has eight miles of trails. On Baker Bay to the east the **Coastal Forest Trail** is an enjoyable 1.5-mile loop through old-growth woods. From the parking area for North Head Lighthouse you can take the

Camping

The best campgrounds in the Long Beach Peninsula area are in **Cape Disappointment State Park,** which has 220 sites total, 180 of them located in the campground between North Head Lighthouse and Benson Beach, the rest along O'Neil Lake. Sixty are full hookups ($45), 18 have water and electricity only ($40), 137 accommodate tents or RVs with no hookups ($35), and 5 are primitive walk-in sites ($12). There are eight restrooms and 14 showers. Reservations can be made by phone (888/226-7688) or online (http://washington.goingtocamp.com) for an $8 fee.

The park also has 14 **yurts** (http://parks.state.wa.us/425, $69) that are 16 feet in diameter, and three 13-by-13-foot **cabins** (http://parks.state.wa.us/409, $69). Both options can, in a pinch, accommodate up to six people. Cabin- and yurt-dwellers bring their own bed linens and share bathroom facilities with the campers.

Transportation

Cape Disappointment is a well-marked 10-minute drive south from the town of Long Beach. It's 115 miles (2.25 hrs.) northwest of Portland on U.S. 30 and 180 miles (3 hrs.) southwest of Seattle on I-5 and U.S. 101.

ILWACO

Ilwaco (pop. 900) is located on Baker Bay, to the northeast of Cape Disappointment State Park. It feels very sleepy, on some blocks verging on a ghost town, but there are two reasons to make a stop here: It has one of the best small-town museums in the state, and its harbor is the peninsula's hub for commercial and recreational fishing, with a picturesque dock.

Columbia Pacific Heritage Museum

The **Columbia Pacific Heritage Museum** (115 SE Lake St., 360/642-3446, http://columbiapacificheritagemuseum.org, Tues.-Sat. 10am-4pm, $5) rivals the Lewis and Clark Interpretive Center as the most engaging and informative museum on the Long Beach Peninsula. A visit here steeps you in the area's history, with exhibits on Chinook Indian culture, early settlers' lives, and Cape Disappointment shipwrecks and rescues. Of particular interest are a detailed scale model of the Columbia River estuary and a coach from the "Clamshell Railroad" that once ran between Ilwaco and Nahcotta, 13 miles north on the peninsula.

Fishing

Ilwaco has a smaller fleet of deep-sea fishing charters than Westport, but if you're staying on the peninsula and looking for an expedition you won't have a problem finding one. Good options include **Sea Breeze Charters** (185 Howerton Way, 360/642-2300, www.seabreezecharters.net) and **Pacific Salmon Charters** (191 Howerton Way, 360/642-3466, http://pacificsalmoncharters.com). Rates run around $130 for salmon and sturgeon trips, $240 for halibut, and $360 for albacore.

Food

Ilwaco's best dining option is **Serious Pizza** (103 1st Ave. N, 360/642-3060, http://capedisappointmentstore.com, Mar.-Apr. and Oct. Fri.-Sun. 9am-7pm, May-Sept. Wed.-Sun. 9am-7pm, $10-14). The simple dining room doesn't look like anything out the ordinary, but the restaurant's wood-fired oven turns out the best Neapolitan-style pizzas on the Washington coast. Almost 30 varieties are on offer, including vegetarian and vegan, along with sandwiches, mac and cheese, and standout clam chowder.

Accommodations

At the **Inn at Harbour Village** (120 Williams Ave. NE, 360/642-0087, http://innatharbourvillage.com, $129-189), 11 guest rooms and one suite occupy a beautifully restored 1928 Presbyterian church.

Under the same ownership as the Shelburne Inn in Seaview, **China Beach Retreat** (222 Robert Gray Dr., 360/642-2442, www.chinabeachretreat.com, $199-289 d) is a lovely 1907 house with a view across marshland to the mouth of the Columbia. A full breakfast comes with your room, but it's served 2.5 miles away at the Shelburne.

LONG BEACH AND SEAVIEW

Seaview and Long Beach are two beach towns with a combined population of 1,800 that blend into one another as you drive the main road, Route 103. This is the tourism center for the peninsula, with more dining, lodging, and diversions than anywhere else. You're a stone's throw from the shoreline, but the beach area is separated from the towns by dunes; as a result, it retains a rugged, undeveloped feel.

Sights

Sightseeing isn't a big part of the experience here, but there are a few places to spend your time on a rainy day. Flying kites is a popular activity on breezy Long Beach, and the **World Kite Museum and Hall of Fame** (303 Sid Snyder Dr., Long Beach, 360/642-4020, http://kitefestival.com, May-mid-June Wed.-Sun. 11am-5pm, mid-June-mid-Sept. daily 11am-5pm, mid-Sept.-Apr. Fri.-Tues. 11am-5pm, $5) does a good job of capturing the color and energy of kites and taking it inside. There are over 1,500 kites on display, including intricate examples from Japan, China, and Indonesia. Exhibits explain the history of kite-making and different ways kites have been put to use, including as vehicles for aerial cameras and as a means of transporting messages during World War II.

To capture the essence of frivolous beach-town amusements, visit **Marsh's Free Museum** (409 Pacific Ave., Long Beach, 360/642-2188, www.marshsfreemuseum.com, daily 9am-6pm, free). It's part gift shop, part carnival sideshow, and 100 percent kitsch. Amid the trinkets, T-shirts, and seashells for sale are displays of the unusual and the macabre, from the world's largest frying pan to a two-headed calf to the throne of love, where you can measure your passion quotient. The museum's star is Jake the Alligator Man; judge for yourself whether he merits his decades of acclaim.

Cranberries are a significant crop in the boggy regions inland from the coast, with over 600 acres on the Long Beach Peninsula area dedicated to their cultivation. The **Cranberry Museum** (2907 Pioneer Rd., Long Beach, 360/642-5553, http://cranberrymuseum.com/museum, Apr.-mid-Dec. daily 10am-5pm, free), run by the Pacific Coast Cranberry Research Foundation, celebrates the bitter fruit with displays about its history, cultivation, and uses. This may not sound like the most engaging topic, but it turns out cranberries have some novel and interesting characteristics. Outside is a 10-acre demonstration bog you can visit even when the museum is closed. The best times to come are June, the peak blossom season, and October, when the berries are harvested.

The Beach

The 28-mile beachfront stands apart from the rest of the peninsula, separated from the towns and other development by grassy dunes, with access points every 10 to 20 blocks. Automobiles are permitted on the beach, with the exception of the area between the Seaview access point at 38th Street and the Long Beach access at Bolstad Road, where vehicles aren't allowed between April 15 and Labor Day. As elsewhere on the Washington coast, the beach isn't for swimming. There are no lifeguards, and signs warn against the dangers of rip currents and bone-chilling water temperatures.

While swimming is strongly discouraged, you're welcome to surf in the chilly waters. Rent gear and get lessons from Ilwaco-based **Skookum Surf Co.** (147 Howerton Ave., 360/301-2233, www.skookumsurf.com, May-Sept. daily 10am-5pm, Oct.-Apr. most weekends but call to confirm).

The most popular activity on the beach, and one that's ideally suited to it, is kite-flying. If you've come without a kite, pick one up from the large selection at **Above It All Kites** (312 Pacific Ave., Long Beach, 360/665-5483, www.aboveitallkites.com).

Hiking

There are a couple of walkways through the dunes that are the result of major civic development efforts. The longer one, **Discovery Trail,** follows the path that William Clark took in 1805, when he wandered up Long Beach from Cape Disappointment. It's almost entirely paved and runs 8.2 miles from Ilwaco into the state park and then up the beach to the 26th Street access point. Along the way it passes several sculptures inspired by Clark's recounting of his hike, including a whale skeleton and a bronze re-creation of the cedar tree that he carved his name into at the point where he turned back—which is the present-day trail's northern terminus.

While the trail is a handy way to travel along the lower peninsula by foot or, especially, by bike, it has one shortcoming: views of the ocean are often blocked by the dunes and the grass. If you're walking, you may be happier on the beach.

The other path of note is **Long Beach Boardwalk,** which goes for half a mile between the Sid Snyder Drive and Bolstad Road access points. The Discovery Trail and the boardwalk parallel one another, which makes the boardwalk's advantage readily apparent: it's elevated, giving you a view of the water.

Food

It's not hard to eat well in the Long Beach/ Seaview area. Restaurants vary in atmosphere but tend to feature local seafood.

On the top floor of the Adrift Hotel, ★ **Pickled Fish** (409 Sid Snyder Dr., Long Beach, 360/642-2344, www.pickledfishrestaurant.com, daily 9am-noon and 3pm-10pm, $16-34) is the only restaurant in Long Beach with ocean views. The kitchen breathes new life into classic beach-resort comfort food, whipping up delicious, creative fish-and-chips, burgers, steaks, salmon, and pizza. There's the same youthful vibe here that you get at Adrift, but it's the kind of place where even stodgy old-timers will concede the kids are doing something right.

The Cottage Bakery (118 Pacific Ave., Long Beach, 360/642-4441, daily 4am-7pm, $5-10) is downtown Long Beach's go-to place for pastries, cookies, and cakes. It also has a deli counter that serves up eggs in the morning and sandwiches throughout the day. And that opening time is correct: You can scarf back a maple bar before the break of dawn.

The captain keeps things simple at **Captain Bob's Chowder** (609 Pacific Ave., Long Beach, 360/642-2082, www.captain-bobschowder.com, Mon.-Tues. and Thurs.-Sat. 11am-7pm, Sun. 11am-5pm, $6-8.50). It's all about the chowder—clam every day, plus two other varieties from a rotating menu that could include crab, tuna, or scallops. For variety there are also crab cakes, crab rolls, and deep-fried hot dogs.

The Australian influence at **Lost Roo** (1700 Pacific Ave., Long Beach, 360/642-4329, http://lostroo.com, daily 11:30am-9pm, $11-26) comes through more in its easygoing attitude than on the menu, which offers a mix of burgers and sandwiches, seafood (fish tacos, cioppino, crab cakes), and meat (grilled steaks, Thai peanut chicken). It's the type of place that's family friendly (with a children's menu) but that adults enjoy with or without the kids in tow.

The restaurant at the **Shelburne Inn** (4415 Pacific Way, Seaview, 360/642-4150, www.theshelburneinn.com, daily 8am-8pm, $18-32) matches the old-fashioned style of the inn with a short selection of traditional high-end cuisine, such as roasted duck breast and cioppino. There's also a more casual pub ($12-17) serving burgers and fish-and-chips.

42nd St. Cafe and Bistro (4201 Pacific Way, Seaview, 360/642-2323, http://42ndstcafe.com, Wed.-Sun. 8am-2pm and 4:30pm-9pm, $10-28) is a comfort-food place that doesn't get too casual. They may serve pot roast and fried chicken, but you can still feel underdressed here if you show up in a ragged T-shirt and flip-flops. They specialize in omelets at breakfast, and the dinner menu also has sandwiches and seafood, including the local delicacy, razor clams.

Chef Michael Lalewicz serves an eclectic menu at **The Depot Restaurant** (1208 38th Pl., Seaview, 360/642-7880, http://depotrestaurantdining.com, daily 5pm-9pm, $19-29): You can get Southern barbecued pork shoulder, Greek meatballs, Thai calamari, and Peruvian scallops. He's been pulling it all off for years, cementing a reputation as one of the finest cooks on the peninsula. The restaurant converts Seaview's old depot, which saw its last train in 1930, into a warm, intimate setting.

Accommodations

The variety of lodging choices in Long Beach and Seaview is pretty impressive. There are good options for families, hipsters, history buffs, and couples on a romantic getaway.

The Breakers (210 26th St. NW, Long Beach, 360/642-4414, http://breakerslongbeach.com, $139-199 d) rents condos in a

144-unit complex north of downtown Long Beach. The privately owned condos vary in furnishings and design, but generally meet or exceed the standards of chain hotels in the same price range. Many rooms have kitchens, there's direct access to the beach, and facilities include playground areas, barbecue grills, and an indoor pool—all of which make the Breakers a good choice for families.

Anchorage Cottages (2209 Ocean Beach Blvd. N, Long Beach, 360/642-2351, www.theanchoragecottages.com) consist of 10 condo cottages built in the 1950s. Four have one bedroom ($119-143) and the remaining six have two ($153-160). All have fully equipped kitchens, and most have wood-burning fireplaces.

The owners of **Adrift Hotel** (409 Sid Snyder Dr., Long Beach, 360/642-2311, www.adrifthotel.com, $150-220 d) bought a run-down lodging and gave it a modern makeover that mixes spare industrial style with some touches of beach chic. The result may not be for everyone—it's comfortable but not cozy, and it feels aimed at a younger market. The location, along one of the beach access roads, is prime, and free use of bikes is a nice perk.

Inn at Discovery Coast (421 11th St. SW,

Long Beach, 360/642-5265, www.innatdiscoverycoast.com, $179-277 d) is the higher-end sister hotel of neighboring Adrift. It's designed with romantic getaways in mind. Guest rooms are decorated with the kind of restrained style you'd find in a Crate and Barrel catalog. All have ocean views that get better the higher you go in the three-story main building. (Prices go up story by story accordingly.) Most have gas fireplaces and two-person jetted tubs.

The ★ **Shelburne Inn** (4415 Pacific Way, Seaview, 360/642-2442, www.theshelburneinn.com, $149-199 d) has been in operation since 1896, and it has the charm of a favorite grandparent—it's unabashedly old-fashioned and wears its age well. The 15 guest rooms are all different, and the least expensive are tiny, but they're comfortable and full of character. When you factor in that room rates include an elaborate breakfast, the Shelburne is one of the area's best deals. The location, on the main road through Seaview, is convenient, but it means the charm evaporates when you step out the front door.

For accommodations with personality, check out **The Sou'wester** (728 J Pl., Seaview, 360/642-2542, www.souwesterlodge.com). It has several lodging options,

Leadbetter Point State Park

all of which qualify as "vintage." The lodge is a big old house dating from 1892 with suites upstairs ($113-143) and smaller rooms with shared bath downstairs ($80). Outside are 1950s-era cabins ($133-173) and refurbished old trailers ($113-183), all with bathrooms, most with kitchens. To top it off there are also RV hookups ($50-55) and tent sites ($45). If "hippie meets hipster" sounds appealing, you'll probably like it here.

Information and Services

Pick up information and get guidance at the **Long Beach Peninsula Visitors Bureau** (3914 Pacific Way, 360/642-2400, http://fun-beach.com, Mon.-Fri. 9am-6pm, Sat.-Sun. 9am-5pm), located at the intersection of U.S. 101 and Route 103 in Seaview.

Transportation

Seaview and Long Beach are a couple of miles north of Ilwaco and Cape Disappointment State Park on U.S. 103.

OYSTERVILLE AND VICINITY

On the tip of the Long Beach Peninsula, oyster farming has been the main order of business for generations. Tiny Oysterville was a hub of activity in the 1800s, and the entire town, with its preserved church, one-room schoolhouse, and old homes, is now in the National Register of Historic Places.

Leadbetter Point State Park

Keep going to the far northern end of the peninsula and you hit **Leadbetter Point State Park** (360/642-3078, http://parks.state.wa.us/537, Discover Pass required for parking) and the Willapa National Wildlife Refuge. The park is day-use only, and it's much quieter than Cape Disappointment State Park, but it is a great spot for bird-watching and beachcombing. There are seven miles of hiking trails and beautiful ocean and bay views from the along the shore.

Food

The one retail establishment for picking up seafood in Oysterville is **Oysterville Sea Farms** (34300 1st St., 360/665-6585, daily 9:30am-5pm). It's a charming shop with great selection and prices, and a deck overlooking Willapa Bay where you can eat on-site.

Transportation

Oysterville is 15 miles, about a 20-minute drive, north on U.S. 103 from Long Beach; it's another few miles and 5 minutes to Leadbetter Point State Park.

Eastern Olympic Peninsula

In the little-visited eastern corner of **Olympic National Park,** accessible from **Dosewallips** and **Staircase,** ancient stands of Douglas fir and cedar cloak the steep ridges of the Skokomish River valley, and the river's raging waters teem with rainbow and bull trout. Though it feels remote, this region is the park's closest major access point to Seattle and Tacoma.

STAIRCASE

The Staircase area is the main point of entry into the southeast portion of Olympic National Park. This "forgotten" corner of the park is a place for adventurous explorers, with trails running deep into primitive forest along the Skokomish and Dosewallips Rivers. Paths pass Pacific rhododendrons, vibrant mossy old growth, waterfalls, and small alpine lakes. Storms can cause road closures in this area. Always check weather and road reports before venturing into this part of the park.

Hiking

Hidden in the shadow of Mount Lincoln and behind Lake Cushman, Staircase offers many nature trails. To enter the park, follow the signs to Lake Cushman and turn left at the end of the road, twisting along the dirt road to Staircase Ranger Station. There are no stairs, but there once were: An 1890 expedition built a cedar stairway to get over the rock bluff. **Shady Lane Trail** marks the location; it's a 1.5-mile stroll through mossy undergrowth, offering vistas of Mount Rose and the North Fork of the Skokomish River and passing a few bridges and an abandoned mine.

For a good look at rapids, take the longer loop trail running along the Skokomish River. The **North Fork Skokomish Trail** is about a 4-mile trek to Flapjack Lakes; you can continue from there and make a complete 15-mile loop, passing a beautiful waterfall and glimpsing rare views of the ragged Sawtooth Range of the Olympics. A steep three-mile climb to Wagonwheel Lake gains nearly 4,000 feet in subalpine forest, where bobcats, deer, and elk roam.

Camping

Staircase Campground (360/565-3131, www.nps.gov/olym, $20), in a deeply wooded area away from the river, is a great starting point for hikes into the Skokomish River valley. There are no RV hookups. Toilets and drinking water are available only in the summer.

Transportation

From Seattle drive south on I-5 through Tacoma, then north on U.S. 101, for a drive of about 100 miles (2 hrs.).

DOSEWALLIPS

The 425-acre **Dosewallips State Park** (306996 U.S. 101, 360/796-4415, http://parks. state.wa.us/499) is the site of Camp Parson, the oldest Boy Scout camp west of the Mississippi. It's just north of the tiny town of Brinnon, between Hood Canal and the Dosewallips River. There's a great viewing platform and large flats where clamming is popular (seasonal, permit required).

The river originates in two forks, which join about five miles from the headwaters near Mount Anderson. The Dosewallips once teemed with salmon, but conditions severely deteriorated due to logging and farming. Restoration efforts are underway to reconnect the river to its original delta and improve salmon habitat. The entire Dosewallips River estuary is located within the state park, where you can watch seasonal salmon spawning.

Hiking

The park's trails are unmarked, but don't let that stop you from exploring. The **Steam Donkey Loop Trail,** beginning behind the park entrance, is an easy three-mile trail through ferns and maple, traversing bridges and following the old Izett Railroad grade before descending back to the main road. The short **Rocky Brook Trail** begins just after crossing Rocky Brook Bridge. It leads through wooded brush and green foliage to a spectacular 229-foot waterfall.

Climbing

Mount Anderson (elev. 7,330 feet) and **Mount Constance** (elev. 7,756 feet) are rewarding challenges for experienced climbers. They both have steep, jagged cliffs and areas of crumbling rock, but offer commanding vistas over forests and waterways, with the Cascade Range towering in the distance. The Wilderness Information Center (360/565-3100) based in Port Angeles provides climbing-related information, including a list of permitted guides.

Camping

Dosewallips State Park Campground (360/796-4415, http://parks.state.wa.us/499) is open year-round and has tent ($25-35) and utility sites ($35-45), as well as platform tents sites ($59) and cabins ($69).

Transportation

Dosewallips is about 30 miles northeast of Staircase via Route 119 and U.S. 101, an hour's drive.

Olympia

Olympia, the capital of Washington, is located at the southwest edge of the Olympic Peninsula, at the far southern end of the Puget Sound. It has a relatively small population—around 50,000—but a big dome, the largest of any state capitol in the United States. Its beautiful capitol campus gives it an elegant air that's enhanced by tall shade trees, attractive old residential areas, creative restaurants, and numerous art galleries.

Much of Olympia's economy runs on government jobs, with over 40 percent of Thurston County workers employed in the public sector. Things really hum during the legislative session. The town's port is primarily used for shipping lumber harvested from the peninsula.

CAPITOL CAMPUS

Olympia's Capitol Campus covers 55 acres and includes an arboretum, a sunken rose garden, a replica of Denmark's Tivoli fountain, memorials to war veterans, and historic buildings dating back to the early 1900s. In the spring

there's the added spectacle of Japanese cherry trees in full bloom.

Legislative Building

The imposing **Legislative Building** (360/902-8880, www.des.wa.gov, Mon.-Fri. 7am-5:30pm, Sat.-Sun. 11am-4pm), aka the capitol, is hard to miss: It bears a strong resemblance to the U.S. Capitol, with a 287-foot dome, completed in 1928, that makes it the fifth-largest masonry-domed building in the world. It's Washington's third state capitol building. The first, a simple log structure, stood on this site until 1903, when the legislature moved into the Thurston County Courthouse. Construction on the present building began in 1921, but it took seven years to gain adequate funding for completion.

The rotunda is the focal point, with a 25-foot-long Tiffany chandelier suspended overhead, enormous bronze doors, busts of George Washington and Martin Luther King Jr., Belgian marble steps, and gargoyle-capped draperies. Entrances to the senate and house

Olympia's Legislative Building

Olympia

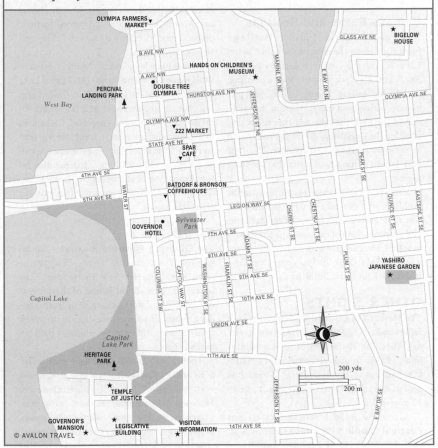

West Bay

OLYMPIA FARMERS MARKET

GLASS AVE NE

★ BIGELOW HOUSE

B AVE NW

HANDS ON CHILDREN'S MUSEUM ★

A AVE NW

● DOUBLE TREE OLYMPIA

PERCIVAL LANDING PARK

THURSTON AVE NW

OLYMPIA AVE NE

OLYMPIA AVE NW

▼ 222 MARKET

STATE AVE NE

▼ SPAR CAFE

4TH AVE SE

6TH AVE SE

BATDORF & BRONSON COFFEEHOUSE

LEGION WAY SE

● GOVERNOR HOTEL

Sylvester Park

7TH AVE SE

8TH AVE SE

9TH AVE SE

YASHIRO JAPANESE GARDEN ★

10TH AVE SE

UNION AVE SE

Capitol Lake

Capitol Lake Park

11TH AVE SE

HERITAGE PARK

0   200 yds

0   200 m

★ TEMPLE OF JUSTICE

GOVERNOR'S MANSION ★

★ LEGISLATIVE BUILDING

★ VISITOR INFORMATION

14TH AVE SE

© AVALON TRAVEL

of representatives gallery chambers are on the 4th floor. From there you can watch the legislature in session from January to early March in even-numbered years and January to mid-April in odd-numbered years.

Guided tours of the capitol are conducted year-round, every hour on the hour 10am-3pm on weekdays and 11am-3pm on weekends. To join one of the free tours go to the **visitor services desk** (360/902-8880, www. des.wa.gov) by the main entrance. Tours are capped at 25 participants and are first come, first served.

Other Capitol Campus Buildings

Just to the west of the capitol, the Georgian-style redbrick **Governor's Mansion** is the oldest building on the campus, completed in 1908. Inside is a fine collection of antique furniture, including pieces by Duncan Phyfe. Free tours are conducted on most Wednesdays and require a reservation; call capitol visitor services at 360/902-8880.

Facing the capitol building to the north is the **Temple of Justice,** dating from 1912, where the state supreme court meets. It's open year-round for free self-guided tours on week-days 8am-5pm.

Campus Parks and Grounds

North of the Temple of Justice, **Heritage Park** runs along the eastern shore of Capitol Lake. There are cherry blossoms here in April, and it's a popular site for swimming, sunbathing, sailing, hiking, biking, and pic-nicking throughout the year. From the north end of the park the lake is a fine reflecting pool for the Legislative Building. Just north of the park, across Fifth Avenue, Heritage Park Fountain has jets of water that kids love to play in.

East of the capitol there are administrative buildings in a parklike setting that includes war memorials, sculpture, flower gardens, and a reproduction of the Copenhagen's Tivoli fountain. You can get a map and directions for a self-guided tour at the visitor services desk inside the Legislative Building.

OTHER SIGHTS

The **Hands On Children's Museum** (414 Jefferson St. NE, 360/956-0818, www.hocm.org, Tues.-Sat. 10am-5pm, Sun.-Mon. 11am-5pm, $13) is an attractive two-story struc-ture with nine galleries and over 150 exhibits geared toward children from infant age to 10-year-olds.

Along the Budd Inlet, the waterfront **Percival Landing Park** (405 Columbia St. NW, 360/753-8380) is a favorite local hang-out with a mile-long boardwalk where you can watch pleasure boats come and go and also get a nice view of the capitol dome.

The **Yashiro Japanese Garden** (1010 Plum St. SE, 360/753-8380, 8am-dusk, free), near Union Avenue, was built in cooperation with Olympia's sister city of Yashiro, Japan. This small, peaceful park has a pond, a water-fall, a garden lantern of cut granite, a bamboo grove, and an 18-foot-tall pagoda.

The gingerbread-style **Bigelow House** (918 Glass Ave. NE, no phone, http://olym-piahistory.org, Fri. and Sun. 1pm-4pm, $5 suggested donation), overlooking Budd Inlet

just off East Bay Drive, is the oldest house in Olympia and one of the oldest frame buildings in Washington. It was built in 1854 by Daniel and Ann Bigelow and is still owned by their descendants. It's open for tours on Friday and Sunday afternoons.

About 10 miles south of Olympia, 80-acre **Wolf Haven International** (3111 Offut Lake Rd. SE, 360/264-4695, http://wolfhaven.org, Fri.-Mon. by appointment, $12) is a sanctuary for displaced, captive-born wolves. Call ahead to make a reservation and a volunteer will lead you on a 50-minute tour. The experience can be a thrill or a disappointment, depending on the disposition of the wolves. When you re-serve, ask about timing your visit to maximize wolf sightings.

FOOD

The **Olympia Farmers Market** (700 N. Capitol Way, Apr.-Oct. Thurs.-Sun. 10am-3pm, Nov.-Dec. Sat.-Sun. 10am-3pm, Jan.-Mar. Sun. 10am-3pm) is one of the biggest and best in the state. Along with fresh pro-duce, meats, and fish, there's lots of prepared food, making this a great place to pick up lunch to go.

They take their coffee seriously at **Batdorf & Bronson Coffeehouse** (516 S. Capitol Way, 360/786-6717, www.batdorfcoffee.com, Mon.-Fri. 6:30am-6pm, Sat.-Sun. 7am-6pm), a comfortable downtown cafe that also serves pastries. For the full experience, attend a tasting at their roastery (200 Market St. NE, 360/753-4057, Wed.-Sun. 9am-4pm).

Spar Café (114 4th Ave. E., 360/357-6444, www.mcmenamins.com/Spar, Sun.-Thurs. 7am-midnight, Fri.-Sat. 7am-1am, $14-22) is a beloved 1950s-era diner that's successfully made the transition to own-ership by the hip Pacific Northwest chain McMenamins. You get three squares here of good-quality diner food, including burgers, fish-and-chips, and pizza.

222 Market (222 Capitol Way N, www.222market.com) is a creative reimag-ining of a food hall, with multiple din-ing options under one roof. The primary restaurants are fish-focused **Chelsea Farms Oyster Bar** (360/915-7784, Tues.-Fri. 11am-10pm, Sat. 10am-10pm, Sun. 9am-9pm, $16-28) and **Bread Peddler Bistro** (360/352-1175, https://breadpeddler. com, Thurs. 5pm-9pm, Fri.-Sun. 9am-3pm and 5pm-9pm, $13-31), which specializes in sustainably raised meats in simple, classic preparations. The latter is an offshoot of **Bread Peddler** (daily 7am-5pm, $7-11), a sophisticated bakery serving breakfast and lunch. Another market highlight is **Broth Bar** (360/352-1175, https://saltfireandtime. com, Tues.-Sun. 10am-5pm, $7-14), which makes carefully crafted soups.

ACCOMMODATIONS

The draw of the **Governor Hotel** (621 Capitol Way S, 360/352-7700, www.coasthotels.com, $119-144 d) is the prime location near the Capitol Campus. The seven-story building has the look and feel of a 1970s-era chain motel, but reasonable prices make up for style shortcomings.

You get a more polished experience at the **DoubleTree Olympia** (415 Capitol Way N., 360/570-0555, http://doubletree3.hilton.com, $139-179 d). It's not as close to the capitol, but it's still right in town, a block from Percival Landing Park.

INFORMATION

Olympia's **Visitor Information Center** (103 Sid Snyder Ave. SW, 360/704-7544, www.visitolympia.com, Mon.-Fri. 9am-5pm), on the Capitol Campus near the intersection of 14th Avenue SE and Capital Way South, has maps, brochures, and tour information.

TRANSPORTATION

Olympia is located along I-5, about 60 miles southwest from Seattle, about an hour's drive.

You can get intercity bus service between Olympia and Tacoma, Seattle, Portland, and other cities along the north-south I-5 corridor with **Greyhound** (800/231-2222, www.greyhound.com). The station is at 107 7th Avenue SE, within easy walking distance of the capitol and downtown.

Amtrak (800/872-7245, www.amtrak.com) stops at Olympia on its Coast Starlight line running between Seattle and Los Angeles. The train station is in east Olympia at 6600 Yelm Highway, eight miles from the Capitol Campus.

Intercity Transit (360/786-1881, www.intercitytransit.com) runs daily bus service in Olympia and throughout most of Thurston County, including a free downtown shuttle between the capitol and the farmers market that operates on weekdays year-round and also on Saturdays in summer.

San Juan Islands and North Puget Sound

The San Juan Islands are the Pacific Northwest's answer to Cape Cod and the Maine coast: an enormously popular summer destination where city dwellers go to experience a laid-back, old-school version of the good life.

From Seattle, a 1.5-hour drive north plus an hour's ferry ride puts you in the middle of the San Juan archipelago, a cluster of some 400 islands (the total changes significantly from high to low tide). One hundred and seventy-two of them are big enough to have names, and three—San Juan, Orcas, and Lopez—see the vast majority of the tourist activity.

San Juan Island is the most populated and second-largest island in the San Juan archipelago. When you say "San Juan," Washingtonians know you mean the individual island; add an "s"—"the San Juans"—and you're talking about all 400 of them. The main town on San Juan, Friday Harbor, is the only place in the archipelago that could ever be referred to as bustling, and the entire island has a greater level of development than its neighbors, with more lodging options and a wider variety of tourist activities as well as a more colorful history.

The islands are like siblings, each with a different personality but possessing some fundamental similarities. Those shared traits are decidedly old-fashioned. There isn't a chain restaurant or hotel to be found on the San Juans. Nor is there a single traffic light (though Friday Harbor might benefit from one). Many lodgings consider it a point of pride not to have TVs or telephones in their guest rooms. Cell phone service can be spotty, though it's inevitably getting better year after year. If you want the kind of summer getaway that your grandparents might have had back in the day (if they were lucky), the San Juan Islands are about as close as you can get.

The surrounding destinations of the northern Puget Sound area live more in the present day but hold plenty of appeal in their own right. Whidbey Island features two charming nautical towns and miles of pretty shoreline within commuting distance of Seattle. In spring the fertile Skagit Valley is a gorgeous sight, carpeted with acres of tulips. Venture

---

Previous: Lime Kiln Point lighthouse; Skagit Valley Tulip Festival. **Above:** orca.

Highlights

★ **Ebey's Landing National Historical Reserve:** At the heart of Whidbey Island, this large swath of preserved land includes gorgeous coastline and the charming old town of Coupeville (page 209).

★ **Skagit Valley Tulip Festival:** Every April the Skagit Valley is awash in a gorgeous display of color (page 216).

★ **Chuckanut Drive:** One of the most scenic stretches of highway in the state winds along wooded bluffs above Puget Sound to the south of Bellingham (page 220).

★ **Lime Kiln Point State Park:** The best on-land location for spotting orcas in the San Juans also has easy coastal hiking paths (page 232).

★ **San Juan Island National Historical Park:** The contrasting English and American camps, relics of the Pig War, add a dose of local history to scenic coastline and prairie (page 232).

★ **Whale-Watching on San Juan Island:** Resident orca whales are a star attraction of the San Juans, and tour operators can get you out on the water to meet them (page 238).

★ **Moran State Park:** With beautiful lakes, miles of majestic trails, and the best campgrounds in the San Juans, this 5,500-acre park is the highlight of Orcas Island (page 249).

★ **Kayaking Around Orcas Island:** Kayaking is great all around the San Juans, but Orcas has the best opportunities for

exploring small outer islands that teem with wildlife (page 255).

★ **Iceberg Point and Watmough Bay:** At these two remote spots on the south end of Lopez Island, you'll feel like you've left the world behind (page 265).

★ **Bicycling Lopez Island:** The flat, pretty landscape and a laid-back sensibility make Lopez an ideal spot to tour by bicycle (page 268).

San Juan Islands and North Puget Sound

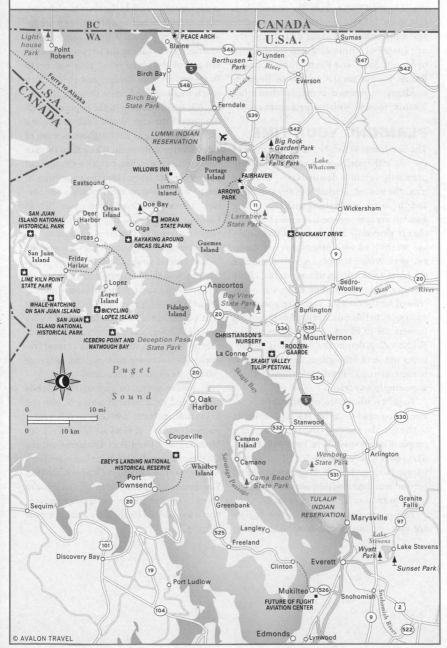

© AVALON TRAVEL

farther north along Chuckanut Drive—a picturesque stretch of winding coastal road—and you'll land in Bellingham, the region's biggest town. It has a hip, laid-back sensibility and a prime location along a bay facing the San Juans but within easy striking distance of Mount Baker and the northern Cascade Range. It's not surprising that Bellingham residents are obsessed, even more than other Washingtonians, with the great outdoors.

PLANNING YOUR TIME

The San Juans, Whidbey Island, and most of the rest of the northern Puget Sound area are primarily summer destinations—days are long, the weather is reliably sunny and mild, and the towns are bustling with life. Spring and fall are less crowded, and on clear days they're gloriously beautiful—but those days are intermixed with others that are damp and gray. Winter is appealing only if you like the bleak romanticism of long nights, chilly weather, and signs in shop windows saying "closed for the season." There are a couple of exceptions to this rule. April, when the spring flowers are in bloom, is prime time in the Skagit Valley, despite the fact that it's sometimes wet. And Bellingham, the biggest town in the region, has a laid-back urbanity that's appealing in any season.

To get a really rewarding **San Juans** experience you need to devote at least 3-4 nights to the islands, and you could easily spend a couple of happy weeks here. For a stay of a few days you're wise to pick one island and devote yourself to it exclusively. If you stick around beyond four days, consider moving from one island to another for a change of pace.

The other destinations in the region are more accessible and demand less time.

Whidbey Island is a popular weekend getaway for Seattleites. To take advantage of the convenience and avoid the crowds, visit midweek. Whidbey and **Skagit Valley** work together as a nice loop: if you're coming from Seattle, start by taking the ferry to the southern end of the island, work your way north to Deception Pass Bridge, and then return south by the inland route through the valley. (Or make the loop in the opposite direction, north through Skagit Valley and south through Whidbey.) **Bellingham** is more of a destination unto itself. It's close to the San Juans as the crow flies, but it's a roundabout trip by car and ferry. More than anything, at least for out-of-state tourists, it's a way station between Seattle and Vancouver, British Columbia—a pleasant stop for lunch or possibly an overnight if you're not in a rush.

Traveling through the region is best done by car. Inland you can get around by intercity bus, and there's Amtrak service through Mount Vernon and Bellingham, but touring by car is part of the reason for visiting in the first place. Whidbey, San Juan, and Orcas Islands all have local bus service. It's most viable on San Juan, where service is most frequent, distances are shortest, and points of interest are closest to the routes.

If you're going to any of the islands you'll need to familiarize yourself with the Washington **ferry system** (www.wsdot. wa.gov/Ferries). It runs to Whidbey from Mukilteo and from Port Townsend on the Olympic Peninsula, and to the San Juans from Anacortes. You can reserve space on the Port Townsend and Anacortes ferries, and if you're going to the San Juans in summer a reservation is as essential for the ferry as it is for your lodging.

Whidbey Island

While the San Juans are known internationally as a tourist destination, many Seattle residents spend leisure time on Whidbey Island, which is only about an hour (including 20 minutes on the ferry) from downtown Seattle. Whidbey may not be quite as scenic as the San Juans, but it has the same laid-back appeal, with beautiful coastline and countryside and mild, dry summers. There are fewer tourists packing the ferries and competing for space in restaurants and campgrounds (especially midweek), and there's a stronger sense of community, established by families that have been coming here year after year, in some cases for generations.

Whidbey is long and narrow, measuring 45 miles north to south with no point more than five miles from the water. Three towns function as the hubs for three roughly defined segments of the island: **Langley,** a tiny, gallery-filled hamlet at the south end; **Coupeville,** an old fishing village on Penn Cove in the middle; and **Oak Harbor** (population 22,000, almost 10 times that of the other two towns combined), site of the largest naval air base in the Pacific Northwest, to the north. At the far northern tip is **Deception Pass State Park,** the island's most popular leisure destination.

There are three ways to reach Whidbey from the mainland. To the south a ferry runs from Mukilteo, at the center of the island there's another ferry from Port Townsend on the Olympic Peninsula, and to the north Whidbey's only bridge—a beautiful one—connects the island to Fidalgo Island and Anacortes.

LANGLEY AND SOUTHERN WHIDBEY

From the ferry landing it's 6.5 miles to the cluster of boutique- and gallery-lined streets that make up Langley. About eight miles to the west another small town, **Freeland,** also has some worthwhile shops and restaurants; from there it's seven miles north to postage-stamp-sized **Greenbank.**

Those are the towns of southern Whidbey, but the area's greatest pleasures come from traveling the country roads that surround them—either by car or by bike—making stops at farm stands, wineries, parks, and the waterfront. The gentleman farmers, retirees, and second-home professionals who reside here give an idyllic, affluent air to the place. Sometimes it can feel like everyone here does yoga at sunrise and eats only organic heirloom produce.

Sights
DOWNTOWN LANGLEY
Langley is a good place for a leisurely stroll. Within a few blocks there's a concentration of galleries, boutiques, and restaurants, and by crossing the street you can get a view over the waters of Saratoga Passage to Camano Island. The life-size bronze *Boy and Dog* is a local landmark that makes for a cute photo op. Stairs next to the sculpture lead down to **Seawall Park,** which has a waterfront footpath. The park also has a "whale bell" that's rung whenever there's a whale sighting, so keep your ears peeled. To learn more about the Southern Resident orcas who live in the area and the dozen or so gray whales who migrate through Saratoga Passage each spring, check out the exhibits at the **Langley Whale Center** (117 Anthes Ave., 360/221-7505, www.orcanetwork.org, Thurs.-Sun. 11am-5pm, free).

The most eye-catching spot in town is **Callahan's Firehouse** (179 2nd St., 360/221-1242, https://callahansfirehouse.com, daily 9am-5pm), a glassblowing studio (located in Langley's former firehouse) with colorful displays inside and out. Here you can watch glass being made, purchase finished products, and, by appointment, blow your own.

Whidbey Island

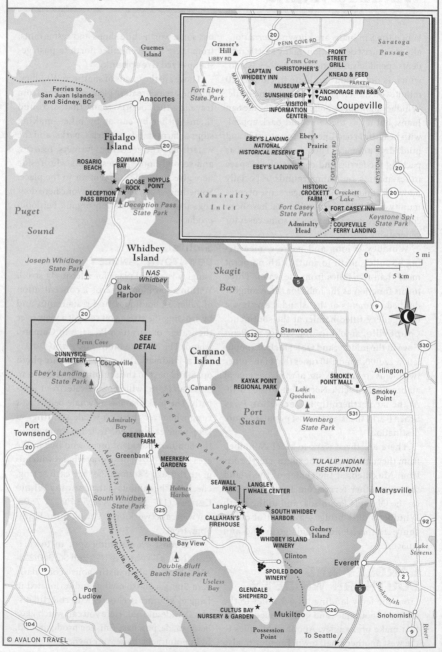

Guemes
Island

Ferries to
San Juan Islands
and Sidney, BC

Anacortes

Fidalgo
Island

ROSARIO
BEACH

BOWMAN
BAY

GOOSE
ROCK

HOYPUS
POINT

DECEPTION
PASS BRIDGE

Deception Pass
State Park

Puget
Sound

Joseph Whidbey
State Park

Whidbey
Island

NAS
Whidbey

Oak
Harbor

Skagit
Bay

SEE
DETAIL

Penn Cove

SUNNYSIDE
CEMETERY

Coupeville

Ebey's Landing
State Park

Admiralty
Bay

Port
Townsend

GREENBANK
FARM

Greenbank

MEERKERK
GARDENS

Holmes
Harbor

South Whidbey
State Park

SEAWALL
PARK

LANGLEY
WHALE CENTER

Langley

CALLAHAN'S
FIREHOUSE

SOUTH WHIDBEY
HARBOR

Freeland

Bay View

WHIDBEY ISLAND
WINERY

Clinton

Double Bluff
Beach State Park

Useless
Bay

SPOILED DOG
WINERY

GLENDALE
SHEPHERD

CULTUS BAY
NURSERY & GARDEN

Mukilteo

Possession
Point

To Seattle

Port
Ludlow

Camano
Island

Camano

KAYAK POINT
REGIONAL PARK

Lake
Goodwin

Port
Susan

Stanwood

Wenberg
State Park

TULALIP INDIAN
RESERVATION

Marysville

Gedney
Island

Everett

Snohomish
River

Snohomish

Lake
Stevens

SMOKEY
POINT MALL

Arlington

Smokey
Point

Saratoga   Passage

0   5 mi

0   5 km

Detail inset (Coupeville):

PENN COVE RD

Saratoga
Passage

Grasser's
Hill

LIBBY RD

Fort Ebey
State Park

Penn Cove

FRONT
STREET
GRILL

CAPTAIN
WHIDBEY INN

CHRISTOPHER'S

KNEAD & FEED

MADRONA WAY

MUSEUM

SUNSHINE DRIP

ANCHORAGE INN B&B

CIAO

Coupeville

VISITOR
INFORMATION
CENTER

PARKER
RD

EBEY'S LANDING
NATIONAL
HISTORICAL RESERVE

Ebey's
Prairie

KEYSTONE RD

EBEY'S LANDING

FORT CASEY RD

Admiralty
Inlet

HISTORIC
CROCKETT
FARM

Crockett
Lake

FORT CASEY INN

Fort Casey
State Park

Admiralty
Head

COUPEVILLE
FERRY LANDING

Keystone Spit
State Park

Seattle-Victoria, BC Ferry

© AVALON TRAVEL

The Boeing Experience

Two miles south of the Mukilteo ferry landing is a major sight for aeronautics buffs, the **Future of Flight Aviation Center & Boeing Tour** (8415 Paine Field Blvd., Mukilteo, 800/464-1476, www.futureofflight.org). Before the days of Microsoft and the tech boom, Seattle was known as Jet City due to the major role that aviation giant Boeing played in the area's economy. Its corporate headquarters moved to Chicago in 2001, but Boeing's primary commercial aviation factory remains, and the company continues to be the largest private employer in the state.

Visiting the facility is an awe-inspiring experience—and also a significant commitment of time and energy. The first stop is the Future of Flight Aviation Center, a hands-on museum where you can examine the materials used to make planes, learn about the evolution of aeronautics design, and experience what it's like to sit on the flight deck of a 727. The real highlight, though, begins when you take a bus to the factory for a tour, on which you witness the assembly of 747, 777, and 787 planes. Seeing sophisticated technology put to use on such a mammoth scale is enough to awaken a sense of wonder in virtually anyone. The factory structure itself is a marvel—measured by volume it's the largest building in the world (and by square feet it's the second largest).

From start to finish the tour takes 90 minutes and requires walking a third of a mile and climbing 21 steep steps. (With advance notice accommodations can be made for visitors with disabilities.) Kids under four feet tall aren't allowed on the tour, though they're welcome at the Aviation Center. Cameras, cellphones, and other personal items such as purses and backpacks are prohibited on the tour. There are lockers available for you to stow your belongings.

The facility is open 8:30am-5:30pm year-round except for Thanksgiving, Christmas, and New Year's Day. Factory tours are conducted 9am-5pm in summer and 9am-3pm the rest of the year. Tickets include both the Aviation Center and tour. Buy them in advance on the website or by calling the 800 number; prices are $25 for adults, $15 for kids 15 and under. The tour is impressive whenever you go, but the ideal time is on a weekday when the factory is in full operation.

SAN JUAN ISLANDS AND NORTH PUGET SOUND

WHIDBEY ISLAND

FARMS

Southern Whidbey is an agrarian community, with small farms blanketing the landscape. Some of them welcome visitors, offer tours, and sell their products on-site. Stopping in and chatting with the proprietors is one of the best ways to get a feel for the character of the area. There's a map of visitor-friendly farms available online (www.whidbeycamanois-lands.com, click on "things to do") and at the Langley Chamber of Commerce (208 Anthes Ave., 360/221-6765). Call ahead before any farm visit. Even during posted "open" hours you're likely to get a warmer reception if they know you're coming.

Among Whidbey's rural highlights are **Glendale Shepherd** (7616 Glendale Heights Rd., 360/593-9935, http://glendaleshepherd. com), where award-winning sheep's milk cheese is made, and **Cultus Bay Nursery and Garden** (7568 Cultus Bay Rd., 360/579-2329, www.cultusbaynursery.com), where the lush grounds are inspired by the great gardens of England.

The most conspicuous farm in the area is no longer a farm at all. **Greenbank Farm** (765 Wonn Rd., 360/678-7700, greenbank-farm.biz) was once the largest producer of loganberries in the world. In the 1990s, faced with the possibility of the land being turned into a housing development, local residents persuaded the county to buy the property. It's now a multipurpose community center. Its big red barn, dating from 1904 and now an event space, is the island's second-most famous landmark (after the bridge at Deception Pass). The surrounding buildings make up a small shopping arcade, with art galleries, stores selling local cheese and wine, and a cafe specializing in berry pies. The main outdoor activity for visitors is taking a short trail through tallgrass to the ridgeline, from where you get a double view: the Strait of Juan de Fuca and the

Olympic Range to the west, Saratoga Passage and the Cascades to the east. This is an off-leash area for dogs, so expect some canine companionship.

WINERIES

Whidbey's location in rain shadow of the Olympic Range makes it a viable location for growing cooler-climate wine grapes, particularly the white varietals madeleine angevine and siegerrebe. Local vintners add variety by also sourcing grapes from elsewhere in the state.

Of the island's half-dozen winemakers, the oldest and largest is **Whidbey Island Winery** (5237 Langley Rd., 360/221-2040, www.whidbeyislandwinery.com), which has its tasting room and vineyard, along with a pleasant picnic area, two miles south of Langley. Another fun stop, just off State Route 525 four miles from the ferry terminal, is **Spoiled Dog Winery** (5881 Maxwelton Rd., 360/661-6226, www.spoileddogwinery.com), where there are actually two spoiled Australian shepherds. Hours for tasting rooms vary with the season and circumstances. It's best to call ahead, though you can count on most places being open weekend afternoons.

MEERKERK RHODODENDRON GARDENS

In April and early May, 1,500 varieties of natural and hybrid rhododendrons come into bloom at **Meerkerk Rhododendron Gardens** (3531 Meerkerk Ln., 360/678-1912, www.meerkerkgardens.org, daily 9am-4pm, $5), making it a must-see attraction for garden lovers. But even when the spring fireworks are over, this is still a pleasant place to visit. The 10-acre garden is surrounded by a 43-acre wooded nature preserve with more than four miles of well-maintained trails. It's a beautiful place for a stroll or a picnic. Guided tours are available for groups of 10 or more; call three weeks in advance to schedule one.

Entertainment and Events

The **Whidbey Island Center for the Arts** (565 Camano Ave., 360/221-8262, www.wica-online.org) in Langley is a surprisingly sophisticated performing arts facility that presents a full calendar of theater and music, with occasional ventures into dance, stand-up comedy, and readings. Every September it hosts **Djangofest Northwest,** a major event for fans and practitioners of the gypsy jazz guitar style made famous by Django Reinhardt.

Greenbank Farm

Shopping

You can take in Langley's flourishing art-gallery scene simply by strolling the few blocks of town and window-shopping—you'll find paintings, photography, and sculpture in a wide range of styles. **Museo** (215 1st St., 360/221-7737, www.museo.cc) is a standout, with innovative, regularly changing exhibits. On the first Saturday of each month Langley's galleries stay open late and for the popular evening **art walk,** where residents and visitors take in the exhibitions and mingle over glasses of chardonnay.

Another prime stop for shopping is **Bayview Corner** (5603 Bayview Rd., www.goosefoot.org/bayview_corner.html), a collection of galleries, shops, and restaurants in and around the renovated Bayview Cash Store, just off Route 525 roughly halfway between Langley and Freeland.

Sports and Recreation
DOUBLE BLUFF BEACH PARK

The most popular beach on this end of the island is at **Double Bluff Beach Park** (South Double Bluff Rd. and East Shore Ave.), three miles south of Freeland. Nestled along bluffs at the west end of Useless Bay, the park is ideal for beachcombing. Gentle tides and long shallows make it easy to explore tidepools, and there's lots of picturesque driftwood for kids to climb on. The mild characteristics that make the beach child friendly also make it dog friendly—it's a popular off-leash area. Locals are vigilant about cleaning up after their dogs and keeping the beach tidy in general.

HIKING

South Whidbey State Park (4128 South Smugglers Cove Rd., 360/331-4559, http://parks.state.wa.us, Discover Pass required for parking), halfway between Freeland and Greenbank, is a great place for hiking, picnicking, and camping. The highlight of the park is its 85 acres of old-growth Douglas firs and cedars, which are home to abundant wildlife, including black-tailed deer, foxes, raccoons, rabbits, bald eagles, osprey,

and pileated woodpeckers. The path through these majestic woods, **Wilbert Trail,** is a 1.5-mile loop that starts at the park entrance. The park also has a narrow, sandy beach, reached by a long staircase from the bluff above, where you can take in views of the Olympics and go crabbing and clamming (licenses available at fishhunt.dfw.wa.gov). Reach the park from Route 525 by turning onto Bush Point Road, which becomes Smugglers Cove Road and after seven miles reaches the park entrance.

BICYCLING

Southern Whidbey's country roads make for pleasant cycling. You can pick up a bicycle touring map and rent bikes for $35 a day at **Bayview Bicycles** (5603 Bayview Rd., 360/331-7980, http://halflinkbikes.com).

KAYAKING

Whidbey Island Kayaking Company (201 Wharf St., 360/221-0229, www.whidbeyislandkayaking.com), based at the Langley marina, conducts two-hour ($59) and four-hour ($99) guided tours and rents boats to experienced kayakers ($35 first hour, $20 additional hours, $75/day).

Food
BREAKFAST AND LUNCH

A hot spot in Langley for both breakfast and lunch is **Braeburn Restaurant** (197 2nd St., 360/221-3211, www.braeburnlangley.com, Mon.-Fri. 8am-3pm, Sat.-Sun. 7am-3pm, $7-15). It dishes out creative variations on classics, such as egg-topped veggie hash and grilled cheese made with bacon and extra-sharp cheddar on raisin bread.

Mukilteo Coffee Roasters (3228 Lake Leo Way, 360/321-5270, www.mukilteocoffee.com, Mon.-Sat. 8am-4pm, $7-12) is a laid-back oasis set in the woods near a little airfield southwest of Langley. The colorful cafe serves hearty, healthy breakfasts and lunches, along with first-rate coffee roasted on-site. The commercial roasting operation ships coffee throughout the Pacific Northwest.

Another hip spot for house-roasted coffee

is **Useless Bay Coffee Company** (121 2nd St., 360/221-4515, http://uselessbaycoffee.com, daily 7:30am-4:30pm, $8-12), located in Langley next to Callahan's Firehouse. Get a cup to go or settle in for a full breakfast or lunch, with burgers, omelets, and tacos among your options.

AMERICAN

Situated inconspicuously in a shopping plaza three miles north of the Clinton ferry landing, **Pickles Deli** (11042 SR 525, 360/341-3940, www.picklesdeliwhidbey.com, Mon.-Sat. 9am-7pm, $8-10) makes two dozen kinds of sandwiches and wraps—everything from Reubens to *bahn mi* to simple turkey and mayo—that are head and shoulders above standard sandwich-shop fare. It's a good choice if you're hungry coming straight off the boat.

At Greenbank Farm, **Whidbey Pies & Cafe** (765 Wonn Rd., 360/678-1288, www.whidbeypies.com, daily 11am-5pm, $10-12) has a menu of salads, soups, and sandwiches to go with a dozen or so varieties of fruit pie. Whole pies are also available to go.

If you're looking for a beer or a creative cocktail to go with some solid pub grub, your place is **Spyhop Ale House** (317 2nd St., Mon.-Fri. 4pm-10:30pm, Sat.-Sun. noon-10:30pm, $8-15). The seasonal patio seating has a Puget Sound view.

FRENCH

From a 2nd-floor location above Langley's Star Store Market, **Prima Bistro** (201 1/2 1st St., 360/221-4060, www.primabistro.com, daily 11:30am-9pm, $15-30) specializes in classic French comfort food—the long menu includes steak frites, onion soup, and duck confit.

PIZZA

Village Pizzeria (106 1st St., 360/221-3363, daily 11:30am-9pm, $7-16) is an unpretentious joint serving handcrafted Neapolitan (thin-crust) and Sicilian (thick) pies. Snag a window table for the best water views of any restaurant in Langley.

resident chickens at Orchard Kitchen

FINE DINING

Whidbey's priciest, most refined cuisine is served at **The Inn at Langley** (400 1st St., 360/221-3033, http://innatlangley.com, Sept.-June Fri.-Sat. 7pm and Sun. 6pm, July-Aug. Thurs.-Sat. 7pm and Sun. 6pm, $155 prix fixe). There's one seating a night for the prix fixe dinner, with a seasonal menu that emphasizes local ingredients. Expect fresh seafood and produce to play a starring role in elegant, modern preparations.

Orchard Kitchen (5574 Bayview Rd., 360/321-1517, www.orchardkitchen.com, Thurs.-Sat. 7pm, $75 prix fixe), just down the road from Bayview Corner, serves "field to fork" cuisine in an intimate setting that feels more like a dinner party than a restaurant. There's one seating a night; diners share an hors d'oeuvre before settling in at a communal table for a set-menu meal that changes from week to week. You can count on four courses of local ingredients prepared in sophisticated but hearty style, with a meat course likely to be the centerpiece.

MARKETS AND GROCERIES

The place in Langley for one-stop shopping is the **Star Store Market** (201 1st St., 360/221-5222, www.starstorewhidbey.com, Mon.-Sat. 8am-8pm, Sun. 8am-7pm), which functions like an old-fashioned general store with a hip attitude. It sells groceries, beer, wine, and local produce, along with clothes, housewares, and souvenirs.

Another way to experience the bounty of the land is at the local **farmers markets,** which are a big part of day-to-day life on the south end of the island. Weekly seasonal markets are held Thursdays in **Clinton,** just off the ferry landing (6411 Central Ave., 3pm-7pm), Fridays in **Langley** (221 2nd St., 3pm-7pm), Saturdays at **Bayview Corner** (5603 Bayview Rd., 10am-2pm), and Sundays at **South Whidbey Tilth** (2812 Thompson Rd., 11am-2pm) and **Greenbank Farm** (765 Wonn Rd., 11am-3pm).

Accommodations
$100-150

Lodging in the area is pricey, making the no-frills **Harbor Inn Motel** (1606 E. Main St., 360/331-6900, harborinn.us, $117-138 d) in Freeland a relative bargain. The facilities are well worn but clean, the staff is friendly, and dogs are welcome.

The **Langley Motel** (526 Camano Ave., 360/221-6070, www.langleymotel.com, $115-175 d), a few blocks from the center of town, has five pleasant, 1950s retro-style rooms with full kitchens.

Situated on five secluded acres just south of Greenbank, **Yoga Lodge on Whidbey** (3475 Christie Rd., 360/222-3749, www.yogalodge.com, $110-125 d) is a tranquil place to spend a night surrounded by gardens and trees. Four simple guest rooms—three with shared bath—are outfitted with organic linens. You have use of a wood-fired sauna and

can take part in midweek yoga classes ($15 per person) or have a private class on the weekend ($70).

$150-200

Comforts of Whidbey (5219 View Rd., 360/969-2961, www.comfortsofwhidbey.com, $185) is a boutique winery perched on a slope overlooking Puget Sound, with six B&B guest rooms on the floor above its tasting room and event space. It's an attractive, contemporary setting, and rooms have stylish design touches, including plush bedding. Kids and pets aren't allowed, but friendly dogs are in residence.

$200-250

Right in town, a block away from Langley's bluffs overlooking Saratoga Passage, the **Saratoga Inn** (201 Cascade Ave., 360/221-5801, http://saratogainnwhidbeyisland.com, $215-255 d) has 15 rooms, all with gas fireplaces, done up in quaint B&B style.

OVER $250

Boatyard Inn (200 Wharf St., 360/221-5120, www.boatyardinn.com, $220-325 d) is located on the waterfront near Langley's marina, and the water is the star attraction. The 13 spacious studios, suites, and two-story lofts all have decks with views of Saratoga Passage. They also come with full kitchens, and the lofts have two sleeping areas and two bathrooms.

If you like minimalist sophistication and aren't on a budget, the stylish **Inn at Langley** (400 1st St., 360/221-3033, http://innatlangley.com) may be the place for you. Rooms ($325-399), suites ($399-599), and cottages ($499) all have jetted tubs, wood-burning fireplaces, and patios overlooking Saratoga Passage. Complimentary breakfast includes scones, granola, yogurt, and quiche. From the street, the inn isn't a conspicuous presence, but what you're paying for is on the other side—beautiful, private views stretching to the Cascades.

Getting to Know the Salish Sea

As you travel through Whidbey and up to the San Juans, you're likely to hear the surrounding waters referred to as the Salish Sea. It's a relatively new name, officially adopted by the U.S. Board of Geographic Names and the Geographic Names Board of Canada in 2009, and it refers to the area encompassed by Puget Sound, the Strait of Juan de Fuca, and, to the north in Canada, the Strait of Georgia.

The prime motivation for the change is to recognize that these bodies of water constitute a single ecological environment—one that biologists and natural-resource managers had previously given the cumbersome title "Georgia Basin Puget Sound Ecosystem." There's a cultural component to the change as well: the waters now have a name linked to the region's indigenous tribes, who share the Coast Salish language.

The new name doesn't replace the old ones, but instead serves as an umbrella term—Puget Sound is now part of the Salish Sea. While the change met with some initial resistance, "Salish Sea" is increasingly acknowledged as a commonplace term.

Information

The office of the **Langley Chamber of Commerce** (208 Anthes Ave., 360/221-6765, www.visitlangley.com) is open daily in summer 11am-4pm.

Transportation

The **state ferry** (206/464-6400, www.wsdot.wa.gov/Ferries) between Mukilteo and Clinton runs every 30 minutes 5am-midnight. The trip takes about 20 minutes. Fares are $11.15 per car and driver, $5.05 for each additional passenger and for walk-ons. There's a $1 additional charge for a walk-on with a bicycle. Passengers and walk-ons pay only going from Mukilteo to Clinton—the trip the other way is no charge. Vehicles pay the same fare going both ways.

Island Transit (360/678-7771, www.islandtransit.org) runs free bus service on Whidbey. Route 7 runs roughly hourly on weekdays between the Clinton ferry terminal and Langley 5:40am-7:20pm. There are no weekend buses.

COUPEVILLE AND EBEY'S LANDING RESERVE

The middle of Whidbey is sometimes called its waist because the land becomes so narrow, giving the island an hourglass figure. The cinch is the tightest at **Penn Cove,** a calm inlet famous for producing the tastiest mussels on Puget Sound. On the south side of the cove is **Coupeville,** a port town founded in 1852 by Captain Thomas Coupe, the first non-native to sail through Deception Pass. Coupeville is the second-oldest town in Washington (after Steilacoom, just southwest of Tacoma). Its 19th-century charm draws tourists to a harbor-front downtown lined with shops and restaurants. The town's long wharf, once used to ship lumber and produce to the mainland, now houses a display of marine mammal skeletons, a gift shop, and a cafe, and provides basic boating services and moorage.

A 17,400-acre swath of central Whidbey, including Coupeville, Penn Cove, Fort Casey State Park, and Fort Ebey State Park, makes up **Ebey's Landing National Historical Reserve.** The reserve is managed by the National Park Service with the aim of maintaining the area's rural character through scenic easements, land donations, tax incentives, and zoning. Roughly 85 percent of the land remains in private ownership.

Sights

ISLAND COUNTY HISTORICAL SOCIETY MUSEUM

At the foot of downtown Coupeville's wharf is the **Island County Historical Society**

Museum (908 NW Alexander St., 360/678-3310, www.islandhistory.org, Mon.-Sat. 10am-4pm, Sun. 11am-4pm, $4), where you can pick up a brochure outlining a walking tour that encompasses some 40 of the town's historic Victorian buildings. Inside the museum are pioneer relics, newsreels from the 1930s, and changing exhibits. Outside is the 1855 Alexander Blockhouse, one of Whidbey Island's first fortifications, along with a garden of native plants.

PENN COVE SCENIC DRIVE

One of the best ways to take in Penn Cove is on a scenic drive. Head northwest from Coupeville along **Madrona Way,** which cuts a path through distinctive, red-barked madrona trees above the shores of the cove. Along the way you pass attractive old homes and the historic **Captain Whidbey Inn,** which is worth a look even if you have no plans to stay there. You can get a drink and a bite to eat at the inn's tavern and take advantage of the outdoor seating that overlooks the cove. Out on the water you'll see dozens of rafts used for mussel farming, and beyond on the northwest shore is Grasser's Hill, an area of hedgerows and open fields that's restricted from development.

★ EBEY'S LANDING NATIONAL HISTORICAL RESERVE

Because of its large size and varied terrain, it's hard to think of **Ebey's Landing National Historical Reserve** (Coupeville office: 162 Cemetery Rd., 360/678-6084, www.nps.gov/ebla) as a single entity. It's better understood as an embodiment of the goals of preservation—an attempt to maintain both the natural beauty of the area and remnants of the limited development from the 19th and early 20th centuries that's now part of the region's history. The result is an expanse of farmland, densely wooded ridges, and steep coastal bluffs. Several useful brochures and maps, available on the reserve's website and in the Coupeville Chamber of Commerce Visitor Information Center (905 NW Alexander St., 360/678-5434), can help you get the lay of the land.

For a scenic tour by car or bicycle, turn west onto Hill Road, two miles south of Coupeville, and follow it through a stand of second-growth Douglas fir trees. The road emerges on a high bluff overlooking Admiralty Inlet before dropping to the shoreline at tiny **Ebey's Landing State Park.** A Discover Pass is required to use the waterfront parking lot, but there's also some space to park at no charge along the side of the road.

Ebey's Landing State Park

From the parking area, hike the 1.5-mile loop trail along the bluff above **Parego Lagoon** for the single most beautiful view on the island, encompassing the coastline, the Olympics, and the Strait of Juan de Fuca. The lagoon is also a good place to watch for migratory birds. From there, follow the loop back along the beach, or continue two miles north to Fort Ebey State Park.

Another trail leads 1.4 miles from Ebey's Landing to **Sunnyside Cemetery,** where on a clear day you can see Mount Baker to the north and Mount Rainier to the south. The cemetery is also accessible by car or bike from Cook Road. The **Davis Blockhouse,** built to defend against Indian attacks, stands on the edge of the cemetery, where it was moved in 1915.

FORT CASEY STATE PARK

The greatest virtue of family-friendly **Fort Casey State Park** (1280 Engle Rd., 360/678-4519, http://parks.state.wa.us/505/Fort-Casey, Discover Pass required for parking) is the variety of things to do there. It has novel military batteries to explore, a lighthouse to climb, two miles of beach, hiking trails, beautiful views of the Olympics, a small museum, campsites, picnic areas, boat ramps, and good fishing in remarkably clear water. The location is south of Coupeville, adjacent to the landing for the ferry to Port Townsend on the Olympic Peninsula.

The fort was built in the 1890s as part of the "triangle of fire," along with Fort Worden and Fort Flagler, to protect the entrance to Puget Sound and the Bremerton Naval Shipyard. Fort Casey's primary weapons were ingenious 10-inch disappearing guns; the recoil sent them swinging down out of sight for reloading. By 1920 advances in naval warfare had made the guns obsolete, so they were melted down. The fort was closed after World War II and was turned into a state park in 1956.

Much of the fort is open for viewing, including ammunition bunkers, observation points, and dungeonlike underground storage facilities. The biggest attractions are two 10-inch disappearing guns, brought in to replace the originals (for show purposes only) in 1968. Another highlight is the **Admiralty Lighthouse Interpretive Center** (June-Aug. daily 11am-5pm, Sept.-Dec. and Mar.-May variable hours, primarily on weekends). The lighthouse has been out of use since 1927, but you can climb to its top for good 360-degree views amid cramped quarters. At its base the interpretive center has displays of fort and lighthouse memorabilia.

FORT EBEY STATE PARK

Located west of Coupeville along Whidbey's western shore, **Fort Ebey State Park** (400 Hill Valley Dr., 360/678-4636, http://parks.state.wa.us/507/Fort-Ebey, Discovery Pass required for parking) has campsites, picnic areas, 3 miles of mostly pebble beach, 28 miles of hiking trails, and 25 miles of bike trails, all on the grounds of a 645-acre World War II fort complex that never saw action.

Like at Fort Casey Park, here there are the remnants of batteries to explore and beautiful westward views of the Strait of Juan de Fuca and the Olympics. The feeling, though, is more woodsy and rugged, with more camping facilities and many more miles of trails. And at the northern end of the park is tiny **Lake Pondilla,** formed by a glacial sinkhole, which is a great spot for swimming and bass fishing. The most scenic hike is along **Bluff Trail,** a level six-mile path along cliffs above the driftwood-littered beach.

Entertainment and Events

Coupeville's biggest annual event is the **Penn Cove Mussel Festival** (360/678-5434, http://thepenncovemusselsfestival.com), held the first weekend in March, which includes cooking demonstrations, off-shore mussel-farm tours, live music, activities for kids, and lots and lots of mussels to eat. Another worthwhile event is the **Penn Cove Water Festival** (www.penncovewaterfestival.com) in mid-May, which celebrates the area's Indian heritage with canoe races on the cove.

Kayaking

The calm waters of Penn Cove make for easygoing kayaking. **Harbor Gift N' Kayak Rental** (26 Front St., 360/678-3625), located at the end of the wharf, has a limited supply of boats available by the hour ($30/hr.).

Diving

One of the top spots for diving in North Puget Sound is the **Keystone Underwater Park,** next to the ferry landing at the south end of Fort Casey State Park. The main resource on Whidbey for diving supplies and information is Oak Harbor's **Whidbey Island Dive Center** (1020 NE 7th Ave., Ste. #1, 360/675-1112, www.whidbeydive.com).

Food
BREAKFAST AND LUNCH

For three generations, little waterfront **Knead & Feed** (4 NW Front St., 360/678-5431, http://kneadandfeed.com, Mon.-Fri. 9am-3pm, Sat.-Sun. 8am-3pm, $8-15) has been baking breads, pies, and cinnamon rolls for Coupeville residents and visitors. They also serve simple sit-down breakfasts (pancakes, scrambled eggs) and lunches (soups, salads, and sandwiches) from a dining room with water views.

The cute little coffee shop **Sunshine Drip** (306 N. Main St., 360/682-6201, www.sunshinedrip.com, Mon.-Fri. 7am-5pm, Sat. 8am-4pm, Sun. 9am-2pm, $4-10), located between Route 525 and the waterfront, serves baked goods and grilled breakfast and lunch sandwiches to go along with its espresso drinks.

AMERICAN

Toby's Tavern (8 NW Front St., 360/678-4222, www.tobysuds.com, $8-22) has all the makings of a classic waterfront bar: warm paneling, nautical bric-a-brac hanging from the ceiling, booths with sagging seats, and million-dollar views of Penn Cove. Food includes chili, fish-and-chips, and the ubiquitous mussels—all prepared in a no-frills style that may leave foodies unimpressed. It's guaranteed to taste better when washed down with one of the regional microbrews on tap. Note

that because Toby's is a bar, no minors are allowed.

If you want to eat on Coupeville's waterfront and you're after something a little nicer than pub grub, look to the **Front Street Grill** (20 NW Front St., 360/682-2551, http://frontstreetgrillcoupeville.com, Mon.-Thurs. 11am-9pm, Fri.-Sat. 11am-10pm, $11-27). It serves lots of classic bar-and-grill options—burgers, steaks, pasta, salads—but the claims to fame here are the views and the mussels, prepared nine ways.

In the midst of historic Coupeville, but not on the water, **Christopher's on Whidbey** (103 NW Coveland St., 360/678-5480, www.christophersonwhidbey.com, Wed.-Mon. 11:30am-2pm and 5pm-close, $16-26) has a casual, contemporary air, with a large, open dining room and patio seating in fair weather. The food is fresh and creative, with a varied-enough selection to please diners of all stripes—there's plenty of seafood, along with grilled meats, salads, pasta, and, at lunch, sandwiches.

PIZZA

If you're feeding a family, a good bet is **Ciao** (701 N. Main St., 360/678-0800, http://ciaocoupeville.com, Mon.-Sat. 11am-8pm, $8-20), where a Naples-trained chef makes a wide selection of thin-crust pizza, along with pastas and salads. The good food and pleasant two-story dining area make the place appealing even if you don't have kids in tow.

FINE DINING

For a first-class meal in a pleasant, unpretentious setting, your best bet on Whidbey is Coupeville's ★ **Oystercatcher** (901 Grace St., 360/678-0683, www.oystercatcherwhidbey.com, Fri.-Mon. noon-3pm, Thurs.-Sun. 5pm-8:30pm, $30-36). The seasonal menu is short and inventive—it won't have something to suit everyone's taste every night, so it's worth checking out what's on offer before you make a reservation. Seafood always has a significant presence—the mussels are, not surprisingly, a standout—and chef Tyler

Hansen likes working with rich, gamy meats like duck and rabbit.

Accommodations

Lodging options in and around Coupeville consist primarily of B&Bs that fill up fast in summer. If you're looking to save money and not interested in camping, you'll probably have better luck finding a hotel in Oak Harbor, about 15 minutes to the north.

$100-150

Anchorage Inn B&B (807 N. Main St., 360/678-5581, http://anchorage-inn.com, $119-179) has the look of a Victorian-era home, from the gables to the floral wallpaper. In fact, it's a 1989 construction, built in an old-fashioned style but minus old-fashioned quirks like creaky floors and drafty rooms. The location is a block up from Coupeville's Front Street, making it convenient to the town's restaurants and shops, and the owners are kind and professional.

    The Coupeville Inn (200 NW Coveland St., 360/678-6668, http://thecoupevilleinn.com, $105-175), located a block and a half from the Coupeville wharf, has clean and comfortable motel-style rooms. Ask for one with a water view.

$150-200

The landmark **Captain Whidbey Inn** (2072 W. Captain Whidbey Inn Rd., 360/678-4097, www.captainwhidbey.com) is a special place, though that doesn't necessarily mean you want to stay here. The original two-story inn, built in 1907 from madrona logs, has loads of rustic charm and a great location overlooking Penn Cove, but the guest rooms ($110-120) are small and worn, and even the suite ($197) shares a bathroom down the hall. Newer cabins ($220-250) and a row of lagoon rooms located away from the cove ($185-199) give you private baths and more space but still feel like relics from another era.

    If you're traveling with a family or two couples, a good option is the **Fort Casey Inn** (1124 S. Engle Rd., 360/678-5050, http://

dock at Captain Whidbey Inn

fortcaseyinn.com). It consists of nine two-story cottages ($170-200) that were originally World War I-era officers' quarters. Each has two bedrooms, a living room, and a full kitchen, and though you can feel their age, they're well maintained and comfortable. The location is on the northern edge of Fort Casey State Park, a stone's throw from the water.

    Two neighboring houses, both in the register of historic places, make up the **Blue Goose Inn** (702 N. Main St., 360/678-4284, http://bluegooseinn.com, $169-209), a luxe, antique-filled B&B in downtown Coupeville.

CAMPING

The small and crowded campground at **Fort Casey State Park** (1280 Engle Rd., 360/678-4519, http://parks.state.wa.us/505/Fort-Casey, $35 for tents, $45 with utilities, Discover Pass required for parking) is open year-round, and sites can be reserved online (http://washington.goingtocamp.com) or by phone (888/226-7688) for stays May 15-September 15. The 35 sites are right on the water next to the ferry terminal.

If you're looking for more of a classic woodsy camping experience, a better option is **Fort Ebey State Park** (400 Hill Valley Dr., 360/678-4636, http://parks.state.wa.us/507/Fort-Ebey), which has 50 sites and follows the same rates and reservation practices as Fort Casey. Both Fort Casey and Fort Ebey have flush toilets, showers, fire pits, and picnic areas.

Information
The office of the **Coupeville Chamber of Commerce** (905 NW Alexander St., 360/678-5434, www.coupevillechamber.com) is open Monday-Saturday 10am-4pm in summer and 10am-3pm in the off-season.

Transportation
The **state ferry** (206/464-6400, www.wsdot.wa.gov/Ferries) between Port Townsend on the Olympic Peninsula and Keystone Landing next to Fort Casey State Park runs every 1.5 hours, with the first boat leaving Port Townsend at 3:30am and the last leaving Keystone at 9pm. The trip takes 35 minutes. Fares are $14.45 per car and driver, $3.35 for each additional passenger and for walk-ons. There's a $0.50 additional charge for a walk-on with a bicycle. Fares are the same for travel in both directions. You can reserve a place on this ferry through the system's website or by phone. Twenty percent of vehicle spaces are set aside for travelers without reservations, but in order to ensure a space it's always a good idea to reserve.

Island Transit (360/678-7771, www.islandtransit.org) runs free bus service on Whidbey. Route 1 between Clinton and Oak Harbor runs approximately once an hour 5am-8pm, with stops in Freeland, Greenbank, and Coupeville. There are no weekend buses.

OAK HARBOR
With one road through Whidbey, every tourist who passes through the island encounters Oak Harbor, far and away the biggest town.

Much like Coupeville, it was founded as a seaport in the 1850s, but it took a different path in 1942 when it became the home of the Whidbey Island Naval Air Station, which remains the largest naval air base in the Pacific Northwest. The result is a stretch of island that isn't tourist-oriented, but Oak Harbor can be a welcome break from "quaint" if you find yourself hankering for a drive-through hamburger and a cup of Starbucks coffee without the tourist prices. Many in-state travelers use Oak Harbor as a gateway town for Deception Pass State Park.

Food and Accommodations
Seabolt's Smokehouse (31640 Rte. 20, 360/675-6485, www.seabolts.com, Mon.-Sat. 11am-9pm, Sun. 10am-8pm, $11-19) is an Oak Harbor institution that specializes in smoked fish to go and fried fish to eat in—there are eight kinds of seafood on offer from the deep fryer, all accompanied by a side of chips.

You can find Whidbey's best deals on lodging here along Route 20, putting you about 15 minutes north of Coupeville and 15 minutes south of Deception Pass by car. If you're just looking for a place to rest your head for the night at a reasonable price, a good option is the clean, no-frills **Acorn Motor Inn** (31530 Rte. 20, 360/675-6646, www.acornmotorinn.com, $99-139 d). For a few dollars more you can upgrade to the **Coachman Inn** (32959 Rte. 20, 360/675-0727, www.thecoachmaninn.com, $114-160 d), which has modern rooms and a pool and hot tub.

Information
The **Oak Harbor Visitor Center** (32630 Rte. 20, 360/675-3755, http://oakharborchamber.com) is open Monday-Friday 8am-7pm and Saturday noon-5pm.

Transportation
Island Transit (360/678-7771, www.islandtransit.org) runs free bus service on Whidbey. Route 1 between Clinton and Oak Harbor runs approximately once an hour 5am-8pm,

with stops in Freeland, Greenbank, and Coupeville. There are no weekend buses.

DECEPTION PASS STATE PARK

From Oak Harbor, continue on Route 20 north about 10 miles to reach **Deception Pass State Park** (41020 Rte. 20, 360/675-3767, http://parks.state.wa.us/497/Deception-Pass, Discover Pass required for parking), the most popular park in the Washington State system. It's 4,134 acres of woods, cliffs, and shoreline, with Deception Pass, and the handsome bridge that crosses it, at its center. Features include two lakes with swimming, four miles of shoreline, 38 miles of hiking trails, six miles of horse trails, fresh- and saltwater fishing, boating, picnicking, scenic vistas, an environmental learning center, and several hundred campsites.

The pass was given its name by Capt. George Vancouver, who sighted it in 1792. At first, he thought it was an inlet and dubbed it Port Gardner. When he realized it was in fact a tidal passage he changed the name to Deception Pass, thus immortalizing his mistake. Because of the strong tidal currents, sailing ships avoided the passage until 1852, when Capt. Thomas Coupe sailed through in a fully rigged, three-masted vessel. Others followed suit, and navigability of the pass enabled Coupe's namesake town, Coupeville, to flourish as a shipping port.

Sights

Completed in 1935, **Deception Pass Bridge** is the only bridge connecting Whidbey Island with the rest of the world. The steel cantilever-truss structure, which crosses over the pass to Fidalgo Island, was built primarily by the Civilian Conservation Corps (CCC). The bridge towers 182 feet above the pass. It's estimated that each year three million people stop here to peer over the edge at the turbulent water below and take in the more peaceful longer views, which can be spectacular at sunset. A scenic trail leads down from the southwest side of the bridge to a beautiful beach. Along the way you get a good look at the bridge's intricate undercarriage.

A mile south of the bridge is the turnoff to Coronet Bay Road, which ends after three miles at **Hoypus Point.** This is a popular location for bike riding and salmon fishing, with striking views of Mount Baker.

Just north of the bridge on the west side of the highway is **Bowman Bay,** which has campsites, a boat launch, and a fishing pier, and is the site of the **CCC Interpretive Center** (360/675-3767, mid-May-Labor Day daily 10am-6pm, free). The building, originally a bathhouse built by the CCC, now has three rooms of displays illustrating the corps' accomplishments during the 1930s.

Rosario Beach, just northwest of Bowman Bay, has a picnic ground with attractive CCC-built stone shelters. A half-mile hiking trail navigates Rosario Head, the wooded point of land that juts into Rosario Bay. The shoreline is a fine place for exploring tidepools. Along the beach is the **Maiden of Deception Pass story pole,** commemorating the legend of a Samish girl who becomes the bride of the water spirit. Offshore, an underwater park is popular with scuba divers.

Hiking

A 15-minute hike to 400-foot **Goose Rock,** the highest point on the island, provides views of the San Juans, Mount Baker, Victoria, and Fidalgo Island. The trail starts at the south end of Deception Pass Bridge. Head east, taking the wide trail that follows the course of the pass, and then turn off on any of several spur trails that head up to the top.

The park is laced with other hiking trails, ranging from easy walks—like the ones down to the beach southwest of the bridge and out along **Rosario Head**—to unimproved trails for experienced hikers only.

Water Sports

There are beaver dams, muskrats, and mink in the marshes on the south end of shallow **Cranberry Lake,** located to the southwest of the bridge. It's a good spot for trout fishing, the warm water makes it a popular swimming hole, and there's a seasonal concession stand. Only human-powered boats and boats with electric motors are allowed on the lake.

North of the bridge, **Pass Lake** is busy fly-fishing destination. No motorized boats are permitted.

Camping

Deception Pass State Park (41020 Rte. 20, 360/675-3767, http://parks.state.wa.us/497/ Deception-Pass, $25-35 tents, $35-45 utility sites) has some of the finest camping in this part of the state, with many sites bordered by tall Douglas firs and some set on or near water. The largest campground is at **Cranberry Lake,** open April-October with 147 tent sites and 83 utility sites. **Bowman Bay** has 18 tent sites and 2 utility sites, also open seasonally. The only year-round camping is at **Quarry Pond**, which has 7 tent sites and 54 utility sites. Reservations are essential in summer and can be made by phone (888/226-7688) or online (http://washington.goingtocamp.com).

Skagit Valley and Chuckanut Drive

The mainland's Skagit (SKA-jit) Valley, which runs north-south parallel to Fidalgo Island and northern Whidbey, consists of acres of flat, lush farmland. Cruising through here on I-5, you see fields of peas, potatoes, cauliflower, broccoli, cucumbers, strawberries, raspberries, and corn.

One claim to fame here is that the valley produces more than half of the world's commercially sold spinach and cabbage seeds. A bigger claim to fame, and a prime reason to get off the highway and spend some time in the region, is its flower production. In March and April, more than 2,000 acres of the valley are carpeted with flowering daffodils, irises, lilies, and, above all, tulips. It's a stunning sight, and it's duly celebrated with the Skagit Valley Tulip Festival, one of Washington's biggest annual events.

The valley's largest town is **Mount Vernon** (pop. 32,000), where an attractive downtown of brick-fronted buildings is festooned with flowers every spring. The biggest tourist destination is tiny **La Conner** (pop. 900). Its waterfront main drag, lined with cute shops and restaurants, looks like it could have been designed by Norman Rockwell.

Heading north toward Bellingham, you can stick to the interstate, but if you can afford a little more time you're amply rewarded for taking the scenic route, **Chuckanut Drive,** one of the most beautiful stretches of road in the state, winding through the woods along the bluffs above Bellingham Bay.

MOUNT VERNON AND VICINITY

Located along an S-curve in the Skagit River, Mount Vernon has evolved from a 19th-century river port into a rail and interstate hub. For tourists it's a pleasant, lower-key alternative to La Conner as a base while touring the Skagit Valley countryside. To the north Mount Vernon blends nearly seamlessly into **Burlington,** which attracts out-of-towners mainly for its outlet malls.

Farms, Gardens, and Nurseries

With its rich soil and mild weather, the Skagit Valley is Washington's flower garden, producing more than 40 million bulbs annually. The first commercial tulips were test-planted here in 1908, but the business didn't start to flourish until after World War II, when Dutch immigrants brought their floral know-how to the valley. One was William Roozen, who started Washington Bulb Company, now the largest producer of bulbs in the nation and one of the valley's biggest employers.

If you come here in April for the Skagit

Valley Tulip Festival you'll see fields awash in color. Things are more subdued other times of year, but it's still lush territory. Some farms open their display gardens to the public and have retail stores where you can purchase bulbs, plants, vegetables, and gardening paraphernalia. The biggest of these is **RoozenGaarde** (15867 Beaver Marsh Rd., 360/424-8531, www.tulips.com, Mon.-Sat. 9am-6pm, Sun. 11am-4pm), the display garden for Washington Bulb Company, easily identified by its Dutch-style windmill. It's open year-round—you can picnic in the summer and buy bulbs in the fall.

Christianson's Nursery (5806 Best Rd., 360/466-3821, www.christiansonsnursery.com, daily 9am-6pm) has rose and perennial display gardens surrounding an 1888 schoolhouse.

The **Washington State University Volunteer Display Gardens** (16650 Rte. 536, 360/848-6120, mtvernon.wsu.edu/volunteer-gardens.html, daily dawn-dusk) are intended to be an educational tool for the general public, with 10 acres divided into three gardens—one for native plants, one for fruit, and one for exhibits of potential home-gardening strategies.

★ Skagit Valley Tulip Festival

The entire month of April is designated the **Skagit Valley Tulip Festival** (www.tulip-festival.org). A full calendar of events includes a daily salmon barbecue, the five-mile Tulip Run on the first weekend, and a bike ride in the middle of the month. Mount Vernon marks the occasion with a street fair, also on a weekend in the middle of the month.

The reason everyone is here, of course, is to take in the beautiful fields of flowers, which you can get a glimpse of simply by criss-crossing the country roads between Mount Vernon and La Conner. Centers of festival activity are Washington Bulb Company's **RoozenGaarde** (15867 Beaver Marsh Rd., 360/424-8531, www.tulips.com, $7) and Skagit Valley Bulb Farm's **Tulip Town** (15002 Bradshaw Rd., 360/424-8152, www.tuliptown.com, $7), which has a platform for elevated viewing.

Some strategies can help you make the most of the experience. Keep an eye on the weather: April can be rainy; try to visit on a clear day for the best viewing. You also benefit by coming on a weekday. Festival weekends are notoriously crowded—traffic becomes a snarl, and it can be hard to snap a picture that doesn't include a fellow

Skagit Valley Tulip Festival

festivalgoer. And though the festival spans all of April, the fields are commonly more spectacular earlier in the month. If you want to see flowers without the festival trappings, come in the last week of March, when early blooms are popping into view.

Bicycling

The farm country of the Skagit Valley is a great place for relaxed bicycling, with good, flat roads, views of mountains on the horizon, and not a lot of traffic—except during the Tulip Festival, when, especially on weekends, navigating the roads can feel like riding in Seattle at rush hour.

Tulip Country Bike Tours (13391 Avon Allen Rd., 360/424-7461, www.country-cycling.com) conducts guided tours both in summer and in tulip season; from May through September they also rent bikes, $30 for a half day and $40 for a full. Another local resource for bike equipment and rentals is **Skagit Cycle** (1704 S. Burlington Blvd., 360/757-7910, http://skagitcyclecenter.com, Mon.-Sat. 10am-6:30pm, Sun. noon-5pm), located among the malls of Burlington a couple of miles north of Mount Vernon. Rental rates are $10 an hour or $40 a day.

Food

Mount Vernon's favorite breakfast place is **Calico Cupboard Cafe and Bakery** (121 Freeway Dr., 360/336-3107, www.calicocupboardcafe.com, daily 7am-4:30pm, $9-14). There's lots to choose from, including eggs done a dozen ways, plus sandwiches, soup, and salads at lunch.

Chuck Wagon Drive-In (800 N. 4th St., 360/336-2732, daily 11am-9pm, $5-9) is a decades-old local favorite specializing in novelty burgers, including, most famously, the peanut butter burger. The place looks a little run-down from the outside, but it's very family friendly. The toy trains running along the ceiling are a guaranteed hit with kids.

Rachawadee Thai Cafe (410 W. Gates St., 360/336-6699, www.rachawadeethaicafe.com, Mon.-Fri. 11am-3pm and 5pm-8pm, $11-16)

has a cult following for its authentic Thai cuisine, served in a narrow old lunch counter. Note that "authentic" means very spicy. Go beyond the one-star heat level at your own peril.

For well-executed bar food, the region's star is **Train Wreck Bar & Grill** (437 E Fairhaven Ave., 360/755-0582, www.trainwreckbar.com, Sun.-Thurs. 8am-11pm, Fri.-Sat. 8am-midnight, $11-24) in Burlington, a couple of miles north of Mount Vernon. Its narrow, exposed-brick room is a warm, boisterous setting for noshing on burgers, fish-and-chips, and fried oysters, washed back with a microbrew. Note that no minors are allowed.

Skagit Valley Food Co-op (202 1st St., 360/336-9777, www.skagitfoodcoop.com, Mon.-Sat. 8am-9pm, Sun. 9am-9pm) is a big, lively operation occupying a prominent block in downtown Mount Vernon. Along with groceries it sells fresh, organic prepared foods, coffee, juice, and house-made ice cream. There's a dining area upstairs and sidewalk seating.

Schuh Farms (15565 Rte. 536, 360/424-6982, www.pugetsoundfresh.org/farm/schuh-farms) is a classic stop for direct-from-the-field produce. They have a farm stand open daily, 9am-6pm, from April through December, and U-pick for the same hours from June through October. Get asparagus and rhubarb in spring, berries and vegetables in summer, and apples and pumpkins in fall.

Accommodations

In and around Mount Vernon you can choose between basic accommodation at motels—both chains and local establishments—and those with a little more character at B&Bs. Reservations, as far in advance as possible, are crucial during the Tulip Festival in April, the busiest time of the year.

You feel like a houseguest when you stay at **Highland Garden House B&B** (501 E. Highland Ave., 360/419-7292, http://highlandgardenhouse.wordpress.com, $56-72 d). That's because it's small, with two rooms that share a bath, and because the good-natured owner lives on the premises. It's also remarkably inexpensive, but don't let the low price mislead you—this is an attractive, well-maintained 1930s house. Breakfast is included in the price.

Whispering Firs Bed and Breakfast (9357 Kanako Ln., 360/428-1990, www.whisperingfirs.com, $85-125 d) is a large, modern home tucked within 250 wooded acres three miles south of Mount Vernon. It feels very remote, up on a hill at the end of a winding dirt road, but seclusion is a big part of the appeal. The four guest rooms have private baths, and there's a hot tub on the deck.

Among the motels, the bargain option is the no-frills **Tulip Inn** (2200 Freeway Dr., 360/428-5969, www.tulipinn.net, $93-110 d).

Information

The **Mount Vernon Chamber of Commerce** (301 W. Kincaid St., 360/428-8547, www.mountvernonchamber.com) is open weekdays 8:30am-5pm and weekends 10am-2pm.

Transportation

Greyhound (360/336-5111, www.greyhound.com) has long-haul bus service in and out of Mount Vernon's Skagit Station (105 E. Kincaid St.).

Amtrak (800/872-7245, www.amtrak.com) has daily service between Seattle and Vancouver, British Columbia, stopping at Mount Vernon's Skagit Station.

Skagit Transit (360/757-4433, www.skagittransit.org) has bus service throughout the valley. The fare is $1 per ride. Route 615 connects Mount Vernon's Skagit Station (105 E. Kincaid St.) with La Conner. This route has buses running approximately once every three hours on weekdays and once every two hours on Saturday. There is no Sunday service.

LA CONNER

Ten miles west of Mount Vernon, little La Conner is an unlikely tourist town. It flourished as a fishing and shipping port until overfishing and the Great Depression triggered a decline. Cheap property in a pleasant setting brought about its rebirth as an artists' colony, and in the 1970s locals started promoting it as a quaint place to escape from city life. Tourists have been coming ever since.

The town is a popular destination for romantic getaways and girls' weekends, and is filled to capacity during the April Tulip Festival. The appeal rests on a combination of factors: there are still remnants of the artists' colony days, in the form of several interesting small museums and galleries; the waterfront is picturesque, crested by the distinctive bright orange Rainbow Bridge; there are good dining and lodging options; and if shopping is a leisure activity for you, you'll be able to while away a happy afternoon browsing on 1st Street.

Sights

A highlight of La Conner is the **Museum of Northwest Arts** (121 S. 1st St., 360/466-4446, www.monamuseum.org, Tues.-Sat. 10am-5pm, Sun.-Mon. noon-5pm, free), a distinctive two-story building along the main drag housing a permanent collection and changing exhibits of contemporary regional art. The gift shop is a good place to find unique glass, textiles, and jewelry by area craftspeople.

The **Skagit County Historical Museum** (501 S. 4th St., 360/466-3365, www.skagitcounty.net/museum, Tues.-Sun. 11am-5pm, $5) sits high on a hill, with a panoramic view from its observation deck across the fields of Skagit Valley. Exhibits cover Indian history and culture, early industry, and pioneer homelife. Hours are extended during the Tulip Festival.

The **Pacific Northwest Quilt & Fiber Arts Museum** (703 S. 2nd St., 360/466-4288, www.qfamuseum.org, Wed.-Sun. 11am-5pm, $7) has diverse, changing exhibits that will broaden most visitors' understanding of what a quilt can be. The museum is located in the restored 1891 **Gaches Mansion,** one of the town's most distinguished buildings.

Little **Pioneer Park** (1200 S. 4th St.,

360/466-3125), at the south end of the **Rainbow Bridge,** is a good place to picnic or just relax and take in the view amid the tall Douglas firs.

Shopping

First Street is the center of commercial activity in La Conner. The main pastime is browsing the boutiques or galleries. A couple of the most appealing are **The Stall** (712 S. 1st St., 360/466-3162, daily 10am-5:30pm), which sells folk art from all over the globe, and **The Wood Merchant** (709 1st St., 360/466-4741, www.woodmerchant.com, daily 10am-5pm), with handcrafted wooden furniture, games, and decorative objects.

Food

For a town of its size, La Conner has remarkably good dining options.

BREAKFAST AND LUNCH

The most popular place for breakfast is **Calico Cupboard Old Town Cafe** (720 S. 1st St., 360/466-4451, www.calicocupboardcafe.com, Mon.-Thurs. 8am-3pm, Fri.-Sat. 8am-4pm, $9-14), which serves the same egg-focused menu as its sister branch in Mount Vernon and also has good soups and sandwiches for lunch.

ECLECTIC

Seeds Bistro and Bar (623 Morris St., 360/466-3280, www.seedsbistro.com, daily 11am-9pm, $11-30) gets its name from the historic Tillinghast Seed Company, which occupied this location for over a century. There's lots to choose from on the menu, including salads, burgers, and bison steak. The fish tacos are a perennial favorite.

Nell Thorn Restaurant and Pub (116 S. 1st St., 360/466-4261, Tues.-Sun. 11:30am-9pm, www.nellthorn.com, $20-38) has something for everyone, from salads and burgers to king salmon and New York strip steak. The interior is comfortably casual, and there's waterfront patio seating.

Reliably good food, five house-brewed beers, and relatively modest prices make **La Conner Brewing Co.** (117 S. 1st St., 360/466-1415, www.laconnerbrewery.com, daily 11:30am-9pm, $11-16) one of the busier places in town. A long list of wood-fired pizzas takes up most of the menu, but there are also salads, quesadillas, and panini.

FINE DINING

The Oyster & Thistle Restaurant & Pub (205 E. Washington St., 360/766-6179, http://theoysterandthistle.com, daily 11:30am-9pm,

La Conner waterfront

$23-42) is an inviting upscale restaurant with an English pub theme, set in a house a couple blocks from 1st Street. Seafood is the main attraction, usually made in rich preparations. The dining room is upstairs and the pub is on the ground floor, serving a less expensive menu ($13-24) that's also seafood-focused.

Accommodations

What's true for the restaurants of La Conner is also true for the hotels: The abundance of good options goes a long way toward explaining why the tiny town is a popular tourist destination. Prices given here are for the summer season and April's Tulip Festival. They go down in fall, winter, and the other months of spring.

$100-150

You get basic, comfortable lodging in a distinctive cedar-shingled building a block off of 1st Street at **La Conner Country Inn** (107 S. 2nd St., 360/466-1500, www.laconnerlodging. com, $139-179 d).

Right in the middle of the main drag, **Hotel Planter** (715 1st St., 360/466-4710, www.hotelplanter.com, $129-169 d) has a dozen quaintly decorated rooms in a 1907 building with a hot tub and a gazebo in the garden courtyard.

Katy's Inn (503 S. 3rd St., 360/466-9909, www.katysinn.com, $129-149 d), located in an 1882 house on a hill three blocks from the waterfront, is a classic, comfortable B&B. Four guest rooms are appointed with floral wallpaper and well-maintained antiques.

The Heron Inn & Day Spa (117 Maple Ave., 360/399-1074, www.theheroninn.com, $129-175 d) is a Victorian-style country inn located on the edge of town adjacent to open country, but still just half a mile from the heart of town. Facilities include a day spa and a backyard hot tub, and a breakfast buffet is included in the rates.

$150-200

At **Wild Iris Inn** (121 Maple Ave., 360/466-1400, http://wildiris.com, $134-199 d), on the outskirts of town next door to the Heron Inn, 12 of the 18 rooms are suites with jetted tubs, gas fireplaces, and decks. There's an outdoor hot tub, and a breakfast buffet is part of the package.

$200-250

La Conner Channel Lodge (205 N. 1st St., 360/466-1500, www.laconnerlodging.com, $218-310 d), under the same ownership as the La Conner Country Inn, is a modern hotel overlooking the waterfront on 1st Street. Rooms have gas fireplaces, small balconies, and, in the more expensive options, Jacuzzi tubs.

Information

The **La Conner Chamber of Commerce Visitors Center** (511 Morris St., 360/466-4778, www.lovelaconner.com) is open March 15-September 15 on weekdays 10am-4pm and Saturdays noon-3pm. The rest of the year it's open weekdays 10am-2pm and Saturdays 10am-1pm.

Transportation

Skagit Transit (360/757-4433, www.skagittransit.org) Route 615 between La Conner and Mount Vernon's Skagit Station (105 E. Kincaid St.) runs approximately once every three hours on weekdays and once every two hours on Saturday. There is no Sunday service. The fare is $1 per ride.

★ CHUCKANUT DRIVE

Heading north up the coast from the Skagit Valley, you enter one of the most scenic stretches of highway in the state—Chuckanut Drive. This 21-mile section of **Route 11** was built as part of the now-defunct Pacific Highway that once stretched along the coastline from Canada to California.

It leaves I-5 just north of **Burlington** on an arrow-straight path across the valley. If you're making the drive from south to north, the first point of interest is the town of **Edison,** a 2.5-mile detour west off the highway. In its way, Edison is a new generation's answer to La

Conner. It's just a few blocks long, basically in the middle of nowhere, but it's become a haven for artists and other creatives. Get out of your car to look around at shops, galleries, and restaurants that look like they could have been airlifted in from hipster Brooklyn. It's a fun and novel place.

A short distance north from the Edison turnoff the highway runs headlong into the **Chuckanut Mountains,** which hover over Puget Sound. It's here that the memorable driving begins. The road doesn't have a straight stretch for seven miles as it swoops and swerves along the bluffs above the water. Much of the way you're surrounded by woods, but there are scenic turnouts and other breaks between the trees where you can take in grand views across the water to Anacortes, Guemes Island, and, farther north, the San Juans. With no shoulder and tight corners, it can be a dicey ride for cyclists, especially on weekends when the traffic is heaviest, but it's a gorgeous trip. Ultimately the road winds up in Fairhaven, a pleasant old section of **Bellingham.**

Larrabee State Park

Seven miles south of Bellingham on Chuckanut Drive, **Larrabee State Park** (245 Chuckanut Dr., 360/676-2093, http://parks.state.wa.us/536/Larrabee, Discover Pass required for parking) covers more than 2,500 acres of mountainous land bordering Samish Bay. You'll find beaches with tidepools, and trails leading to Fragrance and Lost Lakes and the 1,941-foot summit of Chuckanut Mountain, from where you can take in dramatic vistas.

The park has a **campground** with tent ($25) and RV ($35) sites, which can be reserved online at http://washington.goingtocamp.com or by phone at 888/226-7688.

Food

The coast here is prime oyster-farming territory, and Chuckanut Drive is known for its two upscale seafood restaurants where oysters are the star attraction. The farther south of the two is **Chuckanut Manor Seafood and Grill** (3056 Chuckanut Dr., 360/766-6191, www.chuckanutmanor.com, Tues.-Sat. 11:30am-9pm, Sun. 2pm-9pm, $15-42). It's old-school fine dining with lots to choose from even if seafood isn't your thing, including rib eye steak and chicken cordon bleu.

Less than a mile farther north is **The Oyster Bar on Chuckanut Drive** (2578 Chuckanut Dr., 360/766-6185, www.theoysterbar.net, daily 11:30am-10pm, $28-79), wedged on a narrow strip between the road and the bluffs. It began life in the 1930s as an oyster shack and has evolved into a sophisticated, expensive seafood restaurant. About the only thing remaining from the original place is the beautiful view.

If you want to cut out the middleman, take the turnoff near the Oyster Bar that leads down to the beach and **Taylor Shellfish Farms** (2182 Chuckanut Dr., 360/766-6002, www.taylorshellfishfarms.com, daily 9am-5pm), one of the largest seafood purveyors in the Pacific Northwest. You can buy oysters, clams, and crab from the retail counter and consume them on-site. There are picnic tables and barbecue grills; they sell charcoal, but otherwise you have to bring your own equipment and supplies.

Stock up for your picnic in Edison, where **Breadfarm** (5766 Cains Court, 360/766-4065, www.breadfarm.com, daily 8am-6pm) makes a wide array of delicious baked goods. Next door, pick up wine, cheese, and cured meats at **Slough Food** (5766 Cains Court, 360/766-4458, www.sloughfood.com, Wed.-Sat. 11am-6pm, Sun. 11am-5pm).

Bellingham

Bellingham (pop. 82,000) is the closest thing to an urban center that you'll find in the northwestern corner of the state. It's the home of 15,000-student Western Washington University, and it has a relaxed, liberal-leaning college-town vibe. Nineteenth- and early 20th-century development here focused on coal mining and lumber. While the old businesses are gone, they've left behind stately homes and public buildings with an Old West aesthetic.

One of the most pleasant parts of town is the historic district of **Fairhaven,** a neighborhood that in the late 19th century was a rowdy little boomtown of its own. Now its old redbrick buildings make up a lively, eminently strollable retail district south of downtown filled with galleries, boutiques, coffee shops, and restaurants. There's a map with historic sites noted that is available online at www.fairhaven.com and at neighborhood shops.

The city's proximity to both Mount Baker and Puget Sound makes Bellingham popular with outdoor enthusiasts. Many visitors use Bellingham as a home base for day trips to Mount Baker, and every May it hosts the **Ski to Sea** (www.skitosea.com), a seven-sport relay race in which competitors ski (downhill and cross-country), bike (on-road and off), run, canoe, and kayak their way from the slopes of Mount Baker to the waters of Bellingham Bay.

SIGHTS

Western Washington University

It's rewarding to spend time in and around the campus of **Western Washington University** (516 High St., 360/650-3000, http://washington.wwu.edu). The school prides itself on its **Outdoor Sculpture Collection,** consisting of more than 30 pieces found all around campus. Pick up a free annotated sculpture tour booklet while visiting the **Western Gallery** (Fine Arts Building, 360/650-3900, http://westerngallery.wwu.edu, Mon.-Fri. 10am-4pm, Sat. noon-4pm, closed during summer session), which has temporary exhibits of contemporary art and a permanent collection focusing on prints and drawings.

Overlooking Bellingham Bay and accessible via a footpath from the university, the **Sehome Hill Arboretum** (www.wwu.edu/share) provides views of the San Juans and Mount Baker, plus 3.5 miles of paved trails amid 70 acres of Douglas firs, wildflowers, and big-leaf maples.

Whatcom Museum

Bellingham's major museum, the **Whatcom Museum** (360/778-8930, www.whatcommuseum.org, $10), has exhibition spaces in two buildings located a block apart. The **Old City Hall** (121 Prospect St., Wed.-Sun. noon-5pm), occupying the city's ornate 19th-century city hall, has exhibits documenting the history of the town and region and, on the top floor, an arresting collection of more than 500 stuffed and mounted birds. The strikingly modern **Lightcatcher** (250 Flora St., Wed.-Sun. noon-5pm), named for its prominent wall of windows, shows rotating exhibits by Pacific Northwest artists dating from the 19th century to the present day.

Spark Museum of Electrical Invention

Anyone with an interest in science and engineering is likely to get a kick out of **Spark Museum of Electrical Invention** (1312 Bay St., 360/738-3886, www.sparkmuseum.org, Wed.-Sun. 11am-5pm, $8). It displays a world-class collection of artifacts dating back to the 17th century that show the increasingly sophisticated ways in which humans have used electricity. You learn about the obsessive eccentrics who harnessed electrical power, guided by a museum staff that's whatcomsymphony.com) and many other musical and theatrical performances.

Festivals and Events

Every July the two-week-long **Bellingham Music Festival** (360/201-6621, bellinghamfestival.org) brings world-class classical musicians to town for performances primarily at the **Western Washington University Performing Arts Center** (516 High St., 360/650-6146, www.tickets.wwu.edu).

SHOPPING

Fairhaven is Bellingham's most pleasant shopping district. A hub for the area is **Village Books** (1200 11th St., 360/671-2626, www.villagebooks.com, Mon.-Sat. 9am-9pm, Sun. 10am-7pm). This large, first-rate bookstore has a cafe and an event space that gets regular use for readings, lectures, and classes, making it Fairhaven's de facto cultural center.

Other distinctive shops include **Good Earth Pottery** (1000 Harris Ave., 360/671-3998, www.goodearthpots.com, daily noon-6pm), which has been selling pieces by regional potters since 1969; **Bay to Baker Trading Co.** (911 Harris Ave., 360/756-6078, Mon.-Sat. 10am-7pm, Sun. 10am-6pm), a colorful gift shop; and **Gallery West** (1300 12th St., 360/734-8414, www.artgallerywest.com, daily 10am-6pm), where you can find practical and decorative works in a range of mediums.

If you like treasure hunting for antiques, spend a happy afternoon downtown exploring **Penny Lane Antique Mall** (427 W. Holly St., 360/671-3301, daily 10am-6pm) and **Aladdin's Antiques and Records** (427 W. Holly St., 360/647-0066, www.aladdinsantiquesandrecords.com, daily 10am-6pm), conjoined malls selling pieces from over 40 vendors.

SPORTS AND RECREATION

In keeping with the outdoorsy nature of the region, Bellingham has more than 30 parks, trails, and outdoor fitness areas. Get information about all of them at the city's website,

Bellingham's Old City Hall

similarly obsessive. Try to visit on a weekend; at 2:30pm, the sparks fly at the Megazapper Electrical Show, a high-energy demonstration that kids and adults alike will find shocking.

ENTERTAINMENT AND EVENTS
Nightlife

Your best source for nightlife information is the alternative *Cascadia Weekly* (www.cascadiaweekly.com), available for free around town as well as online. For live rock and jazz, with dance nights in between, Bellingham's most well-established performance venue is **The Wild Buffalo** (208 W. Holly St., 360/746-8733, http://wildbuffalo.net).

Theater

The historic **Mount Baker Theatre** (104 N. Commercial St., 360/734-6080, www.mountbakertheatre.com), built in 1927 as a vaudeville and movie palace, hosts the **Whatcom Symphony Orchestra** (360/756-6752, www.

Bellingham

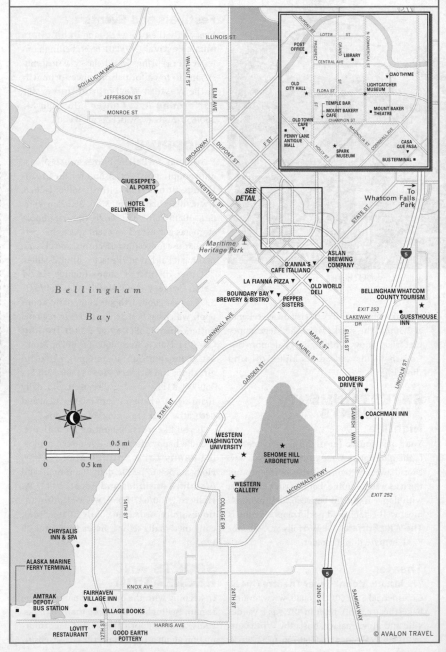

Detail:

DUPONT ST

POST OFFICE

LOTTIE ST

PROSPECT

GRAND ST

N COMMERCIAL AVE

LIBRARY

CENTRAL AVE

CIAO THYME

OLD CITY HALL

FLORA ST

LIGHTCATCHER MUSEUM

TEMPLE BAR

MOUNT BAKERY CAFE

MOUNT BAKER THEATRE

OLD TOWN CAFE

CHAMPION ST

MAGNOLIA AVE

CORNWALL AVE

PENNY LANE ANTIQUE MALL

HOLLY ST

CASA QUE PASA

SPARK MUSEUM

BUS TERMINAL

ILLINOIS ST

WALNUT ST

ELM AVE

SQUALICUM WAY

JEFFERSON ST

MONROE ST

BROADWAY

DUPONT ST

F ST

CHESTNUT ST

SEE DETAIL

To Whatcom Falls Park

STATE ST

GIUESEPPE'S AL PORTO

HOTEL BELLWETHER

Maritime Heritage Park

Bellingham Bay

D'ANNA'S CAFE ITALIANO

ASLAN BREWING COMPANY

LA FIANNA PIZZA

OLD WORLD DELI

BOUNDARY BAY BREWERY & BISTRO

PEPPER SISTERS

BELLINGHAM WHATCOM COUNTY TOURISM

EXIT 253

LAKEWAY DR

GUESTHOUSE INN

CORNWALL AVE

MAPLE ST

ELLIS ST

LAUREL ST

GARDEN ST

BOOMERS DRIVE IN

SAMISH WAY

LINCOLN ST

COACHMAN INN

0   0.5 mi

0   0.5 km

WESTERN WASHINGTON UNIVERSITY

SEHOME HILL ARBORETUM

14TH ST

WESTERN GALLERY

COLLEGE DR

MCDONALD PKWY

EXIT 252

CHRYSALIS INN & SPA

ALASKA MARINE FERRY TERMINAL

KNOX AVE

24TH ST

32ND ST

SAMISH WAY

AMTRAK DEPOT/ BUS STATION

FAIRHAVEN VILLAGE INN

VILLAGE BOOKS

12TH ST

LOVITT RESTAURANT

GOOD EARTH POTTERY

HARRIS AVE

© AVALON TRAVEL

www.cob.org/services/recreation/parks-trails, as well as countywide parks information at www.co.whatcom.wa.us/parks.

Parks and Hiking

Along the water a few blocks from the old city hall, the **Maritime Heritage Park** (500 W. Holly St.) at the mouth of Whatcom Creek is a pleasant urban park that's primarily noted for its salmon ladder, where in mid-October the salmon run draws crowds of onlookers. Within the park there's also a Salmon Art Trail that you can follow past 10 sculptures with salmon themes.

Three miles east of downtown along Whatcom Creek is **Whatcom Falls Park** (1401 Electric Ave.), an idyllic spot with three falls, a trout hatchery, and six miles of paved trails that make for easy, picturesque hiking.

At the south end of town, the **Interurban Trail** follows an old railroad line for six miles above Chuckanut Drive from Fairhaven to Larabee State Park. It's a popular path for walkers, joggers, and cyclists, with several scenic views of Chuckanut Bay and the San Juans. To get there from Harris Street, the main commercial strip of Fairhaven, take 12th Street south to where it veers left and becomes Chuckanut Drive. Continue 1.5 miles to the trailhead parking lot on the left. Along the trail you'll pass through **Arroyo Park,** a practically untouched canyon wilderness with more trails for hiking and horseback riding.

FOOD
Brewpubs

Bellingham has vigorously embraced microbrew culture, with some of its more ambitious breweries offering a full selection of food to go along with the beer. **Boundary Bay Brewery & Bistro** (1107 Railroad Ave., 360/647-5593, www.bbaybrewery.com, Sun.-Wed. 11am-10pm, Thurs-Sat. 11am-11pm, $18-25) is a prime example. It serves hearty meat-and-potatoes meals in an old warehouse that's converted to feel like a classic beer hall.

Aslan Brewing Co. (1330 N. Forest Rd., 360/778-2088, www.aslanbrewing.com,

Mon.-Thurs. 11am-11pm, Fri.-Sat. 11am-midnight, Sun. 11am-10pm, $9-15) has taken a food-cart sensibility into its kitchen, serving a menu of "world street food" that includes tacos, satay, bison burgers, and waffle-fry poutine. The space has a more modern feel than Boundary Bay, but when the tables fill up it achieves a similar kind of warm glow.

Breakfast and Lunch

Mount Bakery Cafe (308 W. Champion St., 360/715-2195, www.mountbakery.com, $8-11, daily 8am-3pm) is a busy little breakfast and lunch place near the Whatcom Museum. The stroke of genius here is eggs Benedict served on a waffle. A second location is in Fairhaven (1217 Harris Ave., 360/778-1261, daily 8am-3pm).

The quirky **Old Town Cafe** (316 W. Holly St., 360/671-4431, www.theoldtowncafe.com, Mon.-Sat. 6am-3pm, Sun. 8am-2pm, $8-10) serves a long list of breakfast classics with health-food variations like tofu scrambles, and there's a similar approach with soups and sandwiches at lunchtime. The line out the door on weekends is a testament to the tasty food.

American

Boomer's Drive In (310 N. Samish Way, 360/647-2666, www.boomersdrivein.com, Sun.-Thurs. 11am-10pm, Fri.-Sat. 11am-11pm, $4-11) is a classic burger joint and a Bellingham institution. The surrounding neighborhood is in a state of decline, but Boomer's is like a time capsule from better days.

Eat in or get it to go at **Old World Deli** (1228 N. State St., 360/738-2090, http://oldworlddeli1.com, Mon. 10am-4pm, Tues.-Wed. 10am-6pm, Thurs.-Sat. 10am-8pm, $7-11), an upscale sandwich shop with Italian and Jewish influences.

★ **Lovitt Restaurant** (1114 Harris Ave., 360/671-7143, Tues.-Sat. 11am-9pm, www.lovittrestaurant.com, $13-25) comes by its farm-to-table sensibility honestly. The husband-and-wife owners moved their operation here from the eastern Washington town of Colville, where they'd succeeded at selling inventive cuisine to a clientele with little interest in hip dining trends. Lovitt's primary focus is on meat, and the owners still buy whole animals from the ranchers they developed relationships with back at their old place. What ends up on your plate is simply but meticulously prepared, using ingredients that aren't just direct from the farm, but top quality.

Eclectic

★ **Ciao Thyme** (207 Unity St., 360/733-1267, http://ciaothyme.com, Tues.-Fri. 11am-3pm, $12-15) is a hybrid cafe, caterer, and cooking school that serves lunch four days a week. The menu is short and variable—main courses one week were tarragon chicken pot pie and Thai beef salad—and you eat at communal tables. It sounds like it could be austere and pretentious, but the genuine dedication to creative, delicious food shines through. They also have prix fixe dinners once or twice a month.

Located along the village green under Fairhaven's Village Books, the **Colophon Cafe** (1208 11th St., 360/647-0092, www.colophoncafe.com, Mon.-Thurs. 9am-8pm, Fri.-Sat. 9am-9pm, Sun. 10am-8pm, $11-16) is a good spot for a snack or a meal throughout the day. It has creative salads, sandwiches, and soups, including rich and delicious African peanut soup. There is also a large selection of cakes, pies, and ice cream.

Italian and Pizza

D'Anna's Cafe Italiano (1317 N. State St., 360/714-0188, www.dannascafeitaliano.com, daily 3pm-10pm, $14-31) is a little trattoria with a big menu of Italian classics—eggplant parmesan, homemade linguine with clam sauce, and some 40 other choices.

You're on the waterfront at classy **Giuseppe's al Porto** (21 Bellwether Way, 360/714-8412, www.giuseppesitalian.com, Mon.-Thurs. 11:30am-8pm, Fri.-Sat. 11:30am-9pm, Sun. 3pm-8pm, $19-39), so it's fitting that the pan-Italian menu emphasizes seafood.

Pizzas at **La Fiamma Wood Fire Pizza** (200 E. Chestnut, 360/647-0060, www.lafiamma.com, Mon.-Thurs. 11am-9pm, Fri.-Sat.

11am-10pm, Sun. 9am-9pm, $11-17) have a chewy, slightly charred crust and come with two dozen topping options, from the traditional (margherita) to the peculiar (curry-roasted vegetables). There are also panini, pasta, and other options on the menu. The dining room is nice enough for a casual date but also kid friendly.

Mexican

Expect big portions and bold flavors at **Casa Que Pasa** (1415 Railroad Ave., 360/756-8226, www.casaquepasarocks.com, $8-15, daily 11am-11pm), including the better-than-it-sounds specialty, the potato burrito. The tequila bar helps keep things lively.

The food at **Pepper Sisters** (1055 N. State St., 360/671-3414, http://peppersisters.com, daily 4:30pm-9pm, $11-17) is labeled Southwestern, which basically means Mexican with a healthy conscience (whole wheat tortillas, a good number of vegetarian and vegan options) and prominent use of green chili sauce.

Fine Dining

If you're up for a gastronomic adventure and money is no object, make the hour's trip (including ferry ride) from Bellingham to Lummi Island's **Willows Inn** (2579 W. Shore Dr., 360/758-2620, www.willows-inn.com, July-Aug. Wed.-Mon., June and Sept. Thurs.-Mon., Apr.-May and Oct.-Dec. Thurs.-Sun., 6:30pm, prix fixe $195). There's one seating a night at 6:30pm for the prix fixe meal, which consists of a dozen or so small courses and can last three hours. The cuisine is rarified farm-to-table, the organic meats and vegetables are mostly island-grown, and local seafood is always featured prominently. Reservations are required and can be hard to come by.

ACCOMMODATIONS

You can tell you're in northwest Washington's largest town when you look at Bellingham's lodging options. While there are no over-the-top luxury hotels, options run the gamut. Inexpensive, sometimes sketchy motels are clustered along North Samish Way near the university. Chain hotels of every stripe are situated near the exits off I-5. Older residential neighborhoods are home to B&Bs. And there are some higher-end boutique hotels along the waterfront.

Under $100

In the bargain category, **Coachman Inn** (120 N. Samish Way, 360/671-9000, www.coachmaninnmotel.com, $65-75 d) is a reasonably clean and comfortable no-frills choice.

Guesthouse Inn (805 Lakeway Dr., 360/671-9600, www.redlion.com/bellingham, $76-108 d) is a newer hotel along I-5 where you can spend relatively little without compromising comfort. Rates include continental breakfast.

$100-150

On a dead-end road in an upscale suburban neighborhood, **Viewmont Manor Bed & Breakfast** (1031 38th St., 360/920-1335, http://viewmontmanor.com, $135 d) is a handsome stone house with two guest rooms, both with private baths and balconies.

$150-200

SpringHill Suites Bellingham (4040 Northwest Ave., 360/714-9600, www.marriott.com, $144-169 d) is an above-average business-oriented hotel with large, comfortable rooms and a good breakfast buffet.

$200-250

Chrysalis Inn and Spa (804 10th St., 360/756-1005, www.thechrysalisinn.com, $219-229 d) is an attractive 43-room hotel facing the water (and also near the sometimes-noisy railroad tracks). Guest rooms are well appointed and include such amenities as down comforters, fireplaces, fridges, and a substantial buffet breakfast.

Fairhaven Village Inn (1200 10th St., 360/733-1311, www.fairhavenvillageinn.com, $239-259 d) is a modern boutique hotel that blends in well with its historic Fairhaven neighbors. Rooms are large and include gas fireplaces and continental breakfast.

Over $250

Hotel Bellwether (1 Bellwether Way, 360/392-3100, www.hotelbellwether.com, $259-319 d) offers Bellingham's most indulgent lodging, with a waterfront location, large rooms, balconies, Italian furnishings, gas fireplaces, marble baths with jetted tubs, and a lavish breakfast buffet.

Just across Bellingham Bay, Lummi Island is technically one of the San Juans, but the only ferry service to it is a 6-minute ride from Gooseberry Point, which is in turn about 30 minutes from downtown Bellingham. A prime reason to make the trip is to stay at **The Willows Inn** (2579 W. Shore Dr., 360/758-2620, www.willows-inn.com, $230-450 d), a luxurious but laid-back retreat with one of the finest restaurants in the Pacific Northwest.

INFORMATION

The visitor information center of **Bellingham Whatcom County Tourism** (904 Potter St., 360/671-3990, www.bellingham.org) is open daily 9am-5pm. **Bay to Baker Trading Co.** (911 Harris Ave., 360/756-6078, Mon.-Sat. 11am-6pm, Sun. 11am-5pm) is Fairhaven's unofficial visitors' center, with maps and other information available at the back of the shop.

TRANSPORTATION

Bellingham is 1.5 hours north of Seattle on I-5 and about the same distance, 90 miles (145 kilometers), south of Vancouver, British Columbia.

Greyhound (360/733-5251, www.greyhound.com) has long-haul bus service in and out of Bellingham's Amtrak station (401 Harris Ave.) in Fairhaven.

Amtrak (800/872-7245, www.amtrak.com) has daily service between Seattle and Vancouver, British Columbia, stopping at the Bellingham Amtrak station (401 Harris Ave.) in Fairhaven.

Whatcom Transit (360/676-7433, www.ridewta.com) provides bus service throughout Bellingham, including a route between downtown and Fairhaven that runs about every 30 minutes, 7am-11pm. The fare is $1.

Anacortes

With a population of 16,000, Anacortes (a-nah-KOR-tis) is one of the bigger and more industrious towns of the northern Puget Sound, with two oil refineries, two seafood-processing plants, and a large shipyard. To most tourists it's best known for its ferry terminal, where you catch your ride to the San Juans, but with a couple of beautiful parks and some first-rate restaurants, it's worth some attention.

SIGHTS

A little over a mile west of the ferry terminal, **Washington Park** has a beautiful wooded loop drive with turnoffs that give you sweeping views of the San Juans and the Olympics.

For more of an adventure, head eight miles south of the terminal to 1,270-foot **Mount Erie,** the highest point on Fidalgo Island. A steep, winding road leads to a partially wooded summit, and from there four short trails take you to vertigo-inducing scenic viewpoints.

Fans of nautical history are likely to enjoy a stop at the **Maritime Heritage Center** (703 R Ave., 360/293-1915, www.cityofanacortes.org, June-Aug. Tues.-Sat. 10am-4pm, Sun. 11am-4pm, Apr.-May and Sept.-Oct. Sat. 10am-4pm, Sun. 11am-4pm, free) at the Cape Sante Marina four miles east of the ferry terminal. Its main attraction is the *W. T. Preston* (tours $5), a historic sternwheeler that operated as a snag boat for the U.S. Corps of Army Engineers 1914-1981.

FOOD

The route from I-5 to the ferry takes you along Commercial Avenue, a major thoroughfare through town. If you keep going a few blocks beyond the ferry turnoff you hit a cluster of good restaurants.

You're likely to find something to suit everyone's tastes at the charming **Adrift Restaurant** (510 Commercial Ave., 360/588-0653, Mon.-Sat. 8am-9pm, Sun. 8am-2pm, $11-34), which serves three meals a day from a diverse menu that includes burgers, soba noodles, and surf and turf.

At lunchtime, a line usually forms at **Gere-A-Deli** (502 Commercial Ave., 360/293-7383, www.gere-a-deli.com, Mon.-Sat. 7am-4pm, $8-11) for its long list of classic sandwiches that you can either eat in or take away.

Another local favorite is **Rockfish Grill & Anacortes Brewery** (320 Commercial Ave., 360/588-1720, www.anacortesrockfish.com, daily 11am-10pm, $10-28), a brewpub serving pizzas, sandwiches, and heartier entrées.

ACCOMMODATIONS

A good option for lodging in Anacortes, particularly if you're planning to catch an

---

Which Island Should I Visit?

If you only have a few days, it's best to pick one of the San Juans and devote yourself to it exclusively. Day trips to other islands usually aren't a great idea—the ferries eat up a lot of time in transit, and visiting the islands' attractions is less fun if you have to keep an eye on the clock. Some basic pointers for choosing an island:

IF YOUR PRIORITY IS:

- **Bicycling:** Visit Lopez.
- **Camping:** Visit Orcas.
- **Hiking:** Visit Orcas.
- **Kayaking:** Visit San Juan or Orcas.
- **Peace and Quiet:** Visit Lopez.
- **Whale-Watching:** Visit San Juan.

San Juan Islands

© AVALON TRAVEL

CANADA
UNITED STATES

WASHINGTON
BRITISH COLUMBIA

Boundary Pass

Satellite Island

Stuart Island

Johns Island

Waldron Island

President Channel

Henry Island

Posey Island Marine State Park

Pearl Island

English Camp

San Juan Island National Historical Park

Haro Strait

WHALE-WATCHING ON SAN JUAN ISLAND

LIME KILN POINT STATE PARK

San Juan Island

Friday Harbor

San Juan Island National Historical Park

American Camp

Griffin Bay

Cactus Islands

Spieden Island

Flattop Island

Jones Island Marine State Park

San Juan Channel

Yellow Is.

Crane Island

Deer Harbor

West Sound

Orcas Village

Turn Island Marine SP

Cedar Rock Biological Preserve

Shaw Island

Canoe Island

Orcas Island

East Sound

Olga

Eastsound

To Sucia Island and Sucia Island State Park

Barnes Island

Clark Island Marine State Park

0   2 km
0   2 mi

FISHERMAN BAY

LOPEZ ISLAND AIRPORT

BICYCLING LOPEZ ISLAND

Lopez Island

Lopez Village

Spencer Spit State Park

Center Island

Decatur Island

Frost Island

Lopez Sound

Upright Channel

Obstruction Pass State Park

KAYAKING AROUND ORCAS ISLAND

Obstruction Island

MORAN STATE PARK

Doe Bay

Doe Island Marine State Park

To Iceberg Point and Watmough Bay

Blakely Island

James Island Marine State Park

Rosario Strait

Cypress Island

Rosario Strait

Allan Island

Burrows Island

Anacortes

Guemes

Guemes Island

Sinclair Island

Vendovi Island

Lummi Island

Portage Island

Bellingham Bay

Eliza Island

Fidalgo Bay

Fidalgo Island

20

early-morning ferry, is the quaint, dockside **Ship Harbor Inn** (5316 Ferry Terminal Rd., 360/293-5177, www.shipharborinn.com, $149-209). You get comfortable accommodations in the heart of town, about 15 minutes from the ferry, at the **Marina Inn** (3300 Commercial Ave., 360/293-1100, www.marinainnwa.com, $124-144) and **Sunrise Inn** (905 20th St., 360/293-8833, www.sunriseinnanacortes. com, $135-199).

TRANSPORTATION

The 80-mile drive from Seattle to Anacortes takes 1.5 hours, mostly north on I-5, with a well-marked exit west onto Route 20 at the end of the trip.

San Juan Island

TOP EXPERIENCE

San Juan is the liveliest and most developed of the islands that make up the San Juans archipelago, with the greatest variety of tourist facilities and activities. The prime motivation for a trip to any of the San Juan Islands is to relax and unwind, but if you want to add some stimulation to your laid-back vacation, this is the island for you.

The hub of the island is **Friday Harbor,** which with a year-round population of 2,300 is the largest town in the San Juans. When the ferry from Anacortes lands here (seven times a day in the summer) there's a burst of action as cars and passengers disembark, and within a half-mile of the dock there's a larger concentration of restaurants, shops, tour operators, and sports outfitters than anywhere else in the archipelago. While it's an appealing town, Friday Harbor is primarily a place where you take care of practicalities—which can mean anything from gassing up the car to booking a whale-watching trip to eating dinner.

A second center of activity is **Roche** (pronounced "Rohsh") **Harbor** at the northwest end of the island, where what was once the company town for a booming lime works has been transformed into a handsome resort complex with a large marina. Beyond that, the island is a mix of parks, woods, farms, and pastures, all encompassed by miles of gorgeous shoreline.

There are opportunities here for beautiful hikes, bike rides, and drives, but Orcas and Lopez are the islands where those activities are the main attractions. San Juan's signature outdoor adventures take place on the water. Kayaking is an easy and exhilarating way to explore the smaller islands nearby and meet the abundant local marinelife. The stars of the waters are the members of the three resident orca (aka killer whale) pods. San Juan is the best-situated island for whale sightings, and it has the largest selection of both whale-watching tours and kayaking outfitters.

SIGHTS
The Whale Museum

If you're planning to go whale-watching while on the San Juans, you'll be amply rewarded by first visiting **The Whale Museum** (62 1st St., 360/378-4710, ext. 30, www.whalemuseum. org, June-Sept. daily 9am-6pm, Oct.-May daily 10am-4pm, $6). The fun, informative exhibits are engaging enough to interest both kids and adults. Along with providing general information about whales, they focus on the three pods of resident orcas that inhabit local waters. You'll see their family trees, hear recordings of their underwater conversations, and learn about the conditions that have put them on the endangered species list.

San Juan Historical Museum

The **San Juan Historical Museum** (405 Price St., Friday Harbor, 360/378-3949, www. sjmuseum.org, June Thurs.-Sat. 10am-2pm, July-Sept. daily 10am-2pm, other months by appointment, $5 suggested donation) is a classic small-town museum. It's located in

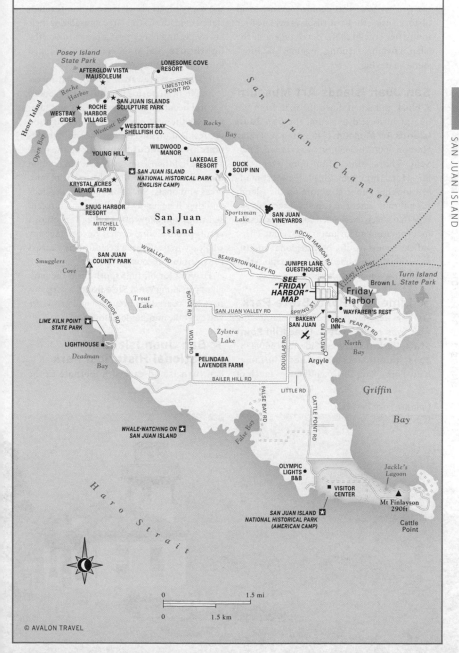

San Juan Island

Posey Island State Park

★ AFTERGLOW VISTA MAUSOLEUM

● LONESOME COVE RESORT

Roche Harbor

LIMESTONE POINT RD

● SAN JUAN ISLANDS SCULPTURE PARK

★ ROCHE HARBOR VILLAGE

★ WESTBAY CIDER

Henry Island

Open Bay

Westcott Bay

WESTCOTT BAY SHELLFISH CO.

Rocky Bay

● WILDWOOD MANOR

★ YOUNG HILL

● LAKEDALE RESORT

● DUCK SOUP INN

★ SAN JUAN ISLAND NATIONAL HISTORICAL PARK (ENGLISH CAMP)

Sportsman Lake

● SAN JUAN VINEYARDS

★ KRYSTAL ACRES ALPACA FARM

● SNUG HARBOR RESORT

San Juan Channel

San Juan Island

MITCHELL BAY RD

W VALLEY RD

ROCHE HARBOR RD

BEAVERTON VALLEY RD

Smugglers Cove

SAN JUAN COUNTY PARK

● JUNIPER LANE GUESTHOUSE

SEE "FRIDAY HARBOR" MAP

Friday Harbor

Turn Island State Park

Brown I.

Trout Lake

BOYCE RD

SAN JUAN VALLEY RD

SPRING ST

● WAYFARER'S REST

WESTSIDE RD

WOLD RD

BAKERY SAN JUAN

ORCA INN

PEAR PT RD

LIME KILN POINT ★ STATE PARK

Zylstra Lake

DOUGLAS RD

North Bay

■ LIGHTHOUSE

ARGYLE RD

Deadman Bay

● PELINDABA LAVENDER FARM

Argyle

Griffin

BAILER HILL RD

LITTLE RD

CATTLE POINT RD

Bay

FALSE BAY RD

Haro Strait

WHALE-WATCHING ON ★ SAN JUAN ISLAND

False Bay

Jackle's Lagoon

OLYMPIC LIGHTS B&B

■ VISITOR CENTER

▲ Mt Finlayson 290ft

SAN JUAN ISLAND ★ NATIONAL HISTORICAL PARK (AMERICAN CAMP)

Cattle Point

0   1.5 mi

0   1.5 km

© AVALON TRAVEL

an 1890s farmhouse and seven surrounding outbuildings, which are filled with old photos and artifacts that cobble together local history. Inside the barn, displays explore four industries crucial to the development of the island: fishing, farming, logging, and limestone quarrying.

San Juan Islands Art Museum

A block and a half down the road from the quaint historical museum, the **San Juan Islands Art Museum** (540 Spring St., Friday Harbor, 360/370-5050, www.sjima.org, May-Sept. Thurs.-Mon. 11am-6pm, Oct.-Apr. Fri.-Mon. 11am-5pm, $10) is the most modern-looking public structure on the island. It's a former emergency medical services garage that's been overhauled with a sleek design incorporating an atrium in the front. Three gallery rooms feature both regional and internationally acclaimed artists in exhibits that change on a quarterly basis.

★ Lime Kiln Point State Park

On the western coast of the island, due west from Friday Harbor, **Lime Kiln Point State Park** (1567 West Side Rd., 360/378-2044, http://parks.state.wa.us/540/Lime-Kiln-Point, 8am-dusk) epitomizes much of

what's appealing about a visit to San Juan. It has 1.5 miles of trails that take you along the rocky bluffs above Haro Strait, through stands of madrona trees (recognizable by their tawny peeling bark), past a postcard-worthy **lighthouse,** and to the hulking abandoned kiln that gives the park its name.

It's an easy, rewarding walk that mixes a couple of historic structures with lots of natural beauty, but it's known first and foremost as the best place on land for sighting the resident orcas. There are several **whale-watching lookout points** along the trail, and the lighthouse serves as a viewing station for statisticians recording the traffic of both orcas and boats. Stick your head in the door and they'll be happy to tell you about recent sightings and show off the orca version of a family photo album. Even if you don't see any whales, you'll still get a beautiful view across the strait to Vancouver Island.

Driving (or biking) south from the park takes you along **West Side Road,** a gorgeous stretch of coastal roadway with pullouts where you can take another look for orcas.

★ San Juan Island National Historical Park

San Juan Island earned a footnote in the

Lime Kiln Point State Park

history books with the Pig War conflict, which ultimately resulted in the San Juans becoming part of the United States instead of British Columbia. Today the outposts of the British and American soldiers during the combat-free standoff, which lasted 1860-1872, make up the **San Juan Island National Historical Park** (www.nps.gov/sajh, free). Though the two sites share a story, they are separate entities: The American Camp is on the southern tip of the island, and British Camp is along the northwest coast at Garrison Bay.

Both camps have visitors centers and a few restored or re-created buildings to give you a sense of their history. In summer there's some sort of ranger-led activity almost every day—check the website for the event calendar, which changes year to year. Even without the historical context or a ranger to guide you, the camps are pleasant places to visit because of their beautiful settings—a stretch of prairieland and sandy beaches at the American Camp, a quiet bay surrounded by wooded hills at the English.

AMERICAN CAMP

The initial conflict between the American farmer and the British pig that would precipitate the Pig War took place on the grounds of what would become the **American Camp** (Cattle Point Rd., daily dawn-11pm, free), and it was here that U.S. forces on land and British ships in the bay to the east faced off during the tense summer of 1859. Today two buildings remain—the officers' quarters, within the long picket fence that surrounds the parade ground, and the laundress's quarters—as well as a redoubt (a defensive fortification). There are artifacts, trail maps, and guides to the camp's wildflowers at the **visitors center** (360/378-2240, ext. 2233, June-Aug. daily 8:30am-5pm, Sept.-May Wed.-Sun. 8:30am-4:30pm).

The camp covers 1,223 acres, including 600 of prairie—one of the few prairielands in the Puget Sound area. From the officers' quarters, near the visitors center and main parking lot, a gentle downward slope runs through the tall grass. There's a spare beauty to the landscape that's enhanced, especially in spring, by wildflowers. You could almost imagine you were on the Dakota plains if you didn't have the Strait of Juan de Fuca glistening before you. As you approach the water you pass the location of the former **Belle Vue Sheep Farm,** the property established by the Hudson's Bay Company in the 1850s that was central to the Pig War conflict.

Haro Strait at American Camp

When you reach the shoreline, you're on a bluff with an expansive view across the strait to Vancouver Island. It's a good place for spotting sea mammals—orcas, harbor seals, porpoises, and sea lions populate the waters. The camp is also a great place to watch for airborne wildlife: It's home to 200 species of birds and 32 of butterflies.

You can hike or drive down to sandy, driftwood-strewn **South Beach,** the longest stretch of public beach on the island and a good place for bird-watching or a sunset stroll. Farther south on Cattle Point Road, another parking area sits at the head of a three-mile loop trail that takes you up to **Mount Finlayson** (a modest 290 ft. in elevation) and down through woods to **Jakle's Lagoon** on Griffin Bay.

Cattle Point Road continues out to **Cattle Point Interpretive Area** at the southern tip of the island, where there is a lighthouse as well as picnic facilities. Cattle Point is state rather than federal property, and the parking area requires a Discover Pass.

English Camp

ENGLISH CAMP

The **English Camp** (West Valley Rd., daily dawn-11pm, free) has a more refined beauty than the American. It's located on tranquil Garrison Bay on the northwestern end of San Juan, 2.5 miles by road (1.5 as the crow flies) from Roche Harbor. Its 529 acres include six re-created structures from the original camp, including the hospital, a barracks, a blockhouse, and a small formal garden. The **visitors center** (June-Aug. daily 9am-5pm), located in the barracks and open only in summer, has a 12-minute video about the Pig War as well as maps of the site.

While much of the American Camp is open, rolling prairie, the English Camp is wooded and hilly. As you climb the switchback path up **Officers' Hill** you get the camp's most photo-worthy view, looking down on the garden, the blockhouse, and the bay. The **Young Hill Trail** brings you to the camp cemetery, where six English marines, all noncombat casualties, lie buried. Continue up the trail through second-growth forest to reach the top of **Young Hill** (690 ft.), from which there's a view of the whole archipelago.

Roche Harbor

On the island's northwest tip at **Roche Harbor** (offices 248 Reuben Memorial Dr., 360/378-2155, www.rocheharbor.com) you get a different experience from anywhere else on San Juan. While most of the island is dotted with small, independent enterprises, Roche Harbor is a self-contained, full-service vacation complex. It's San Juan's most historically rich locale (the Pig War camps not withstanding) as well as its largest resort, with the island's most attractive and harmonious architecture, its prettiest public gardens, and its most picturesque marina.

Hand in hand with those distinctions, it's also the only place on the island that feels a bit contrived and corporate. That's fitting in a way, because Roche Harbor—once the site of the largest lime works west of the Mississippi, founded by Tacoma-based lawyer John S.

McMillin—has long been the island's biggest engine of commerce. Beginning in 1886, a major vein of limestone—a raw material central to the production of concrete, whitewash, and plaster—running through the island was extracted from quarries and refined in towering brick-lined kilns built along the waterfront. The business continued until the 1950s, when the quarries were essentially mined out and the transformation from company town to resort began. Today the historical elements are a key part of the resort's charm.

The **Hotel de Haro,** the centerpiece of the present-day resort, began as a log bunkhouse and evolved during the development of the town into one of Washington's first hotels. It's been restored to maintain its old-timey character. Check out the lobby even if you're staying elsewhere, and while you're there pick up a map with a walking tour of the resort grounds.

Other elements from the past include **two limekilns** to the west of the hotel; **John McMillin's waterfront home,** which has been transformed into a restaurant; **workers' cottages** that now serve as guest accommodations; and the old **company store,** which today supplies provisions to the pleasure boats docked in the 377-slip marina. Even the ground beneath your feet is paved with bricks from disassembled kilns. In keeping with the traditional feel of the place, U.S., British, and Washington flags are lowered every summer night at sunset in a **colors ceremony,** accompanied by music and a cannon blast.

The **Lady of Good Voyage Chapel,** to the east of the hotel, was built in 1892 and changed denominations from Methodist to Catholic in the 1950s to reflect the beliefs of the property's new owners. It remains the only privately owned Catholic church in the United States. It's not generally open to the public, but masses are occasionally held in summer.

A mile farther east—and reachable by a walking path from the resort—is the **Afterglow Vista Mausoleum,** set amid a grove of trees. This open-air temple is the final resting place for McMillin and members of his family. The unusual site consists of a limestone table surrounded by stone chairs that encase the deceased's ashes, all of which is surrounded by Doric columns, one of them deliberately incomplete to symbolize the unfinished nature of life. McMillin was a dedicated Freemason, and the temple is laden with cryptic Masonic symbols.

Down the hill from the mausoleum, just outside the resort grounds, the **San Juan Islands Sculpture Park** (8915 Roche Harbor Rd., 360/370-0035, www.sjisculpturepark. com, daily dawn-dusk, $5 donation) is spread across 20 acres of meadow. From the road the park looks fairly modest, but devote some time to walking the grounds and the experience grows increasingly interesting. The art, all contemporary work by sculptors from the Pacific Northwest, is at times whimsical, poignant, and profound.

Pelindaba Lavender Farm

One of the most flourishing agricultural enterprises on San Juan is the **Pelindaba Lavender Farm** (45 Hawthorne Lane, 360/378-4248, www.pelindabalavender. com), where 20 acres of the aromatic flower are grown and incorporated into a wide range of goods, from beauty products to cookies to jewelry. You're welcome to visit the farm any time of year, but the high season, when the fields are abloom in all their vibrant, scented glory, is July and August. In those months the farm's owner, Stephen Robins, conducts walking tours on Saturday and Sunday (usually at 2pm; call to confirm). Stock up on Pelindaba products at the **farm store** (866/819-1911, May-Sept. daily 9:30am-5:30pm, Apr. and Oct. Wed.-Sun. 9:30am-5:30pm). They also have shops in Friday Harbor and La Conner. The farm is near the center of the island, off of Bailer Hill Road.

Krystal Acres Alpaca Farm

Krystal Acres Alpaca Farm (3501 West Valley Rd., 360/378-6125, www.krystalacres. com, Apr.-Oct. daily 10am-5pm, Nov.-Mar. daily 11am-4pm) is likely to catch your eye along the road south of the English Camp.

The Pig War

San Juan Island occupies a unique place in the annals of American military history. In the so-called Pig War, a conflict between the United States and Great Britain over territorial rights to the island and the archipelago that took place between 1859 and 1872, no battles were fought and no human blood was shed. Though elements of the story are humorous in retrospect, the outcome had significant consequences: It determined the San Juans' national identity.

ORIGINS IN AMBIGUITY

The war had its roots in the Oregon Treaty of 1846, which set a boundary between U.S. and British territory "along the forty-ninth parallel of north latitude to the middle of the channel which separates the continent from Vancouver Island, and thence southerly through the middle of the said channel, and of the Strait of Juan de Fuca, to the Pacific Ocean." The framers of the treaty, sitting far away in London, failed to realize there are two channels that could fit their description—Haro Strait to the west of the San Juans and Rosario Strait to the east.

This ambiguity went unaddressed for a decade, and when negotiations were undertaken they went nowhere. In the meantime, the British Hudson's Bay Company established a sheep ranch on the south end of San Juan, and by 1859 two dozen Americans had laid claim to neighboring farmland.

THIS IS WAR!

The inevitable tensions were a powder keg waiting for a spark, and it came on June 15, 1859. On that day, American Lyman Cutlar shot and killed a pig he found digging up potatoes in his garden. The pig's owner, Charles Griffin, was an employee of the British Hudson's Bay Company. When the two men couldn't agree on proper compensation for the pig (Cutlar offered $10; Griffin wanted $100), the Brits threatened to arrest Cutlar and bring him to Victoria to stand trial.

In response, the Americans requested protection from the U.S. Army's Department of Oregon.

Depending on when they've had their last haircut, the alpacas roaming the grounds may look like long-necked sheep or four-legged dust mops. There are over 70 of the cute, easygoing animals on the farm. They seem to lead an idyllic life, sheared once a year for their luxurious wool and otherwise left to be adored and photographed by passersby. You may stroll around and are encouraged to visit the farm store, which sells all sorts of alpaca knit goods, including coats, sweaters, socks, and plush toys.

Wineries and Distilleries

The island's contribution to the boom in Washington winemaking is **San Juan Vineyards** (3136 Roche Harbor Rd., 360/378-9463, www.sanjuanvineyards.com), located 3.5 miles north of Friday Harbor. The six-acre vineyard produces madeleine angevine and siegerrebe, two white varietals that do well in

cooler climates, but the majority of its wines are made from eastern Washington grapes, including merlot, cabernet sauvignon, cab franc, and chardonnay. The **tasting room** (open daily 11am-5pm in summer, weekends 11am-5pm spring and fall, tasting fee $5) is in a former schoolhouse dating from 1896, fronted by a pleasant deck where you can sit and sip while you take in the surrounding landscape.

San Juan was once a major apple producer, and orchards are making a modest comeback, as evidenced by **Westcott Bay Cider/San Juan Island Distillery** (12 Anderson Ln., 360/378-2606, www.westcottbaycider.com, www.sanjuanislanddistillery.com, tastings Sat. 1pm-4pm or by appointment). Apples grown on-site are turned into small-batch dry ciders, as well as apple brandy and cider-based gin. The showpiece of the facility is the handsome copper still, which the friendly owner-operators, Hawk and Suzi Pingree, like to

On July 27, a 64-man U.S. infantry company arrived under the leadership of Captain George Pickett. What followed was a classic case of conflict escalation: By the end of August, 461 American soldiers were entrenched on the island, and three British warships holding 2,140 men were moored offshore in San Juan Harbor (today's Griffin Bay).

DEFUSING TENSIONS

The military buildup was in part a symptom of the slow pace of mid-19th-century communication. Regional leaders, perhaps a little drunk on power, were responsible for the swelling forces. As higher-ups came to learn what was transpiring, they went to work defusing tensions.

British Rear Admiral Robert Baynes arrived on the scene in August and informed James Douglas, governor of the colony of British Columbia, that he was not going to "involve two great nations in a war over a squabble about a pig." It took six weeks for news of the conflict to reach U.S. president James Buchanan, who sent General Winfield Scott, commander of the army, to negotiate a settlement. Scott and Douglas agreed to reduce forces to fewer than 100 soldiers per side and for San Juan Island to be under joint occupation until a resolution could be reached.

THE KAISER MAKES THE CALL

It was under those terms that the British set up camp on the west side of the island in 1860. As America erupted into Civil War, the soldiers of San Juan were essentially forgotten men. Tensions eased to the point where the two sides peacefully socialized: On the Fourth of July the Americans invited the British to their celebration, and on Victoria Day the Brits returned the favor. Finally in 1871 the two countries agreed that Kaiser Wilhelm I of Germany would arbitrate the dispute. After a year of deliberation, the kaiser ruled in favor of the United States, thus ending the war, with the pig as the only casualty.

have working for visitors to observe during tastings.

ENTERTAINMENT AND EVENTS

Cultural events and nightlife aren't a prime motivation for coming to San Juan, but there are some fun things going on.

Nightlife

Friday Harbor gives you a couple of options for bar-hopping with live music. **Herb's Tavern** (80 1st St., 360/378-7076), sitting in a prime location at the corner of 1st and Spring, is an unpretentious locals' hangout with a pool table in the back and live bands on some weekends. You get a fuller live music schedule, ranging from rock to big band, just down 1st Street at **Rumor Mill** (175 1st St., 360/378-5555, www.rumor-millsanjuan.com), which also has 20 beers on tap and a full kitchen.

Up at the Roche Harbor Resort the **Madrona Bar and Grill** (360/378-7954, ext. 405) has live music—usually rock or blues—and dancing on Friday and Saturday nights in the summer. For something completely different, head to the **English Camp** (West Valley Rd., www.nps.gov/sajh, 360/378-2240, ext. 2233) on summer Monday evenings for contra dancing. The event is free; call for details.

Theater

San Juan has two resident theater companies. **San Juan Community Theatre** (100 2nd St., 360/378-3210, www.sjctheatre.org) hosts live productions and musical performances, as well as HD broadcasts of performances from the Met in New York and the National Theatre in London. **Island Stage Left** (1062 Wold Rd., 360/378-5649, www.islandstageleft. org) does a free annual summer Shakespeare-under-the-Stars production that's staged at both Roche Harbor and the company's mid-island open-air stage. The show also travels to Orcas, Lopez, and Shaw Islands.

Twice a week in July and August the Port of Friday Harbor sponsors **Music in the Park** concerts, which take place on Friday at 5pm and Sunday at 2pm in the park facing the harbor. Performers are usually locals, and the music genre varies.

Festivals and Events

San Juan is good about filling the summer calendar with events. For a complete list, go to www.visitsanjuans.com. The launch of the island's busy season is marked by the **boat parade,** sponsored by the San Juan Island Yacht Club (www.sjiyc.com), held on the first Sunday afternoon in May.

Not surprisingly, they do up Independence Day big here. Among the events are the **Roche Harbor Old Fashioned 4th of July** (360/378-2155, www.rocheharbor.com), which includes logrolling and a donut-eating contest, and the **4th of July Pig War Picnic** at the San Juan Historical Museum (405 Price St., 360/378-3949, www.sjmuseum.org). On the last weekend of July there's another Pig War reenactment event, the **Encampment** at the English Camp (West Valley Rd., www.nps.gov/sajh, 360/378-2240, ext. 2233), the highlight of which is the Candlelight Ball.

To get a sense of the island's rural character, check out the mid-August **San Juan County Fair** (846 Argyle Ave., 360/378-4310, www.sjcfair.org) at the fairgrounds south of Friday Harbor. The four-day event includes food stalls, livestock competitions, concerts, and carnival rides.

SHOPPING
Antiques

Lots of small towns have packed-to-the-rafters antique shops. Friday Harbor's **Funk and Junk Antiques** (85 Nichols St., 360/378-2638, www.funkandjunkantiques.com) fits into that category, but it's a cut above what you usually find. It's the clearinghouse for most estate and business liquidations on the

island, which gives it a varied and sometimes valuable inventory.

Art

A standout among Friday Harbor's numerous art galleries is **Waterworks Gallery** (315 Argyle St., 360/378-3060, www.waterworksgallery.com), which has contemporary paintings and sculpture from regional, national, and international artists. **Island Studios** (270 Spring St., 360/378-6550, www.islandstudios.com) is another good spot, selling an attractively displayed selection of paintings, glass, textiles, and other arts and crafts, all made on the islands. In July and August local artisans sell their work at the **Roche Harbor Village Artist Booths** next to the marina.

Bookstores

Friday Harbor has a couple of thriving bookstores. The more prominent is **Griffin Bay Bookstore** (155 Spring St., 360/378-5511, www.griffinbaybook.com), situated on the town's main drag, where you can while away a couple of hours browsing over a cup of coffee. **Serendipity Books** (223 A St., 360/378-2665) is a used bookstore with a large selection and lots of charm, located in an 1890s house.

Specialty Shops

The Toy Box (20 1st St., 360/378-8889, www.toyboxsanjuan.com) is a handy resource for kids and their parents. The lively shop has toys, games, and art supplies for all ages.

Follow your nose to find **Pelindaba Lavender** (45 Hawthorne Ln., 360/378-4248, www.pelindabalavender.com), a shop dedicated to the aromatic products of San Juan's Pelindaba Lavender Farm.

SPORTS AND RECREATION
★ Whale-Watching

Whale-watching is one of the most popular and distinctive activities in the San Juans. Three resident orca pods, comprising about 80 whales, make the area waters their summer home. The staff at the Whale Museum

Haro Strait kayakers

One well-established tour company is **Maya's Legacy Whale Watching** (360/378-7996, http://sanjuanislandwhalewatch.com, $120), operating two quick, six-passenger catamarans out of Snug Harbor, which is closer to the most common sighting areas than is Friday Harbor. That said, Friday Harbor has good options in all sizes: **San Juan Excursions** (360/378-6636, www.watch-whales.com, $99) runs a 65-foot former navy vessel that seats 97, **Western Prince Whale & Wildlife Tours** (360/378-5315, https://or-cawhalewatch.com, $99) takes a maximum of 32 passengers, and **Spirit of Orca** (360/378-0302, www.spiritoforca.com, $115) has a 6-passenger boat run by a guide with decades of experience. From Roche Harbor a good choice is **San Juan Outfitters** (360/378-1962, www.sanjuanislandoutfitters.com, $99), which has a 24-passenger boat and also operates kayak tours.

In summer the chance of seeing orcas is good, but it's never a sure thing. (Tours that "guarantee" sightings aren't any better at finding whales than their competitors—they're simply willing to let you ride again for free if you don't see any.) With or without orcas, a good tour will show you the rich variety of wildlife that inhabits the archipelago.

Kayaking

Sea kayaking runs neck-and-neck with whale-watching as San Juan's most popular on-water activity. Most outfitters offer tours lasting half a day (usually $90-100, with a sunset trip as one option), a full day ($115-125), and multiple days ($400 and up). Multiday trips often have you camping out on small, remote islands you wouldn't have access to otherwise. If you're experienced with a kayak you can rent one and launch out on your own. Most tours include time in Haro Strait, where there's the prospect of orca sightings. Be aware that regulations are the same for kayaks as for larger craft: you are required to remain 200 yards from the whales.

Among the established outfitters, **Discovery Sea Kayaks** (260 Spring St.,

recommends that visitors watch from shore, which has the double advantage of costing nothing and not disturbing the animals. The best viewing points are **Lime Kiln Point State Park** and the **American Camp** of the national historical park, both which have broad vistas overlooking the Haro Strait where the whales often feed.

TOURS

If you choose to take a tour, the museum strongly encourages using an operator that's a member of the **Pacific Whale Watch Association** (www.pacificwhalewatchas-sociation.com) and adheres to federal regulations, which dictate that boats remain at least 200 yards from the whales and stay out of their line of travel. Most tours last three to four hours and cost $100-115 plus tax. When choosing a tour, consider the qualifications of the guide and the size of the boat. Larger boats usually can travel more quickly and smoothly, while smaller ones provide a more personal experience.

Orca FAQs

You can't visit the San Juans without becoming aware of the orcas (aka killer whales) who reside in the surrounding waters. These giants of the sea are the de facto mascots of the islands, and as you learn about their highly developed social lives and gregarious behavior, it's easy to understand the appeal. Sightings are always a thrill—the whales seem to frolic when they come to surface, like oversized black labs in an off-leash area.

How many orcas live in waters around the San Juans?

There are approximately 80 in the group that inhabits the region, known as the Southern Residents. They are divided into three family clans, the J, K, and L pods, and within the pods there are subgroups consisting of mothers and their offspring. Orcas are matrilineal—they stick with mom for life. You might also see transient killer whales in the area. They travel in smaller groups and, as the name indicates, range over a wider territory.

How big are they and how long do they live?

Adult females are 16-23 feet long, weigh anywhere from 3,000 to 6,000 pounds, and typically live to 50 years, though some have made it to 100. Males measure 20-26 feet, weigh 8,000-12,000 pounds, and average a 30-year lifespan, with the oldest reaching 60.

Should I call them orcas or killer whales?

The scientific community usually prefers "killer whale," which has been in use longer, but it's increasingly common to call the Southern Residents orcas and the transients killer whales. They're killers only in the sense that they're carnivores. The diet of the Southern Residents is over 95 percent salmon, with other fish making up the remainder—each whale takes in 100-300 pounds a day. Transients primarily eat other marine mammals, including sea lions, seals, dolphins, porpoises, and even other whale species.

Are they an endangered species?

The Southern Residents have been protected under the U.S. Endangered Species Act since 2006. Their population took a hit in the 1960s and '70s when nearly 50 whales were captured for use in aquariums. In 1995 there were 98 Southern Residents, but since that time the number has dropped by nearly 20 percent. According to the Center for Whale Research, the number one cause of the decline is a reduction in the salmon population, the orcas' main source of food. Other factors are toxins in the water, which poison blubber and mother's milk, and sound disturbance from vessels.

Do whale-watching cruises threaten their well-being?

In 2011 the National Oceanic and Atmospheric Administration issued revised regulations changing the minimum distance boats are required to keep from whales from 100 to 200 yards. The change was made in response to concerns that boat noise causes stress for the orcas and makes it harder

360/378-2559, www.discoveryseakayak.com) is notable for being a full-service kayak shop located in Friday Harbor. Along with the standard tours, **Crystal Seas Kayaking** (40 Spring St., 877/732-7877, www.crystal-seas.com) has multiday trips that incorporate biking and kayaking. The unique twist offered by **Sea Quest Expeditions** (360/378-5767, www.sea-quest-kayak.com) is the option of women-only multiday trips. **San Juan Kayak Expeditions** (360/378-4436, www.sanjuankayak.com) rents

two-person kayaks for a day ($150) or multiple days ($100/day) and will help you plan a self-guided trip.

Bicycling

The terrain on San Juan is good for biking, with open countryside along much of the central and southern parts of the island and hillier woodland to the north and west, particularly along the western coast from **Lime Kiln Point State Park** to the **American Camp.** The downside is that many of the best roads

surfacing orcas

for them to communicate. But according to Ken Balcomb, senior scientist at the Center for Whale Research, "Whale-watching boats for the most part are providing a positive impact by building a constituency of informed and motivated tourists. Whale appreciation is gaining momentum and the ecological awareness of our society is awakening at least a little bit as a result of responsible whale-watching."

When is the best time of year to see them?

Late spring and summer. The J pod stays in the San Juans area year-round, but K and L head out to sea in search of salmon from late fall through early spring. May and June have the heaviest salmon traffic around the San Juans, and where the salmon go the orcas follow.

What's the best way to see them?

A whale-watching tour is the surest way to see the orcas. That said, there's a large degree of serendipity when it comes to sightings, and sometimes you get a better view from shore. The best land-based observation points are on San Juan's west coast along the Haro Strait at the American Camp and Lime Kiln Point State Park.

for cycling are relatively heavily trafficked by cars. Roads are two lanes and sometimes don't have shoulders.

The go-to place for bike rentals on San Juan is Friday Harbor's **Island Bicycles** (380 Argyle Ave., 360/378-4941, www.islandbicycles.com), which has hybrids ($25/2 hr., $40/day), racing bikes ($35/2 hr., $60/day), electric-assist bikes ($35/2 hr., $60/day), and tandems ($45/2 hr., $80/day). You can make bike reservations with them, which is a good idea in summer.

Hiking

Networks of beautiful short trails run through **Lime Kiln Point State Park** and the American and English Camps that make up the **San Juan National Historical Park.** Trail maps are available at both parks.

For a good overview of the islands, head to **Mount Grant,** located five miles west of Friday Harbor along West Valley Road. A one-mile hike on a wide but sometimes steep trail takes you to the highest publicly

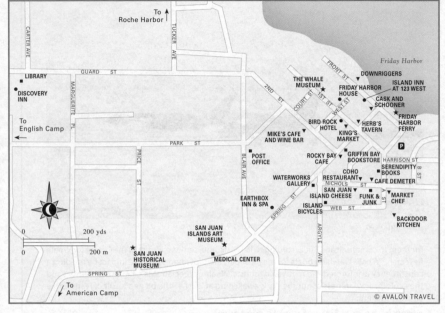

Friday Harbor

accessible point on San Juan, from where on a clear day you can see as far as Mount Rainier.

Boating

Not surprisingly, San Juan is a popular destination for boaters, with the marinas at **Friday Harbor** (360/378-2688, www.portfridayharbor.org) and **Roche Harbor** (800/586-3590, www.rocheharbor.com) the main points of moorage. Both have guest slips available for rent and are fully equipped with everything from fuel to food to showers. They're both also U.S. Customs ports of entry.

If you don't have a boat of your own but you'd like to get out on the water, consider Friday Harbor-based **Schooners North** (360/378-2224, www.sanjuansailcharter.com). From May through October they conduct three-hour ($75) and six-hour ($140) daytime cruises as well as two-hour evening trips ($39) on a handsome 80-foot wooden sailboat. They also have multiday and private charters.

FOOD

The situation with restaurants on San Juan is similar to that of hotels: The combination of a captive market, no chains, and the greater expenses that come with an island location all contribute to higher prices. Fortunately, there are some first-rate restaurants. You may have to pay top dollar, but you'll get something satisfying in return. In summer, dinner reservations are recommended and often essential.

Friday Harbor
BREAKFAST

The classic spot on San Juan for a diner-style breakfast is the **Rocky Bay Café** (225 Spring St., 360/378-5051, daily 6am-2:30pm, $8-13). Most mornings there's a line out the door for giant portions of corned beef hash, biscuits and gravy, omelets, and pancakes. The food is consistently a cut above standard diner fare, with the from-scratch hash browns meriting special mention.

Friday Harbor has two high-quality bakeries, both of which are good options for a quick breakfast or lunch. **Cafe Demeter** (80 Nichols St., 360/370-5443, daily 7am-3pm, $3-10) is especially good with pastries and is a favorite local coffee-klatch gathering spot. **Bakery San Juan** (775 Mullis St., 360/378-5810, www.bakerysanjuan.com, Mon.-Sat. 8am-6pm, $3-9), a couple of blocks south of Spring Street near the airport, has a large selection of creative pizza by the slice as well as sandwiches, bread, and sweets. It's takeout only.

LUNCH

An inventive and varied sandwich menu is the draw at **Market Chef** (225 A St., 360/378-4546, Mon.-Fri. 10am-4pm, $6-11), a stylish deli with pleasant (but tight) indoor and outdoor seating. Most choices are classics with a twist, such as the BLAT (a BLT with avocado) and roast beef dressed with olive salad and horseradish.

San Juan Island Cheese (155 Nichols St., 360/370-5115, www.sjicheese.com, Tues.-Sat. 11am-4pm, $6-18) has a double identity: It's a cheese and wine shop specializing in Pacific Northwest producers, and it also serves light lunches. The feel of the place is sophisticated but casual. Most lunch items, such as the tuna melt and the pastrami and Swiss sandwich, have a cheese component.

AMERICAN

The location of **Cask and Schooner** (1 Front St., 360/378-2922, www.caskandschooner.com, Mon.-Fri. noon-9pm, Sat. 11am-9pm, Sun. 11am-8pm, $14-36) is as central as you can get, at the foot of Spring Street and a 60-second walk from the ferry landing. It's a comfortable setting, with big windows, exposed brick, and a handsome bar, and the menu has a gastropub slant (meat pies, lamb burgers, ploughman's lunch) but also features fresh fish, salads, and burgers—something to satisfy pretty much everyone.

Mike's Cafe and Wine Bar (135 2nd St. S, 360/378-0265, www.mikescafeandwinebar.com, Mon.-Thurs. 4pm-8pm, Fri. 4pm-9pm, Sat. noon-9pm, Sun. noon-8pm, $11-22) feels like it could have been plucked off the streets of Seattle and plopped down in Friday Harbor. Though it calls itself a wine bar, it also serves a variety of microbrews and ciders. The menu sounds like classic pub fare—brats, cheeseburgers, pizzas, steak salad—except that everything is vegan. Carnivores won't be fooled by the faux meats but are likely to find them delicious anyway. There's a streetside patio as well as indoor seating, and while the youthful service isn't always polished, it's usually friendly.

A great waterfront location, well-prepared comfort food, and friendly service make **Downriggers** (10 Front St. N, 360/378-2700, www.downriggerssanjuan.com, daily 11am-9pm, $14-42) a Friday Harbor institution popular with both locals and tourists. The menu is split about evenly between land (burgers, steaks, garlic chicken) and sea (fish-and-chips, seared salmon, fish tacos), and wraparound windows make the most of the harbor views.

FINE DINING

As the name implies, ★ **Backdoor Kitchen** (400 A St., 360/378-9540, www.backdoorkitchen.com, Mon. 11am-2:30pm, Wed.-Thurs. 5pm-9pm, Fri.-Sat. 5pm-10pm, $24-37) doesn't strive to be conspicuous. Its unlikely location, tucked behind a warehouse, gives it an out-of-the-way charm despite being only three blocks from the ferry landing. The menu mixes simplicity and sophistication. Whether you opt for classically prepared scallops, steaks, or chops, or add some international spice with an Indian vegetable platter or Vietnamese duck and prawns, you'll end up getting some of San Juan's most deftly executed cooking. Most tables are outdoors on the patio.

With only nine tables nestled in an old craftsman house, **Coho Restaurant** (120 Nichols St., 360/378-6330, www.cohorestaurant.com, June-Sept. Mon.-Sat. 5pm-9pm, May and Oct. Tues.-Sat. 5pm-9pm,

Feb.-Apr. and Nov.-Dec. Wed.-Sat. 5pm-9pm, $28-34) gives San Juan diners another take on refined intimacy. The approach here is slightly more conservative than at Backdoor Kitchen—menu selections such as grilled hanger steak and pan-seared halibut give a Mediterranean-style treatment to fresh, seasonal ingredients. If you're weighing your options for a dinner splurge, think of Coho as the type of place for a wedding anniversary, while Backdoor is where you might go on an ambitious first date.

MARKETS AND GROCERIES

A fair number of the island's lodging options include full or partial kitchen facilities. Cooking your own meals can save you some money, and if you have access to a grill or a waterfront picnic table it can be just as pleasant an experience as eating out (though you have to do the dishes).

The savviest planners bring their own food, but there are several places where you can stock up once you're on the island. The most conspicuous is **Kings Market** (160 Spring St., 360/378-4505, www.kings-market.com, daily 7am-9pm), right on Friday Harbor's main drag two blocks from the ferry landing. It's a midsize grocery with a deli counter and good selection of produce, prepared foods, and wine. The downside is the prices, which have the expected island markup.

If you travel a few blocks you can save a few bucks at **Friday Harbor Market Place** (515 Market St., 360/378-3238, Mon.-Sat. 8am-6pm), the store where locals do most of their shopping. It doesn't have a sign, but it's easy to recognize—it's the only place in town that resembles supermarkets on the mainland. Prices are lower and the selection of basic supplies is larger, but there's no deli and they don't stock some of the fancier items found at Kings.

Another option is the **San Juan Island Food Co-op** (775 Mullis St., 360/370-5170, www.sanjuancoop.org, Mon.-Fri. 9am-6pm, Sat.-Sun. 10am-5pm), a small store next door to Bakery San Juan that specializes in organic and locally sourced foods and products. Or

go local at the Saturday **farmers market** (150 Nichols St., http://sjifarmersmarket. com, Sat. 10am-1pm), housed in the restored Brickworks community center near the heart of town.

Roche Harbor

The restaurants at Roche Harbor are all under the management of the **Roche Harbor Resort** (www.rocheharbor.com), which means prices are high and you don't have lots of options, but what's there is logically coordinated to meet your dining needs throughout the day.

For simple, order-at-the-counter breakfast and lunch there's the **Lime Kiln Café** (360/378-7954, ext. 1420, daily 8am-3pm, $7-16), located at the end of the marina. It serves pancakes and 10 types of egg dishes in the morning and burgers, sandwiches, and salads at midday.

The next step up on the food chain is the **Madrona Bar and Grill** (360/378-7954, ext. 405, May-Sept. daily 11am-10pm, $14-20), which is open only during the spring and summer season. The long menu includes sandwiches, pizza, and meal-size salads, and includes choices for kids. There's deck seating overlooking the water and a busy bar serving margaritas, martinis, and half a dozen beers on tap.

Roche Harbor's fine-dining option is **McMillin's Dining Room** (360/378-5757, 5pm-10pm daily, $19-47). The house specialty is prime rib, served only on Friday-Sunday nights. The rest of the menu consists largely of grilled and pan-seared seafood, with a burger and a rib eye steak for beef eaters. The food is good, but the highlight here is the location, in the former home of lime works magnate John S. McMillin, which has beautiful views of the water. In summer, window tables give you a prime seat for Roche Harbor's nightly sunset flag-lowering ceremony.

Elsewhere on the Island

Duck Soup Inn (50 Duck Soup Lane, 360/378-4878, www.ducksoupinn.com, May

Fri.-Sun. 5pm-9pm, June and Oct. Thurs.-Sun. 5pm-9pm, July and Sept. Wed.-Sun. 5pm-9pm, Aug. Tues.-Sun. 5pm-9pm, $30-46), a longtime San Juan favorite, came under new ownership and a new chef in 2017. Some of the quirkiness that distinguished the old menu is gone, but the food continues to be high quality, with an emphasis on classic preparations of locally sourced fish, meat, and produce—including seared scallops, grilled rib eye, and gnocchi with tomatoes and goat cheese. The location, out in the woods in a house off Roche Harbor Road, five miles north of Friday Harbor, remains as charming as ever.

Oyster and clam lovers can indulge their passion at **Westcott Bay Shellfish Co.** (904 Westcott Dr., 360/378-2489, www.westcottbayshellfish.com, late May-mid-Sept. daily 11am-5pm), located at the northwest corner of the island between English Camp and Roche Harbor. Eat your bivalves at the picnic tables on site—drinks, salads, bread, and shucking knives are provided—or take them to go.

ACCOMMODATIONS

Your lodging choices on San Juan are almost exclusively small, independently operated hotels, resorts, and B&Bs. That means that, although there are lots of beds, it can take some searching to find a vacancy in the busy summer season. If you're coming in July or August you benefit from booking as far in advance as possible. Also bear in mind that it's a sellers' market. There are a few inexpensive, bare-bones options, but pretty much every place costs a good 25 percent more than what you'd pay for comparable accommodations on the mainland.

Friday Harbor

The advantage of staying in Friday Harbor is your proximity to the ferry terminal and the town's restaurants, shops, and tour outfitters. If your mobility is good you can walk pretty much everywhere in town, and you're at the hub of the island's public transit, making a car-free visit viable (with some patience and planning).

UNDER $100
Wayfarer's Rest (35 Malcolm Street, 360/378-6428, www.hostelssanjuan.com) is San Juan's cheapest lodging option, where you can book a spot in the six-bed hostel room ($40). There are also four private rooms ($70-135) and two cabins ($85). Sleeping quarters are small and bathrooms are shared, but there's a large common area with two full kitchens. The location is 10 minutes by foot from the ferry terminal. For $25 you can rent a bike for the entire length of your stay.

Another low-cost option in Friday Harbor is **The Orca Inn** (770 Mullis St., 360/378-2724, www.orcainnwa.com, $70-115 d). The cheapest rooms are appropriately labeled "micros"—there's barely space enough to turn around—but they come with small private bathrooms, and the location is half a mile from the ferry terminal. If you're looking for nothing more than a clean, inexpensive place to rest your head, this will do the trick.

$100-150
The five guest rooms at ★ **Juniper Lane Guest House** (1312 Beaverton Valley Rd., 360/378-7761, www.juniperlaneguesthouse.com, $90-135 d) are paneled with wood from fallen trees and have names like Mandala and Organic Green Tea. If that sounds like your kind of thing you're in luck, because this place achieves a winning balance between hippie/New Age sensibilities and creature comforts, at a price that makes it San Juan's best bargain. The paneling, along with whimsical (but tasteful) decoration, gives guest rooms a homey warmth. Two of them share a bath, two are big enough to sleep four, and there's also a separate cabin ($225). At 1.5 miles from the ferry dock, the location is on the outskirts of Friday Harbor.

$150-200
Discovery Inn (1016 Guard St., 360/378-2000, www.discoveryinn.com, $169-199 d) is a middle-of-the-road option for travelers who want comfortable, basic rooms for under $200. In other words, it's the closest facsimile

of a good-quality chain hotel you'll find on San Juan. The location, a mile from the center of town, is far enough out that you'll probably want a car if you stay here.

$200-250

From the outside **Bird Rock Hotel** (35 1st St., 360/378-5848, www.birdrockhotel.com, $147-246 d) looks like a classic old inn, but inside the rooms have been updated with modern flair. The character of the 1890s building is maintained in the layout of the rooms, each of which is different; the three cheapest options share a bathroom. Bird Rock is under the same ownership as Earthbox Inn two blocks away, and guests can use the inn's pool and spa facilities.

"Retro chic" is the theme at **Earthbox Inn & Spa** (410 Spring St., 360/378-4000, www.earthboxinn.com, $187-267 d), a rehabbed motor inn. The rooms are done in earth tones and come with microwaves, fridges, and high-end linens. There's a small indoor pool as well as a hot tub and sauna, and cruiser bikes are available at no charge.

OVER $250

Rooms fall into three categories at the sleek and modern **Island Inn at 123 West** (123 West St., 360/378-4400, www.123west.com, $230-420 d). "Euros" are small and have no view (though they share a "view room"), "sweets" are larger and have views, and penthouses ($530-680) are multi-bedroom units suitable for families and groups of up to seven. There's not much of the classic San Juans rustic vibe here, but you do get comfortable, condo-like accommodations in a prime Friday Harbor location.

The location is the star at the swank **Friday Harbor House** (130 West St., 360/378-8455, www.fridayharborhouse.com, $416-469 d), which sits a couple of blocks from the ferry terminal on a bluff overlooking the harbor (and just above the Inn at 123 West). Rooms are large, modern, and equipped with gas fireplaces and jetted tubs.

Roche Harbor Resort

At the north end of the island, **Roche Harbor Resort** (248 Reuben Memorial Dr., 360/378-2155, www.rocheharbor.com) has six distinct lodging options. They all share the resort's facilities, which include a restaurant and two cafes, tennis courts, an outdoor pool, a playground, and a bocce ball court, plus, for an additional charge, boat and bike rentals and guided kayak and whale-watching tours.

$150-200

The most conspicuous, if not the most luxurious, accommodation is the **Hotel de Haro** ($165-295), which sits at the center of the resort, looking out over the gardens and the bay. Guest rooms here have been renovated but maintain the character of the century-old hotel: Floors tend to slope, some furniture is antique, and 15 of 19 rooms have shared bathrooms.

OVER $250

Quarryman Hall ($395-499) is a 21st-century building constructed to mimic the exterior of the adjacent Hotel de Haro while providing more modern accommodations inside. Rooms are big enough for four (with either two queen beds or a king and a sleeper sofa) and have fireplaces, large bathrooms, and views of the bay. The Quarryman is less quaint than the older Roche Harbor lodgings, but it has one feature the others lack: air-conditioning. You don't usually need it in the San Juans, but it's nice to know it's there.

On the east side of the resort the **Historic Cottages** ($410-450) are former company-town laborers' residences. They're comfortable freestanding structures that can sleep up to four, have full kitchens, and are fronted by a large grassy lawn—all of which makes them popular with families.

The four **McMillin Suites** ($500) are Roche Harbor's most deluxe accommodations. They occupy a turn-of-the-20th-century home that's been modernized from top to bottom. Each suite has a fireplace, a balcony with a water view, and a large bathroom with a heated tile floor.

Built in the 1980s in the style of that era, the **Harbor View** and **Lagoon View** condos are an architectural anomaly for the resort, hidden away behind trees on the property's west side. They have fully equipped kitchens, and what you lose in style you gain in savings: one-bedrooms are $285, two-bedrooms $375, and three-bedrooms $600.

On the hill above the marina there are about 20 **Village Homes**—privately owned, freestanding townhouses managed by the resort, done in a period style that blends with the surroundings. They range in size from two bedrooms ($600-800) to four ($1,000), and though they're private houses, they come with daily housekeeping.

Elsewhere on the Island
$150-200
Stay in a restored 1895 farmhouse at ★ **Olympic Lights B&B** (146 Starlight Way, 360/378-3186, www.olympiclights.com, $165-185 d), whose rural setting gives it a casual, comfortable feel. Friendly proprietors Christian and Lea Andrale have nurtured repeat guests with their four sunny, well-maintained rooms and their hospitality. The location is in a meadow on the south end of the island, near the American Camp, giving you an expansive view of the stars at night.

$200-250
★ **Lonesome Cove Resort** (416 Lonesome Cove Rd., 360/378-4477, www.lonesomecove.com, $200-245) is an old-school, rustic resort that hasn't changed much in 70 years. Its six cedar cabins are simple but charming and well equipped. This isn't the sort of place where you come to be pampered: You cook your own meals (if you eat on-site), do your own dishes, and take out the trash. The real draw is the location. In an isolated spot at the end of a gravel road on the northern tip of the island, it's the rare San Juan lodging that sits right along the open water—there's a very real chance of seeing whales pass by as you lounge on your front porch. A five-night minimum stay is required in summer, but if you call and ask they can sometimes fit you in for a shorter visit.

OVER $250
There's something for everyone at **Lakedale Resort** (4313 Roche Harbor Rd., 360/378-2350, www.lakedale.com): a handsome 10-room lodge ($290-300), log cabins ($459), "canvas cabins" (furnished tents, $179-269),

Lonesome Cove Resort

campsites ($50-65), RV sites ($67), even an Airstream trailer ($259). The place has the feel of a high-end summer camp, with grounds that include three small lakes good for kid-friendly swimming and boating.

Snug Harbor Resort (1997 Mitchell Bay Rd., 360/378-4762, www.snugresort.com, $299-499) is a from-the-ground-up overhaul of an old San Juan resort on a quiet bay just south of Roche Harbor and the English Camp. The one- and two-bedroom cabins, built in 2013 and 2014, are stylish and comfortable, and come with full kitchens, barbecue grills, and sofa beds. There are also bayside fire pits, and bikes and kayaks available at no extra cost.

Camping

Camping options are limited on San Juan and usually book up far in advance for the summer months. The only public campground on the island is at **San Juan County Park** (360/378-8420, www.co.san-juan.wa.us/Parks, $32-45, $7 reservation fee), just north of Lime Kiln Point State Park along West Side Road. All sites have full or partial views of Haro Strait—you can launch your kayak from here in the morning and then take in a glorious sunset when evening rolls around. Some sites can accommodate RVs, but there are no hookups. There are restrooms but no showers. (Coin-operated showers can be found at the Roche Harbor marina.) Spaces for campers without motorized vehicles (i.e., hikers, cyclists, and kayakers) are available for $10 per person. You can reserve sites online up to three months in advance; for the peak summer season the entire campground can book up within an hour of becoming available, but if you miss out it's worth checking periodically to see if there have been cancellations. From November through March fees are reduced and reservations aren't accepted.

INFORMATION

The office of the **San Juan Island Chamber of Commerce** (135 Spring St., 360/378-5240, www.sanjuanisland.org) is open daily 10am-4pm.

TRANSPORTATION
Getting There

The **state ferry** (206/464-6400, www.wsdot.wa.gov/Ferries) runs between Anacortes and Friday Harbor 14 or 15 times a day, from about 4am-11pm. The trip takes approximately 1-1.75 hours, depending on whether the ferry stops at other islands en route. Fares are $65.60 per car and driver, $13.50 for each additional passenger and for walk-ons. There's an additional $4 charge for a walk-on with a bicycle. Fares are charged only in one direction, from Anacortes to Friday Harbor; the ride back is free. You can reserve a place on this ferry up to two months in advance through the system's website or by phone. Although places are set aside for vehicles without reservations, you may have to wait for several ferries to come and go before you can get a place if you haven't reserved.

Getting Around

San Juan Transit (360/378-8887, www.sanjuantransit.com) has two daily bus routes, one running north between Friday Harbor and Roche Harbor, the other south and west between Friday Harbor, American Camp, and Lime Kiln Point State Park, both making stops at tourist sites along the way. There are buses about once an hour from late morning to early evening. Fares are $5 one-way or $15 for a day pass. Exact change is required.

Rent cars in Friday Harbor from **M&W Auto Sales & Rental** (725 Spring St., 360/378-2794, www.sanjuanauto.com). Also in Friday Harbor, just up from the ferry landing, **Susie's Mopeds** (125 Nichols St., 360/378-5244, www.susiesmopeds.com) rents cars and distinctive Scoot Coupes (tiny three-wheeled, two-passenger vehicles) as well as mopeds and motor-assisted bicycles.

Friday Harbor Taxi (360/298-4434, www.fridayharbortaxi.com) and **Bob's Taxi and Tours** (360/378-6777, http://bobs-taxi.com) have van service around the island.

Orcas Island

TOP EXPERIENCE

Orcas is the largest and hilliest of the San Juan Islands, as well as the most heavily wooded of the inhabited ones, making it a great place for hiking and camping. It's roughly horseshoe-shaped, with the East Sound running up the middle and nearly dividing the island in two. Ferry access is on the western tip of the horseshoe, which means the farthest reaches on the other side feel very remote. That may explain the appeal the island holds for artists, free spirits, and well-heeled types in search of privacy.

The ferry lands at **Orcas Village,** which consists of little more than a hotel, a restaurant, a market, and a gift shop. From there it's a 15-minute, 8.5-mile drive to **Eastsound,** Orcas's main hub of activity and the second-largest town in the San Juans after Friday Harbor. It's situated at the point where the eastern and western halves of the island connect at the end of East Sound. (Note that the town is one word and the body of water two.) This is the place to stock up on provisions, gas up the car, and bend an elbow with the locals. There are also two little villages on the west side of the island, **West Sound** and **Deer Harbor,** that have marinas and a smattering of tourist facilities.

The island's biggest attraction is Moran State Park, on the eastern side. It's arguably the finest park in the entire state system, with over 5,000 acres of old-growth woods, hiking trails, swimmable lakes, and appealing campsites, capped by Mount Constitution, the highest point on the San Juans. It's beautiful and also novel. While most of the allure of the San Juans relates in some way to the surrounding sea, Moran State Park is landlocked and covered by a blanket of forest.

How that sounds to you should go a long way toward determining how much time you devote to Orcas. If your main goal is a classic island getaway, you'll probably want to make San Juan your primary base and come here for a day or two as a change of pace. If above all you love hiking and camping, with the seaside attractions as an added bonus, you could be happy spending your entire San Juans vacation on Orcas.

SIGHTS
★ Moran State Park

Moran State Park (3572 Olga Rd., 360/376-2326, http://parks.state.wa.us/547/Moran, free, Discover Pass required for parking), about 30 minutes by car from the ferry terminal, strikes a nice balance between accessibility and seclusion. Within its 5,579 acres you can have a satisfying experience touring by car, taking short hikes, or venturing onto demanding, remote trails on the park's west side. Of its five lakes, the larger ones are popular places to swim, boat, and fish, while the smaller are little gems accessible only by foot.

The park's star attraction is **Mount Constitution,** which at 2,409 feet is the highest point on the San Juans. You can reach it the easy way, by car, or the scenic way, along one of several trails, the most picturesque of which is a 3.7-mile climb from **Mountain Lake Landing.** At the summit there's a 52-foot stone observation tower, built in 1936 by the Civilian Conservation Corps and designed in the style of 12th-century watchtowers in eastern Europe's Caucasus Mountains. From the tower you get impressive views stretching north to British Columbia and south to—on a clear day—Mount Rainier.

HIKING

The park has 38 miles of hiking trails, including the 3.7-mile climb to the peak of Mount Constitution. Trail maps are available at the registration booth near the entrance and at the park office on Cascade Lake. In the park's southeast section there are several enjoyable, undemanding walks, including a 0.3-mile

Orcas Island

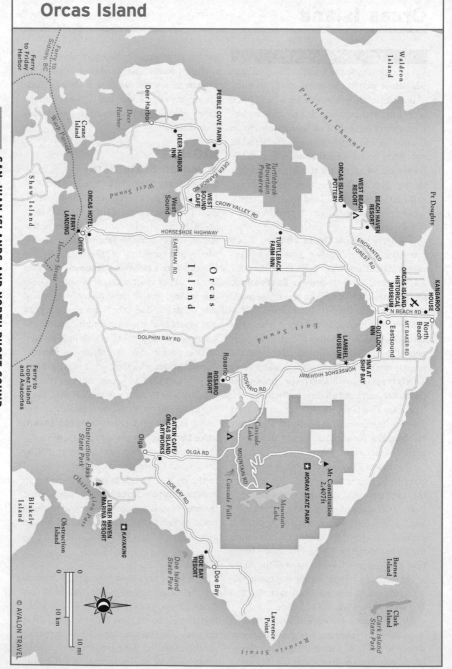

Waldron Island

Ferry to Sidney, BC

Ferry to Friday Harbor

Deer Harbor

PEBBLE COVE FARM

DEER HARBOR INN

Deer Harbor

Crane Island

Shaw Island

Wasp Passage

Deer Harbor

West Sound

President Channel

Turtleback Mountain Preserve

ORCAS ISLAND POTTERY

WEST BEACH RESORT

BEACH HAVEN RESORT

Pt Doughty

WEST SOUND CAFE

West Sound

CROW VALLEY RD

DEER HARBOR RD

ORCAS HOTEL

FERRY LANDING

Orcas

Harney Strait

HORSESHOE HIGHWAY

EASTMAN RD

Orcas Island

TURTLEBACK FARM INN

ENCHANTED FOREST RD

ORCAS ISLAND HISTORICAL MUSEUM

N BEACH RD

KANGAROO HOUSE

MT BAKER RD

North Beach

Eastsound

OUTLOOK INN

INN AT SHIP BAY

DOLPHIN BAY RD

Ferry to Lopez Island and Anacortes

East Sound

LAMBIEL MUSEUM

HORSESHOE HIGHWAY

Rosario

ROSARIO RESORT

ROSARIO RD

Cascade Lake

Cascade Falls

MOUNTAIN RD

MORAN STATE PARK

Mt Constitution 2,407ft

CATKIN CAFE/ ORCAS ISLAND ARTWORKS

Olga

OLGA RD

Cascade Falls

Mountain Lake

Obstruction Pass State Park

Obstruction Pass

DOE BAY RD

LIEBER HAVEN MARINA RESORT

KAYAKING

Obstruction Island

Blakely Island

Barnes Island

Clark Island State Park

Clark Island

Doe Island State Park

DOE BAY RESORT

Doe Bay

Lawrence Point

Rosario Strait

0   10 km
0   10 mi

© AVALON TRAVEL

nature trail near **Cascade Lake** and a quarter-mile trail to 75-foot **Cascade Falls,** which is at its most dramatic in the spring.

Loop trails around **Cascade Lake** and **Mountain Lake** are longer but don't require any climbing; they're both pleasant, with Mountain Lake being more tranquil. If you're up for taking on a little elevation, you can hike from one lake to the other on the **Cascade Creek Trail,** which runs three miles through the woods past giant Douglas firs. From the northern end of Mountain Lake there's another beautiful wooded trail up to the Twin Lakes. (This is the first stretch of the hike to Mount Constitution.)

Eleven miles of trails are open to bikes year-round, and cyclists are permitted on an additional 14 miles from mid-September through mid-May. Six miles are open to horseback riding.

WATER SPORTS

Cascade Lake is the busiest center of activity in the park and the main destination for water sports. The lake is stocked with trout for fishing. You can rent paddleboats and canoes, and there's a popular roped-off swimming area (with no lifeguard). Three of the park's five camping areas are on the lake, as are a snack bar (open Memorial Day to Labor Day) and covered kitchen facilities. **Mountain Lake,** the largest and deepest lake in the San Juans, is also stocked with fish and has boat rentals; you make rental arrangements at the Cascade Lake boathouse. Both lakes have a boat ramp. Only nonmotorized craft are permitted.

Moran Mansion

The centerpiece of **Rosario Resort** (1400 Rosario Rd., 360/376-2222, www.rosarioresort.com), located on the east side of the island, 5.5 miles from Eastsound and 1.5 from Moran State Park, is the **Moran Mansion.** Built in 1908, the mansion is now the site of the resort's reception area, restaurant, bar, and spa, but originally it was the home of Robert Moran, a self-made millionaire shipbuilder and former mayor of Seattle. Much of the space is preserved as a museum dedicated to him.

Despite his success, by the age of 49 business had turned Moran into a self-described nervous wreck. Doctors advised that he retire or risk heart failure. He purchased 7,800 acres on Orcas and spent 1.5 million dollars, the equivalent of nearly $40 million today, building his retirement home. (Much of the acreage he eventually donated to the state of

Mount Constitution observation tower

Washington for what would become Moran State Park.) The change served his heart well—he remained an Orcas resident for over three decades, until his death in 1943.

Today, the 2nd floor of the mansion is open to visitors (daily 9am-9pm, free) and preserves the furnishings from Moran's time. He employed shipwrights as his designers, and there are nautical touches throughout, along with original photos and models from his company's biggest shipbuilding commissions. There's also a strongly felt influence of the arts and crafts style, which Moran championed.

The mansion's centerpiece is the two-story-tall, mahogany-paneled ballroom, which is dominated by an organ composed of 1,972 pipes. Remarkably, the organ is designed to play musical rolls in much the same way as a player piano. Moran wasn't a musician, but he would sit down at the organ's bench, out of sight in the ballroom's balcony, and pump out songs for guests, never letting on that he wasn't actually playing.

Eventually a keyboard was added to the organ, and on most afternoons at 4pm the resort's general manager, Christopher Peacock—who *is* a talented musician, as well as a local historian—plays a recital and narrates a slideshow illustrating the mansion's past. Peacock has been putting on this performance for three decades, making him almost as much a part of the place as Moran himself. Call ahead to confirm that he's playing on the day you visit.

Orcas Island Historical Museum

The **Orcas Island Historical Museum** (181 North Beach Rd., Eastsound, 360/376-4849, www.orcasmuseums.org, Wed.-Sat. 11am-4pm, $5) is housed in six homesteaders' cabins dating from the 1870s to the 1890s that were relocated half a block off Main Street and linked to create a single structure. The collection consists primarily of artifacts and documents of the late-19th-century settlers, along with some Salish Indian objects and 14,000-year-old bison bones discovered in an island peat bog.

Lambiel Museum

For a full immersion into the San Juans art world, head 1.5 miles west of the Eastsound town center to the **Lambiel Museum** (668 Olga Rd., Eastsound, 360/376-4544, www.lambielmuseum.org, by appointment). Owner Leo Lambiel has turned collecting art made in the San Juans into a lifelong obsession; the handsome museum, which is also his home, contains pieces by more 250 artists, all of them from the islands, collected over four decades. Highlights include the world's largest collection of works by Helen Loggie, the San Juans' most esteemed artist, and two architectural follies, a grotto and a faux Grecian temple. The museum is open by appointment only, and visits consist of a two-hour tour led by Lambiel, for which there's a suggested donation of $20 per person. It's not for short attention spans, but if you enjoy art and one-of-a-kind homes you're likely to appreciate Lambiel's passion.

The Funhouse Commons

If you're traveling with kids you might want to check out **The Funhouse Commons** (30 Pea Patch Ln., Eastsound, 360/376-7177, www.funhousecommons.org, July-Aug. weekdays 1pm-5pm, Sept.-June weekdays 3pm-5:30pm). This youth facility was designed with locals in mind, but traveling kids are welcome, and the facilities are impressive, especially considering the size of the community. There's something for everyone from toddlers to teens, including hands-on science exhibits, an arts and crafts yurt, and video and audio recording studios complete with musical instruments. Admission is $10 per child (7 or older) left under staff supervision or $15 per family if a parent sticks around.

ENTERTAINMENT AND EVENTS
Nightlife

Nights are quiet on Orcas, with pretty much

(107 Doe Bay Rd., 360/376-8059, www.doebay.com), the restaurant of the Doe Bay Resort.

Performing Arts

The main site for performing arts on the island is the **Orcas Center** (917 Mt. Baker Rd., 360/376-2281, www.orcascenter.org) in Eastsound, which puts on a varied calendar of events. Every year there are a few nationally known musical acts scheduled, along with lecturers, local performers, and live video broadcasts of world-renowned theater and opera-company productions.

In August—some years rolling over into September—the two-week-long **Orcas Island Chamber Music Festival** (360/376-6636, www.oicmf.org) comes to the Orcas Center. As well as performing, guest musicians with international pedigrees take part in forums and receptions.

SHOPPING

A concentration of shops and boutiques is on and around Eastsound's Main Street, anchored by **Darvill's Bookstore** (296 Main St., 360/376-2135, www.darvillsbookstore.com), which has been in business for over 40 years. It has about everything you could hope for in a resort-town bookshop: a broad and eclectic selection, including lots of titles with local relevance; a friendly, knowledgeable staff; Orcas souvenirs; and a coffee bar in the back.

The island prides itself on its arts and crafts, and it's an especially good place to shop for pottery. The oldest pottery studio in the Pacific Northwest, **Orcas Island Pottery** (338 Old Pottery Rd., 360/376-2813, www.orcasislandpottery.com), is also one of the most fun places on Orcas to visit. Along the island's western side, a turnoff from West Beach Road leads to a quarter mile of unpaved road running through a forest of Douglas firs. At its end there's a clearing with a cluster of buildings and a yard, all filled with colorful, varied ceramics produced by 15 potters. Even if pottery doesn't interest you, it's worth the trip here for the fanciful setting. The yard ends at

Orcas Island Pottery

everything shuttered by 10pm. An exception is **The Lower Tavern** (46 Prune Alley, 360/376-4848, www.lowertavern.com), which pours until 2am. It's an unpretentious locals' hangout with a dozen beers on tap, sports on the TV, and pool tables in the back. It also serves above-average burgers and fish-and-chips.

Craft cocktails are the order of the day at **The Barnacle** (249 Prune Alley, 360/679-5683), a charming little Eastsound bar with nautical decor and a youthful but not aggressively hip vibe.

About a mile north of Eastsound's Main Street, **Island Hoppin' Brewery** (33 Hope Ln., 360/376-6079, www.islandhoppinbrewery.com) is Orcas's contribution to the world of microbrews. The small, homey taproom can fill up fast, but there are picnic tables on the patio to accommodate any overflow.

Casual entertainment on Orcas is primarily do-it-yourself. The Lower Tavern has weekly open-mic and karaoke nights. Over on the eastern lobe of the island there's another open mic on Thursday nights at the **Doe Bay Café** a bluff overlooking President Channel; you're welcome to bring a picnic, relax on a bench, and take in the beautiful vista. Meanwhile your kids will be getting even better views as they levitate on the swing set or climb to the elaborate tree house.

Other good sources for local ceramics are **Crow Valley Pottery & Gallery** (296 Main St., 360/376-4260, www.crowvalley.com), which has a shop in the heart of Eastsound, and, on the east side of the island, **Olga Pottery** (6928 Olga Rd., 360/376-4648, www.olgapottery.com), the studio of Jerry Weatherman, who's been crafting beautiful, functional pieces since the 1970s.

The largest artists' collective on the island, **Orcas Island Artworks** (11 Point Lawrence Rd., 360/376-4408, http://orcasartworks.com) sells paintings, photography, sculpture, jewelry, and furniture, all made on the island. The location is in an old strawberry packing plant on the road from Eastsound to Moran State Park.

SPORTS AND RECREATION
Hiking

Hikers of all stripes naturally gravitate to the great trails in **Moran State Park,** but Orcas has some other attractive hiking options as well.

On the western half of the island, 1,718-acre **Turtleback Mountain Preserve** (360/378-4402, www.sjclandbank.org, daily dawn-dusk) encompasses the second-highest point on the San Juans (after Mount Constitution). Eight miles of primitive wooded trails are accessible from parking areas at the preserve's north end off Crow Valley Road (just south of the Crow Valley Schoolhouse) and south end off Deer Harbor Road (turn at Wild Rose Lane, 2.4 miles west of West Sound). A rocky outcrop at Ship Peak on the south side of Turtleback Mountain provides a beautiful view over the island and beyond. Along with being a pleasant place to hike, the preserve is evidence of the affluence of the San Juans' residents. In

2006 the property, which had been privately owned by the chairman of Weyerhaeuser, was up for sale. In order to fend off developers, islanders purchased it for $18.5 million and designated it a nature preserve. Fires, camping, and motorized vehicles are prohibited. At the north trailhead mountain bikes are permitted on even-numbered days, horses on odd.

For guided hikes through Moran State Park, Natalie Herner of **Gnat's Nature Hikes** (360/376-6629, www.orcasislandhikes. com, $30 per person) is a tried-and-true resource. She picks you up from your lodging and leads you through the park on 2-3-hour walks customized to suit your interests and endurance level.

Beachcombing

For a wonderful combination of hiking and beachcombing, head to **Obstruction Pass State Park** (360/376-2326, http://parks.state. wa.us/553/Obstruction-Pass, daily 6:30am-sunset, Discover Pass required for parking). The remote little park consists of 80 acres of woods and waterfront on the southwest tip of Orcas, three miles beyond the hamlet of Olga. A half-mile trail leads from the parking area to the most picturesque beach on the island, an expanse of soft pebbles covered with bleached driftwood. It's a popular site for launching kayaks, picnicking, and crabbing (licenses available at fishhunt.dfw. wa.gov). There are nine hike-in tent spaces for campers, available on a first-come, first-served basis.

A more centrally located beachcombing option is **Crescent Beach Preserve** (360/378-4402, www.sjclandbank.org, daily dawn-dusk), managed by the same group that oversees Turtleback Mountain. Half a mile east of Eastsound (Main Street turns into Crescent Beach Drive), waterfowl, sand dollars, and eelgrass populate 2,000 feet of beachfront. On the north side of the road there are three small parking lots and a stretch of marshland with a 0.7-mile trail that's also part of the preserve.

Bicycling

Cycling on the winding, often hilly roads of Orcas can be fun and challenging but also requires a good dose of caution. The two-lane roads weren't designed with bicycles in mind, and automobile traffic along the main arteries can move at a dangerously fast clip. The farther you are from the ferry dock and from Eastsound, particularly on the east side of the island, the fewer cars you have to contend with. If you're up for a challenge, the five-mile ascent to the top of Mount Constitution in Moran State Park is a gratifying climb.

Eastsound has a first-rate, full-service bike shop, **Wildlife Cycles** (350 North Beach Rd., 360/376-4708, www.wildlifecycles.com, May-Sept. daily 10am-6pm, off-season hours vary), where you can buy and rent bikes, pick up parts and accessories, and have repairs done. They're also a good resource for maps and route-planning tips. Daily rentals run $40 for hybrids and $60 for higher-end road and mountain bikes. On the western end of the island the moorage office of **Deer Harbor Marina** (360/376-3037, www.deerharbormarina.com) also has bikes for rent.

Skateboarding

A unique attraction of the island is **Orcas Island Skatepark** (off Mt. Baker Rd. in Buck Park, 360/376-7275, www.orcasparkandrec.org/parks/skate-park), one of the premier skateboarding facilities in the Pacific Northwest, with over 30,000 square feet of curves, humps, and bowls. Note that helmets are mandatory. The location is a mile from the center of Eastsound—to get there take North Beach Road north and turn right on Mount Baker Road.

★ Kayaking

Sea kayaking is popular throughout the San Juans, and while the range of outfitters and tours available on Orcas isn't as large as on San Juan, great kayaking opportunities are to be had with less traffic on the water.

The largest and longest-established tour operator is **Shearwater Adventures** (138 North Beach Rd., 360/376-4699, www.shearwaterkayaks.com). It offers a variety of three-hour guided tours for $79 per person starting at four locations around the island—Deer Harbor, Rosario Resort, West Beach Resort, and Doe Bay—and a daylong, $159 tour that takes you to Sucia Island, a state park north of Orcas known for its abundant marinelife. Shearwater uses only two-person kayaks, which give you a stable ride but mean you need to be amenable to paddling with a partner.

Orcas Outdoors (360/376-4611, www.orcasoutdoors.com) specializes in all-inclusive multiday trips ($349 for one night, $549 for two) that explore smaller surrounding islands, with overnight camping usually on Jones Island, one of the area's island state parks, located just west of Deer Harbor.

Have a shorter outing at a reasonable price with **Spring Bay Kayak Tours** (360/376-5531, www.springbayinn.com). For $45 per person, former park rangers Carl Burger and Sandy Playa lead morning and evening two-hour trips starting from the shore off their wooded property just east of Obstruction Pass State Park.

If you're not looking for a guide, try **Outer Island Excursions** (360/376-3711, www.outerislandx.com), which rents kayaks by the day (singles $50, doubles $75). You can launch from its location at Smuggler's Villa Resort (54 Hunt Rd.) on the north end of the island. Or, for $25 per boat, it will deliver kayaks to sites throughout Orcas, including the lakes of Moran State Park.

Boating

The main site on Orcas for docking recreational boats and for boating services is **Deer Harbor Marina** (360/376-3037, www.deerharbormarina.com), located at the southwest end of the island. **Orcas Boat Rentals & Charters** (360/376-7616 www.orcasboatrentals.com), owned by harbormaster Marc Broman, rents a range of small motorized craft, including a 15-foot rigid-hulled inflatable ($225/4 hrs., $300/8 hrs.) and a 19-foot runabout ($300/4 hrs., $375/8hrs.).

Deer Harbor is also the launching point for a couple of worthwhile sailing charters. **Northwest Classic Day Sailing** (360/376-5581, www.classicdaysails.com) takes out groups of up to six ($76 per person) for three-hour tours on a handsome 33-foot sloop dating from the 1940s. Dedicated sailors can indulge in 3-6-day trips around the San Juans, running $1,400-2,400 per person, aboard the 54-foot pilothouse ketch of **Emerald Isle Sailing Charters** (360/376-3472, www.emeraldislesailing.com). The boat is also used for six-hour day sails, which run $145 per person.

On the east side of the island, **Rosario Resort Marina** (360/376-2152, www.rosarioresort.com) has moorage, fuel, showers, and a supply store; when you dock your boat there you get use of the resort's spa and swimming pool. A less luxe option is **Lieber Haven Resort & Marina** (360/376-2472, www.lieberhavenresort.com), located along Obstruction Pass.

Whale-Watching

Sightings of the area's resident orca pods are most frequent along the Haro Strait west of San Juan Island. That said, Orcas does have reputable tour operators—you just might end up spending more time on the water in your quest for whales.

Deer Harbor Charters (360/376-5989, www.deerharborcharters.com) runs daily three-to-four-hour whale-watching trips with experienced naturalists. May-October it operates a 40-passenger boat out of Deer Harbor and a 20-passenger boat from Rosario Resort (both $99 per person). Off-season trips originate from Deer Harbor.

Orcas Island Eclipse Charters (360/376-6566, www.orcasislandwhales.com) sails from the dock by the ferry landing at Orcas Village and times its whale-watching tours to coincide with ferry arrivals. Three-and-a-half-hour trips ($85 pp) run daily May-mid-October on a 56-passenger boat with a heated cabin and an open-air observation deck.

At the north end of the island, **Outer Island Excursions** (360/376-3711, www.outerislandx.com) runs daily afternoon and evening tours (up to 4 hrs., $99 pp) April-October out of Smuggler's Villa Resort (54 Hunt Rd.), due north of Eastsound. Most tours are on high-speed, 30-passenger catamarans.

FOOD

When it comes to interesting and varied dining options, Orcas surpasses San Juan for the title of best restaurant scene in the archipelago. The emphasis is on contemporary farm-to-table cuisine—it's the rare menu that doesn't tout its locally sourced ingredients. Prices, as on the other islands, skew higher than the mainland. Most restaurants take reservations for dinner, and in summer you can have a hard time getting a table without one. The number of ambitious restaurants seems to exceed the availability of experienced waiters and waitresses. Service is usually friendly, but it's not always polished and can be slow.

Eastsound and Vicinity
BREAKFAST AND LUNCH

Brown Bear Baking (29 North Beach Rd., 360/855-7456, Wed.-Mon. 8am-4pm, $3-12) makes alluring, handcrafted baked goods both sweet and savory, from muffins to quiche to croissants. It also serves coffee and soup, so it's easy to make a meal of the offerings. Take your food to a table on the porch to people-watch while you eat.

For diner-style comfort-food breakfasts, the place to go is **Island Skillet** (325 Prune Alley, 360/376-3984, daily 8am-2pm, $6-12). Omelets, pancakes, and eggs Benedict all come in large, satisfying portions. Lunch follows the same formula, featuring soups, salads, and grilled sandwiches.

As the name indicates, there's a double identity at **Roses Bakery & Café** (382 Prune Alley, bakery 360/376-5805, cafe 360/376-4292, www.rosesbakerycafe.com, bakery Mon.-Sat. 10am-5pm, cafe Mon.-Sat. 8:30am-4pm, cafe $9-24). The bakery, set in a former firehouse, makes high-quality breads and pastries and also sells cheese, cured meats, and wine—it's a good place to pick up provisions for a picnic. The cafe serves sophisticated breakfast and lunch in a casual setting. The pizzas are the stars of the lunch menu.

AMERICAN

For good, straightforward bar food (burgers, sandwiches, fish-and-chips), settle into a booth at **The Lower Tavern** (46 Prune Alley, 360/376-4848, www.lowertavern.com, daily 11am-2am, $9-14). It's the only place in Eastsound where on an average summer night you're likely to find more locals than tourists.

ASIAN

From its modest walk-up counter, **The Kitchen** (249 Prune Alley, 360/376-6958, www.thekitchenorcas.com, Mon.-Sat. 11am-8pm, $10-15) serves brightly flavored, Asian-influenced fare, including wraps, pot stickers, and build-your-own noodle bowls. Limited seating is available at covered and open-air picnic tables.

FINE DINING

There's little dispute that the island's classiest restaurant is ★ **Inn at Ship Bay** (326 Olga Rd., 360/376-5886, www.innatshipbay.com, Tues.-Sat 5:30pm-10pm, $25-32). It's located 1.5 miles east of Eastsound in a beautifully restored 1860s farmhouse with 11 dining rooms and a patio where you can eat in fair weather. The seasonal menu takes top-quality ingredients (many of them grown on-site) and gives them classic "new American" preparations, meaning light sauces and creative side dishes—scallops come with a zippy lemon aioli and bacon-potato hash, while fish stew swims in a tomato-fennel-saffron broth.

New Leaf Café (171 Main St., 360/376-2200, www.outlookinn.com/new-leaf-cafe, Mon. and Thurs.-Fri. 8am-11:30am and 5pm-9pm, Sat.-Sun. 8am-12:30pm and 5pm-9pm, $22-42) serves upscale, French-inflected cuisine from the ground-floor dining room of the Outlook Inn, where many tables have views of Fishing Bay. Entrées are typically half a

dozen creative takes on grilled or pan-seared meat and fish, accompanied by a long list of small plates such as duck mac and cheese, crab cakes, and French onion soup. New Leaf is also a popular brunch spot.

No place on the island embraces the farm-to-table sensibility more vigorously than **AElder/Hogstone's Wood Oven** (460 Main St., 360/376-4647, www.hogstone.com, Thurs.-Sun. 5:30pm-close, $50-75 tasting menu). What started as a hip little pizzeria has transformed into a set-menu showplace for locally sourced meats, fish, and produce prepared in wildly creative ways. If you're looking for familiar comfort food this isn't the restaurant for you, but if you're a foodie eager to surrender your palate to an inventive young chef you're likely to be happy here. Pizza is still served on the patio, and indoors in the off-season.

MARKETS AND GROCERIES

The main supermarket for the island is Eastsound's **Island Market** (469 Market St., 360/376-6000, http://orcasislandmarket.com, Mon.-Sat. 7am-10pm, Sun. 8am-8pm), which has the basics for stocking a kitchen.

For organic groceries and produce, much of it locally grown, stop by the **Orcas Food Co-op** (138 North Beach Rd., 360/376-2009, www.orcasfood.coop, Mon.-Sat. 8am-8pm, Sun. 10am-6pm).

May-September, on Saturdays 10am-3pm, the **Orcas Island Farmers Market** (541/306-7084, http://orcasislandfarmersmarket.org) convenes on the Eastsound village green, along North Beach Road, a short walk north of Main Street.

Western Orcas

The restaurant at **Deer Harbor Inn** (33 Inn Ln., 360/376-1040, www.deerharborinnrestaurant.com, Thurs.-Mon. 5pm-9pm, $22-48) has a touch of country-western ambience that signals this isn't a place for trendy, modernist cuisine. What you get instead are the same fresh ingredients found at other Orcas restaurants, prepared simply—king crab is steamed and served with drawn butter, steaks are char-grilled. The results are satisfying, but the island price markup might be a little harder to swallow here than at some of Orcas's more creative restaurants.

Nice water views, a casual atmosphere, and big flavors are the hallmarks of ★ **West Sound Café** (4362 Crow Valley Rd., 360/376-4440, www.kingfishinn.com, Wed.-Sun. 5pm-9pm, $18-27). The menu mixes straightforward dishes like burgers and fish-and-chips with more elaborate meat and fish entrées, all consistently tasty. If you want well-prepared food without foodie pretensions, this is a good choice. It helps that prices are a bargain by island standards.

Octavia's Bistro (18 Orcas Hill Rd., 360/376-4300, www.orcashotel.com, daily 4pm-8:30pm, $14-25), located above the ferry landing in the Orcas Hotel, is a middle-of-the-road option serving dishes such as fried calamari, veggie lasagna, and baby back ribs that all qualify as straightforward comfort food. Water views from the handsome hotel are Octavia's signature appeal.

Eastern Orcas

It's worth making the drive out to Doe Bay Resort to dine at the exceptional ★ **Doe Bay Café** (107 Doe Bay Rd., 360/376-8059, www.doebay.com, July-Aug. daily 8am-2pm and 5pm-9pm, call for variable off-season days and hours, $17-30), which blends the resort's laid-back sensibility with a foodie's devotion to fine ingredients and creative cooking. The menu is short—five or six starters and the same number of entrées, all fish or vegetarian—but everything is delicious, and the warm, wood-paneled dining room with big windows looking out over the bay enhances the experience. The cafe also serves breakfast and lunch, and on Thursday night hosts open-mic performers.

In the back of Orcas Island Artworks gallery, **Catkin Cafe** (11 Point Lawrence Rd., 360/376-3242, www.catkincafe.com, Wed.-Sun. 9am-3pm, $8-16) serves simple, tasty breakfast and lunch dishes with a few creative twists, like baked eggs with a ratatouille-style stew over creamy polenta, and a grilled cheddar cheese and oyster mushroom sandwich. It also bakes cookies, cakes, pies, and scones, which you can include in your meal or order to go.

The most elegant dining room on Orcas belongs to **The Mansion Restaurant** (1400 Rosario Rd., 360/376-2152, ext. 400, www.rosarioresort.com, daily 8am-11am, noon-3pm,

Doe Bay

and 5pm-9pm, $22-40), located in early-20th-century millionaire Robert Moran's former home, now the centerpiece of the Rosario Resort. It also has the largest and most eclectic menu of any high-end restaurant on the island. Locally and regionally sourced ingredients get sophisticated treatments, from flat iron steak with tomato gremolata to tuna crudo with braised rhubarb and Greek yogurt.

Delicious local oysters and clams are available from **Buck Bay Shellfish Farm** (117 EJ Young Rd., 360/376-5280, www.buckbayshellfishfarm.com, Mon.-Sat. 11am-6pm, Sun. noon-5pm) near Olga. Dine on-site and enjoy the view—the farm provides bread and simple salads to go with the shellfish—or take a bag full of bivalves to go.

ACCOMMODATIONS

While visitors to San Juan Island come from far and wide, Orcas tends to get a higher concentration of in-state vacationers who make summer trips here an annual ritual. The range of accommodations reflects this difference: Orcas has more moderately priced, rustic resorts with family-friendly cabins that require multiple-day stays. It's important to book these types of places as far in advance as possible.

Regardless of where you stay, reservations are essential—in the height of summer it can seem like there isn't a vacant bed on the island. If you're having a hard time finding a place, check with the **Orcas Island Chamber of Commerce** (360/376-2273, www.orcasislandchamber.com) or the **Orcas Island Lodging Association** (www.orcas-lodging.com). Both websites allow you to search for availability at multiple locations, and the chamber can provide leads over the phone.

Eastsound and Vicinity
$100-150
The cheapest bed on the island is at the pleasant **Golden Tree Hostel** (1159 North Beach Rd., 360/317-8693, www.goldentréehostel.com), half a mile north of Eastsound. The restored 1890s farmhouse has coed and women's

dorm rooms with bunk beds going for $45 per person. There are also six private rooms ($115 d) and a dome (similar to a yurt, $125 d), all with shared baths. Extensive facilities, including a kitchen, sauna, hot tub, fire pit, and a pool table in the barn, make this a place where you can hang out rather than just bed down.

$150-200
Inn at Ship Bay (326 Olga Rd., 877/276-7296, www.innatshipbay.com, $195 d) is known first and foremost for its fine restaurant, but it also has 11 attractive guest rooms. By island standards they're relatively new (built in 2000), and if you're willing to forgo the lived-in charm that characterizes most Orcas lodgings in exchange for amenities and furnishings more like what you'd find at a good midrange chain hotel, they're a worthwhile option. All rooms have king beds, balconies with water views, and sitting areas with TVs and Franklin stoves. There's one suite ($295), and one standard room is handicapped-accessible. Rates include a continental breakfast.

Kangaroo House B&B (1459 North Beach Rd., 360/376-2175, www.kangaroohouse.com, $175-209 d) does a standout job of creating a casual, comfortable environment while maintaining high standards. The attractive craftsman-style house sits back from the road amid a well-maintained garden that's a state-certified wildlife sanctuary. The five guest rooms vary in size, and it's taken some repurposing to give each a private bath, but they're all attractively, unfussily decorated. Shared facilities include a garden hot tub and a living room with mission-style furniture and a stone fireplace. Friendly owners Jill Johnson and Charles Toxey whip up satisfying multicourse breakfasts and are dependable resources for information about the island.

$200-250
Outlook Inn (171 Main St., 360/376-2200, www.outlookinn.com), right on the main drag in Eastsound, is one of Orcas's most conspicuous and conveniently located lodgings. Rooms here fall into three categories. You can stay

in the quaint original hotel ($94-124), dating from 1888, where you share a bathroom, the floors slant, and some appointments are worn around the edges. The East Wing's rooms ($199-219) are newer and have private baths but aren't luxurious. Bayview suites ($289-319) are the inn's showplaces, with nicer furnishings, beautiful views and, in some cases, Jacuzzi tubs.

At **Smuggler's Villa Resort** (54 Hunt Rd., 360/376-2297, www.smuggler.com), located on the water due north of Eastsound, guests stay in modern two-bedroom townhouses sleeping four to six ($299-325) with full kitchens, fireplaces, and decks facing the water. Amenities include an outdoor pool, a hot tub, a sauna, tennis and basketball courts, and a private beach. Lodgings face west for sunset views.

SeaStar Lodging (360/507-5444, http://seastarorcasisland.com) manages three good lodging options on Orcas, two of them in Eastsound. The SeaStar Lofts ($185-275) are hidden in plain sight along Main Street. Three of the four rooms have views directly over the water, and all are furnished in contemporary style with full kitchen facilities. SeaStar also has a four-bedroom restored early-20th-century home on the water in Eastsound ($510), and a farm cottage that sleeps four located near Turtleback Mountain Preserve ($245).

Western Orcas
$100-150
★ **Beach Haven Resort** (684 Beach Haven Rd., 360/376-2288, www.beach-haven.com) is the epitome of an old-school San Juans retreat. Thirteen cabins and three lodge apartments border a pebbled beach along the northwest shore of Orcas. Six of the accommodations sleep 2 ($125-150), while the rest sleep 4-10 ($185 up to $325 for the beautiful Beachcomber house). All are cedar- or pine-paneled, with kitchens, decks, and barbecues. They're standout sites for a comfortable, laid-back vacation, with location being the key—you're right on the water, ideally situated to take in beautiful sunsets, a short drive from

Eastsound but isolated enough to feel like you've left the everyday world behind. The downside is that mid-June-mid-September, annual repeat guests book up most, if not all, of the spaces. But it's worth calling to double-check, or making a visit in the off-season.

$150-200
The Deer Harbor Inn (33 Inn Ln., 360/376-4110, www.deerharborinn.com) gives you a hodgepodge of places to stay. An eight-unit lodge has small wood-paneled rooms with rustic log furniture ($179 d). The six cottages sleeping four to six ($269-399), some with great views of Deer Harbor, are done in a range of styles. Though the decor varies, the general feel of the place is comfortable but worn. It's a nice property, set around an old apple orchard on a hill above the harbor, where you're likely to see more rabbits and deer than members of the low-key staff.

The first lodging you encounter when you roll off the ferry is the **Orcas Hotel** (18 Orcas Hill Rd., 360/376-4300, www.orcashotel.com, $94-237 d), perched on a hill above the landing. The handsome, porch-lined Victorian building has been housing guests for over a century and has the quirky, lived-in feel of an old B&B. Each of the 12 rooms (eight with private baths) is unique, which accounts for the range of prices—squeeze into the attic on the cheap or splurge on a honeymoon room with a Jacuzzi tub and a private deck. Views are great, but the dockside location is a mixed blessing. The ferry starts operating before 7am and can be hard to sleep through.

One of Orcas's longest-established B&Bs, **Turtleback Farm Inn** (1981 Crow Valley Rd., 360/376-4914, www.turtlebackinn.com, $125-195 d) occupies a restored 19th-century farmhouse located on an 80-acre property just east of Turtleback Mountain Preserve. The seven rooms range from the tiny Nook to the spacious Valley View, which has a private balcony. Throughout the place you find tasteful Victorian decor, claw-foot tubs, and hardwood floors—there's nothing "shabby chic" about it. Down the road an annex, the Orchard House, is a bigger indulgence. The four rooms ($260) all have king beds, fireplaces, large bathrooms, and private decks; breakfast is delivered to your room each morning.

OVER $250

It somehow fits the personality of Orcas that its most lavish lodging is a B&B. An inconspicuous road near Deer Harbor leads to **The Inn on Orcas Island** (114 Channel Rd., 360/376-5227, www.theinnonorcasisland.com, $225-345 d), a tripped-out estate suited to the pages of a design magazine. You're greeted at the door with a glass of champagne and pampered throughout your stay by proprietors John Gibbs and Jeremy Trumble, former gallery owners who have covered the walls with 19th- and 20th-century English art. Whether you stay in a standard room, a suite, or one of two small freestanding houses, your lodging will be lushly appointed and meticulously maintained. All accommodations are intended for adult couples (no kids allowed). Note that a 5 percent gratuity is added to your bill.

★ **Pebble Cove Farm** (3341 Deer Harbor Rd., 360/376-6161, www.pebblecovefarm.com) is an agrarian idyll come to life. A four-person cottage ($350) and three suites ($250-300, sleep 3-4), appointed in comfortable contemporary style, are surrounded by an orchard, an organic garden, and a barnyard. There's also a tiny cabin ($160) with a ladder-accessed loft bed. Guests can pick fruit, vegetables, and even eggs from the henhouse for use in their kitchenettes, and stop to say hello to the resident pony, goats, and potbelly pigs. The location is right on the water at Massacre Bay, where you can take a rowboat to a little island just offshore or launch a kayak expedition.

Eastern Orcas
$100-150

Orcas has its share of quirky places to stay, but **Doe Bay Resort and Retreat** (107 Doe Bay Rd., 360/376-2291, www.doebay.com) is in a category all its own. The 38-acre property, located along the water in a remote setting

19 miles from the ferry landing and 11 miles from Eastsound, offers a variety of lodging options, including 28 cabins, most sleeping 2-4 people ($91-233); 10 two-person yurts ($92-122); a tree house ($233); and 36 campsites ($43-66). Attitude is everything here, and that attitude is decidedly laid-back. A prevailing hippie sensibility means service can range from caring to indifferent, and standards of maintenance and cleanliness are similarly variable. If you're cool with that, your rewards are a gorgeous location, a spa with (clothing optional) saltwater soaking tubs overlooking the bay, and convenient proximity to Moran State Park. The Doe Bay Café is one of the best restaurants on the island, but its prices are steep in comparison to the rest of the resort. You can wind up spending more on a dinner for two than on a night's lodging.

$150-200

Lieber Haven Marina Resort (1945 Obstruction Pass Rd, 360/376-2472, www.lieberhavenresort.com) takes the prize, amid plenty of competition, for Orcas's most barebones, lost-in-time lodging. It's located on Obstruction Pass near the hamlet of Olga and offers beachfront cabins and apartments that sleep four ($200-250), all with full kitchens, as well as studios for two ($160). Facilities are clean but show their age. This is a good option for families who want a quiet, comparatively inexpensive location on the water where they can do their own cooking and take in beautiful views. Kayaks and rowboats are available for rent at the resort's marina.

The **Rosario Resort and Spa** (1400 Rosario Rd., 360/376-2222, www.rosarioresort.com, $169-269 d) is an Orcas landmark and the closest thing on the island to a luxury resort. The centerpiece of the property is the 1908 mansion of shipbuilder Robert Moran, which now houses Rosario's reception area, restaurant, and spa, as well as a museum commemorating Moran. The resort opened in 1960 and has grown over time on the 40-acre grounds around the mansion, with some struggles along the way, including being sold at auction in 2008. Lodging options vary from standard-issue, midrange hotel rooms to well-appointed suites, with locations along the water and on the hill above it. (The most remote hillside rooms are a 15-minute walk from the facilities at the mansion.) By the standards of high-end, amenities-rich resorts Rosario falls short, but it's a pretty and peaceful property that's well suited to the unpretentious, old-fashioned mindset that prevails throughout the San Juans.

Camping

Orcas Island's main destination for camping is **Moran State Park** (3572 Olga Rd., 360/376-2326, http://parks.state.wa.us/547/ Moran), which has 151 tent sites. There are four campgrounds, three on Cascade Lake and one on Mountain Lake, with a range of utilities ($25-40), and a fifth between the lakes on Mount Constitution Road with primitive sites ($12) for use by cyclists and hikers. Reservations are essential in summer and can be made by phone (888/226-7688) or online (http://washington.goingtocamp.com).

West Beach Resort (90 Waterfront Way, 360/376-2240, www.westbeachresort.com), on the water three miles west of Eastsound, is a classic old-school resort with campsites

($33-45) and RV hookups ($38-49). It also has an array of cabins ($189-309) that are rented by the week in summer.

Among the variety of lodging options at funky **Doe Bay Resort and Retreat** (107 Doe Bay Rd., 360/376-2291, www.doebay. com) are 9 drive-in ($56-66) and 27 walk-in ($43-66) campsites. The walk-in sites have water views.

Tiny **Obstruction Pass State Park** (360/376-2326, http://parks.state.wa.us/553/ Obstruction-Pass), along a beach at the southeast end of the island, has nine primitive walk-in tent sites ($12) with gorgeous water views, available on a first-come, first-served basis.

INFORMATION

Tourist information is available in Eastsound at the office of the **Orcas Island Chamber of Commerce** (65 N. Beach Rd., 360/376-2273, http://orcasislandchamber.com), Monday-Saturday 10am-3pm.

TRANSPORTATION
Getting There

The **state ferry** (206/464-6400, www.wsdot. wa.gov/Ferries) runs between Anacortes and Orcas Island 10-12 times a day, from 5:30am to as late as 10:30pm, usually stopping at

Obstruction Pass campsite

Shaw and Lopez Islands along the way. The trip takes 1-1.5 hours. Fares are $55.20 per car and driver, $13.50 for each additional passenger and for walk-ons. There's a $4 additional charge for a walk-on with a bicycle. Fares are only charged in one direction, from Anacortes to Orcas. The trip back is free. You can reserve a place on this ferry up to two months in advance through the system's website or by phone. Although places are set aside for vehicles without reservations, you may have to wait for several ferries to come and go before you can get a place if you haven't reserved.

Getting Around

Late June-Labor Day **San Juan Transit** (360/378-8887, www.sanjuantransit.com) has a bus running Friday, Saturday, and Sunday between the ferry landing and Moran State Park, with stops at points in between. There are six buses a day, the earliest departing the landing at 9am, the latest finishing service at the landing at 5pm. Fares are $5 one-way or $15 for a day pass. Exact change is required.

Rent cars from **Orcas Island Shuttle** (725 Spring St., 360/376-7433, www.orcasislandshuttle.com), which, despite the name, is a rental facility and not a shuttle service.

Orcas Island Taxi Service (360/376-8294, http://orcasislandtaxi.com) takes passengers around the island. The fare from the ferry landing to Eastsound is $30.

Lopez Island

In the hierarchy of the San Juans archipelago, Lopez Island happily plays third fiddle behind San Juan and Orcas. Life here is decidedly low key. You don't come to "Slow-pez" to have an adventure; you come to relax and unwind.

Lopez has an elongated north-south orientation and a flat, pastoral landscape—it's the most heavily farmed island in the San Juans—with beautiful bays and short, wooded hiking trails. Bicycling is Lopez's signature outdoor activity. Thanks to the level terrain you can virtually make it from one end of the island to the other without shifting gears, and the smaller population, both of locals and tourists, compared to San Juan and Orcas means there are fewer cars to share the roads with.

The Lopez coastline features a series of picturesque bays and points, and while much of the waterfront is privately owned, there are enough beautiful exceptions to keep you from resenting the fortunate landowners. (Most notable among them is Microsoft cofounder Paul Allen, who has a retreat on Sperry Peninsula at the island's southeast end.) Some of the best sites can be reached only by foot along wooded trails, which adds to the secluded charm but creates barriers for visitors with limited mobility.

Lopez Village is the center of activity for the island's 2,400 residents, but it consists of just a few blocks of modest buildings. It's easy to cruise right by while looking for "town." Boat traffic moors at two marinas in Fisherman Bay, about a mile south of the village.

SIGHTS
Odlin County Park

Coming off the ferry on the northern tip of the island, the first public waterfront area you hit, a mile from the landing, is **Odlin County Park** (148 Ferry Rd., 360/468-2496, www.sanjuanco.com/495/Lopez-Island). It has two miles of sandy beaches and is well equipped with facilities, including campsites, a boat launch, picnic tables, and restrooms. Hiking paths lead through old-growth woods and up to a bluff-top vista.

Spencer Spit State Park

Four miles from the ferry landing, on the eastern side of the island, 138-acre **Spencer Spit State Park** (Spencer Spit State Park Rd.,

Lopez Island

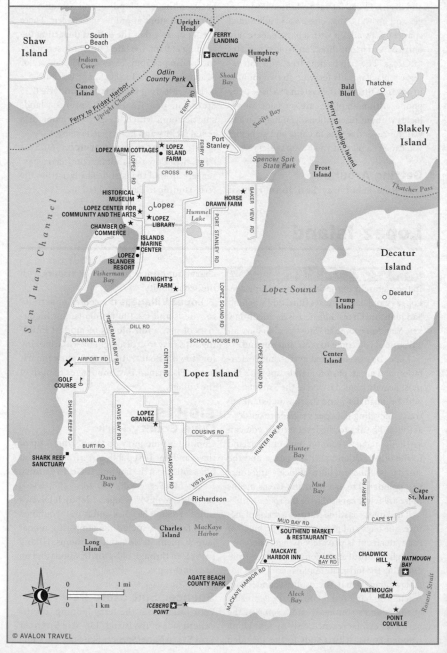

Shaw Island

South Beach

Indian Cove

Canoe Island

Upright Head

FERRY LANDING

BICYCLING

Humphrey Head

Odlin County Park

Shoal Bay

Swifts Bay

Bald Bluff

Thatcher

Blakely Island

Ferry to Friday Harbor

Upright Channel

FERRY RD

Port Stanley

Thatcher Pass

Ferry to Fidalgo Island

LOPEZ FARM COTTAGES

LOPEZ ISLAND FARM

CROSS RD

Spencer Spit State Park

Frost Island

HISTORICAL MUSEUM

Lopez

LOPEZ CENTER FOR COMMUNITY AND THE ARTS

LOPEZ LIBRARY

HORSE DRAWN FARM

BAKER VIEW RD

Decatur Island

CHAMBER OF COMMERCE

Hummel Lake

PORT STANLEY RD

San Juan Channel

ISLANDS MARINE CENTER

LOPEZ ISLANDER RESORT

Fisherman Bay

MIDNIGHT'S FARM

Lopez Sound

Trump Island

Decatur

LOPEZ SOUND RD

DILL RD

Center Island

CHANNEL RD

SCHOOL HOUSE RD

AIRPORT RD

GOLF COURSE

Lopez Island

FISHERMAN BAY RD

DAVIS BAY RD

LOPEZ GRANGE

CENTER RD

COUSINS RD

Hunter Bay

SHARK REEF RD

BURT RD

HUNTER BAY RD

SHARK REEF SANCTUARY

RICHARDSON RD

Davis Bay

VISTA RD

Mud Bay

SPERRY RD

Cape St. Mary

Richardson

CAPE ST

Charles Island

MacKaye Harbor

MUD BAY RD

SOUTHEND MARKET & RESTAURANT

CHADWICK HILL

WATMOUGH BAY

Long Island

MACKAYE HARBOR INN

ALECK BAY RD

WATMOUGH HEAD

AGATE BEACH COUNTY PARK

MACKAYE HARBOR RD

Aleck Bay

POINT COLVILLE

Rosario Strait

ICEBERG POINT

0   1 mi

0   1 km

© AVALON TRAVEL

360/468-2251, http://parks.state.wa.us/687/ Spencer-Spit, Mar.-Oct., Discover Pass required for parking) is a popular, well-equipped park with a public beach. In addition to campsites, picnic facilities, and restrooms, there's a concession renting kayaks ($20 first hr., $9 additional hrs.) and bicycles ($25/day).

Among the many great places on the island for wildlife sightings, this is one of the best, with rabbits and deer populating the woods and abundant birds on the water and in the air. The namesake spit creates a brackish lagoon that's a particularly good area for clamming and crabbing. Purchase mandatory fishing licenses at the Islands Marine Center on Fisherman Bay (2793 Fisherman Bay Rd., 360/468-3377) or online (fishhunt. dfw.wa.gov).

Shark Reef Sanctuary

Down on the southwest corner of the island, an easy half-mile hike from a parking area off Shark Reef Road takes you through old-growth forest to **Shark Reef Sanctuary**. When you reach the water a jagged promontory gives you beautiful views of the coast and San Juan Island across the channel. Despite the name, no sharks live here. Instead the main attraction is the abundant seal population usually found lounging on the rocks below, sometimes joined by sea lions and otters. Bring binoculars to get up-close views of the marine mammals, as well as bald eagles who make their nests in the trees above the shore.

Agate Beach County Park

Agate Beach County Park (MacKaye Harbor Rd.), on the south end of Lopez, is a rare stretch of roadside public beach on the island. There's not a lot to it—the only facilities are a picnic table and outhouses—but it provides the simple pleasures of waves crashing on the shore and pretty sunset views over Outer Bay. The beach is mainly rocks and pebbles, but at low tide you can stroll out onto sand.

★ Iceberg Point

Iceberg Point is a 76-acre, publicly owned, protected marine bluff jutting out at the far southern end of the island. On it is a circuit of trails totaling three miles, running past native grasses, rare wildflowers, and 500-year-old Douglas firs. At the waterfront, glacial striations are scored into the bluffs. Stand atop them and you get views that, on a clear day, encompass Mount Baker and the Cascades to the east and the Olympics to the southwest. This is a favorite spot with bird-watchers, and a great place for viewing the sunset.

Iceberg Point is under the control of the Bureau of Land Management, but to reach it you need to follow a path through private property, which feels illicit but is perfectly legal. To get there, park your car in the Agate Beach lot and continue by foot south about 100 yards on MacKaye Harbor Road, past the "End of County Road" sign. Turn right at the driveway with a green metal gate. (There may or may not be a sign there indicating the way to Iceberg Point.) Go around this gate and then another, then head left at the fork in the road. After a few hundred yards you'll be back on public land.

★ Watmough Bay

Watmough Bay, at the southeast end of Lopez, is just as remote as Iceberg Point, and just as beautiful. A pebble beach stretching 200 yards gives access to gentle, sun-warmed waters that make for good swimming in summer. (Note that there is no lifeguard. Don't stray too far from shore or leave kids unattended.) On either side of the beach wooded cliffs surround the bay and frame a view of Mount Baker jutting up over the horizon.

This is also a good spot for hiking. At the south end of the beach, a trail leads up to the ridge of **Watmough Head.** At the beach's north end, and also from the parking lot, you can join a trail making the steep ascent up **Chadwick Hill,** from where you get a vista over the bay. If you continue a half mile past the parking lot entrance along Watmough

The Lopez Wave

It's a tradition and a habit among Lopez residents: when they pass someone on the street—whether they're in a car, on a bike, or on foot—they give a little wave. It can vary from the lift of an index finger (for strangers) to a vigorous hand flap (for friends and family).

The gesture is part-and-parcel with Lopez's self-proclaimed identity as "the friendly isle," and to outsiders it may feel a little contrived. Bear in mind, though, that this is something locals do even when the tourists aren't looking. It's a genuine by-product of a small, close-knit community, and if they include visitors in the ritual, all the better. So, when you arrive here, be prepared to do some waving. It's the friendly thing to do.

Head Road you reach the **Point Colville** trail. (Trail access is marked by trees arranged in a tepee formation.) The flat two-mile loop takes you around a marsh and past a small, rocky public beach.

Watmough Bay is managed by the Bureau of Land Management. To get here, take Mud Bay Road down into the southeast spur of the island, then turn south (right) onto Aleck Bay Road for half a mile, to where Watmough Head Road branches off to the left. Follow this road through the woods for a mile until, at the base of a hill, you reach a "Watmough Bay" sign marking a driveway on the left that leads to a parking lot. From the lot it's a flat quarter-mile walk through the woods to reach the bay.

Lopez Island Historical Museum

The **Lopez Island Historical Museum** (28 Washburn Pl., 360/468-2049, http://lopezmuseum.org, May-Sept. Wed.-Sun. noon-4pm, donation requested) in Lopez Village has the sort of hodgepodge collection that's typical of such small-town institutions—a mix of old farming equipment, fishing gear, and photos from yesteryear. There's usually a special exhibit focusing on a particular aspect of life on the island, such as "Lopez Women." You can also pick up a map of historic island homes (also available on the museum's website, along with background information on each house featured).

Watmough Bay

Farms

Lopez is blanketed with farmland, much of it devoted to small, family-run operations practicing organic, sustainable agriculture. While these are working farms, many of them are happy to give tours provided you make arrangements in advance. The handy **Lopez Island Farm Products Guide,** available at the historical museum, at the chamber of commerce, and online (www.lopezclt.org/farm-products-guide), provides a map, descriptions, and contact information for some 30 such farms, including orchards, livestock ranches, and a goat dairy.

Some places have self-serve farm stands, among them **Horse Drawn Farm** (2823 Port Stanley Rd., 360/468-3486), where, just like the name says, produce and livestock are raised the old-fashioned way, using animal-powered implements. The farm's tours, by advance arrangement, are a hit with animal-loving kids. Drop by the farm stand at **Lopez Island Farm** (193 Cross Rd., 360/468-4620, www.lopezislandfarm.com) and you're likely to meet pasture-raised pigs and sheep. In addition to its farm stand, **Midnight's Farm** (3042 Center Rd., 360/468-3269, www.midnightsfarm.com) has a bakery, yoga studio, and guesthouse for rent.

ENTERTAINMENT AND EVENTS
Nightlife

For nightlife you have two options, both local hangouts with friendly, somewhat divey atmospheres. **The Tiki Lounge** (2864 Fisherman Bay Rd., 360/468-2233, www.lopezfun.com) at the Lopez Islander Resort has half a dozen beers on tap and two pool tables; there's live music or karaoke some weekends. Just down the road, **The Galley Restaurant and Lounge** (3365 Fisherman Bay Rd., 360/468-2713, www.thegalleylopez.com) also has a pool table, along with a couple of old arcade games and a surprisingly long wine list.

Festivals and Events

Sleepy Lopez livens things up with a few annual celebrations and cultural activities. The **Lopez Center for Community and the Arts** (204 Village Rd., 360/468-2203, www.lopezcenter.org), in the village, is the main performing arts venue, staging occasional music, theater, and community-related events.

Just east of town, housed in a red school-house dating from 1894, **Lopez Library** (2225 Fisherman Bay Rd., 360/468-2265, http://lopezlibrary.org) is the island's standout civic institution. It's a comfortable space with a surprisingly deep collection, and it hosts frequent lectures, readings, and concerts. On the south end of the island the 1918 **Lopez Grange** (452 Richardson Rd.) is a general-use space where there are occasional musical performances and dances.

A rite of spring is the annual **Tour de Lopez,** held the last Saturday in April. The noncompetitive bicycle ride has four routes to choose from, with distances of 5, 12, 17, and 31 miles. Registration is through the **Lopez Chamber of Commerce** (360/468-4664, www.lopezisland.com).

The biggest day of the year on Lopez is the **Fourth of July,** which is celebrated with a morning fun run (register through the chamber of commerce website), a parade, a barbecue, and one of Washington's biggest fireworks displays, set off over Fisherman Bay. It's the one day when the island can feel crowded and hectic; if you're planning on being here, be aware that ferries fill up far in advance of departure, and lodging needs to be booked well ahead of time.

SHOPPING

The island's shopping is concentrated in **Lopez Village.** Hours and days of operation for virtually every shop are seasonal and change frequently, sometimes based on the owner's whims on a given day. On the upside, the village is small enough that no place is more than a five-minute walk from anyplace else.

The primary place to pick up local art is **Chimera Gallery** (211 Lopez Rd., 360/468-3265, www.chimeragallery.com), an artists' cooperative where you can browse an array of island-made arts and crafts, including paintings, ceramics, and jewelry. Local art is also frequently for sale at **Lopez Center for Community and the Arts** (204 Village Rd., 360/468-2203, www.lopezcenter.org).

Stock up on reading material at **Lopez Bookshop** (211 Lopez Rd., 360/468-2132, www.lopezbookshop.com), where the owners are happy to help you sort through a diverse selection of new and used titles.

SPORTS AND RECREATION
★ Bicycling

One of the most popular activities on Lopez is cycling the **30-mile loop** around the island. Except for a climb coming off the ferry dock, the going is easy, with occasional rolling hills. Hop off and do some exploring on the way. It can take getting used to—a little like waving to everyone you pass on the road—but the local practice is to leave bikes unlocked.

The island has three primary resources for bike rentals. **Lopez Bicycle Works** (2864 Fisherman Bay Rd., 360/468-2847, www.lopezbicycleworks.com) has a large and varied selection, with most bikes renting for $7/hour, $30/day, and tandems, recumbent bikes, and

trailer carts also available. The fleet is large enough that reservations aren't necessary, but you do have to call ahead if you want your bike waiting for you at the ferry (for a $5 fee). It operates May-September.

Village Cycles (9 Old Post Rd., 360/469-4013, www.villagecycles.net), a full-service bike shop in Lopez Village, has the advantage of being open year-round. Basic rental rates, including the charge for ferry delivery, are the same as Lopez Bicycle Works, with higher-end hybrids and performance bikes available for $10-13/hour and electric bikes for $16. Reservations are recommended, especially on summer weekends. It also offers two-, four-, and six-hour guided tours.

You can also rent bikes from the stand on the beach at Spencer Spit State Park run by **Outdoor Adventure Center** (425-883-9039, http://outdooradventurecenter.com). Rates are $25/day, and it's open daily June-August and on weekends in May and September.

Kayaking

As elsewhere in the San Juans, sea kayaking is a great way to get out on the water here. The primary launch locations are Odlin County Park, Spencer Spit Sate Park, Fisherman Bay, MacKaye Harbor, and Hunter Bay.

kayaks at Spencer Spit State Park

Rent kayaks at **Lopez Kayaks** (2864 Fisherman Bay Rd., 360/468-2847, www.lopezkayaks.com, May-Sept.), which operates out of the same offices as Lopez Bicycle Works at the Islander Resort on Fisherman Bay. Singles are $20-30/hour, $40-60/day, doubles $30-35/hour, $60-70/day. They will deliver kayaks anywhere on the island.

The stand on the beach at Spencer Spit State Park run by **Outdoor Adventure Center** (425/883-9039, http://outdooradventurecenter.com) rents kayaks. Rates are: single $20/first hour, $9/additional hours, $55/day; double $25/first hour, $11/additional hours, $75/day. The stand is open daily June-August and on weekends in May and September. Three-hour guided tours are $79 per person.

For a range of tour options, check with **Cascadia Kayak Tours** (135 Lopez Rd., 360/468-3008, http://cascadiakayaks.com). Half-day tours are $69 per person, full-day tours are $99, and they also offer multiday, all-inclusive trips where you camp on small outer islands ($330/two days, $490/three days).

Whale-Watching

Outer Island Excursions (360/376-3711, www.outerislandx.com), operating out of Orcas Island, picks up passengers for its whale-watching tours at Lopez Islander Resort on Fisherman Bay. Rates are $109 per person for a three-to-five-hour tour.

FOOD

Whether you're looking for fine dining or groceries, most of your food choices are in Lopez Village. Hours for restaurants in the off-season are casual; management may close early if business is slow or take days off to tend to other priorities.

Coffee

Next door to Holly B's Bakery in the heart of the village, **Lopez Coffee Shop** (Lopez Plaza, 360/468-3533, http://lopezcoffeeshop.com, daily 7am-5pm, $2-10) serves up bagels and soup along with its espresso drinks. The other option for a caffeine fix is **Isabel's Espresso** (308 Lopez Rd., 360/468-4114, http://isabelsespresso.com, daily 7am-5pm, $2-10), which has a fun, funky atmosphere and a deck looking out over the village.

American

A four-decade-old Lopez institution, ★ **Holly B's Bakery** (Lopez Plaza, 360/468-2133, www.hollybsbakery.com, June-Aug. Wed.-Sun. 7am-4pm, May and Sept. Thurs.-Sun. 7am-4pm, Oct.-Apr. days variable, $2-10) makes a wide assortment of first-class baked goods. Cinnamon rolls and ham-and-gruyere croissants are especially popular, but everything from pizzas to rye bread to marionberry cheesecake bars is consistently satisfying.

Located in the Homestead Building at the south end of the village, **Vortex Cafe and Juice Bar** (135 Lopez Rd., 360/468-4740, www.vortexonlopez.com, Wed.-Sat. 10am-3pm, $4-11) serves primarily vegetarian wraps and salads with a Southwestern accent, along with fresh-made fruit and vegetable juices, coffee, tea, and a soup of the day. Most of the business is takeaway, but there's limited seating both inside and out.

The Galley Restaurant and Lounge (3365 Fisherman Bay Rd., 360/468-2713, www.thegalleylopez.com, daily 8am-8:30pm, $11-30), located by the marinas along Fisherman Bay, is an unpretentious, three-squares-a-day kind of place that serves oversized omelets for breakfast, double bacon cheeseburgers for lunch, and three kinds of steak (including chicken-fried) for dinner. There's outdoor seating with views of the bay, and a private dock in case you're arriving by boat.

Eclectic

High-end prepared foods, suitable for a fancy picnic or dinner on your deck, are on the offer in Lopez Village at **Vita's Wildly Delicious** (77 Village Rd., 360/468-4268, http://vitasonlopez.com, May-Sept. Tues.-Sat. 11am-5pm, Fri. 11am-8pm, Sat. 11am-3pm, occasional off-season opening hours, $10-25). Deli cases are filled with everything you need to make a satisfying meal—the changing selection often includes shrimp cakes, Asian noodle salad, and grilled flank steak, among the dozens of options, all prepared in-house. There's limited seating indoors and out, but business is primarily takeaway. Vita's also has a good selection of wine.

Haven Restaurant & Bar (9 Old Post Rd., 360/468-3272, www.lopezhaven.com, Wed.-Sat. noon-3pm and 5pm-8pm, $14-19) serves bar-and-grill menu items with creative touches, such as Asian noodles and burrata cheese with heirloom tomatoes, at prices that feel like a bargain by island standards. The waterfront location has the village's best sunset views.

Lopez gets its own hip farm-to-market restaurant with **Ursa Minor** (210 Lopez Rd., 360/622-2730, www.ursaminorlopez.com, Thurs.-Sun. 5pm-9pm, $21-42). The painstakingly prepared small plates take full advantage of the bounty from the island's farms. While the most out-there options (raw lamb heart with spruce tips) may have you doing double takes, there are enough more conventional dishes to satisfy most diners.

Mexican

The south end of the island has one establishment for both groceries and sit-down meals, **Southend Market and Restaurant** (3024 Mud Bay Rd., 360/468-2315, www.southendmarket.net, daily 8am-8pm, $12-17). Wednesday-Sunday the restaurant at the back of the store serves a full menu of Mexican classics—tacos, burritos, enchiladas, fajitas—for lunch and dinner.

Markets and Groceries

Lopez Village Market (162 Weeks Rd., 360/468-2266, http://lopezvillagemarket.com, daily 7:30am-7pm) is a full-service supermarket, complete with a beer and wine department and an ATM. A couple of blocks south in the village, **Blossom Grocery** (295 Village Rd., 360/468-2204, www.blossomgrocery.com, daily 9am-7pm) specializes in organic foods, including local produce and meats. For a wide selection from the island's bounty, head

to the **farmers market** (www.lopezfarmersmarket.com), held mid-May through mid-September next door to the Lopez Center for Community and the Arts (204 Village Rd.) on Saturdays 10am-2pm.

On the sleepy southern end of the island, pick up provisions at **Southend Market and Restaurant** (3024 Mud Bay Rd., 360/468-2315, www.southendmarket.net, daily 8am-8pm). The selection includes lots of basic supplies—sort of like a well-stocked convenience store—and a deli counter with sandwiches and other prepared foods.

ACCOMMODATIONS

While tourism is a big part of Lopez's economy, the focus is more on vacation home owners than travelers, as indicated by the fact that there are fewer than 100 guest rooms on the island available for rent by the night. Your choices boil down to one motel-like resort, a couple of B&Bs, and numerous single-unit cabins, apartments, and rental homes.

Many of the options in the last category require a minimum one-week stay, but they'll sometimes waive the requirement in order to fill vacancies—it's worth checking. Find listings through **Lopez Village Properties** (360/468-5055, www.lopezvillageproperties.com), which manages two dozen homes, with rates ranging from $125 to $475 a night; **Vacasa** (503/345-9399, www.vacasa.com), a rental agent with properties throughout the Pacific Northwest; and the **Lopez Island Chamber of Commerce** (360/468-4664, www.lopezisland.com), the website of which has information on about a dozen cabins and cottages, most renting for under $200 a night.

$100-150

Lopez Lodge (37 Weeks Point Rd., 360/468-2816, www.lopezlodge.com, $85-155) offers three comfortable guest rooms in a building behind a cluster of shops in Lopez Village. All of the rooms have private decks and TVs (not the norm on the San Juans), and the largest one has a full kitchen.

$150-200

The largest lodging on the island is the **Lopez Islander Resort** (2864 Fisherman Bay Rd., 360/468-2233, http://lopezfun.com, $139-179 d), with 30 rooms in a two-level, motel-style structure. The location is first-rate, overlooking Fisherman Bay, where the resort has its own marina with slips for rent. Amenities include a restaurant and lounge, bike and kayak rentals, a hot tub, and the only pool on the island. Don't take the name "resort" to mean luxury: rooms are well worn, with some retro charm, and while service on a good day is friendly, you aren't going to feel pampered here. The best rooms are on the 2nd floor, with decks that provide views of the bay.

Located between the ferry landing and the village, **Lopez Farm Cottages & Tent Camping** (555 Fisherman Bay Rd., 360/468-3555, www.lopezfarmcottages.com, $185-225 d) has five cozy, two-person cottages done in a Scandinavian-inspired design, along with two furnished tents on carpeted wood platforms ($98) and a dozen tent sites ($48-52). You have minimal interaction with the proprietors here—you pay in advance, do self-check-in and checkout, and get breakfast delivered to your door in a basket. What you will see lots of are sheep in the adjacent pasture.

$200-250

Edenwild Inn (132 Lopez Rd., 360/468-3238, www.edenwildinn.com, $195-270 d) is a hybrid between a bed-and-breakfast and a small hotel. Set on a large plot in the heart of Lopez Village, its modern, Victorian-style building has the atmosphere of a quaint house but was built as a commercial lodging, meaning it lacks the quirks of a more typical home-to-B&B conversion—which can be both a plus and a minus. The eight guest rooms are all comfortable and individually appointed, some with fireplaces.

For a secluded stay at the south end of the island, try **MacKaye Harbor Inn** (949 MacKaye Harbor Rd., 360/468-2253, www.mackayeharborinn.com, $185-265 d), near Agate Beach and Iceberg Point. It's an old-school B&B with five guest rooms in a 1904 farmhouse across the road from the water. Along with a full breakfast, guests get free use of bikes for touring the island. One downside of the location is that you're nine miles from the island's best dining options in Lopez Village.

Camping

Lopez has four choices for camping, two in public parks and two on privately managed property. The parks don't have showers, but you can shower at the public restrooms near Lopez Village Market and at Islands Marine Center on Fisherman Bay.

Odlin County Park (148 Ferry Rd., 360/468-2496, www.sanjuanco.com/495/Lopez-Island, $22-27, $7 reservation fee), a mile south of the ferry landing, has 30 sites, including 10 beach sites. They're available year-round but can be reserved only in summer; reservations can be made up to three months in advance on the park website or by phone. Sites have picnic tables and fire rings, with firewood available for purchase.

Spencer Spit State Park (Spencer Spit State Park Rd., 360/468-2251, http://parks.state.wa.us/687/Spencer-Spit, $25-35), four miles from the ferry landing, has 37 tent spaces, including 7 walk-in beach sites. The park is open March-October, and you can reserve sites May 15-September 15, online at http://washington.goingtocamp.com or by phone at 888/226-7688.

Lopez Farm Cottages & Tent Camping (555 Fisherman Bay Rd., 360/468-3555, www.lopezfarmcottages.com, $48-52) has 12 walk-in tent sites in a wooded area surrounded by fields and sheep pasture. Amenities include a table, hammock, and Adirondack chairs at every site, free coffee in the morning, and showers. The downside is that this is the only camping facility on the island that isn't located by the water. Note that the facility is geared toward couples and singles looking for a quiet getaway. No kids under 14, pets, RVs, or non-acoustic music are allowed.

Lopez Islander Resort (2864 Fisherman Bay Rd., 360/468-2233, http://lopezfun.com) has tent camping ($28) in an open field and the island's only RV sites ($38) in a wooded area, both adjacent to the resort's other facilities along Fisherman Bay. Coin-operated showers are next to the pool and hot tub (which you can use with a $6 day pass).

INFORMATION

The office of the **Lopez Island Chamber of Commerce** (6 Old Post Rd., 360/468-4664, www.lopezisland.com) in Lopez Village holds variable hours—call to check if it's open. There's always a rack with maps and brochures out front.

TRANSPORTATION
Getting There

The 30-square-mile island is the first stop for the ferry coming from Anacortes. The **state ferry** (206/464-6400, www.wsdot.wa.gov/Ferries) runs between Anacortes and Lopez Island about 10 times a day, from about 6am-11pm. The trip takes 50 minutes. Fares are $46 per car and driver, $13.50 for each additional passenger and for walk-ons. There's a $4 additional charge for a walk-on with a bicycle. Fares are only charged in one direction, from Anacortes to Lopez. The trip back is free. You can reserve a place on this ferry up to two months in advance through the system's website or by phone. Although places are set aside for vehicles without reservations, you may have to wait for several ferries to come and go before you can get a place if you haven't reserved.

Getting Around

From late June-Labor Day, **San Juan Transit** (360/378-8887, www.sanjuantransit.com) has a bus running Friday-Sunday between the ferry landing and the Southend Market and Restaurant, with stops at points in between. (Note that not every bus makes every stop.) There are six buses a day, the earliest departing the landing at 9am, the latest finishing service at the landing at 6pm. Fares are $5 one-way or $15 for a day pass. Exact change is required.

North Cascades

Look for ★ to find recommended
sights, activities, dining, and lodging.

Highlights

★ **Heather Meadows Trails:** Heather Meadows is a spectacular driving destination and the starting point for beautiful hiking trails ranging from easy strolls to strenuous treks (page 285).

★ **North Cascades Highway (Newhalem to Washington Pass):** The road through the national park is the state's finest mountain drive (page 290).

★ **Ross Lake:** This lake running up to the Canadian border is tough to get to and largely undeveloped—and that's where its great allure lies (page 293).

★ **Shafer Museum:** The sculpture-like beauty of the old mining and agricultural machinery makes this establishment a cut above other small-town museums (page 300).

★ **Cross-Country Skiing the Methow Valley:** Ski this network of more than 120 miles of trails, the most of any cross-country skiing area in the United States (page 302).

★ **Stehekin:** At the northern end of 50-mile-long Lake Chelan, this remote little community is a beautiful spot at arm's length from the rest of the world (page 310).

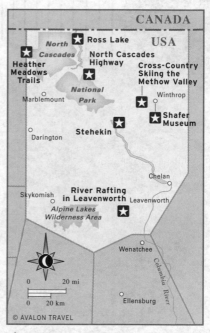

★ **River Rafting in Leavenworth:** The Wenatchee River running past Leavenworth is Washington's top rafting destination (page 320).

The first White explorers to visit the North Cascades dubbed them the American Alps. The nickname stuck, for good reason.

This part of the Cascade Range is filled with jagged, snowcapped peaks that form rows of spires across the skyline. For serious climbers it's a playground filled with substantial challenges and magnificent rewards. Even from a car seat the view is spectacular.

Route 2, which serves as the region's southern border, runs east from Everett (just north of Seattle) over Stevens Pass to Wenatchee, on the banks of the Columbia River near the middle of the state. From here north to the Canadian border and beyond there's not another road across the Cascades that's open year-round. This is truly one of the wildest places in the United States. At its heart is the 684,000-acre North Cascades National Park Complex, which consists of the park and bordering Ross Lake and Lake Chelan National Recreational Areas. Almost all of it is protected land, surrounded by hundreds of thousands of acres of designated wilderness and national forest.

To the east side of the mountains, three vacation destinations are extremely popular with Washington residents. Along Route 20 in the Methow Valley is Winthrop, a former mining town that's taken on a second life as a Western-themed village ideally situated for travelers who have just driven through the national park. A little farther south, the southern end of Lake Chelan is a classic resort area where families come to swim, water-ski, and bask in the sun. Southwest of that, along Route 2, the town of Leavenworth has done itself up to resemble a Bavarian alpine village. Visitors flock here to eat sausage and drink beer, but once you get past the novelty, the real appeal, as elsewhere, is the natural beauty.

PLANNING YOUR TIME

Unless you're a road-hardened cyclist, a car is essential for getting around the North Cascades. Some portions of the area are popular day trips from elsewhere in the state. The Mountain Loop Highway is an easy drive from Seattle, and many visitors to Mount Baker are day-trippers from Bellingham.

A popular and effective way to explore

Previous: Diablo Lake in North Cascades National Park; Mount Baker area. **Above:** Stehekin's Red Bus.

North Cascades

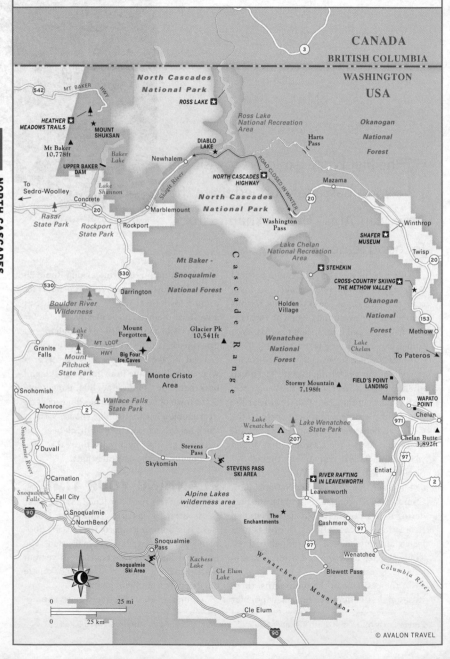

CANADA
BRITISH COLUMBIA

WASHINGTON
USA

North Cascades
National Park

ROSS LAKE

Ross Lake
National Recreation
Area

Okanogan

National

Forest

Harts
Pass

HEATHER
MEADOWS TRAILS

MOUNT
SHUKSAN

MT BAKER

542

Mt Baker
10,778ft

Baker
Lake

DIABLO
LAKE

Newhalem

Lake
Shannon

NORTH CASCADES
HIGHWAY

Mazama

ROAD CLOSED IN WINTER

20

To
Sedro-Woolley

UPPER BAKER
DAM

Concrete

Marblemount

North Cascades
National Park

Washington
Pass

Winthrop

SHAFER
MUSEUM

Twisp

20

Rasar
State Park

Rockport
State Park

Rockport

20

Mt Baker -
Snoqualmie

Lake Chelan
National Recreation
Area

STEHEKIN

CROSS-COUNTRY SKIING
THE METHOW VALLEY

530

Darrington

National Forest

Holden
Village

Okanogan

National

Forest

153

Methow

Boulder River
Wilderness

Lake
22

MT LOOP

Mount
Forgotten

Glacier Pk
10,541ft

Wenatchee

National

Forest

Lake
Chelan

To Pateros

Granite
Falls

Mount
Pilchuck
State Park

HWY

Big Four
Ice Caves

Monte Cristo
Area

Stormy Mountain
7,198ft

FIELD'S POINT
LANDING

Snohomish

Wallace Falls
State Park

Manson

WAPATO
POINT

Monroe

2

Lake
Wenatchee

Lake Wenatchee
State Park

Chelan

971

Duvall

Snoqualmie River

Stevens
Pass

2

207

Chelan Butte
3,892ft

Carnation

Skykomish

STEVENS PASS
SKI AREA

Entiat

97

Snoqualmie
Falls

Fall City

Snoqualmie

NorthBend

90

Alpine Lakes
wilderness area

The
Enchantments

RIVER RAFTING
IN LEAVENWORTH

Leavenworth

Cashmere

97

2

Wenatchee

Columbia River

Snoqualmie
Pass

Snoqualmie
Ski Area

Kachess
Lake

Cle Elum
Lake

97

Blewett Pass

Wenatchee

Mountains

0   25 mi

0   25 km

Cle Elum

90

© AVALON TRAVEL

more of the region is to follow the **Cascade Loop,** a circular route that, traveling clockwise starting from the Seattle area, takes you through North Cascades National Park on Route 20, continues south through the Methow Valley to Chelan, and heads back west on Route 2 with a stop in Leavenworth. Trip-planning ideas and links to travel resources along the loop can be found at **www. cascadeloop.com.** The trip can be made late spring-early fall; at the first sign of snow portions of Route 20 close for the season.

The region is busiest in summer, when you can hike, bike, kayak, and camp surrounded by spectacular mountain scenery, but it's also a winter destination. Mount Baker, at the western edge of the range, has challenging slopes especially popular with snowboarders. The Methow Valley has an extensive network of cross-country ski trails. And Leavenworth makes the most of the Christmas season with an impressive display of lights and a month's worth of festivities.

Because of the seasonal nature of the region, it's valuable to plan ahead. Accommodations, whether you're camping or staying at a luxury lodge, are in high demand during the glorious summer months.

Mountain Loop Highway

About an hour north of Seattle via I-5, the Mountain Loop Highway (not to be confused with the much larger Cascade Loop) is the easiest way to get a taste of the North Cascades on a day trip from the city. It doesn't take you deep into the mountains, but It's a beautiful wooded drive. The entire loop, which runs through the towns of Granite Falls and Arlington to the west and Darrington to the east, is 95 miles long; the main attraction is the scenic 54-mile segment on the loop's south and east sides, between Granite Falls and Darrington. The road goes through a corner of the massive Mount Baker-Snoqualmie National Forest, with turnouts along the way for camping, picnic sites, and some wonderful mountain hiking trails.

DRIVING THE LOOP

Heading east out of **Granite Falls,** the road is paved for the first 30 miles as it follows the South Fork of the Stillaguamish River to its headwaters at Barlow Pass. At about the 11-mile point you reach the tiny town of **Verlot** (pop. 285), which marks the entry into **Mount Baker-Snoqualmie National Forest.** Over the next 19 miles you pass turnoffs for more than 10 campgrounds and 20 trails, which constitute the primary recreational sites along the loop.

At **Barlow Pass** the road turns north and switches from pavement to gravel, and it remains that way for the next 14 miles. It's impassible in snow and is closed throughout the winter, but when the weather is fair you won't have trouble making the drive in a standard road car—you just have to be patient enough to travel 15 to 25 miles an hour the whole way, and be ready to pull over if you encounter traffic from the other direction on the many narrow stretches. Going slow shouldn't be a problem; the curving road is the highlight of the loop. It has the scenic virtues of a hiking trail, with old-growth forest, creeks, lakes, rocky bluffs, and looming peaks all visible from your car seat. You're deep in the woods here.

The last nine miles to **Darrington** are paved. From there the loop turns west, out of the national forest and into a wide valley bisected by the North Fork of the Stillaguamish River. For the rest of the way back to Granite Falls the landscape is less spectacular but still pleasant, filled with farmland, big red barns, lumber mills, patches of clear-cut, and regenerating stands of trees. Along the way you hit **Arlington** (pop. 18,000), by far the largest town on the loop and the place with the most options if you want to stop for a meal. You can pick up I-5 here instead of taking the final segment of the loop back to Granite Falls.

You can also travel the most scenic stretches of the loop as part of your route to or from North Cascades National Park. North from Darrington, Route 530 intersects with Route 20, the road that runs through the park.

HIKING

There are more than 300 miles of trails accessible from the Mountain Loop Highway, ranging from multiday backwoods climbs to comfortable strolls leading to waterfall viewpoints. Most of the trailheads are located in the southern part of the loop, between Verlot and Barlow Pass, and the most popular of them can get crowded in summer. For less congestion, visit on a weekday. The parking areas at the trailheads have a history of break-ins, so don't leave any valuables in your car.

The trailhead parking areas require a **Northwest Forest Pass** ($5 day pass, $30 annual pass). Buy it online (www.discovernw.org/store) or at the **Forest Service Centers** in Verlot (33515 Mountain Loop Hwy., 360/691-7791, June-Sept. Thurs.-Mon. 8am-4pm, Oct.-May Sat.-Sun. 8am-4pm) and Darrington (1405 Emens Ave. N., 360/436-1155, Mon.-Sat. 8am-4:30pm). Annual passes are good on all national forest land in Washington and Oregon. The Discover Pass used for state parks isn't accepted.

Mount Pilchuck

Just east of Verlot, 5,324-foot **Mount Pilchuck** (360-902-8844, http://parks.state.wa.us/548) is a challenging day hike that offers dramatic 360-degree views of the Cascades and Puget Sound from the summit. Reach the trail by taking the loop highway a mile east of Verlot's Forest Service Center and turning onto Forest Road 42. It's a seven-mile trip up the rock-strewn road to the park entrance at an abandoned ski area. Allow five hours for the six-mile out-and-back hike, and be prepared for a 2,200-foot gain in elevation and some boulder hopping at the end. At the summit there's a restored fire lookout station with interpretive plaques that identify the surrounding terrain. Note that Mount Pilchuck is part of the state park system, but the trailhead parking area isn't. You still need a Northwest Forest Pass to park there.

Heather Lake and Lake 22

A little farther east are two popular trails

Lake 22 trail off the Mountain Loop Highway

The Mountain Loop's Ghost Town

In 1889 veins of gold and silver were discovered east of Barlow Pass, giving rise to the little boomtown of **Monte Cristo.** A railroad line, funded in part by John D. Rockefeller, was constructed running west from Monte Cristo over the pass, down the canyon created by the South Fork of the Stillaguamish River, through the town of Granite Falls, and on to Everett along Puget Sound. The depression of the 1890s hobbled investors, and the ore never materialized in the quantity or quality anticipated. By 1907 the mines had gone bust.

The train line continued to run, as the natural beauty of the area began attracting tourists. Business flourished in the 1920s, with hotels erected catering to a wealthy clientele, but the Great Depression brought an end to Monte Cristo's second life as a leisure destination. The railroad shuttered in 1936, and the old railroad grade became the scenic highway that now constitutes the southern segment of the mountain loop.

You can explore the area by driving 19 miles east from Verlot to Barlow Pass, where the four-mile side road to Monte Cristo begins. Floods have made it impassable to cars, but it's a popular place for mountain bikers and hikers in the summer, and cross-country skiers and snowmobilers in the winter. You'll find a few remnants of the ghost town of Monte Cristo, most notably the fireplace and foundation of the Big Four Inn, a luxurious resort that burned to the ground in 1949. Check at the Forest Service offices in Darrington or Verlot for current road and bridge conditions.

Glacier Basin Trail is a steep, rocky two-mile hike from Monte Cristo into nearby high country. The trail follows an old railroad grade for the first half mile, then climbs past Glacier Falls, around Mystery Hill, and into gorgeous Glacier Basin, gaining 1,300 feet in elevation. The route passes all sorts of rusting mining equipment, pieces of the cable tramway, and old mine shafts.

leading to lakes. The subalpine forests and meadows are as much the attractions as the clear mountain lake on the four-mile round-trip hike to **Heather Lake.** To reach the trailhead, take Forest Road 42 for 1.5 miles, then hike up an old logging road before reaching the forest and then open meadows. Allow three hours; elevation gain is 1,100 feet.

The hike to **Lake 22** is a little longer (2.7 miles one-way) and a little steeper (1,400-foot elevation gain) than the Heather Lake trail, with a few patches of jagged rubble to cross along the way, but it's also a little prettier. The trail starts from a parking area just off the loop road two miles east of the Verlot Service Center. It passes through old-growth hemlock and cedar forest, with several waterfalls along the way, and then enters a clearing with mountain views. You go back into woodland for a stretch before reaching Lake 22 at the base of Mount Pilchuck's steep northern face. The lake is circled by a path that extends the hike an additional 1.1 miles. Allow four hours for the whole trip.

Big Four Ice Caves

The trail to the **Big Four Ice Caves** is the most popular on the loop, both because it's easy and because it has a novel attraction—but that attraction also makes it dangerous if you ignore safety regulations. The two-mile round-trip hike starts 26 miles from Granite Falls at the Big Four Picnic Area. It begins on boardwalks over a beaver-created marsh, and then heads through a dense forest and across the South Fork of the Stillaguamish River to ice caves and a view of 6,135-foot Big Four Mountain. The caves, which are created when water channels under a small glacier, are prone to collapse in hot summers; in 2011 and 2015 hikers who disregarded the warning signs were killed when the ice gave way.

Goat Lake

Along the gravel road 3.5 miles north of Barlow Pass is the turnoff for **Goat Lake Trail.** At 10.4 miles round-trip it's a full-day excursion, but it's relatively easygoing and suitable for the whole family, with a varied landscape that includes a creek, waterfalls, wild berries, and lovely woods. For much of the way there are two parallel trails, Upper Elliot and Lower Elliot, so you can either make it a loop hike or take the same way out and back. Lower Elliot is more scenic; Upper Elliot, which follows an old road, is a flatter, quicker trip. Your destination, Goat Lake, is one of the largest and most picturesque lakes in the region, surrounded by snowcapped mountains.

North Fork Sauk Falls

If you're driving through and want a quick blast of natural beauty, make a stop at **North Fork Sauk Falls.** At about the midpoint of the unpaved portion of the Mountain Loop Highway, seven miles north of Barlow Pass near the Bedal Campground, turn onto Sloan Creek Road and take it for a mile. You'll come to a trailhead for the quarter-mile path that descends to a viewpoint for the falls, which make a thunderous 45-foot drop.

FOOD

Three towns on the loop are your resources for picnic supplies or a sit-down meal. Granite Falls and Darrington have the most convenient locations, at either end of the portion of the loop running through the national forest, while Arlington is the biggest of the three and has the greatest variety of options.

Granite Falls

Fill your stomach and your gas tank in one stop at **Mark's Country Store** (108 W. Stanley St., 360/548-3462, www.markscountrystore.com, daily 7am-8pm, $7-10), a classic all-purpose place that serves pancakes and eggs in the morning and sandwiches and fries the rest of the day. It also specializes in ice cream treats and has a large selection of beer.

Other options include decent Mexican food in a colorful setting at **Playa Bonita** (206 E. Stanley St., 360/691-3152, www.playabonitarestaurant.com, daily 11am-9pm, $10-21), ribs and brisket at the no-frills **Barbecue Bucket** (402 E. Stanley Ave., 360/691-1215,

Thurs.-Sun. noon-7pm, $9-15), and pizza and Greek food at **Omega Pizza and Pasta** (102 S. Granite Ave., 360/691-4394, daily 11am-9pm, $10-20).

Darrington

Darrington has the fewest dining options of the towns on the loop. The place for your morning coffee and a pastry is **Mountain Loop Books and Coffee** (1085 Darrington St., 360/630-7673, Mon.-Fri. 8am-5pm, Sat. 9am-5pm, Sun. 10am-4pm), where the locals linger to shoot the breeze. For a sit-down meal there's **4 Corners Cafe** (1080 Seeman St., 360/436-9757, daily 8am-5:30pm, $8-13), which has a straightforward menu of sandwiches, soups, and salads, with breakfast served all day. The highlights at the hole-in-the-wall **Burger Barn** (1020 Emens Ave. N., 360/436-2070, daily 11am-7pm, $6-11) are satisfying shakes in a dozen flavors.

Arlington

Arlington is in the less scenic northwestern corner of the Mountain Loop Highway, 13 miles north of Granite Falls and 28 miles west of Darrington, but if you're traveling the full circle it makes sense to plan for a meal here at either the beginning or the end of your tour.

For burgers and shakes, stop by **Nutty's Junkyard Grill** (6717 204th St. NE, 360/403-7538, Tues.-Sun. 11am-9pm, $7-9), a cute automotive-themed restaurant where everything is prepared fresh to order. **Moose Creek BBQ** (3617 172nd St. NE, 360/651-2523, www.moosecreekbbq.com, Sun.-Thurs. 11am-7pm, Fri.-Sat. 11am-8pm, $11-25) draws homesick Texans with its slow-smoked meats. Quirky, Tolkien-themed **Mirkwood Public House** (117 E. Division St., 360/403-9020, www.mirkwoodshirecafe.com, Mon.-Thurs. 11am-11pm, Fri.-Sat. 11am-1am, Sun. 11am-8pm, $8-14) serves burgers and pizza, with some vegetarian options and good selection of microbrews. It also does tattoos and piercings.

For a sophisticated dinner, look to **Bistro San Martin** (231 N. Olympic Ave., 360/474-9229, www.bistrosanmartin.com, Tues.-Sat.

5pm-9pm, $18-44). A menu consisting primarily of steaks and seafood is prepared with finesse that goes well beyond what you'd expect from a small-town restaurant.

CAMPING

The Forest Service operates 14 campgrounds ($14-24) along the Mountain Loop. You can make reservations six months in advance at www.recreation.gov ($9 fee) or by calling 877/444-6777 ($10 fee). Campgrounds are generally open mid-May-September.

Neighboring **Turlo** and **Verlot** campgrounds near the Verlot Service Center are open year-round and are nicely situated along the South Fork of the Stillaguamish River. Seven miles east of the service center is another good riverside option, **Red Bridge Campground.** Eighteen miles south of Darrington, **Bedal Campground** puts you just a mile from the short trail to beautiful North Fork Sauk Falls.

INFORMATION

The main information resources for the Mountain Loop Highway are the two **Forest Service Centers,** one east of Granite Falls in **Verlot** (33515 Mountain Loop Hwy., 360/691-7791, June-Sept. Thurs.-Mon. 8am-4pm, Oct.-May Sat.-Sun. 8am-4pm), the other in **Darrington** (1405 Emens Ave. N., 360/436-1155, Mon.-Sat. 8am-4:30pm). As well as selling trailhead parking passes, the service centers have maps and brochures, and rangers there can provide hiking recommendations and information about road and trail conditions. Your online resource is the **National Forest Service** website, www.fs.fed.us—but for up-to-the-minute information you're better served by calling one of the service centers or visiting in person.

TRANSPORTATION

From the Puget Sound area to the west you reach the Mountain Loop Highway via I-5. It's a little less than an hour drive from central Seattle to Granite Falls, and a little under an hour from Bellingham to Arlington. Approaching from the north on Route 20, turn onto Route 530 at Rockport and drive 18 miles south to Darrington, about a 25-minute drive.

Mount Baker

If it weren't for Mount Rainier, Mount Baker would be Washington's iconic peak. At 10,778 feet, the northernmost of the Cascade volcanoes towers over the surrounding hills and has a dramatic presence on the horizon in Bellingham, the San Juans, and Vancouver, British Columbia. From elevated points in Seattle—such as the Space Needle or Columbia Center—you can take it in along with Rainier in one sweeping vista.

The area around Mount Baker is a prime location for outdoor recreational activities. In summer hiking is the main attraction, with scores of trails ranging from scenic strolls to challenging climbs, and there are also river-rafting opportunities. Come winter, the slopes around Mount Baker have the longest ski season in the state, with unpretentious facilities that attract free-spirited snowboarders.

There are a few small towns with minimal facilities and services along the Mount Baker Highway from Bellingham, but because of how the road is situated, Mount Baker is essentially Bellingham's big, spectacular backyard. Many visitors are day-trippers from Bellingham or the surrounding region, and travelers from farther afield looking to spend the night most often bed down there, if they aren't camping.

SIGHTS
Mount Baker Highway

There's one way in to the Mount Baker region:

Mount Baker

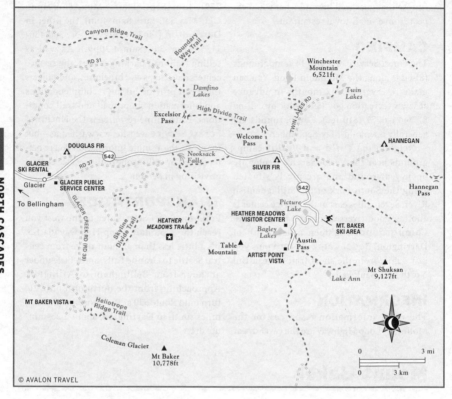

Route 542, also known as Mount Baker Highway, which starts in Bellingham and ends 57 miles to the east at the parking lot for Artist Point. The road is one of the North Cascades' most spectacular drives. Simply making the trip out and back, with a couple of possible detours along the way and a few stops to breathe in the fresh air and linger over the mountain scenery, is a day well spent.

As it works its way east from Bellingham, the Mount Baker Highway goes from suburbs to countryside, passing the little towns of Deming, Kendall, Maple Falls, and Glacier, none of which has a population over 350. Just past Glacier the road enters Mount Baker Wilderness and National Recreation Area. At this point you'll find the **Glacier Public**

Service Center (10091 Mt. Baker Hwy., 360/599-2714, June-mid-Oct. daily 8am-4:30pm, mid-Oct.-May Fri.-Sun. 9am-3pm, hours can vary depending on funding). It's a good idea to stop here to get oriented. You can buy required parking passes, pick up maps and trail descriptions, check out a scale model of the region, and consult with the rangers on staff.

From this point east the road is designated a National Forest Scenic Byway. It starts out as a fairly straight path running through old-growth forest with mild elevation gains. Three-quarters of a mile past the Public Service Center, you hit your first prime detour opportunity: After turning right onto **Glacier Creek Road** (Forest Rd. 39), drive nine miles to reach **Mount Baker Vista.** The pretty drive on mostly paved road takes about 30 minutes each way. At the end, if the weather is clear, you'll get what's arguably the most spectacular road-accessible view of the mountain. (The view from Artist Point is the other contender for this title.) If you venture out a little on the Heliotrope Ridge Trail the vista gets even more impressive.

Back down on Mount Baker Highway, seven miles east from the Public Service Center is the turnoff to the right for Forest Road 33, leading to **Nooksack Falls.** After a two-thirds-of-a-mile descent you reach a parking area just before a bridge over the North Fork of the Nooksack River. Across the road are the falls, which drop 88 feet in two cascades down a narrow crevasse. It's impossible to get a full view of the falls—over the years at least 10 people have died trying. The viewing area is now fenced in, but that won't keep you from getting a good look. Signage explains how the remote falls were once dammed to harness hydroelectric power.

As the road continues east it gets more and more impressive. Curves increase, and through the woods you can catch glimpses of the river running below you and peaks towering above. Then you begin a steeper,

ear-popping climb and emerge from the woods to full mountain views on both sides. At that point you reach the ski area, beyond which the road is closed for most of the year, but when it's clear of snow in summer it continues for another six miles of tight switchbacks. Along the way you circle around **Picture Lake,** which you can get to on a half-mile loop trail. It's one of the most photogenic spots in all of the Cascades, with Mount Shuksan reflected in the water.

Heather Meadows

Mount Baker Highway ends at 5,140-foot **Artist Point,** 23 miles east of Glacier. It's the only alpine area in the North Cascades accessible by car, and the surrounding area, Heather Meadows, delivers incredible vistas, enjoyable picnic sites, and a multitude of hiking trails to explore in late summer. At the handsome stone **Heather Meadows Visitor Center** (no phone, July-Sept. daily 10am-4pm), built in 1940, rangers provide information and advice.

HIKING

More than 200 miles of hiking trails meander through the Mount Baker area, providing enough scenic options to satisfy everyone

Nooksack Falls, off Mount Baker Highway

from high-mileage backpackers to families with small children.

The trailhead parking areas require a **Northwest Forest Pass** (day passes $5, annual pass $30). Buy them online (www.discovernw.org/store) or at the **Glacier Public Service Center** (10091 Mt. Baker Hwy., 360/599-2714, June-mid-Oct. daily 8am-4:30pm, mid-Oct.-May Fri.-Sun. 9am-3pm, hours can vary depending on funding). Annual passes are good on all national forest land in Washington and Oregon.

Trails off Mount Baker Highway

In summer it's tempting—and a perfectly good idea—to drive to the end of the highway and choose one of the trails in Heather Meadows, but there are attractive trails all along the way there as well. They can be less crowded, and in the nonsummer months when the last part of the highway to Heather Meadows is closed they're your only option.

If you take Glacier Creek Road to Mount Baker Vista, you can continue on foot from there along the **Heliotrope Ridge Trail.** It's a demanding 3.7-mile, 2,000-foot ascent amid stretches of forest and meadows to the edge of Coleman Glacier, the largest glacier on Mount Baker. It's impressive to see the blue ice and the moraine—and to hear the glacier groaning. Note that in early summer creeks along the trail can be impassable due to snowmelt.

At the turnoff for Glacier Creek Road you can also access Forest Road 37, which after 13 miles reaches the trailhead for the **Skyline Divide Trail,** a seven-mile round-trip with a 1,500-foot elevation gain. This is another trail with great views of Mount Baker. On clear days you can make out the San Juans to the west and innumerable peaks of the North Cascades to your east. Throughout summer the meadows are awash with wildflowers. Sunsets here are spectacular, though you have to be okay with finishing your hike by moonlight.

A little farther along the highway, where it crosses the North Fork of the Nooksack 1.7 miles east of the Public Service Center, you can take the easy, flat, three-mile out-and-back **Horseshoe Bend Trail.** There are no mountain views here; instead you follow the river through shady woods with undergrowth of moss and ferns.

view of Mount Shuksan from Heather Meadows

★ Heather Meadows Trails

The Heather Meadows area is an immensely popular late-summer hiking destination. From Artist Point, trails branch out in all directions. The easiest is the **Artist Ridge Trail,** a mile-long loop with interpretive signs and views to Mount Rainier on clear days. The first 200 feet are wheelchair-accessible. Another easy path, the **Fire and Ice Trail,** is a paved half-mile loop with views of the Bagley Lakes.

The 8.5-mile round-trip **Lake Ann Trail** begins with a descent before climbing to a pass above one of the Cascades' most beautiful high-country lakes. This is the main approach for climbers of 9,127-foot Mount Shuksan, which rises up before you. The trail often has snow cover well into summer.

For a short but vigorous hike take the 1.5-mile switchback climb up lava cliffs to the appropriately named, flat-topped **Table Mountain.** The unencumbered views of Mount Baker and Mount Shuksan are unique and spectacular.

The 6.5-mile **Chain Lakes Loop** skirts the base of Table Mountain, passes a series of alpine lakes, climbs over Herman Saddle into the Bagley Lakes basin, and then picks up the **Wild Goose Trail** back to Artist Point. It's another high-country classic with beautiful meadows and, at the Herman Saddle high point, 360-degree mountain views.

RIVER RAFTING

Several rafting companies, including **Wild and Scenic River Tours** (360/599-3115, www.wildandscenic.com, $80-90 pp), offer eight-mile white-water trips down the Nooksack from Glacier to Deming June-August. It's a Class II-III trip; the first half has narrow, technically challenging passages, and then things mellow out on the lower river delta, where you can take in a view of Mount Baker and watch for wildlife.

SKIING

Mt. Baker Ski Resort (Mt. Baker Hwy., 52 miles east of Bellingham, 360/734-6771, www. mtbaker.us, $60 weekends, $55 weekdays) is usually open from November through April, the longest season in the state. It's famous for its abundant snow, averaging over 600 inches a year, and is especially popular with snowboarders. There are 1,500 vertical feet of slope with 10 lifts and 38 runs, about half intermediate, 20 percent beginner, and 30 percent expert. There's no overnight lodging, but there's a big day lodge, a ski school, rentals, a restaurant, and a bar. Most skiers come in for the day from Bellingham, some on the **Baker Bus** (360/599-3115, www.bakerbus.org, $14 round-trip), which runs on weekends and holidays.

Cross-country and backcountry skiers will find plenty of trails in the area around Mount Baker. For rentals, contact **Glacier Ski Shop** (9966 Mt. Baker Hwy., 360/599-1943, www. glacierskishop.com).

FOOD

There aren't a lot of dining options near Mount Baker, but the ones you'll find are surprisingly good, with an emphasis on substantial meals to fuel hikers and skiers. Start the day with coffee and pastries at **Wake 'n' Bakery** (6903 Bourne St., 360/599-1658, www.getsconed.com, daily 7:30am-5pm), in Glacier behind Milano's.

You have two choices for Italian: In Demming, **Rifugio's** (5415 Mt. Baker Hwy., 360/592-2888, http://ilcafferifugio.com, Thurs.-Fri. 4pm-9pm, Sat.-Sun. 10am-9pm, $18-25) serves its pasta and other traditional specialties with some hip bohemian style, while in Glacier **Milano's Restaurant** (9990 Mt. Baker Hwy., 360/599-2863, daily 4pm-8pm, $14-26) has been dishing out healthy portions of good-quality Italian cuisine for over a quarter century.

Across the street from Milano's, **Grahams Restaurant** (9989 Mt. Baker Hwy., Glacier, 360/599-9883, Mon.-Thurs. 2pm-10pm, Fri. noon-10pm, Sat.-Sun. 8am-10pm, $8-14) is a big, rustic bar and grill where you can get burgers, meatloaf, and fried fish, washed down with a microbrew. Pick up snacks for the road in the adjoining general store.

The last place to eat before you enter the national forest is **Chair 9 Woodstone Pizza and Bar** (10459 Mt. Baker Hwy., 360/599-5211, www.chair9.com, daily noon-10pm, $9-23), another pub-grub stop with burgers, steaks, and salmon as well as creative pizzas.

North Fork Brewery (6186 Mt. Baker Hwy., 360/599-2337, www.northforkbrewery.com, Mon.-Fri. 4pm-9pm, Sat.-Sun. noon-9pm, $10-15) is a local institution serving its own beers and barley wine alongside pizza and grinders. Beyond the log-cabin-style dining room there's a beer shrine and a wedding chapel.

ACCOMMODATIONS

For a full-service hotel, your closest options are in Bellingham. Accommodations near Mount Baker are mostly cabins and condos, available primarily through the rental service **Mount Baker Lodging** (800/709-7669, www.mtbakerlodging.com). Many places require a two-night minimum on weekends and have higher rates around Christmas and New Year's. One dependable choice is **The Logs at Canyon Creek** (7577 Canyon View Dr., 360/599-2711, www.thelogs.com, $135 d, $15 each additional person), located between Maple Falls and Glacier. It has five cozy cabins that sleep up to six, each with a fireplace, an equipped kitchen, and two bedrooms.

Camping

The 411-acre **Silver Lake County Park** (9006 Silver Lake Rd., 360/599-2776, www.whatcomcounty.us/1937), three miles north of Maple Falls, has a beautiful day lodge/information center and year-round camping with RV hookups ($25-31), showers, swimming, and six lakeside cabins ($78-120).

There are two Forest Service campgrounds in the Mount Baker area, both situated in the woods along the Nooksack River just off of Mount Baker Highway, and both open mid-May-mid-September. **Douglas Fir Campground** ($18-20) is two miles east of Glacier; **Silver Fir Campground** ($16) is farther down the road, 13 miles east of Glacier. You can make reservations six months in advance online at www.recreation.gov ($9 fee) or by calling 877/444-6777 ($10 fee).

Dispersed camping is free on Forest Service land below milepost 52 of the Mount Baker Highway. Check with the **Glacier Public Service Center** (10091 Mt. Baker Hwy., 360/599-2714, June-mid-Oct. daily 8am-4:30pm, mid-Oct.-May Fri.-Sun. 9am-3pm, hours can vary depending on funding) regarding camping regulations, including approved methods of waste disposal and regulations regarding campfires.

INFORMATION

Glacier Public Service Center (10091 Mt. Baker Hwy., 360/599-2714, June-mid-Oct. daily 8am-4:30pm, mid-Oct.-May Fri.-Sun. 9am-3pm, hours can vary depending on funding) is staffed with rangers who can answer your questions and share information. In summer the **Heather Meadows Visitor Center** (no phone, July-Sept. daily 10am-4pm) is also open at the end of Mount Baker Highway near Artist Point.

TRANSPORTATION

Except for the Baker Bus in ski season, the only way to get to Mount Baker is by car, and there's only one way in: **Route 542,** also known as Mount Baker Highway. The trip east from Bellingham is 57 miles (1.5 hrs.). Mount Baker is 95 miles (2.5 hrs.) southeast from Vancouver, British Columbia, and 140 miles (3 hrs.) northeast of Seattle.

North Cascades Highway and National Park

The portion of Route 20 running between Burlington to the west and Mazama to the east is known as the North Cascades Highway, and it's the only road crossing North Cascades National Park. At its western end, it follows the Skagit River through flat farmland, but you can see your craggy destination in front of you—the sawtooth peaks of the North Cascades.

What most casual visitors think of as **North Cascades National Park** is actually a national park complex totaling 684,000 acres, made up of North Cascades National Park as well as **Ross Lake** and **Lake Chelan National Recreational Areas.** Driving through the **North Cascades National Park Complex** is the region's most popular tourist activity, largely because most of it is accessible only on foot or by boat. Make the effort to venture into the remote reaches, though, and you'll discover beautiful lakes, rewarding day hikes, and great trails into the mountains for multiday backpacking expeditions.

As the North Cascades Highway climbs into the park area it becomes a spectacular scenic drive through the heart of the northern Cascades range. One hundred and twenty miles later you'll find yourself on the other side, having navigated the beautiful curves of the well-maintained highway up through the North Cascades National Park Complex, into the Okanogan National Forest, over 5,477-foot Washington Pass, and down to the Methow Valley.

Note that this is a seasonal trip. When there's a risk of avalanches, usually November-April, the road closes from Ross Dam to the eastern side of Washington Pass.

NORTH CASCADES HIGHWAY
Sedro-Woolley to Marblemount

Heading east from I-5 on **Route 20** you encounter the Skagit Valley towns of Sedro-Woolley, Concrete, and Marblemount. None are tourist draws, but they're useful pit stops along the way to the mountains, and surrounding them are some worthwhile outdoor attractions.

Sedro-Woolley (pop. 10,600) is a former lumber town that was hit hard by the decline of logging in the area, but it remains a commercial center and is a base for outfitters serving the North Cascades. Fading **Concrete** (pop. 700) was home for many years to the largest cement plant in the state, the source for cement used in building the Grand Coulee Dam, as well as the Ross and Diablo Dams. It has a couple of places to eat and spend the night, as well as a quiet, lost-in-time Main Street and a giant cement silo by the side of the road that's a local landmark. Entering **Marblemount** (pop. 200) from the west, you'll see signs warning "Last Gas for 69 Miles" and "Last Tavern for 89 Miles." The little town is a good place to stock up on essentials, and to get information and backcountry permits for North Cascades National Park.

BAKER LAKE

Off Route 20 north of Concrete, nine-mile-long **Baker Lake,** created by the Upper Dam on the Baker River, is popular with campers, swimmers, motorboaters, and water-skiers. It has multiple campgrounds, and it's also the starting point for a couple of nice hikes.

At the south end of the lake, across the dam off the main road, is the **Baker Lake Trail,** which goes all the way up the lake's eastern

North Cascades Highway and National Park

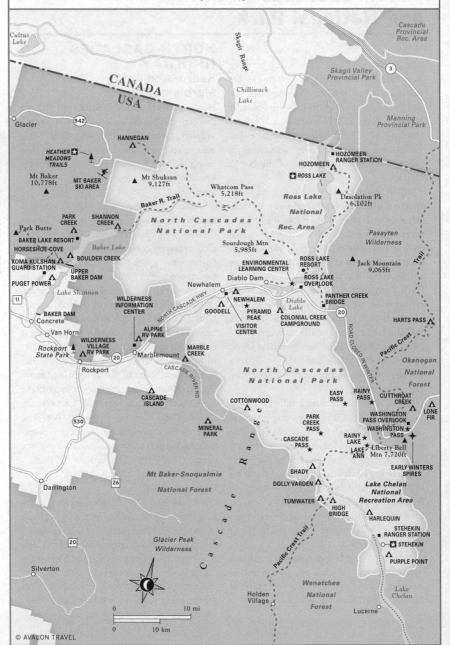

Cultus Lake

Skagit Range

Cascade Provincial Rec. Area

Skagit Valley Provincial Park

CANADA
USA

Chilliwack Lake

Manning Provincial Park

Glacier 542

HANNEGAN

HEATHER MEADOWS TRAILS

Mt Baker 10,778ft

MT BAKER SKI AREA

Mt Shuksan 9,127ft

Whatcom Pass 5,218ft

Baker R. Trail

HOZOMEEN RANGER STATION

HOZOMEEN

ROSS LAKE

Ross Lake

Desolation Pk 6,102ft

National

Rec. Area

PARK CREEK

SHANNON CREEK

North Cascades National Park

Park Butte

BAKER LAKE RESORT

HORSESHOE COVE

KOMA KULSHAN GUARD STATION

BOULDER CREEK

Baker Lake

Sourdough Mtn 5,985ft

Pasayten Wilderness

Jack Mountain 9,065ft

ROSS LAKE RESORT

ENVIRONMENTAL LEARNING CENTER

ROSS LAKE OVERLOOK

UPPER BAKER DAM

PUGET POWER

Lake Shannon

Newhalem

Diablo Dam

11

WILDERNESS INFORMATION CENTER

NORTH CASCADE HWY

NEWHALEM

GOODELL

PYRAMID PEAK

Diablo Lake

PANTHER CREEK BRIDGE

20

BAKER DAM

Concrete

Van Horn

ALPINE RV PARK

VISITOR CENTER

COLONIAL CREEK CAMPGROUND

ROAD CLOSED IN WINTER

HARTS PASS

Pacific Crest

Rockport State Park

WILDERNESS VILLAGE RV PARK

20

Marblemount

MARBLE CREEK

CASCADE RIVER RD

North Cascades National Park

Okanogan National Forest

Rockport

530

CASCADE ISLAND

COTTONWOOD

EASY PASS

RAINY PASS

CUTTHROAT CREEK

WASHINGTON PASS OVERLOOK

LONE FIR

26

MINERAL PARK

PARK CREEK PASS

WASHINGTON PASS

CASCADE PASS

RAINY LAKE

Liberty Bell Mtn 7,720ft

LAKE ANN

EARLY WINTERS SPIRES

Mt Baker-Snoqualmie

National Forest

Cascade Range

SHADY

DOLLY VARDEN

Lake Chelan National Recreation Area

Darrington

TUMWATER

HIGH BRIDGE

HARLEQUIN

STEHEKIN RANGER STATION

20

STEHEKIN

Glacier Peak Wilderness

PURPLE POINT

Pacific Crest Trail

Silverton

0   10 mi

0   10 km

Holden Village

Wenatchee National Forest

Lake Chelan

Lucerne

© AVALON TRAVEL

shore. You can also drive to the far north-eastern end of the lake (Baker Lake Rd. will turn into Forest Rd. 11) and pick up the **Baker River Trail,** a mostly flat 2.5-mile trip that takes you through old-growth cedar forests and past a beaver pond, with Cascade views along the way.

A more demanding Baker Lake hike takes you to **Park Butte,** a 5,450-foot summit with incredible views of Mount Baker glaciers. This summer-only trek is seven miles round-trip, but with an elevation gain of over 2,200 feet it takes the better part of the day to complete. To get there, go north for 12.5 miles on Baker Lake Road; turn left on Forest Road 12 and take it for 3.5 miles, and then turn right onto Forest Road 13 and continue for 5 miles to the road's end. The trail is west of the road, crossing Sulphur Creek and then ascending switchbacks.

ROCKPORT STATE PARK

Rockport State Park (51095 Rte. 20, 360/853-8461, parks.state.wa.us/574, Discover Pass required), about seven miles east of Concrete, covers 670 acres and has five miles of wooded hiking trails beneath incredible 250-foot-high old-growth Douglas fir trees, as well as Skagit River steelhead fishing. The paved and wheelchair-accessible **Skagit View Trail** leads down to the riverbank, a good lookout point for bald eagles in winter.

Immediately west of the park is the start of **Sauk Mountain Road,** a 7.5-mile gravel road that takes you most of the way up this 5,537-foot peak, ending at a trailhead. The steep, switchback-filled trail climbs another 1.5 miles to the summit, where you're treated to views of the North Cascades and the Skagit and Sauk River valleys.

SKAGIT RIVER BALD EAGLE NATURAL AREA

The Skagit River is a great place to watch wintering bald eagles. The 2,450-acre **Skagit River Bald Eagle Natural Area** (360/445-4441, wdfw.wa.gov/lands/wild-life_areas/skagit), overseen jointly by the Nature Conservancy and the Washington Department of Fish and Wildlife, preserves the wooded habitat at the confluence of the Skagit and Sauk Rivers as a haven for the ea-gles, which come by the hundreds to feed on salmon. December and January are the best times to spot them. There's a viewing area just east of Rockport State Park, on the south side of Route 20. Turn off onto Route 530; continue until you cross the bridge over the Skagit, then turn left on Martin Road (the first road past the bridge) and take it to the parking area. From there a short trail leads to the river's edge. A Discover Pass is required for parking.

On weekends in December and January the volunteer-run **Skagit River Bald Eagle Interpretive Center** (52809 Rockport Park Rd., 360 853-7626, skagiteagle.org) conducts guided eagle-watching hikes starting at 11am. From November through February **Pacific Northwest Float Trips** (360/719-5808, www.pacificnwfloattrips.com) leads eagle-watching raft excursions on the Skagit lasting 1.5 hours ($45) or 3 hours ($87).

FOOD

Concrete's **5B's Bakery** (45597 Main St., 360/853-8700, http://5bsbakery.com, daily 7am-5pm, $9-15) will have you doing a dou-ble take—it's like a hip Seattle shop that's been teleported to small-town Skagit Valley. It sells a wide range of breads, cakes, muf-fins, and pastries, as well as simple breakfasts and lunches, and there's a soda counter where you can get shakes, egg creams, and root beer floats. Everything, miraculously, is gluten-free.

Out on Route 20, **Annie's Pizza Station** (44568 Rt. 20, 360/853-7227, www.anniespiz-zastation.net, Tues.-Sat. 11am-9pm, Sun. 2pm-8pm, $9-12) is another appealing place to eat in Concrete. It's a colorful, casual joint occupying a former gas station. Handmade pizzas come with a wide variety of toppings, and the menu also has subs, salads, and pasta.

ACCOMMODATIONS AND CAMPING

Lodging is scarce in these parts. If you're coming across the Cascades from the east and looking for a hotel, you may want to continue on to Burlington, where there are some chains, or a few miles past that to Mount Vernon, where there are additional options. That said, a viable option south of Concrete is **Ovenell's Heritage Inn** (46276 Concrete Sauk Valley Rd., 360/853-8494, www.ovenells-inn.com), which has five fully equipped log cabins that sleep up to four ($150-160) and two larger guesthouses ($240-260) situated on a working ranch along the banks of the Skagit. The lodgings have a rustic feel but are relatively new structures with full kitchens, living rooms, TV, air-conditioning, and barbecue grills.

If you're camping, your prospects are better. There are a dozen campgrounds around the perimeter of **Baker Lake** ($12-18) with nearly 200 sites, many of which accommodate RVs. They're all well situated to take advantage of the lake's recreational activities on and off the water. The most picturesque is Panorama Point, which has views of Mount Baker and Mount Shuksan. Those looking for peace and quiet might opt for Maple Grove on the eastern shore, which can be reached only on foot or by boat, and which, unlike the other sites, is free of charge, can't be reserved, and is open all year. For the rest, you can make reservations six months in advance online at www.

recreation.gov ($9 fee) or by calling 877/444-6777 ($10 fee). These campgrounds are open mid-May through September.

★ Newhalem to Washington Pass

Heading east from Marblemount, Route 20 enters the **North Cascades National Park Complex** after five miles. This area marks the beginning of the most beautiful portion of the North Cascades Highway. While the designation "North Cascades Highway" technically applies to all of Route 20 between Burlington and Mazama, most visitors use the name to refer to this truly spectacular part of the road running through the park complex between Newhalem and Washington Pass.

After entering the park area, in quick succession the road passes Goodell Creek and Newhalem campgrounds, the turnoff to North Cascades Visitor Center, and the little settlement of **Newhalem,** where the **Skagit General Store** (Rt. 20 milepost 120, 206/386-4489, mid-May-Oct. daily 10am-5pm, Nov.-mid-May Mon.-Fri. 10am-5pm) is your one stop in the park for snacks and camping supplies. Newhalem is a quiet company town with one focus: producing electricity at nearby Gorge, Diablo, and Ross Dams.

North Cascades Highway

Parklike grounds are surrounded by trim clapboard homes. Next to the general store is **Old Number Six,** a 1928 Baldwin steam locomotive that hauled passengers and supplies to the Skagit River dams in the days before the highway. If you're driving through and want to get out into the open air for a little while, take a short, easy walk along the **Trail of the Cedars,** a 0.3-mile loop that starts in Newhalem and goes through an old-growth cedar forest that includes trees over 1,000 years old.

East of Newhalem the highway begins a serious climb into the forested Cascades, passing a series of three dams and reservoirs—Gorge, Diablo, and Ross—that constitute the centerpiece of **Ross Lake National Recreation Area.** Tours of **Diablo Dam and Lake** are a popular attraction. Near milepost 123 is an overlook for **Forge Creek Falls** as it plunges into the gorge below. Colonial Creek Campground is along the highway near Diablo Lake, and a mile east is an overlook where you can peer down on the turquoise lake waters and across to the jagged summits of **Pyramid Peak** and **Colonial Peak.**

Continuing eastward, the highway passes **Ross Lake Overlook.** Soon after that it leaves the national park and enters Okanogan National Forest. It climbs along Granite Creek before cresting two passes, 4,855-foot **Rainy Pass** and 5,477-foot **Washington Pass.** Both are great places for taking in views of the Cascades; a short paved trail leads from Washington Pass to over-the-highway viewpoints of the 7,720-foot peak **Liberty Bell**—the symbol of the North Cascades Highway—and **Early Winter Spires.** From there the highway spirals downward to the Methow Valley and the town of Winthrop, 30 miles to the east and 3,600 feet lower in elevation.

Before you begin this drive be sure you have a full tank of gas and, if you're going to make a day (or more) of it, bring along sufficient food—you won't find either along the way. Also be aware that this is a seasonal trip. Every year the highway shuts down between Ross Dam and the east side of Washington Pass with the first winter snow. It's usually closed mid-November-April. If you travel the highway from west to east (as described here), you can spend the night in the tourist-friendly Methow Valley at the end of your journey. When going the other way you don't have as many options for places to stay or eat after you've descend.

NORTH CASCADES NATIONAL PARK

North Cascades National Park is significantly less developed than Washington's other two national parks, Olympic and Mount Rainier. There's no admission fee and there are few services—no food is available other than a convenience store, and lodging is limited to the small facilities on Ross Lake and Lake Chelan, neither of which is accessible by car. As you drive the highway, there's little to distinguish the national park from the Okanogan National Forest to the east. Both have beautiful mountain scenery, and trails (including the Pacific Crest Trail) cross from one into the other.

Within the park there are over 300 glaciers, by far the greatest concentration of them anywhere in the continental United States. Rugged peaks, mountain lakes, and waterfalls greet the determined backcountry hiker. For the casual day-tripper, though, one of the most popular attractions is a man-made feature: beautiful turquoise-blue Diablo Lake, the result of the Diablo Dam on the Skagit River.

Park Information
VISITOR INFORMATION
The park's main **visitors center** (Rte. 20, milepost 120, 206/386-4495, ext. 11, www.nps.gov/noca, mid-Apr.-mid-May and Oct. Sat.-Sun 9am-5pm, mid-May-Sept. daily 9am-5pm), near the little township of Newhalem, contains natural history exhibits, a large relief model of the region, a gift shop, and a theater with slide shows, movies, and other presentations. It's the best place to get a museum-like

overview of the park and to get general information.

To the west of the park, just west of the town of Marblemount, there's a turnoff from Route 20 at milepost 105.5 for the **Wilderness Information Center** (7280 Ranger Station Rd., 360/854-7245, May-June and Sept. daily 8am-5pm, July-Aug. daily 7am-6pm). This center has information about backcountry camping, climbing, and other activities. It's where you go to get backcountry permits.

The park's main administrative offices in Sedro-Woolley are the site of the **Park and Forest Information Center** (810 Rte. 20, 360/854-7200, June-Sept. daily 8am-4pm, Oct.-May Mon.-Fri. 8am-4pm). There are resources here for visitors to both the national park and the surrounding national forests, including some backcountry passes. It's a year-round resource that's invaluable when the other centers are closed.

WEATHER

The park complex is open year-round, but the segment of Route 20 from Ross Dam to the east side of Washington Pass closes every winter, usually late November-April, because of the risk of avalanches. The lower elevations are appealing sites for spring and fall hikes in the woods, but late June through September is the prime time to visit the North Cascades. Summer is the driest season, but there's still the possibility of showers, so bring rain gear if you're going out on a trail. Precipitation in spring and fall is steadier, and from November through April the western slopes of the Cascades are one of the snowiest places on earth.

FEES

There is no admission fee for the park, and there's also no charge for backcountry passes. Unlike in the surrounding national forest areas, there's no pass required for parking at trailheads or anywhere else in the national park. A site at one of the campgrounds that provides water and services costs $16.

Cascade River Road and Cascade Pass

For a journey deep into the national park, with many scenic rewards, at Marblemount turn off of Route 20 onto **Cascade River Road,** which runs 23 miles through forest and mountains to the trailhead of the Cascade Pass Trail. The first half of the road is paved, the rest of the way gravel, with narrow, steep segments, tight switchbacks, and areas with

Diablo Dam

North Cascades Environmental Learning Center

North Cascades Environmental Learning Center (1940 Diablo Dam Rd., 206/526-2599, ncascades.org), administered by the North Cascades Institute and backed by funding from Seattle City Light, is an impressive multipurpose facility with varied programs for kids, families, and adults.

The lake's most popular activities are two tours administered by the Learning Center. Both tours frequently sell out; reserve a spot online or by calling the Learning Center. **Diablo Lake Tour** (360/854-2589, July-mid-Sept. Thurs.-Mon., $42 including lunch) is a four-hour guided boat ride around the lake, taking you to otherwise inaccessible spots on the water, with views of waterfalls, the surrounding peaks, and Ross and Diablo dams. The **Insiders Powerhouse Tour** (360/854-2589, July-Sept. Sat.-Sun, $20 including lunch) begins with a walk through the town of Newhalem, followed by a look inside the Gorge Powerhouse.

The center also hosts overnight activities, including kids' programs, three- and four-day family getaways, and themed adult events ranging from birding to mushroom hunting to journaling. When facilities aren't otherwise in use the center welcomes overnight guests through its Base Camp program, which includes meals and a morning activity with a naturalist. Get program schedules and make reservations online.

★ Ross Lake

The northeast corner of the park complex is the site of 24-mile-long, 2-mile-wide, 12,000-acre Ross Lake, which is the product of a 540-foot-high hydroelectric dam completed in 1949 by Seattle City Light. You can see the reservoir from the Ross Lake overlook at Route 20 milepost 135, but the only vehicle access is far away at the lake's north end, reached via a 40-mile gravel road from Canada.

The isolation makes Ross Lake alluring and elusive. It takes effort to get to there, but your reward is a pristine mountain lake with quiet coves, waterfalls, boat-in campsites, and scenic trails accessible from the shore.

the potential for washouts. It's a demanding drive, but it's manageable with a standard road car. Before you begin, check in at the Wilderness Information Center to make sure the road is passable. From late autumn through spring the road is frequently closed due to snow.

Most people who make the trip do so to hike the trail to **Cascade Pass.** The 7.4-mile round-trip is one of the finest day hikes in the North Cascades, starting in dense forest and ascending steadily into alpine meadows. When you reach the pass you have a 360-degree view of peaks, glaciers, and valleys carpeted in summer with wildflowers. The hike has an 1,800-foot elevation gain and can take 3.5 to 4.5 hours to complete. You can extend your hike by heading north up the challenging Sahale Arm Trail. In the other direction the Cascade Pass Trail leads all the way to Lake Chelan and Stehekin, 30 miles to the south.

Diablo Lake

Along the northern shore of Diablo Lake, the

It's a paradise for peaceful kayaking. The waters are chilly, but swimming is viable in July and August.

The hub of activity is **Ross Lake Resort** (206/386-4437, http://rosslakeresort.com) near the southern end. Booking one of its cabins is probably the most difficult reservation in the entire state, but the resort is also an accommodating place for day-trippers and campers, with canoes, kayaks, motorboats, and fishing equipment to rent, and a water taxi service that will take you to trailheads and campsites along the lakeshore.

Getting to the resort is a multistep process. You can take the **Diablo Lake Ferry** (runs twice daily at 8:30am and 3pm, $20 round-trip), which leaves from a dock next to a parking lot reached by crossing over the Diablo Dam from Route 20 and turning right. It goes to the northwest corner of Diablo Lake, from where a shuttle run by the resort ($8 round-trip) takes you to the southern tip of Ross Lake. From there a short boat ride delivers you to the resort on the opposite shore. The entire journey lasts about an hour.

Alternatively, park at the lot along Route 20 at milepost 134, hike the Ross Dam Trail for a mile to where it meets with a gravel road, and continue a short way on the road to the waterfront, where there's a phone from which you can call for a boat (the number is 18-31974) to take you across the water to the resort. The ride is $2 one-way.

Hiking
DAY HIKES
There are trails of all difficulty levels in and around the park complex, but the rugged, steep terrain means that more experienced and durable hikers have more options. Before you start out on a day hike, it's smart to stop in at the visitors center near Newhalem to get information and advice from the rangers.

If you're up for a challenge, consider climbing the **Sourdough Mountain Trail.** Turn off Route 20 at milepost 126 to reach the trailhead, which is near the lodging for Diablo Dam workers. It's a steep, difficult climb with many switchbacks, rising 5,000 feet in a little over five miles to reach Sourdough's summit, but the views of the lakes and the surrounding peaks are extraordinary.

You'll find easier access to good views on trails around the grounds of the North Cascades Environmental Learning Center. **Diablo Lake Trail** leads 3.8 miles to Ross Dam; you can hike in one direction and take the Diablo Lake Ferry in the other. A one-mile

Diablo Lake Trail

hike up the **Sourdough Creek Trail** takes you to several good viewpoints and a pretty waterfall.

There's another undemanding trail at the east end of the Cascade Highway—flat, mile-long, fully accessible **Rainy Lake Trail** at Rainy Pass. Along the path there are waterfalls and signs identifying plants and describing the natural processes at work. At the end you reach the namesake glacier-fed lake.

At the same trailhead you can take the more demanding 3.1-mile out-and-back **Lake Ann Trail** or the challenging 7.5-mile **Maple Pass Loop Trail,** the latter with a 2,200-foot elevation gain. The Maple Pass Trail includes portions of the Rainy Lake and Lake Ann trails. This area is in the Okanogan National Forest, which means you need a Northwest Forest Pass to park at the trailhead.

Also popular is an easy trail to **Blue Lake** starting at a trailhead a half-mile west of Washington Pass. It leads two miles through subalpine meadows to the emerald waters of the mountain lake surrounded by a trio of spectacular summits: Liberty Bell, Whistler Mountain, and Cutthroat Peak.

BACKCOUNTRY TREKS

For experienced campers a multiday backpacking trip is the ideal way to experience the remote North Cascades—you get to explore beautiful, varied terrain that's beyond the reach of a day hike. If you're new to the region it's best to have a hiking companion who knows the turf, but if that's not the case it's essential to consult with a ranger at the **Wilderness Information Center** (7280 Ranger Station Rd., 360/854-7245, May-June and Sept. daily 8am-5pm, July-Aug. daily 7am-6pm). For preplanning, call ahead and talk on the phone. There's also a thorough rundown of procedures, regulations, and backcountry strategies at the park's website, www.nps.gov/noca.

A free **backcountry permit** is required for all overnight trips into the park. Between March 15 and May 15, you can reserve permits and backcountry campsites for the summer

season online (www.nps.gov/noca/planyour-visit/backcountry-reservations.htm). Though permits are free, a $20 nonrefundable reservation fee applies. If you don't have a reservation, get a permit in person no more than a day in advance of your trip. Permits are available from the Wilderness Information Center in Marblemount. You can also get them at the information or ranger stations in Newhalem, Hozomeen, Sedro-Woolley, Winthrop, Twisp, Chelan, or Stehekin, but these locations issue permits only to the areas for which they are the nearest station. (Permits for the Cascade Pass area are available only at the Wilderness Information Center; the Sedro-Woolley office issues passes only for trips starting at the Baker River Trail and Hozomeen).

There are limits on the number of permits the park issues at any one time, so if you're hoping to take a popular trail on a busy summer weekend it's a good idea to have a backup plan; rangers can suggest less busy areas. There are some 140 backcountry campgrounds in the park complex. If you're flexible, there will almost always be a place for you.

Among the many multiday backpacking options, one appealing choice is to hike through the Ross Lake area on the **East Bank Trail.** The trailhead is at the Panther Creek Bridge, along Route 20 at milepost 138. Heading north, the generally flat trail leads through low forest and along the lakeshore for 18 miles, at which point you have the option to ascend 6,102-foot **Desolation Peak.** The hike to the peak is 4.5 miles almost straight up, with an elevation gain of 4,400 feet. At the top are views of Mount Baker, Mount Shuksan, Jack Mountain, Hozomeen Mountain, and the Pickets.

You can continue farther north, as the trail turns inland and passes several little alpine lakes before returning to the shore at Hozomeen campground. If you do choose to go the whole distance—31 miles total from Panther Creek Bridge to Hozomeen—you need to figure out a way back. One option is to plan for a water taxi from Ross Resort to meet you; the ride costs $175 regardless

Desolation Angel

Beatnik fans will appreciate that **Jack Kerouac** spent the summer of 1956 as a fire lookout on Desolation Peak, overlooking Ross Lake. He got the idea from a friend, poet **Gary Snyder,** who had manned other North Cascades lookouts in earlier years. Kerouac would describe his excruciatingly lonely experience in two novels, *Dharma Bums* and *Desolation Angels*.

Three months after Kerouac came down from the mountain his groundbreaking novel *On the Road* was published, transforming him from a thoughtful drifter into a cultural icon. The station at the top of Desolation Peak that he called home for two months is still there, and is still occupied by a lookout every summer.

of the number of passengers. You can also have someone pick you up by car. This is the only part of the lake accessible by car, but it's a tough trip on a 40-mile gravel road from Canada.

Another excellent point-to-point hike goes through the southern portion of the park. Start at the Colonial Creek Campground, near Route 20 along Diablo Lake, and follow the Thunder Creek and Park Creek Trails over 6,100-foot **Park Creek Pass.** You wind up on the Old Wagon Trail, which takes you to High Bridge Campground, for a total hike of 35 miles. From High Bridge you can catch the shuttle bus to Stehekin, and then ride the boat down Lake Chelan to the town of Chelan.

If you can handle a long uphill slog, **Easy Pass** makes a fine overnight hike. The trailhead is in the Okanogan National Forest, on Route 20 six miles west of Rainy Pass and 46 miles east of Marblemount. The inappropriately named Easy Pass Trail climbs steadily for 3.7 miles to a 6,500-foot summit, at which point you enter North Cascades National Park. The magnificent vista includes sawtooth mountaintops and active glaciers. From here you can continue deeper into the wilderness on **Fisher Creek Trail.** The Easy Pass Trail is usually open late July-late September.

Food

If you're planning on being in the park complex long enough to get hungry, bring food with you. The only place where you can

buy something to eat is in Newhalem at the **Skagit General Store** (Rte. 20 milepost 120, 206/386-4489, mid-May-Oct. daily 10am-5pm, Nov.-mid-May Mon.-Fri. 10am-5pm). It has standard convenience-store merchandise, along with coffee, soup, and sandwiches. There's also a cafeteria at the **North Cascades Environmental Learning Center** (1940 Diablo Dam Rd., 206/526-2599, ncascades.org), but it's open only to people participating in its overnight programs.

Accommodations

There are only a couple of lodging options in the park complex, and they're not designed to serve a large number of guests.

★ **Ross Lake Resort** (206/386-4437, http://rosslakeresort.com), open mid-June-October, is one of the most novel and appealing places to bed down in Washington. Everything here is literally on the water, with cabins and bunkhouses built on log floats. Stay in a modern cabin ($220 d), a smaller 1950s-era cabin ($195 d), a two-story cabin that sleeps up to nine ($370), or a 10-person bunkhouse ($280). The resort has rental motorboats, kayaks, and canoes to get you out on the beautiful lake, and there are fantastic views up to 8,300-foot Mount Hozomeen at the Canadian border. Getting a reservation here is a challenge: You can book online or by phone a year in advance, and usually all cabins are reserved immediately upon availability. There are often cancellations, though, so it's sometimes possible to find availability close to your date of arrival. Note that there are no telephones (either land lines or cell), Wi-Fi, groceries, or food service. You have to bring your own food; all the cabins have full kitchens, and there are shared barbecue grills.

Another option, available on a limited basis, is a dorm-style room at the **North Cascades Environmental Learning Center** (1940 Diablo Dam Rd., 206/526-2599, ncascades.org). June-October, when rooms aren't in use for one of the center's programs they're made available to overnight guests. Each room can sleep up to four ($160 for one person, $220 for two, $264 for three, $300 for four) in two bunk beds, with shared bathrooms down the hall. Along with lodging you get three meals and can take part in a naturalist-led activity in the morning.

CAMPING

What the park complex lacks in lodging it makes up for in campsites. Some sites at all of these car-accessible campgrounds, except Hozomeen, can be reserved up to 360 days in advance, either by phone (877/444-6777, $10 fee) or online (www.recreation.gov, $9 fee).

Campgrounds accessible by car on the North Cascades Highway include **Goodell Creek** (Rte. 20 milepost 119, 19 sites, year-round, no services or fee Oct.-Apr.), **Newhalem Creek** (Rte. 20 milepost 120, 111 sites, mid-May-mid-Oct.), and **Colonial Creek** (Rte. 20 milepost 130, 142 sites, mid-May-mid-Oct). Sites at all three campgrounds cost $16 a night. All have potable water, toilets, garbage pickup, and dump stations, but no showers or hookups. In summer there are

naturalist activities at Colonial Creek and Newhalem Creek.

You can also reach tiny **Gorge Lake Campground** (Rte. 20 milepost 126, 6 sites, year-round) by car; it's free but has no services or facilities beyond pit toilets. **Hozomeen Campground** (Silver/Skagit Rd., 75 sites, mid-May-Oct.) at the north end of Ross Lake is accessible by car, but only from Canada, over a rough 40-mile gravel road from Hope, British Columbia. It's free and has water May-September.

There are about 140 **backcountry campgrounds** throughout the park complex. All of them have some sort of toilet facilities (usually pit), and they're all free, but they require a backcountry permit. Between March 15 and May 15 you can reserve permits and backcountry campsites for the summer season online (www.nps.gov/noca/planyour-visit/backcountry-reservations.htm). Though permits are free, a $20 nonrefundable reservation fee applies. If you don't have a reservation, choose your site from the ones available at the time you pick up your permit in person. Note that all sites require some method for keeping food out of the reach of bears and other wildlife. Some locations have bear boxes or wires for hanging food, but others require you to bring a hard-sided canister with you.

Transportation

Driving options in the park complex are limited to the North Cascades Highway (Rt. 20), and rugged Cascade River Road. From Seattle to Newhalem it's a 125-mile drive, heading north on I-5 and exiting east onto Route 20, which takes about 2.75 hours.

The Methow Valley

In the Methow (MET-how) Valley the forested eastern slopes of the Cascades transition into irrigated pastures surrounded by hills covered with sage, grass, and scattered pines. Route 20 sheds its identity as the North Cascades Highway as it follows the Methow River past the towns of Mazama, Winthrop, and Twisp. These three small towns, especially Western-themed Winthrop, were transformed into tourist destinations by the completion of Route 20 over the mountains in 1972.

They continue to be popular destinations for North Cascades travelers, but in the 2010s they've had to contend with the brutal consequences of the worst wildfires in Washington history. The dry, warm climate east of the Cascades means that fire in this region is inevitable, which is not entirely a bad thing—wildfire has always had a role in the region's ecosystem. The recent fires, though, have been of an unprecedented scale. The towns have survived the blazes, but hundreds of homes have been lost and hundreds of thousands of acres have gone up in flames.

For leisure travelers, visits thus carry a caveat. The tourism infrastructure remains intact, and when circumstances are fire-free this is a fun part of the state to visit, with a laid-back charm, good restaurants and hotels, and appealing trails for hiking, mountain biking, and cross-country skiing. But if another major blaze erupts, tourism will be an afterthought as the region contends with fundamental issues of survival.

MAZAMA

If you're traveling west to east on the North Cascades Highway, tiny Mazama is the first sign of civilization you encounter as you descend from the mountains. Given its small size, Mazama has a lot to offer: a couple of good lodging options, a few restaurants, and a first-rate general store where you can get gas and stock up on food.

Harts Pass

If you haven't had your fill of mountain driving, consider a trip up to **Harts Pass** (6,197 ft.). From Mazama it's a 19-mile drive northwest along a gravel road that passes the 2,000-foot slopes of glacially carved **Goat Wall** along the way. The road splits at the pass. Turning left (south) and continuing for nine downhill miles leads to the ghost towns of **Barron** and **Chancellor,** once home to 2,000 miners. Turning right (north) and climbing three steep miles brings you to the highest point you can reach by car in all of Washington, **Slate Peak Lookout** (7,440 ft.). It's a short walk to the lookout tower, from where you get spectacular 360-degree views of the entire Cascade Range.

Harts Pass Road is steep and narrow; RVs and trailers are prohibited, and it's a demanding mountain bike ride. The road is not

Methow Valley fire danger status

Food and Accommodations

The town's claim to fame is the ★ **Mazama Store** (50 Lost River Rd., 509/996-2855, www.themazamastore.com, daily 7am-6pm). Technically it qualifies as a convenience store, with gas (available 24 hours a day), packaged food, and basic necessities. But it doubles as an oasis of good taste: The store bakes its own breads and pastries, sells organic local produce, makes delicious sandwiches and espresso drinks, and stocks an impressive selection of Washington wine and beer. You can also rent bikes and buy outdoor gear and Mazama souvenirs. If you're heading west into the mountains this is your last chance for supplies. It's likely to be the classiest "last chance" shop you've ever encountered.

Freestone Inn & Cabins (31 Early Winters Dr., 509/996-3906, www.freestone-inn.com, $209-319 d) has a modern, rustic-luxury lodge and restored historic cabins set on the edge of a small lake. The hotel organizes lots of outdoor activities for guests, including horseback riding, mountain biking, backcountry skiing, and fly-fishing. On-site there's a high-end **restaurant** (Wed.-Sun. 5pm-9pm, $25-34).

Accommodations are less luxurious but eminently comfortable at **Mazama Country Inn** (15 Country Rd., 509/996-2681, www.mazamacountryinn.com, $115-180 d), located near the Mazama Store. Along with its main lodge the inn rents numerous cabins around Mazama, ranging from a small studio ($88) to a four-bedroom ($400). The inn's **restaurant** ($11-25) serves breakfast daily and dinner on a seasonal schedule. Facilities include a pool, a tennis court, and the only squash court within a hundred-mile radius.

WINTHROP

Located 13 miles southeast of Mazama near the junction of the Methow and Chewuch (CHEE-wuk) rivers, Winthrop began as a mining settlement in the late 19th century and struggled through lean times as a cow town for much of the 20th. Things changed when the North Cascades Highway opened in 1972,

Mazama Store

plowed beyond Lost River in the winter. Near Harts Pass, you can camp at two free Forest Service campgrounds with gorgeous alpine settings: **Meadows** and **Harts Pass.** They are usually open mid-July to late September; there's no potable water.

HIKING

The high-alpine country around Harts Pass offers some of the most popular day hiking in this part of the state. The **Windy Pass Trail** begins 1.5 miles up Slate Peak Road from Harts Pass and follows the Pacific Crest Trail for 3.5 miles to Windy Pass. The hike begins at 6,800 feet; there's little additional elevation gain, but you get striking views of peaks and meadows all along the route. A second fun hike with little change in elevation begins at Harts Pass and proceeds along the PCT south to **Grasshopper Pass.** The round-trip distance is 11 miles, and the route follows the crest of the mountains to beautiful meadows at Grasshopper Pass. Because of the high elevation, these trails are often covered with snow into July.

funneling hundreds of thousands of travelers into the Methow Valley.

The successful transformation of Leavenworth, 100 miles to the south, into a Bavarian theme town motivated locals to try something similar. They decided to give Winthrop a Wild West makeover, inspired in part by the fact that Owen Whistler, author of the iconic Western novel *The Virginian,* had spent time in town and was thought to have based parts of the book on his experiences here.

By the time the first carloads of tourists crossed Washington Pass on the new highway, Winthrop had given its buildings Old West facades, laid down boardwalks on top of the cement sidewalks, and put in hitching posts. Today its shops are filled with Western art, apparel, and trinkets, and saloons share the street with upscale restaurants and espresso bars.

The area is home to about 2,000 year-round residents, most of whom make it their business to serve the half-million tourists who pass through annually. The layout is unapologetically contrived, but it does have a ring of truth. While Leavenworth was never a part of Bavaria, Winthrop was in fact once part of the Western frontier.

Outside of town, you'll discover the area is more than a Western theme park. This part of the Methow Valley is crisscrossed with mountain-biking and hiking trails, and come winter it's the most active location in the state for cross-country skiing.

Shafer Museum

★ Shafer Museum

For proof of Winthrop's pioneer past, pay a visit to the **Shafer Museum** (285 Castle Ave., 509/996-2712, http://shafermuseum.com, buildings Memorial Day-Sept. daily 10am-5pm, grounds year-round dawn-dusk, donation requested). The indoor/outdoor site has as its centerpiece an 1896 log home, cheekily nicknamed the Castle, built by the town's founder, Guy Waring. On display are pioneer farming and mining tools, bicycles, furniture, an impressive rifle collection, and other relics from the early days in the Methow Valley, including hundreds of old photographs.

A dozen more buildings are on the grounds, including a general store, print shop, homestead cabin, schoolhouse, and assay office. The 1923 Rickenbacker automobile here is one of just 80 still in existence. All in all it's an impressive display that goes well beyond what you find at a typical small-town museum. Some of the old equipment has the beauty of sculpture, making for good photo ops.

Riverside Avenue

The main diversion in town is strolling the boardwalks along Riverside Avenue, Winthrop's main street. It's lined with Western-themed establishments where you can buy souvenirs and authentic arts and crafts, get your picture taken in old-time garb, and knock back a shot of whiskey. One of the busiest places along the street is usually **Sheri's Sweet Shoppe** (207 Riverside Ave., 509/996-3834, www.sherissweetshoppe.com, June-Sept. daily 6:30am-10pm, Apr.-May and

Oct.-Dec. Sat.-Sun. 6:30am-8pm). It's a cute multipurpose hangout where you can snack on homemade ice cream and other sweets, lounge in a saddle stool on the deck, and get in a round of miniature golf.

Other well-established institutions on the main drag include **Three-Fingered Jack's** (176 Riverside Ave., 509/996-2411, www.3fingeredjacks.com, daily 7am-close), which purports to be the oldest saloon in the state, and **Trail's End Bookstore** (241 Riverside Ave., 509/996-2345, Sun.-Thurs. 10am-7pm, Fri.-Sat. 9am-8pm), which has an impressive selection of regional titles.

Winthrop National Fish Hatchery

A mile south of town at the **Winthrop National Fish Hatchery** (453A Twin Lakes Rd., 509/996-2424, www.fws.gov/winthropnfh, daily 8am-4pm, free), where they raise 1.5 million spring chinook salmon and 750,000 trout annually, you can look over the large, covered raceway ponds and peer at the fish through an underwater window.

North Cascades Smokejumper Base

Halfway between Winthrop and Twisp, get insights into the world of forest fire management at the **North Cascades Smokejumper Base** (Methow Valley State Airport, 23 Intercity Airport Rd., 509/997-2031, www.northcascadessmokejumperbase.com, June-Sept. daily 10am-5pm, free). It was here in the fall of 1939 that the first tests were conducted to determine the safety and effectiveness of parachute jumps as a means of reaching remote mountain fires. A year later the strategy was put to use in an actual fire situation, and it continues to be used today, with nine bases now in operation throughout the western United States.

Drop in for a tour in summer when the base is active. One of the jumpers will show you around the facilities—you'll inspect their equipment, climb aboard one of their planes, learn when and why smoke jumping is used

to manage fires, and hear stories from your guide's personal experience as a jumper. It's fun to get a firsthand look at the operation, and it's hard not to be impressed with the raw courage of the jumpers. To get here take East County Road, which parallels Route 20 between Winthrop and Twisp.

Sports and Recreation

While Winthrop has some amusement-park characteristics, when it comes to outdoor sports the surrounding area is a 100 percent authentic pleasure, particularly for mountain bikers in summer and cross-country skiers in winter. There are two invaluable resources for trail information, not matter whether you're on foot, on a bike, or on skis. One is the U.S. Forest Service, which operates the **Methow Valley Ranger Station** (24 West Chewuch Rd., 509/996-4003, www.fs.usda.gov/okawen, Mon.-Fri. 7:45am-4:30pm). Online or at the station, located just to the northwest of town, you can get descriptions and learn about current conditions for scores of trails maintained by the Forest Service.

The second resource is the privately run nonprofit **Methow Trails** (309 Riverside Ave., 509/996-3287, www.methowtrails.org, Mon.-Fri. 9am-3:30pm), which maintains cross-country skiing trails and has information about a wide range of biking and hiking trails, as well as road-biking routes.

BICYCLING

Winthrop is a summer mecca for cyclists, with an impressive range of trails and country roads spreading through the valley and into the surrounding mountains. There are routes for every ability level. Rent bikes and get trail recommendations from **Methow Cycle & Sport** (29 Rte. 20, 509/996-3645, http://methowcyclesport.com, Mon.-Sat. 9am-6pm, Sun. 9am-5pm, $35-50/day), located just northwest of town near the Methow Valley Ranger Station.

A good place for mountain bikers to access the trail system is from the Sun Mountain Lodge parking lot. There's a network of trails at **Sun Mountain** that includes a variety of terrain and difficulty levels. Other exceptional rides are **Buck Mountain,** to the north of Winthrop, and the challenging, full-day adventure on **Angel's Staircase** to the south of town.

★ CROSS-COUNTRY SKIING

In winter, when the Methow Valley often has two or three feet of powdery snow on the ground and sunshine in the sky, outdoor recreation changes from biking and hiking to cross-country skiing. **Methow Trails** (309 Riverside Ave., 509/996-3287, www.methowtrails.org, Mon.-Fri. 9am-3:30pm) maintains over 120 miles of cross-country ski trails throughout the valley, making this the largest such ski area in the nation. Fees are $24 for one day and $60 for three days; kids 17 and under ski for free. Rent equipment at **Cascades Outdoor Store** (222 Riverside Ave., 509/996-3480, http://cascadesoutdoorstore.com, Mon.-Fri. 10am-6pm, Sat.-Sun. 9am-6pm) or **Winthrop Mountain Sports** (257 Riverside Ave., 509/996-2886, www.winthropmountainsports.com, Mon.-Fri. 9:30am-6pm, Sat. 9am-6pm, Sun. 9am-5pm).

Backcountry skiers will be interested in **Rendezvous Huts** (509/996-8100, www.rendezvoushuts.com), which provides hut-to-hut skiing opportunities along the Methow Trails system. There are six huts, all of which sleep up to eight and have full kitchens, woodstove heating, and outhouses. They go for $150-200 a night.

Food

For casual dining in a funky, eclectic atmosphere, stop in at downtown's **Duck Brand Cantina** (248 Riverside Ave., 509/996-2408, www.duckbrandhotel.com, May-Oct. daily 7am-9pm, Dec.-Apr. Wed.-Sat. 8am-9pm, Sun. 8am-2pm, $12-25). The menu is mainly Mexican but takes detours all over the globe: You can get curries, pasta, and grilled salmon as well as chile rellenos and carne asada. This is a busy breakfast spot, and it also has five simple guestrooms upstairs.

Rocking Horse Bakery (265 Riverside Ave., 509/996-4241, www.rockinghorse-bakery.com, daily 7am-4pm, $5-10) makes high-quality breads and pastries. A cinnamon roll and a coffee from here is one of the town's most popular ways to start the day. It serves sandwiches, soups, pizza, and salads at lunchtime.

Behind the red facade of the **Old Schoolhouse Brewery** (155 Riverside Ave., 509/996-3183, www.oldschoolhousebrewery.com, daily noon-10pm, $12-15) there's a comfortable bar that opens out onto an expansive deck along the Methow. Crowds flock here for microbrews and classic pub grub—burgers, salads, nachos—in a friendly setting. There's live music most weekends.

Just outside of town, casually sophisticated **Arrowleaf Bistro** (207 White Ave., 509-996-3919, www.arrowleafbistro.com, Wed.-Mon. 4pm-9pm, $22-49) is Winthrop's most satisfying restaurant. The seasonal menu is largely French-influenced but isn't precious about it—there are lots of grilled meats and hearty game dishes.

Sun Mountain Lodge (604 Patterson Lake Rd., 509/996-4707, www.sunmountainlodge.com) has a beautiful dining room (daily 5:30pm-9pm, $29-51) with mountain views and a classic meat-and-potatoes menu. The resort's Wolf Creek Bar and Grill (daily 11:30am-10pm, $13-18) has sandwiches, pasta, and individual pizzas.

Accommodations

One of Winthrop's greatest virtues is a good selection of places to stay. Along the Methow River and in the surrounding hills are a number of well-run small to midsize accommodations, most of which play off of Winthrop's Western theme.

A half-mile south of town the ★ **Mt. Gardner Inn** (611 Rte. 20, 509/996-2000, www.mtgardnerinn.com, $104-149 d) sets the standard for good-quality, reasonably priced lodging in the Winthrop area. Some Western touches, like knotty-pine bed frames, add charm, but the inn's appeal is that it gets the basics right—rooms are comfortable and well maintained, and service is professional and friendly. Rooms at the higher end of the price range have decks with mountain views.

Winthrop Inn (960 Rte. 20, 800/444-1972, www.winthropinn.com, $95-140 d), one mile southeast of town, has a two-level motel-style setup. Eight rooms all have a microwaves and fridges, and outdoor facilities include a small pool, a hot tub, volleyball courts, and a picnic area with barbecue grills.

Just south of downtown Winthrop is **Hotel Rio Vista** (285 Riverside Ave., 509/996-3535, www.hotelriovista.com, $129-154 d), a pleasant, well-maintained four-room lodge done in Old West style with views overlooking the Methow River.

Chewuch Inn and Cabins (223 White Ave., 509/996-3107, http://chewuchinn.com) has 11 guest rooms ($105-210 d) and seven cabins ($140-260) in the hills west of town. Nice touches here include a hot tub, high-end linens, and a substantial breakfast that's included in the rate.

★ **Sun Mountain Lodge** (604 Patterson Lake Rd., 509/996-2211, www.sunmountain-lodge.com, $259-345) set atop a 5,000-foot peak with panoramic views into the North Cascades and Methow Valley, is one of the premier destination resorts in Washington. In keeping with the spirit of the region, rooms deliver luxury in a casual, rustic style, with lots of exposed wood and stone. Amenities include three hot tubs and a swimming pool with a mountain view, and you can partake in abundant activities, from fly-fishing to horseback riding to wine tasting in a handsome stone cellar.

Information and Services

Stop in at the **Winthrop Chamber of Commerce Information Station** (202 Riverside Ave., 509/996-2125, www.winthrop-washington.com, daily 10am-5pm) for maps, brochures, and one-on-one travel advice.

Transportation

There's no public transportation into Winthrop or the rest of the Methow Valley. In summer most visitors from the west come over Route 20, the North Cascades Highway. In winter you have to come from the south, over Stevens Pass on Route 2 and then up from Wenatchee on Routes 97 to Pateros, 153 to Twisp, and 20 into Winthrop.

TWISP

Twisp doesn't have a comparable tourism infrastructure to Winthrop, nine miles to the

view from Sun Mountain Lodge

north, but it's an appealing little town with a growing arts community. The heart of it consists of a few blocks along Glover Street, where there's an impressive art gallery, a good bakery, and a couple of nice shops. It's worth a stop for a meal and a look around, and if you have an artsy sensibility you might find it a more appealing option than Winthrop for an overnight stay.

Sights

Just off of Route 20, **TwispWorks** (502 S. Glover St., 509/997-3300, twispworks.org) is a complex of buildings that for much of the 20th century was a National Forest Service workstation made up of offices and garage and warehouse space for equipment. It's been transformed into an arts-focused multipurpose center that includes studios, gallery space, gardens, and offices of creative entrepreneurs. What you get out of a visit here depends a lot on timing. On Saturday afternoons the studios are open to the public, and on weekends the **Methow Valley Interpretive Center** (509/997-4904, www.methowvalleyinterpretivecenter.com) is open, with displays about the ecology, geology, and history of the region. Even if you're here on a weekday you can have a rewarding visit checking out the gardens, the sculpture, and the New Deal-era architecture. If you plan ahead (by looking on the TwispWorks website) you can attend one of the regular art classes or lectures.

Along Glover Street is Twisp's cultural hub, **Confluence Gallery & Arts Center** (104 N. Glover St., 509/997-2787, www.confluencegallery.com, Wed.-Fri. 10am-5pm, Sat. 10am-3pm). It has six exhibits a year of local and regional artists, and it also hosts classes, musical performances, lectures, and film screenings.

Hiking

To visit an old fire tower with mountain vistas in all directions, take the Alder Creek Road about five miles southwest from Twisp to Lookout Mountain. At the end of the road a trail leads 1.3 miles to **Lookout Mountain Lookout.**

Twisp River Road west of town provides access to the north side of the 145,667-acre **Lake Chelan-Sawtooth Wilderness,** with a dozen different paths taking off from the valley. A fine loop trip of approximately 15 miles begins just southwest of War Creek Campground on Forest Road 4420. The **Eagle Creek Trail** starts at an elevation of 3,000 feet and climbs steadily through Douglas fir forests and meadows, reaching 7,280-foot Eagle Pass after seven miles. Here it meets the **Summit Trail,** with connections to the Stehekin end of Lake Chelan or to other points in the wilderness. To continue the loop hike, follow it south a mile to the **Oval Creek Trail.** This path leads back down to the trailhead, passing beautiful West Oval Lake on the way; a two-mile detour climbs to two additional cirque lakes.

Food

Cinnamon Twisp Bakery (116 N. Glover St., 509/997-5030, daily 6am-3pm) makes first-rate organic breads and pastries, and true to their name they're masters of the cinnamon twist. This is the place to go in town for coffee and a light breakfast, and it's also good for sandwiches and pizza at lunch.

You get the sense that Twisp isn't a typical small town when you drop in at **Glover Street Market** (124 N. Glover St., 509/997-1320, www.gloverstreetmarket.com, Mon.-Sat. 9am-6pm). It's a natural-foods store that wouldn't feel out of place in Seattle—its all-organic selection feels a little precious and a little pricey, but the quality is top-of-the-line. There is also sit-down breakfast and lunch ($9-13) and an extensive wine cellar.

You get good renditions of Mexican specialties, along with a few pasta dishes, at local favorite **La Fonda Lopez** (125 Rte. 20, 509/997-0247, www.lafondalopez.com, daily 11:30am-8pm, $10-20).

Accommodations

Twisp River Suites (140 Twisp Ave.,

855/294-4758, www.twispriversuites.com) is a stylish modern structure a block off of Glover Street. There are standard rooms ($139), but most of the lodgings are one-bedroom ($209-259) or two-bedroom ($308-388) suites with living rooms, full kitchens, and private decks overlooking the river. The experience is more like staying in a furnished apartment than a typical hotel. Breakfast comes with the room.

Southwest of town, **Methow Suites B&B** (620 Moody Ln., 509/997-5970, www.methowsuites.com, $125) has two guest rooms with private decks looking out over the surrounding hills. They're set in a comfortable late-20th-century home overseen by a friendly couple, a former teacher and a former smokejumper.

Information and Services

Learn about local events and activities at the **Twisp Visitor Information Center** (201 Rte. 20 S., 509/997-2020, www.twispinfo.com, Mon.-Fri. 9am-5pm, Sat. 9am-2pm).

Transportation

Twisp is nine miles south of Winthrop on Route 20, about a 15-minute drive, and 52 miles north of Chelan via Routes 153 and 97, an hour's drive. The drive to Chelan takes you through the farm town of Pateros, where the Twisp River feeds into the mighty Columbia.

Lake Chelan

Long and narrow Lake Chelan (sheh-LAN) makes a wormlike squiggle across the middle of the Washington map. Its novel shape—50 miles long but seldom more than 2 miles wide—is the result of a trough carved by ice age glaciers. The glaciers also made the lake very deep, 1,486 feet below the waterline and 450 feet below sea level at the deepest point. In the United States only Lake Tahoe and Oregon's Crater Lake are deeper.

The developed southern end of the lake is a very popular recreational area. A big part of the appeal is the water temperature, which reaches the 70s in summer, making it one of the few major bodies of water in Washington that's comfortable for swimming. The town of Chelan is dominated by lakefront resorts where families from all over the state come to swim, boat, fish, water-ski, paddleboard, and sunbathe. The surrounding hills constitute Washington's most recently developed wine region. Whether or not you're interested in wine, the area is a pleasant place for a drive or a bicycle ride through rolling countryside. And keep your eyes on the sky: Chelan has an international reputation as an excellent place for experienced hang gliders and paragliders

(when the winds are right, some gliders make it all the way to Idaho).

Fifty miles away, the north end of the lake, Lake Chelan National Recreation Area, is part of the North Cascades National Park Complex. It's notable for Stehekin, its primary hub of activity, reachable only by hiking trail or boat from Chelan. Most visitors are day-trippers who make the boat ride up to have lunch and take in the natural beauty, but there are a couple of lodging options. Spend the night and you'll get a serious dose of peace and quiet.

CHELAN AND VICINITY

The town of Chelan at the south end of the lake is a full-service tourist destination, where you can get out on the water during the day and bed down in comfort at night. The town itself feels like a relic of the 1950s, with a couple of blocks of storefronts, a few quirky little local restaurants, and an old-time movie palace. Because of its central location and its uncommonly pleasant waters, Chelan is a magnet for Washingtonians from all over the state. It's a rare place where you could be standing in line for coffee with residents of

Lake Chelan

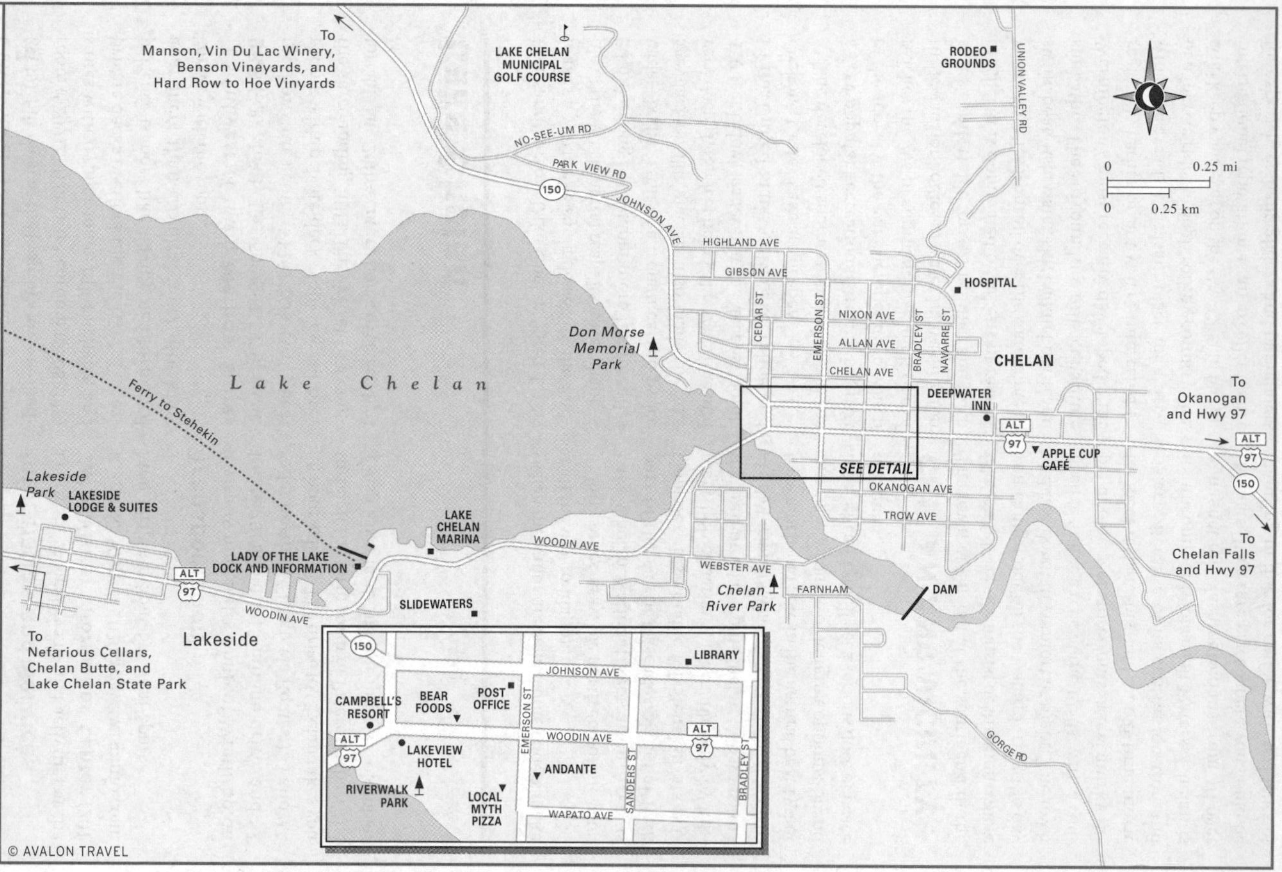

© AVALON TRAVEL

Lakeside Park

LAKESIDE LODGE & SUITES

To
Nefarious Cellars,
Chelan Butte, and
Lake Chelan State Park

Lakeside

WOODIN AVE

ALT 97

Ferry to Stehekin

Lake Chelan

To
Manson, Vin Du Lac Winery,
Benson Vineyards, and
Hard Row to Hoe Vinyards

LADY OF THE LAKE DOCK AND INFORMATION

SLIDEWATERS

LAKE CHELAN MARINA

WOODIN AVE

Don Morse Memorial Park

LAKE CHELAN MUNICIPAL GOLF COURSE

150

NO-SEE-UM RD

PARK VIEW RD

JOHNSON AVE

HIGHLAND AVE

GIBSON AVE

CEDAR ST

EMERSON ST

CHELAN AVE

ALLAN AVE

NIXON AVE

BRADLEY ST

NAVARRE ST

HOSPITAL

RODEO GROUNDS

UNION VALLEY RD

CHELAN

DEEPWATER INN

ALT 97

APPLE CUP CAFE

To
Okanogan and Hwy 97

To
Chelan Falls
and Hwy 97

150

ALT 97

WEBSTER AVE

FARNHAM

Chelan River Park

OKANOGAN AVE

TROW AVE

DAM

GORGE RD

SEE DETAIL

Detail inset

ALT 97

150

CAMPBELL'S RESORT

RIVERWALK PARK

LAKEVIEW HOTEL

BEAR FOODS

POST OFFICE

LOCAL MYTH PIZZA

EMERSON ST

WOODIN AVE

JOHNSON AVE

ANDANTE

WAPATO AVE

SANDERS ST

ALT 97

LIBRARY

BRADLEY ST

0   0.25 mi
0   0.25 km

Spokane, Seattle, and the Tri-Cities. Both sides of the lake offer scenic drives and wine-tasting opportunities. Along the north shore the little town of **Manson,** seven miles from Chelan, gives the area added character.

Scenic Drives

While most visitors come to Chelan to hang out in or along the water, many of them discover that there's beautiful scenery in the surrounding hillsides. The most popular scenic drive is the 12-mile **Manson Loop.** It starts in Manson, and goes up among the vineyards, apple orchards, and smaller lakes in the foothills, with striking views all along the way. From Manson, drive west on Lakeshore Drive and Summit Boulevard, north on Loop Avenue, east on Wapato Lake Road, and then south on Swartout Road and back along the water to Manson.

There's another scenic drive on the south shore of the lake. Follow Route 97 to the **Chelan Butte Lookout** sign across the street from the Park Lake Motel. The road curves upward for seven miles, with pullouts for photos of the lake and surrounding hills, the Columbia River almost directly below, the wheat fields of eastern Washington, and acres of apple orchards. The 3,892-foot butte is also one of the state's best launching pads for hang gliders.

Stormy Mountain has views across Lake Chelan, into the North Cascades, and over into the arid wheat country. Reach it by driving up Lake Chelan's South Shore Road to its end at 25-Mile Creek State Park and then taking Forest Service Road 2805 to its end at Windy Camp. The view here is wonderful. A half-mile hike to the summit of 7,198-foot Stormy Mountain provides an even better one.

Wine-Tasting

The hills around Lake Chelan are relatively new to winemaking, but the conditions—warm summer days and cool nights, volcanic soil—are well suited to growing grapes. More than two dozen winemakers are here; primary varietals are syrah, merlot, malbec, and pinot noir among the reds, and chardonnay, pinot gris, riesling, and gewürztraminer among the whites.

On the south side of the lake, one of the best wineries to visit is **Nefarious** (495 S. Lakeshore Rd., 509/682-9505, http://nefariouscellars.com, June-Oct. daily noon-5pm, Apr.-May Sat.-Sun. noon-5pm). They make high-quality syrah and riesling, and their tasting room has a patio with a beautiful view

Lake Chelan

over the lake. They also rent out a two-bedroom guesthouse ($300).

Across the water on the lake's north shore, **Vin du Lac Winery** (105 Route 150, 509/682-2882, http://chelanwine.com, daily noon-5pm) has an indoor-outdoor tasting area with a nice laid-back vibe. It produces a full range of varietals but has an affinity for cabernet franc. In summer, the winery opens up a farm-to-table restaurant, and there's live music on most Saturday nights.

Up in the hills between Chelan and Manson, **Benson Vineyards** (754 Winesap Ave., 509/687-0313, www.bensonvineyards. com, daily 11am-5pm) has a spectacular view and a luxe—if a little McMansion-like—winery facility.

For something more down-to-earth, drop in at **WineGirl Wines** (222 E. Wapato Way, 509/293-9679, www.winegirlwines.com, June-Sept. daily noon-7pm, Oct.-May Sat.-Sun. noon-7pm). It's a modest, warehouse-style facility along the road to Manson where the young, irreverent winemaker produces some delicious wines made with grapes sourced from throughout the state. You're likely to meet a couple of friendly winery dogs here.

There's a playful atmosphere up in the hills off of the Manson Loop drive at **Hard Roe to Hoe Vineyards** (300 Ivan Morse Rd., 509/687-3000, www.hardrow.com, daily noon-6pm), where the tasting room is decorated in an Old West bordello style.

Hiking

For an easy, pretty stroll take **Riverwalk Park Loop,** which runs a mile along the Chelan River adjacent to town. The park has restrooms, a picnic area, and a boat launch. From the boat launch you can continue on the three-mile round-trip **Chelan River Trail,** which has signage describing the workings of the Chelan Dam.

The prime spot for longer hikes is the **Echo Ridge Trail System,** nine miles north of Chelan along Boyd Road. There are 25 miles of trails through mostly open hill

patio at Nefarious winery

country with views of the lake and mountains in the distance.

Boating

There are lots of ways to get on the water at Lake Chelan—sailboarding, waterskiing, Jet Skiing, kayaking, canoeing, rowing, and paddleboarding are all popular. You can bring your own craft or rent personal watercraft, sailboats, canoes, and waterski boats from several local companies: for canoes, kayaks, and paddleboards, **Lake Rider Sports** (509/885-4767, http://lakeridersports. com); for motorboats and personal watercraft, **Shoreline Watercraft** (509/682-1515, www. shorelineofchelan.com); and for parasails and crafts of all sorts, **Chelan Parasail and Watersports** (509/682-7245, http://chelan-parasail.com).

Bicycling

Chelan has good options for both road cycling and trail riding. Both highways that go up-lake from Chelan are popular, as are several roads with lighter traffic such as the **Manson Loop.** North of the lake you can ride on the **Echo Ridge Trail System,** and numerous Forest Service roads and trails are open to mountain bikes. Check with the **Chelan Ranger District** (428 W. Woodin Ave., 509/682-4900, www.fs.fed.us, Mon.-Fri. 7:45am-4:30pm) for information and maps of roads and trails. The forest road winding out past 25-Mile Creek Campground and up a steep mountainside is a good workout and offers fantastic views of the upper reaches of Lake Chelan. Trails can be found branching off into the mountains from this road, which eventually comes out of the woods at the town of Entiat.

Conventional bike rental services have struggled to find a foothold in Chelan, but you can get a bike with a boost from **Chelan Electric Bikes** (204 E. Wapato Ave., 509/683-2125, http://chelanelectricbikes.com, $40/2 hrs.). Along with rentals, it leads electric-bike tours.

Water Parks

Slidewaters at Lake Chelan (102 Waterslide Dr., 509/682-5751, www.slidewaterswaterpark.com, June-Sept. daily 10am-7pm, $23), one of Chelan's most popular places for children, is a short walk from the downtown area. Ten waterslides overlook the town and lake, and there are also kiddie slides, a 60-person hot tub, a swimming pool, an inner tube ride, a picnic area, video arcade, and concession stand.

Food

Dining options in and around Chelan tend to fall into two categories: old standbys that have been serving visitors for years and ambitious newcomers trying to lure in diners with something a little different.

Apple Cup Cafe (804 E. Woodin Ave., 509/682-5997, www.applecupcafe.com, daily 6am-9pm, $8-24) is one of Chelan's dining institutions. It's an unpretentious, straightforward diner that's most popular at breakfast time, when it serves substantial portions of all the classics—bacon and eggs, biscuits and gravy, and the house specialty, cottage cheese pancakes.

Along the main drag in Chelan **Bear Foods Market and Creperie** (125 E. Woodin Ave., 509/682-5535, http://bearfoodsmarket.com, Mon.-Sat. 9am-6pm, Sun. 9:30am-5pm) serves double duty. It's a natural-foods store where you can get picnic supplies or stock up if you're cooking on your own, and in an adjoining dining room decorated with northwestern-themed murals you can sit down for a sweet or savory crepe (daily 9:30am-2:30pm, $7-13). The crepes are heartier than you might expect, and you can also get soups and salads.

The busiest restaurant in town is ★ **Local Myth Pizza** (122 S. Emerson St., 509/682-2914, http://localmythpizza.com, Tues.-Sun. 11:30am-9pm, $9-19), which serves creative pizzas in a lively setting that manages to be both hip and family friendly. Options range from classic margherita to Canadian bacon and pineapple, all of which can be made gluten-free or as a calzone. Also available is a good selection of Washington beer and wine.

Your best option for a romantic dinner is the candlelit trattoria **Andante** (113 S. Emerson St., 509/888-4855, http://bob1185.wix.com/andantechelan, daily 5pm-10pm, $20-25). The menu features Italian classics like chicken marsala, lasagna, and Tuscan seafood stew.

At Campbell's Resort, **Campbell's Pub and Veranda** (104 W. Woodin Ave., 509/682-2561, www.campbellsresort.com, daily 7am-9pm, $16-42), located in the original, century-old hotel, serves three meals a day, with a seasonal dinner menu that includes grilled meats, pasta, and big salads.

Lake Chelan Winery (3519 Rte. 150, 509/687-9463, http://lakechelanwinery.com), located along the lake's north shore, was the first winemaker in the area, and it's a vigorous self-promoter with a folksy tasting room and gift shop. Its best feature is out back, where you can get barbecued ribs, burgers, and salmon straight off the grill (Mon.-Fri.

4pm-8pm, Sat.-Sun. noon-8pm, $14-30) and eat at picnic tables with views of the vineyard and the hills.

In Manson, family-run **El Vaquero** (75 W. Wapato Way, 509/687-3179, daily 11:30am-9:30pm, $8-18) serves from-scratch Mexican food. There's no cheesy Tex-Mex here, just fresh, authentic cuisine made from family recipes and served in a tidy, pleasant dining room.

Accommodations

Chelan gets packed with visitors in summer, which means you need to book well in advance and you're going to pay premium prices. Off-season rates are often as much as 50 percent lower.

The dominant player in Chelan lodging is ★ **Campbell's Resort** (104 W. Woodin Ave., 509/682-2561, www.campbellsresort. com, $249-349 d), which has sprawling grounds in a prime location, with 170 waterfront rooms, a 1,200-foot sandy beach, boat moorage, kayak and paddleboard rentals, two pools, kids' activities in summer, a day spa, and two restaurants. Most standard rooms can accommodate up to four people with two queen beds or a king and a sofa bed. They're well maintained, with some midcentury-modern design touches, and they all have balconies or patios.

Chelan's best bargain option is **Deep Water Inn** (531 E. Woodin Ave., 509/888-5461, www.deepwaterinn.com, $90-120), a clean, no-frills motel located in town half a dozen blocks from the lake.

Lakeview Hotel (104 E. Woodin Ave., 509/682-1334, http://chelanhotel.com, $229-325) is an adults-only boutique property just down the street from Campbell's. It caters to guests who want a quieter, more elegant experience than what family-focused Campbell's provides. The 13 rooms have jetted tubs and fireplaces, and some have balconies, but the name is misleading—there are only partial water views.

Chelan has a couple of old-style resorts—small, rustic places with fully equipped facilities that are well suited to families wanting to unwind for a few days (and probably do some of their own cooking). **Watson's Harverene Resort** (7750 S. Lakeshore Rd., 509/687-3720, www.watsonsresort.com), along the south shore 10 miles west of Chelan, has large beachfront accommodations that require a week's stay in prime summer months. There are four lodges that can sleep up to six ($335-380), plus a cabin and two duplex units that sleep four ($235-280). Along with the private beach there's an outdoor pool and a hot tub, and they have boat moorage.

Three miles farther up the lake from Watson's is **Kelly's Resort** (12800 S. Lakeshore Rd., 509/687-3220, http://kellysresort.com), which has 11 pine-paneled cabins with one to three bedrooms ($245-310) and four lakeside condos with one or two bedrooms ($270-310). There's a sandy beach and boat moorage, and guests have use of kayaks and canoes.

Transportation

Chelan is 60 miles south of Winthrop on a well-marked 1.25-hour drive that follows Routes 20, 153, and 97. It's 40 miles south on Route 97 Alternate from Chelan to Wenatchee. From Seattle it's a 180-mile, 3.5-hour trip east to Chelan along I-90, Route 2, and Route 97 Alternate.

★ STEHEKIN

The isolated hamlet of Stehekin (steh-HEE-kin) sits at the northwest end of Lake Chelan, where it can be reached only by boat, foot, or private plane. Without four wheels, you'll need to develop an understanding of Stehekin's unique transportation logistics, which can require some patience and strategizing. But the fact that Stehekin isn't reachable by car is part of what makes a trip here so appealing: It's a beautiful place that feels removed from the rest of the world. Thousands of visitors each year take the 50-mile boat trip—a core part of the experience in itself—up-lake from Chelan for lunch or an overnight stay at one of Stehekin's rustic resorts. The town is also a launching point for treks into the heart of the North Cascades National Park Complex.

The name Stehekin (an Indian term meaning "the way through") is a good fit for this mountain gateway. The town came into existence in the late 1880s when prospectors arrived in search of gold and silver. They didn't find enough to establish a large mine, and as a result there wasn't the impetus to connect Stehekin to the outside world by road. Today it's home to fewer than 100 permanent residents, but it has all the basics, including a post office, convenience store, restaurant, and grade school, as well as a bakery and an outdoor supply shop that operate only in summer.

Sights

A couple of historic sites are part of the Stehekin experience. Three and a half miles up the main road you'll encounter the **Old Stehekin Schoolhouse,** a character-rich log building that functioned as Stehekin's school from 1921 to 1988. A side road near the schoolhouse leads to **Buckner Homestead and Orchard** (http://bucknerhomestead. org), where 15 structures, the oldest dating from 1889, sit in the midst of an apple orchard that still bears fruit.

Hiking

The Stehekin area is popular with hikers of all levels, with trails running along the water and up into the mountains. The Red Bus shuttle makes it easy to get from the boat landing to the trailheads and back again. While many of the trails aren't physically taxing, even the easiest ones can have a few rough patches. You'll always be happier wearing hiking boots.

A first stop for most hikers during the season is the National Park Service's **Golden West Visitor Center** (509/699-2080, ext. 14, www.nps.gov/noca, May-Oct. daily 8:30am-5pm), located by the landing. At the center you can peruse a relief map of the area, get advice from rangers, and pick up maps of hiking trails.

Located near the landing, just behind the visitors center, is the **Imus Creek Nature Trail,** a three-quarter-mile-long loop hike that climbs a hill overlooking the lake. The **Lakeshore Trail** also starts near the landing. It's a level, waterside hike that connects Stehekin with Moore Point, seven miles away.

Spectacular **Rainbow Falls,** a towering two-level cataract that plummets 312 feet, is just off the road amid tall western red cedar trees. Get there by walking (or biking, or catching the tour bus) 3.5 miles up the road.

view from the deck of the North Cascades Lodge at Stehekin

Take the shuttle to High Bridge for a beautiful day hike to **Howard Lake** (formerly named, and sometimes still referred to as, Coon Lake). A 1.2-mile trail leads uphill to the lake, which offers views of Agnes Mountain and good bird-watching. From High Bridge another scenic option is the 2.5-mile **Agnes Gorge Trail,** which ends at a springtime waterfall and has beautiful gorge views. (Don't confuse this with the less impressive Agnes Creek Trail, which runs parallel.)

There are over a dozen more trails, including one of the steepest hikes in the state—the tortuous climb to the 8,122-foot summit of **McGregor Mountain**—and multiday backpacking trips taking you into North Cascades National Park.

Food

North Cascades Lodge at Stehekin (509/682-4494, http://lodgeatstehekin.com), located next to the boat landing, serves three meals a day mid-May-mid-October, and for the rest of the year has lunch on the days when the boat is running from Chelan. Meals are the sort of palatable institutional food you'd expect in such a remote location—burgers, sandwiches, and salads for lunch ($8-11), and steak, chicken, fish, and pasta for dinner ($15-26).

The restaurant at **Stehekin Valley Ranch** (509/682-4677, http://stehekinvalleyranch.com, $12-24) welcomes nonguests at dinner, with reservations required. The menu includes steak, chicken, salmon, burgers, and a vegetarian plate, plus a nightly special. A dinner shuttle runs to and from the landing.

Two miles up from the boat dock is Stehekin's biggest culinary attraction, ★ **Stehekin Pastry Company** (509/682-7742, http://stehekinpastry.com, mid-May-mid-Oct. daily, variable hours), commonly just called "the bakery." Given the isolated location, the high quality of the baked goods is a wonder—the giant cinnamon rolls are especially popular. It also serves sandwiches, soup, salads, ice cream, and espresso. Though precise hours vary through the season, you can count on them being open for breakfast and lunch.

Accommodations

To get the most out of a visit to Stehekin you need to experience the peace and quiet that come with spending a night here. Reservations are a must in the summer.

Located by the landing, the **North Cascades Lodge at Stehekin** (509/682-4494, http://lodgeatstehekin.com) has standard lodge rooms ($145-210) and units with kitchens ($210-250) that can sleep from three to seven. Amenities include a restaurant, a convenience store, and kayaks available for rent. Standard rooms are available from May through October, while kitchen units are available year-round; you need to bring your own food in the off-season, when the restaurant has limited service.

The main alternative to the North Cascades Lodge is **Stehekin Valley Ranch** (509/682-4677, http://stehekinvalleyranch.com), nine miles up the road from Stehekin. Most of the lodgings here are primitive tent cabins ($100 per person) with kerosene lamps, no running water or electricity, and shared bathrooms in the main lodge building. A few nicer cabins ($135 per person) have private baths and electricity. Three hearty meals and local transportation are included in the price of your stay. The ranch is open mid-June-early October.

Silver Bay Inn at Stehekin (509/670-0693, http://www.silverbayinn.com), two miles from the landing at the far northern point of the lake, rents a cabin sleeping up to four ($339), a house sleeping up to four ($425), and a single guest room ($225). The facilities are well appointed—they feel like nice time-shares. The house and cabin require a five-night minimum stay.

CAMPING

Stehekin has good camping options. There's no charge for sites, but they require permits, which are available on a first-come, first-served basis from Golden West Visitor Center. (Park administrators say they will

Hiding Out in Holden Village

If you want to up the isolation factor, disembark the *Lady of the Lake II* (which carries passengers from Chelan to Stehekin) when it stops at Lucerne. From there, take a bus 12 miles uphill to **Holden Village** (www.holdenvillage.org), which like Stehekin is an old copper- and gold-mining town that's off the main road system. The mine closed in 1957, but the historic buildings remain and are now part of a Lutheran retreat. You don't have to be religious to stay here. You can take part in classes of all sorts, covering topics from interpersonal relations to the environment to craft-making, or simply use the village as a base for exploring the spectacular mountain-rimmed setting. Guests stay in simple lodges with bunk rooms that accommodate 2-4 people and bathrooms down the hall. Three wholesome meals are included in the rate of $90 per person per night. A sauna, hot tub, pool hall, bowling alley, and snack bar are also in the village.

find a site for every camper.) **Purple Point Campground** is the most accessible, just a third of a mile from the boat landing in Stehekin. Its sites overlook the lake, and it has flush toilets and running water. Campers can also ride the shuttle bus from Stehekin to **Harlequin, High Bridge,** and **Tumwater,** and there are additional campgrounds accessible by trail only. **Weaver Point Campground** is a popular boat-access location at the north end of the lake across from Stehekin.

Information

Just up from the boat landing, the National Park Service's **Golden West Visitor Center** (509/699-2080, ext. 14) is open 8:30am-5pm daily May-October.

Transportation

GETTING THERE

Unless you're backpacking through the national park or using a private plane, the only way to reach Stehekin is by water. **Lake Chelan Boat Company** (1418 W. Woodin Ave., 509/682-4584, http://ladyofthelake.com) has two boats that make the voyage between Chelan and Stehekin: the 285-passenger *Lady of the Lake II,* which makes the trip in 4 hours, and the 130-passenger *Lady Express,* which gets there in 2.5 hours.

Lady of the Lake II operates daily May-mid-October, leaving from a dock a mile south of Chelan at 8:30am and arriving at Stehekin at

12:30pm. The return trip departs at 2pm and arrives back at Chelan at 6pm. The fare is $24 one-way, $40.50 round-trip.

The *Lady Express* runs daily mid-June-mid-September, and on a more limited schedule varying 3-5 days a week, mid-October-April. In summer it leaves Chelan at 8:30am, arrives in Stehekin at 11am, and heads back at noon, arriving in Chelan at 2:45. In the off-season departure is at 10am from Chelan and 1:30pm from Stehekin. In summer the fare is $37 one-way, $61 round-trip. In the off-season it's $24 one-way, $40.50 round-trip.

For day-trippers the boat ride leaves a fairly short window of time to be in Stehekin—90 minutes if you take *Lady of the Lake II,* an hour if you take the *Lady Express.* You can extend your visit to three hours by taking the express up and the slow boat back.

GETTING AROUND

Once you arrive at the boat landing you can go it on foot—there are a couple of easily accessed trails, and the deck of the North Cascades Lodge, just a few steps away, is a pretty place to have lunch and take in waterside views.

To get the most out of your visit, it helps to make use of the limited transportation options. June-October a shuttle, commonly known as the **Red Bus,** makes four trips a day along Stehekin Valley Road, which goes up the valley the 11 miles to High Bridge. The schedule is timed to correspond with boat arrivals and departures, and there are stops along the way at trailheads, campsites, and the bakery. The fare is $8 one-way. There's also a shuttle that runs 3.5 miles up the road to Rainbow Falls. It costs $10 round-trip and takes 50 minutes, making it perfectly timed for day-trippers.

Another option for getting around is cycling. A five-minute walk from the landing takes you to **Discover Bikes** (http://stehekindiscoverybikes.com), where you can rent bikes by the hour ($5) or day ($25). Note that there are only four miles of paved road. When the road to High Bridge turns to gravel, it's rough going.

Wenatchee

With a population of 32,000, Wenatchee is the biggest town in central Washington. It sits in the eastern foothills of the Cascades at the confluence of the Wenatchee and Columbia Rivers, an ideal location for both growing and shipping apples, which have been the central to the town's economy and culture from its earliest days. Wenatchee bills itself as the Apple Capital of Washington—or, depending on who you ask, the Apple Capital of the World.

For most leisure travelers Wenatchee is a convenience stop. It's at the southwest corner of the Cascade Loop on the road between Chelan and Leavenworth, and while it doesn't have the tourism focus of those two towns, there are good places to eat, some pleasant diversions, and lots of chain hotels.

OHME GARDENS

Located just north of town on a bluff overlooking the Wenatchee Valley, **Ohme Gardens** (3327 Ohme Rd., 509/662-5785, www.ohmegardens.com, Memorial Day-Labor Day daily 9am-7pm, Apr. 15-Memorial Day and Labor Day-Oct. 15 daily 9am-6pm, $8) is a testament to over half a century of dedicated horticulture on the part of the Ohme family, who transformed a barren hillside of sagebrush into a highly acclaimed garden. They originally intended it for their private use, but opened it to the public when interest grew; it 1991 the original owners' son sold the property to the state, and it's now managed by Chelan County.

The nine acres of manicured gardens resemble alpine scenery: evergreens, grass, ponds, and waterfalls blend in with the existing rock. Several lookout points provide broad views of the valley, the Cascades, and the Columbia. The garden is located at the junction of Routes 2 and 97.

OTHER SIGHTS

The **Wenatchee Valley Museum and Cultural Center** (127 S. Mission St., 509/888-6240, www.wenatcheevalleymuseum.org, Tues.-Sat. 10am-4pm, $5) is a step up from your usual small-town museum. It has engaging exhibits about local history and culture, including a thorough examination of the world of apples, as well as temporary displays that focus on art, history, or science. Hands-on activities and a model train diorama are hits with kids.

The 4,800-foot-long **Rocky Reach Dam** (6151 Rte. 97A, 509/663-7522, http://chelan-pud.org/visitor-center.html, daily 9am-6pm, free), seven miles north of Wenatchee, makes a point of being visitor friendly. It has 18 acres of landscaped grounds, a fish ladder with a viewing area, and a visitors center with a museum focusing on life along the Columbia throughout history. A 90-minute tour (usually three times a day; call for schedule), gives an up-close look at the workings of the dam.

SPORTS AND RECREATION

The **Apple Capital Loop Trail** is a 10-mile paved path that makes for a good waterfront stroll or bike ride. The trail goes along

Ohme Gardens

both sides of the Columbia River, connecting a series of parks, including **Wenatchee Confluence State Park** (which has hiking trails and good bird-watching), **Riverfront Park** (with a skating rink and a miniature steam train), and **Walla Walla Point Park** (with a swimming beach).

Bike rentals ($30-50/day) are available along the trail from **Arlberg Sports** (3 N. Worthen Ave., 509/888-7433, www.arlbergsports.com, Mon.-Sat. 10am-5pm, Sun. noon-5pm), located in Pybus Public Market.

FOOD

A good place to start in Wenatchee, especially if you're not sure what you're hungry for, is **Pybus Public Market** (3 N. Worthen Ave., 509/888-3900, www.pybuspublicmarket.org, daily 8am-9pm), a riverside former steel mill that's been transformed into a hip, food-centric mall. Inside are Mexican, French, and Italian restaurants, as well as a brewpub, coffee shop, wine-tasting room, butcher, baker, produce vendor—and half a

dozen more specialty shops. When things get busy there's a fun collective energy to the big, open building.

A destination spot for breakfast is **The Wild Huckleberry** (302 S. Mission St., 509/663-1013, http://wildhuck.com, Mon.-Fri. 7am-3pm, Sat.-Sun. 8am-3pm, $8-15). Set in an old downtown house, it has a comfortable atmosphere that feels a little more refined than a diner. The food—pancakes, eggs Benedict, biscuits and gravy—is also a cut above typical diner fare.

Take a nostalgia trip at **Owl Soda Fountain** (25 N. Wenatchee Ave., 509/664-7221, Mon.-Thurs. 9:30am-6pm, Fri.-Sat. 9:30am-8pm, Sun. noon-5pm, $7-10), a downtown institution dating back to 1926. The standard lunch options (burgers, grilled cheese) are really just an excuse for indulging in one of the milk shakes or other ice cream treats.

For good pub grub in a casual setting, try **McGlinn's Public House** (111 Orondo Ave., 509/663-9073, www.mcglinns.com, Mon.-Thurs. 11am-11pm, Fri. 11am-midnight, Sat. 8am-midnight, Sun. 8am-10pm, $12-20), a bar and grill that accommodates an after-work drinking crowd while remaining family friendly. The large menu includes pizza, pasta, sandwiches, and steaks, along with choices for kids. The location, in a historic building that originally housed a social club, is a big part of the appeal.

Inna's Cuisine (26 N. Wenatchee Ave., 509/888-4662, www.innascuisine.com, Tues.-Fri. 11am-2pm and 4:30pm-9pm, Sat. noon-9pm, $15-28) bills itself as a European restaurant. It serves dishes from all over the Continent, but its heart is in Russia and Ukraine. Come for the pierogies, cabbage rolls, and beef stroganoff, served in a candlelit dining room. This is a family-run operation, and you can sense it in the personable service.

The Windmill (1501 N. Wenatchee Ave., 509/665-9529, www.thewindmillrestaurant.com, daily 4:30pm-9pm, $14-46) is Wenatchee's classic stop for old-school, small-town fine dining. That means steaks and prime rib, with house-made marionberry pie for dessert.

ACCOMMODATIONS

Wenatchee's role as a business hub for the surrounding countryside has attracted national chain businesses of all sorts, giving the central commercial area an "Anytown USA" vibe. That phenomenon holds true for lodging. Along North Wenatchee Avenue there are more than a dozen chain hotels delivering comfortable but generic accommodations. There's not much else to choose from.

The nicest of the lot is **Coast Wenatchee Center Hotel** (201 N. Wenatchee Ave., 509/662-1234, www.coasthotels.com, $139-179). It's located next door to the convention center and attracts primarily business travelers, but vacationers also appreciate the well-appointed rooms and the river and mountain views.

Get a luxe B&B experience along the Wenatchee River north of town at **Warm Springs Inn and Winery** (1611 Love Ln., 509/662-5683, www.warmspringsinn.com, $220-260), where six guest rooms occupy a renovated colonial-style mansion on a 10-acre property. There's a romantic feel to the place that makes it a popular wedding location.

TRANSPORTATION

Because of the way the highway system navigates around the mountains, a drive between Chelan and Leavenworth takes you past Wenatchee. The city is 40 miles south of Chelan via Route 97 Alternate and 23 miles southeast of Leavenworth on Route 2, a half-hour drive.

Leavenworth

Few places have embraced the "if you build it, they will come" sensibility more successfully than the little town of Leavenworth, situated on the eastern slopes of the Cascades. Leavenworth faced a dire future in the 1960s, after being stripped bare by the lumber industry and abandoned by the railroad. Its response was to bet all-in on tourism by transforming the city into a faux Bavarian village. The mountain backdrop was a good start, and city leaders enlisted the help of architect Karl Heinz Ulbricht, an East German refugee who was a stickler for authenticity.

Half a century later Leavenworth is going strong. The novelty of the quaint, kitschy Bavarian theme is a big part of the allure, but after a day or two of soaking up the atmosphere, many Leavenworth tourists revert to the habits of travelers elsewhere in the Cascades—they take to the wilds to enjoy the natural beauty. There's good hiking on the surrounding slopes, and the Wenatchee River, which runs along the south side of town, has some of the best rafting in the state.

SIGHTS

The main activity in Leavenworth is strolling around town—checking out the shops, eating some sausage, drinking some beer. There is, however, one cultural institution that merits a visit: the **Nutcracker Museum** (735 Front St., 509/548-4573, www.nutcrackermuseum. com, May-Dec. daily 1pm-5pm, Jan.-Apr. call for hours, $5), perched in a 2nd-story space above the shops of Front Street. As you look through the museum's display cases you realize that the nutcracker is the perfect object for the obsessive collector. Across cultures and across time people have come up with a remarkable variety of ways to crack a nut, and the museum's collection has thousands of examples from all over the world, dating back to the 16th century. They're by turns ingenious, whimsical, weird, and beautiful. A visit here is a quirky, one-of-a-kind experience.

For a respite from shopping, idle awhile in **Front Street Park,** located between Front Street and Route 2, the highway into town. It's a sunny spot with a central gazebo that's

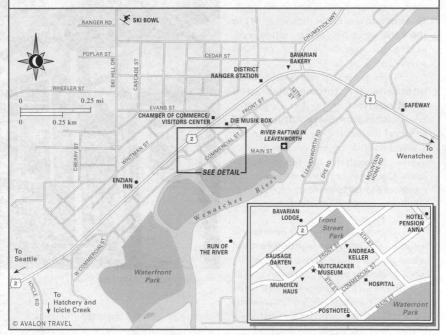

Leavenworth

the site for community events such as dance performances and art exhibits. There are also public restrooms.

To get a little farther away from the hubbub of town, take a walk through **Waterfront Park,** on the cottonwood-shaded banks of the Wenatchee River off 8th and Commercial Streets. There are paths over and around the river, views of the peaks surrounding Icicle Canyon, and benches for lingering.

Two miles south of town off of Icicle Road, the **Leavenworth National Fish Hatchery** (12790 Fish Hatchery Rd., 509/548-7641, www.fws.gov/leavenworth, Mon.-Fri. 8am-4pm, Sat.-Sun. call for seasonal hours, free) is the birthplace of well over a million Chinook salmon each year. Only a few thousand will eventually return to spawn, having navigated seven dams on the way upstream. The hatchery was the largest such facility in the world when it was completed in 1940. Stop by to watch fish swimming through the raceways

and step inside to see displays and educational videos. Exhibits reveal how Columbia River dams and development have impaired natural salmon and steelhead runs and how the hatchery attempts to mitigate some of that damage. The biggest attraction here is an outdoor aquarium where you can watch rainbow trout in the eye-level concrete stream.

FESTIVALS AND EVENTS

Leavenworth is always finding something to celebrate—festivals and fairs fill the calendar. Most are managed by the chamber of commerce; the website for its **visitors center** (904 Rte. 2, 509/548-5807, www.leavenworth.org) has complete event details.

Mid-January brings the **Bavarian IceFest,** with snowshoe and cross-country ski races, dogsled pulls, a tug-of-war, and fireworks. The next big event is **Maifest,** held on Mother's Day weekend, when costumed Bavarian dancers circle the maypole. There are also concerts, a parade, and a Saturday-night street dance accompanied by oompah music. This weekend also marks the start of **Art in the Park,** which features area artists every weekend from May through October in Front Street Park.

Summer festivals include mid-June's **International Accordion Celebration** and **Kinderfest** on the Fourth of July. The **Washington State Autumn Leaf Festival** takes place the last weekend of September, with a grand parade, evening dancing in the streets, and pancake breakfasts. The following three weekends are given over to **Oktoberfest,** where a keg-tapping ceremony each Saturday afternoon launches the revelry.

Christmas is Leavenworth's most festive holiday. The **Christmas Lighting Festival** is held the first three weekends in December, when all the Christmas lights go on at dusk and Mr. and Mrs. Claus appear in their house in the park. Caroling, sleigh rides, concerts, and food booths are all part of the holiday festivities. The lights stay lit till February.

SHOPPING

Shopping is a conspicuous part of the Leavenworth experience. The tiny town has over 50 retail stores, most of them located on **Front Street,** where they sit alongside restaurants and beer gardens—all nicely decorated with carved wood, flower boxes, and murals. Even the automated teller machine is surrounded by a painted alpine scene. Once you get past the facades, Leavenworth's shops are more diverse than you might expect. What you primarily find are specialized boutiques selling casual and outdoor clothes, housewares, souvenirs, and food. Playing off the general international theme, shops specialize in products from Australia, Russia, and the developing world.

Only a few have a Bavarian connection: the **Nussknacker Haus** (735 Front St., 509/548-4708, www.nussknackerhaus.com, daily 10am-7pm), located under the Nutcracker

Leavenworth's Nutcracker Museum

Museum, showcases imported collectibles, including hundreds of German nutcrackers; **Die Musik Box** (933 Front St., 509/548-6152, www.musicboxshop.com, daily 10am-7pm), stocks thousands of intricate music boxes from around the globe, including German creations.

There's also a concentration of wine-tasting rooms. A standout among them is Yakima Valley-based **Kestrel Vintners** (843 Front St., 509/548-7348, http://kestrelwines.com, daily 11am-5pm).

SPORTS AND RECREATION
Hiking

At Wenatchee National Forest's **Leavenworth Ranger District** (600 Sherbourne St., 509/548-2550, www.fs.usda.gov/okawen, Mon.-Sat. 7:45am-4:30pm), along Route 2 a couple of blocks from the heart of town, you can get literature and ranger advice about nearby day hikes. Two prime hiking areas worth exploring are along

Icicle Creek to the southwest of town and Lake Wenatchee to the north.

ICICLE CREEK

Just east of town, a turn south from Route 2 onto Icicle Road leads to a variety of good hiking options. Starting from the Leavenworth National Fish Hatchery, the **Icicle Creek Interpretive Trail** is a mile-long loop; pick up one of the informative trail brochures before heading out to see the sights along the creek, including a wildlife viewing blind. Nearby, a two-mile climb on the demanding **Icicle Ridge Trail** leads to a lovely ridge-top viewpoint.

Farther down Icicle Road, a turnoff onto a stretch of unpaved roadway leads to two trails that have lakes as their destinations. The easier **Eightmile Lake Trail** is a seven-mile round trip; in summer the lake water is warm enough for swimming. There's more of a climb on the nine-mile round-trip **Lake Stuart Trail,** but for your efforts you get spectacular views of Mount Stuart. Farther still along Icicle Road is **Icicle Gorge Trail,** a four-mile loop that takes you up one side the Icicle Creek and down the other, with vistas over the rushing water and abundant wildflowers in spring and summer.

LAKE WENATCHEE

The **Lake Wenatchee** area at the north end of Route 207 has an extensive system of hiking trails. Popular with hikers and photographers is the **Dirtyface Trail,** a steep 4.5-mile one-way hike from the Lake Wenatchee Ranger Station to the Dirtyface Lookout at 6,000 feet, where you get views of the lake and surrounding scenery. Backpackers may want to try the **Nason Ridge Trail,** a 22-mile one-way scenic trail along the length of the Nason Ridge, starting at South Shore Road off Route 207.

The upper Chiwawa River drainage north of Lake Wenatchee is one of the most popular access points for the Glacier Peak Wilderness. Several trails take off near the end of this road, including the heavily used **Phelps Creek Trail,** which follows the creek for five miles to mountain-rimmed Spider Meadows inside the wilderness.

THE ENCHANTMENTS

The **Enchantments** area south of Leavenworth holds Shangri-La status for Washington hikers. Its clear alpine lakes and craggy peaks have a singular, otherworldly beauty that leaves viewers at a loss for superlatives, and the hike's challenges add to its near-mythic allure. It's best seen on a two-day

along the Icicle Gorge Trail

(or longer) trip, but mandatory overnight permits are hard to come by—each year they're awarded through a lottery in March, with a small number held back for same-day distribution from the Leavenworth Ranger District office. Once on the trail, you're faced with significant ascents and an often-rugged path. Few regret the effort.

The 18-mile hike runs between Snow Lakes and Stuart Lake trailheads, which are eight miles apart by car off Icicle Road. (You either need to have another car waiting at the finish line or hope to hitch a ride with another hiker who does.) Starting at Snow Lakes is the classic route: Over the first 10 miles you gain more than 7,000 feet in elevation, ascending from the lower to upper Enchantments basins before crossing Aasgard Pass. Starting from Stuart Lake means 1,000 feet less elevation gain but a steeper initial climb, and arguably a less dramatic experience—you see the Upper Enchantments first, and it's all downhill from there, literally and metaphorically.

Go to the Wenatchee National Forest website (www.fs.usda.gov/okawen) to learn about the lottery for overnight permits. Applications are accepted in the last two weeks of February, and the drawing is conducted mid-March. Some trail-hardened hikers make the trip in a day, but it's a 12-hour slog not undertaken lightly.

★ River Rafting

Many rivers in the central Cascades are good for rafting, but the Wenatchee is easily the top rafting river in the state. Above Leavenworth it drops through rugged Tumwater Canyon, navigating several Class IV stretches before calming down to more manageable Class III rapids below town. Leavenworth is the most common put-in point, with white-water trips covering 16-24 miles depending upon the take-out spot. Conditions change through the year; high spring runoff creates excellent white-water conditions April-mid-July, and sometimes longer.

Gentler float trips begin at Lake Wenatchee and cover the stretch of easy water before the river enters Tumwater Canyon near Tumwater Campground (the take-out point). These are especially popular when flow levels drop during August and September. Inner tubers often float down slower parts of the Icicle and Wenatchee Rivers to Blackbird Island near Leavenworth's Waterfront Park.

Resources for guided rafting trips and kayak, paddleboard, and inner tube rental are **Osprey Rafting** (9342 Icicle Rd., 509/548-6800, http://ospreyrafting.com), **Blue Sky Outfitters** (900 Front St., 800/228-7238, www.blueskyoutfitters.com), and **Leavenworth Outdoor Center** (321 9th St., 509/548-8823, www.leavenworthoutdoorcenter.com).

FOOD
German Cuisine
Classy **Mozart's** (829 Front St., 509/548-0600, www.mozartsrestaurant.com, Mon.-Fri. noon-8pm, Sat.-Sun. noon-9pm, $17-59) sits above the fray of the village, with a subdued dining room one story above Front Street. The menu has German touches, such as schnitzel and spaetzle, but the emphasis is equally on classic American upscale cuisine—blackened salmon, twice-baked potatoes, and four kinds of steak.

In the basement of the same building as Mozart's, ★ **Andreas Keller** (829 Front St., 509/548-6000, www.andreaskellerrestaurant.com, daily 11:30am-8:30pm, $13-30) offers a thorough take on German fare, with a long menu that includes wursts, schnitzels, smoked pork chops, pickled herring, and potato salad. Comfortable wooden booths, murals on the walls, and frequent live music add to the lively spirit of the place, making it one of the most popular, and most fun, places to eat in Leavenworth.

Beer Halls and Gardens
Beer is served in restaurants all over town, but for the German beer garden experience, head to **Munchen Haus** (709 Front St., 509/548-1158, www.munchenhaus.com, Sun.-Thurs. 11am-9pm, Fri.-Sat. 11am-11pm, $6-7) or

Sausage Garten (636 Front St., 509/888-4959, www.viscontis.com/sausage-garten, Sun.-Thurs. 10am-9pm, Fri.-Sat. 10am-10pm, $7-10). Both show some New World influences, including regional microbrews on tap and grilled rather than boiled sausages, but the busy, boisterous atmosphere has a touch of Bavarian spirit.

Another lively place to drink beer is **Icicle Brewing Company** (935 Front St., 509/548-2739, www.iciclebrewing.com, Mon.-Wed. noon-10pm, Thurs.-Fri. 11am-11pm, Sun. 11am-10pm), Leavenworth's own microbrewery. It has a pleasant indoor-outdoor setting and a menu of snacks ($2-11) with a few gestures toward the German theme—pretzels and landjaeger—as well as turkey sandwiches and cheese and meat platters.

Bakeries and Delis

Leavenworth has several appealing bakeries. In the heart of town, **The Gingerbread Factory** (828 Commercial St., 509/548-6592, www.gingerbreadfactory.com, summer daily 8am-8pm, variable hours in other seasons) specializes in gingerbread cookies and houses and also has a deli counter selling soups and sandwiches. Along Front Street, **The Danish Bakery** (9731 Front St., 509/548-7514, Mon.-Fri. 9am-6pm, Sat.-Sun. 9am-8pm) sells pastries and cookies along with fresh soft pretzels. Down Route 2 a few blocks beyond the village, **The Bavarian Bakery** (1330 Rte. 2, 509/548-2244, Thurs.-Mon. 7am-5pm) sticks to German specialties, including Christmas *stollen*.

For something to go with your bread, check out **Cured** (636 Front St., 509/888-0424, daily 10am-8pm), which sells high-quality European-style cured meats, including landjaeger, several kinds of salami, and German and Italian sausages.

Latin American

South (913 Front St., 509/888-4328, www.southrestaurants.com, Sun.-Thurs. 11:30am-9pm, Fri.-Sat. 11:30am-11pm, $14-27) does creative takes on Latin American (primarily Mexican) cuisine. In the pleasant back garden it feels like you've left Bavaria and been transported to a charming hacienda.

New American

For casually sophisticated farm-to-table dining, Leavenworth has **Watershed** (221 8th St., 509/888-0214, Thurs.-Mon. 5pm-9pm, $25-30). The menu features creative preparations of regionally sourced meat and fish, with a vegetarian option and local veggies playing a significant role in every dish. The location, in the Bavarian village but removed from Front Street, has an intimate, romantic feel, and there's outdoor seating with a mountain view.

ACCOMMODATIONS

Leavenworth has lots of lodging options, but it can be hard to find a room over a summer weekend or during a festival, so it pays to book in advance. Most places have higher rates at busy times and often require a two-night minimum stay. Complimentary breakfast is standard here; some hotels have elaborate buffets. The website of the chamber of commerce **visitors center** (509/548-5807, www.leavenworth.org) has a complete list of lodgings. Call them for help in finding a place to stay when vacancies are hard to come by.

Along Route 2 across the highway from the village there are several larger hotels that all deliver a comfortable stay with Bavarian touches. **Enzian Inn** (590 Rte. 2, 509/548-5269, www.enzianinn.com, $140-265 d) has over 100 rooms with themed furnishings. The owner gets you in the spirit of things by playing an alpenhorn every morning. The hotel has indoor and outdoor pools, hot tubs, and an exercise facility. Next door and under the same ownership is **Linderhof Inn** (690 Rte. 2, 800/828-5680, www.linderhof.com, $125-185 d), where for slightly lower rates you get comfortable rooms without the perks of a pool and a workout room.

The nicest of the hotels along Route 2 is **Bavarian Lodge** (810 Rte. 2, 888/717-7878, www.bavarianlodge.com, $153-224 d), located right across from the village. It's well maintained and professionally run, with 50 nicely appointed rooms, a small outdoor heated pool, and two hot tubs.

Within the village, cozy, quiet **Hotel Pension Anna** (926 Commercial St., 509/548-6273, www.pensionanna.com, $179-309 d) captures the Bavarian spirit with authentic furnishings and friendly, efficient service.

There's a different twist on the Bavarian concept at the high-end **Posthotel** (309 8th St., 509/548-7678, https://posthotelleavenworth.com, $355-415 d), located in a prime village spot overlooking the Wenatchee River. Here the goal is to emulate a modern German spa, with bright, clean design, multiple pools and steam rooms, and a full array of wellness treatments.

In the countryside to the north of the village, **Abendblume Pension** (12570 Ranger Rd., 509/548-4059, www.abendblume.com, $188-262 d) has seven elegant, individually decorated rooms with balconies and fireplaces imported from Germany. You're a mile from town, but you're still steeped in the Bavarian aesthetic.

Ditch the Bavarian theme for rustic luxury at a couple of places outside of town. Up in the mountains three miles south of the village, **Mountain Home Lodge** (8201 Mountain Home Rd., 800/414-2378, www.mthome.com, $170-320 d) is a wooded retreat made up of ten lodge rooms and two cabins. It's a great base for hiking in summer and cross-country skiing and snowshoeing in winter.

Run of the River (9308 E. Leavenworth Rd., 509/548-7171, www.runoftheriver.com, $249-289 d), across the Wenatchee half a mile upstream from town, has six suites and one house that change decor to match the seasons.

INFORMATION

Given that tourism is the lifeblood of Leavenworth, it's fitting that the town has a first-rate **visitors center** (940 Rte. 2, 509/548-5807, www.leavenworth.org, Mon.-Thurs. 8am-6pm, Fri.-Sat. 8am-8pm, Sun. 8am-4pm). Representatives, both in person and over the phone, are eager to help you plan your visit. Check the website for thorough listings of hotels, restaurants, shops, and events.

TRANSPORTATION

Leavenworth is due east of Seattle, about a 2.25-hour drive whether you go via I-90 over Snoqualmie Pass to Route 97 or along Route 2 over Stevens Pass. Getting to Leavenworth from Chelan along the Cascade Loop takes a little over an hour, first heading south on Route 97 and then turning northwest onto Route 2 in Wenatchee.

Mount Rainier and the South Cascades

Look for ★ to find recommended
sights, activities, dining, and lodging.

Highlights

★ **Snoqualmie Falls:** The biggest—and most easily accessible—waterfall in the state is just a short drive from Seattle (page 328).

★ **Crystal Mountain Summit:** The gondola of Crystal Mountain ski resort whisks you up to a jaw-dropping vista of Mount Rainier and the surrounding Cascades (page 344).

★ **Paradise Area, Mount Rainier National Park:** You'll get the full Rainier experience here, with a classic national park inn, an excellent visitors center, scores of trails, and the majestic peak towering above you (page 352).

★ **Sunrise Area, Mount Rainier National Park:** Get close to the peak of Mount Rainier on fabulous trails, from easy meadow strolls to demanding ascents (page 355).

★ **Johnston Ridge Observatory:** This visitors center has first-rate exhibits along with great views of Mount St. Helens's crater (page 362).

★ **Ape Cave:** It's an adventure hiking through this 2.5-mile lava tube, one of the longest caves of its kind in the nation (page 364).

The South Cascades, from Snoqualmie Pass down to the Columbia River Gorge, are Washington's favorite mountain playground.

Among numerous attractions, star billing goes to snowcapped Mount Rainier, which looms over the landscape as the tallest and most visually striking volcanic peak in America's Lower 48.

One of the reasons the area is so popular is its accessibility. Interstate 90, which heads east out of Seattle over Snoqualmie Pass and all the way to Spokane (and, eventually, Boston), is the biggest and busiest road through the Cascades. Long-haul semis share the highway with city dwellers in hybrids and SUVs on their way to hiking trails and ski slopes often less than an hour from home.

To the south of the interstate are three giant volcanoes with three different personalities. Towering Mount Rainier dominates the scene—it's the centerpiece of a national park that draws more than 1.5 million visitors a year. South from there is Mount St. Helens, which in 1980 had the most destructive eruption in U.S. history, in the process boiling lakes, charring forests, and sending up ash that could be detected over a third of the nation. It's a remarkable experience to tour the violently altered terrain and witness the early stages of what will be a centuries-long healing process.

Rainier and St. Helens are both easily reached by well-traveled roads and have top-of-the-line visitors centers. The third volcano, Mount Adams, receives a fraction of the attention of the other two. Located to the east of St. Helens, it's an off-the-beaten-path colossus crisscrossed with remote trails.

PLANNING YOUR TIME

The sort of experience you have in the South Cascades depends on the season. Summer is prime time all over: In July and August well over a million visitors explore Mount Rainier National Park, and nearly that many head to Mount St. Helens. Meanwhile Puget Sound-area residents head up toward Snoqualmie Pass on I-90, where it seems like every exit along the way leads to a rich and varied selection of hiking trails.

Previous: view of the South Cascades from Crystal Mountain Summit; Mount St. Helens. **Above:** trees on Twin Falls Trail near North Bend.

Mount Rainier and the South Cascades

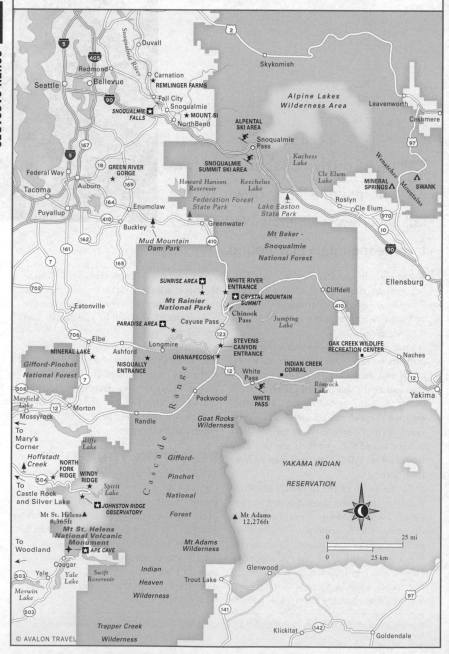

© AVALON TRAVEL

Winters are long and snowy. Smaller mountain passes and many surrounding roads close down for the season, but skiers take to the slopes at Snoqualmie Pass, Crystal Mountain, and White Pass. While most of Mount Rainier National Park shuts down, the Paradise area—one of the snowiest places on earth—stays open for cross-country skiing, snowshoeing, and tubing.

Summer or winter, the slopes around the I-90 corridor are an easy day trip from the Seattle area. The biggest challenge is contending with traffic on busy weekends; it's best to travel on a weekday if you can. Mount Rainier National Park is theoretically doable on a day trip from Seattle—it's about a two-hour drive—but requires a couple of days at minimum to do it justice. Lodging within the park consists of two charmingly rustic, but pricey, inns, and three large campgrounds. Good alternative accommodations can be found outside the park, particularly around Ashford at the southwest corner near the Nisqually entrance.

Mount St. Helens is usually treated as one day in a larger summer itinerary—possibly coming or going from Rainier or the Columbia Gorge—or as a day trip from Portland, an hour away. On the road in from the west, taken by a vast majority of travelers, there are more visitors centers than overnight accommodations.

The I-90 Corridor: Snoqualmie Falls to Cle Elum

You can get in your car in downtown Seattle, head east through the mountains at 70 miles an hour on I-90, and reach the town of Cle Elum on the other side in less than 1.5 hours. The trip over Snoqualmie Pass is about as pleasant a drive as you're likely to find on an eight-lane interstate, but for the leisure traveler the point of coming here is to get off the highway and explore.

What you find at virtually every exit are hiking trails—scores of them, from easy strolls to rugged scrambles, taking you through forests, past rivers and lakes and waterfalls, into a world of diverse wildlife, and up to ridges with panoramic views. There are also opportunities for mountain biking and camping, and come winter visitors trade in their hiking boots for skis and snowshoes.

There are some attractions here that don't require you to break a sweat, too. Viewpoints for Snoqualmie Falls, the biggest and arguably most impressive waterfall in the state, are easily accessible. Fans of the TV cult favorite Twin Peaks will recognize the falls and the adjacent lodge from the show. The tiny town of Roslyn is a charmingly rustic spot to stop for lunch and a stroll, and it also has a place in TV history as the location for another1990s hit, Northern Exposure.

SNOQUALMIE AND NORTH BEND

The neighboring towns of Snoqualmie and North Bend draw visitors from the Seattle area and farther afield primarily for two attractions: one of Washington's most popular sights, Snoqualmie Falls, and one of its most popular hiking trails, the path up Mount Si.

Increasingly this region is also drawing tech workers as a place to live. Snoqualmie Ridge, a planned community developed by Weyerhaeuser beginning in the late 1990s, has attracted over 10,000 new residents to the area, many of them employees of Microsoft, which has its Redmond home office just 20 miles away. Ridge dwellers now far outnumber locals in the old Snoqualmie, which has a population hovering around 2,000, but it's still the original town that gives character to the place. North Bend, three miles away, doesn't have the same managed development, but it's also increasingly becoming a bedroom community.

★ Snoqualmie Falls

A mile north of downtown Snoqualmie, massive **Snoqualmie Falls** (6501 Railroad Ave., daily 7am-dusk, free) plunges 270 feet—a hundred feet farther than Niagara. It's Washington's most famous waterfall, attracting some 1.5 million visitors annually, and identifiable from the opening credits of TV show *Twin Peaks.*

A century ago the falls attracted the attention of civil engineers as a potential source of electricity. In 1899 a 1,215-foot tunnel was excavated through the rock above the falls to divert water into the world's first totally underground generating facility. Visitors may not even realize the power plant is there, but it's still operational. It's been the subject of controversy since its inception, both because Snoqualmie Indians consider it a desecration of a sacred site and because it diminishes the majesty of the falls by diverting most of the water that would otherwise flow over it.

Even with the reduced flow, the falls are an impressive sight. A paved, wheelchair-accessible path leads less than 100 yards from the parking lot to the upper viewing platform. A wide but sometimes steep 0.7-mile trail leads down to another viewing area at the base of the falls—it's a pleasant walk, with informative signage along the way, courtesy of Puget Sound Energy. Once you're down there it's impossible to miss the massive workings of a second power plant, built along the river in 1910. Back up at the parking lot there's a gift shop and espresso stand, and you're right next door to the **Salish Lodge,** known as the Great Northern Hotel to *Twin Peaks* fans, where you can have an indulgent meal or spend the night.

Northwest Railway Museum

Snoqualmie's main commercial strip runs along the railway tracks across from the old depot, which now serves as the **Northwest**

Snoqualmie Falls

Railway Museum (38625 SE King St., 425/888-3030, www.trainmuseum.org, daily 10am-5pm, free). The restored 1890 structure is well maintained, with a couple of rooms of exhibits and some preserved railcars outside. On weekends from April through October you can take a leisurely 75-minute ride to North Bend and back in an antique train, following a route that includes a view of Snoqualmie Falls (adults $20, children 2-12 $10).

Remlinger Farms

Eleven miles north of Snoqualmie, outside of the town of Carnation, is **Remlinger Farms** (32610 NE 32nd St., 425/333-4135, www.remlingerfarms.com, mid-May-mid-June Sat.-Sun. 10am-4:30pm, mid-June-Labor Day daily 10am-4:30pm, Labor Day-Oct. Sat.-Sun. 10am-4:30pm, $14.75). It's a farm in name, with some produce for sale and U-pick fields including a pumpkin patch in the fall, but primarily it's a countrified amusement park aimed at small children. Attractions include pony rides, a mini-roller coaster, and half-size train. Everyone over a year in age pays full admission; the price includes all of the rides and activities.

Shopping
North Bend Premium Outlets (461 S. Fork Ave. SW, 425/888-4505, Mon.-Sat. 10am-9pm, Sun. 10am-7pm) has more than 50 shops, including such familiar names as Nike, Banana Republic, and Eddie Bauer. What makes it noteworthy, though, is its location—surrounded by the foothills of the Cascades, it is both surprisingly picturesque and convenient for day-trippers who want to combine hiking and bargain hunting.

Hiking
Exits 32 and 34 off of I-90 lead to a variety of satisfying hiking trails. Because of the proximity to the Seattle area, they're well used, especially on sunny weekends.

MOUNT SI
The climb up Mount Si is believed to be the most popular trail in the state. That doesn't mean it's an easy hike. The four-mile path has a 3,100-foot elevation gain, with many switchbacks and rocky patches along the way. It's heavily wooded, meaning there isn't much in the way of views—until you get to the top, where your two-hour ascent is rewarded with a panorama that stretches as far as Puget Sound and Mount Rainier, and the sensation that you've genuinely climbed a mountain. To reach the actual summit you need to continue up a near-vertical haystack that requires serious rock-climbing skills. Most hikers are content getting to the end of the trail.

Because the view is so central to the experience, this isn't a hike for a cloudy day, and when you go expect company. To reach the trailhead from I-90, take exit 32 and turn north onto 436th Avenue SE. From there take a left onto North Bend Way and in a quarter mile turn right onto Mount Si Road. In 2.5 miles the entrance to the parking area is on the left. You need a Discover Pass to park in the lot.

LITTLE SI
An easier alternative to Mount Si is Little Si, just up the road. The 2.5-mile trail starts and ends with climbs but is flat in between, and at the top is a good view across the Snoqualmie Valley. To get to the trailhead follow the same route as to Mount Si; you'll come to the parking area just past the bridge, two miles before reaching the Mount Si parking area. As with Mount Si, you need a Discover Pass here.

RATTLESNAKE LEDGE
Rattlesnake Ledge is another Mount Si alternative—a relatively easy two-mile hike ending with a terrific view. From the parking area beside Rattlesnake Lake it doesn't *look* like it would be easy to reach the top of the prominent ledge, but the trail is a well-maintained switchback that increases your distance while lessening your workload. The ledge is an exposed rock above a sheer cliff, and it merits due caution when approaching, especially if you have children or dogs with you. Once you're there you have views of the lake far below, the Snoqualmie Valley, and neighboring Mount Si. To get to the parking area and trailhead, take exit 32 off of I-90 and head south along 436th Avenue SE (also known on this stretch as Cedar Falls Rd. SE). Continue four miles to reach the Rattlesnake Lake parking lot. A Discover Pass isn't required here.

TWIN FALLS
The Twin Falls Trail is an appealing hike that follows the south fork of the Snoqualmie River as it drops 300 feet over a series of falls. It's accessible year-round and is a good option in winter, when the water flow over the falls is at its most vigorous. The location is south of I-90 exit 34, five miles east of North Bend. The exit puts you on Edgewick Road, off of which you turn left onto SE 159th Street; continue a half mile to the parking area and trailhead at **Olallie State Park** (51350 SE Homestead Valley Rd., 425/455-7010, http://parks.state. wa.us/555, daily dawn-dusk, Discover Pass required). A 1.3-mile path leads to Twin Falls. From there you can cross a footbridge

The Trail Across the Cascades

Though it's part of Washington's park system, **Iron Horse State Park** (509/656-2230, http://parks.state.wa.us/521) is, by anyone's definition, a trail—and a long one at that. It stretches 113 miles, with one end near North Bend and the other across the Cascades on the banks of the Columbia River. The route extends along property where the Milwaukee, St. Paul, and Pacific Railroad ran electric trains from 1912 until its bankruptcy in 1980. It's now open to hikers, skiers, mountain bikers, and horseback riders, but closed to motorized vehicles.

The western end of the trail starts in Olallie State Park, south of I-90's exit 34. From there it climbs the west slope of the Cascades to Snoqualmie Pass, and then descends past Cle Elum and Ellensburg to its eastern end near Vantage along the Columbia. The gravel trail has a maximum 2 percent grade, taking advantage the leveling work done to make train passage viable, including 30 substantial trestles and four tunnels. The longest tunnel, through Snoqualmie Pass, goes on for 2.3 miles. (Bring flashlights and warm clothes.) There are trail access points near many I-90 exits along the way, including at Snoqualmie Pass, Easton, South Cle Elum, and Thorp.

and continue uphill another 1.6 miles to the Homestead Valley trailhead near exit 38.

Food

SNOQUALMIE

The **Dining Room at Salish Lodge** (6501 Railroad Ave. SE, 800/272-5474, www.salishlodge.com, daily 7am-2pm and 5pm-9pm, $38-75) combines a sophisticated menu with an elegant but comfortable setting that includes window tables overlooking the top of Snoqualmie Falls. (If you want the view, book in advance and request it.) Half of the dinner menu is dedicated to grilled meat and fish, and the rest consists of seasonal appetizers and entrées. A lavish brunch is also served daily. This is among the most expensive restaurants in Washington outside of Seattle, a money-is-no-object indulgence.

For a comparable view in a more casual setting, head upstairs to Salish's **Attic** (6501 Railroad Ave. SE, 800/272-5474, www.salishlodge.com, daily 11am-10pm, $16-22). It

Rattlesnake Ledge

serves pizzas, sandwiches, and appetizers to go with creative cocktails and microbrews.

You get an old-school take on fine dining at **Woodman Lodge** (38601 SE King St., 425/888-4441, http://woodmanlodge.com, Tues.-Sun. 4pm-9pm, $16-61), located in a former loggers' guildhall behind the Snoqualmie depot. From the grand bar to the potbelly stove to the abundant animal mounts, the place is thick with atmosphere. Grilled steaks are the main attraction, and there are gamy options such as wild boar osso bucco and bacon-wrapped elk medallions. Keep the tab down by dining at the bar during the weekday happy hour (4pm-6pm).

Snoqualmie Brewery and Taproom (8032 Falls Ave. SE, 425/831-2357, http://fallsbrew.com, Mon.-Sat. 11am-10pm, Sun. 11am-9pm, $11-17) may be a brewpub, but it's also the most family-friendly place to eat in town, with a colorful, casual dining room and a large menu of sandwiches, salads, and pizza. And they take their beer seriously, brewing seasonal selections to go with nine varieties available year-round, from kolsch to stout to root beer.

NORTH BEND

Georgia's Bakery (127 W. North Bend Way, 425/888-0632, http://georgiasbakerycafe.com, Tues.-Sun. 7am-5pm) is locally famous for its doughnuts and apple-cinnamon bread. It's a good choice when you want to take in a few extra calories to fuel a day of hiking.

Diehard *Twin Peaks* fans will want to visit **Twede's Cafe** (137 W. North Bend Way, 425/831-5511, www.twedescafe.com, Mon.-Fri. 8am-8pm, Sat.-Sun. 6:30am-8pm, $11-15), which plays the role of the Double R Diner in the TV show. The food is typical diner fare—the claim to fame is 50 varieties of burgers, all enormous, with unlimited fries on the side. Dale Cooper groupies may find the cherry pie and coffee not quite as "damn fine" as they would have hoped.

If you're seeking beer, bar food, and some local color after a day of hiking, check out **Mount Si Pub** (45530 SE North Bend Way, 425/831-6155, Mon.-Thurs. noon-midnight, Fri.-Sat. noon-2am, Sun. noon-11pm, $8-10). It's a former loggers' bar that's been in business since the 1930s. Food options are limited to burgers, chicken sandwiches, and simple pizzas, but it's a comfortable spot to unwind, with a fireplace roaring when it's chilly outside and a beer garden open when it's warm.

Accommodations

Most visitors to Snoqualmie and North Bend are day-trippers, and there isn't much in terms of overnight accommodations in the area. The one striking exception is **Salish Lodge** (6501 Railroad Ave. SE, 425/888-2556, www.salishlodge.com, $309-509), perched in a prime location above Snoqualmie Falls. It aims for a rustic elegance, with lots of exposed beams and a wood-burning fireplace in each of the 84 guest rooms. The lodge is a special-occasion destination for many Washingtonians, with a first-class restaurant and a full-service spa. There are some 300 weddings performed here annually.

Outside North Bend, **Roaring River Bed and Breakfast** (46715 SE 129th St., 425/888-4834, www.theroaringriver.com, $139-219) is a comfortable, woodsy retreat with pretty views of the middle fork of the Snoqualmie River. The four rooms and one cabin all have private entrances, baths, and decks. Breakfast comes in a basket delivered to your door.

Information and Services

The **North Bend Visitor Information Center** (250 Bendigo Blvd. S, 425/292-0260, http://northbendwa.gov, Wed.-Thurs. 10am-4pm, Fri.-Sun. 10am-5pm) is a resource for information and advice.

The **North Bend Ranger Station** (902 SE North Bend Way, 425/888-1421, Tues.-Sat. 8am-12:30pm and 1:30pm-4:30pm), about half a mile southeast of the center of town, has information on local trails, mountain bike routes, and campgrounds.

Transportation

The area is about 30 miles from downtown

Seattle, a 30-minute drive heading eastbound on I-90. Take exit 25 for Snoqualmie and exit 32 for North Bend. The **King County Metro Bus Line** (206/553-3000, http://kingcounty.gov) route 208 runs from North Bend through Snoqualmie and terminates in Issaquah, where you can catch buses to and from Seattle.

SNOQUALMIE PASS

Snoqualmie Pass, a little less than an hour east of Seattle, is first and foremost a ski destination. The peaks on either side of I-90, at exits 52 through 54, make up Washington's oldest downhill skiing area, collectively known as the Summit at Snoqualmie. The area also includes over 30 miles of cross-country and snowshoeing trails. In summer the ski facilities sit quiet, but hikers launch out onto some beautiful trails accessing parts of the Alpine Lakes Wilderness.

Skiing and Snowboarding

The Summit at Snoqualmie (general info 425/434-7669, snow line 206/236-1600, www.summit-at-snoqualmie.com) has four downhill areas: **Alpental** to the north of I-90 and **Summit West, Summit Central,** and **Summit East** to the south. The season usually lasts from early December to late April, and full-day lift tickets, good for all four areas, cost $66-79. (You can travel from one area to another on a free shuttle bus.) In total the areas have 25 lifts and over 100 trails, 15 percent of which are suitable for beginners and the rest evenly split between intermediate and advanced. Vertical drops range from 750 feet at Summit West to 2,200 feet at Alpental. Snoqualmie has one of the country's biggest nighttime ski areas.

The **Summit Nordic Center** (425/434-6778), with its base near Summit East, maintains 23 trails for cross-country skiing and snowshoeing; full-day passes are $24 for skiers, $18 for snowshoers. The **Summit Tubing Center** (425/434-6791), open on weekends only, divides each day into five two-hour sessions and charges $22 to $25 per session.

Summit at Snoqualmie services include ski shops, equipment rentals, ski schools, day lodges, food service, and childcare. On winter weekends **Seattle Ski Shuttle** (206/697-9611, www.seattleskishuttle.com) has service to the pass with pickups in West Seattle, downtown Seattle, Bellevue, and North Bend. Reservations are required, and the round-trip fare is $45.

Hiking

Snoqualmie Pass is an access point for the **Alpine Lakes Wilderness,** a beautiful 393,000-acre stretch of high Cascades country bordered by I-90 to the south and Route 2 to the north, which gets its name from its 700 or so lakes, ponds, and tarns. The area is part of the Mount Baker-Snoqualmie National Forest and requires a **Northwest Forest Pass** (day pass $5, annual pass $30) in order to use the parking lots. Passes are usually *not* available at trailheads. Order passes online (www.discovernw.org) or pick them up at gas stations and convenience stores in the area. On the way to Snoqualmie Pass from Seattle you can get one at the North Bend Chevron station (425/888-4393) at I-90 exit 31. They're also available at the **Snoqualmie Pass Visitor Center** (69805 SE Snoqualmie Pass Summit Rd., 425/434-6111), located off of I-90 exit 52. It's open Thursday-Sunday June-August and mid-December-mid-March.

Among the many trails in the Alpine Lakes, a couple of the easiest to reach are on the turnoff for the Alpental ski area. From I-90 take exit 52 if you're coming from the west, or exit 53 from the east. Head north and take the first right into the Pacific Crest Trail (PCT) North parking lot. From the trailhead at the east end of the lot you join the PCT—the long-distance trail running all the way from Mexico to the Canadian border. Hiking north on the trail for 5.5 miles brings you to one of the most striking points on the PCT, the **Kendall Katwalk.** You get there on a gradual, steady wooded ascent that, after a few miles, opens up to views of Cascade peaks. The Katwalk is a 150-yard segment of the trail that was blasted out of the side of steep Kendall Peak. As you walk along it you have views usually reserved for mountain goats and eagles.

Two and a half miles along the PCT toward Kendall Katwalk there's a junction where, if you take the fork to the left, you can instead hike through the meadows of **Commonwealth Basin** and then climb a switchback trail to **Red Pass** for more spectacular views. From the trailhead to the pass is five miles.

If you drive past the PCT access point and to the parking lot of the Alpental ski area, you'll find another trailhead into the Alpine Lakes Wilderness. One of the best hikes from this location is the three-mile trek to **Snow Lake,** one of the largest of the Alpine Lakes, nestled among the peaks. The hike is mostly through open meadows but requires climbs to get in and out of the lake basin.

Food

The Snoqualmie ski areas have indoor concession stands and modest restaurants where, during the ski season, you can warm up with a cup of coffee and some institutional cuisine.

One tasty food oasis is **Aardvark Express** (521 Rte. 906, 425/578-4456, daily 6am-6pm, $9-12), a takeaway stand that brings to the slopes some of the energy and innovation associated with urban food trucks. Curry is the specialty, but there's a range of things to choose from, including creative soups and sandwiches and fresh juice.

Commonwealth (1001 Rte. 906, 425/434-0808, http://thepasslife.com/common-wealth-restaurant, Wed.-Fri. 11am-9pm, Sat. 8am-10pm, Sun. 8am-8pm, $11-23) in the Pass Life condo development at the base of Summit West, serves hearty pub grub—burgers, chili, potpie—in an attractive dining room with a fireplace and an open kitchen. On weekend mornings you can get coffee and pastries.

For a no-frills meal, check out **Pie for the People NW** (741 Rte. 906, 425/518-7799, Sun.-Thurs. 11am-8pm, Fri.-Sat. 11am-10pm, $12-16), which serves New York-style pizza out of a modest space within Lee's Summit Grocery. Next door to Commonwealth,

microbrewery **Dru Bru** (10 Pass Life Way, 425/434-0700, www.drubru.com, Wed.-Thurs. noon-9pm, Fri.-Sat. 11am-10pm, Sun. 11am-9pm) pours 10 or so varieties of German- and Belgian-style beer. You're welcome to bring in food, making this a good spot to eat curry from Aardvark Express or pizza from Pie for the People NW, washed back with a pale ale.

Red Mountain Coffee (773 Rte. 906, 425/434-7337, daily 7am-7pm) is a reliable spot for espresso drinks and baked goods.

Accommodations

The Summit at Snoqualmie doesn't maintain any overnight lodging—an indication of the high percentage of skiers who return home at the end of the day. There's one independently run hotel at the base of the slopes, **Summit Inn** (603 Rte. 906, 425/434-6300, http://snoqualmiesummitinn.com, $139-179), but it has a less-than-stellar reputation and is recommended only as a last resort. A popular alternative for overnighters, especially in groups of four or more, is to rent a privately owned vacation home. (Browse through listings at www.vrbo.com.) Skiers also stay at hotels in the vicinity of Snoqualmie and Cle Elum, both of which are a half-hour drive away.

Information and Services

Snoqualmie Pass Visitor Center (69805 SE Snoqualmie Pass Summit Rd., 425/434-6111), located off of I-90 exit 52, is open from Memorial Day through Labor Day and from mid-December to mid-January. For both seasons the hours are Thursday-Sunday 8:30am-4pm. Stop in here to purchase Northwest Forest Passes and maps and to get information on trail conditions. In winter there are occasional ranger-led snowshoe treks—call the center for details.

Transportation

I-90 runs through Snoqualmie Pass; exits for the pass are 52, 53, and 54. When traffic is clear the 55-mile drive east from downtown Seattle takes less than an hour, and driving the 90 miles northwest from Yakima on I-82 and I-90 takes about 80 minutes.

ROSLYN, CLE ELUM, AND VICINITY

On the east side of Snoqualmie Pass two neighboring towns sit 3.5 miles apart at the foot of the Cascades: little Cle Elum (pop. 1,800) and even littler Roslyn (pop. 900). Both are former coal-mining towns that saw their heydays in the late 19th and early 20th centuries. They now function as bases for stocking up on supplies, having a meal, and perhaps spending the night while visiting the surrounding mountain wilderness.

Roslyn qualifies as a tourist draw in its own right. The couple of blocks that make up the heart of town are lined with restaurants and shops and have an Old West ambience that's both quaint and rough around the edges. If the scene looks familiar, it's probably because Roslyn was the location for the popular 1990s TV series *Northern Exposure*. Fans still make pilgrimages to the town, and a few of the sets remain intact.

The biggest draw here, though, is the sprawling **Suncadia Resort,** which occupies 6,300 acres of former mining and logging land just south of Roslyn and west of Cle Elum. It opened in 2005 and has been growing ever since, with a 254-room lodge on a bluff above the Cle Elum River, three golf courses, a spa, a fitness center, and nine planned neighborhoods with upward of 2,000 vacation homes, primarily owned by Seattle-area residents. On summer weekends the population of Suncadia easily outnumbers that of Cle Elum and Roslyn combined.

Sights

Roslyn and Cle Elum are contrasts in 19th-century urban planning. Cle Elum dreamed big, envisioning itself as the Pittsburgh of the West. Its main commercial streets reflect that ambition—they're four lanes wide, and they feel a little oversized for the small town Cle Elum turned out to be. Roslyn's streets are narrower and more walkable; cars navigate them with caution and tend to yield to pedestrians instinctively.

NORTHERN EXPOSURE SIGHTS

You don't have to be a *Northern Exposure* fan to enjoy a stroll through Roslyn, but it adds to the experience. Aficionados will recognize at least a dozen different locations where the program was filmed, from the doctor's office to the dump. **Central Sundries** (101 W. Pennsylvania Ave., Roslyn, 509/649-2210, http://inlandnet.com/~sundries, Mon.-Sat. 10am-6pm) was the location of Ruth-Anne's General Store and now sells souvenirs from the show. Across the street, *Northern Exposure*'s favorite watering hole, **The Brick** (100 W. Pennsylvania Ave., Roslyn, 509/649-2643, www.bricksaloon.com), is the oldest licensed tavern in Washington. It opened in 1889 and is famous for its 23-foot-long running-water spittoon, which remains operational.

ROSLYN HISTORICAL MUSEUM

The **Roslyn Historical Museum** (203 W. Pennsylvania Ave., Roslyn, 509/649-2355, http://www.roslynmuseum.com, call for hours, $2) has irregular hours depending on volunteer availability, but it's worth checking out if you have a chance. It does a good job of evoking the bygone coal-mining days of the region, when the town was four times its current size.

ROSLYN CEMETERY

Even more evocative is the **Roslyn Cemetery** (Memorial Dr., Roslyn, www.roslyncemetery. org), set on a hill half a mile west from the center of town. The beautiful, partially wooded landscape holds 5,000 graves, which are divided into 25 small adjoining cemeteries representing the different religious, ethnic, and social groups that constituted Roslyn's population during the coal-mining era. It's a striking testament to the diversity of the miners and their high mortality rate. The cemetery is a focus of civic pride; it's well maintained, and respectful visitors are welcome.

CLE ELUM HISTORICAL TELEPHONE MUSEUM

Cle Elum was the last town in America to use a manually operated switchboard, and the last to institute the touch-tone dial system. The old phone building is now the **Cle Elum Historical Telephone Museum** (221 E. 1st St., 509/674-5702, www.nkcmuseums.org, May-Sept. Tues.-Sun. noon-4pm, free), a surprisingly engaging little museum with switchboard exhibits, photos of early Cle Elum, and other memorabilia.

LAKE EASTON STATE PARK

About 15 miles west of Cle Elum, just off I-90 at exit 70, **Lake Easton State Park** (150 Lake Easton State Park Rd., 509/656-2230, http://parks.state.wa.us/532, Discover Pass required) consists of 516 forested acres on the west and north sides of Lake Easton. The most popular feature is the mile-long reservoir, which is good for swimming, boating, and trout fishing. There are also six miles of hiking and biking trails, and in winter you can cross-country ski and go snowmobiling. Within the park there's access to the Iron Horse State Park trail.

Food

Suncadia has reasonably good resort dining for a premium price, and Cle Elum has a couple of prime spots for picking up provisions if you're doing the cooking yourself. But for a variety of appealing restaurants with some genuine character, your best bet is to head into Roslyn.

SUNCADIA

The main dining room at the Suncadia Lodge is **Portals** (3600 Suncadia Trail, 509/649-6473, www.suncadiaresort.com, daily 6:30am-3pm and 5pm-10pm). Dinner entrées ($21-39) include pasta dishes and grilled or pan-seared fish, fowl, and beef. It's the only place in the resort for breakfast ($10-18), which features egg dishes and pancakes. The lodge's bar, **Fifty-6 Degrees** (509/649-6473, Sun.-Thurs. 3pm-10pm, Fri.-Sat. 11am-11pm, $14-27), has a full menu that includes a burger and crab mac and cheese.

Up the road from the lodge, **Swiftwater Cellars** (301 Rope Rider Dr., 509/674-6555, www.swiftwatercellars.com, daily 11:30am-close, $13-75) plays three roles: winery, clubhouse for one of the resort's golf courses, and restaurant. The menu covers similar turf to Portals in a larger, more casual dining room. It serves steaks, chops, pasta, and seafood, along with less expensive flatbreads.

ROSLYN

Roslyn provides more restaurant options than your typical town of under 1,000. One of its dining landmarks is ★ **Roslyn Cafe** (201 W. Pennsylvania Ave., 509/649-2763, http://theroslyncafe.com, Sun.-Tues. 7am-3pm, Thurs.-Sat. 7am-9pm, $9-16), which has a large mural outside that was prominently featured in *Northern Exposure*. Inside, the cafe is both cute and rough-hewn, capturing the essence of what makes the town appealing. The menu takes diner standards and creatively twists some of them, as with the Buffalo chicken spring rolls and banh mi burgers. Parmesan fries and the tater-tot-of-the-month special are a cut above your average spuds. This is also a popular spot for hearty breakfasts, which are served into the afternoon.

Another *Northern Exposure* icon is **The Brick** (100 W. Pennsylvania Ave., 509/649-2643, www.bricksaloon.com, Mon.-Thurs. 11:30am-close, Fri. 11:30am-2am, Sat. 11am-2am, Sun. 11am-close, $11-15), a bar and grill that anchors one corner of Roslyn's main intersection. The oldest licensed watering hole in Washington, it maintains an old-timey atmosphere, with a century-old bar, a running-water spittoon, and a potbelly stove; neon beer signs and TVs keep it from feeling precious. Every tourist who comes to town pays a visit to this big, busy place, and many stay for a meal or a drink. The food is a respectable rendition of standard pub grub, with burgers, sandwiches, and salads.

You get less atmosphere but tasty food at **Village Pizza** (105 W. Pennsylvania Ave., 509/649-2992, Wed.-Fri. 4pm-9pm, Sat. 2pm-9pm, Sun. 2pm-8pm, $11-14). It serves

16 varieties of pie, all with lots of cheese and crust that includes a touch of honey.

If you're thirsty for a beer and don't want to deal with crowds at The Brick, walk a block down the main drag and duck into **Roslyn Roadhouse** (204 W. Pennsylvania Ave., 509/649-3125, Sun.-Thurs. 8am-10pm, Fri.-Sat. 8am-2am), a locals' hole-in-the-wall that also serves burgers, sandwiches, and breakfast in the morning. Next door is the taproom of the local microbrewery, **Roslyn Brewing Company** (208 W. Pennsylvania Ave., 509/649-2232, http://roslynbrewery.com, Fri.-Sat. noon-8pm, Sun.-Mon. noon-6pm), where you can sample craft beer creations.

CLE ELUM

Across the street from one another are two Cle Elum culinary institutions. Since 1887 **Owens Meats** (502 E. 1st St., 509/674-2530, www.owensmeats.com, Mon.-Sat. 8am-6pm, Sun. 9am-5pm) has been selling high-quality sausages, jerky, and fresh and cured meat. If you're planning to grill while camping or to use the kitchen that comes with your room at Suncadia, this is a great place to get your meats.

Across the way, **Cle Elum Bakery** (501 E. 1st St, 509/674-2233, Mon.-Sat. 7am-5:30pm, Sun. 7am-3pm) has been making breads, pastries, and doughnuts since 1906 (and claims that, in all that time, the oven has never been cool). It also sells prepared sandwiches and serves light lunches in a dining room behind the bakery.

For a sit-down dinner, **Parlour Car Bistro** (105 Pennsylvania Ave., 509/260-0722, www.parlourcar.com, Wed.-Sat. 5pm-10pm, $16-32) is a friendly small-town take on fine dining, with a menu featuring creatively prepared steaks, ribs, and pasta.

For a simple, healthy breakfast or lunch a good option is **Stella's** (316 1/2 W. 1st St., 509/674-6816, daily 7am-4pm, $6-10), which serves breakfast wraps and oatmeal in the morning and four variations on a turkey sandwich at midday.

Accommodations
SUNCADIA
Suncadia Lodge (3600 Suncadia Trail, 509/649-6400, www.suncadiaresort.com, $228-428 d) is the focal point of the giant Suncadia Resort, which includes over 2,000 private vacation houses. The lodge sits on a bluff overlooking the Cle Elum River, with views of the mountains framed by the picture window in the lounge area behind the lobby. You can hike down to the water and elsewhere along the

Roslyn Cafe

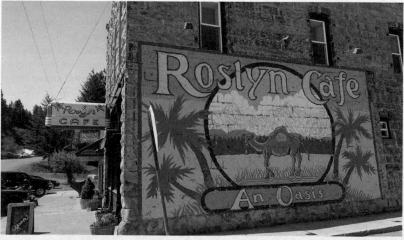

resort's 40 miles of trails; other features include two 18-hole golf courses, indoor and outdoor pools, a spa, a winter skating rink, and a winery. The lodge's guest rooms are actually condos. They maintain a uniform décor but are more fully equipped than most hotel rooms—there are kitchens with dishes and utensils, laundry machines, and a high percentage of two-bedroom suites. The lodge is family-focused, with kid-friendly facilities and children's programs.

CLE ELUM

The **Iron Horse Inn B&B** (526 Marie Ave., 509/674-5939, www.ironhorseinnbb.com, $80-145 d) was built in 1909 as a lodging for railroad workers. It's been restored and decorated with railway memorabilia. Four rooms in the original house share two bathrooms, while four rooms in a 1920 addition have private baths. Outside, the train theme continues with four antique cabooses that have been transformed into suites. The Iron Horse State Park trail is just a few feet from here, making this a good stop for multiday trail trekkers.

Horse lovers are likely to delight in the vast open spaces of the **Flying Horseshoe Ranch** (3190 Red Bridge Rd., 509/674-2366, http://flyinghorseshoeranch.com). It's a genuine working ranch where you can ride one of the resident horses or board your own. There's a variety of lodging for humans, including a large log cabin that sleeps six ($285), a smaller cabin for two ($175), bare-bones bunkhouses that sleep eight ($110), and tepees that sleep four ($100). The latter two categories have shared bathrooms, and there's also a shared cookhouse.

CAMPING

Lake Easton State Park (150 Lake Easton State Park Rd., 509/656-2230, http://parks.state.wa.us/532, Discover Pass required) has 90 tent sites ($35) and 45 hookups ($45), all set amid the woods, with the tent sites primarily along the Yakima River and the RV sites near the lake. You can reserve sites by phone (888/226-7688) or online (http://washington.goingtocamp.com).

Transportation

To reach Roslyn and Suncadia from I-90, take exit 80, head north on Bullfrog Road, and follow the signs. Suncadia is to the left at the first roundabout. Roslyn is straight ahead through that roundabout and another. At the second roundabout, a right will take you into Cle Elum. Reach Cle Elum more directly from I-90 by taking exit 84. The area is about 90 minutes, 85 miles due east, from Seattle.

Suncadia Lodge

Roads to Mount Rainier

Mount Rainier National Park is the undisputed star attraction of the southern Cascades. The park has three primary entrances—White River, Nisqually, and Stevens Canyon. Deciding which to use depends on a number of factors, including where you're coming from, what you want to see, and the time of year. **Nisqually,** the busiest entrance and the only one open year-round, is at the park's southwest corner and the most convenient to I-5; **White River** (summer only) is to the northeast and slightly closer if you're coming from Seattle; **Stevens Canyon** (usually open May-Nov.) makes sense if you're coming from Yakima or other points southeast.

Each route in and out of the park has attractions that, depending on your interests, may be worth stopping for, and each has lodging and dining options that are good alternatives to what's available in the park. Come winter Crystal Mountain, just to the east of the White River entrance, is Washington's biggest and busiest ski destination. Farther south there's a more laid-back skiing scene at White Pass, with fewer slopes and fewer facilities.

APPROACHING THE NISQUALLY ENTRANCE

The busiest entrance to the park is Nisqually at the southwest corner. It falls on **Route 706,** which branches off from north-south-running **Route 7** 14 miles west of the park. Once through the entrance, you're 6.5 miles from Longmire and 17.5 miles from Paradise, two of the park's most visited areas and the sites of its lodges. Nisqually is the only entrance that's open year-round, though severe weather in winter leads to occasional closures. It's also the entrance closest to the southern Puget Sound area, an hour and 15 minutes from both Tacoma and Olympia. And it's the most convenient entrance from I-5, the interstate running between Seattle

and Portland—Seattle is 2 hours away, Portland 2.5.

If you enter the park at Nisqually you'll travel through the towns of **Ashford, Elbe,** and, if you're coming from the north, **Eatonville.** They all are viable places for Mount Rainier visitors to spend the night—particularly Ashford, which is just 10 minutes from the entrance and has the best hotel and restaurant options of any location bordering the park. Tiny Ashford and Elbe's existence depends upon the thousands of park visitors who pass through every year. Slightly larger Eatonville is a former logging town with an identity of its own, though Rainier is still a conspicuous presence on the horizon.

Eatonville

Heading to the national park from Seattle, you hit Eatonville (pop 2,750) along Route 161 about an hour and 20 minutes into the drive and 40 minutes before reaching the Nisqually entrance. It's a decent place to make a pit stop, and its wildlife park draws lots of visitors, especially those traveling with kids.

NORTHWEST TREK WILDLIFE PARK

Just north of Eatonville, you're guaranteed animal sightings at **Northwest Trek Wildlife Park** (11610 Trek Dr. E, 360/832-6117, www.nwtrek.org, July-Aug. daily 9:30am-6pm, mid-Mar.-June and Sept. Mon.-Fri. 9:30am-4pm, Sat.-Sun. 9:30am-5pm, Oct.-mid-Mar. Sat.-Sun. 9:30am-3pm, adults $22.25, kids 5-12 $14.25, kids 3-4 $10.25, kids under 3 free). Two experiences are included in the admission price. One part of the 600-acre grounds is essentially a zoo (although the park doesn't use that term) for animals native to the region. There are sections for bears, birds, canines, cats, and other native animals such as beavers, badgers, and otters, all of whom live in roomy habitats filled with natural features.

The second part of the park is an open

animal preserve where bison, elk, deer, moose, sheep, and mountain goats roam. Visitors experience the area on an hour-long guided tram ride with lots of stops for photos along the way. Throughout the park you will see more animals if you come early; many of them lie low in the warmer afternoon. Also note that closing times indicate the time of last entry; those already in the park can stick around for another 90 minutes.

The park has an additional section, **Zip Wild** (open daily June-Aug., open weekends May and Sept.) with five zip line courses through the neighboring woods. The courses have varying degrees of complexity, and they're priced accordingly ($22-70).

PACK FOREST

You can have a novel hiking experience just west of Eatonville at **Pack Forest** (9010 453rd St. E, 360/832-6534, www.packforest. org, daily dawn-dusk, free). The 4,300-acre property is used for research by the University of Washington's School of Forestry Services and includes areas in various stages of reforestation, as well as a preserve of old-growth Douglas fir, cedar, and hemlock—a rarity in this heavily logged region. Short hiking trails crisscross the forest; there are waterfalls, and a moderate climb takes you to Hugo Peak, with nice views along the way. Pick up a trail map at the entrance or print one online. The forest is open to the public year-round, and it's a good place for winter hikes. Note that hunting is allowed Friday through Sunday in the hunting season, roughly from September through January.

FOOD

The biggest and busiest place to eat in town is **Bruno's Family Restaurant & Bar** (204 Center St. E, 360/832-7866, www.eatbrunos. com, Mon.-Thurs. 8am-10pm, Fri. 8am-11pm, Sat. 7am-11pm, Sun. 7am-10pm, $11-28). It's an all-purpose small-town restaurant with paneled booths, sports pennants decorating the bar, and a long menu that includes bison burgers, grilled salmon, and chicken-fried steak.

You get more of an old-school, homey experience at **Cruiser Cafe** (106 Washington Ave. S, 360/832-8646, http://cruisercafe.biz, daily 6am-9pm, $8-19), a little spot with a primarily local clientele. Burgers are big sellers, but you can also get fried fish and home-cooking classics like pot roast, meatloaf, and liver and onions.

For a quick bite, stop at **Cottage Bakery and Cafe** (212 N. Washington Ave., 360/832-1959, Mon.-Fri. 7am-5pm, Sat.-Sun. 8am-4pm, $6-9) for pastries, cookies, espresso drinks, and sandwiches. Indoor and outdoor seating is available if you want to linger.

ACCOMMODATIONS AND CAMPING

Eatonville's one lodging option is **Mill Village Motel** (210 Center St. E, 360/832-3200, http:// whitepasstravel.com, $130-140). It's a reasonably well-maintained two-story exterior-corridor motel with prices that are a little inflated because of the proximity to Mount Rainier.

There's year-round camping seven miles south of Eatonville at **Alder Lake Park** (50324 School Rd., 360/569-2778, www. mytpu.org), which has both tent sites ($24) and full RV hookups ($35) along with restrooms and coin-op showers. You can reserve online or by calling 888/226-7688. The seven-mile-long lake is the result of a hydroelectric dam managed by Tacoma City Light. It has a sandy beach that's popular for swimming.

Elbe

Elbe, with a population at last count of 29, is barely a clearing along Route 7, 14 miles west of the national park's Nisqually entrance. You'll know you're there when you see the railroad cars by the side of the road. Elbe was once a stop on the Tacoma & Eastern Railway, and it's now the terminus for a tourist train.

SIGHTS

On May-October weekends **Mount Rainier Scenic Railroad** (54124 Mountain Hwy. E, 360/569-7959, http://mtrainierrailroad.com, $44-57) runs antique steam-driven trains from Elbe to the town of Mineral, a seven-mile trip that takes 40 minutes each way. The ride travels through woods and over the Upper Nisqually River, with views of Mount Rainier on clear days. In Mineral you have 40 minutes to tour the railroad's museum, which displays the world's largest collection of steam logging locomotives.

The other attraction in Elbe is the historic **Evangelical Lutheran Church,** erected in 1906 to serve the German immigrant community. The spare but handsome structure is most noteworthy for its tiny size—it measures 18 by 24 feet. From March through November there are services on the third Sunday of the month, and in summer it's open to tourists on an irregular schedule, depending on the availability of volunteers. The building is such a landmark that it doesn't have a street address, but the location is right along the highway—you can't miss it.

FOOD

The restaurant for the Hobo Inn is the **Mount Rainier Railroad Dining Co.** (54106 Mountain Hwy. E, 888/773-4637, www.rrdiner.com, daily 9am-9pm, $10-26), located in an old train dining car. The novelty of the location is the main draw. The food is typical greasy-spoon fare—burgers, sandwiches, fried fish. It serves three meals a day, and of them breakfast is probably your best bet.

Across the road from Elbe's depot and the Hobo Inn, summer-only **Scaleburgers** (54109 Mountain Hwy. E, 360/569-2247, June-August daily 11am-8pm, $7-10) occupies a former weigh station where you can get burgers, fries, and shakes for a quick, filling meal. There are picnic tables for diners who want to eat on-site.

ACCOMMODATIONS

The railroad theme prevails in Elbe's dining and lodging. The one hotel in town is the **Hobo Inn** (54106 Mountain Hwy. E, 888/773-4637, www.rrdiner.com, $115 d), which consists of seven remodeled cabooses. They're a fun novelty for train lovers, though they can

Elbe's Evangelical Lutheran Church

feel musty because the windows don't open. (There is air-conditioning.)

At Mineral Lake, three miles south of Elbe, **Mineral Lake Lodge** (195 Mineral Hill Rd., 360/492-5253, www.minerallakelodge.com, $119-157) has quaint, rustic accommodations in a sturdy cedar building dating from 1906. Of the eight rooms, half have private baths and half share a bathroom. You get great views of Mount Rainier from here, with the trout-filled lake in the foreground.

Another option on the lake is **Mineral Lake Resort** (148 Mineral Hill Rd., 360/492-5367, http://minerallakeresort.com), which has RV hookups ($20-30), camping cabins that sleep up to six ($85-105), and a bunkhouse that sleeps eight ($175-189). These are rudimentary facilities: You bring your own bed linens and towels, and while the bunkhouse has a bathroom, the cabins share an outside bathroom, and you have to go off-site to take a shower. Most guests are here to fish on the lake, and the lodgings have kitchens for cooking up your catch.

Ashford

Located 10 miles from Mount Rainier's Nisqually entrance, Ashford doesn't need any sights of its own to qualify as a tourist town, though with a population of only 217 it barely makes a dent in the surrounding woods. There are dozens of places to stay here, primarily small, independently owned operations. Most are better bargains than the two national park lodges, and some more appealing as well (though for location there's no beating the park's Paradise Inn).

FOOD

Since the 1940s Rainier visitors have been filling up on the home cooking at **Copper Creek Restaurant** (35707 Rte. 706 E, 360/569-2326, www.coppercreekinn.com, June-Aug. daily 7am-9pm, Sept.-May call for off-season hours, $12-27). The building is charmingly rustic and the menu long—soups and stews are standouts, but the real star is the blackberry pie. This is also a good choice for breakfast, available throughout the summer and on weekends the rest of the year.

For something unexpected, it's hard to beat **Wildberry** (37718 Rte. 706 E, 360/569-2277, www.rainierwildberry.com, daily 11am-8pm, $9-20). It's an unassuming diner serving American comfort food—burgers, steaks, milk shakes, huckleberry pie—but there's also a separate menu of tasty and substantial Nepalese cuisine, perfect fuel if you're preparing to channel your inner Sherpa on the trails of Mount Rainier.

To get a dose of youthful, outdoorsy energy head to **BaseCamp Bar & Grill** (30027 Rte. 706 E, 360/569-2727, www.basecamp-grill.com, $9-13), part of the cluster of facilities that includes Whittaker's Historic Bunkhouse and BaseCamp Cottages. It specializes in burgers and pizzas made with all-natural ingredients and offers vegan and gluten-free options. Most of the seating is at outdoor picnic tables.

ACCOMMODATIONS

Whittaker's Historic Bunkhouse and Motel (30204 Rte. 706 E, 360/569-2439, www.whittakersbunkhouse.com, $90-130 d) was originally a lodging quarters for loggers, and it retains a no-frills, backwoods feel, offering 18 basic, well-maintained rooms available year-round and a hostel-style bunkhouse that sleeps six ($35 per person) May-September. It's owned by local mountaineering legend Lou Whittaker and is part of the Base Camp area that includes the offices of Rainier Mountaineering Inc.

Neighboring Whittaker's, **BaseCamp Cottages** (30005 Rte. 706 E, 360/569-2682, www.basecampcottages.com, $135-150) gives you a little more room and a little more privacy in three homey freestanding cottages. Note that there's a two- or three-night minimum stay, depending on the season.

Nisqually Lodge (31609 Rte. 706, 360/569-8804, http://nisqually.whitepasstravel.com, $170-190 d) is a reliably comfortable standard motel with good-size rooms and complimentary hot breakfast in the morning and wine in the evening.

Wellspring Spa & Retreat (54922 Kernahan Rd. E, 360/569-2514, http://wellspringspa.com, $95-195 d) has a wide assortment of woodsy accommodations, from log cabins to a tree house to a lodge that can sleep 14. The place has a lot of charm; it's a remote, deep-in-the-woods experience.

Deep Forest Cabins (33823 Rte. 706 E, 360/553-9373, www.deepforestcabins.com, $140-350 d) has seven guesthouses ranging from modern and functional to large and luxurious. All have kitchens and are convenient to local restaurants despite the location off the main road. A two-night minimum stay applies.

Ashford's most indulgent lodging option is ★ **Stormking Spa and Cabins** (37311 Rte. 706 E, 360/569-2964, http://stormkingspa.com, $220-260 d). The five rustic but luxurious cabins are set on a wooded 10-acre property, and each comes with its own hot tub, deck, and barbecue grill. Stormking caters to couples—children aren't allowed, and many guests come here for honeymoons or anniversaries. Given the quality of the accommodations and proximity to Mount Rainier, it's a good value.

APPROACHING THE WHITE RIVER ENTRANCE

Rainier's White River entrance off **Route 410** is less than two hours from Seattle, making it slightly closer to the city than Nisqually. From the entrance it's another 45 minutes on a switchback road to reach the Sunrise area, one of the park's main destinations and the highest point on Rainier reachable by car. Coming from the east, it's about an hour and 45 minutes to the White River entrance from Yakima.

This is a summer-only route for visits to the park: Sunrise is usually open only from early July through early September, and Route 410 shuts down at Chinook Pass with the winter weather, usually from mid-November through May. (Check the road's status at www.wsdot.com/traffic/passes.) Throughout the year Route 410 is open as far as the turnoff just north of the park's border that leads to Washington's biggest ski area, Crystal Mountain.

Enumclaw

The dairy-farming town of Enumclaw (pop. 11,600) sits in the valley west of the mountains, along Route 410 at its junction with Route 169 from the north and Route 164 from the west. It's not a destination in itself, but it has a pleasant downtown area lined with shops and some good places to eat, making it an appealing stop on the way to or from the park. Enumclaw is about an hour and 15 minutes from the park's Sunrise area, making it a viable place for park visitors to spend the night.

GREEN RIVER GORGE

About six miles north of Enumclaw off of Route 169, the **Green River Gorge** Conservation Area is a 14-mile stretch of protected river with white-water rapids running through narrow gorges with wildflowers and caves along the banks. It's bookended by two small state parks, **Kanaskat-Palmer** (32101 Cumberland-Kanaskat Rd., 360/886-0148, http://parks.state.wa.us/527) upriver at the eastern end, and **Flaming Geyser** (23700 SE Flaming Geyser Rd., 253/735-8839, http://parks.state.wa.us/504) downriver to the west.

You can take pleasant hikes along the river on the trails found in either of the state parks, but the highlight lies in between, along the fern-covered bluffs known as the **Hanging Gardens.** Getting there is tricky—access is off of Franklin-Enumclaw Road, a turnoff from Route 169 2.5 miles north or Enumclaw. The trailhead is unmarked; your surest way to find it is to track down a ranger or a knowing local in one of the state parks and ask for directions. The hike from the road to the Hanging Gardens is about a mile.

In April and May the gorge is a beautiful spot for invigorating Class III-IV white-water rafting. **Alpine Adventures** (800/723-8386, www.alpineadventures.com) and **River Recreation** (800/464-5899, http://riverrecreation.com) lead guided trips.

FOOD

The Kettle (1666 Garrett St., 360/825-7033, Tues.-Sat. 5am-2pm, Sun. 7am-2pm, $9-13) is Enumclaw's favorite place for breakfast, serving hefty portions of classic diner fare, including scrambles, French toast, cinnamon rolls, and blueberry muffins.

The original century-old bar is the centerpiece of the **Rainier Bar & Grill** (1623 Cole St., 360/825-6363, www.rainierbarandgrill.com, Mon.-Thurs. 11am-10pm, Fri.-Sat. 11am-11pm, Sun. 11am-8pm, $10-27), a casual but classy joint with a long list of beers on tap and burgers, steaks, and clam chowder coming out of the kitchen.

You get a similar experience across the street at **The Mint** (608 Cole St., 360/284-2517, www.thehistoricmint.com, Sun.-Thurs. 11am-10pm, Fri.-Sat. 11am-11pm, $11-27),

view of Mount Rainier from Crystal Mountain

Crystal Mountain

In winter this resort area off of Route 410, just outside the northeast corner of Mount Rainier National Park, is Washington's top ski destination, with more acreage and higher elevation than any other slopes in the state. Come summertime you can hike and go horseback riding. It may seem crazy to spend summer days here when the national park is next door, but the resort's lodging is a good option for park visitors, and there are some rewarding activities. It's worth a visit just for the gondola ride up to the top of the mountain, from where you get spectacular views of Mount Rainier and the Cascades.

Along with hiking, featured summer activities at the resort are horseback riding, disc golf, and ridge-top yoga. The golf and yoga are casually organized. Find out about current plans by calling the resort (888/754-6199) or checking its website (http://crystalmountainresort.com). For information about horseback riding contact **Crystal Mountain Outfitters** (509/653-2633, www.crystalmountainoutfitters.com).

SKIING AND SNOWBOARDING

Crystal Mountain Resort (general info 888/754-6199, road conditions 800/695-7623, http://crystalmountainresort.com) has a good variety of runs and state-of-the-art snow grooming. There are 2,600 acres of skiable terrain, with a top elevation of 7,002 feet, a vertical drop of 3,100 feet, and 11 lifts, including Washington's only gondola. The season usually lasts from early December to late April, though in some years the slopes have stayed open as late as June. Full-day lift tickets are $74. Over half the runs are intermediate, 10 percent beginner, and 35 percent advanced. Services at Crystal Mountain include rentals, ski and snowboard schools, day care, and numerous food and lodging venues.

Crystal Mountain is 80 miles from Seattle. The **Crystal Mountain Express** (206/838-7129, www.mtrwestern.com) provides bus service from Seattle, Bellevue, and Tacoma on weekends and holidays from late December

housed in another historic downtown building. The menu here is more eclectic; along with steaks, entrée options include green curry, flatbreads, and jambalaya.

Enumclaw is a good place to indulge your sweet tooth. **The Pie Goddess** (1100 Griffin Ave., 360/625-8568, Sun.-Thurs. 11am-7pm, Fri.-Sat. 11am-9pm) is a tiny shop with a big reputation for delicious from-scratch pies in two dozen varieties, from marionberry to butterscotch, many available by the slice. For ice cream and candy there's **Sweet Necessities** (1215 Griffin Ave., 360/802-5475, Sun.-Thurs. 10am-9pm, Fri.-Sat. 10am-10pm), where the owner makes his own caramels, truffles, and fudge.

ACCOMMODATIONS

Enumclaw has two older, no-frills motels: the **Cedars Inn** (1334 Roosevelt Ave. E, 360/825-1626, http://cedarsinnenumclaw.com, $79-89 d) and the **GuestHouse Inn** (1000 Griffin Ave., 360/825-4490, www.redlion.com/enumclaw, $120-130 d).

through February. A round-trip ride costs $48, and you can get a bus-and-lift-ticket package for $98, with discounted rates for kids and seniors. On weekdays **Seattle Ski Shuttle** (206/697-9611, www.seattleskishuttle.com) operates buses to Crystal Mountain with pickups in West Seattle, downtown Seattle, Mercer Island, Bellevue, Auburn, and Enumclaw. Reservations are required. The round-trip fare is $50, or $115 with a lift ticket.

★ **CRYSTAL MOUNTAIN SUMMIT**

On a clear day the summit of Crystal Mountain provides a phenomenal view of the Cascades, with Mount Rainier towering before you, Mount Adams looming on the southern horizon, and a distant Mount Baker to the north. The quick and easy way to make the 2,200-foot ascent from the resort's base is to take the **gondola** ($23, kids 4-12 $12). It's an expensive but worthwhile trip. The gondola runs throughout the ski season, on weekends Memorial Day-June, and daily from the last week of June to late September. At the top are trails along the ridge, the Summit House restaurant, and a viewing area where you can relax in an Adirondack chair and admire Rainier.

If you have the time and the energy, you can **hike to the summit.** Trail maps are available at the resort and on its website; take one with you because signage is minimal. The full trip is a loop of about 12 miles that strings together three named trails: **Silver Creek, Crystal Mountain,** and **Northway.** There are some dull patches at the beginning and end, including 2.5 miles along the road to the resort, but they're more than compensated for by the forests and alpine fields along the ridgeline, where it's possible to forget you're in the midst of a ski area. In late summer you can pick huckleberries along the way.

If the full loop is too big a commitment, you can hike one way and take the gondola the other. You have to pay full fare if you take the gondola up. If you hike up and take the gondola down the ride costs $10.

FOOD

The Crystal Mountain gondola deposits riders a few steps from the highest-elevation restaurant in Washington, **Summit House** (360/663-3085, winter daily 10:30am-2:45pm, summer Sun.-Thurs. 10:30am-4:30pm, Fri.-Sat. 10:30am-6:30pm, $14-28). The attractive paneled dining room has a vaulted ceiling and two walls of windows to take in the views, but when the weather's warm you can't beat the large deck, with sky above you and mountains to every side. The menu is basic bar-and-grill: steaks, burgers, tacos, and salads, all for prices that reflect the remote and beautiful location. Service is often slow, but few diners are in any rush.

Down at the base, the main restaurant is the dining room at the **Alpine Inn** (360/663-7798, fall-spring daily 7:30am-9:30am and 5pm-9:30pm, summer daily 7:30am-9:30am and 11am-9:30pm, $13-28), which serves some alpine-inspired dishes to match the setting—wiener schnitzel, goulash—along with pasta, steak, chicken, and vegetarian curry. Downstairs the **Snorting Elk** (360/663-7798, winter daily 11am-close, summer Mon.-Fri. 3pm-10pm, Sat.-Sun. 2pm-10pm, $10-13) is the resort's center for nightlife, with frequent live music and a bar that can get hopping, but you can also fill up here on pizza and sandwiches. The Alpine Inn and Snorting Elk are the only places to eat at the base that operate in both summer and winter. During the ski season other options are a cafeteria, an open-air grill, and another bar. Up on the mountain there's a restaurant at Campbell Basin.

Halfway between Enumclaw and Crystal Mountain along Route 410, it's hard to miss **Naches Tavern** (58411 Rte. 410 E., 360/663-2267, Mon.-Thurs. 4pm-2am, Fri. noon-2am, Sat.-Sun. 10am-2am, $11-20), an inviting old shingled pub that looks like it could have come out of a Frank Capra movie. Inside it's a little more divey, and the bar food is run-of-the-mill, but it's still a character-rich place to stop for a bite and a beer—and one of the few options in this neck of the woods.

Naches Tavern

ACCOMMODATIONS

At the base of the ski area are three lodging choices, all managed by **Crystal Mountain Hotels** (33818 Crystal Mountain Blvd., 360/663-2262, www.crystalhotels.com). None are luxurious and all are well worn, but for a reasonably comfortable place to spend the night they do the trick. The largest and least expensive option is the ski-in **Alpine Inn** ($115-235), which is decorated with alpine touches but more than anything feels like a college dorm. Most double rooms are small but functional (no TV or phone); there are larger rooms with bunk beds that can sleep four or six. **The Village Inn** ($175-240) and **Quicksilver Lodge** ($205-290) are closer to what you'd expect from midrange, middle-aged chain hotels, with more amenities and less communal spirit. Quicksilver has loft rooms that are well suited to families. Prices are 20 to 30 percent lower in the summer season.

Ten to 15 minutes from the slopes, but closer to the park entrance, is the most appealing lodging in the area: **Alta Crystal Resort** (68317 Rte. 410 E., 360/663-2500, www.altacrystalresort.com, $250-365). It has 24 suites, all big enough to accommodate families of four. The feel is more rustic than elegant, which fits the wooded location; the rooms are well appointed and have full kitchens. A heated swimming pool and nightly bonfires are popular with kids.

TRANSPORTATION

Crystal Mountain is about 80 miles southeast of Seattle via Routes 169 and 410, and 85 miles northwest of Yakima via U.S. 12 and Route 410. Both drives take just under two hours. In most years Chinook Pass and Cayuse Pass close November-April because of avalanche risk, making Crystal Mountain inaccessible from Yakima and other points to the south and east.

Chinook and Cayuse Passes

The highest of the Cascade passes, Chinook Pass rises more than a mile above sea level (5,440 feet) on Route 410, providing access from the east to the park's White River entrance. This is a fair-weather route, closed in winter and often dusted with snow as late as June. Heading west on a twisting 3.5 miles of road brings you to Cayuse Pass (4,694 feet), where Route 123 from the south merges with Route 410. At Chinook Pass you enter the park, but there's no entrance gate or admission charge here because Route 123 and Route 410 are through roads used by non-park visitors.

Between the two passes the highway crosses into parkland, skirting **Tipsoo Lake,** one of the most beautiful and easily accessed Cascade alpine lakes. A lakeside picnic here affords striking views of Mount Rainier. There's a good hike here as well, the **Naches Peak Loop**, a 3.5-mile trip that follows the lakeshore and then circles the peak. Part of the path follows the Pacific Crest Trail.

APPROACHING THE STEVENS CANYON ENTRANCE

At the southeast corner of Mount Rainier National Park, Stevens Canyon is the entrance most remote from Washington's population centers along Puget Sound, and it's also the farthest from the park's biggest draws, the Paradise and Sunrise areas. Located off of **Route 123,** it's a seasonal entrance, usually open May-November, depending on the snowfall.

It makes sense to enter the park this way if you're coming from Yakima, the Tri-Cities, or other points to the southeast. You also might consider using the Stevens Canyon entrance if you're approaching from the southwest and you like picturesque drives. **U.S. 12,** which runs south of the park and intersects with Route 123, is also known as White Pass Scenic Byway. At points it takes you along the banks of the Cowlitz River, through stands of old-growth Douglas firs, and past viewpoints for Mount Rainier and Mount St. Helens.

To the east of the turnoff for the national park, the road crosses White Pass, the only passage over the Cascades between I-90 and the Columbia Valley that's open year-round. At White Pass there's a ski area with a lodge that's also a viable place to stay for summertime park visitors.

White Pass Scenic Byway

The 1.5-hour drive east from I-5 along **U.S. 12** (White Pass Scenic Byway) to White Pass begins in farmland and forest, with the Cascades on the horizon. Five miles east of I-5 a turnoff at Marys Corner leads to **Lewis and Clark State Park** (4583 Jackson Hwy., Winlock, 360/864-2643, http://parks.state.wa.us/538, Discover Pass required), an impressive 621-acre parcel of land that holds one of the few remaining major stands of old-growth forest in Washington. Several short trails provide loop hikes through the tall Douglas fir, western red cedar, western hemlock, and grand fir trees.

Continuing east you hit Mayfield Lake,

bordered by **Ike Kinswa State Park** (873 Rte. 122, Silver Creek, 360/983-3402, http://parks.state.wa.us/519, Discover Pass required), and Riffe Lake, bordered by **Mossyrock Park** (202 Ajlune Rd., Mossyrock, 360/983-3900, www.mytpu.org, $5 parking fee), both popular spots for swimming, boating, and especially trout fishing. Mossyrock Dam, which created Riffe Lake, is the tallest dam in the state (even taller than Grand Coulee) and one of the primary sources of power for Tacoma.

East of Riffe Lake there's a turnoff for **Hopkins Hill Viewpoint,** from where you can see Mount St. Helens in the distance. At the town of Randle the road starts to parallel the Cowlitz River, and after another 15 miles you reach Packwood, another little town that's an overnight option for national park visitors. Past the turnoff for the park at the junction with Route 123 there are two more roadside outlooks, **Palisades Viewpoint** and **Mount Rainier Viewpoint,** before you reach White Pass.

Packwood

Packwood is an unassuming little town 15 minutes from the Stevens Canyon entrance with some good bargain lodging options for park visitors.

FOOD

As with accommodations, dining options in Packwood aren't numerous or fancy, but you can get some decent food. **Mountain Goat Coffee Co.** (105 Main St. E, 360/494-5600, daily 7am-5pm) is the locals' favorite place to share gossip over a cup of joe and a pastry. **Cliff Droppers** (12968 U.S. 12, 360/494-2055, Wed.-Mon. 11am-7pm, $9-15) is a quirky little place with above-average burgers, fries, and shakes. **Blue Spruce Saloon & Grill** (13019 U.S. 12, 360/494-5605, Mon.-Thurs. 11am-midnight, Fri.-Sat. 6am-2am, Sun. 6am-midnight, $9-18), the local tavern, serves typical pub grub along with breakfast on the weekends.

ACCOMMODATIONS

For a step back in time, bed down at **Hotel Packwood** (104 Main St., 360/494-5431, www.packwoodwa.com/Hotel Packwood. htm, $35-49 d). It's a renovated 1912 hotel with a big veranda and tiny, immaculately maintained guest rooms, two with private baths, seven with shared. It's definitely nothing fancy, but the management is caring and kind, and the rates are a bargain from another era.

Crest Trail Lodge (12729 U.S. 12, 800/477-5339, http://whitepasstravel.com, $130-140 d) is another good choice, with comfortable standard motel rooms and a free hot breakfast. **Mountain View Lodge** (13163 U.S. 12, 360/494-5555, www.mtvlodge.com, $95-150 d) is older and feels more bare bones, but it's also well maintained and well priced. In addition to the standard doubles there are bigger rooms ($145-190) that can sleep 4-6.

White Pass Ski Area

Twelve miles southeast of where it intersects Route 123 and 55 miles west of Yakima, U.S. 12 crosses 4,500-foot White Pass. There you find **White Pass Ski Area** (48935 U.S. 12, 509/672-3100, http://skiwhitepass.com), a more modest alternative to Crystal Mountain that has the virtue of being more easily accessible to skiers from east of the Cascades. It has a 2,000-foot vertical drop, 1,500 acres of skiing, eight lifts, and 45 runs (20 percent are beginner, 60 percent intermediate, 20 percent advanced). Amenities include ski and snowboard lessons and rentals, childcare, a bar, and several cafes. Full-day lift tickets are $63 for adults, $43 for kids ages 7-15.

ACCOMMODATIONS

Near the ski area, **White Pass Village Inn** (48933 U.S. 12, 509/672-3131, http://whitepassvillageinn.com) has condos in a range of sizes; studios sleep 1-4 ($159 winter, $89 summer), larger units 4-8 ($212-318 winter, $143-179 summer), though if you have the maximum suggested occupancy it's going to be tight quarters. Facilities are pretty well worn; these are places to crash after spending a day in the mountains. All units have kitchens, which is crucial in summer when none of the ski area's dining facilities are open.

Mount Rainier National Park

TOP EXPERIENCE

Mount Rainier is the most impressive geographical landmark in the Pacific Northwest. With an elevation of 14,410 feet, it's the tallest peak in the row of volcanic mountains stretching from California to Canada that make up the Cascade Range. It has the fifth-highest elevation of any mountain in America's Lower 48 states, and it's by far the most topographically prominent. That means, in layman's terms, that it has the greatest rise in elevation from its base—over 3,000 higher than the second peak on the list, California's Mount Whitney. It's also the most heavily glaciated, with 25 glaciers covering 35 square miles, giving it a stately white cap.

The sheer size of Mount Rainier can take your breath away. Flying over en route to Sea-Tac you're struck by how enormous it looks from the perspective of your plane window. On land the white peak is visible all the way from Oregon and Canada. Throughout much of Washington it dominates the horizon, and is such an integral part of the state's identity that it's emblazoned on the license plates. Seattleites celebrate clear, sunny weather by saying, "The mountain is out today."

One of the main reasons for visiting Mount Rainier National Park is to ramp up that level of awe the peak inspires. When you're at the Paradise and Sunrise areas—the two highest points in the park reachable by car—the

Mount Rainier National Park

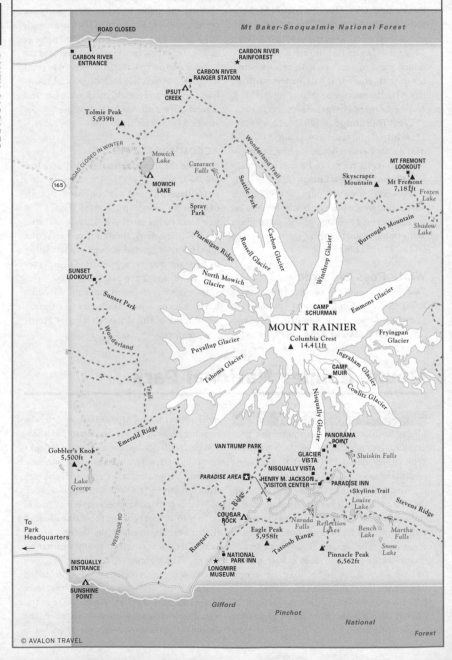

ROAD CLOSED

Mt Baker-Snoqualmie National Forest

CARBON RIVER
ENTRANCE

CARBON RIVER
RAINFOREST

CARBON RIVER
RANGER STATION

IPSUT
CREEK

Tolmie Peak
5,939ft

MT FREMONT
LOOKOUT

Mowich
Lake

Cataract
Falls

Skyscraper
Mountain

Mt Fremont
7,181ft

Frozen
Lake

165

ROAD CLOSED IN WINTER

MOWICH
LAKE

Spray
Park

Seattle Park

Wonderland Trail

Burroughs Mountain

Shadow
Lake

SUNSET
LOOKOUT

Ptarmigan Ridge

Russell Glacier

Carbon Glacier

Winthrop Glacier

Sunset Park

North Mowich
Glacier

CAMP
SCHURMAN

Emmons Glacier

Wonderland

Puyallup Glacier

MOUNT RAINIER

Columbia Crest
14,411ft

Fryingpan
Glacier

Trail

Tahoma Glacier

CAMP
MUIR

Ingraham Glacier

Cowlitz Glacier

Emerald Ridge

Gobbler's Knob
5,500ft

VAN TRUMP PARK

PANORAMA
POINT

GLACIER
VISTA

Sluiskin Falls

Lake
George

NISQUALLY VISTA

PARADISE AREA

HENRY M. JACKSON
VISITOR CENTER

PARADISE INN

Skyline Trail

Stevens Ridge

WESTSIDE RD

Ridge

COUGAR
ROCK

Louise
Lake

To
Park
Headquarters

Rampart

Eagle Peak
5,958ft

Narada
Falls

Reflection
Lakes

Bench
Lake

Martha
Falls

NATIONAL
PARK INN

Tatoosh Range

Pinnacle Peak
6,562ft

Snow
Lake

NISQUALLY
ENTRANCE

LONGMIRE
MUSEUM

SUNSHINE
POINT

Gifford

Pinchot

National

Forest

© AVALON TRAVEL

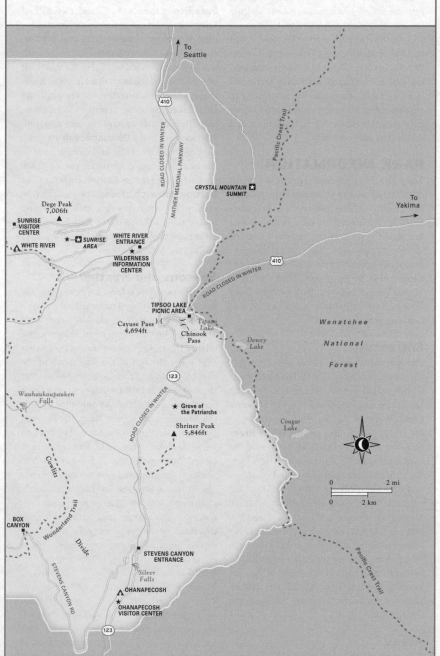

towering summit feels just beyond your grasp, just one flower-filled meadow away, despite the fact that it's still 8,000-9,000 feet above you. Within the park is abundant and varied natural beauty—old-growth forests, waterfalls, alpine lakes, fields of brilliant wildflowers—all reached by idyllic hiking trails and twisting mountain roads. But wherever you go, even when it's not in view, Rainier's peak is a constant presence. It's the fulcrum around which the park revolves.

PARK INFORMATION

The park is 369 square miles, with the summit of Mount Rainier near the center. It's roughly square-shaped. Those who drew its boundaries in 1899 followed the same protocol used to create the borders for America's western states—straight lines and right angles predominate, with an occasional squiggly concession made to topography. Most visitors to Mount Rainier National Park get here using their own vehicle, whether it be a car, RV, motorcycle, or bicycle.

Entrances

There are three entry points where you pay admission to the park: the **Nisqually** entrance at the southwest corner, near the Longmire and Paradise areas; the **Stevens Canyon** entrance at the southeast corner, in the Ohanapecosh area; and the **White River** entrance to the northeast, at the base of the road leading to the Sunrise area. Nisqually is the only entrance open year-round.

Two main roads are within the park. One runs through the southern portion, with the Nisqually entrance at the west end and the Stevens Canyon entrance at the east. There it intersects with the primary north-south road, which runs up the park's eastern side, with a turnoff halfway up at Cayuse Pass for Route 410 leading out of the park, and another turnoff 3.5 miles farther north leading to the Sunrise area.

Areas

The park has five developed areas that are the centers of activity. The main areas are **Paradise** to the south of Rainier's peak and **Sunrise** to the northeast, both elevated locations with great views, large parking lots, sophisticated visitors centers, and many trailheads. Eleven miles downhill to the southwest of Paradise is the **Longmire** area, which was the original headquarters for the park and still makes use of the century-old facilities, including a hotel, restaurant, and museum. Development in the **Ohanapecosh** area consists of a visitors center and campground in the heavily wooded southeast corner of the park near the Stevens Canyon entrance. The **Carbon/Mowich** area in the park's rainy northwest corner gets very little traffic and is essentially a backcountry destination, with hiking and bicycling trails and one gravel road leading to Mowich Lake.

Seasons and Weather

The park experiences long, harsh winters—the Paradise area averages more annual snowfall than any other place on earth where records are kept. The vast majority of visitors come during the mild summer season (late June-Sept.). For the rest of the year much of the park closes down. From October or November through May or June the only entrance that's open is Nisqually, and the only road open is the 18-mile stretch from Nisqually through Longmire and up to Paradise. The road to Paradise closes every night, and can remain closed during the day if it's unplowable. Seasonal openings and closures vary depending on the conditions. To check the current status, call 360/569-2211 or go to www.nps.gov/mora and search "road status." All vehicles entering the park during the winter season are required to carry tire chains.

Fees

It costs $25 per automobile, $20 per motorcycle, and $10 per bicyclist or pedestrian for a pass that gives you access to the park for one week. You can buy a one-year pass for $50. The road along the eastern side of the park accommodates through traffic and doesn't require an admission fee, but to access the park's primary attractions you have to turn off at the Stevens Canyon or White River entrance. The minimally accessible Carbon/Mowich area doesn't have an entry gate; you pay admission on the honor system in a drop box.

Food and Accommodations

There are two hotels in the park: **National Park Inn** at Longmire, which is open year-round, and **Paradise Inn** at Paradise, which is usually open from mid-May to mid-October. There are three campgrounds, all open only for the summer season: **Cougar Rock,** along the road between Longmire and Paradise; **Ohanapecosh,** south of the Stevens Canyon entrance; and **White River,** along the road to Sunrise.

National Park Inn and Paradise Inn have **restaurants,** and **snack bars** are in Paradise and Sunrise.

Information and Services

Delve into the details of park procedures and rules on the National Park Service website (www.nps.gov/mora). Among other things, you can find out the status of seasonal openings of roads and facilities, which vary from year to year. Another good way to get park information is to talk to a ranger. The park's general-information phone line (360/569-6575) will connect you with one who nine times out of ten will be able to answer even your most obscure questions.

There is **no gasoline available in the park;** you need to arrive with enough gas in the tank to get you out again. From Seattle you can take a daylong guided tour with **Discover Nature** (253/777-8226, www.tourmtrainier.com) or **Tours Northwest** (888/293-1404, www.toursnorthwest.com), but such tours give just a glimpse of the park's glory.

LONGMIRE AREA

Longmire is seven miles from the Nisqually entrance in the southwest corner of the park. This area is home to the **Longmire Museum**

(360/569-6575, May-Sept. daily 9am-5pm, off-season hours vary), one of the oldest national park museums in existence. The small facility, located in the original park headquarters, contains displays on the park's natural history, along with exhibits of basketry, a small totem pole, and photos from the early days of the park.

At Longmire's **Wilderness Information Center** (360/569-6650, mid-May-mid-Oct. daily 7:30am-5pm), get passes for and information about backcountry hiking and camping, as well as suggestions for hikes around the area.

Hiking

Though visitors gravitate more toward hikes in other areas of the park, nearby trails cover the gamut, from easy walks through the woods to steep mountain climbs. Less than a mile in length, the **Trail of the Shadows** takes you on a stroll around the meadow where Longmire's resort stood, with views of the mountain. A longer loop hike continues from here up Rampart Ridge to a majestic view over the Nisqually River far below, and then joins the Wonderland Trail. Follow this back to Longmire for a total distance of five miles.

More adventurous hikers can climb the many switchbacks to the summit of 5,958-foot **Eagle Peak,** a distance of seven miles round-trip. The route passes through a wide range of vegetation, from dense old-growth stands along the Nisqually River to flowery alpine meadows offering vistas across to Mount Rainier. The mountain-encircling Wonderland Trail also passes through Longmire, making this is a favorite starting point for backcountry hikes of varying lengths.

Food

The **National Park Inn Dining Room** (360/569-2411, www.mtrainierguestservices.com, daily 7am-11am, 11:30am-4:30pm, 5pm-7pm, $19-35) serves three meals a day throughout the year. The food could be classified as "upscale institutional"—there are some alluring dinner entrées, such baked halibut and bison stew, but don't expect sophisticated cuisine.

Pick up snacks at the area's **General Store** (360/569-2411, mid-June-Aug. daily 9am-8pm, Sept.-mid-June daily 10am-5pm).

Accommodations

National Park Inn (360/569-2411, www. mtrainierguestservices.com, $126-218) was the original lodge in the park. It has 25 small, simply furnished guest rooms, some of which share bathrooms. It's the only lodging in the park that's open year-round. In summer you can sit on the porch and admire the view of Rainier, and in winter you can warm up in front of the large stone fireplace in the lounge.

CAMPING

A few miles up the road from Longmire on the way to Paradise is **Cougar Rock Campground** (360/569-2211, mid-May-mid-Sept., $20). It has 173 sites suitable for RVs or tents, with flush toilets, drinking water, fire rings, and a dump station. You can reserve sites at www.recreation.gov.

★ PARADISE AREA

The 13-mile drive from Longmire to Paradise is a beautiful climb through evergreen forests where periodic openings provide down-valley and up-mountain vistas. Three miles before you reach Paradise is a pullout overlooking **Narada Falls,** where a steep trail leads to the plunge pool at its base.

At an elevation of 5,400 feet, with glacier-clad Rainier standing before you front and center, Paradise is a gorgeous and understandably popular spot. When Virinda Longmire, daughter of park founding father James Longmire, first visited here in the summer of 1885 she's said to have exclaimed, "Oh my, what a paradise!" thus establishing the area's name. Late July and August is the prime time for viewing the peak framed by fields of wildflowers. Visit then and you won't be alone. This is the busiest place in the park,

Paradise area of Mount Rainer

and on weekends the large parking lot can be entirely full.

Paradise's **Henry M. Jackson Visitor Center** (360/569-6571, May-mid-June and Sept. daily 10am-5pm, mid-June-Aug. 10am-7pm, Oct.-Apr. Sat.-Sun. 10am-5pm), erected in 2008, is a handsome building that's a modern take on traditional alpine design, with a steep-pitched roof, a 60-foot-high ceiling, and giant fir and cedar doors. Inside you can watch an introductory film about the park, consult with rangers about hikes and other activities, and have a bite at the snack bar. The visitors center is the starting point for ranger-led daily nature walks in summer and weekend snowshoe treks in winter, all free of charge.

Hiking

A spiderweb of trails spreads out over the subalpine forests and high-country meadows at Paradise. Trail maps are available at the visitors center. Easiest is the **Nisqually Vista Trail,** a 1.2-mile loop hike that leads through flamboyantly floral high-country meadows west of the visitors center. The popular **Skyline Trail** is a 5.5-mile loop with 1,700 feet of elevation gain, taking you above the timberline to impressive views from Glacier Vista and Panorama Point. The full hike lasts over four hours; you can knock off an hour by taking a shortcut on the Golden Gate Trail. Carry water with you and expect some steep sections going both up and down.

Heading east from Paradise toward Stevens Canyon, the road passes **Reflection Lakes,** where on a calm and clear day the mirrorlike surface reflects Mount Rainier and a rim of forest. The **Pinnacle Peak Trail** starts at the Reflection Lakes parking lot; hike this 1.5-mile trail to the saddle between Pinnacle and Plummer Peaks for more great Rainier views. You'll gain 1,100 feet in elevation along the way.

An easier trail takes you uphill to **Bench and Snow Lakes.** The trailhead is a mile east of Reflection Lakes on Stevens Canyon Road, and the path goes 1.25 miles each way, through meadows that in late summer fill with bear grass and flowers.

Food

The **Paradise Inn Dining Room** (360/569-2413, www.mtrainierguestservices. com, mid-May-early Oct. daily 7am-9:30am, noon-2pm, and 5:30pm-8pm, $17-35) is a big, attractive, open space that shares the rustic grandeur found in the hotel's lobby. The food doesn't live up to the setting, but that's par for the course for national park restaurants. The simpler dishes at lunch, such as burgers and fish-and-chips, are less of an investment and often more satisfying than the dinner entrées.

Pick up sandwiches, soups, and salads at **Paradise Camp Deli** (www.mtrainierguest-services.com, May-mid-June daily 10am-4:45pm, mid-June-Sept. daily 10am-6:45pm, Oct.-Apr. Sat.-Sun. 10am-4:45pm) in the Jackson Visitor Center.

Accommodations

Erected in 1916, **Paradise Inn** (360/569-2413, www.mtrainierguestservices.com) is an imposing timber lodge built in the style of many national park hotels, with the highlights found in the public spaces. The lobby is impressive, with high ceilings, stone fireplaces, and mountain views. The original guest rooms ($123-185 d) feel like a step back in time, with shared bathroom facilities, tight quarters, and well-maintained but spare furnishings. Come here to unplug: You won't

Paradise Inn

find TVs, phones, or Wi-Fi. The inn is open mid-May-early October. Its annex, which has rooms with private bathrooms, is undergoing a major renovation and is scheduled to reopen in summer 2019.

OHANAPECOSH AREA

East of Paradise, 19-mile **Stevens Canyon Road** is arguably the most beautiful drive in the park. (The other candidate, the road to Sunrise, is gorgeous too.) It's open only in summer and early fall—usually June through October. Check its status by calling 360/569-2211 or going to www.nps.gov/mora and searching "road status." You begin by passing Reflection Lakes and then wind through forests and past more small lakes, with views of Mount Rainier and the Cascades appearing between the trees.

There's a pullout along the way for viewing **Martha Falls,** but it gives you only a side view of the multi-tiered falls, which end with a 145-foot plunge. For a closer look, pull off the road where it intersects with the Wonderland Trail, half a mile west of the falls pullout, and take the trail for two-thirds of a mile to the bridge at the falls' base.

The road cuts across the slopes of Stevens Canyon as it follows Stevens Creek downhill. It then reaches **Box Canyon,** where a short trail leads to a footbridge spanning the deep, narrow gorge created by the Muddy Fork of the Cowlitz River. By the time you get to the junction with Route 123 the road is deep within old-growth forests of Douglas fir and western hemlock at an elevation of just 2,200 feet.

You're now in the Ohanapecosh area, the location of the Stevens Canyon entrance and the **Ohanapecosh Visitor Center** (360/569-6581). Because the center gets less traffic than Paradise or Sunrise it operates on a less regular schedule. It's usually open from June through September, but days and hours vary from year to year depending on staffing and funding; call to find out the current status. In summer rangers lead nature walks from the center several times a week, and you can pick

Grove of the Patriarchs Trail

up trail maps and consult with rangers about the best ways to explore the area.

Hiking

One of the highlights of the area is the **Grove of the Patriarchs Trail,** which starts just west of the Stevens Canyon entrance station. It's an easy 1.5-mile round-trip that follows the crystalline Ohanapecosh River and crosses a suspension bridge onto an island of virgin forest. It's like strolling through a museum of old-growth trees, with thousand-year-old Douglas firs, western hemlocks, and western red cedars towering over a fern-filled understory.

A longer hike, the **Silver Falls Trail,** begins at the Ohanapecosh Campground and follows the river in a three-mile loop through more old-growth forest to the 75-foot Silver Falls. Along the way a side trail leads to the site of Ohanapecosh Hot Springs Resort, which was a vacation destination in the Roaring '20s. It was closed in the 1960s and eventually torn down by the Park Service.

For something more rigorous, consider the **Shriner Peak Trail.** It's an eight-mile hike—about five hours round-trip—with significant ascents and almost no shade, ending up at the lookout station on Shriner Peak (5,834 feet). It's not a hike for a warm summer day, but if you can hit it when the temperatures begin to drop in the fall, the beautiful 360-degree views from the peak make it worth the effort. The trail starts from Route 123, 3.5 miles north of the Stevens Canyon entrance; park on the west side of the road about a half mile north of the Panther Creek Bridge.

Camping

Next to the visitors center, amid the woods along the Ohanapecosh River, **Ohanapecosh Campground** (360/569-2211, mid-May-early Oct., $20) has 188 sites suitable for RVs or tents, with flush toilets, drinking water, fire rings, and a dump station. You can reserve sites at www.recreation.gov.

★ SUNRISE AREA

The Sunrise area occupies a subalpine plateau with spectacular views of the northeast side of Mount Rainier. It's one of the most popular destinations in the park, but the window for visiting is narrow—the road up is usually open only from late June or early July through early September. At 6,400 feet, Sunrise is the highest point in the park reachable by car, and getting there is part of the fun. Starting at the White River entrance station off of Route 410, you climb for 11 miles on a series of switchbacks lacing through evergreen forests and then emerge into meadows with all-encompassing vistas.

Because of the rain-shadow effect, this side of Mount Rainier gets far less precipitation than the western side, and the vegetation reflects this: grasses, sedges, and even whitebark pine are common here. The Sunrise area is also home to large numbers of elk during the summer and fall. Elk are not native to the park; they were brought here from Yellowstone and other parts of the West between 1903 and 1933. Around 1,500 of them inhabit the park.

The log cabin **Sunrise Visitor Center** (360/663-2425, July-early Sept. daily 10am-6pm) houses natural history displays and has telescopes you can use to check out Mount Rainier's glaciers, including massive Emmons

Sunrise area of Mount Rainier

Glacier, largest in the Lower 48. Rangers answer questions and lead daily nature walks; stop by the information desk for times and destinations. Across the parking lot, **Sunrise Day Lodge** has a gift shop and a cafeteria.

Hiking

Many trails head out from the Sunrise area, including sections of the Wonderland Trail and shorter hikes to nearby lakes and mountains. Get maps and advice from rangers at the visitors center. The **Shadow Lakes Trail** is one of the most popular hikes; it's a three-mile round trip that starts at Sunrise parking lot, drops to a rim overlooking the White River valley, and then follows that ridge to Shadow Lake, returning via Frozen Lake and Sourdough Ridge.

If you want to gain some elevation, head to **Mount Fremont Lookout.** From the Sunrise parking lot follow the trails to Sourdough Ridge and Frozen Lake and then branch off to the north. The old fire lookout is at an elevation of 7,181 feet and there's a 900-foot gain over the course of the hike. The well-marked 5.6-mile path takes about 3.5 hours round-trip.

A gentle climb to **Dege Peak** (elevation 7,006 feet) starts at the north end of the Sunrise parking area and follows Sourdough Ridge east. After 1.7 miles you're at the peak, where on a clear day you can see as far as Mount Baker to the north and Mount Adams to the south.

Food

The **Sunrise Day Lodge Snack Bar** (late June-early Sept. daily 10am-7pm) has a grill for flipping burgers and also offers deli sandwiches, soups, and soft-serve ice cream.

Camping

The **White River Campground** (360/569-2211, late June-late Sept., $20) is reached via the turnoff four miles past the entrance station on the road to Sunrise; after the turn it's another mile to the campground. There are 112 sites suitable for RVs or tents, with flush toilets, drinking water, and fire rings. You can't reserve sites here.

CARBON/MOWICH AREA

The remote Carbon/Mowich area in the far northwest corner is a separate world from the rest of the park. Because it's to the west of Mount Rainier it receives more rainfall than the park's other areas, resulting in the **Carbon River Rainforest.** Reach it by taking Route 165, which runs south from Enumclaw, and exiting onto Carbon River Road. At the park's border the road turns into a trail and you have to go it from their either on foot or bicycle. Four miles in, the trail meets up with the Wonderland Trail; if you take that southeast for about 3.5 miles you reach the base of **Carbon Glacier,** the lowest-elevation glacier in the United States outside Alaska.

A little farther to the south is a glacial basin containing the largest and deepest body of water in the park, **Mowich Lake,** which is surrounded by meadows. To get there, stay on Route 165, which crosses into the park and becomes Mowich Lake Road. After three miles the pavement turns to gravel; from there it's another three miles of rough road to reach the lake. The road is usually open from June through September. From Mowich Lake a three-mile trail leads past pretty Eunice Lake and on to the historic **Tolmie Peak** fire lookout at 5,939 feet in elevation.

Camping

The primitive **Mowich Lake Campground** (early July-early Oct., free) has 10 tent sites. There are vault toilets and no potable water. Fires are prohibited.

BACKCOUNTRY HIKING AND CAMPING

Some 300 miles of hiking trails crisscross Mount Rainier National Park. Many of them are suitable for day hikes, but you can also go deeper into the park on a multiday hiking trip. Doing so, though, can be a challenge—even before you take your first step on the trail.

Overnight hikes require a **wilderness**

permit—one per group, not per individual. A limited number of permits are issued each year. The park accepts permit reservations on-line starting March 15. There is a $20 charge to reserve. Forms and instructions are available online at www.nps.gov/mora (search for "wilderness permits"). Forms received between March 15 and April 1 are processed in random order, and typically all permits issued for the most popular summer dates are taken by this group. You can submit a reservation form after April 1, but the odds are stacked against you.

There is, however, a second way to get a permit: simply show up. The park holds back 30 percent of permits for distribution at the time of use—you can get them on the same day or a day before you begin your trip, but no earlier. Permits must be requested in person and are available at the Longmire and White River Wilderness Information Centers, the Jackson Visitor Center at Paradise, and the Carbon River Ranger Station. If you try this approach you stand a chance of not getting a permit, but you will save a few bucks because you don't have to pay a reservation fee. There's no charge for the permit itself, only for the reservation.

Backcountry Logistics

Rainier's hiking season is short: Most trails are snow-free only from late June to mid-October, though trails at the lower elevations may open earlier and remain open later. It's always advisable to dress for *all* seasons when hiking in the Cascades, and to carry rain gear.

Fires are not allowed in the backcountry, but you can bring a stove along. Be sure to filter or otherwise treat any drinking water, since the protozoan *Giardia* and other harmful microorganisms may be present. Always practice no-trace camping and haul out any garbage. Hikers in backcountry meadows should stay on the trails at all times. Plants here have only a brief growing season, and damaged areas take a long time to recover.

There are three types of backcountry camps within the park. **Trailside camps** are located every 3-7 miles along backcountry trails, including the mountain-circling Wonderland Trail. These camps all have a nearby water source and pit toilet, and five people (in two tents) are allowed at an individual campsite. The vast majority of hikers use these established sites. If you choose to camp away from these, you'll need to stay at a **cross-country camp**—a site of your own selection, located a quarter-mile away from the trail and other camps and at least 100 feet from water sources. **Alpine camps,** used primarily by climbers, are in areas above 6,000 feet and have their own rules. Broadly speaking, you're not allowed to disturb the terrain (by, for instance, building a windbreak using materials found on the mountain).

Wonderland Trail

The biggest draw for backcountry hikers is the Wonderland Trail—a 93-mile loop circling the mountain, traversing passes, forests, streams, and alpine meadows. The trail has lots of ups and downs, including 3,500-foot changes in elevation in several stretches. Other trails intersect the Wonderland, and it passes through the busiest areas of the park, so you may well find yourself using a segment of it for a day hike. Typically it takes 10 days to two weeks to make the entire trip.

CLIMBING

Because of its many glaciers and rocky faces, Mount Rainier has long been one of the premier training peaks for American climbers. About 5,000 people reach the summit every year, and a similar number set out to reach it but turn back. Two days are usually required for the trek: The first day involves hiking 4-5 hours over trails and snowfields to Camp Muir, the south-side base camp at 10,000 feet, or Camp Schurman, on the northeast side at 9,500 feet. Reservations are not accepted for the high camps, so be prepared to camp outside: Muir has a shelter with a 25-person capacity that's frequently filled, and Schurman has no public shelter—your only luxury is a pit toilet. The second day starts early (about 2am) for the summit climb. Above the high camps climbers are roped, using ice axes and crampons to inch their way over glaciers to the summit.

To hike at elevations above 10,000 feet you need to pay a **climbing cost recovery fee** ($47, $32 if you're under 26 years old, good for one calendar year). Payment must be made in advance online; go to www.nps.gov/mora and search for "climbing." Once you're in the park, you must also obtain a free **climbing permit**, available at the Longmire and Paradise areas, White River Wilderness Information Center, and Carbon River Ranger Station.

Guided Climbs

Inexperienced climbers in top physical condition can conquer the mountain with some help from the pros. **Alpine Ascents International** (206/378-1927, www.alpineascents.com), **International Mountain Guides** (360/569-2609, www.mountainguides.com), and **Rainier Mountaineering Inc.** (888/892-5462, www.rmiguides.com) all lead park-approved guided climbs to Rainier's summit and conduct classes in basic climbing techniques.

WINTER IN THE PARK

When the snow starts to fall in October or November most of the park shuts down, and it stays that way through May or June. The exception is the park's southwest corner: the Nisqually entrance and the 18 miles of road from Nisqually through Longmire and up to Paradise remain open year-round. The road to Paradise closes every night, and can remain closed during the day if conditions make it unplowable. Call 360/569-2211 to check road conditions. Note that all vehicles entering the park during the winter season are required to carry tire chains.

Come for a winter visit and you'll experience a wonderland. Paradise averages 643 inches of snow a year—the most of any place on earth where annual snowfall is recorded. The Paradise Inn is closed, but the National Park Inn at Longmire remains open, and Paradise's Jackson Visitor Center is open on weekends.

Cross-Country Skiing

Mount Rainier is famous for its abundant backcountry, and in winter the cross-country skiing is fantastic. Many beginners head to the Paradise parking lot to ski up the unplowed road, or out on the trails to Nisqually Vista, Narada Falls, or Reflection Lakes. None of these are groomed, but it generally doesn't take long for skiers to set down tracks in the new snow.

Rent skis, avalanche beacons, snowshoes, and other winter gear from the **Longmire General Store** (360/569-2411, daily 10am-5pm in winter). There you can also arrange ski lessons and tours. Ski rentals are not available at Paradise.

Other Winter Activities

Facilities are open for winter sports at Paradise from December to April. The park constructs a supervised snow-play area here in early December; to protect vegetation, no snow sliding is allowed before that time. You can slide on inner tubes, saucers, and other soft sliding toys—you need to bring your own, as none are available for rent. Wooden toboggans and sleds with metal runners are not allowed.

Ranger-led **snowshoe walks** (free) are offered at the Jackson Visitor Center on winter weekends and holidays. Snowshoes are free to use during these walks, and can be rented from the lodge gift shop or the Longmire General Store.

Mount St. Helens

TOP EXPERIENCE

Visitors come to Mount Rainier to revel in nature's tremendous beauty. They come to Mount St. Helens to marvel at nature's tremendous destructive power.

Prior to May 18, 1980, Mount St. Helens was known primarily for having the most perfectly shaped cone in the Cascades volcanic chain. It was thought of as a sleeping beauty, dormant for well over a century. At 9,677 feet in elevation it was diminutive in comparison to neighboring Mount Rainier and Mount Adams, making it a popular first ascent for novice climbers.

On that May day Mount St. Helens awoke from its sleep. Set off by an earthquake, it erupted, sending ash 15 miles into the sky and triggering the largest landslide in recorded history. The impact was like a blitz of atomic bombs, and the devastation was total—lakes boiled and forests burned as if they were kindling, leaving behind a wasteland. In one day the volcano had lost 1,300 feet in elevation.

Decades after the eruption, St. Helens and the surrounding area are still in the early stage of recovery. After you've surveyed the scorched earth, a big part of the experience here is imagining what exactly happened—the before, during, and after of the eruption—and grasping the scale of its geological, ecological, and human impact.

Visiting Mount St. Helens

In 1982 the 110,000-acre **Mount St. Helens National Volcanic Monument** was created, and the area gradually opened to the public as roads, bridges, visitors centers, and trails were built. The government still keeps parts of it off-limits to serve as a natural laboratory for scientists, who have found that plants and animals are returning more quickly than expected. Yet every visitor to the volcano immediately senses that the landscape has undergone a massive and violent transformation.

If there's any natural environment that benefits from a good visitors center, this is it. Here you've got not just one but four of them. They're independently operated, but they coordinate well, highlighting different facets of the story.

Because the area around Mount St. Helens is a mix of federal, state, and private lands, there isn't one master online resource for getting background on the destination. The website of the **U.S. Forest Service** (www.fs.usda.gov/mountsthelens) is a good place to start—there's lots of information, though it can be a challenge to sort through. The site of the **Mount St. Helens Science and Learning Center** (www.mshslc.org) gives a good overview, with a predictable emphasis on science.

Entrances

There are three approaches to Mount St. Helens: from the west, east, and south. The vast majority of visitors, close to a million a year, use the **western route,** which has a wide highway along which the visitors centers are located. Coming from the **east** you get a good view of the huge divot in the side of the mountain, but the road in is rough, and you miss out on the interpretive facilities available to the west. The **southern approach** is for visitors who want to climb Mount St. Helens rather than examine it; the impact of the eruption was much less significant on the south side than on the north.

Regardless of which route you take, you won't find a lot of tourist facilities other than the visitors centers. There are some trails and campgrounds, but restaurants and lodging are thin on the ground. That reflects the nature of the destination. For most visitors Mount St. Helens is a day trip or a half-day stop in a larger itinerary. Despite the unique and remarkable nature of St. Helens, unless you're a geologist it's likely to be a "one and done" experience.

Mount St. Helens

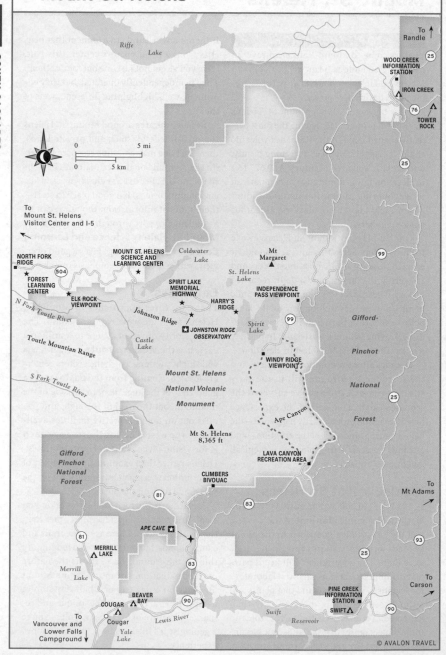

To
Randle

To
Mount St. Helens
Visitor Center and I-5

WOOD CREEK
INFORMATION
STATION

IRON CREEK

TOWER
ROCK

Riffe
Lake

NORTH FORK
RIDGE

FOREST
LEARNING
CENTER

ELK ROCK
VIEWPOINT

N Fork Toutle River

Toutle Mountian Range

S Fork Toutle River

MOUNT ST. HELENS
SCIENCE AND
LEARNING CENTER

Coldwater
Lake

SPIRIT LAKE
MEMORIAL
HIGHWAY

Johnston Ridge

HARRY'S
RIDGE

JOHNSTON RIDGE
OBSERVATORY

Castle
Lake

Mt
Margaret

St. Helens
Lake

INDEPENDENCE
PASS VIEWPOINT

Spirit
Lake

WINDY RIDGE
VIEWPOINT

Gifford-

Pinchot

National

Forest

Mount St. Helens

National Volcanic

Monument

Ape Canyon

Mt St. Helens
8,365 ft

Gifford
Pinchot
National
Forest

CLIMBERS
BIVOUAC

LAVA CANYON
RECREATION AREA

To
Mt Adams

APE CAVE

MERRILL
LAKE

Merrill
Lake

COUGAR

Cougar

BEAVER
BAY

Yale
Lake

Lewis River

Swift

Reservoir

PINE CREEK
INFORMATION
STATION

SWIFT

To
Carson

To
Vancouver and
Lower Falls
Campground

0   5 mi

0   5 km

504

81

81

83

83

90

90

90

93

25

25

26

99

99

25

25

76

© AVALON TRAVEL

Mount St. Helens Blows its Top

At 8:32am on May 18, 1980, triggered by an earthquake measuring 5.1 on the Richter scale, Mount St. Helens exploded. The quake sent a massive avalanche of rock, snow, and ice down the mountain's north slope at 200 miles an hour, filling Spirit Lake—the surface of which was instantly raised by 200 feet—and cresting over a 1,200-foot ridge. A second debris avalanche blasted down the North Fork of the Toutle River, and additional flows sent muddy water, rocks, and logs down the river, destroying bridges and homes along the way.

The landslide allowed pressure inside the volcano to escape explosively in an eruption that blew 1,312 feet (8.8 billion cubic yards) off the volcano's summit. A lateral blast shot northeast at 670 miles an hour, searing surrounding forests and flattening them for as far as 15 miles. Temperatures 15 miles away reached 572 degrees Fahrenheit, and the blast sent a plume of ash 15 miles up into the atmosphere. The explosion, coupled with the intense heat, landslides, and falling trees, killed 57 people within the blast zone and destroyed more than 220 homes and 17 miles of railroad. The wildlife death toll was upward of 5,000 black-tailed deer, 1,500 Roosevelt elk, 200 black bears, and millions of birds and fish. The economic loss included 4.5 billion board feet of usable timber on 96,000 acres.

The damage wasn't limited to the area of the blast itself; 60,000 acres not destroyed by the blast were covered with more than eight inches of ash. Six hours after the eruption, river water at Castle Rock, 40 miles downstream, was over 100 degrees Fahrenheit, and towns in eastern Washington, 150 miles away, were coated with up to three inches of ash, clogging carburetors and shrouding the towns in darkness at noon. Traces of ash were detected as far away as central Montana; Vancouver, British Columbia; and Denver.

In the six years following the blast, Mount St. Helens experienced 21 additional eruptions, resulting in a new lava dome within the crater. Things were quiet until 2004, when thousands of tiny earthquakes led to a slow, three-year-long eruption that created additional domes, depositing 121 million cubic yards of lava on the crater floor. The activity from 1980 to 1986 and from 2004 to 2008 has replaced about 7 percent of the volume lost in the 1980 eruption.

WEST SIDE ACCESS

The west side of Mount St. Helens has the easiest access, on **Route 504,** known as the Spirit Lake Memorial Highway. The drive in provides great views and takes you past the four visitors centers. Starting from the town of Castle Rock (exit 49 from I-5), the road makes a scenic 54-mile climb into the heart of the ravaged landscape, ending at the Johnston Ridge Observatory—the visitors center you should choose if you're going to stop at only one. From Hoffstadt Bluffs at milepost 27 the road gets steep, with wide shoulders for bikes and numerous turnouts to take in the scenery. You shouldn't pull a trailer on this trip, as the highway has some 7 percent grades.

Mount St. Helens
Visitor Center

Silver Lake, five miles east of I-5 on Route 504, is the site of the comprehensive **Mount St. Helens Visitor Center** (Rte. 504 milepost 5, 360/274-2100, http://parks.state. wa.us/245, mid-May-mid-Sept. daily 9am-5pm, Mar.-mid-May and mid-Sept.-Oct. daily 9am-4pm, Nov.-Feb. Thurs.-Mon. 9am-4pm, $5). This cathedral-like building opened in 1987 and was the first visitors center built after the eruption. The focus is on the eruption and its impact. The highlights are a walk-in volcano that displays geological forces at work, and a 10-minute slide show and a 22-minute movie that alternate every half-hour throughout the day. Other exhibits include models comparing the 1980 eruption with others throughout history (it was puny compared to the blast that created Crater Lake), images of the volcano in action, and a seismograph recording the latest tremors. The mountain is 30 miles away, but

On the Brink of Disaster

Near milepost 27 you cross the Hoffstadt Creek Bridge, one of 14 bridges that had to be reconstructed on Route 504 after the eruption of Mount St. Helens. It rises 370 feet above the canyon and stands near the edge of the blast zone, 15 miles from the volcano. The explosion killed everything from here to the crater.

From this point on you can see the contrast between how private companies and the U.S. Forest Service handled the aftermath of the eruption. Weyerhaeuser, the lumber industry giant, salvage-logged its lands and immediately replanted millions of trees. With fertilization, the new stands have come back surprisingly fast. As a public agency, the Forest Service had a different mandate, and no logging or replanting took place within the national volcanic monument boundaries. Instead the land has become a place where scientists can study the natural recovery process.

One example of adaptation in the wild can be seen in the upper Toutle River valley, which hundreds of Roosevelt elk call home. Despite harsh conditions, the elk survive on grasses and clover that were deposited in the valley by the mudflow following the eruption. You can often get a good look at them by hiking two miles down Road 3100 near the Hoffstadt Creek Bridge.

on a clear day you can see it through telescopes outside.

Seaquest State Park (3030 Rte. 504, 360/274-8633, http://parks.state.wa.us/581, Discover Pass required) is right next to the visitors center. It's situated within a beautiful stand of gigantic old-growth Douglas firs and hemlocks and includes a mile of shoreline on Silver Lake. You can camp here year-round.

Forest Learning Center

For the lumber industry's perspective on the eruption, stop in at the **Forest Learning Center** (17000 Rte. 504, 360/274-7750, www. weyerhaeuser.com, mid-May-mid-Sept. Fri.-Tues. 10am-4pm, free), located near milepost 33 on North Fork Ridge, a 2,700-foot-high bluff over the North Fork of the Toutle River. Weyerhaeuser funds the center, and the exhibits focus on the company's lumber salvage and recovery efforts after the eruption. Walk through a diorama of the forest prior to 1980, enter an "eruption chamber" with a you-are-there multimedia program, and check out displays explaining Weyerhaeuser's approach to reforestation. The center is popular with kids, who can climb aboard a toy helicopter and play outside in a seven-foot-high rubber volcano. Telescopes provide a chance to watch elk in the valley below, and a one-mile trail

descends into the valley. Other facilities include a gift shop and picnic area.

A little less than four miles up the road, stop at the **Elk Rock Viewpoint,** at the entrance to Mount St. Helens National Volcanic Monument, for magnificent views of the crater to the south and the river valley below, filled with a 700-foot-deep layer of rock, ash, and debris. You might also spot elk when you're here.

Mount St. Helens Science and Learning Center

Located 43 miles east of I-5, Coldwater Ridge is the site of the Forest Service's **Mount St. Helens Science and Learning Center** (19000 Rte. 504, 360/274-2114, www.mshslc. org, Nov.-Apr. Sat.-Sun. 10am-4pm, free). It's open to the public only on winter weekends when Johnston Ridge Observatory is closed due to snow, but in summer it's the base for educational events run by the Mount St. Helens Institute. On the Learning Center website you can sign up for guided hikes and single-day and overnight educational camps for kids.

★ Johnston Ridge Observatory

Spirit Lake Memorial Highway ends eight

miles uphill from Coldwater Lake at the 4,300-foot-elevation **Johnston Ridge Observatory** (24000 Rte. 504, 360/274-2140, www.fs.usda.gov/mountsthelens, mid-May-mid-Oct. daily 10am-6pm, $8). This facility emphasizes the geology of Mount St. Helens and ongoing scientific research, and is named for Dr. David Johnston, a geologist who was working here in 1980 and died in the eruption. His last radio transmission, sent out as the mountain was giving way, captured both the excitement and the horror of the moment: "Vancouver, Vancouver, this is it, this is it!"

The observatory has a prime location looking directly into the crater just five miles away. After spending an hour or more driving the highway and watching Mount St. Helens grow steadily closer, this is the payoff—a front-and-center view of the volcano, with the side facing you dramatically caved in and moonscape-like desolation all around it. It's an awesome, sobering sight, and it would be worth the drive to see it even if the observatory didn't exist. Fortunately, though, it does: Inside are first-rate exhibits, including a large model of the volcano that shows how the eruption progressed, geological equipment monitoring current activity, and displays about the geology, geography, and biology of the area

before and after the explosion. A large theater shows two short, engaging films. Every visitor should plan to see at least one.

HIKING

Mount St. Helens isn't a national park, but the observatory has park-like features, including a staff of rangers who lead interpretive walks. Even if you've studied the exhibits at all of the visitors centers, it's invaluable to have a knowledgeable guide explain the nuances of what you see as you walk along the trails near the observatory.

Longer treks require you to head out on your own. Get even closer to the crater by taking the **Truman Trail,** a 12-mile round-trip that can be shortened simply by turning around when you've seen enough. That path has no shade, so bring a hat, water, and sunscreen.

For a spectacular hike with commanding views into Spirit Lake, begin at the observatory and follow the **Boundary Trail** four miles to Harry's Ridge. For an overnight hike, continue along this path to the summit of Mount Margaret and then descend via the 5.5-mile **Lakes Trail.** You can camp at several small high-country lakes here (permit required). This is a research area, and scientists

Johnston Ridge Observatory

are attempting to keep human impacts to a minimum, so hikers need to stick within 10 feet of the trails.

Food

The only dining option along Route 504 is **Fire Mountain Grill** (9440 Rte. 504, 360/957-1025, http://fmgrill.com, Apr.-mid-May Thurs.-Mon. 11am-4pm, mid-May-Sept. daily 11am-7pm, Oct. daily 11am-4pm, $12-21), located in a big old house with a wraparound porch at milepost 19. It serves diner-style food—burgers are the specialty, and you can also get fried fish and sandwiches.

Accommodations

Eco Park Resort at Mount St. Helens (14000 Rte. 504, 360/274-6542, www.ecoparkresort.com) has the only accommodations within the St. Helens blast zone. It is located at milepost 24, about halfway between I-5 and the Johnston Ridge Observatory. There are six log cabins ($140-150) along with RV hookups ($25) and tent sites ($25), all of which share bathroom facilities. Bring a flashlight for nighttime trips to the bathroom.

CAMPING

There's limited camping allowed at designated sites in the Mount Margaret backcountry area within the boundaries of Mount St. Helens National Volcanic Monument. You need to get a permit to camp; to get one and learn about camping requirements, go to www.recreation.gov and search for "Mount Margaret," or call 877/444-6777.

There's a year-round campground on Silver Lake at **Seaquest State Park** (3030 Rte. 504, 360/274-8633, http://parks.state.wa.us/581). It has 55 tent sites ($30); 33 RV sites, some with hookups ($40); and 5 yurts ($69) that accommodate up to six. Make reservations at http://washington.goingtocamp.com or by calling 888/226-7688.

SOUTH SIDE ACCESS

The south side of Mount St. Helens was not impacted nearly as much by the 1980 eruption as the north side. It's best known as the access route for climbing the summit as well as exploring Ape Cave. Trailheads are here for various hikes, including the Loowit System that circles the mountain. The main route in is Lewis River Road east of I-5.

★ Ape Cave

This 12,810-foot-long lava tube is the third-longest such cave in the nation, and one of the most popular attractions near Mount St. Helens. From the entrance a staircase leads down to a chamber where you have two route options. The downhill arm ends after an easy three-quarter-mile walk, while the uphill route is more difficult and rocky, continuing 1.5 miles to an exit where an aboveground trail leads back to the starting point. Forest Service interpreters lead half-hour tours of Ape Cave twice a day in the summer.

The cave is located 10 miles northeast of the town of Cougar at the junction of Forest Roads 83 and 90 and is open at all times. Be sure to bring drinking water and two flashlights and extra batteries. Wear hiking boots, gloves, and warm clothes (the air is a steady 42 degrees Fahrenheit all year). A small **visitors center** (Memorial Day-Sept. daily 10am-5:30pm) near the cave entrance and parking area can provide assistance, publications, and lantern rentals ($5). A Northwest Forest Pass ($5) is required for access to the cave. The road is plowed to the Trail of Two Forests, a half-mile away from the cave entrance, in the winter.

Hiking

The easy **Trail of Two Forests** is a brief boardwalk path that takes you past the molds left when trees were immersed in lava flows 2,000 years ago. You can even crawl through two of these ancient impressions. The trail is across from Ape Cave on Road 8303.

One of the most interesting hikes on the south end of Mount St. Helens is the 2.5-mile **Lava Canyon Trail,** which drops 1,400 feet along the Muddy River. This canyon was scoured out by a mudflow during the 1980 eruption, revealing sharp cliffs and five tall waterfalls. The upper end is wheelchair-accessible; the lower part crosses a long suspension bridge and then descends a cliff face via a steel ladder. To get to the trail, follow Forest Road 83 nine miles (paved the entire way) beyond Ape Cave to the trailhead.

For an enjoyable loop hike, head to the end of Forest Road 8123 on the southwest side of the mountain and the start of the **Sheep Canyon Trail** (No. 240). This path climbs through old-growth forests and drainages that were ravaged by volcanic mudflows, and then enters a flower-filled alpine meadow before returning downhill on the Toutle Trail (No. 238), which connects to the Sheep Canyon Trail and your starting point. Total distance is approximately seven miles.

The **Lewis River Trail** (No. 31) follows along its beautiful namesake river from Curly Creek Falls to Lower Falls (a fun swimming hole), a distance of more than 10 miles. Between Curly Creek Falls and Lower Falls on Road 99 is **Big Creek Falls,** plummeting 125 feet into a pool that is a popular place for a summer dip. Above Lower Falls, you can follow the road to a series of roadside falls, including the scenic Middle Falls and Upper Falls.

Climbing Mount St. Helens

Mount St. Helens is the second-most climbed peak on the planet (exceeded only by Japan's Mount Fuji), with 16,000 people making the trip each year. All climbing routes start from the south side of the peak, and a **permit** ($22 Apr.-Oct., free the rest of the year) is required for travel above the 4,800-foot level. Purchase a permit, find out the logistics of making the climb, and learn about guided climbs at the website of the **Mount St. Helens Institute** (www.mshinstitute.org).

Camping

The Forest Service's **Lower Falls Campground** has views of three large falls along the Lewis River and a hiking trail that heads downriver for 10 miles. The campground has tent and RV sites ($15-30). It's located 15 miles east of the Pine Creek Information Station on Forest Road 90 and is open mid-May to mid-October. You can reserve sites at www.recreation.gov or by calling 877/444-6777.

EAST SIDE ACCESS

Visitors to Mount St. Helens's eastern flanks will discover narrow, winding one-lane roads, simple information stations, and minimal facilities. This is the wild side of the mountain. Access is on **Forest Road 25,** which heads south from the town of Randle. This paved but steep one-lane road (with turnouts) continues all the way to Pine Creek Ranger Station on Swift Creek Reservoir, south of the mountain. It is closed late October-Memorial Day weekend and is not recommended for trailers or RVs.

Windy Ridge

The primary destination on the east side is **Windy Ridge,** from where you can see Spirit Lake and get an up-close view of the volcano. Take Forest Roads 25 and 99 to reach the viewpoint. Windy Ridge stands at the end of Road 99, 4,000 feet above sea level and 34 miles southwest of Randle. It's just five miles from the crater of Mount St. Helens. Climb the 361 steps for an incredible view into the volcano, across the devastated pumice plain, and over the log-choked Spirit Lake. Forest Service interpretive personnel are here daily from May through October, providing frequent talks about the volcano from an amphitheater.

Mount Adams

If it stood alone, 12,276-foot Mount Adams would be a prime recreation site, but from the population centers of Puget Sound, Adams is geographically behind and below its more popular volcanic siblings, Mount Rainier and Mount St. Helens. Those willing to go the extra distance will find in the relative isolation of Mount Adams varied hiking trails, unusual geologic formations, and scenic areas. If your goal is to get away from it all, this is the place to do it.

MOUNT ADAMS WILDERNESS

This 42,280-acre wilderness encompasses the summit of Mount Adams along with its eastern and northern flanks. The east side of the peak lies within the Yakama Reservation and is termed "Tract D." Trails, including the Pacific Crest Trail, provide a semicircular path through the heart of the wilderness.

Hiking

The most heavily used trail in the Mount Adams Wilderness is **South Climb.** It runs 2.2 miles from Cold Springs Campground to the timberline, from where climbers depart for routes to the summit. Those who prefer to stay low can follow the **Around the Mountain Trail** (No. 9) northwest for about six miles to the **Pacific Crest Trail** (PCT).

The 21 miles of the PCT that pass through the Mount Adams Wilderness are accessible on the south from Forest Service Road 23, near its intersection with Forest Service Road 8810. On the north the PCT crosses Forest Service Road 5603 near Potato Hill. Adventurous hikers are rewarded with subalpine meadows, glacial streams, dense forest, wildflowers, and scenic viewpoints.

Beginning at Morrison Creek Horse Camp on the south side of Mount Adams, the 2.7-mile **Crofton Butte Trail** (No. 73) follows the mountain's lower slopes for scenic views of the butte. Take Forest Roads 80 and 8040 for about 10 miles from Trout Lake.

Climbing Mount Adams

Mount Adams is one of the easiest Northwest volcanic peaks to climb and is often used as a first climb by area mountaineering clubs. Before you begin you're required to register with the **Mount Adams Ranger Station** (2455 Rte. 141, Trout Lake, 509/395-3400), where you need to purchase a Cascades Volcano Pass ($10 for weekday climbs, $15 for weekends).

The south slope route is the least difficult. It begins at an elevation of 6,000 feet at the end of Forest Roads 8040 and 500 at Cold Springs Camp. Follow the old road for two miles to Timberline Camp. From there take the **South Climb Trail** (No. 183) to a large snowfield. Bear right across the snowfield to the ridge, following the ridge to the false summit at 11,500 feet. A zigzag trail leads through pumice to the summit. In total it's a six-hour one-way trip. Climbers should carry an ice ax, rope, crampons, warm clothing, and sunglasses, along with basic hiking supplies.

Camping

The Mount Adams Ranger District has 17 developed campgrounds on the south side of Mount Adams. Some are free, but there is a $16 fee at the larger ones, including **Moss Creek** and **Peterson Prairie.**

Other Forest Service campgrounds line Forest Road 23, the route that connects the town of Randle with the northwest side of Mount Adams. These are managed by the **Cowlitz Valley Ranger District** (10024 U.S. 12 in Randle, 360/497-1103, Mon.-Fri. 8am-noon and 1pm-4:30pm), and range from free to $18 a night. Closest to the

Mount Adams Wilderness Area are Olallie Lake, Takhalakh Lake, and Horseshoe Lake Campgrounds. Takhalakh Lake Campground affords a fine view of Mount Adams.

TROUT LAKE

Trout Lake is a tiny agricultural settlement with dairy and horse farms found approximately 30 miles north of the Columbia Gorge town of White Salmon. It's the main access point for the Mount Adams area. Though there are limited services—a pair of restaurants, a grocery store, and a gas station—it maintains a reputation for welcoming hikers and other travelers. For more dining variety and other services, head south to the Columbia Gorge.

The town has the Forest Service's **Mount Adams Ranger Station** (2455 Rte. 141, Trout Lake, 509/395-3400, Mon.-Sat. 8am-noon and 1pm-4:30pm), where you can get maps, camping information, and current trail conditions. Mountain climbers must register here to climb Mount Adams.

Food

Trout Lake's go-to diner and espresso bar, **Station Cafe & Espresso** (2374 Rte. 141, 509/395-2211, daily 7am-8pm, $7-14) serves up satisfying breakfasts, including huckleberry pancakes and smoothies in season, and pizza and burgers at lunch and dinner.

There's a friendly roadhouse vibe at **Trout Lake Country Inn** (15 Guler Rd., 509/395-3667, http://troutlakecountryinn.net, Mon. 5pm-9pm, Thurs. and Sun. 11:30am-9pm, Fri.-Sat. 11:30am-11pm, $8-11), a century-old restaurant and bar that serves burgers and some creative sandwiches, such as Thai yam

tuna salad. On many nights there's live music and dancing.

Pick up provisions for a day of hiking at the homey **Trout Lake Grocery** (2383 Rte. 141, 509/395-2777, daily 8am-7pm). It's a popular stop for hikers on the Pacific Crest Trail.

Accommodations

Kelly's Trout Creek Inn Bed and Breakfast (25 Mt. Adams Rd., Trout Lake, 509/395-2769, www.kellysbnb.com, $75-100) has three guest rooms in a restored 1940s farmhouse. Breakfast consists of muffins, toast, and coffee.

Trout Lake Valley Inn (2300 Rte. 141, 509/395-2300, www.troutlakevalleyinn.com, $100-110) is a clean, comfortable motel with some character added by pine furniture. Continental breakfast is included in the price.

Transportation

You can approach the Mount Adams area from Seattle in two ways. For a slightly quicker 4.5-hour, 250-mile trip, take I-5 South to I-205 South near Vancouver, then turn onto Route 14 heading east. At Underwood, take Route 141 north to Trout Lake. An alternative is to drive I-5 South past Chehalis, head east on Route 12 to Randle, and take Randle Road (Forest Rd. 23) south for 56 miles to Trout Lake. It's an isolated, scenic route, but the entire length is paved. The 195-mile trip takes about 5 hours total.

Approaching from the east, you can drive down Route 97 to Goldendale and west on Route 142 to Klickitat and take the Glenwood-Trout Lake Road, or follow Route 14 from Maryhill to Underwood and drive north. The roads into the Mount Adams area are closed each winter due to heavy snowfall.

Columbia River Gorge and Wine Country

Great mountains make great rivers, and one of America's greatest is the mighty Columbia, fed by runoff from the Cascades and the Rockies.

The river's 1,200-mile course begins in Canada. At the Washington-Oregon border it delivers the largest flow into the Pacific of any river in North America. Everywhere it runs, the Columbia is the defining force behind the geography, economy, and culture of the land that surrounds it.

Nowhere is that force more evident than in the Columbia River Gorge and Washington's wine country. The Columbia River Gorge National Scenic Area, which slices through the Cascade Range along the Washington-Oregon border, is the site of natural beauty on a grand scale, with abundant waterfalls and 30-mile vistas over towering bluffs. To the Gorge's northeast, the valleys between the towns of Yakima and Walla Walla are the heart of Washington's rapidly growing wine industry, where the Columbia and its tributaries are the main source of the irrigation water that has transformed a desert into flourishing farmland.

The Gorge is both a weekend getaway for Portland residents and a destination for travelers from around the world. There's a multitude of ways to enjoy yourself here. Almost everyone devotes some time to the Historic Columbia River Highway, a scenic route on the west end of the Oregon side that leads past the greatest concentration of waterfalls in North America. Hiking trails crisscross both sides, and the stretch of water near the town of Hood River is one of the best spots in the world for windsurfing and kiteboarding.

One of the most fascinating experiences in the Gorge is simply driving its length and witnessing the change in landscape. Over the course of 40 miles from Cascade Locks to The Dalles the average annual rainfall drops dramatically, and the lush green terrain turns brown and austere. The two areas are strikingly beautiful in very different ways.

The center of Washington's booming winemaking production is the territory bookended by Yakima and Walla Walla. The region is still in its winemaking adolescence, and in many ways that's a good thing. A few large producers are mixed in with scores of ambitious

Previous: vineyard in Walla Walla; view of the Columbia River Gorge from the Portland Women's Forum State Scenic Viewpoint. **Above:** Columbia Hills State Park petroglyph.

Look for ★ to find recommended
sights, activities, dining, and lodging.

Highlights

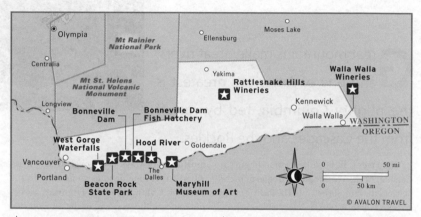

★ **Beacon Rock State Park:** Take a short, fun hike up the switchback trail on this 848-foot-tall rock for spectacular views of the Gorge (page 374).

★ **Bonneville Dam:** The 1980s addition accessible from Washington is more fun to visit than the historic section on the Oregon side, with a better fish-ladder viewing area and more up-close tour (page 375).

★ **West Gorge Waterfalls:** The Oregon side of the Gorge is like a waterfall theme park, with some falls visible from the historic highway and many more accessible via hiking trails (page 380).

★ **Bonneville Dam Fish Hatchery:** Hatcheries can be found up and down the Columbia, but this early example is the most elaborate and most fun to visit (pages 383).

★ **Hood River:** The liveliest town along the Gorge is a mecca for outdoor sports enthusiasts and craft beer lovers. (page 384).

★ **Maryhill Museum of Art:** Deemed "the loneliest museum in the world," this isolated gem has a wide-ranging collection that includes everything from Rodin sculptures to miniature mannequins wearing French haute couture (page 391).

★ **Rattlesnake Hills Wineries:** A picturesque slope in Yakima Valley is the perfect setting for sampling the region's wine and meeting its friendly, unpretentious winemakers (page 397).

★ **Walla Walla Wineries:** High standards of quality and a diverse group of colorful producers make Walla Walla the place to experience Washington wine at its best (page 409).

Columbia River Gorge and Wine Country

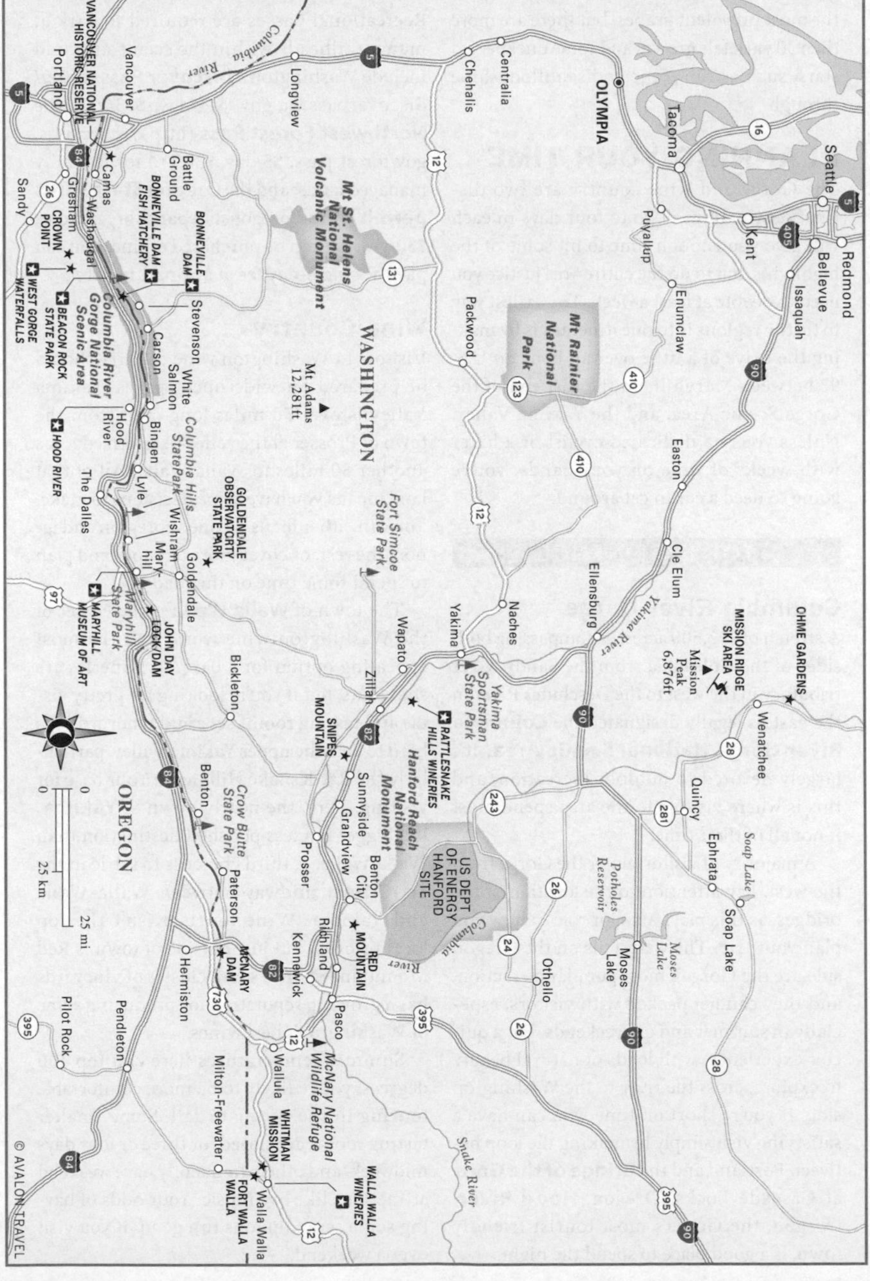

WASHINGTON
OREGON
OLYMPIA
Seattle
Redmond
Bellevue
Issaquah
Kent
Tacoma
Puyallup
Enumclaw
Centralia
Chehalis
Longview
Vancouver
VANCOUVER NATIONAL HISTORIC RESERVE
Portland
Gresham
Sandy
Camas
Washougal
Battle Ground
Columbia River
Mt St. Helens National Volcanic Monument
Mt Rainier National Park
Packwood
Mt Adams 12,281ft
Easton
Cle Elum
Ellensburg
Yakima River
MISSION RIDGE SKI AREA
Mission Peak 6,876ft
OHME GARDENS
Wenatchee
Quincy
Ephrata
Soap Lake
Potholes Reservoir
Moses Lake
Othello
Naches
Yakima
Yakima Sportsman State Park
Wapato
Fort Simcoe State Park
Zillah
RATTLESNAKE HILLS WINERIES
SNIPES MOUNTAIN
Sunnyside
Grandview
Prosser
Hanford Reach National Monument
US DEPT OF ENERGY HANFORD SITE
Benton City
RED MOUNTAIN
Richland
Kennewick
Pasco
McNary National Wildlife Refuge
Wallula
WHITMAN MISSION
WALLA WALLA WINERIES
FORT WALLA WALLA
Walla Walla
Milton-Freewater
Pendleton
Pilot Rock
Hermiston
MCNARY DAM
Paterson
Crow Butte State Park
Benton
Bickleton
Goldendale
GOLDENDALE OBSERVATORY STATE PARK
Maryhill
Maryhill State Park
MARYHILL MUSEUM OF ART
JOHN DAY LOCK/DAM
Wishram
Columbia Hills State Park
Lyle
The Dalles
Bingen
White Salmon
Hood River
HOOD RIVER
Carson
Stevenson
Columbia River Gorge National Scenic Area
BONNEVILLE DAM
BONNEVILLE DAM FISH HATCHERY
BEACON ROCK STATE PARK
CROWN POINT
WEST GORGE WATERFALLS
Snake River
5
12
16
405
410
123
90
131
82
24
26
28
243
281
395
730
84
97
0
25 mi
25 km
© AVALON TRAVEL

small wineries devoted to discovering what works best with the terrain. Cabernet sauvignon, merlot, chardonnay, and riesling are the most prevalent grapes, but there are more than 30 varietals grown, and some unexpected stars, such as cab franc and semillon, shine through.

PLANNING YOUR TIME

The Gorge and wine country are two distinct destinations. Two to four days in each will give you enough time to hit some of the highlights, but to do the entire area justice you need to devote at least a week. The easiest way to tie the regions into one itinerary is by making the drive of a little over an hour on U.S. 97 between Maryhill, on the east end of the Gorge Scenic Area, and the Yakima Valley. Unless you're a dedicated cyclist or a hiker with weeks of time on your hands, you're going to need a car to get around.

TOP EXPERIENCE

Columbia River Gorge

A stretch of 292,500 acres, encompassing both sides of the Columbia from the Sandy River tributary in the west to the Deschutes River in the east, is legally designated the **Columbia River Gorge National Scenic Area.** It's largely devoted to outdoor recreation, and this is where visitors to the area spend most if not all of their time.

A majority of visitors enter the Gorge from the west. Pay attention to the location of the bridges, as this plays a major role in how you plan your trip. The waterfalls on the Oregon side are the Gorge's most popular attraction, and they can get packed with visitors, especially in summer and on weekends. For a quieter experience, with loads of natural beauty to explore, cross the river to the Washington side. If you're short on time, you can have a satisfying visit simply by making the loop between Portland and the **Bridge of the Gods** at Cascade Locks, Oregon. **Hood River,** Oregon, the Gorge's most tourist-friendly town, is a good place to spend the night.

The Friends of the Columbia Gorge website (http://gorgefriends.org) is a useful resource for nuts-and-bolts visitor information. Recreational passes are required to park at many trailheads within the scenic area and include Washington's **Discover Pass** (http://discoverpass.wa.gov, $11/day, $33/yr.), the **Northwest Forest Pass** (https://store.usgs.gov/forest-pass, $5/day, $30/yr.) for federally managed lands, and the **Oregon State Parks permit** (http://oregonstateparks.org, $5/day, $30/yr.). All can be purchased online. You can pay the single-day fee at any parking area.

Wine Country

Visitors to Washington wine country should be prepared for wide-open spaces. Yakima Valley is over 50 miles long, and from the town of Prosser at the valley's eastern edge it's another 80 miles to Walla Walla. All of that land means you have some decisions to make. You can either focus on one subregion and ignore the rest, or cover more territory and plan to spend some time on the road.

The town of **Walla Walla** is the center of the Washington wine world and the most appealing option for a base. Its wineries are standouts, but if you're looking for pretty vistas and tasting rooms set amid vineyards, it's hard to beat the upper Yakima Valley, particularly the Rattlesnake Hills area. Your base for visiting there, the nearby town of **Yakima,** is a bigger but less polished destination than Walla Walla. A third choice is to settle in the **Tri-Cities,** midway between Walla Walla and Yakima. Wine tourism isn't the top local priority, but just outside of town is Red Mountain, where a small cluster of vineyards has a growing reputation for producing some of Washington's best wines.

Summer temperatures here can top 100 degrees; you're likely to be more comfortable touring in the spring or fall. Some smaller tasting rooms are closed for three or four days midweek, and others frequently have weekend attractions like live music. Your odds of having some serendipitous fun go up if you visit over a weekend.

Western Gorge, Washington Side

The waterfalls and surrounding woods on the Oregon side are the top attractions of the western Gorge, but there are good reasons to travel along the Washington side, which is traced by **Route 14** (also known as the Lewis and Clark Highway). First among them is that in Washington near the Bridge of the Gods you find more dining and lodging options. If you're planning on spending a night or two in the western Gorge area, it's a good strategy to make your initial drive on the Washington side, get situated at your hotel, and then cross the bridge to see the falls.

The gateway towns of Camas and Washougal, at the west end of the Gorge, both possess their own brands of small-town charm. Farther east there's a high-quality regional museum, and great hikes and vistas are found throughout the area, highlighted by towering Beacon Rock, one of the Gorge's most distinctive landmarks. On the way, the towns of North Bonneville, Stevenson, and Carson, with fewer than 5,000 residents between them, aren't much more than reduced-speed zones along the highway, but they support facilities for travelers that belie their size. In the vicinity there are two resorts, several other lodging options, and a handful of good casual restaurants.

CAMAS AND WASHOUGAL

Camas (pop 20,500) and Washougal (pop 14,500), located just a couple of miles apart along Route 14, are small industrial towns that double as Washington's west-end gateways to the Columbia River Gorge Scenic Area. Take the highway east along the state border and you won't hit another metropolis with a population over 4,000 until you reach Walla Walla, 230 miles away. Downtown Camas sits right next door to the Georgia-Pacific paper mill that's the town economic engine, but the tree-lined streets manage to maintain a step-back-in-time charm.

As you wind your way east on Route 14 from Camas and Washougal, keep your eyes peeled for the **Cape Horn Viewpoint** at milepost 25. It's just a turnoff at the side of the road, but it's your first spectacular view over the Columbia River Gorge.

Shopping

Washougal's top draw is the **Pendleton Woolen Mill Outlet Store** (2 Pendleton Way, 360/835-1118, www.pendleton-usa. com, Mon.-Fri. 8am-5pm, Sat. 9am-5pm, Sun. 11am-5pm). Pendleton blankets and clothes are sturdy Western icons, and the outlet here is housed in the same building as the factory—which you can tour for free on weekdays at 9am, 10am, 11am, and 1:30pm.

Food

The most creative restaurant in the area is Washougal's hip little **OurBar** (1887 Main St., 360/954-5141, www.our-bar.com, Tues.-Sun. 9am-2pm, $5-10), a breakfast and lunch spot that prides itself on simply prepared farm-to-table cuisine and an interesting wine and beer selection. Stop in for huckleberry pancakes or a spicy steak sandwich. Across the street, **Amnesia Brewing** (1834 Main St., 360/335-1008, www.amnesiabrewz.com, Mon.-Tues. 3pm-9pm, Wed.-Fri. 11am-9pm, Sat. noon-10pm, Sun. noon-9pm, $11-18) has a similarly clean-lined design and serves up hearty sandwiches, barbecued ribs, and mac and cheese to go with its collection of microbrews.

Accommodations

If you're looking for a bargain and you don't mind being a ways down the road from the Gorge's main attractions, the **Camas Hotel** (405 NE 4th Ave., 360/834-5722, www.camashotel.com, $75-175) is a good option. It's tucked into a corner building in the quaint

Western Columbia River Gorge

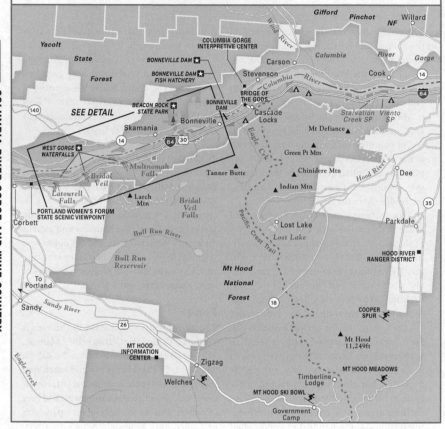

downtown district, with 20 simple rooms accented with stylish touches; half have shared bathrooms.

Transportation

Camas is 180 miles (3 hrs.) southeast of Seattle and 22 miles (0.5 hr.) northeast of Portland via I-5 and Route 14.

★ BEACON ROCK STATE PARK

Beacon Rock, the 848-foot-tall core of an ancient volcano along the northern shore of the Columbia, was given its name in 1806 by Lewis and Clark as they traveled the river

on their Corps of Discovery Expedition. It had formed some 50,000 years earlier when magma cooled and solidified inside a volcanic vent. Between 15,000 and 13,000 years ago the massive Missoula Floods blasted across the landscape, eroding the softer outer shell but leaving the hard basalt core. Today it's the centerpiece of **Beacon Rock State Park** (34841 Route 14, 509/427-8265, http://parks.state. wa.us/474/Beacon-Rock, daily 8am-dusk, parking pass available on-site).

The rock is interesting to look at, but the real fun is hiking it. What looks like a daunting ascent is surprisingly easy. The vertical face is crisscrossed by a mile-long trail that

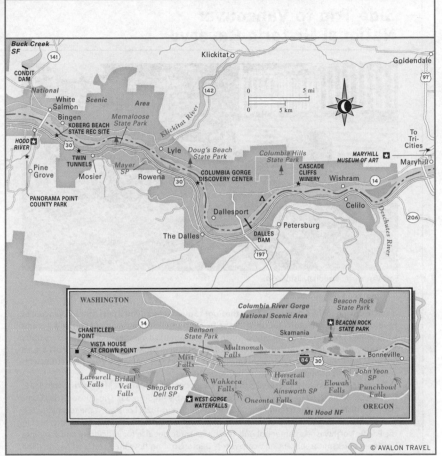

Buck Creek SF
141
CONDIT DAM
National
White Salmon
Bingen
HOOD RIVER
Pine Grove
TWIN TUNNELS
30
Mosier
PANORAMA POINT COUNTY PARK
Scenic
KOBERG BEACH STATE REC SITE
Memaloose State Park
Mayer SP
Rowena
30
Area
Klickitat
142
Klickitat River
Lyle
Doug's Beach State Park
COLUMBIA GORGE DISCOVERY CENTER
Dallesport
The Dalles
DALLES DAM
197
Columbia Hills State Park
CASCADE CLIFFS WINERY
Petersburg
Wishram
14
Celilo
Klickitat
Goldendale
97
To Tri-Cities
MARYHILL MUSEUM OF ART
Maryhill
206
Deschutes River

0   5 mi
0   5 km

WASHINGTON
14
CHANTICLEER POINT
VISTA HOUSE AT CROWN POINT
Benson State Park
Mist Falls
Latourell Falls
Bridal Veil Falls
Shepperd's Dell SP
WEST GORGE WATERFALLS
Wahkeena Falls
Oneonta Falls
Columbia River Gorge National Scenic Area
Skamania
Multnomah Falls
Horsetail Falls
Ainsworth SP
84
30
Beacon Rock State Park
BEACON ROCK STATE PARK
Bonneville
John Yeon SP
Elowah Falls
Punchbowl Falls
OREGON
Mt Hood NF

© AVALON TRAVEL

incorporates 52 switchbacks and 22 bridges, resulting in a short, safe, exhilarating hike with many spectacular views up and down the Gorge. The trail exists thanks to the vision of Henry Biddle, a retired engineer and geologist who bought Beacon Rock for a dollar in 1915 and spent the next three years carving the path into the stone. The hike takes about an hour, including stops for photographs.

★ BONNEVILLE DAM
Washington Visitors Center
Bonneville Dam Washington Shore Visitors Complex (Route 14, 2 mi. east of North Bonneville, 509/427-4281, http://www.

nwp.usace.army.mil/bonneville, daily 9am-5pm, free) gives you access to the workings of the dam's Powerhouse 2, which was opened in 1981, and the accompanying fish ladder. The structure doesn't have the same historical significance as the original dam, which you can visit across the river in Oregon, but it has the benefits of being designed to accommodate visitors. On this side of the river you'll find better informational displays, superior views of the fish ladder, and guided tours that provide a more up-close look at the generators. Tours are conducted at 10am, 1:30pm, and 3:30pm daily June-August and on weekends throughout the year.

Side Trip to Vancouver National Historic Reserve

Fort Vancouver National Historic Site

If you're driving to the Gorge on I-5 from the Puget Sound region, you'll pass through Vancouver (pop. 160,000), Washington's fourth-largest city and a satellite community of Portland (I-5 and I-205 connect Portland and Vancouver, which are only about 20 minutes apart). For history buffs it's worthwhile to stop at the **Vancouver National Historic Reserve** (Exit 5C off of I-5; turn left on E. Mill Plain Blvd. and then right on Fort Vancouver Way), a pleasant park-like setting with several sites that played key roles in the region's history.

The main attraction in the reserve is the **Fort Vancouver National Historic Site** (612 E. Reserve St., 360/816-6230, www.nps.gov/fova, Tues.-Sat. 9am-5pm, $5). The Hudson's Bay Company, a British-owned fur-trading giant, founded the fort in 1825. Looking at the reconstructed version, it's amazing to think that for its first 20 years this was the most important settlement in the Pacific Northwest—a center not only for the fur trade but also for agriculture and shipping. You'll see blacksmiths, bakers, and carpenters demonstrating how their crafts were practiced at the fort.

On a slope just above the fort is the **Vancouver Barracks,** a major U.S. Army outpost in the late 1800s that also played roles in both World Wars. There's not much currently going on there, but just across the road is the handsome **Officers Row,** with 22 Victorian houses that were home to the barracks leadership. You can tour the **Marshall House** (1301 Officers Row, 360/693-3103, Mon.-Sat. 10am-5pm, free), where General George Marshall of Marshall Plan fame lived from 1936 to 1938. There's a good midrange restaurant in the **Grant House** (1101 Officers Row, 360/906-1101, Mon.-Fri. 11am-8pm, $15-31), the oldest of the row's homes, built in 1849. Ulysses S. Grant never lived here, but he was quartermaster of the fort from 1852 to 1853.

East of the fort is **Pearson Airfield**, which dates from 1905 and is still an active airstrip. The **Pearson Air Museum** (1115 E. 5th St., 360/816-6232, www.nps.gov/fova, Tues.-Sat. 9am-5pm, free) has exhibits about the airfield, Vancouver Barracks, and military aviation in the Pacific Northwest during World War I.

the path up Beacon Rock

The fish ladder here, with its underwater viewing area where workers painstakingly count the number of fish migrating upstream, provides a telling illustration of the huge ecological impact that dams along the Columbia have had. Statistics point to growing fish populations over the past decade, but there's no denying that humans have messed with Mother Nature along this powerful river—with results both good and bad.

STEVENSON AND CARSON

The little towns of Stevenson (10 miles east of Beacon Rock) and Carson (5 miles east of Stevenson) are centers for tourism services on the Washington side of the western Gorge.

Columbia Gorge Interpretive Center

Outside of Stevenson, across the road from the Skamania Lodge, the **Columbia Gorge Interpretive Center** (990 SW Rock Creek Dr., 509/427-8211, www.columbiagorge.org,

daily 9am-5pm, $10) has a much more impressive collection of displays than you would expect from a small-town museum. The centerpiece is the Grand Gallery, which focuses on fishing and logging and features a waterfall, a 37-foot-tall fish wheel, and a massive steam engine once used to power a sawmill. The museum isn't as large or as broadly focused as the Columbia Gorge Discovery Center, located near The Dalles, but if you don't plan to go that far east this is a more-than-adequate alternative.

Hiking

Beautiful waterfalls aren't found exclusively on the Oregon side of the Columbia. One of the Gorge's best waterfall hikes is along the **Falls Creek Falls Trail.** To reach the trailhead, make the turnoff five miles past Stevenson along Route 14 for Wind River Road (Route 30), take that for 15 miles, and then turn right onto Road 3062 and follow the signs for another 2.5 miles. It takes some work to get there, but it's worth it. A little under two miles in on the trail you reach the gorgeous three-tiered, 200-plus-foot Falls Creek Falls. The full loop trail runs six miles, taking you above Falls Creek Canyon and through old-growth forest.

Food

The Skamania Lodge has two dining options. The **Cascade Dining Room** (Mon.-Sat. 7am-2pm and 5pm-9pm, Sun. 9am-2pm and 5pm-9pm, $22-42), the lodge's main restaurant, is a large, attractive space, with a wall of windows looking toward the Gorge. The menu focuses on upscale versions of regional specialties, including grilled salmon, pork chops, and steaks. **River Rock** (Mon.-Thurs. 2pm-10pm, Fri. 2pm-11pm, Sat. 11am-11pm, Sun. 7am-10pm, $13-26) has a more casual, bar-and-grill feel, with food to match, including burgers, pizza, and mac and cheese.

For a spot with more on the menu than a brewpub and a homier atmosphere than Skamania, there's Stevenson's **Big River Grill** (192 SW 2nd St., 509/427-4888, www.

thebigrivergrill.com, Mon.-Fri. 11:30am-9pm, Sat.-Sun. 8am-9pm, $14-23). The eclectic menu ranges from meatloaf to Thai chicken.

Brewpubs are big throughout the Pacific Northwest, and in this area of the Gorge they make for a couple of the best casual-dining options. **Walking Man Brewing** (240 1st St., 509/427-5520, www.walkingmanbeer.com, Wed.-Mon. noon-9pm, $8-16) in Stevenson has been around the longest and has received international accolades for its beer. The bar/dining room has a hole-in-the-wall feel, but when the weather's nice diners flock to the pleasant patio for burgers, pizza, and fish tacos. You have to go around to the back of a small retail complex in Carson to find **Backwoods Brewing Company** (1162B Wind River Rd., 509/427-3412, www.backwoodsbrewingcompany.com, daily 11:30am-9pm, $11-13), but the dining room and patio are pleasant and surprisingly large. The food is predictable brewpub fare—salads, sandwiches, and pizza—and there's a youthful, friendly vibe to the place.

Accommodations

The closest thing to a large luxury resort in the Gorge area is **Skamania Lodge** (1131 SW Skamania Lodge Way, 509/314-4177, www.skamania.com, $239-349). It's not over-the-top swanky, but it has comfortable rooms, good dining options, and extensive grounds that include a golf course and hiking trails. The design pays homage to national park lodges, an influence you feel most strongly in the stately Gorge Room looking out at the river.

For more secluded lodging, a great choice is the ★ **Resort at Skamania Coves** (45932 Route 14, 509/427-4900, www.skamaniacoves.com). It has six two-bedroom rental homes ($275-350), a novel one-bedroom tree house ($285), and 17 RV sites with full hookups ($42), all immaculately maintained on a prime riverside property. Guests have access to five acres of woods and three idyllic coves with pebbled beachfront and fire pits.

Carson Ridge Cabins (1261 Wind River Rd., 509/427-7777, www.carsonridgecabins.com, $275-435) has B&B touches, such as elaborate breakfasts and cookies in the afternoon, but each guest room is a separate cabin with a fireplace, a porch, and knotty-pine furnishings.

The **Carson Hot Springs Golf Spa & Resort** (372 St. Martin's Springs Rd., 509/427-8296, www.carsonhotspringresort.com, $105-199) is a century-old local landmark that's

Columbia River Gorge from Beacon Rock

been rehabilitated and expanded in fits and starts. Guest rooms have no more character than a typical bargain motel, but rates are cheaper than most other options in the area, and you get access to a mineral pool. At the rustic 1930s-era spa, which is open to walk-ins as well as overnight guests, a soak and a wrap are $30 weekdays, $35 weekends.

Western Gorge, Oregon Side

The Columbia River Gorge National Scenic Area officially begins at the Sandy River, a Columbia tributary 15 miles west of Portland. While I-84 cuts a straight, quick path along the Oregon side, to appreciate the scenery you need to take the parallel Historic Columbia River Highway, also designated **Route 30.** It was built between 1913 and 1922 as America's first planned scenic roadway, and though much of it is now closed to traffic, you can still drive the 22-mile portion from Troutdale east nearly to Bonneville. Every year millions of visitors make this trip to take in the Gorge's most iconic sights: majestic bluff-top vistas and dozens of roaring waterfalls.

In 2017 the Eagle Creek Fire ravaged the Oregon side of the Gorge, burning 49,000 acres, much of it within the National Scenic Area. Consequences were both immediate and long-term. Patches of scorched forestland surrounding the area's famous waterfalls are ghosts of their former selves and will take decades to recover. Landslides are likely to reroute trails or make them impassable. Damage was most severe along the Eagle Creek Trail to Punchbowl Falls. Check on area conditions via the **Forest Service** (www.fs.usda. gov/recmain/crgnsa/recreation).

TROUTDALE

The small town of Troutdale comes by its name honestly: It's situated at the mouth of the Sandy River, one of the region's premier trout-fishing destinations. Main Street has some spots to eat and shop, but if you're not here to fish you're probably stopping to visit McMenamins Edgefield, a sort of hipster resort just outside of town.

Fishing

Winter is the peak season for steelhead trout fishing along the Sandy, but there are steelhead and chinook salmon in summer as well. **Dabney State Recreation Area,** and **Dodge Park** and **Oxbow Park** farther upstream, are all popular access points. **Mark's Snack N Tackle** (1208 E. Historic Columbia River Hwy., 503/489-5649, 8am-5pm daily) is the go-to resource for gear and tips, as well as barbecue. If you want a guide try **Team Hook-Up** (503/206-8285, www.hookup-guideservice.com), a father-and-son operation that's been fishing the Sandy and the Columbia for over 40 years.

Food

In the main building at Edgefield, the **Black Rabbit Restaurant** (2126 SW Halsey St., 503/492-3086, www.mcmenamins.com, daily 7am-10pm, dinner $17-36) offers a more high-end menu than you usually find at McMenamins establishments. Artfully presented seasonal dishes can range from delicate steamed halibut to hearty smoked boar. Edgefield's **Power Station Pub** (daily 11am-10pm, $10-17) and **Loading Dock Grill** (daily 11am-midnight, $10-16) serve more typical pub grub, featuring burgers and pizza.

Accommodations

★ **McMenamins Edgefield** (2126 SW Halsey St., 503/669-8610, www.mcmenamins. com), located on the site of the former county poor farm, isn't your typical resort experience. The original 1911 buildings and 74-acre grounds have been restored with care and whimsy. Murals throughout the interiors illustrate the history of the place and region, and garden paths lead to a spa, movie theater, and two par-3 golf courses. Rooms ($140-200 d) are creatively decorated but simple: None have phones or televisions, and all but the most expensive have shared baths. For a true bargain, a bed in the hostel area runs $30. Though you don't have to be a drinker to enjoy yourself, booze is part of the experience here: A brewery, winery, and distillery are all on-site, and with 10 bars to choose from, a libation is never far away.

Transportation

Troutdale is 15 miles east of Portland via the scenic Historic Columbia River Highway (Route 30) or the faster I-84. From Troutdale, follow the Columbia River Highway east for 22 miles to reach Bonneville.

HISTORIC COLUMBIA RIVER HIGHWAY

This winding scenic roadway is perched on the bluffs above I-84 and the river. You can have a fulfilling experience from the seat of your car here, simply taking in the rich green woods and the bird's-eye views of the Gorge, and then making a few stops at the roadside waterfalls. If you have more time and energy, you can easily spend half a day or more on hiking trails that put you within feel-the-spray distance of numerous falls. This is the area that made the Gorge famous.

Viewpoints

Heading east, the highway's first beautiful vista comes at the **Portland Women's Forum State Scenic Viewpoint,** nine miles outside of Troutdale. This is the signature view of the Gorge from the Oregon side—miles of river weaving between basalt bluffs. It's similar to what you see from Crown Point a short distance down the road, but you have two advantages here: because it's less of a landmark you're less likely to encounter crowds, and the lovely Vista House at Crown Point is part of the panorama, like a jewel embellishing the landscape. (The viewpoint's name comes from an organization that

bought the land in order to ensure its maintenance and preservation. The group eventually gifted the property to the Oregon Parks and Recreation Department.)

A rewarding detour comes half a mile down the highway at the turnoff for **Sherrard Point** on Larch Mountain, which is accessible only when the road up is clear of snow, usually from April or May until November. It's a 14-mile drive and a steep quarter-mile hike from the parking lot to the viewpoint. What you see when you get there makes it worth the time and effort: an awesome view of the Cascades that, on a clear day, includes Mounts Rainier, St. Helens, Adams, Hood, and Jefferson. If you want to make a day of it, you can also reach Sherrard Point via a seven-mile hiking trail from Multnomah Falls.

Back down on the historic highway, the next scenic stop is **Crown Point,** 1.5 miles past the Women's Forum Viewpoint. The draws here are that the promontory juts far out above the river, and that it's capped by **Vista House** (503/695-2240, www.vistahouse.com, 9am-6pm daily, mid-Mar.-Oct.). This beautiful art nouveau observatory and rest stop was built between 1915 and 1918 at the instigation of Samuel Lancaster, the chief engineer for the Columbia River Highway, who proclaimed that it would be "an observatory from which the view both up and down the Columbia could be viewed in silent communion with the infinite." Some less idealistic Oregonian taxpayers labeled it the "$100,000 Outhouse." A hundred years later, both interpretations still have a ring of truth to them.

★ West Gorge Waterfalls

Of all its natural wonders, the Columbia River Gorge's greatest claim to fame is the series of waterfalls along the historic highway between Crown Point and the Bonneville Dam. The renown results from a combination of factors: abundance (there's a higher concentration of falls here than anywhere else in North America), grandeur, variety, and accessibility. There are lots of hiking trails to choose from if you want to do off-road exploring, but there's

Multnomah Falls

plenty to see on a simple driving tour. If you stick to the highway, you'll encounter these falls traveling west to east.

Heading east from Crown Point the road descends to the base of the bluffs. After 2.5 miles you reach **Latourell Falls,** which makes a 249-foot drop from a basalt cliff. It's partially visible from the parking lot; a short but steep path leads up to a viewpoint, and another descends to the base.

From there it's two miles down the highway to **Bridal Veil Falls,** which requires a quarter-mile hike down a gentle switchback path. This two-tiered, 118-foot horsetail fall is the only one situated below the highway.

Next up, three miles farther along the highway, is **Wahkeena Falls,** which skips down a series of plateaus in its 242-foot descent. You get a good view from the parking area, and if you walk the 0.4-mile round-trip up to the bridge facing the falls you'll be close enough to feel the spray on your face.

From there it's a half mile to the crown jewel of Gorge waterfalls, **Multnomah Falls**—there's

a trail that you can take from Wahkeena if you don't feel like getting back in the car. At 635 feet, with an uninterrupted free fall of 542 feet, this is one of the tallest continually flowing falls in the United States. It's also the most visited natural attraction in the state of Oregon. For most of the year the base of the falls is crowded with onlookers, and parking can be a trial.

There's one more roadside stop before the Historic Columbia River Highway merges onto I-84: **Horsetail Falls,** which makes a single 176-foot drop into a pool. The highway's lead engineer, Samuel Lancaster, was so impressed by Horsetail that it was one of his priorities for the road to run by it. It's close enough that mist often dampens the windows of passing cars.

WATERFALL HIKES

Hikes around the falls are abundant and rewarding, and many of the trails connect, making it easy to tailor an excursion to the time and difficulty level that suits you. Below are some highlights, but if you're going to devote several days to hiking it's worthwhile to get a specialized guide, such as *Moon Outdoors Oregon Hiking.*

At the west end of the falls area, a 2.4-mile loop hike starts at the **Latourell Falls** parking lot and heads up a steep initial grade and over four bridges to Upper Latourell Falls. From there you descend stairs into Guy Talbot Park (where there are picnic tables) and continue under the highway to the base of the falls. A short, paved path leads back to the parking lot.

Starting from a roadside parking area about a mile east of Bridal Veil Falls, it's a winding five-mile round-trip on the out-and-back trail to **Angels Rest.** When you arrive at the lookout you're rewarded with 270-degree views over the Gorge.

The highlight of the five-mile **Multnomah-Wahkeena Loop Hike** is the abundance of falls you pass on the way—10 in total. If you start at Multnomah Falls and do the loop counterclockwise, you begin with a half-mile path just above the road to Wahkeena Falls. From there take the Wahkeena Trail (No. 420) on a fairly steep switchback climb that passes a beautiful outlook at Lemmon's Viewpoint. The next highlight, after more switchbacks, is the fan-shaped Fairy Falls. As you continue you hit two trail intersections; stick with No. 420. Eventually you reach the turnoff for the Larch Mountain Trail, which will take you past several more falls as you make the descent to Multnomah. Be sure to make the short side trip to the spectacular Multnomah Falls Upper Viewpoint.

The **Horsetail Falls Loop Hike** is a relatively flat 2.5 miles that takes you past three falls. Start in the Horsetail Falls parking area and follow the trail of the same name, No. 438. After a little over half a mile you dip into the valley containing Ponytail Falls. You then come to Oneonta Canyon; as you cross the bridge there you have Middle Oneonta Falls above you and Lower Oneonta Falls below. Farther along you hit a junction with the Oneonta Trail, which you take down to the historic highway. It's a half-mile walk along the roadside to get you back to the Horsetail Falls Trailhead.

Past the point where the historic highway merges back onto I-84, there's an easy 1.5-mile out-and-back hike, suitable for kids and dogs, to **Elowah Falls.** To reach the trailhead approaching from the west, take exit 35 off I-84 and continue two miles on the frontage road. The 220-foot waterfall descends into a large amphitheater. You can extend the hike by climbing an additional half mile to McCord Falls (a double falls), where there's a good view of the Gorge and Mount Adams.

Food

Your one dining option on waterfall row is the historic **Multnomah Falls Lodge** (53000 E. Historic Columbia River Hwy., 503/695-2376, www.multnomahfallslodge. com, daily 8am-9pm, dinner $16-25), situated in an ideal spot at the base of Oregon's most famous falls. The food—burgers, salads, pasta, steaks—isn't exceptional, but the view

from the window-filled dining room is the main attraction.

Camping

At the eastern end of the historic highway you can camp at **Ainsworth State Park** (59700 E. Historic Columbia River Hwy., 503/695-2261, mid-Mar.-Oct.), which has 40 full-hookup sites ($24) and six walk-in tent sites ($17); reserve by calling 800/452-5687. You don't get backwoods isolation, but you're within hiking distance of the waterfalls.

BONNEVILLE DAM AND CASCADE LOCKS

The first passage across the Columbia within the National Scenic Area has a grand name— the **Bridge of the Gods**—and a modest $2 toll. On the Oregon side it's accessed through the town of Cascade Locks (pop. 1,149), where there are basic services but not a lot more. Four miles downstream, though, there's a substantial attraction: the Bonneville Dam, a New Deal project that was the first federal dam on the Columbia. Including a second powerhouse completed in 1981, it generates five billion kilowatt-hours of electricity a year, enough to power half a million homes.

Bonneville Dam
OREGON VISITORS CENTER

The Bonneville Dam opened to great fanfare in 1938. It was one of the biggest projects executed by the Public Works Administration, part of Franklin Roosevelt's New Deal aimed at pulling the United States out of the Great Depression. Today at the dam's **Bradford Island Visitors Center** (Dam Rd., Exit 40 off I-84, 541/374-8820, www.nwp.usace.army. mil/bonneville, daily 9am-5pm, free) you can visit historical exhibits and the fish ladder viewing area throughout the day, but it's worthwhile to take a guided tour. A ranger will give you a look at the generators, each of which is harnessing enough electricity to power a midsize town. Tours are conducted at 11am, 1pm, and 3pm on weekends throughout the year and daily June-August.

The Bridge of the Gods

The Bridge of the Gods, which crosses the Columbia from Oregon's Cascade Locks to Washington's Skamania County, gets its name through a combination of geology and legend. At this point some 600 years ago a massive landslide created a natural dam (and bridge). Eventually, possibly as recently as the Cascadia Earthquake of 1700, the river broke through. The debris that remained turned this stretch of river into the perilous Cascade Rapids, which in turn were tamed by the Bonneville Dam.

That's the geology part. Several legends among local Indian tribes explain things roughly this way: The chief of the gods created the bridge as a crossing for his two sons, who resided on either side of the river. Subsequently the brothers fell in love with the same maiden and battled over her so violently that the bridge collapsed. As punishment, the chief turned his sons into stone. One became Mount Hood, the other Mount Adams. The beautiful maiden didn't fare any better. She was transformed into the hotheaded Mount St. Helens.

Bridge of the Gods

The cantilevered bridge that stands here today was completed in 1926. Its greatest claim to fame involves a stunt executed by Charles Lindbergh. In 1927 he flew his *Spirit of St. Louis* up the Columbia from Portland, passed over the bridge, and then turned tail and flew under it on his way back.

You can get what's arguably an even better experience by crossing the Bridge of the Gods and visiting the dam's **Powerhouse 2** on the Washington side, which was completed in 1981. The site isn't as historically significant, but it was designed with visitors in mind and gives you a closer look at the dam's workings.

★ Bonneville Dam Fish Hatchery

Just up the road from the dam on the Oregon side is the **Bonneville Dam Fish Hatchery** (70543 NE Herman Loop, 541/374-8393, www.dfw.state.or.us/resources/visitors, Mar.-Oct daily 7am-8pm, Nov.-Feb. daily 7am-5pm, free). It was built in 1909, thus predating the dam, but its main purpose is to help counteract the negative impact that human intervention on the river has had on the fish population. Over nine million fish are raised here annually—mostly chinook salmon but also coho and steelhead.

The hatchery's vast rearing pools are busiest during the fall spawning season, but this is a rewarding place to visit any time of year. It's in a pretty setting with ornamental ponds and well-maintained gardens. The star of the show is Herman, a 10-foot-long, 70-plus-year-old sturgeon who patrols a pond that has an underwater viewing area. Because it's open late in summer, the hatchery is a good place to finish the day after viewing the nearby waterfalls or touring the dam.

Cascade Locks

Before there was the dam there were the locks, an engineering triumph of the late 19th century that allowed for safe passage through the particularly treacherous stretch of the Columbia dubbed the Cascade Rapids. The dam left the locks underwater, but you can still see evidence of them from the **Cascade Locks Marine Park.** To get one of the Gorge's best water-level views, stroll out onto the park's little Thunder Island. You can also get out on the water here by taking a ride on the **Columbia Gorge Sternwheeler** (503/224-3900, www.portlandspirit.com, May-Oct Thurs.-Tues., $25-30), which makes one- and two-hour trips along the river and also has full-day, dinner, and Sunday brunch cruises.

Hiking

The **Eagle Creek Trail,** between Bonneville Dam and Cascade Locks, is one of the most beautiful, and most popular, hiking paths in the Gorge. There are multiple options for hiking the trail, which continues for 13 miles before joining the Pacific Crest Trail, the famous 2,600-mile path that runs all the way from Canada to Mexico. An easy, beautiful hike is the 3.8-mile out-and-back to **Punchbowl Falls,** which takes you through a narrow valley, into lush woods, and past several falls before reaching its destination. The path to Punchbowl Falls isn't physically taxing, but it is narrow at points with steep drops, so it's not a good option for small children.

To get to the Eagle Creek Trailhead from the west take Exit 41 off of I-84, then turn right and follow the road half a mile to the trailhead, where there's a large parking area. (If you're coming from the east you need to continue to Exit 40 and turn around; Exit 41 is accessible only to eastbound traffic.) A **Northwest Forest Pass** is required for vehicles in the parking area; you can purchase a $10 day pass on-site. Car break-ins are common here, so take valuables, including the car documents with personal information that are commonly stowed in the glove compartment, with you.

Accommodations

Just east of the Bridge of the Gods in Cascade Locks, the **Best Western Plus Columbia River Inn** (735 WaNaPa St., 541/374-8777, www.bestwestern.com, $160-215) has an enviable location right on the water and clean, well-maintained rooms. The downside: It's also right on the railway tracks, and trains rumble through at all hours. Rooms facing the road are quieter but have no river view. Earplugs are provided. More lodging options are just across the river in Washington.

Hood River and the Central Gorge

In the 20 miles between the Bridge of the Gods and the Hood River Bridge you get a sense of how rapidly the climate shifts along the Gorge. In that short span temperatures rise, precipitation drops, and vegetation becomes less dense. It's just a hint of the more dramatic transformation farther east.

It's not just the weather that changes. The whole attitude toward vacationing is different. In the western Gorge most visitors are there to admire the scenery, either from the roadside or a hiking trail. Here the emphasis is on vigorous outdoor sports. Many of the most popular activities, from kiteboarding to mountain biking to snowboarding, barely existed a generation ago. If you think "hipster machismo" sounds like an oxymoron, you haven't been to Hood River.

★ HOOD RIVER

Regardless of whether outdoor sports are your thing, you're likely to find Hood River offers the most fun of the towns along the Gorge. It feels like a ski resort—which it is for much of the year, serving as a base for those heading to the slopes of Mount Hood—with a youthful counterculture vibe supplied by the Portlanders who flock here.

The town's claim to fame comes from the winds. All of the Columbia River is effectively a wind tunnel through the Cascades,

Hood River

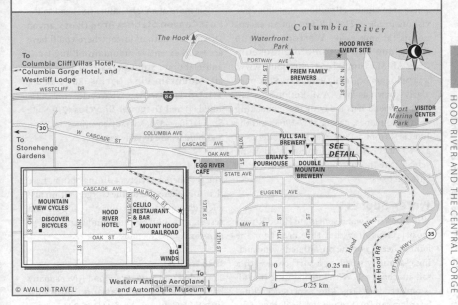

and the additional gusts at this point, where the Hood River feeds into the Columbia from the south and the White Salmon River from the north, make the waters here especially blustery. In the 1980s the area became a mecca for the young sport of windsurfing, and it's now also a hot spot for kiteboarding and paddleboarding, as well as mountain biking and hiking.

Scenic Drives

If you want to have a good time in the Hood River area without breaking a sweat, there are some appealing sightseeing options. One of the most popular drives is the **Fruit Loop** (www.hoodriverfruitloop.com), which takes you south of town through 35 miles of picturesque farmland, past visitor-friendly produce stands, U-pick orchards, cideries, wineries, and petting zoos. The Loop takes you out on Route 35 and brings you back on Dee Highway, aka Route 281. Maps are available at the **Hood River Visitor Center**

(720 East Port Marina Dr., 541/386-2000, Mon.-Fri. 9am-5pm, Sat.-Sun. 10am-4pm).

A short drive up to **Panorama Point County Park** (Eastside Rd., off Rte. 35), just three miles from downtown, gives you a good overview of Hood River valley farm country, with Mount Adams and Mount Hood bookending the panorama.

Mount Hood Railroad

Another way to see the valley is by train. The **Mount Hood Railroad** (110 Railroad Ave., 541/386-3556, www.mthoodrr.com, mid-Apr.-Oct., $35-55 base fare) has been running between Hood River and Parkdale since 1906, and though it's now mainly tourist-focused it continues to haul produce and timber. A four-hour round-trip ride takes you through farmland and up into the forested base of Mount Hood. You can also opt for a two-hour ride and take excursions where meals are served and there are Old West-style reenactments.

Western Antique Aeroplane and Automobile Museum

There aren't many attractions that can draw visitors inside in Hood River, but an exception is the impressive **Western Antique Aeroplane and Automobile Museum** (1600 Air Museum Rd., 541/308-1600, www. waaamuseum.org, daily 9am-5pm, $16), popularly known as WAAAM. Enthusiasts can happily spend half a day or more checking out the 75 planes, dating 1917-1963, and the 100 cars, from a 1909 Franklin Model D to a 1963 Chevy Bel Air. Remarkably, all of the vehicles are in working order and are regularly put to use.

Water Sports

Wind-powered water sports are Hood River's most famous draw, but they aren't for the faint of heart. For the uninitiated, windsurfing essentially is riding a surfboard with a sail attached to it. With kiteboarding the sail is replaced by a large kite; experienced kiteboarders can fly through the air doing tricks skateboarders wouldn't dare dream of. A more sedate option available in the area is stand-up paddleboarding.

Whether you're an experienced boarder or an intrepid novice, **Big Winds** (207 Front St., 541/386-6086, www.bigwinds.com) is a reliable resource for rental equipment and windsurfing or paddleboarding lessons. The technical demands of kiteboarding mean that instruction lasts for hours and costs hundreds or even thousands of dollars. If you want to give it a go, you can get lessons at **Kite the Gorge** (541/490-9426, www.kitethegorge. com) and **Cascade Kiteboarding** (541/392-1212, www.cascadekiteboarding.com).

Bicycling

A great spot for an easy, beautiful bicycle ride is the 4.5-mile **Columbia River Highway Trail** running between Hood River and Mosier. This stretch of road is part of the original scenic highway built through the Gorge starting in 1913. It's been closed to automobile traffic since 1960 and was turned into a state trail in the 1980s.

For more of an adrenaline fix, head to the **Post Canyon Staging Area** (Post Canyon Drive) just south of town, where you'll have access to extensive mountain-biking trails and elaborate stunt parks. For bike rentals, **Mountain View Cycles** (205 Oak St., 541/386-2453, www.mtviewcycles.com, $75-100/day) and **Discover Bicycles** (210 State St., 541/386-4820, www.discoverbicycles.com, $50-80/day) are reliable resources.

Food

You get a better variety of dining options here than anywhere else on the Gorge. Within just a few downtown blocks there are higher-end restaurants, quirky cafes, and a mind-boggling array of brewpubs.

BREWPUBS

The oldest and largest of Hood River's many brewpubs is **Full Sail Tasting Room and Pub** (506 Columbia St., 541/386-2247, www. fullsailbrewing.com, daily 11am-9pm, $12-15). It's also the most family friendly: there's a kids menu, and it gets lots of use. The bright, cheery dining room has a nice view of the Columbia, and the food is solid, occasionally creative pub grub: salads, sandwiches (including a couple of veggie options), and salmon fish-and-chips. Brewery tours are held daily at 1pm, 2pm, 3pm, and 4pm.

Double Mountain Brewery (8 4th St., 541/387-0042, www.doublemountainbrewery. com, Sun.-Thurs. 11am-10pm, Fri.-Sat. 11am-11pm, $9-22) has a warm glow to it that comes from low lights, a wood-fired pizza oven, and scores of happy customers quaffing delicious beer. The pizzas—made in the style of the legendary New Haven, Connecticut, pizzerias—are the kitchen's stars.

In the more newly developed area along Waterfront Park, **pFriem Family Brewers** (707 Portway Ave., 541/321-0490, www. pfriembeer.com, daily 11:30am-9pm, $12-23) has a bright, lively taproom. And the food menu is more wide-ranging than your typical brewpub—you can find everything from brats and burgers to crab rolls and mushroom-stuffed squash.

BREAKFAST AND LUNCH

A good spot to start the day is **Egg River Cafe** (1313 Oak St., 541/386-1127, www.eggriver-cafe.com, daily 6am-2pm, $10-20), where the booths and the large portions are classic diner, but the kitchen has embraced the contemporary "fresh and local" sensibility.

Broder Ost (102 Oak St., 541/436-3444, daily 7am-3pm, $9-13), adjacent to the Hood River Hotel, serves Scandinavian-style breakfast and lunch, including items such as baked eggs with smoked trout, Norwegian potato crepes, Swedish meatballs, and a gravlax sandwich. It's a fun change of pace—the food is tasty, and the dining room has a pleasant, clean design that's in keeping with the Nordic theme.

FINE DINING

Celilo Restaurant and Bar (16 Oak St., 541/386-5710, www.celilorestaurant.com, Mon.-Fri. 5pm-9pm, Sat.-Sun. 11:30am-3pm and 5pm-9pm, $25-31) is firmly established as Hood River's fine-dining destination; it's wise to get a reservation if you plan to eat here. The French-trained chef creates meals that are meticulously prepared but not overly elaborate. The flat iron steak arrives with potatoes and spinach. Vegetarian risotto comes with leeks, cremini and porcini mushrooms, and a drizzle of fennel chive oil.

Up a gravel road not far from the Columbia Gorge Hotel, **Stonehedge Gardens** (3405 Wine Country Ave., 541/386-3940, www.stonehedgeweddings.com, daily 5pm-9pm, $12-32) is a nice alternative to the busier, trendier places in town. The menu and the atmosphere feel like they haven't changed in decades, but they're old-fashioned in a good way. Within the charming old house or out on the expansive patio you can dine on classics like steak Diane and scampi Provençal.

It's easy to understand why the romantic setting is popular for weddings.

Accommodations

There's an old-timey elegance to the historic **Columbia Gorge Hotel** (4000 Westcliff Dr., 541/386-5566, www.columbiagorgehotel.com, $229-329), located west of town on the river bluffs. The building is a handsome Italianate structure dating from the 1920s, the views over the river are beautiful, and the well-maintained grounds even have their own 200-foot waterfall. Guest rooms are old-fashioned in a way that may not satisfy everyone: They're comfortable but on the small side, with floors that occasionally let out a creak. You stay here for the charm, not for the creature comforts.

Next door, the **Columbia Cliff Villas** (3880 Westcliff Dr., 866/912-8366, www.columbiacliffvillas.com, $249-499) is part of a condo complex and functions essentially like a new wing of the Columbia Gorge Hotel. The design mimics the hotel, and though the villas have no restaurant or other public facilities, guests are welcome to use the hotel's. The appointments are high-end, and you can get suites with kitchens and multiple bedrooms.

For a waterfront location in a lower price category, there's **Westcliff Lodge** (4070 Westcliff Dr., 541/386-2992, http://westcliflodge.com, $96-179), set just down the road from the Columbia Gorge Hotel. It's a no-frills motel on a pleasant property, with rooms in the back that look out over the river.

Hood River's second historic lodging is in the middle of town. The **Hood River Hotel** (102 Oak St., 541/386-1900, www.hoodriverhotel.com, $91-160) doesn't hide its age: rooms are small, climate control is erratic, and bathroom facilities occupy what were formerly closets. But everything is clean and well maintained, the staff is friendly, and the location is right in the heart of things.

The area's big chain hotel, **Best Western Plus Hood River Inn** (1108 E. Marina Way, 541/386-2200, www.hoodriverinn.com, $220-300), has modern, well-maintained furnishings and a great riverfront location. A mile-long walking path takes you into town.

Transportation

Hood River is 230 miles from Seattle; it's reached by going south on I-5 and east on I-84, a drive of 3.5 hours. It's about 65 miles east and an hour's drive from Portland on I-84.

WHITE SALMON

Across the Columbia from Hood River, the little town of White Salmon is a base for activities on the White Salmon River, which is one of the top white-water rafting spots in the Pacific Northwest. Hardcore rafters come here to take on the Class V rapids of the Little White Salmon—some of the most dangerous in the United States—but non-daredevils can find less risky options, too.

White-Water Rafting and Kayaking

The popularity of rafting here has resulted in the establishment of several good-quality guide companies that lead both novices and experienced rafters downriver. It's a thrill ride that's popular with families; most trips are suitable for kids 10 and older.

One of the best guides is **Wet Planet Whitewater** (860 Hwy. 141, 509/493-8989, www.wetplanetwhitewater.com), which offers half- and full-day rafting trips as well as kayak lessons. Other well-regarded options include **All Rivers Adventures** (1256 Hwy. 141, 509/998-8545, www.alladventuresrafting.com), **River Drifters** (856 Hwy. 141,

800/972-0430, www.riverdrifters.net), and **Zoller's Outdoor Odysseys** (1248 Hwy. 141, 509/493-2641, www.zooraft.com). Rates are similar for all of the guides: about $70 for a half day and $130 for a full day.

Food

White Salmon is close enough to Hood River that you can easily cross the Columbia for meals and other diversions, but there are couple of good options in town as well. The local entry in the region's brewpub bonanza, **Everybody's Brewing** (151 E. Jewett Blvd., 509/637-2774, www.everybodysbrewing.com, Sun.-Thurs. 11:30am-10pm, Fri.-Sat. 11:30am-10:30pm, $10-17), has a nice paneled bar, a big patio, and a menu with a few surprises, such as roasted spaghetti squash and a falafel sandwich.

Henni's Kitchen and Bar (120 E. Jewett Blvd., 509/493-1555, www.henniskitchenandbar.com, daily 4:30pm-9pm, $17-25) is the most acclaimed restaurant in the area. It features grilled meats and fish, along with an eclectic selection of small plates with international influences, including South African beef curry, papadum, and asparagus risotto.

Accommodations

The Inn of the White Salmon (172 W. Jewett Blvd., 509/493-2335, www.innofthewhitesalmon.com, $89-189) was built in the 1930s, and while it's been thoroughly renovated in clean-lined, modern style, it shows its age in its tiny bathrooms. If you're looking for modest but comfortable lodgings, this will do the trick.

The Eastern Gorge: The Dalles and Maryhill

As you head east from the Hood River Bridge the terrain turns semiarid. Trees disappear. The bluffs surrounding the Columbia wear a coat of green in spring but turn desert brown by June. It's beautiful in a lonesome, haunting way.

It's not the kind of landscape that makes you want to jump out of your car and start exploring, but there are a few carrots to keep the curious traveler moving forward. On the Oregon side of the river just outside The Dalles is the Columbia Gorge Discovery Center, a large, first-rate museum devoted to the region's geology and history. Continue east, crossing over to Washington via either The Dalles or the Sam Hill Bridge, and you reach the oddly situated Maryhill Museum of Art. When you encounter it here, in what would fit almost anyone's definition of "the middle of nowhere," you feel like you've entered an episode of *The Twilight Zone*. The art collection inside is vast, varied, and suitably quirky.

THE DALLES

The Dalles (pop. 14,000) is a regional trade hub and the largest town for many miles. Its name comes from the French word for "flagstone," reflecting the rock formations that created strong currents in the Columbia here before The Dalles Dam was built in the 1950s. It's not a tourist magnet, but there are some sights around town that merit a visit.

Columbia Gorge Discovery Center

A couple of miles west of The Dalles, the **Columbia Gorge Discovery Center-Wasco County Historical Museum** (5000 Discovery Dr., 541/296-8600, www.gorgediscovery.org, daily 9am-5pm, $9) is the kind of place small-town museum curators dream about. Its large, handsome building has two wings separated by a marble-floored hall with a picture window at one end framing a beautiful view of the Columbia. One wing contains the Discovery Center, which uses dioramas, video, and artifacts to tell the story of the Gorge, from its ice age birth to its controversial present-day damming. Across the hall the Historical Museum features re-created storefronts from the early days of The Dalles. The whole complex is kid friendly yet sophisticated enough to engage adults. There are picnic tables outside and a cafe with a patio.

Fort Dalles Museum

For some on-site local history, stop by the **Fort Dalles Museum** (500 W. 15th St., 541/296-4547, www.fortdallesmuseum.org, Apr.-Oct. daily 10am-5pm, Nov.-Mar. call for hours, $8). It's located inside the 1856 surgeon's quarters, the only building of the fort that remains standing, and has served as a museum since 1905. You'll learn here about the important role The Dalles played for pioneers on the Oregon Trail.

Sunshine Mill Winery

The husband-wife team of James and Molli Martin are a local success story. They came up with the concept of packaging wine in single-serving plastic cups, and the resulting company, Copa di Vino, quickly became one of Oregon's largest wine producers. Their tasting room is another feat of inventive packaging. **Sunshine Mill Winery** (901 E. 2nd St., 541/298-8900, www.sunshinemill.com, Sat.-Thurs. noon-6pm, Fri. noon-7pm), the largest building in the Gorge, was once a mill for the Sunshine Biscuit Company. It's been repurposed using industrial design elements, creating an inviting space where you can nibble appetizers while sampling Copa di Vino and the traditionally bottled wines of the higher-end Quenett label.

Columbia Hills State Park

A short drive across the Dalles Bridge into Washington and 2.5 miles west on Route 14 takes you to **Columbia Hills State Park** (85 Hwy. 14, 509/767-1159, http://parks.state.wa.us/489, Apr.-Oct. daily 6:30am-dusk). For locals this is a popular place to fish and camp, but what makes it unique are the Indian petroglyphs and pictographs. Next to the main parking area there's a row of petroglyphs (images carved in stone) that were salvaged from land permanently flooded by the Dalles Dam. They're interesting, but to get the most from your visit you need to go into the surrounding hills on a **ranger-guided tour** (reservations 509/439-9032, Apr.-Oct. Fri. and Sat. 10am, free). On it you see pictographs (paintings on stone) in their original locations, as well as *She Who Watches,* an especially striking petroglyph. The origins of these images are largely lost to the ages, but there's an intimate quality to them that's striking.

Food

Petit Provence (408 E. 2nd St., 541/506-0037, www.provencepdx.com, daily 7am-3pm, $10-15) is the far-flung branch of a Portland-area bakery. Breakfast and lunch selections have a French accent, from omelets to monte cristos, and make good use of the freshly baked bread. You can pick up pastries and breads to take with you.

For a dose of Old West atmosphere, check out the historic **Baldwin Saloon** (205 Court St., 541/296-5666, http://baldwinsaloon.com, Mon.-Sat. 11am-10pm, $11-33), which has a handsome paneled dining room. The long menu includes salads, sandwiches, steaks, pasta, and seafood.

Accommodations

From the outside the **Celilo Inn** (3550 E. 2nd St., 541/769-0001, www.celiloinn.com, $129-309) looks like a nondescript motel. Its appeal comes from the way it defies outward

Sunshine Mill Winery

appearances. They sweat the small stuff here: attention to detail shows through in the nicely appointed midcentury-modern-style rooms and the friendly, professional service. The pricier rooms come with great views of the Gorge, while the less expensive ones are tiny.

The Dalles also has a few chain hotel options, including a **Fairfield Inn & Suites** (2014 W. 7th St., 541/769-0753, www.marriott.com, $159-189) and a **Comfort Inn** (351 Lone Pine Dr., 541/298-2800, www.choicehotels.com, $139-169).

Transportation

The Dalles is 100 miles (2 hrs.) south of Yakima on I-84 and U.S. 97. From Yakima it's another 140 miles (2.5 hrs.) northwest to Seattle on I-82 and I-90. Walla Walla is 160 miles (2.5 hrs.) east on I-84, U.S. 730, and U.S. 12.

MARYHILL

Sometimes if you build it, they won't come. That's the case with Maryhill, a town that was the singular vision of Seattle business-man Sam Hill. In 1907 he bought property along the Washington side of the Gorge with the hopes of creating a Quaker community, but no Quakers followed his lead, and the initial structures he built were eventually leveled by fire.

What remains are a mansion along the bluffs that Hill built for his wife but that they never lived in, and a replica of Stonehenge he had erected to honor the fallen soldiers of World War I. The mansion was converted into the Maryhill Museum of Art, which houses an impressive and varied collection that's well worth going out of your way to see. Hill would hopefully find some solace in knowing that while his Quaker colony failed, his museum continues to thrive.

★ Maryhill Museum of Art

Your first reaction upon seeing the **Maryhill Museum of Art** (35 Maryhill Museum of Art Drive, 509/773-3733, www.maryhillmuseum.org, Mar. 15-Nov. 15 daily 10am-5pm, $9) is likely to be bewilderment. The building is a classic example of the kind of place an early-20th-century captain of industry such as Sam Hill would build for his palace, but the location—on a lonely bluff at the parched,

treeless end of the Columbia River Gorge—defies reason. Its nickname, Castle Nowhere, couldn't be more apt. (Its actual name, Maryhill, comes from Hill's wife, daughter, and mother-in-law, all of whom were Mary Hills. None of them wanted anything to do with the place.)

Many of the exhibits inside reflect Sam Hill's personal history. He was friends with Queen Marie of Romania, who presided over the museum's dedication in 1926 and donated to it her coronation gown and crown along with 15 crates of additional memorabilia, much of which is now prominently displayed. Another exhibit is dedicated to the modern dancer Loïe Fuller, another friend of Hill's and the person who convinced him to turn Maryhill into a museum. On the lower level is large collection of sculptures and drawings by Auguste Rodin, bought by Hill, possibly thanks to Fuller's persuasion, on a trip to Paris.

That's just the tip of the iceberg. Other exhibits include art nouveau glass; a wide-ranging collection of European and American paintings; Eastern European Orthodox icons; American Indian artifacts; hand-carved chess sets; and miniature mannequins wearing French haute couture. There are also

Maryhill Museum of Art

temporary exhibits. When museum fatigue sets in you can get a snack at the cafe and sit out on the patio, which has a beautiful view of the Gorge.

Stonehenge Memorial

Three miles east of the museum, the **Stonehenge Memorial** (Hwy. 14, www.maryhillmuseum.org, daily 7am-dusk, free) was erected by Sam Hill between 1918 and 1929 and stands as a tribute to soldiers of Klickitat County who died in World War I. Hill was a man with unique and grand ideas. It was commonly believed at the time that the original Stonehenge had been the site of human sacrifices; Hill intended his replica to honor the sacrifices made by the fallen soldiers and highlight the "incredible folly" of war. The structure is meant to represent how Stonehenge originally appeared, before the millennia of decay.

Wineries

Two wineries along the Washington side of the Gorge between the Dalles Bridge and the Maryhill Museum give you a look at contrasting approaches to winemaking. As you head east, you first encounter **Cascade Cliffs** (8866 Hwy. 14, 509/767-1100, www.cascadecliffs.com, daily 10am-6pm). In some ways this is a classic small producer: the owner, Bob Lorkowski, is also the winemaker, and the wines—primarily Italian varietals done in a bold, high-alcohol style—are stamped with his personality. Stop here for a tasting and you'll interact with someone involved in making the wine, as opposed to a tasting-room employee. You'll also be in the middle of the vineyard. Unlike most smaller wineries, Cascade Cliffs grows most of its own fruit, in a striking setting along the river with Mount Hood looming on the horizon.

Nine miles down the road to the east is **Maryhill Winery** (9774 Hwy. 14, 877/627-9445, www.maryhillwinery.com, daily 10am-6pm), the 10th-biggest producer in the state, making more than 20 times the volume of wine that Cascade Cliffs does. Not surprisingly, it's a much more polished operation, with a large tasting room and gift shop and a pergola-shaded patio that looks down over the vineyards and the Gorge. Maryhill produces nearly 40 wines, growing some of its own grapes but also sourcing fruit from elsewhere in the state; a tasting here will give you an introduction to Washington wine as a whole. There's also a 4,000-seat amphitheater

Stonehenge Memorial

on the property that hosts major musical acts in the summer.

GOLDENDALE
Goldendale Observatory

A turn north off Route 14 onto U.S. 97 gets you out of the Gorge area and heading in the direction of Yakima Valley, about an hour's drive away. If you're an astronomy buff you'll want to make a stop in Goldendale, 13 miles from the Maryhill Museum, to check out the **Goldendale Observatory** (1602 Observatory Dr., 509/773-3141, www.goldendaleobservatory.com, Apr.-Oct. Wed.-Sun. 10am-11:30pm, Nov.-Mar. Fri.-Sun. 1pm-9pm, free). Some of the largest publicly accessible telescopes in the United States are found here, and the interpretive center has afternoon and evening presentations about the stars and the equipment used to view them. The observatory is part of a state park, and its hilltop location provides beautiful views. It's worth visiting even during daylight hours.

Food

If you're not a stargazer, your other reason for stopping in Goldendale is to eat at **The Glass Onion Restaurant & Gallery** (604 S. Columbus Ave., 509/773-4928, www. theglassonionrestaurant.com, Wed.-Sat. 11:30am-9pm, $11-20). The setting, a renovated old house, is casual and unpretentious, and the menu is a mix of American standards (grilled meats and fish) and a few surprises (including Indian curries), as well as brick-oven pizza. Evident care goes into the dining experience, from the food to the service to the decor.

Yakima Valley

Yakima Valley dubs itself the "Fruit Bowl of the Nation," and with good reason—Yakima County produces more apples and sweet cherries than any other county in the United States. It also leads the country in mint production and grows an impressive 75 percent of the nation's hops.

The region was transformed into a major agricultural producer by the introduction of widespread irrigation in the early 1900s, but wine grapes are relatively new on the scene. They started getting a foothold in the 1980s and really took off starting at the turn of the 21st century. Statewide, the acreage devoted to vineyards has doubled since 2000, and more of those acres are in the Yakima Valley AVA (American Viticultural Area) than anywhere else.

The valley is still adjusting to the tourism expectations that come with being "wine country." There are some good restaurants in the town of Yakima but not many choices out in the countryside, and lodging options aren't much different than they were before the wine business started to flourish. Fortunately, the winemakers themselves do a good job of accommodating visitors. Drive east from Yakima on **I-82**, and you'll find that the hills around the valley are filled with interesting and varied tasting rooms pouring creative, high-quality wine. It's one of the best places in the state for a wine-tasting tour.

YAKIMA

The town of Yakima (pop. 90,000) is the valley's commercial hub. It's been through the ups and downs common to American towns that depend on agribusiness; you'd be more likely to mistake it for Cedar Rapids than for Napa. The downtown area has some attractive early-20th-century architecture, including a 1912 train depot that's now home to a coffee bar and a 1920 theater where you can see live performances, but the only real sightseeing destination is the Yakima Valley Museum, located in a pretty residential neighborhood a couple of miles north of the town center.

Yakima Valley

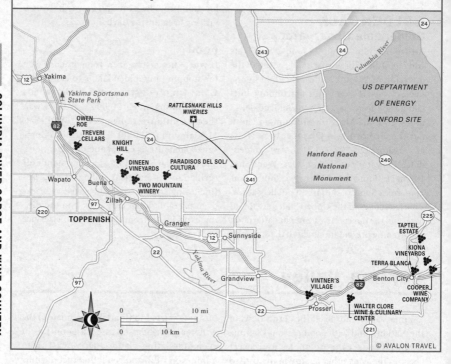

Sights

The **Yakima Valley Museum** (2105 Tieton Drive, 509/248-0747, yakimavalleymuseum. org, Mon.-Sat. 10am-5pm, $5) strikes a good balance between regional history and civic pride. There are exhibits about geology and the Yakama Indians, but the main emphasis is on 19th- and 20th-century settlement and the importance of agriculture in the area. Things are brightened up by the Neon Garden (a collection of vintage signs), and the Children's Underground provides history-related hands-on activities for kids.

Airplane enthusiasts might want to check out the **McAllister Museum of Aviation** (2008 S. 16th Ave., 509/457-4933, www.mcallistermuseum.org, Thurs.-Fri. 10am-4pm, Sat. 9am-4pm, free), located at the Yakima Air Terminal. It has that small-town museum feel, with lots of local memorabilia and a staff of friendly volunteers. No planes are in the collection, but the museum has two flight simulators, and on some summer Saturdays historic planes stop in for a visit.

Naches Heights Wineries

The tiny AVA of Naches Heights to the northwest of town isn't technically part of the valley, but it sits on a perch with a sweeping view over it. The existence of Naches Heights as an AVA is a testament to the determination of the winemakers here to forge their own identity. The region is definitely distinctive, thanks to its elevation and its windblown soil, but the first grapes weren't planted here until 2002, and when it received the AVA designation in 2012 there were only 40 acres of vineyards.

The region's two main producers, Naches Heights Vineyard (http://nhvwines.com) and Wilridge Winery (https://wilridgewinery.

com), share **The Tasting Room Yakima** (250 Ehler Rd., 509/966-0686, summer Fri.-Mon. 11am-6pm, call for hours off-season). It's set in a pleasant farmhouse surrounded by vineyards on a hillside spot that provides a magisterial view of Yakima Valley. Riesling, sauvignon blanc, and syrah are the main varietals, but a lot of experimentation is going on as the winemakers discover what grapes like this *terroir* best. A fun strategy is to incorporate your visit into a hike on the Cowiche Canyon Trail, taking the signed Wine Trail detour, which leads to the tasting room.

Hiking and Bicycling

The most popular thing to do here on a sunny day is visit wineries, but there are also some satisfying hikes with varying degrees of difficulty. The easiest and most accessible is the **Yakima Greenway** (www.yakimagreenway.org), a paved walking and biking path that runs a 15-mile route mostly along the Yakima River. The western end is at Myron Lake, across from Harlan Landing; you can access it all along the river as well as at Sarg Hubbard Park and the **Yakima Area Arboretum** (1401 Arboretum Drive, www.ahtrees.org, daily dawn-dusk, free). Incorporating the arboretum into your walk takes you through 46 acres of gardens, lawns, and woodland.

A few miles to the northwest of town you can reach the **Cowiche Canyon Trail** by turning off Route 12 at Cowiche Canyon Road. Take the road two miles to its end, where you'll find the trailhead. The easy-to-moderate three-mile trail follows Cowiche Creek through scrubland and interesting rock formations—it feels a little like a set for a spaghetti western. A marked turnoff for the Wine Trail leads up to the Naches Heights tasting room. The area is maintained by the **Cowiche Canyon Conservancy** (509/248-5065, www.cowichecanyon.org), which can provide maps and information about other trails in the canyon.

Auto Racing

As you drive along I-82 it's hard to miss Yakima's main spectator-sport venue, the **Yakima Speedway** (1600 Pacific Ave., 509/248-0647, www.yakimaspeedway.us). From April through September there are events most Saturdays, mainly late-model stock car races, with a demolition derby on Fourth of July weekend. This may not be what brings you to Yakima, but it's definitely a slice of the local culture.

Entertainment and Events

The ornate **Capitol Theatre** (19 S. 3rd St., 509/853-2787, www.capitoltheatre.org) is a Yakima landmark and a point of civic pride. Opened as a vaudeville house in 1920, it eventually became derelict and was gutted by fire in 1975. Thanks to a major local fundraising effort it reopened in 1978 with a gala featuring Bob Hope. Today it's home to the Yakima Symphony Orchestra and has a regular schedule of touring musicians, speakers, and theatrical productions.

Hackett Ranch (2620 Draper Rd., 509/249-9049, ext. 7, www.gilbertcellars.com), 10 miles from downtown, is the picturesque winery for Gilbert Cellars and doubles as an entertainment venue. There are summer concerts at the ranch's amphitheater as well as monthly free performances with accompanying food trucks. The Gilbert Cellars tasting room is downtown, but if you arrange ahead you can have a tasting and a tour out at the ranch ($25 pp, $15 pp for groups of 10 or more).

The biggest event of the year in Yakima is the **Central Washington State Fair,** held at **State Fair Park** (1301 S. Fair Ave., 509/248-7160, www.statefairpark.org). Carnival rides, livestock shows, concerts, food stands, and wine-tasting draw more than a quarter-million attendees for a week in mid-September. The park also hosts events at other times during the year, from pop music acts to monster-truck rallies.

Food

Yakima dining choices include reliable, mid-priced bar-and-grills, a few more ambitious restaurants, and numerous takes on Mexican cuisine. In downtown's **North Front Street** historic district there's a cluster of good dining options.

BREAKFAST

Your best bet for a well-made breakfast is the quaint **White House Café** (3602 Kern Rd., 509/469-2644, www.whitehouseinyakima. com, Mon.-Fri.8am-2pm, Sat.-Sun. 9am-2pm, $10-14), located in a residential neighborhood a couple of miles south of downtown. The menu sticks to the basics—several egg options, oatmeal, breakfast breads—all prepared with care. You can also get a good lunch from a simple menu of sandwiches, soups, and salads. In the summer the White House makes a couple of upstairs rooms available as a B&B.

At **North Town Coffeehouse** (32 N. Front St., 509/895-7600, www.northtowncoffee.com, Mon.-Fri.6am-midnight, Sat.-Sun. 7am-midnight) espresso drinks, high-quality pastries, and gelato are served in what was once the waiting room of the old train depot. It's a good spot for a light breakfast or an afternoon pick-me-up.

WINE BARS

Gilbert Cellars (5 N. Front St., 509/249-9049, www.gilbertcellars.com, Mon.-Thurs. 1pm-7pm, Fri.-Sat. 1pm-9pm, Sun. 1pm-6pm) is officially the tasting room for the winery of the same name, but in practice it's Yakima's most stylish wine bar. Order a cheese plate to accompany the varied selection of wines.

AMERICAN

It's hard to miss the **Sports Center** (214 E. Yakima Ave, 509/453-4647, Mon.-Sat. 11am-2am, $9-24)—look for the neon duck hunter spinning around out front. Inside the decor has a split personality: The front room has a retro diner vibe, while farther in it morphs into a sports bar. It's one of the liveliest nightspots in town, and the menu is mainly pub grub—burgers and fries, wraps, salads—that's surprisingly good. If you want something simple but tasty, washed back with a local microbrew, you'll be well served here.

The hippest place in town for a meal is just down the block from the Sports Center at **Cowiche Canyon Kitchen + Icehouse** (202 E. Yakima Ave, 509/457-2007, www.cowichecanyon.com, Sun.-Mon. 11am-9pm, Tues.-Thurs. 11am-10pm, Fri.-Sat. 11am-11pm, $13-37). In the large, bustling, warmly lit dining room they offer a pointedly eclectic menu that ranges from burgers to prime rib to Asian noodles. The adjacent bar pours 20 types of craft cocktails.

Miner's (2415 S. 1st St., 509/457-8194, daily 8am-3am, $6-12) is an institution in Union Gap, a few miles east of Yakima. Its oversized drive-in-style burgers, curly fries, and thick shakes have been a hit with generations of customers.

ITALIAN

Gasperetti's (1013 N. 1st St., 509/248-0628, www.gasperettisrestaurant.com, Mon.-Thurs.11am-11pm, Fri. 11am-midnight, Sat. 2pm-midnight, $14-35) is a 50-year-old standby that's serious about its food but serves it with a playful, slightly louche attitude. The menu leans toward old-school Italian, with meat dishes such as pork Milanese and filet mignon with gorgonzola sauce, and lots of pasta options. There's a lively bar scene here.

There's a bigger menu and a more contemporary atmosphere at Yakima's other high-end Italian restaurant, **Zesta Cucina** (5110 Tieton Dr., 509/972-2000, http://zestacucina. com, Mon.-Thurs. 11am-9pm, Fri.-Sat. 11am-10pm, $11-33). Along with classically prepared steaks, seafood, and pasta, it offers pizzas and a kids menu.

MEXICAN

Among the Mexican options, two places stand out. **Antojitos Mexicanos** (3512 Summitview Ave, 509/248-2626, Tues.-Sat. 9am-8pm, Sun 8am-4pm, $7-15), housed in a spruced-up former fast-food joint in the southwest part of town, is a local favorite. It serves a full range of regional specialties, from burritos and tortas to camarones and carne asada, and every meal comes with six varieties of salsa.

If you like tamales, make a visit to the satellite town of Union Gap, a few miles east of Yakima, where they're the only thing on the menu at **Los Hernandez** (3706 Main St., 509/457-6603, Sun.-Fri. 11am-6pm, Sat. 10am-7pm, $3-6). The asparagus tamales, available in season, may be Yakima's single greatest culinary claim to fame.

FRENCH

A good option for a fancy meal is east of town at the **Birchfield Manor** (2018 Birchfield Rd., 509/452-1960, www.birchfieldmanor.com, Thurs.-Sat. one seating 7pm, five courses $42-55), which has mastered a French-inspired prix-fixe menu. The lamb chops and the pastry-wrapped salmon have been satisfying diners for decades.

At **Carousel** (25 N. Front St., 509/248-6720, http://carouselfrenchcuisine.com, Tues.-Sat. 4:30pm-10:30pm, Sun. 10am-2pm, $17-40), steps lead down from street level to several small, intimate rooms where you can dine on classic French cuisine, including escargot, coq au vin, and filet mignon in a cognac cream reduction.

Accommodations

Yakima lodging consists primarily of chain hotels and a couple of good B&Bs. Most of the chains are located just off I-82, near the river and a few blocks east of downtown, in a safe but nondescript area. On weekends from spring through fall they're often filled with families attending youth sports tournaments.

The **Oxford Inn** (1603 E. Yakima Ave., 509/457-4444, www.oxfordinnyakima.com, $89-115) and its more nicely appointed neighbor, **Oxford Suites** (1701 E. Yakima Ave., 509/457-9000, www.oxfordsuitesyakima.com, $129-159), are both comfortable, well-managed options. They're located along the Yakima Greenway trail, which is a good spot for a morning or evening stroll.

Things are a little swankier at **Hotel Maison** (321 E. Yakima Ave., 509/571-1900, www.thehotelmaison.com, $179-229), located in the impressive old Masonic temple building in the middle of town. The rooms feel a bit generic, particularly given the interesting building they're housed in, but this still ranks as one of Yakima's nicer lodging options.

Among the B&Bs, **Rosedell Bed & Breakfast** (1811 W. Yakima Ave., 509/961-2964, www.rosedellbb.com, $125-160) is a classic, set in a stately early-20th-century house in a pleasant residential neighborhood just south of the heart of town. There's an old-timey feel to the place, but rooms are comfortable and well maintained.

Transportation

It's a 2.5-hour drive and about 145 miles from Seattle to Yakima going east on I-90 and I-82. Yakima is about 80 miles west of the Tri-Cities on I-82, a little over an hour's drive.

RATTLESNAKE HILLS

A lot of Washington wine country is flat and not exceptionally picturesque, but the Rattlesnake Hills, to the southeast of Yakima along I-82, are an exception.

TOP EXPERIENCE

★ Rattlesnake Hills Wineries

This AVA has the key ingredients for good wine touring. The rolling hills are nice to look at and conducive to growing high-quality grapes. Winemakers with different philosophies and goals are situated near one another, so you can get interesting, contrasting experiences just by crossing the road. Many small producers are here, which means there's a good chance you'll be greeted in the tasting room by someone who has a direct hand in making the wine. And the wineries usually sit in the midst of vineyards where their grapes are grown. That's far from a given in Washington, where it's common for winemakers to source fruit from vineyards that may be 50-100 miles away.

Heading southwest along I-82, before

What Is an AVA?

If you're wine touring you're bound to hear frequent reference to AVAs—American Viticultural Areas. This designation is given to wine-growing regions by the Alcohol and Tobacco Tax and Trade Bureau of the U.S. Department of Treasury. It's vitally important to winemakers because it dictates how they're allowed to label their wine.

For a region to receive an AVA designation, it has to demonstrate that it has its own distinct grape-growing conditions and that its name and borders are already established informally within the wine community. There are over 200 AVAs in 33 states within the United States, 13 of them in Washington. To complicate things, one AVA can exist inside another. For example, Washington's huge Columbia Valley AVA encompasses about a third of the state. Within it are most of the state's other AVAs, including Yakima Valley. And within Yakima Valley there are three smaller AVAs—Rattlesnake Hills, Snipes Mountain, and Red Mountain.

This system takes its inspiration from the highly regulated appellations found in Europe, and it has the same goal: to help consumers understand what they're getting. The characteristics of where the grapes are grown—from the soil to the elevation to the climate—impact the character of the wine. Listing the AVA on the label will, at least theoretically, tell you what to expect inside the bottle. The winemaker also hopes the AVA will confer status. Just maybe future connoisseurs will prize a bottle from Naches Heights the same way they now do one from Bordeaux or Barolo.

you're eight miles outside Yakima you hit two worthwhile, very different wineries. In a region where robust red wines tend to be the stars, **Treveri Cellars** (71 Gangl Rd., 509/877-0925, www.trevericellars.com, Mon.-Thurs. noon-5pm, Fri.-Sat. noon-6pm, Sun. noon-4pm) makes nothing but sparkling wine. That doesn't keep winemaker Juergen Grieb from offering a wide range of choices: Treveri produces eight different wines, including sparkling riesling, müller-thurgau, and syrah. Tasting the unconventional sparklers can be a revelation.

Just down the road, **Owen Roe** (309 Gangl Rd., 509/877-0454, www.owenroe.com, daily 11am-5pm) is a completely different experience. While friendly and informal, it's also deadly serious about the craft of making fine wine, with a primary focus on bordeaux and rhone varietals. Owner David O'Reilly says a tasting should ideally be "a two- or three-hour experience." This is the sort of place where you'll never find a gift shop or a party limo parked outside.

Owen Roe may well make the AVA's finest wine, but for the full Rattlesnake Hills experience you need to go one exit down the highway, where the cluster of wineries on the slopes above the little town of Zillah make up the heart of the region. A good place to start is ultracasual **Two Mountain Winery** (2151 Cheyne Rd., 509/829-3900, www.twomountainwinery.com, daily 10am-6pm), operated by two brothers who grow grapes in what used to be their grandfather's orchard. The tasting room and winery occupy a big, stylish barn; it's the kind of place where an old dog sleeps in the corner and kids make chalk drawings on the floor while their parents chat with the charismatic young proprietors. When it comes to wine, they're daring enough to try anything from cab franc to lemberger. The riesling is a standout.

You get a different sort of casual experience a mile away at **Paradisos del Sol** (3230 Highland Dr., 509/829-9000, www.paradisosdelsol.com, daily 11am-6pm). The place looks more like a hippie's farmhouse than a winery: chickens roam the yard, a vegetable garden looks semi-feral, and cats gaze longingly into a koi pond. But a sign along the walkway assures you, "Yes! This is a tasting room." Each wine is paired with a tiny sample of food, and you're instructed to "sip, sip, taste, sip." One of the pleasures here, as at other small wineries in the region, is discovering unusual limited-production wines you're unlikely to have experienced before.

Across the road, **Cultura** (3601 Highland Dr., 509/829-0204, www.culturawine.com, Fri.-Sun. 11am-5pm) mixes the youthful energy of Two Mountain Winery with a dose of big-red gravitas. Cabernet sauvignon, cab franc, merlot, and zinfandel are all well rendered here.

There are about 20 more wineries in the AVA, each one different from the next. **Dineen Vineyards** (2980 Gilbert Rd., 509/829-6897, www.dineenvineyards.com, Apr.-Oct. Fri.-Sun. noon-5pm) makes bordeaux varietals in an attractive facility, and on some Saturdays serves pizza from a wood-fired oven (call to see if they're baking). **Knight Hill** (5330 Lombard Loop Rd., 509/865-5654, www.knighthillwine.com, Feb.-Nov. daily 11am-5pm) is a modest place producing some uncommon wines, from an earthy mourvedre to a creamy verdelho, out of a winery with the highest elevation, and the best views, in the region.

Teapot Dome Service Station

The town of Zillah's most famous tourist attraction is the **Teapot Dome Service Station** (117 First Ave.). This piece of Americana no longer pumps gas, but the teapot-shaped structure, complete with handle and spout, remains a great photo op. It was built in 1922 as a reminder of the infamous Teapot Dome Scandal, in which members of the Harding administration took bribes in exchange for no-bid leases to publicly held oil land.

Food

Among the limited options for dining in Zillah, **The Chop House at the Old Warehouse** (705 Railroad Ave., 509/314-6266, Mon.-Fri. 11am-10pm, Sat.-Sun. 9am-10pm, $10-18) does a reputable job with bar-and-grill fare. The restaurant is in one corner of a used-furniture warehouse, where an auction takes place every Saturday evening.

El Porton (905 Vintage Valley Pkwy., 509/829-9100, daily 11am-9pm, $7-17) dishes up hearty portions of Mexican standards—the long menu features tacos, burritos, fajitas, and carne asada, and includes a good selection of vegetarian options. Friendly service and a simple, pleasant dining room contribute toward making a meal here a satisfying experience.

Paradisos del Sol

Accommodations

The **Cherry Wood Bed Breakfast and Barn** (3271 Roza Dr., 509/829-3500, www.cherrywoodbbandb.com, $285) is a truly unique B&B experience. It consists of six tepees erected amid a ranch for rescued horses, surrounded by a cherry orchard on the slopes of the Rattlesnake Hills. If you come at it with the right attitude it's a fun experience—the tepees are nicely appointed with Old West-style furnishings, and each has a private outdoor area with a beautiful view of the valley. It's not for everyone, however. Getting in and out of the tepees can be awkward, and bathrooms consist of well-scrubbed portable toilets and open-air sinks and showers. And you have to take the price for what it really is: a donation to help maintain the horses. Cherry Wood also conducts horseback wine-tasting tours.

TOPPENISH

The Yakama Indian Reservation occupies a 2,100-square-mile rectangle of land that's bordered on its northeast side by I-82. It has a population of about 25,000 (80 percent of which is non-Indian). Toppenish, four miles from Zillah, is the reservation's largest town, with about 9,000 residents. There are two main reasons for putting your wineglass aside and making a visit to Toppenish: its murals, which cover many of the exterior walls in the center of town, and its three museums, dedicated to the Yakama history, rail travel, and hops.

Sights

Toppenish is best known for its **historical murals**—there are more than 80 of them decorating walls in the center of town, and a new one is added every year. The concept could be gimmicky, but persistence and talent have created something truly impressive. Paintings can vary in subject from iconic images of traditional Indian dances and early sodbusters to portraits of prominent citizens. It's striking just to walk around and take them in, but you can get more from the experience by picking up an annotated map explaining each picture's significance from the office of

Teapot Dome Service Station

the **Chamber of Commerce** (504 S. Elm St., 509/865-3262, www.visittoppenish.com). Office hours depend on volunteer availability, but when no one's there you can get a map from the box outside the front door.

One of the mural-covered buildings is the **American Hop Museum** (22 South B St., 509/865-4677, May-Sept. Wed.-Sat. 10am-4pm, Sun. 11am-4pm, www.americanhopmuseum.org, $3), where you can learn pretty much everything there is to know about hops, a key ingredient in beer. Seventy-five percent of the hops grown in the United States come from the Yakima Valley; it's hard to miss the fields filled with row after row of 10-foot-tall trellised hopvines. The museum has exhibits about the growing and harvesting process, the history of hop cultivation, and the use of hops in brewing. If you enjoy beer, you're likely to get a kick out of a visit here.

A block from the Hop Museum, the **Northern Pacific Railway Museum** (10 S. Asotin Ave., 509/865-1911, www.nprymuseum.org, May-mid-Oct. Tues.-Sat.

Wine-Tasting Tips

Here are a few subjective suggestions for ways to get the most from a wine country tour:

- **It's about the people.** Wine-tasting as it's done in most wineries isn't the best way to taste wine. Drinking a bunch of tiny samples is like going to the movies and watching only the previews—you're missing out on most of what makes the experience pleasurable and rewarding. What wine-tasting *is* good for is learning about wine, by getting to know the place where it's made and, most importantly, by engaging with the people who make it. Who's pouring can be just as important as what goes in the glass.

- **Think small.** The smaller the winery, the more likely it is that you'll end up talking to someone who's part of the winemaking process rather than a staffer. That's not always a good thing (some staffers are engaging and knowledgeable, while some winemakers are awkward or curmudgeonly), but usually it is.

- **Strange is good.** On an afternoon devoted to tasting, you're going to sample a lot of chardonnay and syrah and cabernet sauvignon, and no matter how good it is your palate is likely to get a little bored. If the winery has a bottle open of something you've never heard of before, don't be shy about trying it. Whether you like it or not, you'll be giving your taste buds a new sensation and broadening your wine experience. And the weird stuff is often something the winemaker has a special affection for. It might just be delicious.

- **Ask about the wine.** Sometimes to get the person pouring to open up you need to send a signal that you're interested. Asking a basic question, like "Do the grapes in this blend change from year to year?" or "Why does the winemaker prefer unoaked chardonnay?" could trigger a more wide-ranging conversation.

- **Ask about other wineries.** When you find a pourer you hit it off with, ask him or her to recommend other wineries to visit and you're likely to get some good leads. If you then say at your next stop, "Jim from XYZ Vineyards suggested I come by," you've opened up a new dialogue there.

- **Keep an eye out for special events.** Winemakers in Washington are good at bringing something extra to the tasting experience, whether it's by firing up a grill or bringing in a guitar player. If you know ahead of time where you want to visit, call or check on the web to see if they've got anything going on, and once you're on the ground ask around about what's happening. You can also plan your visit to correspond with one of Yakima Valley's two big annual events, the spring barrel tasting at the end of April and the harvest celebration at the end of September. (For Walla Walla it's the spring release at the beginning of May and the fall release at the beginning of November.)

- **Use the spit bucket.** Most people aren't going to do this, for good reasons: it's awkward, it can feel crass, and plainly put, you've got to swallow to get a buzz. But if you're in it for a full day, by the time you've reached your fourth or fifth winery not having a buzz is a good thing. Your palate and your mind will be better equipped to appreciate the flavors you're experiencing, and you won't feel like you need a nap. Also, the person pouring the wine may think you're a hotshot. Most spitters are wine-industry professionals or serious aficionados.

10am-4pm, Sun. noon-4pm, $5) occupies Toppenish's old 1911 depot. There's a bittersweet feel to the place. It's filled with memorabilia from a bygone era when trains ran through town; when service was discontinued in the 1960s it was a significant hit to the local economy and culture. Outside the depot old train cars in various stages of restoration are on display.

To the west of town is the Yakama Nation Cultural Heritage Center, a complex that includes the **Yakama Nation Museum** (Spiel-yi Loop, 509/865-2800, ext. 1, www.yakamamuseum.com, daily 8am-5pm, $6).

The museum contains 12,000 square feet of dioramas, artifacts, and interactive displays illuminating Yakama culture and history. You learn about everything from the nation's spiritual underpinnings to the lives of present-day members.

It's well off the beaten path, but if you're a military-history buff and the weather's nice it can be worth it to make the 30-mile drive west from Toppenish to **Fort Simcoe State Park** (5150 Fort Simcoe Rd., 509/874-2372, http://parks.state.wa.us/509/Fort-Simcoe, May-Oct. daily 6:30am-dusk, free). The fort was used for three years in the mid-19th century as an army outpost before being converted into an Indian school and the headquarters for the Yakama Indian Agency. The five remaining original fort buildings are filled with period furnishings, and other fort structures have been re-created. An interpretive center (May-Oct. Wed.-Sun. 9:30am-4:30pm) focuses on relations between Indians and settlers. The pleasant park setting is a great spot for a picnic.

Food

There's a large Mexican presence in Toppenish, and it's reflected in the town's numerous Mexican restaurants. One of the best is **Taqueria Mexicana** (105 S. Alder St., 509/865-7116, Mon.-Sat. 10am-9:30pm, Sun. 8:30am-9:30pm, $6-14). You can tell this is a family-run place: the friendly owner is often waiting tables, and the meals have from-scratch flavor. If menudo is your thing, this is a good place for it.

SNIPES MOUNTAIN TO PROSSER

As you travel farther down the Yakima River you get a strong reinforcement of the difference between a vineyard and a winery. To your right off of I-82, roughly between the exits for Granger and Sunnyside, the hill known as Snipes Mountain is another of Washington's tiny AVAs. It's one of the oldest areas in the state for growing wine grapes,

with still-active muscat vines dating back to 1917, and it's dominated by one grower, Upland Vineyards. While Upland makes a small amount of its own wine, sold from a tasting room in Woodinville just outside Seattle, its real business is farming. Grapes from the company's 800 acres are sold to some 30 wineries, including two of Washington's biggest, Chateau Ste. Michelle and Hogue.

There are no tasting rooms to visit on Snipes Mountain, but 15 miles down the road the town of Prosser more than makes up for that. It represents the other half of the vineyard-winery divide. Here over 30 wineries, most of which source grapes from vineyards like Upland, are making wine and happily welcoming retail customers.

Prosser Wineries

The epicenter for the Prosser wine trade is **Vintner's Village** (100 Merlot Dr., 509/786-7401, www.prosservintnersvillage.com), which is essentially an upscale open-air shopping mall for wine. A dozen winemakers have tasting rooms here, which also function as wine bars; on weekends they're busy with consumers unwinding over a glass or a bottle.

All the tasting rooms have handsome layouts, but the prize for most distinctive goes to **Airfield Estates** (509/786-7401, www.airfieldwines.com, daily 11am-5pm), built to resemble an airplane hangar, complete with tower. Another notable member of the group is **Milbrandt Vineyards** (509/788-0030, www.milbrandtvineyards.com, daily 10am-5pm), which, as the name indicates, grows its own grapes—over 2,000 acres of them, on 12 vineyards throughout the state. Smaller producers include **Martinez & Martinez** (509/786-2392, www.martinezwine.com, daily 11am-5pm), which makes cabernet sauvignon from the Horse Heaven Hills AVA south of the Yakima Valley, and **Thurston Wolfe** (509/786-3313, www.thurstonwolfe.com, Apr.-Dec. Thurs.-Sun. 11am-5pm), which specializes in less common varietals such as albariño, petite sirah, and lemberger.

Two and a half miles farther along I-82, the **Walter Clore Wine and Culinary Center** (2140 Wine Country Rd., 509/786-1000, www.theclorecenter.org, daily 11am-5pm) takes a unique, holistic approach to Washington wine education and promotion. It has a tasting room that every month features a different AVA in the state, and it hosts blind tastings and wine-focused cooking classes.

Food

The liveliest dining option between Yakima and Prosser is **Snipes Mountain Brewery** (905 Yakima Valley Hwy., 509/837-2739, www.snipesmountain.com, Mon.-Fri. 11am-10pm, Sat.-Sun. 8am-10pm, $12-29), a big, attractive space where they make their own beer, grill burgers, and bake pizzas in a wood-fired oven.

In Prosser's Vintner's Village, **Wine O'Clock** (548 Cabernet Court, 509/786-2197, Thurs. and Sun.-Mon. noon-8pm, Fri.-Sat. noon-9pm, www.bunnellfamilycellar.com, $12-32), run by the Bunnell winery, also serves pizza, along with salads and grilled meats. The difference between this place and Snipes Mountain Brewery is the difference between wine and beer: one's a little more sophisticated, the other a little more down-to-earth.

Accommodations

There are several chain motels around the town of Sunnyside, about 20 minutes northwest of Prosser on I-82. The location puts you between Rattlesnake Hills and Prosser, so you have lots of options nearby for winery visits, but when the sun goes down on Sunnyside there's not a lot to do.

In Prosser, the **Inn at Desert Wind** (2258 Wine Country Rd., 509/786-7277, www.desertwindwincry.com, $245-295) has four guest rooms in an attractive, adobe-style winery. The well-appointed rooms aren't over-the-top swank, but they're the most luxurious lodging in the area. Breakfast, delivered to your door, is part of the package.

THE TRI-CITIES

The Tri-Cities are three neighboring towns— **Richland, Pasco,** and **Kennewick**—located at the point where the Yakima River from the west and the Snake River from the east flow into the Columbia. They were once separate communities, but in the second half of the 20th century they expanded at a rapid rate and melded into one metropolitan area with a population of a quarter million. That growth was sparked by of one of the most fascinating, if sobering, events in the history of

Airfield Estates

modern Washington State: In 1942, the small nearby town of Hanford was chosen as one of two sites in the country that would produce nuclear material for the development of an atomic bomb. While the Tri-Cities aren't tourism-focused, their size and prosperity have resulted in good-quality business hotels and some good restaurants. They're a good overnight base for touring the nearby Red Mountain wineries.

The REACH

If you're curious about the history of Hanford and the surrounding area, it's worth stopping by **The REACH** (1943 Columbia Park Trail, 509/943-4100, www.visitthereach.org, Tues-Sat. 10am-4:30pm, $8) even if you aren't planning to linger in the Tri-Cities. This regional museum covers a wide range of topics in intelligent, creative ways. A gallery devoted to the Manhattan Project uses artifacts and displays to capture a sense of what it was like to live in the Tri-Cities during the massive push to build the atomic bomb, and what the consequences were for the rest of the world. Another emphasis is agriculture; there's a fascinating giant mural that drives home the enormous significance of irrigation in eastern Washington.

Hanford Tours

To get an up-close look at the Hanford site you can go on a Department of Energy-run **Hanford B Reactor Tour** (www.hanford. gov, free). Tours are conducted several times a month in the spring and summer and fill up months in advance. You sign up on the Hanford website; to take part you have to be a U.S. citizen and at least 18 years old. On the four-hour tour, you're taken by bus past the townsites that were abandoned to make way for the facility; 300 Area, where uranium fuel rods were fabricated; and 100 Area, where fuel rods were irradiated to produce nuclear weapons. You're then given a guided walking tour of B Reactor, the world's first full-scale plutonium production reactor.

Another way to experience Hanford is along the Columbia by boat on a **Hanford Reach National Monument Tour** (509/734-9941, www.columbiariverjourneys.com, $90). The national monument designation was given to the restricted-access area surrounding the site. Because there hasn't been any development, this stretch of river looks more like what Lewis and Clark saw on their travels than any other part of the Columbia—except for the nuclear reactors on the horizon. Wild animals roam freely along the shores; the

Columbia River bluffs within Hanford Reach National Monument

The Tri-Cities' Atomic History

In 1942 the United States was embroiled in World War II and working frantically to develop an atomic bomb. Toward the end of the year scientists executed the first controlled nuclear chain reaction, and the government quickly settled on two sites for the production of nuclear material—Oak Ridge, Tennessee, and Hanford, a tiny town just west of the Tri-Cities. Both locations had the required combination of isolation, railroad access, and abundant sources of river water for cooling nuclear reactors.

In the ensuing months, the thousand or so residents of Hanford and the surrounding area were given 30 days to vacate their homes. They were replaced by a temporary construction camp that would grow to a population of 51,000. Within the same time period the town of Richland went from 200 residents to 17,000. The resulting nuclear facility produced the plutonium used for the bomb dropped on Nagasaki, Japan.

During the Cold War the Hanford site expanded, becoming the primary plutonium source for America's nuclear arsenal and transforming the Tri-Cities into southeastern Washington's largest metropolitan area. When the Cold War came to an end, Hanford was decommissioned. What remained was two-thirds of the radioactive waste found within the United States and the country's most nuclear-contaminated site. Plutonium production once drove the economy of the Tri-Cities, but now the nation's largest environmental cleanup does, with costs running into the tens of billions of dollars.

What does all this mean for the leisure traveler? First, be aware that the most recent couple of generations of Tri-Cities residents have lived in the area without suffering ill effects from the nuclear site; being here isn't a health risk. And if you're fascinated by the Hanford site, you can learn more about it and even take a tour.

guide is great at spotting them, and is also a font of information on the history of Hanford. The tour lasts four hours. You're encouraged to bring along water and a snack.

TOP EXPERIENCE

Red Mountain Wineries

Washington wine's biggest small-AVA success story is Red Mountain, located about 10 miles west of the Tri-Cities. Its southwest-facing slope (which no one would mistake for a mountain) sits on a bend of the Yakima River, above the town of Carson City (which no one would mistake for a city) and about 15 miles from the Yakima's confluence with the Columbia. The area's calcium-carbonate-rich soil and its desert climate—with only five inches of rain a year and a large variation in daily temperatures—produce excellent wine grapes, especially bordeaux varietals, which are the vineyards' mainstays. The proof is in the price: Grapes sourced from Red Mountain cost three times more than the state

average. You'll have the best luck visiting Red Mountain on a weekend. Some of the wineries have irregular hours, but every place that has a tasting room is open on Saturday and Sunday, and most are open on Friday as well.

As you climb the hill from I-82 the first winery you encounter is at **Terra Blanca Estate** (34715 Demoss Rd., 509/588-6082, www.terra-blanca.com, daily 10am-6pm), one of the oldest, biggest, and most polished winemakers on Red Mountain. With beautiful landscaping and a stately winery that would look at home in the hills of Tuscany, it's a lovely place to while away a few hours. That's an easy thing to do: In the summer, Friday-Sunday noon-5pm, the tasting room serves pizzas, salads, and sandwiches. The focus here, like elsewhere on Red Mountain, is primarily bordeaux varietals, along with chardonnay and syrah.

Farther up the hill you hit North Sunset Road, which has Red Mountain's greatest concentration of wineries. The first place you come to is **Cooper Wine Company** (35306 N. Sunset Rd, 509/588-2667, www.

cooperwinecompany.com, daily 11am-5pm), which falls on the other end of the spectrum from Terra Blanca: It's a fledgling operation with a winery in a barn and an ambitious young winemaker at the helm.

A few doors down is venerable **Kiona Vineyards and Winery** (44612 N. Sunset Rd., 509/588-6716, www.kionawine.com, daily noon-5pm). Kiona was Red Mountain's first vineyard, breaking ground in 1975. Today it has a beautiful, modern winery with a tasting room looking out over the estate vines and Yakima Valley beyond them. Despite the elder-statesman status, Kiona prides itself on a plainspoken, unpretentious approach to winemaking.

At the end of Sunset Road and down a dirt drive, **Tapteil Estate** (20206 E. 583 PR NE, 509/588-4460, www.tapteil.com, Apr.-Dec. Fri.-Sun. 11am-5pm) is a modest establishment that's been in operation since 1985. Ninety-five percent of the grapes grown here are sold to other wineries, but the owner-winemaker saves a few for himself. Producing a minuscule 400 cases a year and under no commercial pressures, he can follow his whims. That leads to curiosities you won't find in any other tasting room, like two bottles of the same syrah, one aged in American oak and the other in Hungarian.

A little farther up the slope are two impressive estates producing premium wine. **Hedges Family Estate** (53511 N. Sunset Rd., www.hedgesfamilyestate.com, 509/588-1355 Sat.-Sun. 11am-5pm) resembles a French chateau and makes primarily cabernet sauvignon and syrah. **Col Solare** (50207 Antinori Rd., 509/588-6806, www.colsolare.com, Wed.-Sun. 11am-5pm), a partnership between two winemaking giants, Washington's Chateau Ste. Michelle and Italy's Antinori, is perched near the top of the hill in a sleek facility. It also focuses on cab and syrah.

Food

Located in a former A&W drive-in, **Atomic Ale Brewpub & Eatery** (1015 Lee Blvd., Richland, 509/946-5465, www.

desert-dry vines at Red Mountain's Tapteil Estate

atomicalebrewpub.com, Mon.-Thurs. 11am-10pm, Fri.-Sat. 11am-11pm, Sun. 11am-9pm, $9-16) is a Richland institution. It's a lively place with a large, ever-evolving selection of beers made on-site and a menu featuring sandwiches, pizza, soups, and salads.

For something more sophisticated, head to **Tulip Lane** on the west end of Richland, where three side-by-side wineries have opened full-service restaurants. Each is different, but they all serve good food and have tasting rooms. With some strategic ordering you can graze your way through all in one visit. **Taverna Tagaris** (844 Tulip Ln., 509/628-0020, www.tagariswines.com, Mon.-Sat. 11am-9pm, Sun. 11am-3pm, $14-46) takes a Spanish approach, featuring tapas and grilled meats. **Fiction @ J. Bookwalter** (894 Tulip Ln., 509/627-5000, www.book-walterwines.com, Mon.-Sat. 11am-10pm, Sun. 4pm-10pm, $14-37) also specializes in grilled meats along with pizza and salad. **The Kitchen at Barnard Griffin** (878 Tulip Ln., 509/627-0266, www.barnardgriffin.com,

Tues.-Sat. noon-9pm, $11-18) has a nice patio out back and a lighter menu of pizzas, sandwiches, and charcuterie.

Accommodations

Among the dozens of mid-priced chain hotels in the Tri-Cities, the **Hampton Inn Richland** (486 Bradley Blvd., Richland, 509/943-4400, www.hamptoninn.com, $149-194) and the **Courtyard Richland Columbia Point** (480 Columbia Point Dr., Richland, 509/942-9400, www.marriott.com, $159-199) stand out for their attractive locations overlooking the Columbia.

Walla Walla

During the Idaho gold rush of the 1860s Walla Walla (pop. 31,000) became a boomtown, supplying miners with equipment and provisions at hefty markups. A century and a half later there's still an air of prosperity here. Despite its relative isolation, 60 miles east of the Tri-Cities in the southeast corner of the state, and the fact that the surrounding AVA produces one-fifth as many grapes as the Yakima Valley, it's become the center of the booming Washington wine trade—Yakima may have more grapes, but Walla Walla has more wineries. With pedestrian-friendly, tree-lined streets, cute locally owned shops, and an abundance of inventive restaurants, Walla Walla is unquestionably Washington wine country's most tourist-friendly town.

What makes wine-tasting here particularly enjoyable is the wide range of experiences you can have. Some wineries have boutique-like tasting rooms downtown, while others are set in vineyards with views of the Blue Mountains on the horizon. Some are elegant and sophisticated, while others are homey and unpretentious, and a few like to strike an irreverent, rock-and-roll attitude. No matter the atmosphere, the wine you're sampling is likely to be good. The bar for quality is set high here.

SIGHTS

Pick up a downtown walking-tour map and get other information about local points of interest at the **Walla Walla Visitors Kiosk** (26 E. Main St., 509/525-8799, www.wallawalla. org, May-Sept. daily 10am-4pm, Oct.-Apr. Thurs.-Sun. 10am-4pm).

Walla Walla's two main non-wine attractions are sites from the region's pioneer days, the Whitman Mission and the Fort Walla Walla Museum.

Whitman Mission

A defining moment in the history of the settlement of the Pacific Northwest occurred eight miles west of downtown at what's now the **Whitman Mission National Historic Site** (328 Whitman Mission Rd., 509/522-6360, www.nps.gov/whmi, daily 8am-4:30pm, visitors center June-Aug. daily 9am-4pm, Oct.-Nov. and Jan.-May Wed.-Sun. 9am-4pm, free). Here in 1836 Dr. Marcus Whitman and his wife, Narcissa, established a mission with the goal of converting the native Cayuse Indians to Christianity. In 1843 Whitman led the first large wagon train along the Oregon Trail, and the mission developed a second role as a trail way station.

As part of his missionary work Whitman practiced medicine on the natives. In 1847 he was unable to stem a measles epidemic among the Cayuse, who came to believe he was inflicting the disease on the tribe. On November 29 a group of them attacked the mission, killing the Whitmans and 11 other white mission residents. The event was a national scandal. It helped prompt Congress to establish the Oregon Territory in 1848 and triggered the Cayuse War, which left the tribe decimated by the time the conflict ended with a treaty in 1855.

All that remains of the mission are some foundation stones. A paved path leads past

Walla Walla

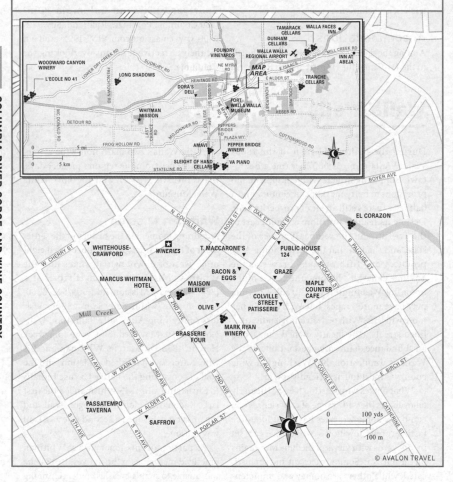

the Whitmans' grave site, through the mission grounds, and up a hill to an obelisk honoring the missionaries. It's a pleasant but somber walk, and the hilltop provides a good view of the surrounding countryside. A visitors center displays artifacts and dioramas depicting mission life. It has the tough task of interpreting an event that remains the subject of dispute to the present day. Though the center is kid friendly, it could be a challenge for parents to explain to younger children the complex, conflicting interpretations of what went on here.

Fort Walla Walla Museum

The name is a little misleading at the **Fort Walla Walla Museum** (755 Myra Road, 509/525-7703, www.fortwallawallamuseum. org, Mar.-Oct. daily 10am-5pm, Nov.-Feb. daily 10am-4pm, $8). There were three Fort Walla Wallas, and the museum is located on the grounds of the third one, which was active 1858-1910, but it doesn't include any of the fort's structures or specifically address the fort's history.

Instead it's a good-quality general local

Whitman Mission National Historic Site

and many have tasting rooms along downtown's quaint streets. There's also a group of about 20 wineries that occupy the grounds of Walla Walla's old World War II-era military airport, which makes for a novel touring destination.

With so many wineries to choose from, it can be tough to decide which ones to visit. Below are some good options, but you can also learn a lot by discussing the subject with locals. Hotel clerks, restaurant servers, bartenders—everyone has a favorite winery.

Downtown

The tasting rooms in town are essentially wine shops—you aren't out among the vines here, but on the upside, within a couple of blocks you have the opportunity to sample wine from a dozen different makers. In the heart of downtown, **Mark Ryan Winery** (26 E. Main St., 509/876-4577, www.markryanwinery. com, Sat.-Thurs. 11am-5pm, Fri. 11am-8pm) and **Maison Bleue** (20 N. 2nd Ave., 509/525-9084, www.mbwinery.com, Wed.-Mon. 11am-5pm) are among the most highly esteemed.

A couple of blocks off Main Street you get a down-to-earth experience at **El Corazon** (37 S. Palouse St., 509/520-4408, www.elcorazonwinery.com, by appointment). The little storefront winery is run by two young, charismatic winemakers who fearlessly experiment with unusual varietals and blends. You may not like everything you taste, but odds are you'll enjoy the tasting. Technically you need to call ahead for an appointment, but usually that means one of the winemakers saying, "I can meet you there in half an hour"; if you pass by and they're open, they'll welcome you in.

East of downtown but still within city limits is **Foundry Vineyards** (1111 Abadie St., 509/529-0736, www.foundryvineyards.com, Thurs.-Sun. 11am-5pm), an unusual amalgam: The owners also run a world-renowned sculpture-fabricating business, and their tasting room includes a gallery and sculpture garden. Check Foundry's website for its frequent events, including music recitals, winemaker dinners, and yoga classes.

history museum with a focus on early pioneer settlement and agriculture. There are five exhibition halls. The first has conventional displays about Lewis and Clark, Indians of the region, and military history. The other four are filled old farm equipment, primarily vehicles. The most striking is a large hall dedicated exclusively to a giant 1919 wheat combine, complete with fiberglass replicas of the 33-mule team that pulled it. Down a slope from the halls there's the open-air Pioneer Village, consisting of 17 vintage buildings brought here from locations around Walla Walla. Among the structures are a log cabin, railway depot, jail, and blacksmith shop.

TOP EXPERIENCE

★ WALLA WALLA WINERIES

When Walla Walla Valley was designated an AVA in 1984 it had four wineries. Today there are well over 100, most within easy driving distance of town. Some actually are *in* town,

The Airport

Walla Walla's old military airport east of downtown had been derelict for years when enterprising winemakers got the idea to convert the grounds into winemaking facilities. Of the older and more highly regarded winemakers there now, **Dunham Cellars** (150 E. Boeing Ave., 509/529-4685, www.dunhamcellars.com, daily 11am-4pm) is notable for its pleasant tasting room and colorful event space, while **Tamarack Cellars** (700 C St., 509/526-3533, http://tamarackcellars.com, daily 10am-4pm) keeps things simple in the unadorned old firehouse. The airport also has five "incubator" spaces where new, small producers—including brewers and distillers as well as winemakers—set up shop for up to four years. It can be fun to see what they're coming up with.

Another good place to stop east of town is **Tranche Cellars** (705 Berney Dr., 509/526-3500, http://tranche.wine, daily 11am-5pm), which is noted for its rhone varietals. The handsome, modern winery is in an idyllic spot overlooking a sheep farm.

L'Ecole No. 41

West of Town

You can spend a pleasant half-day west of town visiting the following wineries and the Whitman Mission. Bring along lunch—you can picnic at the mission, Woodward Canyon, or L'Ecole No. 41.

Woodward Canyon Wineries (11920 U.S. 12, 509/525-4129, www.woodwardcanyon.com, daily 10am-4:30pm) was started in 1981, making it one of Walla Walla's earliest wine producers. It remains one of the most respected, and with an annual output of about 15,000 cases it's stayed small enough to maintain the owners' personal character. The tasting room, in an 1870s farmhouse, is pleasant and unpretentious. Cabernet sauvignon gets top billing, but the chardonnay is also a standout.

Right next door to Woodward Canyon, **L'Ecole No. 41** (41 Lowden School Rd., 509/525-0940, www.lecole.com, daily 10am-5pm) is another Walla Walla wine pioneer, having been in business since 1983. It's a bigger, more polished operation than Woodward, but it shares a similarly unpretentious sensibility. The tasting room occupies a restored old schoolhouse (hence the name). Grapes are sourced from vineyards throughout Walla Walla and the Columbia Valley, allowing L'Ecole to produce a wide variety of wines.

Long Shadows (1604 Frenchtown Rd., 509/526-0905, www.longshadows.com, by appointment) is an all-star project put together by Allen Shoup, the former president and CEO of wine giant Chateau Ste. Michelle. He matches European varietals grown in Washington with esteemed winemakers from around the world. Thus a bordeaux blend is made under the supervision of French celebrity winemaker Michel Rolland, and a syrah is overseen by Australian shiraz master John Duval. The tasting room fits with the high-end concept: Instead of standing at a bar you sit in a cushy chair beneath a Dale Chihuly chandelier, and the wine is brought to you. A tasting reservation is required, but Long Shadows welcomes visitors seven days a week.

South of Town

While the area west of Walla Walla is home to the AVA's oldest wineries, to the south are some younger rising stars. It's also an attractive landscape, with vineyards surrounding the wineries and the Blue Mountains studding the horizon.

A prime example of the area's new generation of winemakers is **Sleight of Hand Cellars** (1959 JB George Rd., 509/525-3661, www.sofhcellars.com, daily 11am-5pm), which produces carefully crafted, highly sought-after bordeaux blends while maintaining a whimsical attitude evident on every label. Adding to the experience, you can be your own DJ while you taste, choosing from the thousands of records in the owner's collection.

Just down the road, **Pepper Bridge Winery** (1704 JB George Rd., 509/525-6502, www.pepperbridge.com, daily 10am-4pm) has been around a while longer and takes itself a little more seriously. It's a rare Walla Walla

winery that uses exclusively estate-grown grapes, all bordeaux varietals. The tasting room is a little house in the vineyard with a patio and lovely views, and the staff is knowledgeable and friendly, if a bit more formal than the neighbors.

Other places south of town worth a stop include the beautifully situated **Va Piano** (1793 JB George Rd., 509/529-0900, www.vapianovineyards.com, daily 11am-5pm), where the winemaker is a talented Walla Walla native, and **Amavi** (3796 Peppers Bridge Rd., 509/525-3541, hwww.amavicellars.com, daily 10am-4pm), an offshoot of Pepper Bridge that also has a patio with a view.

FOOD

Most visitors come to Walla Walla for the wine, but they're often just as impressed by the food. For a town this small, the number and variety of good restaurants is impressive. Don't expect small-town prices though. Tabs are along the lines of comparable restaurants in Portland and Seattle.

Bakeries

Downtown's **Colville Street Patisserie** (40 S. Colville St., 509/301-7289, www.colvillestreetpatisserie.com, Mon.-Thurs.

Pepper Bridge Winery tasting room

9am-8pm, Fri.-Sat. 9am-9pm, Sun. 9am-6pm, $2-6) is a good spot for a morning coffee, an afternoon gelato, or a pastry any time.

Breakfast and Lunch

Breakfast and lunch get the locavore treatment at **Bacon & Eggs** (57 E. Main St., 509/876-4553, www.baconandeggswallawalla. com, Thurs.-Tues. 8am-2pm, $9-15), a hip diner with a menu that sways a little Mexican (huevos rancheros, carne asada) and a little Southern (shrimp and grits, crab cakes). Start the day off with a bang with one of the craft cocktails.

Maple Counter Cafe (209 E. Alder St., 509/876-2527, http://maplecountercafe.com, daily 7am-3pm, $9-15) serves up a long menu of breakfast and lunch classics—eggs, pancakes, burgers, salads—done with touches of sophistication. The pancake batter is made from scratch, and eggs aren't fried here but basted in clarified butter.

Eclectic

For something quick and delicious, locals and visitors alike rely on centrally located **Olive** (21 E. Main St., 509/526-0200, www.olivemarketplaceandcafe.com, daily 8am-9pm, $10-16).

Head for the main counter to order substantial breakfasts, sandwiches, pizzas, and salads, prepared with a touch of creativity. There's a large, comfortable dining room and seating outside along the sidewalk.

Graze (5 S. Colville St., 509/522-9991, www.grazeevents.com, Mon.-Sat. 10am-7:30pm, Sun. 10am-3:30pm, $8-12) is a sandwich shop with an attitude. Along with standards like pastrami and turkey with cheese, it offers banh mi sandwiches, pulled pork tortas, and a "sexy time" panini, with chicken, bacon, brie, and caramelized onions.

Public House 124 (124 E. Main St., 509/876-4511, www.ph124.com, Tues.-Sat. 3pm-10pm, $16-31) is Main Street's gastropub. Pair your craft cocktail or microbrew with anything from a bowl of cashews to a German dumpling to a full steak-and-potatoes dinner.

Walla Walla's most beautiful dining room belongs to **Whitehouse-Crawford** (55 W. Cherry St, 509/525-2222, www.whitehousecrawford.com, Wed.-Mon. 5pm-9pm, $26-43), which occupies an old mill that's been smartly restored with exposed brick and high whitebeamed ceilings. The regularly changing menu is a mash-up of new American cooking

The Inn at Abeja

with East Asian, Indian, and Italian influences. If something sounds too weird to be good, you might be right, but you can rely on the grilled meats and pasta dishes.

French

The menu at ★ **Brasserie Four** (4 E. Main St., 509/529-2011, www.brasseriefour.com, Tues.-Sat. noon-10pm, $15-30) ticks off one French standard after another: escargot, vichyssoise, bouillabaisse, steak frites. That might sound pretentious, but what comes out of the kitchen is consistently delicious and not overly fussy. Throw in a casually romantic dining room and friendly, polished service, and you have what's arguably Walla Walla's best restaurant.

Italian

With Seattle-based pasta guru Mike Easton overseeing the menu and local cocktail legend Jim German managing the bar, **Passatempo** (215 W. Main St., 509/876-8822, www.passatempowallawalla.com, Thurs.-Mon. 3pm-10pm, $18-43) opened to unprecedented fanfare in 2017 and continues to be Walla Walla's most coveted dinner reservation. The menu consists of half a dozen pasta dishes and a few grilled meats. In keeping with the spirit of Italian cuisine, cooking here starts with high-quality ingredients and lets them shine with simple, meticulously executed preparations.

T. Maccarone's (4 N. Colville St., 509/522-4776, www.tmaccarones.com, Mon.-Fri. 11am-9pm, Sat.-Sun. 3pm-9pm, $22-44) is an upscale Italian restaurant, but don't expect marinara sauce and waiters in tuxes. This is modern Italian, with lots of seafood choices and a few surprising ingredients like mango and green curry. If there's a shortcoming, it's that some dishes are a little more complicated than they need to be.

Mediterranean

There's an inviting, intimate feel to **Saffron** (125 W. Alder St., 509/525-2112, www.

saffronmediterraneankitchen.com, Tues.-Sun. 2pm-9pm, $14-42), a small place with a Mediterranean-focused menu. Dishes like kibbeh and lamb tagine may seem exotic, but what they're serving here is international comfort food—rich, satisfying, and made with care.

Mexican

If you're south or west of town visiting wineries or the Whitman Mission, the go-to restaurant, and practically your only option, is **Dora's Deli at the Worm Ranch** (1186 Wallula Ave., 509/529-3629, daily 9am-6pm, $6-12). The unappetizing name has a perverse charm to it (Dora's is located in a bait and tackle shop), but the delicious, straightforward Mexican food makes eating here more than a novelty. Burritos, tacos, and tamales are standouts. Be aware, though, that the deep-fried dishes can be grease bombs.

ACCOMMODATIONS

The **Marcus Whitman Hotel** (6 W. Rose St., 509/525-2200, www.marcuswhitmanhotel.com, $129-249) is the classic place to stay in Walla Walla. The 10-story building towers over the rest of downtown. It's been restored to its early-20th-century splendor, with grand chandeliers, scrolled woodwork, and a fireside parlor. Guest rooms in the original building include handsome suites with large tiled bathrooms. There's a newer wing with smaller but equally well-appointed rooms available for lower rates.

Walla Faces Inn (254 Wheat Ridge Ln., 877/301-1181, www.wallafaces.com, $145-345) has three suites and a guesthouse, all done in a clean, contemporary style, on the grounds of a vineyard east of town. The units share a pool, which can be a nice bonus in Walla Walla's summer heat.

Set on a working winery that once was a farm, ★ **The Inn at Abeja** (2014 Mill Creek Rd., 509/522-1234, www.abeja.net, $325-625) looks like it's ready for a *Travel + Leisure* photo shoot. The farm's outbuildings have been tripped out with high-end rustic decor, including fully equipped kitchens.

TRANSPORTATION

Walla Walla is 260 miles (4.5 hrs.) southeast of Seattle via I-90, I-82, and I-182. It's 150 miles (2.75 hrs.) south of Spokane via I-90 and Route 261. Be sure you have gas in your tank and food in your stomach when driving to Walla Walla. Services are few and far between.

You can catch daily flights to Seattle from the **Walla Walla Regional Airport** (45 Terminal Loop, 509/522-5211, www.wallawallaairport.com), located four miles east of downtown.

Eastern Washington

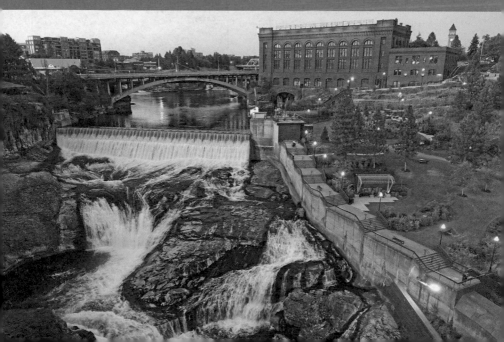

Look for ★ to find recommended
sights, activities, dining, and lodging.

Highlights

★ **Wild Horse Renewable Energy Center:** Learn about how humans are harnessing wind and solar power, and actually go inside a wind turbine (page 422).

★ **Gorge Amphitheatre:** Catch a concert in Washington's most majestic outdoor performance venue, situated on the banks of the Columbia River (page 423).

★ **Grand Coulee Dam:** This enormous dam—the result of the largest construction project in U.S. history—transformed eastern Washington's geography, ecology, and economy. It's an engineering marvel (page 424).

★ **Sun Lakes-Dry Falls State Park:** The largest waterfall the world has ever known has now sat dry at the south end of Grand Coulee for millennia, a prime example of eastern Washington's stark, severe beauty (page 428).

East of the Cascade Range, Washington takes on an entirely different character. Instead of mountains, forest, and coastline, you'll find vast open prairie and the stark northern reaches of the Great American Desert.

Locals have dubbed this part of the state the Inland Northwest. This may not be the kind of terrain you associate with Washington, but it has some impressive sights. The most popular attraction is the Grand Coulee Dam, which draws visitors from all over the world to marvel at its enormous size and the gargantuan effort that went into building it. The dam is the centerpiece of the Columbia Basin Irrigation Project, which supplies water to 670,000 acres of farmland, making it the largest such enterprise in the U.S.

Two lakes created by the dam, Roosevelt and Banks, are popular destinations for water sports and camping. Just south of Banks Lake is Dry Falls, a geological wonder that, when water flowed over it during the last ice age, was the largest falls on earth. Farther downstream along the banks of the Columbia River is the Gorge Amphitheatre, one of America's most spectacular outdoor music venues.

To the west, near the Idaho border, is Spokane, Washington's second-largest city and the urban hub for the Inland Northwest. It strikes a nice balance, with the laid-back charm of a big town and sophistication of a small city, with beautiful parks, a lively downtown, and a good mix of hip and old-school restaurants.

PLANNING YOUR TIME

The climate of eastern Washington is basically the opposite of what you find on the western side of the Cascades. Most of the region gets over 300 sunny days a year, with little precipitation. Summers are hot; winters are cold. For travelers, that means the shoulder seasons of late spring and early fall are the most pleasant times for exploring.

You can incorporate the Grand Coulee Dam area and Spokane into a big loop tour of the state, along with a pass through the North Cascades and a visit to wine country

Previous: Wild Horse Renewable Energy Center; Spokane Falls. **Above:** Gonzaga University's bulldog mascot.

Eastern Washington

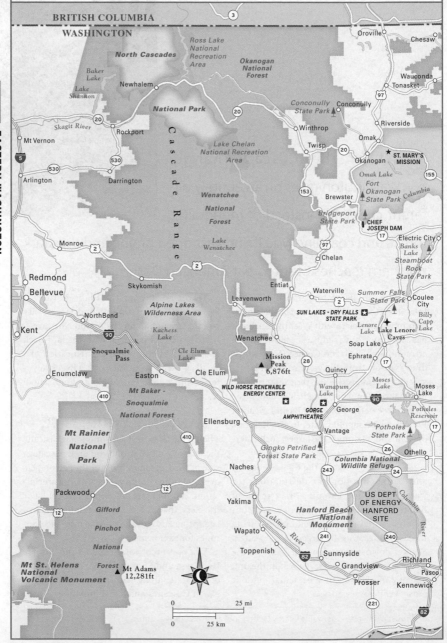

BRITISH COLUMBIA

WASHINGTON

North Cascades

Ross Lake
National
Recreation
Area

Okanogan
National
Forest

Baker
Lake

Lake
Shannon

Newhalem

National Park

Oroville

Chesaw

Wauconda

Tonasket

Conconully
State Park

Conconully

Riverside

Skagit River

Rockport

Mt Vernon

Arlington

Darrington

Winthrop

Twisp

Omak

Okanogan

ST. MARY'S
MISSION

Omak Lake

Fort
Okanogan
State Park

Columbia

Brewster

Bridgeport
State Park

CHIEF
JOSEPH DAM

Electric City

Banks
Lake

Steamboat
Rock
State Park

C
a
s
c
a
d
e

R
a
n
g
e

Lake Chelan
National Recreation
Area

Wenatchee

National

Forest

Lake
Wenatchee

Monroe

Skykomish

Redmond

Bellevue

NorthBend

Kent

Enumclaw

Snoqualmie
Pass

Alpine Lakes
Wilderness Area

Kachess
Lake

Cle Elum
Lake

Easton

Cle Elum

Leavenworth

Entiat

Waterville

Chelan

Coulee
City

Summer Falls
State Park

SUN LAKES - DRY FALLS
STATE PARK

Lenore
Lake

Lake Lenore
Caves

Billy
Capp
Lake

Wenatchee

Soap Lake

Ephrata

Mission
Peak
6,876ft

Quincy

WILD HORSE RENEWABLE
ENERGY CENTER

Wanapum
Lake

George

Moses
Lake

Potholes
Reservoir

GORGE
AMPHITHEATRE

Moses
Lake

Mt Baker -
Snoqualmie
National Forest

Ellensburg

Vantage

Potholes
State Park

Othello

Mt Rainier
National
Park

Gingko Petrified
Forest State Park

Naches

Columbia National
Wildlife Refuge

US DEPT
OF ENERGY
HANFORD
SITE

Packwood

Gifford

Pinchot

National

Mt St. Helens
National
Volcanic Monument

Forest

Mt Adams
12,281ft

Yakima

Wapato

Toppenish

Hanford Reach
National
Monument

Yakima River

Columbia River

Sunnyside

Grandview

Prosser

Richland

Pasco

Kennewick

0   25 mi

0   25 km

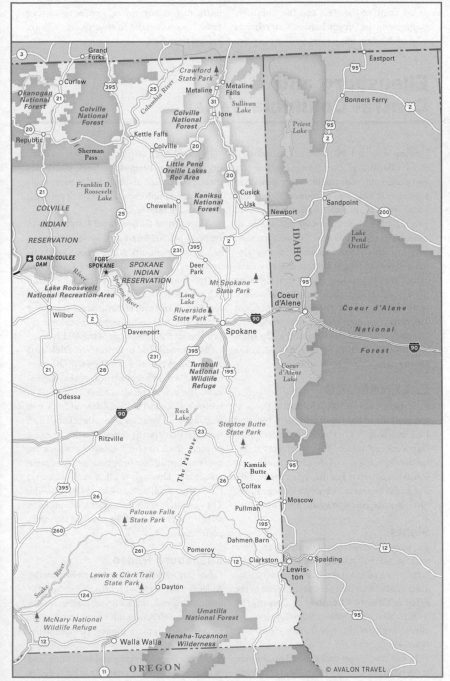

© AVALON TRAVEL

in the south of the state and the Columbia Gorge along the Oregon border. That requires a lot of driving, but unless you already live in the region, any itinerary covering eastern Washington is going to require many hours behind the wheel.

Ellensburg and Central Columbia Valley

Driving west on I-90 over the Cascades toward Ellensburg, the change in weather and geography is dramatic. From Seattle to Snoqualmie Pass, you encounter forests and snowcapped peaks, often under a thick cloud cover. By the time you're 20 miles west of Ellensburg, the clouds have thinned, the temperature rises in summer and drops in winter, and the landscape flattens to low, rolling hills. From Ellensburg it's 30 miles west to the Columbia River, where along the eastern banks the Gorge Amphitheatre is the most spectacular outdoor music venue in the state and one of the finest in the country. The nearest town, a few miles farther up I-90, is the goofily named George, Washington.

ELLENSBURG

Ellensburg (pop. 18,000) is located in the eastern foothills of the Cascades where I-90 and I-82 intersect. It's best known for its Labor Day weekend rodeo, which attracts thousands of spectators and top rodeo talent from across the country. For the rest of the year it's a regional business hub and a college town, the home of Central Washington University.

Sights

The streets of downtown Ellensburg are lined with Victorian-style buildings that you can take in on a pleasant stroll. Pick up a map for a self-guided tour online or at the office of the **Kittitas County Chamber of Commerce** (609 N. Main St., 509/925-2002, www.my-ellensburg.com, Mon.-Fri. 9am-5pm, Sat. 10am-4pm).

In downtown, get background on the area at the **Kittitas County Historical Museum** (114 E. 3rd Ave., 509/925-3778, www.kchm.org, Mon.-Sat. 10am-4pm, free), which has displays of Indian artifacts and pioneer tools as well as an impressive collection of petrified wood and gemstones.

The **Clymer Gallery and Museum** (416 N. Pearl St., 509/962-6416, www.clymermuseum.com, Mon.-Fri. 10am-5pm, Sat. 11am-3pm, free) displays the work of Ellensburg native John Ford Clymer (1907-89), who achieved renown for his illustrations in *Field and Stream* and over 80 *Saturday Evening Post* covers. His most enduring works are his carefully researched paintings of the Old West.

At the south end of downtown, **Dick and Jane's Spot** (101 N. Pearl St., www.reflector-art.com) is a different sort of local arts treasure. The private residence has a yard full of whimsical, colorful "outsider art." As you walk around, you can sense the energy and devotion that's been poured into this ongoing project, which has been evolving for four decades and includes contributions from some 40 artists. Through it all, a real Dick and Jane—two local artists—have lived inside. They ask that visitors respect their privacy; all of the art can be seen by strolling the yard's perimeter.

Ellensburg Rodeo

Labor Day weekend's **Ellensburg Rodeo** (N. Alder St., 800/637-2444, http://ellensburgrodeo.com) is one of the biggest such events in the nation, attracting top competitors to vie for $400,000 in prize money. Held annually since 1923, it features the classic cowboy contests including calf roping and bull riding, and barrel racing for the cowgirls. The rodeo is

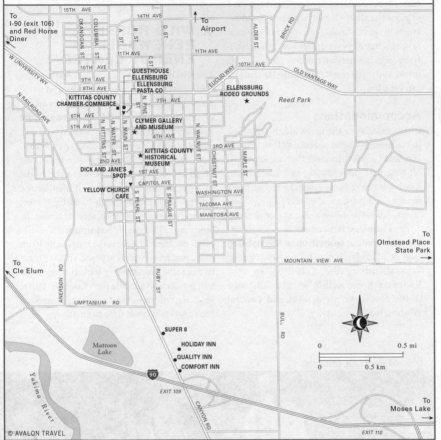

Ellensburg

held in conjunction with the **Kittitas County Fair** (509/962-7639, www.kittitascountyfair. com), another classic of its kind, highlighted by livestock and cooking competitions.

Food

Ellensburg's most appealing restaurants get a lot of mileage out of small-town nostalgia. An old gas station is now a burger joint, and an old church is a cute casual restaurant.

Located in a former gas station, **Red Horse Diner** (1518 W. University Way, 509/925-1956, http://redhorsediner.com, daily 7am-9pm, $9-12) has held on tightly to a retro automotive theme, with vintage signs on the walls and diner classics—mainly burgers and sandwiches—on the menu. It's a favorite with car clubs and motorcycle enthusiasts.

Yellow Church Cafe (111 S. Pearl St., 509/933-2233, www.theyellowchurchcafe. com, Mon.-Thurs. 11am-9pm, Fri.-Sun. 8am-9pm, $13-27) is a former Lutheran church that's been converted into a cozy, casual restaurant serving creative comfort food, including entrée-size salads, sandwiches, and grilled meats.

Ellensburg Pasta Company (600 N. Main St., 509/933-3330, www.ellensburgpasta. com, Mon.-Sat. 11am-9pm, $9-24) is the kind of place the Olive Garden wishes it could be: an inviting, reasonably priced family restaurant serving 20 pasta dishes and other satisfying Italian American entrées. There's a kids menu, and if you're not feeling like Italian, you can get a burger.

Accommodations

Chain motels are the main lodging options in Ellensburg—Super 8, Holiday Inn, Quality Inn, and Comfort Inn line Canyon Road just off I-90, with more choices in a similar vein nearby. If you're coming for the rodeo, book months in advance and expect to pay a premium, often double the standard rate or more.

For a homier stay, book one of two well-appointed rooms at **Guesthouse Ellensburg** (606 N. Main St., 509/962-3706, www.guesthouseellensburg.com, $145-175), an 1888 Victorian home within walking distance of the downtown attractions and Central Washington University.

Transportation

Ellensburg is a 1.75-hour, 110-mile drive southeast of Seattle on I-90.

★ WILD HORSE RENEWABLE ENERGY CENTER

The windy, open land of central Washington is ideal for harnessing wind power, and you'll see turbines throughout the region. For an up-close look, visit the **Wild Horse Renewable Energy Center** (25905 Vantage Hwy., 509/964-7815, www.pse.com, Apr.-mid.-Nov. daily 9am-5:30pm, free), 16 miles east of Ellensburg off I-90. It's set in the midst of a giant wind farm run by Puget Sound Energy—149 turbines, each standing 351 feet tall and weighing 223 tons, stretch across the landscape. The center has informative displays, but the highlight is the tour (daily 10am and 2pm, free), which gets you inside an active turbine. You'll never look at these massive modern windmills the same way again. In spring wildflowers carpet the hills, making it an especially good time to visit.

Dick and Jane's Spot, Ellensburg

GINGKO PETRIFIED FOREST STATE PARK

Fifteen to 20 million years ago, this part of central Washington was covered by lush forests, which were subsumed by molten lava that poured out of fissures in the earth's crust. Some logs were preserved intact by the lava cover; water eventually leaked through to the logs, and minerals replaced the natural structure of the wood. The result—259 species of petrified trees—was exposed by the tremendous erosion of the last ice age. You can explore the trees at **Gingko Petrified Forest State Park/Wanapum Recreational Area** (4511 Huntzinger Rd., 509/856-2700, http://parks.state.wa.us/288, Discover Pass required for parking), along the Columbia River about 30 miles east of Ellensburg, at Exit 136 of I-90.

An **interpretive center** (mid-May-mid-Sept. daily 10am-6pm, donation requested) displays exhibits on the geologic history of the area and a collection of petrified wood. Outside there's more wood as well as a viewing area with a spectacular vista overlooking the Columbia. Two miles west of the center the **Trees of Stone Interpretive Trail**, a one-mile loop, goes through a fossil bed with more than a score of petrified logs.

★ GORGE AMPHITHEATRE

Located along the Columbia River Gorge, 43 miles east-northeast of Ellensburg and 7 miles northwest of the little town of George, the **Gorge Amphitheatre** (754 Silica Rd., 509/785-6262, www.gorgeamphitheatre.net) is an outdoor amphitheater seating 20,000 along the bluffs overlooking the river canyon. It takes some effort to get here, but it's worth it—it's a beautiful natural setting for a show,

especially when enhanced by a summer sunset, and the acoustics are great. Each summer the venue hosts music festivals and headliner rock and pop acts. Major events fill motels as far away as Wenatchee, so reserve ahead.

Food and Accommodations

Camping and RV spaces are available on adjacent grounds (make reservations at www.GorgeCamping.com), and there's food service at the theater.

Overlooking the Columbia next door to the Gorge Amphitheatre is the area's high-end lodging option, **Cave B Inn & Spa** (344 Silica Rd. NW, 509/787-8000, www.cavebinn.com). Its several kinds of accommodations are all done up in rustic-luxe style: inn rooms built into the bluffs ($229-479), freestanding suites ($289-619), and yurts ($179-429) sitting out in the adjacent vineyard. The wide price ranges reflect markups on nights when there are events at the amphitheater.

Cave B bottles its own wine and has a large tasting room. Even if you're not staying at the inn, this is a good place to visit—you can sample the wine and take a hike down to the river. **Tendrils Restaurant** (344 Silica Rd. NW, 509/787-8000, www.cavebinn.com, Mon.-Sat. 7:30am-8pm, Sun. 9am-8pm, $29-58) at Cave B has beautiful sunset views (ask for a window table) and a menu that mixes Italian starters and pastas with classic meat entrées—rack of lamb, beef tenderloin, rosemary chicken.

Transportation

The Gorge Amphitheatre is on the eastern bank of the Columbia, 7 miles north of I-90 via a well-marked exit. From Seattle, it's a straight shot 150 miles east on the interstate. It's a 2.5-hour drive.

Grand Coulee Dam Region

If you've been driving through the desert country of central Washington, the area in the immediate vicinity of Grand Coulee Dam can seem like a mirage. Instead of barren sage, grass, and rock, you find a cluster of small lakeside towns with green lawns and split-level homes. And, in what feels like the middle of nowhere, you come upon the largest construction project ever undertaken in the United States—the Grand Coulee Dam.

To its southwest the dam flooded a portion of Grand Coulee to create 27-mile-long Banks Lake, a reservoir that's the source of irrigation water for some 670,000 acres of central and southern Washington farmland. Upriver the dam created Lake Roosevelt, a reservoir that meanders for 130 miles, to near the Canadian border.

Several little towns with similar names serve the dam region. Clustered around the dam are **Electric City** and **Grand Coulee,** just to the south, and **Coulee Dam** just to the north, each with a population that hovers around a thousand. Thirty miles to the south,

Coulee City (pop. 600) sits adjacent to **Dry Falls Dam** on Banks Lake.

★ GRAND COULEE DAM

The **Grand Coulee** is a 50-mile-long gorge carved by the Columbia River during the ice ages, when glaciers forced the river south of its current path. At its north end the **Grand Coulee Dam** stands 550 feet tall and spans almost a mile, with a spillway that's more than a quarter-mile wide. It was initiated as a New Deal project of the 1930s, and it transformed the landscape to a degree that rivals the impact of the ice ages. The dam became the biggest source of electricity for the Northwest. It's by far the largest generator of hydroelectric power in the United States, and one of the largest in the world. Its isolated location means that, if you're willing to put in the miles driving, you'll get to see a truly remarkable feat of engineering without having to contend with large crowds.

The hub for sightseers is the **visitors center** (Rte. 155 just north of dam, 509/633-9265, www.usbr.gov/pn/grandcoulee, daily

Grand Coulee Dam

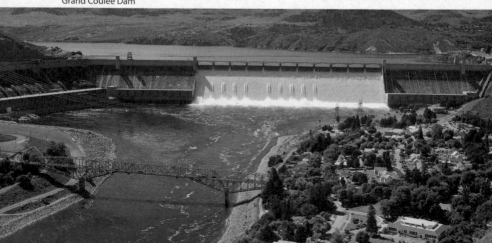

Grand Coulee Dam

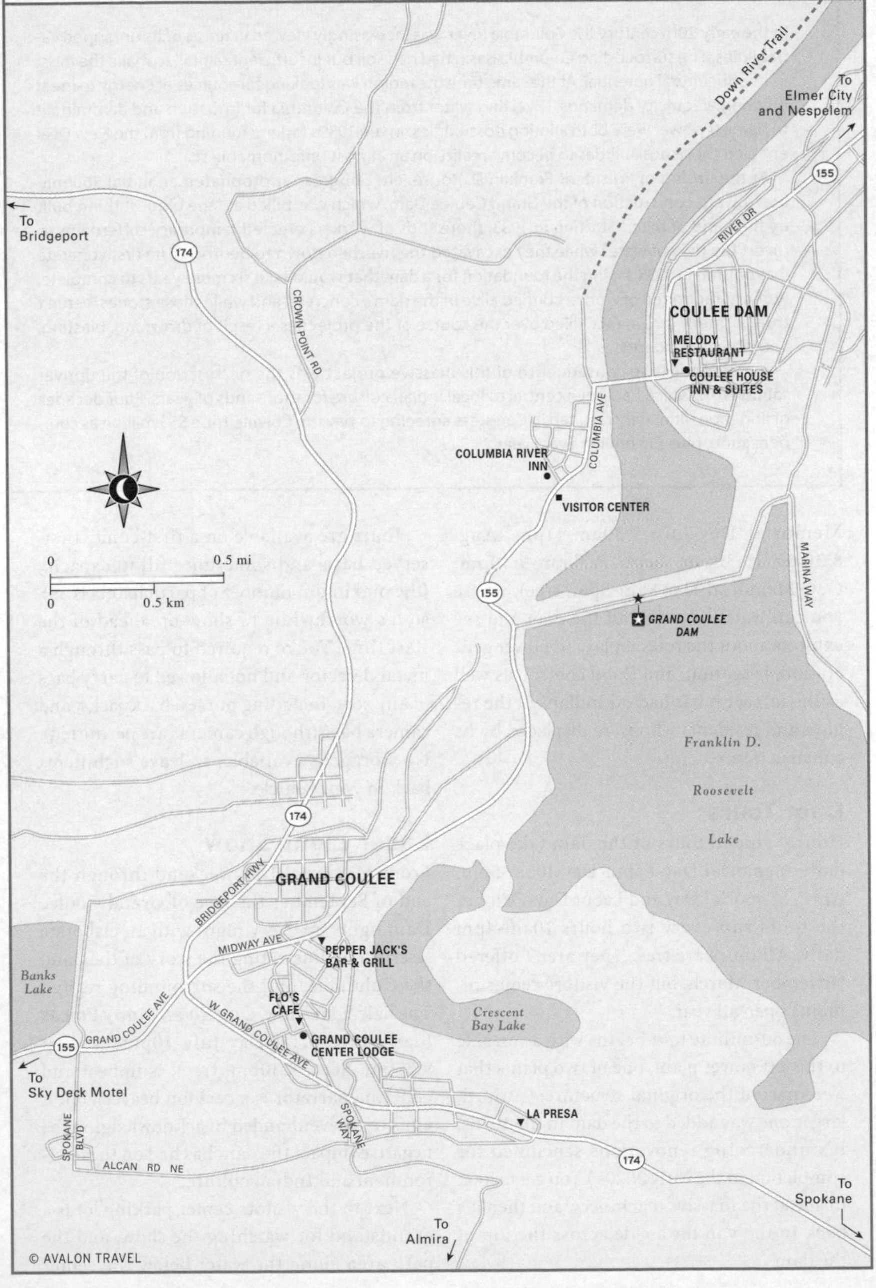

To Bridgeport

174

CROWN POINT RD

Down River Trail

To Elmer City and Nespelem

155

RIVER DR

COULEE DAM

MELODY RESTAURANT

COULEE HOUSE INN & SUITES

COLUMBIA AVE

COLUMBIA RIVER INN

VISITOR CENTER

155

MARINA WAY

⭐ GRAND COULEE DAM

Franklin D.

Roosevelt

Lake

174

BRIDGEPORT HWY

GRAND COULEE

MIDWAY AVE

PEPPER JACK'S BAR & GRILL

FLO'S CAFE

GRAND COULEE CENTER LODGE

Banks Lake

GRAND COULEE AVE

W. GRAND COULEE AVE

155

To Sky Deck Motel

Crescent Bay Lake

SPOKANE BLVD

SPOKANE WAY

ALCAN RD NE

LA PRESA

174

To Spokane

To Almira

0   0.5 mi

0   0.5 km

© AVALON TRAVEL

The Birth of a Dam

In the early 20th century the Columbia River was increasingly viewed in terms of its untapped capabilities. The surrounding Columbia Basin had rich soil but insufficient rainfall to make the most of its agricultural potential. At the same time the region was looking for sources of energy to meet growing electricity demands. Diverting water from the Columbia for irrigation and damming it to harness power were both alluring possibilities. In the 1930s federal funding from the New Deal enabled those possibilities to become reality on an almost unfathomable scale.

At the urging of President Franklin D. Roosevelt, Congress appropriated an initial $60 million toward construction of the Grand Coulee Dam, which was billed as "the biggest thing built by the hand of man." Starting in 1933, thousands of workers erected temporary cofferdams to divert the flow of water while they excavated the riverbed down to bedrock. The first concrete was poured in 1935, laying the foundation for a dam that would take six more years to complete. Rumors abounded of workers buried alive in the dam's concrete, and while those stories weren't true, 77 men were in fact killed over the course of the project as a result of drowning, blasting, and vehicle accidents.

A major negative consequence of this massive project was the destruction of the upriver salmon run, which had been central to local Indian culture for thousands of years. Four decades of litigation ultimately resulted in Congress agreeing to pay the Colville Tribe $53 million as compensation, plus $15 million every year.

Memorial Day-July 8:30am-11pm, Aug. 8:30am-10:30pm, Sept. 8:30am-9:30pm, Oct.-Memorial Day 9am-5pm, free), where you can watch films about the dam and see exhibits about the roles it plays in power generation, irrigation, and flood control, as well as the impact it has had on Indians of the region and residents who were displaced by its construction.

Dam Tours

Hourly guided tours of the dam take place daily Memorial Day-Labor Day 10am-5pm. April-Memorial Day and Labor Day-October the tours run every two hours 10am-4pm daily. All tours are free. They aren't offered November-March, but the visitors center remains open all year.

The 50-minute tour begins with a van ride to the left power plant, one of two plants that were part of the original structure. (A third, larger one was added to the dam in the 1970s. It's undergoing renovations scheduled for completion in the early 2020s.) You get to look inside at the massive machinery, and then it's back in the van for a ride across the top of the dam.

Tours are available on a first-come, first-served basis and sometimes fill to capacity (the maximum number of participants is 35), so it's worthwhile to show up ahead of the start time. You're required to pass through a metal detector and not allowed to carry bags of any sort, including purses, backpacks, and camera bags (though cameras are permitted). No storage is available, so leave such items back in your vehicle.

Laser Light Show

From Memorial Day weekend through the end of September the face of Grand Coulee Dam lights up every night with an elaborate laser show illustrating the story of the dam, the Columbia, and the surrounding region. The half-hour show, *One River, Many Voices* (daily Memorial Day-July 10pm, August 9:30pm, Sept. 8:30pm, free), is upbeat and cute (the narrator is a cartoon beaver), but it aims to be evenhanded in acknowledging the negative impact the dam has had on the environment and Indian culture.

Next to the visitors center parking lot is a grandstand for watching the show, and the park area along the water below the center is another good viewpoint; both locations have speakers. The parking lot area draws the biggest crowds, so if you want to watch from there on a weekend night, arrive early to claim your space.

Food

★ **The Melody Restaurant** (512 River Dr., Coulee Dam, 509/633-8113, Tues.-Sat. 11am-9pm, $9-21) is a diamond in the rough. It's a modest-looking place, but you can tell when your food arrives that a creative, caring chef is at work. The wide-ranging menu has something to please a variety of tastes, from sandwiches to entrée salads to shrimp scampi to grilled rib eye, and there are often inventive specials.

Little **Flo's Cafe** (316 Spokane Way, Grand Coulee, 509/633-3216, Wed.-Mon. 5am-1pm, $5-10) is a cozy, friendly, quirky small-town diner serving healthy portions of breakfast and lunch classics.

For another taste of small-town life, head to **Pepper Jack's Bar and Grill** (113 Midway Ave., Grand Coulee, 509/633-8283, http://pepperjacks.webs.com, daily 7am-9pm, $8-16). The food is standard diner—eggs in the morning, burgers and sandwiches the rest of the day—and so is the setting, with worn Naugahyde booths and a bar in the back that's a popular local hangout.

La Presa (515 E. Grand Coulee Ave., 509/633-3173, Mon.-Sat. 11am-9pm, $12-24) is a favorite for reliable Mexican food, with a long menu that includes burritos, enchiladas, and grilled and fried meat and fish entrées.

Accommodations

Near the dam are a few basic, independently owned motels. On summer weekends they fill up, so booking in advance is pretty much mandatory.

Less than a quarter mile from the dam visitors center, **Columbia River Inn** (10 Lincoln Ave., Coulee Dam, 509/633-2100, www.columbiariverinn.com, $118-129 d) is the nicest choice. The rooms are comfortable and have refrigerators, microwaves, and private decks.

Facilities include an outdoor pool, a hot tub, and a sauna.

The best deal near the dam is **Grand Coulee Center Lodge** (404 Spokane Way, Grand Coulee, 509/633-2860, http://grandcouleecenterlodge.com, $70-110). It's a simple, old-fashioned motel, and the location isn't scenic, but it's well maintained by a friendly, professional staff. All rooms come with refrigerator and microwave, and some have full kitchens.

Coulee House Inn and Suites (110 Roosevelt Way, Coulee Dam, 509/633-1103, http://couleehouse.com, $100-120) could use a renovation, but it has a prime location near the dam, with views of the laser show from the property grounds.

Three miles south of the dam, **Sky Deck Motel** (138 Miller Ave., Electric City, 509/633-0290, www.skydeckmotel.com, $80-120) is a modest place with a nice location. It's the only full-service lodging on the shores of Banks Lake.

Transportation

Grand Coulee Dam is about 25 miles north of U.S. 2, the nearest major highway. Coming from the west, exit onto Route 155, which follows the shore of Banks Lake up to the dam. The drive is 125 miles (2.5 hrs.) from Ellensburg and 230 miles (4 hrs.) from Seattle, with both trips via I-90 and Routes 283 and 17. From Spokane, take I-90, Route 2, and then Route 174 at the little town of Wilbur; the 90-mile drive takes about 1.75 hours.

BANKS LAKE

Banks Lake defines the landscape as you drive to Grand Coulee Dam from the west. It's a 27-mile-long, clear-blue reservoir surrounded by the steep sides of the coulee. Since the early 1950s it's been dammed at both ends and filled with water that's pumped 280 feet uphill from Lake Roosevelt through enormous pipes visible on the west side of Grand Coulee Dam. Canals drawing water from the reservoir irrigate farmland stretching south to the Oregon border. The banks of the coulee are gorgeous in a parched way, and the area is busy with camping and boating. Many visitors to the dam stay here.

★ Sun Lakes-Dry Falls State Park

Sun Lakes-Dry Falls State Park (34875 Park Lake Rd. NE, 509/632-5583, http://parks.state.wa.us/298, Discover Pass required for parking), at the south end of massive Banks Lake, seven miles southwest of Coulee City on Route 17, is famous for the giant waterfall that once flowed here. Dry Falls was the earth's largest known fall, reaching 400 feet high and over 3.5 miles across. It was one of the results of the Missoula Floods that occurred some 17,000 years ago, when ice dams that restrained massive Lake Missoula, in what's now northern Idaho, repeatedly gave way. The flooding was of biblical proportions—imagine a 200-foot-high wall of water stretching as far as the eye can see. It carved out the landscape of much of Washington, from Dry Falls and the surrounding coulees in this area, known as the Channeled Scablands, all the way to the Columbia Gorge that marks the Washington-Oregon border. The water is gone, but the massive falls remain. They're a prime example of the region's beauty, and are especially picturesque at dusk. It's hard to take in the scene without feeling a sense of awe at the forces of nature.

The park covers 4,000 acres and has year-round camping plus horse trails, boating, swimming, and rainbow trout fishing. Concessions offer snacks, fishing supplies, horse rentals, and groceries. Ten or so smaller lakes dot the park; they're ancient plunge pools from the once-stupendous falls. A road leads east from Park Lake along the basalt cliff walls lining Meadow Creek to Deep Lake, and hiking trails provide access to other parts of the park.

Four miles north of the main park entrance along Route 17 is **Dry Falls Interpretive Center** (Mar.-mid-Sept. daily 9am-6pm). The center has information about the incredible geologic history of this area; outside, from cliff-edge viewpoints, you can gaze down at a cluster of lakes set at the base of the stark basalt falls. A steep path leads a half-mile down from the overlook to Dry Falls Lake.

Camping

Sun Lakes-Dry Falls State Park is open year-round for camping with 152 tent sites ($25-35), 39 utility spaces ($35-45), one dump station, six restrooms, and 12 showers. All

Sun Lakes-Dry Falls State Park

sites have fire pits. Sites can be reserved April 15-September 15 (888/226-7688, www.washington.goingtocamp.com, $7 reservation fee).

At the north end of the Banks Lake, **Steamboat Rock State Park** (51052 Rt. 155, 509/633-1304, http://parks.state.wa.us/590, Discover Pass required for parking) features the namesake rock, a striking landmark rising 800 feet above the water. The state park has a big, busy campsite often used by visitors to the dam, which is just eight miles away. The lake is used for swimming, fishing, and boating, and the area is starkly scenic, surrounded by stratified bluffs that look straight out of a John Ford Western. The park is open year-round and has 26 tent sites ($25-35), 136 utility spaces ($35-45), three cabins ($75), 12 boat-in sites ($25-35), one dump station, six restrooms, and six showers. Sites can be reserved April-October (888/226-7688, www.washington.goingtocamp.com, $7 reservation fee).

Transportation

The northern end of Banks Lake is 4 miles west of Grand Coulee Dam on Route 155. Sun Lakes-Dry Falls State Park is 40 miles (1 hr.) southwest of Grand Coulee Dam via Route 155, U.S. 2, and Route 17.

LAKE ROOSEVELT NATIONAL RECREATION AREA

Lake Roosevelt is the 130-mile-long segment of the Columbia River located above Grand Coulee Dam that was transformed into a reservoir when the dam was built. Most of it is part of the sprawling **Lake Roosevelt National Recreation Area** (509/633-9441, www.nps.gov/laro), a popular boating, waterskiing, fishing, camping, and swimming destination. The reservoir backs up not just the Columbia River waters, but also parts of the Spokane, Kettle, Colville, and Sanpoil Rivers.

Lake Roosevelt is primarily used by residents of Spokane and the smaller towns within the region. Most people out on the lake are either here on a day trip, camping,

or spending the night in a private home, and as a result the area is short on restaurants and overnight accommodations. For a meal or a motel, the towns around Grand Coulee Dam are your best bet.

Fort Spokane

The main historic site within the recreation area is **Fort Spokane,** located along Route 25 where the Spokane River meets Lake Roosevelt. From 1880 to 1898 the fort was a U.S. Army outpost, growing by the 1890s to have 45 buildings. It later served as the home office for the Bureau of Indian Affairs and as a tuberculosis sanatorium and Indian hospital before being abandoned in 1929.

In 1960 the fort was transferred to the National Park Service. It restored the four remaining structures, which can be viewed on a self-guided walking tour. The brick guardhouse is now the **Fort Spokane Visitor Center and Museum** (44150 District Office Ln., 509/754-7893, Memorial Day-Labor Day daily 9:30am-5pm), where you can see exhibits and a 10-minute film about the fort. Most summer weekends there's some sort of ranger-led activity—call or check www.nps.gov/laro to learn what's going on. The **Sentinel Trail** leads from the fort up to a bluff with expansive views.

Scenic Drives

If you enjoy exploring beautiful terrain by car along back roads, you can spend a happy half day behind the wheel here. A three-hour, 140-mile loop takes you along the shore of the lake from **Inchelium** to **Kettle Falls** on Route 25, west over **Sherman Pass** (Washington's highest year-round-accessible pass) to the mining town of **Republic** on Route 20, south on Route 21 to the junction with Route 68, and east on 68 back to Inchelium.

As well as skirting the lake, the drive takes you past farm- and pastureland, forests, and high scenic outlooks, with numerous opportunities to stop and stretch your legs on a short trail. If you're coming from Grand Coulee Dam you can access the loop via Manilla Creek Road and Route 21, which adds another 50 minutes to the drive each way.

Sports and Recreation

SWIMMING

No lifeguards patrol the lake, but popular swimming beaches are found at **Spring Canyon** and **Keller Ferry** in lower Lake Roosevelt, and at **Fort Spokane** and **Porcupine Bay** on the Spokane River arm. The water in the Spokane River arm tends to be five to eight degrees warmer than the rest of the lake, where it averages in the 60s in June, rising to the 70s in August.

BOATING

Twenty-two public boat launches line Lake Roosevelt, but some are closed when water levels are low; call the Bureau of Reclamation (800/824-4916) to find out the current status. All boats must have a launch permit ($8 for seven consecutive days, $45 for a year, available at the launches).

FISHING

A state fishing license is required to fish in the recreation area; pick one up—along with current fishing regulations—at area marinas and hardware and sporting goods stores. The 30-plus species of fish inhabiting these waters include walleye (more than 90 percent of the annual catch), rainbow trout, and enormous white sturgeon, which can weigh upward of 300 pounds. Other residents include kokanee salmon, yellow perch, bass, cutthroat trout, perch, and pike.

The best months for fishing are May, June, and September to November. In midsummer the fish retreat to cooler waters deep in the lake or in neighboring streams. Popular fishing spots are at the points where rivers and streams meet the lake—the Sanpoil River, Wilmont Creek, Hunters Creek, Kettle River, and others—and the waters near high shoreline cliffs, such as those near Keller Ferry.

Camping

Campers can stay at one of 27 campgrounds (11 of these are accessible only by boat) that line Lake Roosevelt. None of the campgrounds offer hookups or showers, but all of them have restrooms and most have running water. There's no charge for the boat-in sites; for the rest you pay $18 per night from May through September and $9 the rest of the year. No reservations are accepted. For a list of campgrounds check out the recreational area's website, www.nps.gov/laro.

Transportation

Grand Coulee Dam is the southwest terminus of Lake Roosevelt, but most of the recreational activity takes place farther up lake. From the dam to Fort Spokane it's a 50-mile drive south on Route 174, east on U.S. 2, and back north on Route 25, requiring a little over an hour. It's a 60-mile drive northwest from Spokane to Fort Spokane via U.S. 2 and Route 25, and also takes just over an hour.

Spokane

Spokane's population of 215,000 makes it the second-largest city in Washington. Like Seattle, it was leveled by a great fire in the 19th century and rebuilt using brick. Also like Seattle, it has an impressive park system, and hosted a world's fair (in 1974; Seattle's was in 1962) that made a permanent impact on the city's landscape.

Despite the similarities, no one would confuse the two cities. Spokane, located just 18 miles from the Idaho border, is the main urban center for the largely rural Inland Northwest (roughly the region between the Cascades and the Rockies). It has the friendly, laid-back atmosphere of an overgrown town, with an easily walkable downtown surrounded by quiet

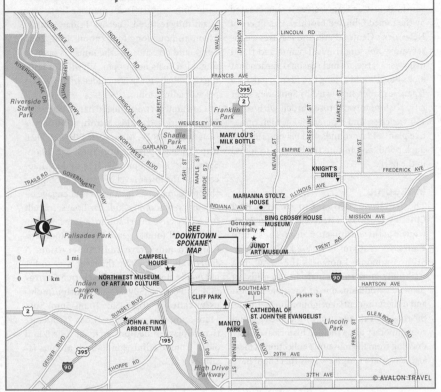

Greater Spokane

residential neighborhoods and, beyond that, the vast countryside.

SIGHTS
Riverfront Park

The city's centerpiece is **Riverfront Park** (507 N. Howard St., 509/625-6601, http://my.spokanecity.org/riverfrontpark, daily 5am-midnight), the 100-acre site of the Expo '74 World's Fair located along the Spokane River where it runs through the heart of downtown. In 2014 Spokane initiated a major five-year redevelopment for the park focused primarily on improving existing features. When the work is completed in 2019 the SkyRide gondola over **Spokane Falls** will be extended, the **U.S. Pavilion** will be a large-events space, a new rotunda will house the

hand-carved 1909 **Looff Carousel,** and the skating rink will be enhanced by an adjoining ice ribbon—an ice-covered path looping through the park.

As work proceeds, much of the park will remain open. Stroll around flower-bedecked paths, follow a sculpture walk that takes you past more than 20 works of art, cross a suspension bridge to Canada Island, and snap a photo of the park's most distinctive landmark, the riverside clock tower that for many years was part of the Great Northern Railroad depot.

Manito Park

While Riverfront Park is Spokane's most conspicuous green space, **Manito Park** (1702 S. Grand Blvd., 509/625-6200, www.

manitopark.org, daily 8am-dusk, free), in a residential neighborhood two miles to the south, is just as impressive. It was created by the famed Olmsted brothers, designers of New York's Central Park, and features a conservatory housing tropical plants and floral displays; a large, formal seasonal garden that looks like it could belong to a French palace; a Japanese garden supported by Spokane's sister city, Nishinomiya; a rose garden with some 150 varieties; and a perennial garden of native plants. Playgrounds and playing fields, a duck pond, and hiking trails are also found in the park.

Museums

The **Northwest Museum of Arts and Culture** (2316 W. 1st. Ave., 509/456-3931, www.northwestmuseum.org, Tues. and Thurs.-Sun. 10am-5pm, Wed. 10am-8pm, $10), commonly known as the MAC, is a strikingly modern anomaly in the midst of Browne's Addition, one of Spokane's oldest and toniest residential neighborhoods. Inside, the rotating exhibits usually include regional contemporary art, a themed historical display drawing from the museum's collection of local artifacts, and a traveling show that could have an art or a history focus. A highlight of the MAC is the **Campbell House** next door, an early-20th-century Tudor mansion that's been beautifully restored. Tuesday-Friday, you can go on an hour-long tour (noon, 1pm, 2pm, 3pm), and on Saturday the house is open to unguided visits noon-4pm. Viewing or touring Campbell House is included in the MAC's price of admission.

Downtown, two affiliated hands-on museums are targeted at kids. **Mobius Children's Museum** (808 W. Main Ave., 509/321-7121, http://mobiusspokane.org, Tues.-Sat. 10am-5pm, Sun. 11am-5pm, $8, free under 1), located on the lower level of River Park Square shopping mall, has play areas that engage elementary-school-age kids for hours, including a play city, an art studio, a stage, and an "enchanted forest" geared toward toddlers. Children must have adult supervision. A short walk away, along the river next to the old power station, **Mobius Science Center** (331 N. Post St., 509/321-7133, http://mobiusspokane.org, Tues.-Sat. 10am-5pm, Sun. 11am-5pm, $8, free under 1) has 75 interactive displays aimed primarily at kids 8 and older. Combo admission to both Mobius facilities is $12.

Riverfront Park

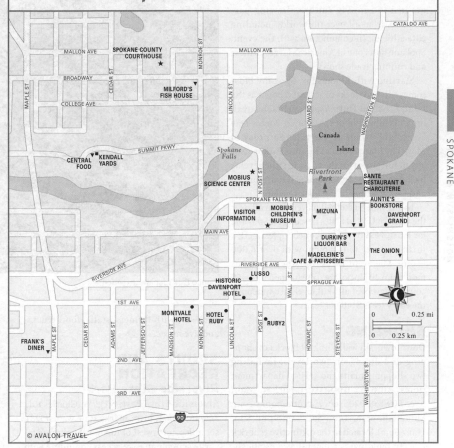

Downtown Spokane

© AVALON TRAVEL

Historic Buildings

Spokane has a couple of landmark buildings worth a look. Just north of the river, a couple of blocks from the Kendall Yards area, is the **Spokane County Courthouse** (W. Broadway at Jefferson St.). Built in 1895 and modeled after a pair of French chateaus, the ornate courthouse was designed by W. A. Ritchie, a 29-year-old at the time who, amazingly, had no previous design experience. His architectural training came from a correspondence course.

At the south end of downtown, **Cathedral of St. John the Evangelist** (1125 S. Grand Blvd., 509/838-4277, www.stjohns-cathedral. org, Mon.-Sat. 9am-4pm, free) is an impressive example of Gothic architecture, complete with stained glass windows and stone carvings. Free 45-minute guided tours are available on the first, third, and fifth Fridays and second and fourth Saturdays of every month 11am-2pm. The cathedral also hosts occasional concerts.

FESTIVALS AND EVENTS

On the first Sunday of every May, Spokane draws over 40,000 runners for the 12K **Lilac**

Bloomsday Run (www.bloomsdayrun.org). Over four decades the event has become ingrained in running culture, drawing participants from all over the world, including elite athletes. In conjunction with the event, Spokane hosts one of America's largest fitness and running trade shows.

Starting with Bloomsday, Spokane blossoms with two weeks of activity known as the Lilac Festival (http://spokanelilacfestival.org), culminating in the Armed Forces Day Torchlight Parade on the third Saturday of May. The lilac garden at Manito Park is usually in full bloom for the festival. Other events include concerts, an amateur golf tournament, and the crowning of the Lilac Queen.

In late June basketball players from all over the western United States descend on Spokane for Hoopfest (www.spokanehoopfest.net), a three-on-three tournament with over 6,000 teams. The event takes over the streets, as more than 40 blocks are transformed into 450 courts. Players of all skill levels are welcome; the entry fee is $140 per team.

Manito Park's Japanese garden

SHOPPING

Downtown, skywalks link 14 blocks of shopping and dining on two levels, including two shopping malls and several department stores. Auntie's Bookstore (402 W. Main Ave., 509/838-0206, www.auntiesbooks.com, Mon. 9am-6pm, Tues.-Sat. 9am-9pm, Sun. 11am-6pm), located in the distinctive redbrick Liberty Building, is a much-loved establishment. The spacious shop sells new and used titles, hosts frequent readings, and also stocks games, puzzles, and Spokane souvenirs.

On the north side of the river, across from downtown, the residential and retail development Kendall Yards (www.kendallyards.com) has transformed an old rail yard into a hip neighborhood. A stroll here takes you past boutiques, galleries, and wine, beer, and cider tasting rooms, along with viewpoints over the river and lots of public art. On Wednesday evenings May-early October a night market (http://kendallnightmarket.org) fills the main commercial road, Summit Parkway, with farmers' stalls, food trucks, and live music.

SPORTS AND RECREATION
Riverside State Park

Riverside State Park (9711 W. Charles Rd., 509/465-5064, http://parks.state.wa.us/573), six miles northwest of town, is Spokane's favorite spot for an easy-access commune with nature. The 14,000-acre park sits along the Spokane River and encompasses open ponderosa pine forests with a grassy understory. It's a popular place for camping, hiking, cycling, bird watching, and boating. From mid-May through mid-September kayaks and canoes are available for rent at the park's Nine Mile Recreation Area. Most visitors reach the park via Nine Mile Road on the north side of the river, though there are also several convoluted routes along the south shore.

A favorite hiking destination in the park is the Bowl and Pitcher area. A trail leaves the parking area and crosses a suspension

Bing Crosby and Gonzaga

Spokane's most famous native son, the best-selling crooner Bing Crosby, has close ties to Gonzaga University. He grew up in a house on the edge of campus, and when he came of age enrolled in the school as a pre-law student. The official record contends that he dropped out a semester short of earning his degree to pursue his singing career, but an alternative story has him getting kicked out for pushing a piano through a 4th-floor window.

Crosby wound up receiving an honorary doctorate from Gonzaga in 1937, after he'd achieved worldwide fame. Today his boyhood home is the **Bing Crosby House Museum** (508 E. Sharp Ave., 509/313-3847, Mon.-Fri. 9am-4:30pm, Sat. 1pm-4pm, free), which displays some original furniture and hundreds of mementos from his career, including gold records and a replica of his 1945 Best Actor Academy Award for *Going My Way*.

Regardless of whether you're a Crosby fan, Gonzaga is a pleasant place to visit, with an idyllic campus on the north shore of the Spokane River, 5 minutes by car or 20 by foot from downtown. It has a sculpture garden along the waterfront, and in front of its athletic center is a bronze statue of the school's bulldog mascot—a popular photo op, especially for young fans of the basketball team. The university's **Jundt Art Museum** (200 E. Desmet Ave., 509/313-6843, www.gonzaga. edu, Mon.-Sat. 10am-4pm, free) is home to a Dale Chihuly chandelier and three exhibition rooms showing temporary exhibits and pieces from permanent collection, which includes a Rodin sculpture and European prints.

bridge to connect with a network of paths. The giant volcanic formations that give Bowl and Pitcher its name stand along the fast-flowing river and are visible from the bridge and from a dramatic overlook. Get here by heading northwest from town on Route 291 (Nine Mile Rd.) and turning left onto Rifle Club Road, then left again on Aubrey L. White Parkway after a half mile. The park entrance and the Bowl and Pitcher are on the right after 1.7 miles.

Mount Spokane State Park

The 14,000-acre **Mount Spokane State Park** (N. 26107 Mt. Spokane Park Dr., 509/238-4258, parks.state.wa.us/549, Discover Pass required for parking), 30 miles northeast of the city on Route 206, encompasses 5,881-foot Mount Spokane and 5,306-foot Mount Kit Carson. Here you can hike, mountain bike, and camp in the summer, and downhill and cross-country ski in the winter.

A narrow, winding road (no RVs) climbs to the summit of Mount Spokane, where you can stop for a picnic at the Civilian Conservation Corps-built Vista House. The 360-degree view encompasses the entire region, including parts of Idaho, Montana, British Columbia, and Alberta. Dirt roads lead to other areas, and hiking trails crisscross the park.

FOOD

Spokane's dining choices include a mix of lost-in-time old-school classics and of-the-moment farm-to-table restaurants.

Breakfast and Lunch

Knight's Diner (2909 N. Market St., 509/484-0015, www.knightsdiner.com, Tues.-Sat. 6:30am-2pm, Sun. 7:30am-2pm, $9-14) is in a nondescript commercial area four miles northeast of downtown, but it's worth going a little out of your way for breakfast at this 70-year-old landmark. The setting is an old railroad car with a long mahogany counter, from where you can exchange banter with speedy, friendly waitresses and watch the cook work a mountain of hash browns. The menu is classic diner food. Look for the huckleberry pancakes in season.

You get a similar experience in a more central location at **Frank's Diner** (1516 W. 2nd Ave., 509/747-8798, http://franksdiners.com, daily 7am-9pm, $8-18), which also occupies an old train car. It's a bigger, busier operation—an addition to the car with booths accommodates more diners—but the food is the same style as Knight's, right down to the huckleberry pancakes.

In the heart of downtown, **Madeleine's Café & Patisserie** (415 W. Main Ave., 509/624-2253, Mon.-Fri. 7:45am-5pm, Sat.-Sun. 8:30am-5pm, $8-12) is a busy, hip bakery where you can pick up a pastry and coffee or take a table and choose from a menu that mixes American classics (corned beef hash, BLT) with some French influences (crepes, croque madame).

Mary Lou's Milk Bottle (802 W. Garland Ave., 509/325-1772, Tues.-Sat. 11am-8pm, Sun.-Mon. 11am-4pm, $5-9) is another local institution that's a little off the beaten path. It's been serving burgers, shakes, and homemade ice cream in a distinctive milk-bottle-shaped building on the north end of town since 1932.

Eclectic

Next door to Auntie's Bookstore, **Santé Restaurant & Charcuterie** (404 W. Main St., 509/315-4613, http://santespokane.com, daily 9am-9pm, $24-35) doubles as a hangout where you can linger over a cup of coffee or a glass of wine, and a sophisticated restaurant specializing in locally sourced meats, usually paired in creative ways with seasonal vegetables.

Despite the name, **Durkin's Liquor Bar** (415 W. Main Ave., 509/863-9501, www.durkinsliquorbar.com, Mon.-Wed. 11am-11pm, Thurs.-Sat. 11am-1am, $14-27) is a full-service restaurant. The lively open kitchen turns out farm-to-table cuisine that's a little more down-to-earth than Santé across the street—along with fancier meat and seafood options, the menu includes fish-and-chips, a burger, and a fried baloney sandwich. In the basement there's a faux speakeasy bar pouring craft cocktails.

Mizuna (214 N. Howard St., 509/747-2004, www.mizuna.com, Mon.-Sat. 11am-10pm, Sun. 4pm-10pm, $20-36) presents you with two menus, one vegetarian and one predominantly meat, both featuring simple but creative preparations that emphasize fresh ingredients. The brick dining room in an old downtown building is a comfortable place for a low-key, laid-back meal.

Just north of the river in the Kendall Yards development, **Central Food** (1335 W. Summit Pkwy., 509/315-8036, http://eatcentralfood.com, Mon.-Sat. 8am-9pm, Sun. 8am-3pm, $15-24) does a nice job of balancing New American-style food with a French bistro sensibility. It's a casual neighborhood restaurant serving three meals a day with a menu varied enough to suit most tastes, whether you're hankering for a burger, kale salad, or cassoulet. Patio seating has a view of the water.

Seafood

For an old-fashioned indulgence, try **Milford's Fish House** (719 N. Monroe St., 509/326-7251, Mon.-Sat. 5pm-9pm, Sun. 4pm-8pm, $24-31). It's the kind of place where you dine in a paneled booth with a white tablecloth while Sinatra plays in the background. The fresh grilled and roasted seafood is dependably good, and if you're not feeling like fish you can opt for steaks or chops.

ACCOMMODATIONS

Strictly in terms of lodging, Spokane is one of the best destinations in the state. There are lots of choices, from the luxurious to the quaint to the hip, all at rates that are half (or less) of what you'd pay in Seattle. Along with the places listed here there are many reliable chain hotels.

Under $100

Hotel Ruby (901 W. 1st Ave., 509/747-1041, www.hotelrubyspokane.com, $80-140) takes a standard motel and jazzes it up with some design touches to give it a hip attitude. At the end of the day it's a comfortable place to stay—in a good location five blocks from Riverfront Park—for a reasonable price. **Ruby2** (123 S. Post St., 509/838-8504, www.hotelruby2.com, $78-102) applies the same concept to a refurbished old motor court a block away from its sister hotel.

$100-150

Spokane's oldest lodging, the **Montvale Hotel** (1005 W. 1st Ave., 509/747-1919, http://montvalespokane.com, $96-147), isn't a luxurious spot like the Davenport down the street, but for half the price you get character and a fair amount of comfort, with savvy, professional management from the same owners who run the Ruby hotels.

The B&B **Marianna Stoltz House** (427 E. Indiana Ave., 509/483-4316, www.mariannastoltzhouse.com, $95-125) occupies a classic American foursquare home built in 1908, located on a tree-lined street near Gonzaga University. The four antiques-furnished guest rooms all have private baths, and a wide veranda and spacious parlor add to the homey appeal.

$150-200

Hotel Lusso (808 W. Sprague Ave., 800/899-1482, www.davenporthotelcollection.com, $129-204), under the same management as the Davenport Hotel, is a luxurious boutique lodging dating from 1890. The 48 rooms are in two adjacent buildings joined by an attractive lobby.

$200-250

Spokane residents take pride in having what may be the grandest hotel in the state, the century-old ★ **Historic Davenport Hotel** (10 South Post St., 800/899-1482, www.davenporthotelcollection.com, $159-264 d). It's been thoroughly renovated, adding contemporary features to classic design. From the lobby to the guest room showers there's marble everywhere. Given the level of luxury, it's a bargain.

The biggest of the downtown Davenport hotels, the **Davenport Grand** (333 W. Spokane Falls Blvd., 800/918-9344, www.davenporthotelcollection.com, $154-244 d), has over 700 rooms in a prime location across the street from Riverfront Park. The design here is sleekly modern, and from the higher floors you get a view over the city.

INFORMATION AND SERVICES

Get information downtown in the River Front Square mall at the information kiosk of **Visit Spokane** (808 W. Main Ave., 888/776-5263, www.visitspokane.com, Mon.-Thurs. 10am-5pm, Fri.-Sat. 10am-6pm, Sun. 11am-4pm). Request maps and brochures by phone or on the website.

TRANSPORTATION
Air

Spokane International Airport (9000 W. Airport Dr., 509/455-6455, www.spokaneairports.net), seven miles west of town, is served by major airlines including Alaska, Delta, Southwest, American, and United.

Train

Amtrak's Empire Builder (509/624-5144 or 800/872-724, www.amtrak.com) has daily service to Spokane from Chicago and Minneapolis, continuing west to Ephrata, Wenatchee, Everett, Edmonds, and Seattle or southwest to Pasco, Wishram, Bingen, Vancouver, and Portland. Spokane's train station is located at 221 West 1st Avenue.

Bus

Greyhound (509/624-5251 or 800/231-2222, www.greyhound.com) provides nationwide bus connections from the terminal at 221 West 1st Avenue.

Spokane Transit (509/328-7433, www.spokanetransit.com) serves downtown Spokane and the Cheney area. Routes and schedules are on the website. Get information at the Visit Spokane information kiosk.

Car

It's a straight 280-mile, 4-hour drive east on I-90 from Seattle to Spokane. Spokane is 90 miles from Grand Coulee Dam, heading south on Route 174 and then east on Route 2, about a 1.75-hour drive.

Background

The Landscape

GEOGRAPHY AND CLIMATE

Visitors expecting only old-growth forest, snowcapped mountains, and a steady drizzle will be surprised to find that when it comes to geography and climate, Washington has a split personality. The Cascade mountain range, which extends 600 miles from Canada to Oregon, runs through the middle of the state and acts as the great dividing line. The image of Washington as a land of evergreens and moss holds true to the west of the mountains, but much of the territory to the east resembles the Great Plains, with big sky and mile after mile of scrub and irrigated farmland. The mountains wring the moisture out of weather systems, dumping precipitation on their western flanks and leaving the east side dry and sunny.

The Salish Sea and Puget Sound take a bite out Washington's top left corner and help isolate the Olympic Peninsula, the most idiosyncratic part of the state. It's the northwesternmost region in the contiguous United States, and also the rainiest. At its heart are the Olympic Mountains, a smaller and less volatile range than the Cascades.

The Olympics are among the world's youngest mountains, just one to two million years old. Though not exceptionally tall (Mount Olympus is the highest at 7,965 feet), the Olympics are the root cause of the peninsula's dramatically varied weather. Storms coming in from the Pacific dump 70-100 inches of annual rainfall on the coastal plains, and 150 inches or more (with a record of 184 inches at the Wynoochee River oxbow) in the rain forests on the western and southwestern slopes. Northeast of the range, in the rain shadow, is the driest area in western Washington.

Western Washington

Aside from the Olympic rain forests, most of the "wet side of the mountains" doesn't get an unusually large amount of rain. Seattle averages 37 inches annually—less than New York or Houston. What makes the area distinctive is the way the rain comes down. There are almost never thunderstorms or torrential downpours. Instead you get an intermittent light rain that can persist for weeks at a time. By some measures Seattle has the fewest sunny days of any major city in the United States.

Most of the precipitation comes from November through April. When you factor in the region's northern latitude, resulting in days with less than nine hours of light in December and January, winter can feel pretty gloomy. If there's an upside, it's that in Seattle and the lowlands of western Washington winters are mild, with little snowfall and temperatures that seldom drop below freezing.

For a dose of wintry weather you just have to head for the mountains. Mount Rainier and Mount Baker are two of the snowiest places on earth. In the winter of 1971-1972, Mount Rainier's Paradise Ranger Station received a record 1,122 inches of snow. (In 2014-2015 it hit a record low, 266 inches.) Cascade ski areas usually open in November and remain open through early spring; Mount Baker typically has the longest ski season in the state.

In spring, the clouds give way to partly sunny days, and it's not unusual to have six weeks of clear skies in July and August. Summer daytime temperatures are usually in the 70s and 80s, with perhaps half a dozen 90-degree days each year. Surprisingly, given western Washington's reputation for moisture, the humidity is low. If winter in western Washington is gloomy, summer is glorious.

Previous: Columbia Hills State Park petroglyphs; Grove of the Patriarchs Trail in Mount Rainier National Park.

The one shortcoming of summer is that coastal waters never warm up enough for comfortable swimming. Water temperatures along the Pacific Coast and in the Strait of Juan de Fuca and Puget Sound average in the mid-40s in winter, rising to the mid-50s at the height of summer; some small coves and bays get into the 60s. Most swimming and waterskiing is done in the region's lakes.

Eastern Washington

Compared with western Washington, the "dry side of the mountains" has hotter summers, colder winters, more snow, and less rain. The area from the Cascade Range east across the Columbia River Basin to the Palouse hills has hot, dry weather with anywhere from 7 to 15 inches of annual rainfall. Summer daytime temperatures are typically in the 90s, with many days each year over 100; the state's record high of 118 degrees occurred at Ice Harbor Dam near Pasco in 1961. The upside is that it's not humid. July and August are the driest months, often devoid of any precipitation; what rain there is generally comes in the form of thunderstorms. Winters bring 10-35 inches of snowfall and daytime temperatures in the 20s and 30s.

The Okanogan and Methow Valleys, in the north-central part of the state, have ideal winter conditions for cross-country skiing. Annual snowfalls range 30-70 inches, beginning in November and staying on the ground through March or April. January high temperatures hover around 30, with some nights dropping below zero.

Much of Washington from the Columbia River east to the Spokane area and the Palouse hills gets less than 12 inches of rainfall a year, technically qualifying the region as desert. It is in fact the northern end of the Great American Desert, which runs from the Mexican border almost all the way to Canada. Today it doesn't resemble Death Valley because of a vast irrigation system drawing water from the mighty Columbia and its tributaries. There are well over half a million acres of irrigated fields, divided neatly into uniform squares.

Near the state's eastern boundary with Idaho the elevation gradually rises and the weather moderates slightly. The clouds are forced upward, and as they cool they drop some of their precipitation: Rainfall averages 10-20 inches per year, with 20-40 inches of snow.

western Washington's Hoh Rain Forest

Plants and Animals

Washington has widely varied flora and fauna that reflect its diverse climate and geography. The Pacific coast, Puget Sound, Olympic Peninsula, Cascades, and arid eastern Washington each support a unique population of birds, animals, and plants.

FORESTS

Washington's state tree, the western hemlock, is widely used in the lumber industry for pulpwood; it and the Douglas fir are two of the most abundant low-elevation trees in the state. Above 3,000 feet, Pacific silver fir and mountain hemlock predominate. A couple of eye-catching varieties are the big-leaf maple, with leaves that can span up to a foot across, and the Pacific madrone, or madrona, characterized by waxy evergreen leaves and peeling reddish bark. Other common trees are the western red cedar, Sitka spruce, grand fir, black cottonwood, red alder, and vine maple. Northeast Washington and parts of the Cascades are also home to lodgepole pine, western larch, western white pine, ponderosa pine, and Engelmann spruce.

Old-Growth Forest

The lumber industry has harvested and replanted large parts of Washington's timberland, but old-growth forest is protected in Washington's three national parks (Olympic, Mount Rainier, and North Cascades) and is found in patches elsewhere. "Old growth" is defined as at least 250 years old, but some stands are far older, approaching 1,000 years.

Because the tall trees moderate temperatures and hold much of the snow, original forests are more stable than cutover areas and less susceptible to climatic extremes. This helps the survival of forest animals by allowing them to roam throughout the year and by creating a multilayered understory of trees, bushes, and herbs that support a large variety of animal life. Defects in the old trees and standing dead trees, called snags, provide nesting sites for birds, squirrels, and other animals, and fallen trees create nutrient-rich mulch as they decay.

Olympic Rain Forest

In Olympic National Park, the Hoh, Queets,

eastern Washington scrubland

and Quinault River valleys are all part of the Olympic rain forest, an area unique in the world. It averages more than 150 inches of rain annually and produces some of the world's biggest trees. The largest known western hemlock and Sitka spruce grow in the Quinault Valley, the largest Douglas fir is in Queets, and the largest red alder is in the Hoh. The four major species here—the Sitka spruce, western red cedar, Douglas fir, and western hemlock—all grow very tall, averaging 200 feet, with many topping 300.

The height of the trees isn't the only fascinating aspect of the rain forest. You're immediately struck by how green everything is, and how pristine. These areas have never been logged; what you see is nature in essentially an unaltered state. Enormous trees spring out of the long-since-decayed "nursery logs" that gave them life, with club moss eerily draping the branches. Ferns and mosses cover the ground in a thick carpet. Though most rainfall occurs fall-spring, even summer days feel damp from high humidity and ocean fog.

the rhododendron, Washington's state flower

RHODODENDRONS

The state flower, the coast rhododendron, is a regular feature in western Washington gardens. About 500 pure rhododendron species are hardy to the region's climate, along with several hundred more greenhouse varieties, which are cross-pollinated to produce thousands of hybrids. Impressive public rhododendron gardens are on Whidbey and Bainbridge Islands and in the towns of Federal Way and Brinnon. They're at their peak in spring and early summer.

MARINELIFE
Salmon

There's no creature more central to the ecology and the character of Washington than the salmon. For thousands of years they populated every waterway in the region in unfathomable numbers. Throughout that time they've been a mainstay in the diets of humans and many other creatures, from orcas to eagles to bears.

In the 20th century human encroachment, in the form of dammed rivers, water pollution, and overfishing, had a devastating effect on the salmon population. By the end of the century wild salmon were no longer found in 40 percent of their historic breeding habitat in the Pacific Northwest, and 17 species traditionally common to Washington were identified as threatened or endangered under the Endangered Species Act.

Federal and state salmon recovery efforts in recent years have been varied and far-reaching. The many-pronged endeavor includes establishing pollution controls, decreasing fishing, maintaining habitats, breaching dams, and building fish ladders. Salmon hatcheries, which populate Washington rivers with millions of fry every year, have been a mixed blessing, as the hatchery-raised fish have taken on characteristics damaging to the wild population. All told, the recovery efforts have started showing positive outcomes, but it's a complicated attempt to balance human and natural needs, often with unanticipated results.

Washington has five salmon species: chinook, sockeye, coho, pink, and chum. Chinook, also known as king, are the largest, growing up to 125 pounds. Pink are the smallest and most abundant.

Orcas (Killer Whales)

The orca, or killer whale, is the largest member of the family Delphinidae, a classification that includes toothed whales and dolphins. They are highly social, traveling in groups known as pods consisting of up to 40 individuals. Families stay together, protecting the young and mourning their dead. Females are typically 16-23 feet long and weigh 3,000-6,000 pounds, while males measure 20-26 feet and weigh 8,000-12,000 pounds, with dorsal fins up to 6.5 feet high and tail flukes spanning 9 feet. Unencumbered by their size, orcas can travel at speeds upward of 30 mph.

The name "killer whale" derives from the fact they consume warm-blooded prey. Transient pods, which range for hundreds of miles, eat anything from seals and otters to seabirds, dolphins, fish, and squid. Resident pods, which remain within a more limited range (such as Puget Sound), generally eat only fish—mostly salmon, rockfish, and cod. Although there have been rare instances of transient orcas attacking people, they don't treat humans as prey.

Three resident pods, totaling about 80 members and collectively known as the J clan, live in Puget Sound and along the Washington coast. The most frequent sightings are around the San Juan Islands, especially in Haro Strait to the west of San Juan Island. The clan's small population, declining prey, and threats from pollution have placed it on the endangered species list. Transient pods also occasionally swim into the area but don't stay long.

Gray Whales

Every spring, tour boats leave the docks at Westport and a few other coastal towns for a close-up look at the migrating California gray whales. These enormous animals, which can grow 42 feet long and weigh upward of 30 tons, migrate from the Bering and Chukchi Seas to the breeding lagoons off Baja California in winter, passing the Washington coast southbound in November and December and northbound from April to June. They're easily identified by their gray color, the absence of a dorsal fin, and bumpy ridges on their backs; their faces are generally covered with patches of barnacles and orange whale lice. Occasionally a group of gray

BACKGROUND
PLANTS AND ANIMALS

Leavenworth salmon hatchery

whales comes into Puget Sound, but most follow the outer coastline.

Porpoises

Visitors often think that the black-and-white sea creatures riding the bow waves of their ferry or tour boat are baby killer whales, but these playful characters are **Dall's porpoises.** They're commonly seen in the Strait of Juan de Fuca and frequently travel south through the Admiralty Inlet, occasionally getting as far south as Tacoma. Dall's porpoises reach lengths of 6.5 feet and weigh up to 330 pounds. They feed primarily on squid and small fish.

In summer and early fall, schools of up to 100 **Pacific white-sided dolphins** enter the Strait of Juan de Fuca, traveling as far east as Port Angeles. They reach up to seven feet in length and 200 pounds, and are common off Japan and along the continental shelf from Baja California to the Gulf of Alaska. They have black backs, white shoulders and bellies, and hourglass-shaped streaks that run from their foreheads to their tails; the rear halves of their dorsal fins are light gray. Like Dall's porpoises, white-sided dolphins enjoy riding bow waves and often leap out of the water alongside a boat.

Seals and Sea Lions

Harbor seals are abundant throughout the Salish Sea. They can be seen at low tide sunning themselves on rocks in isolated areas. Though they appear clumsy on land, the 100- to 200-pound seals are graceful underwater, flipping and gliding beneath the surface for as long as 20 minutes.

The **California sea lion** is a seasonal visitor to the Strait of Juan de Fuca and northern Puget Sound, though on some mornings in winter and early spring their barking can be heard in shoreline communities as far south as Tacoma. The dark brown sea lions breed off the coast of California and Mexico in the early summer, and then some adventurous males migrate as far north as British Columbia for the winter.

Lighter-colored **Steller sea lions** are more numerous in the Puget Sound area, numbering up to several hundred in winter, primarily around Sucia Island, north of Orcas Island in the San Juans. Males grow to almost 10 feet in length and weigh over a ton, while females are commonly 6 feet long and 600 pounds. Both are almost white when wet; the male has a yellow mane.

Other Marine Creatures

Puget Sound is home to the largest species of **octopus** in the world, growing to 12 feet across and weighing 25 pounds or more. It's not dangerous and often plays with divers.

Another peculiar Puget Sound inhabitant is the **geoduck** (pronounced GOOee-duk, from the Indian word *gweduck,* meaning "dig deep"). These large clams can burrow five feet into the sand and usually weigh 4-5 pounds, with some reported to exceed 15 pounds. The fleshy part of the body is so large that neither it nor the siphon can completely withdraw into the shell. They're considered a delicacy; look for them on the menu at sushi bars and some high-end restaurants.

LAND ANIMALS

Washington is home to a wide variety of land mammals. Get out into the wilds of the state and you stand a chance of encountering mule deer, the rare Columbian white-tailed deer, Rocky Mountain and Roosevelt elk, bighorn sheep, mountain goats, black bears, and many smaller mammals, such as marmots, beavers, badgers, muskrat, nutrias, rabbits, and squirrels.

Endangered Species

There are several species of larger mammals fighting for survival in Washington. In the greatest peril are the **woodland caribou**—the last remaining herd in the Lower 48, consisting of only 12 members, lives in the isolated Selkirk Mountains of northeast Washington.

The **gray wolf,** exterminated from

Washington in the 1930s, made a reappearance in the 1990s, with small numbers moving into the North Cascades and Selkirks from British Columbia. There are now over 100 in 20 known packs. Most live in the northeast corner, but a pack has made it as far south as Walla Walla, and another lives in the Wenatchee area.

Lewis and Clark were the first explorers to comment on the **Columbian white-tailed deer,** a subspecies of mule deer that looks much like its cousins but is smaller and has a slightly longer tail and a white underside. It has a limited range along the lower Columbia River between Vancouver and the Pacific. The population in Washington is estimated at under 1,000, while approximately 6,000 live across the Columbia in Oregon.

Elk

One of the most impressive mammals on the Olympic Peninsula is the **Roosevelt elk**. About 5,000 of them live mostly inside the boundaries of Olympic National Park, where hunting them is forbidden. Washington has about 10 times more **Rocky Mountain elk,** another subspecies of North American elk with bigger antlers and a smaller body than the Roosevelt elk. Most live east of the Cascade crest.

Cougars

Washington has 2,000-2,500 cougars, also called mountain lions. They're the largest cats in North America, ranging 90-180 pounds and 6-8 feet in length (including the tail), and they've evoked mixed reactions over the years. From 1935 to 1960 the state paid a bounty to hunters for them. After the bounty was lifted they became subject to restrictive game-hunting regulations. In 1996 Washington voters enacted a ban on the use of hounds to hunt them for recreation. Cougars are predators who pose a threat to humans and to livestock, but they're also nocturnal loners who live primarily in undeveloped, unpopulated areas, making them a rare risk to people.

Bears

Black bears are fairly common throughout Washington, with a population of 25,000 to 30,000. The largest concentrations are on the Olympic Peninsula and in the northeast corner of the state. All of the black bears on the Olympic Peninsula are black; in other areas they may be black, brown, or honey colored. They'll eat anything, from carpenter ants to berries to salmon to elk corpses. They also have an appetite for anything edible you bring with you into the wilderness.

Grizzly bears are very rare in Washington—fewer than 10 are in the North Cascades and 25-30 are in the Selkirk Mountains along the Washington-Idaho border. Grizzlies once roamed throughout the Western states. Now an estimated 1,800 live in the Lower 48, mostly in remote parts of Wyoming, Idaho, and Montana.

BIRDS

The Washington State office of the **National Audubon Society** (206/652-2444, wa.audubon.org) has detailed information on birds and bird-watching in the state.

Bald Eagles

In 1978, when bald eagles came under the protection of the Endangered Species Act, there were just over 100 nests in Washington. Today the number is nearing 10 times that. In winter the year-round residents are joined by over a thousand migrating eagles, drawn to rivers throughout the state—particularly the Skagit, Sauk, Nooksack, and Stillaguamish—to feed on the carcasses of spawned-out salmon.

The adult bald eagle's distinctive white head and tail make it easy to spot. It takes four years to acquire the markings, so immature eagles are more difficult to identify. Their large nests, sometimes measuring over 8 feet wide and 12 feet high, are often found in old-growth spruce and fir; snags are popular for sunning, resting, and watching for the next meal.

The state's largest concentration of breeding bald eagles is on the San Juan Islands, where they tend to congregate amid the warm updrafts around Mount Constitution on Orcas Island and Mount Findlayson and Mount Dallas on San Juan Island. They're also commonly found along the Strait of Juan de Fuca.

Spotted Owls

Washington's most famous nighttime aerial hunter is the northern spotted owl, which lives in old-growth forests along the Pacific coast—forests filled with snags and broken trees that provide ideal nesting spots, and smaller, sheltered trees for young owls who can't yet fly properly and must climb from tree to tree. These forests are full of prey for spotted owls: flying squirrels, snowshoe hares, and wood rats.

Spotted owls are big eaters requiring large territories: 2,200 acres of forest will support only a single pair. The spotted owl's numbers are diminishing due to reduction in suitable forest and competition for prey from the more populous barred owl. An estimated 11,000 live along the West Coast, with 15 percent of that population in Washington.

Other Birds

Other noteworthy birds in western Washington include the **great blue heron,** frequently seen along harbors or suburban lakes. The **belted kingfisher** is a common year-round resident of Puget Sound and the Strait of Juan de Fuca. **Red-tailed hawks** are often perched along I-5 and other highways, waiting for a meal. Noisy **Steller's jays,** blue with a black head, are common in picnic areas and residential neighborhoods. In the Cascades and east of the mountains, the beautiful **mountain bluebird** is sometimes spotted in snags in open areas, and striking black-and-white **magpies** are frequently seen flitting over the highway.

History

EARLY HISTORY

Several archaeological sites in Washington support the theory that the Pacific Northwest was one of the first areas in North America to be populated by humans.

One of the most fascinating discoveries occurred in 1977, when Emanuel Manis, retired on a farm outside of Sequim, was digging a pond on his land and found two enormous tusks. A Washington State University archaeological team, led by zoologist Carl Gustafson, concluded these were 12,000-year-old mastodon tusks. The group discovered other mastodon bones, including a rib that contained the point of a prehistoric weapon used to kill the animal. The bones are now on display at the Sequim-Dungeness Museum in Sequim.

In the late 1950s and early 1960s, archaeologists uncovered numerous artifacts and partial skeletons in a cave overlooking the Palouse River near its confluence with the Snake River. Dated at more than 10,000 years old, this is one of the earliest known human occupation sites in North America.

Some 500 years ago a village at Ozette in the northwest corner of the Olympic Peninsula was covered by a mudflow, perhaps triggered by an earthquake. More than 50,000 well-preserved artifacts from the site have been found and cataloged; many are now on display at the Makah Cultural and Research Center in Neah Bay. Another noteworthy find was a group of thumbnail-sized quartz knife blades, believed to be 2,500 years old, discovered at a Hoko River site near Clallam Bay.

American Indians

According to one theory, the ancestors of American Indians originally crossed over to Alaska from Asia at the end of the last ice age, when the sea was 300 or more feet below present levels and the Bering Strait was a walkable passage. As these people settled throughout the Pacific Northwest, they adopted significantly different lifestyles on each side of the Cascades. West of the mountains, salmon, shellfish, whales, and other seafood made up a large part of the diet; western red cedars provided ample wood for canoes, houses, and medicinal teas and ointments. A mild climate and plentiful food allowed coastal tribes to stay in one place for most of the year. North-coast tribes became relatively prosperous. They often built longhouses—wooden structures up to 100 feet long and 40 feet wide that were inhabited by several families.

East of the Cascades, particularly near the Columbia River, salmon was an important part of the diet, though dependence on deer, elk, bear, squirrel, and rabbit led these tribes to live seminomadic lives. The introduction of the horse to eastern Washington in the mid-1700s made hunting much easier. Native Americans in eastern Washington lived in caves or rock shelters while hunting, as well as in well-insulated pit houses that could hold several families.

The arrival of Europeans was met with reactions ranging from tolerant acceptance to swift murder. Relations between the races can still be strained today, fueled by disputes over property, water, and fishing rights, as well as the interpretation of peace treaties signed in the 1850s. The majority of Indians don't live on reservations, though there are 28 of them scattered throughout Washington, the largest being the Yakama and Colville.

EXPLORERS ARRIVE

Archeological artifacts point to the possibility that the first foreigners on Washington shores were Chinese and Japanese fishermen whose boats had been blown far off course, but there's no indication that the Asian nations had any interest in exploring the unknown territory. The Europeans who came later were more curious, and more covetous.

Spanish Explorers

In 1592 a Greek explorer using the Spanish name Juan de Fuca sailed along Washington's coast and claimed to have discovered the fabled Northwest Passage, an inland waterway crossing North America from the Pacific to the Atlantic. Later explorers did find a waterway close to where de Fuca indicated, but it led only into Puget Sound.

Spain, hoping to regain some of its diminishing power and wealth, sent an expedition in the 1700s to explore the Pacific Northwest coast. In 1774, Juan Perez explored as far north as the Queen Charlotte Islands off Vancouver Island before he was forced to turn back by sickness and storms. He was the first European to describe the area's coastline and the Olympic Mountains.

In 1775 a larger Spanish expedition set out, led by Bruno de Heceta and Juan Francisco de la Bodega y Quadra. Heceta went ashore at Point Grenville, just north of Moclips on the Washington coast, and claimed all of the Northwest for Spain. Farther south, Bodega y Quadra sent seven men ashore to procure wood and water; they were killed in the first encounter between whites and coastal Indians. The ship departed without further conflict.

Quadra continued as far north as present-day Sitka, Alaska, while Heceta sailed north to Nootka Sound. Heceta failed to note the Strait of Juan de Fuca, but he did come across "the mouth of some great river," presumably the Columbia. The illness or death of much of his crew prevented further exploration.

Russian Voyages

Russian exploration of the Pacific Northwest began in the mid-1700s, when Vitus Bering led two expeditions to determine whether a land bridge connected Russia with North America. Bering sailed as far south as the Columbia River before turning back. The abundance of sea otters and beavers led Russian fur traders to establish posts from Alaska to northern California, sowing seeds for conflict with other nations hoping to stake a claim.

English and American Exploration

England dominated European claims on the

Northwest. In 1787, Charles Barkley and his wife, Frances, explored and named the Strait of Juan de Fuca. In 1788, John Meares named Mount Olympus and other features of the Olympic Peninsula.

An American, Robert Gray, sailed out of Boston to explore and trade along the Pacific Northwest coast in 1792. After stopping at Nootka Sound—the hot spot of trade on Vancouver Island—he worked his way south and spent three days anchored in today's Grays Harbor. Continuing south, Gray discovered the mouth of the Columbia River and traded there with the Chinook people before heading home.

The year 1792 was also when George Vancouver arrived on what would be the most consequential of the English expeditions. His goal was to explore inland waters and make another attempt to find the Northwest Passage. His team charted and described all navigable waterways and named many prominent features. Some of Washington's major geographical landmarks bear the names of Vancouver's lieutenants and crew, including Mount Baker, Mount Rainier, Whidbey Island, and Puget Sound.

Lewis and Clark Expedition

America's most famous overland expedition began in St. Louis in 1804. Meriwether Lewis and William Clark were under orders from President Thomas Jefferson to explore the territory acquired in the Louisiana Purchase, which extended as far west as the Rocky Mountains, and the land beyond all the way to the Pacific. In their final push after crossing the Rockies on foot, they headed down the Snake River in search of the Columbia, which they knew would lead them to the ocean. They found it in October 1805 and traveled downriver for many a "cloudy, rainey, disagreeable morning" before finally reaching the Pacific. They built a winter camp, Fort Clatsop, south of the river and spent a cold, wet winter there, plagued by sickness. In spring they headed for home.

EARLY SETTLERS

During the time between the early exploration and the permanent settlement of the Northwest, British and American trading posts emerged to take advantage of the area's abundant supply of beaver and sea otter pelts. The most influential of the traders, the Hudson's Bay Company, built its temporary headquarters on the north side of the Columbia, 100 miles inland at Fort Vancouver, across the river from the confluence with the Willamette.

The settlers planted crops (including the apples and wheat that are so important to Washington's economy today), raised livestock, and made the fort as self-sufficient as possible. At its peak, 500 people lived at or near the fort. Fort Vancouver served as a model for other Hudson's Bay Company posts at Spokane, Okanogan, and Nisqually. When settlers began arriving in droves and the beaver population diminished in the late 1840s, the Hudson's Bay Company was crowded out and moved its headquarters north to Fort Victoria on Vancouver Island.

Staking Claims

Between 1840 and 1860, 53,000 settlers moved west to Oregon Country to take advantage of the free land they could acquire through the Organic Act of 1843 and the Donation Land Law of 1850. Under the Organic Act of the Provisional Government, an adult white male could own a square mile of land by simply marking its boundaries, filing a claim, and building a cabin on the site. The Donation Land Law put additional restrictions on land claims: 320 acres were awarded to White or half-White males who were American citizens and had arrived prior to 1851; another 320 acres could be claimed by each man's wife. These and other restrictions effectively eliminated claims by Blacks, Asians, single women, and non-U.S. citizens, not to mention Indians who had been living on the land for centuries.

The promise of free land fueled the Great Migration of 1843, in which almost 900 settlers traveled to Oregon Country. Thousands more would follow over the ensuing years, most by way of the Oregon Trail from St. Joseph, Missouri, along the North Platte River, through southern Wyoming and southern Idaho into Oregon, then north to the Columbia River. Soon the route looked like a cleared road; wagon wheels dug ruts in stone that are still there today.

Washington's early settlers congregated around six fledgling cities: Seattle, Port Townsend, Oysterville, Centralia, Spokane, and Walla Walla. Smaller communities developed at Tumwater, Steilacoom, Olympia, and Fairhaven, now part of Bellingham.

The Pig War

By 1846, only the United States and England retained claims to Oregon Country. In that year the two nations agreed to a border at the 49th parallel from the Rockies to the main channel between Vancouver Island and the mainland, continuing through the center of the Strait of Juan de Fuca to the Pacific Ocean.

The "main channel" of the agreement was subject to conflicting interpretations—it could be either the Rosario Strait or the Haro Strait. As a result, the San Juan Islands became disputed territory. The British maintained a Hudson's Bay Company fort on San Juan, while American settlers began establishing farms. In 1859, one of the Americans shot and killed a British-owned pig, sparking a conflict that rapidly escalated. Within three months the English had a force of 2,140 troops, five warships, and 167 heavy guns arrayed against the American army's 461 soldiers and 14 cannons. No further shots were fired, but soldiers from both nations remained on the island for the next 13 years, until in 1872 Germany's Kaiser Wilhelm arbitrated a settlement awarding the San Juans to the Americans, thus ending the "Pig War."

GROWTH OF A NEW STATE

When President James K. Polk created Oregon Territory in 1848 only 304 settlers lived north of the Columbia River. The number quickly grew, and as more settlers ventured north they determined they needed a governmental body of their own.

Delegates met at the Monticello Convention in 1852 to list reasons for separating from the Oregon Territory. When the resulting bill came before Congress there was little opposition. Washington Territory—named, of course, for George Washington—was created in 1853. It initially included much of present-day Idaho and Montana. Idaho Territory was created in 1863, followed by Montana Territory in 1864, using much the same boundaries as the present-day states.

When Washington became a territory, its population was under 4,000. By 1880 it had grown to over 125,000, making it a candidate for statehood. Washington was admitted as the 42nd state in 1889, with Olympia as its capital and a population of over 173,000.

Into the 20th Century

By 1910 Washington's population had reached 1,142,000. Much of the growth was a direct result of the arrival of the Northern Pacific and Great Northern railways in the late 1880s, bringing industry and settlers to Puget Sound and creating new towns along the routes.

The 1880s also brought disaster for Spokane, Ellensburg, and Seattle; each city saw a major portion of its thriving downtown destroyed by fire. The cities rebounded, rebuilding in brick, but the entire state was soon afterward hit hard by a nationwide depression, the Panic of 1893.

A gold rush in the Yukon and the emergence of hydroelectric power helped get the state back on its feet. At the end of this period of growth, the Alaska-Yukon-Pacific Exposition of 1909 brought nationwide attention and over 3.7 million visitors to what is now the University of Washington campus in Seattle to promote the ties between Washington, the far north, and Pacific Rim countries.

The first and second world wars saw Washington's economic base shift from mining, farming, logging, and fishing to manufacturing and ship and airplane building, exemplified by Boeing's B-17: over 13,000 of the "Flying Fortresses" were built in Washington for use in World War II. Boeing continues to be the state's largest private employer.

Seattle's 1962 World's Fair was the first such exposition to be an economic success, drawing almost 10 million people during its six-month run and creating a permanent addition to the city with the Seattle Center. Spokane followed suit 12 years later with Expo '74, which emphasized environmental concerns.

PRESENT-DAY WASHINGTON

The Seattle area, the population center and the economic engine of the state, has tended from its earliest days to be subject to boom-and-bust cycles. The trend continued in the latter part of the 20th century. When Boeing experienced a significant downturn in the late 1960s and early 1970s, the entire city suffered, triggering an exodus of workers. Things got so bad that in 1971 a local real estate agency put up a billboard near Sea-Tac Airport reading, "Will the last person leaving Seattle turn out the lights."

The 1970s ended on a higher note, with Microsoft setting up shop in Bellevue, across Lake Washington from Seattle. The burgeoning software giant would be at the vanguard of a technology boom that continues into the present day. While Boeing is still a major part of the region's economy, tech as a whole is now the biggest business. Amazon has turned Seattle's South Lake Union, once a neighborhood of warehouses and auto repair shops, into its high-rise campus, and familiar names such as Nintendo, T-Mobile, Realnetworks, Expedia, and Zillow are among the scores of tech companies that call the Seattle area home. The most common job in the state is now software developer.

Outside of Seattle the timber industry is still a big, albeit declining business. Agriculture continues to flourish, with the largest crop, apples, exported all over the world. The 21st century has seen an explosion in Washington wine production: The state is the second-largest producer in the United States, after California. In 2000 there were 150 Washington wineries; today there are more than 800.

Local Culture

AMERICAN INDIAN CULTURE

Most out-of-state visitors get their first indication of Washington's deep-rooted American Indian culture by looking at a map. Many place names—including the three largest cities, Seattle, Spokane, and Tacoma—have Indian origins. It's an association that feels both profound and superficial. The names are a sign of the connections the Indians have to the land that predate the arrival of non-Indian settlers by thousands of years. But when you're actually in the places, you have to look hard to find traces of Indian culture—much less Indians themselves.

American Indians in Washington number 130,000—around 2 percent of the total population—and belong to 29 recognized tribes. About 40 percent of them live on 28 reservations spread across the state. Most tribes are based in the Puget Sound area and on the Olympic Peninsula, but the largest reservations are the Yakama in the south-central part of the state and the Colville in the northeast.

In Seattle you can learn about Indian culture at Discovery Park's Daybreak Star

Cultural Center, which holds a powwow in July, and at the Burke Museum and Seattle Art Museum, both of which have collections of artifacts. At the northwest corner of the Olympic Peninsula in Neah Bay there's the exceptional Makah Museum, and farther south along the coast at La Push the Quileute Tribe hosts the Quileute Days festival every July. There's another good museum near Toppenish on the Yakama Reservation, and the Northwest Museum of Art and Culture in Spokane also has a strong collection.

For better or for worse, the most conspicuous presence American Indians have in Washington society at large comes in the form of the 29 casinos around the state under tribal control.

LITERATURE

Something about the atmosphere of western Washington—maybe the presence of dramatic mountains and ocean, or the contrast of dark, damp winter and Eden-like summer—fosters a strong literary culture. Seattle is known as one of the most bookish cities in America, and along with its many readers the region is home to many accomplished writers.

The English department at the University of Washington has employed a few of the state's most heralded literary figures. In the 1950s the school drew the great American poet Theodore Roethke to the Pacific Northwest, where he mentored a younger generation of poets that included Seattle native Richard Hugo. Seattle's Hugo House, named in his honor, is a hub of literary activity in the city. Fiction writer and essayist Charles Johnson rose to prominence while serving on the UW faculty. His novel *Middle Passage* won the 1990 National Book Award, and in 1998 he was named a MacArthur fellow.

The most prominent figure in the current Seattle literary scene is novelist and poet Sherman Alexie, whose work captures the hardships, joys, and irony of contemporary American Indian life. Leading figures among an older generation of writers are poet Tess Gallagher, a Roethke student and Port Angeles native, and exuberant novelist Tom Robbins, a longtime Seattle resident resettled in La Conner.

Literature with a strong Washington connection includes *This Boy's Life*, Tobias Wolff's memoir of growing up in Seattle and the tiny North Cascades town of Newhalem. English expat Jonathan Raban has chronicled Pacific Northwest life with a perceptive outsider's eye in both fiction and essays, including the novel *Waxwings* and the travelogue *Passage to Juneau*. Two popular novels, David Guterson's *Snow Falling on Cedars* and Jamie Ford's *Hotel on the Corner of Bitter and Sweet*, address the experiences of Washington's Japanese Americans sent to internment camps during World War II. Seattle resident Maria Semple's comic novel *Where'd You Go, Bernadette?* takes a wry look at contemporary life in the city.

MUSIC

Washington has made some significant contributions to the world of popular music. Spokane native Bing Crosby was one of the first pop superstars, crooning his way into America's living rooms starting in the 1930s and producing what remains the best-selling single of all time, "White Christmas." He was also one of the most successful crossover performers ever. He appeared in more than 80 movies, winning the 1951 Best Actor Oscar for *Going My Way*.

In the 1960s Seattleite Jimi Hendrix blended rock, blues, and jazz influences into a unique, instantly recognizable guitar style that was one of the signature sounds of the era. A quarter-century later, Kurt Cobain, a disaffected youth from Aberdeen on the Olympic Peninsula, became an era-defining star as the front man for Nirvana, the seminal band of the Seattle-centered grunge rock scene. Hendrix and Cobain were both sensitive nonconformists who struggled with the trappings of fame. Both died at the age of 27, Hendrix from drug-related asphyxiation and Cobain from suicide.

Other major music figures who hail from

Washington include producer, composer, and trumpeter Quincy Jones; 1970s arena-rock stars Heart; heavy metal stalwarts Queensrÿche; grunge rockers Pearl Jam and Soundgarden; indie rock bands Death Cab for Cutie and Modest Mouse; and rappers Sir Mix-a-Lot and, most recently, Macklemore.

There are also some local legends who achieved limited fame. Folk singer Ivar Haglund became best known as the gregarious owner of a chain of seafood restaurants. Tacoma's Wailers are often cited as the first garage-rock band and the inspiration for later Pacific Northwest bands, particularly the Kingsmen, Paul Revere and the Raiders, and another Tacoma product, the Sonics.

You can learn about the region's rock and roll history at Seattle's MoPOP and get a sense of what's happening now by listening to the indie radio station KEXP.

FOOD

Seattle's booming tech-driven economy has resulted in lots of well-paid, trend-conscious residents looking for a good place to have dinner, and as a result the restaurant scene has flowered. Alongside the city's decades-old fish houses and burger joints there are now dozens of hip, sophisticated restaurants doing creative takes on Asian, European, Latin American, and U.S. regional cuisines.

Though the influences come from all over the map, there's a consistent emphasis on local, seasonal ingredients, for which Washington is a bountiful resource. Salmon is a staple found everywhere, and other regional seafood—everything from halibut and cod to oysters and the novel geoduck—is a regular feature on many menus. Washington farms are leading producers of an array of delicious crops, including apples, pears, cherries, berries, grapes, asparagus, onions, herbs, and lentils.

The focus on good food has caught on throughout the state. Spokane, Tacoma, Walla Walla, Orcas Island, and Port Townsend, to name a few prominent examples, all have ambitious restaurants cooking up exceptional food.

Wine and Beer

This is also a good time for drinkers in Washington. Over the past decade winemaking has grown by leaps and bounds. Both in quality and quantity Washington wine has gained in prominence; the state is the second-largest producer in the United States after California, and vineyards are growing good-quality grapes in virtually all of the major European varietals. Walla Walla and the Yakima Valley are the centers of the industry, but there are vineyards throughout the Columbia Valley and in pockets elsewhere in the state. In growing numbers winemakers are establishing production and sales facilities in Woodinville, across Lake Washington from Seattle, and a few are setting up shop within the city itself.

Craft brewers are keeping pace with the winemakers. In Seattle and Bellingham breweries play a significant role in local culture, and it seems like every small town has its own microbrewery. Yakima Valley is the world's largest producer of hops, so when you have a Washington beer you're genuinely drinking local.

Essentials

Transportation

GETTING THERE

Air

The **Seattle-Tacoma International Airport** (SEA, 800/544-1965 or 206/787-5388, www.portseattle.org/seatac) is the state's busiest point of entry, served by about two dozen airlines. Another option, particularly if you're planning to focus on the southern part of the state, is **Portland International** (PDX, 7000 NE Airport Way, Portland, 877/739-4636, www.pdx.com), just across the Oregon border and a 2.5-hour drive from Seattle.

Train

Amtrak (800/872-7245, www.amtrak.com) provides service throughout the country. The **Coast Starlight** connects Seattle, Portland, Sacramento, Oakland, and Los Angeles. Amtrak also operates the **Cascade Line** (800/872-7245, www.amtrakcascades.com), which runs between Eugene, Oregon, and Vancouver, British Columbia, with stops in Portland and Seattle. International visitors can buy a USA Rail Pass, good for unlimited travel for a period of 15, 30, or 45 days.

Bus

Greyhound (800/231-2222, www.greyhound.com) is the largest intercity bus service in the United States, connecting all major cities and many points in between. It offers discounts to students and seniors.

BoltBus (877/265-8287, www.boltbus.com) is the cheapest way to travel south from Vancouver, British Columbia, with stops in Seattle, Portland, and Eugene.

Car

Drivers enter Washington from the north, over the Canadian border; east from Idaho; or south from Oregon. I-5 is the major north-south highway into the state. I-90, the main east-west route, is the road over the Cascades that's least likely to close due to winter weather.

GETTING AROUND

Car

CAR RENTALS

Major international rental car companies are easily found at Sea-Tac airport. Most require drivers to be at least 25 years of age (some allow drivers 21 years of age with an extra fee), possess a valid driver's license, and have a major credit card (debit cards are not acceptable). Expect to pay around $30 per day and up, plus taxes, fees, and insurance (optional). If you are in the military or a member of AAA, AARP, or Costco, discounts may apply. Airports have lower rates, but fees run higher. Hybrid and biofuel rental cars are available, at higher rates, from a few companies, such as **Hertz** (800/654-3131, www.hertz.com), **Enterprise** (800/261-7331, www.enterprise.com), **Avis** (800/331-1212, www.avis.com), **Thrifty** (800/847-4389, www.thrifty.com), and **Budget** (800/527-0700, www.budget.com).

SAFETY ON THE ROAD

For **emergency assistance** and services call **911**. To receive reports on **road conditions,** call **511**. If your phone carrier does not support 511, call toll-free 800/977-6368.

Snow tires or chains are frequently required on the passes across the Cascades, which are sometimes closed during storms because of hazardous road conditions. From late fall to early spring, expect snow at I-90's Snoqualmie Pass, Stevens Pass on U.S. Route

---

Previous: ferry to the San Juan Islands; safety warning on Whidbey Island.

2, and White Pass on U.S. Route 12. Cayuse Pass on State Route 410 and Rainy and Washington Passes on State Route 20 (the North Cascades Highway) are closed after the first snowfall each winter. Skiers and other winter travelers passing through the Cascades should always carry a set of chains and emergency equipment (flares, shovel, blankets, food, and cell phone). Before you set out, check conditions online via the **Department of Transportation Mountain Pass Report** (www.wsdot.com/traffic/passes). The site has live cameras showing conditions at passes and other areas with frequent traffic issues.

Bus
INTERCITY BUSES
Greyhound (800/231-2222, www.greyhound. com) serves most major cities in Washington and provides nationwide connections. Its main routes are along I-5 from Canada to Oregon, along I-90 from Seattle to Spokane, plus I-82 from Ellensburg to Pendleton, Oregon.

Northwestern Trailways (800/366-3830, www.northwesterntrailways.com) has service along three Washington routes between Spokane and Tacoma, Omak and Wenatchee, and Spokane and Boise, all with multiple stops along the way.

PUBLIC TRANSIT BUSES
Washington's local and regional public buses offer a remarkably comprehensive system, with service throughout western Washington. The coverage is less complete east of the Cascades, but still good. Many buses have bike racks. Check the Washington State Department of Transportation website's public transit page (www.wsdot.wa.gov/transit) for a complete listing of buses, trains, and other travel options.

BUS TOURS
A number of companies offer motor coach tours throughout the Pacific Northwest. Seattle-based **Tours Northwest** (888/293-1404, www.toursnorthwest.com) has day trips to Mount Rainier, the San Juans, and the Boeing factory tour in Mukilteo.

Washington State Ferries
The **Washington State Ferry System** (206/464-6400, www.wsdot.wa.gov/Ferries) is the largest mass transit system in the state, carrying more than 23 million passengers and 10 million vehicles each year across Puget Sound.

ROUTES
Washington has the largest ferry fleet in the United States, with 24 vessels, ranging from a 94-foot passenger boat to jumbo-class 460-foot-long ships capable of carrying more than 200 cars and 2,500 passengers. The ferries call at 20 different ports around Puget Sound, from Tacoma to Vancouver Island.

The best sightseeing is on the Anacortes-San Juan Islands route, which has seasonal service continuing to Sidney, British Columbia. Ferries also connect Seattle and Bremerton; Seattle and Bainbridge Island; Port Townsend and Coupeville (Whidbey Island); Clinton (Whidbey Island) and Mukilteo (southwest of Everett); Edmonds and Kingston (on the Kitsap Peninsula); Southworth (southeast of Bremerton), Fauntleroy (West Seattle), and Vashon Island; and Tacoma (at Point Defiance) and Tahlequah (at the south end of Vashon Island). You can get a full rundown of routes, schedules, and fares on the ferry system website.

PRACTICALITIES
The ferry system operates every day, including holidays, but schedules change with the seasons. Most routes take passengers on a first-come, first-served basis. The exceptions are the ferry between Port Townsend and Coupeville, and the ferries servicing Anacortes, the San Juan Islands, and Sidney, all of which take reservations for vehicles (but not walk-ons). For service to Anacortes and the San Juans, 30 percent of spaces are made available two months before sailing, 30 percent two weeks before, and 30 percent two

days before—so even if you're planning just a few days in advance you still have the chance to book a space. You can make reservations by phone (206/464-6400) or online (www.wsdot.wa.gov/Ferries).

The larger ferries have cafeteria-style food service that usually includes packaged sandwiches, chowder, ice cream, beer, and wine. Smaller boats have vending machines.

Pets on leashes are allowed on car decks and exterior passenger decks. Pets in carriers are allowed on interior passenger decks. Bikes, kayaks, and canoes are also allowed on board for a small surcharge.

Other Ferries

The privately owned **Black Ball Ferry Line** (360/457-4491, www.cohoferry.com) runs the *MV Coho* between Port Angeles and Victoria, British Columbia. There are four trips a day from mid-June through early September, with the number tapering off to one in January and February.

Victoria Clipper (800/888-2535, www.clippervacations.com) has passenger-only service daily between Seattle and Victoria, and also runs between Seattle and the San Juan Islands in summer.

Several small ferries provide short local service within the Puget Sound area, including routes between Anderson Island and Steilacoom (near Tacoma), Anacortes and Guemes Island, and Lummi Island and Gooseberry Point (near Bellingham).

Bicycle

Cycling is a popular means of getting around for Seattle locals, but if you want to take to the streets you need to be careful. Traffic is heavy in the city center, and there's a sometimes-tense relationship between cyclists and drivers. For a leisurely ride in the city your best bet is to take the car-free Burke-Gilman Trail or head for one of the beautiful parks.

Elsewhere in the state there are great road-riding experiences to be had, particularly in the Skagit Valley, on the San Juan Islands (especially Lopez), and along the Olympic Discovery Trail, which spans the north end of the Olympic Peninsula. There are off-road biking opportunities in many of Washington's state parks.

The Washington State Department of Transportation website (www.wsdot.wa.gov/bike) is a great resource for cyclists, with dozens of maps showing bike routes throughout the state.

Visas and Officialdom

PASSPORTS AND VISAS

Visitors from other countries must have a **valid passport** and a **visa.** Visitors with current passports from one of the following countries qualify for a **visa waiver:** Andorra, Australia, Austria, Belgium, Brunei, Chile, Czech Republic, Denmark, Estonia, Finland, France, Germany, Greece, Hungary, Iceland, Ireland, Italy, Japan, Latvia, Liechtenstein, Lithuania, Luxembourg, Malta, Monaco, the Netherlands, New Zealand, Norway, Portugal, San Marino, Singapore, Slovakia, Slovenia, South Korea, Spain, Sweden, Switzerland, Taiwan, and the United Kingdom. They must apply online with the Electronic System for Travel Authorization at www.cbp.gov and hold a **return plane ticket** to their home countries less than 90 days from their time of entry. Holders of **Canadian passports** don't need visas or waivers. In most countries, the local U.S. embassy can provide a **tourist visa.** Plan at least two weeks for visa processing, longer during the busy summer season (June-Aug.). More information is available online: http://travel.state.gov.

CUSTOMS

Foreigners and U.S. citizens age 21 or older may import (free of duty) the following: 1L of alcohol; 200 cigarettes (one carton); 50 cigars; and $100 worth of gifts.

International travelers must declare amounts that exceed $10,000 in cash (U.S. or foreign), travelers checks, or money orders. Meat products, fruits, and vegetables are prohibited due to health and safety regulations.

INTERNATIONAL DRIVING PERMITS

International visitors other than Canadians need to secure an **International Driving Permit** from their home countries before coming to the United States. They should also bring the government-issued driving permit from their home countries. They are also expected to be familiar with the driving regulations of the states they will visit. More information is available online: www.usa.gov/Topics/Motor-Vehicles.shtml.

Travel Tips

MONEY

Most businesses accept the **major credit cards** Visa, MasterCard, Discover, and American Express. ATM and debit cards work at many stores and restaurants, and ATMs are available throughout Washington. You can **change currency** at any international airport or bank. Currency exchange is generally easier in large cities than in rural and wilderness areas.

Banking hours tend to be 8am-5pm Monday-Friday, 9am-noon Saturday. There are **24-hour ATMs** not only at banks but at many markets, bars, and hotels. A **convenience fee** of $2-4 per transaction may apply.

INTERNET ACCESS

While many hotels and B&Bs offer free Wi-Fi, some charge a fee. Free Wi-Fi is often available at cafes and public libraries. Do not expect to find Wi-Fi connections in rural areas, parks, or campgrounds.

ACCESS FOR TRAVELERS WITH DISABILITIES

Most hotels, restaurants, museums, and public transit are equipped to accommodate travelers with disabilities, and several state and national parks have paved trails. That said, there are some attractions that pose challenges, such as certain historic sites and wildlife areas.

U.S. citizens with permanent disabilities, including the visually impaired, are eligible for an **Access Pass** (888/275-8747, ext. 3, https://store.usgs.gov/access-pass) providing free admission to national parks and other federally managed recreational sites. You can obtain an Access Pass in person at federal recreation sites or by mailing in an application available for download on the USGS website. (Mailed applications require a $10 processing fee.) The pass does not cover special recreation permits or concessioner fees.

TRAVELING WITH CHILDREN

With the abundance of outdoor wilderness activities in Washington, it's important to take some basic safety precautions with children. As a general rule, parents should keep kids close. Lookout points often don't have guardrails, and trails almost never do. *Never* let a child out of sight on a trail. It's impossible to know what risks might be around the next corner. Animal attacks are extremely rare—historically numbering one or two per decade—but predators have a tendency to target children and to steer clear of groups.

SENIOR TRAVELERS

If you are over 60 years of age, ask about potential discounts. Many attractions, amusement parks, theaters, and museums offer discounts to seniors. Have identification on hand to confirm your senior status.

GAY AND LESBIAN TRAVELERS

By and large Washington is very gay friendly. In 2012 a referendum legalizing same-sex marriage passed with 54 percent of the vote, making Washington the first state to approve gay marriage in a popular vote. (Maryland and Maine share the honor, having passed similar measures on the same day.)

Not surprisingly, urban areas and popular tourist destinations that attract a diverse range of visitors tend to be more progressive, but even in areas that are more socially conservative there seems to be a sense that homophobia belongs to a bygone era.

TOBACCO AND MARIJUANA

Smoking is banned in many places, including all restaurants and bars. Many hotels, motels, and inns are also nonsmoking. Smokers should request a smoking room when making reservations.

Recreational use of **marijuana** is legal in Washington for adults 21 and over. It's for sale at licensed pot shops and must be consumed in a private location. It's illegal to drive under the influence or to transport marijuana to another state. Possession and consumption remain illegal on federal lands, which means no getting high in national forests and parks. Seattle-based **Kush Tourism** (206/587-5874, http://kushtourism.com) conducts pot-related tours (which it models after winery tours) and has recommendations on its website for pot-friendly hotels.

Recreation

The diversity of recreational opportunities is one of Washington's biggest attractions. The Pacific coast has long beaches for playing in the sand, fishing, or beachcombing; state parks and national parks and forests offer spectacular hiking and climbing opportunities; Puget Sound is a haven for kayaking and sailing; the Columbia River Gorge offers some of the finest windsurfing on the planet; anglers love the countless lakes, reservoirs, and rivers; river rafters and kayakers head down the state's white-water rivers throughout the summer; and cyclists discover roads and trails of every description. In the winter, the options shift to snow sports, and Washington has them all, including skiing of all types, snowboarding, sledding, skating, and snowmobiling.

ORGANIZATIONS
The Mountaineers

Established in 1906, **The Mountaineers** (206/521-6000, www.mountaineers.org) is a 15,000-member organization of outdoor enthusiasts with a strong environmental bent. Based in Seattle, the club organizes hiking, climbing, cycling, skiing, snowshoeing, sea kayaking, and other activities and events throughout the year.

Membership costs $75 per year. Members receive *Mountaineer,* a quarterly magazine listing local activities, along with 20 percent discounts on the organization's many books. In addition to Seattle, The Mountaineers have branches in Olympia, Tacoma, Everett, Bellingham, and Wenatchee. They have a bookstore at their Seattle Program Center (7700 Sand Point Way NE, Mon.-Tues. and Thurs.-Fri. 9am-5pm, Wed. 9am-7pm).

Washington Department of Fish and Wildlife

The **Washington Department of Fish and Wildlife** (360/902-2200, wdfw.wa.gov) administers licenses and regulates fishing, hunting, and clamming in the state. Its website is a trove of information—you'll find dates for seasons, other regulations, and all kinds of fishing and hunting tips.

PUBLIC LANDS

Almost 45 percent of Washington's 42.6 million acres are publicly held. The largest landholding agencies are the U.S. Forest Service, Bureau of Indian Affairs, National Park Service, U.S. Fish and Wildlife Service, and various branches of the military. The state (primarily the Department of Natural Resources) owns almost 3.5 million acres.

National Parks

Washington's three major national parks attract millions of visitors each year. **North Cascades National Park Service Complex** (www.nps.gov/noca) covers a half-million acres of wild mountain country that includes more than 300 glaciers, hundreds of miles of hiking trails, and Diablo and Ross Lakes. **Mount Rainier National Park** (www.nps.gov/mora) contains the state's tallest and most iconic summit: 14,411-foot Mount Rainier. Hiking trails circle the peak, and scenic mountain roads provide views of alpine meadows, subalpine forests, and glaciers. **Olympic National Park** (www.nps.gov/olym) is famous for its lush rain forests that include enormous old-growth trees, but it also has dramatic mountain country and miles of undeveloped Pacific coastline. National park fees can change annually; check a national park's website or call ahead to confirm pricing.

In addition to these areas, the Park Service manages the **San Juan Island National Historical Park** (www.nps.gov/sajh), **Lake Roosevelt National Recreation Area** (www.nps.gov/laro) in eastern Washington, **Ebey's Landing National Historical**

Reserve (www.nps.gov/ebla) on Whidbey Island, **Fort Vancouver National Historic Site** (www.nps.gov/fova) in Vancouver, **Whitman Mission National Historical Site** (www.nps.gov/whmi) near Walla Walla, and a small annex of the **Klondike Gold Rush National Historical Park** (www.nps.gov/klse) in Seattle's Pioneer Square (the main park is in Skagway, Alaska).

Forest Service Lands

U.S. Forest Service lands cover more than nine million acres in Washington State within seven national forests. These forests are managed for multiple uses, including recreation, wildlife habitat maintenance, and logging. The national forests of Washington contain 24 wilderness areas that cover more than 2.5 million acres. Over half of the total acreage falls within the three largest: **Glacier Peak Wilderness** (576,900 acres), **Pasayten Wilderness** (530,000 acres), and **Alpine Lakes Wilderness** (393,360 acres). The Forest Service also manages **Mount St. Helens National Volcanic Monument** and the **Columbia River Gorge National Scenic Area**.

Many Forest Service trailheads charge user fees. Day use is generally $5 per vehicle per day, or pay $30 for an annual **Northwest Forest Pass** (www.discovernw.org/store), which can be used in most national forests in Washington. For details on recreation in the forests, stop by a local ranger station or contact the appropriate headquarters office:

- **Colville National Forest,** 765 S. Main St., Colville, 509/684-7000, www.fs.usda.gov/main/colville
- **Gifford Pinchot National Forest,** 1501 E. Evergreen Blvd., Vancouver, 360/891-5000, www.fs.usda.gov/giffordpinchot
- **Columbia River Gorge National Scenic Area,** 902 Wasco Ave., Hood River, Ore., 541/380-1700, www.fs.usda.gov/crgnsa
- **Mount St. Helens National Volcanic Monument,** 42218 NE Yale Bridge Rd,

Amboy, 360/449-7800, www.fs.usda.gov/main/mountsthelens

- **Mount Baker-Snoqualmie National Forest,** 2930 Wetmore Ave., Everett, 425/783-6000, www.fs.usda.gov/main/mbs
- **Okanogan-Wenatchee National Forest,** 215 Melody Ln., Wenatchee, 509/664-9200, www.fs.usda.gov/main/okawen
- **Olympic National Forest,** 1835 Black Lake Blvd. SW, Olympia, 360/956-2402, www.fs.usda.gov/olympic

State Parks

Washington State Parks (360/902-8844, http://parks.state.wa.us) manages 125 parks covering over 230,000 acres. Most encompass a few hundred acres or less, but some, such as Moran State Park in the San Juan Islands and Deception Pass on Whidbey Island, are several thousand acres each and attract throngs of visitors.

State park facilities include several historic forts (Fort Townsend, Fort Flagler, Fort Ebey, Fort Worden, and others), many miles of sandy ocean beaches (including Grayland Beach, Fort Canby, Long Beach, Ocean City, and Pacific Beach), one of the largest public telescopes in the region (Goldendale Observatory), a park devoted to whale-watching (Lime Kiln), a campground where Lewis and Clark spent a night (Lewis and Clark Trail), and an incredible waterfall surrounded by desolate eastern Washington land (Palouse Falls). In addition, the state park system includes numerous historic sites, environmental learning centers for schoolkids, and 40 marine parks, many of which are accessible only by boat.

One of the primary sources of park funding is the **Discover Pass,** which is required for parking within the parks. Annual passes cost $30 and day passes are $10. The busiest parks have automated pass dispensers. You can also buy passes online (www.discoverpass.wa.gov),

and they're often available at gas stations and convenience stores near the parks.

CAMPING
State Parks

Washington State Parks (360/902-8844, http://parks.state.wa.us) maintains more than 80 parks with campgrounds across the state. Tent sites are $25-35, RV hookups (not available in all campgrounds) $35-45. Some state parks also offer primitive campsites accessible to hikers and cyclists for $12. Most park sites include a picnic table, barbecue grill, nearby running water, garbage removal, a flush toilet, and coin-operated hot showers. Some state parks are closed from October through March; those that remain open often have limited winter camping facilities. Most campground gates close at 10pm, so don't plan on a late arrival.

Campground reservations can be made for nearly half of the state parks, and are available as little as two days in advance or as much as 11 months ahead of time. You can reserve sites by phone (888/226-7688, $10 fee) or online (http://washington.goingtocamp.com, $8 fee).

The state also maintains 40 or so marine state parks in the San Juan Islands and around Puget Sound. Continuous moorage is limited to three nights. An annual moorage permit costs $5 per foot, with a minimum fee of $60; the daily fee is 70 cents per foot, minimum $15; buoy moorage costs $15 per night.

The **Cascadia Marine Trail System** includes more than 35 campsites around Puget Sound available to sea kayakers and users of other small human-powered or sailing vessels. Get maps and other information from the **Washington Water Trails Association** (206/545-9161, www.wwta.org).

Other Public Campgrounds

There are campsites in national forests and parks across Washington. Some sites are free, but most campgrounds charge $10-16 per night. Some sites can be reserved up to 180 days in advance by phone (877/444-6777, $10 fee) or online (www.recreation.gov, $9 fee).

Washington's Department of Natural Resources (DNR) manages millions of acres of public lands in the state, primarily on a multiple-use basis—meaning the land is often used for timber harvesting. Not everything has been logged, however, and campsites can be found at DNR forests throughout the state. You can find a helpful map with locations and information about the DNR's 70-plus free campgrounds at its website, www.dnr.wa.gov.

Private RV Parks

Most towns have at least one private RV park, and such parks often have better amenities than public alternatives. You can find links to privately owned parks at www.rvparkhunter.com.

Health and Safety

If immediate help is needed, always **dial 911;** otherwise, go to the nearest 24-hour hospital emergency room.

Carry your **insurance card** and a list of any **medications** you are taking. Keep a **first-aid kit** in your car or luggage, and take it with you when hiking. A good kit should include sterile gauze pads, butterfly bandages, adhesive tape, antibiotic ointment, alcohol wipes, pain relievers for both adults and children, and a multipurpose pocketknife.

Do not ignore **health or safety warnings.** Some beaches and other bodies of water have health warning signs posted due to potential bacteria in the water. You should also never stray from hiking trails.

Whether you're in a city, small town, or wilderness area, take precautions against **theft.** Don't leave valuables in the car. If it's unavoidable, keep them out of sight in the trunk or glove compartment with a lock if available. Keep wallets, purses, cameras, mobile phones, and other small electronics on your person if possible.

Crime is more prevalent in cities. Be alert to your surroundings, just as you would in any unfamiliar place. It's a smart precaution not to use ATMs at night or walk alone after dark.

BACKCOUNTRY SAFETY

The most important part of backcountry travel is to be prepared. Know where you're going; get maps, camping information, and weather and trail conditions from a ranger before setting out. Don't hike alone. Two are better than one, and three are better than two; if someone gets hurt, one person can stay with the injured party while the other goes for help. Bring more than enough food. Tell someone where you're going and when you'll be back.

Always carry the **10 essentials:** map, compass, water bottle, first-aid kit, flashlight, matches (or lighter) and fire starter, knife, extra clothing (a full set, in case you get wet), rain gear, extra food, and sunglasses (especially if you're hiking on snow). An addition to this traditional list is a cell phone; coverage in remote locations is unlikely but not unheard of.

Caution should always trump bravado. Head back or stop for the night when the weather gets bad, even if it's 2pm. Don't press on when you're exhausted. Tired hikers are sloppy hikers, and even a small injury can be disastrous in the woods.

Giardia

Although Washington's backcountry lakes and streams may appear clean, you risk a debilitating sickness by drinking untreated water. The protozoan *Giardia lamblia* is found throughout the state. Symptoms include diarrhea, nausea, cramps, and fatigue. If you believe you've contracted *Giardia,* seek medical attention. The disease is curable with drugs, but it's always best to carry drinking water or to treat water taken from creeks or lakes.

Bringing water to a full boil is sufficient to kill *Giardia* and other harmful organisms. Another option is to use a water filter (available in camping stores). Note, however, that these may not filter out other organisms such as *Campylobacter jejuni,* bacteria that are just 0.2 microns in size. Chlorine and iodine are not always reliable, taste foul, and can be unhealthy.

Hypothermia

Even at temperatures well above freezing, hypothermia—the reduction of the body's inner core temperature—can prove fatal. Hypothermia occurs more often in Northwest summers than winters because people traveling at high elevations fail to take necessary precautions. Weather in the Cascades and Olympics is unpredictable. The temperature can drop dramatically in a matter of hours or even minutes.

In the early stages, hypothermia causes uncontrollable shivering, followed by a loss of coordination, slurred speech, and then a rapid descent into unconsciousness and death. Always travel prepared for sudden changes in the weather. Wear clothing that insulates well and that holds its heat when wet. If you're out in potentially threatening conditions, carry a wool hat, bring a waterproof shell to cut the wind, and put on rain gear *before* it starts raining. If the weather starts to turn, head back or set up camp before conditions get worse.

If someone in your party begins to show signs of hypothermia, don't take any chances, even if the person denies needing help. Get the person out of the wind, strip off his or her clothes, and put him or her in a dry sleeping bag on an insulating pad. Skin-to-skin contact is the best way to warm a person with hypothermia, so someone else should also partially undress and climb into the sleeping bag with the victim. Do not give the victim alcohol or hot drinks, and do not try to warm the person too quickly, which could lead to heart failure.

Once the victim has recovered, get medical help as soon as possible. The best strategy is caution: Keep close tabs on everyone in the group and seek shelter *before* exhaustion and hypothermia set in.

Ticks

Ticks can be an annoyance in parts of Washington, particularly lower-elevation brushy and grassy areas in the spring and early summer. They drop onto unsuspecting humans and other animals to suck blood, and can spread Lyme disease or relapsing fever, although in Washington this is uncommon.

Avoid ticks by tucking pant legs into boots and shirts into pants, using insect repellents containing DEET, and carefully inspecting your clothes while outside. Light-colored clothing (which makes it easier to see the ticks) and broad hats may also help. Check your body while hiking and immediately after the trip. If possible, remove ticks before they become embedded in your skin. If one does become attached, use tweezers to gently remove it, being sure to get the head. Try not to crush the body since this may release more bacteria. Apply a triple antibiotic ointment such as Neosporin to the area, and monitor the bite area for two weeks. You may want to save the tick in a jar with some damp tissue paper for later identification.

Wildlife Encounters

Keep a safe distance from wildlife. Stay at least 300 feet away. Bring binoculars if you want an up-close view. Cougars and bears are the potentially dangerous predators you might encounter in Washington's wilderness. Attacks are extremely rare. You shouldn't let fear of an attack limit your outdoor activities, but in the unlikely event that you have an up-close encounter with a predator you should know the standard precautionary measures to take, and you should treat the situation seriously.

COUGARS

There are 2,000-2,500 cougars in Washington, most living in the isolated mountainous regions in the north of the state. The chances of one attacking are small: Over the last century there have been 15 reported cougar attacks on humans in Washington, one of which was fatal.

As frightening as it is to be stalked by a big cat, wildlife experts say it is unlikely that cougars have mayhem in mind when following or watching humans. Like all cats, they are curious animals. If you come face to face with one, maintain eye contact while backing slowly away. Try to appear larger than you are by raising your arms or by spreading a jacket or shirt. If you have children with you, pick them up. Talk loudly. **Never, ever run.** Wildlife officials say compressed-air horns and pepper spray may ward off cougar attacks, and cougars are less likely to attack groups of two or more people traveling together. Children alone on the trail are the most vulnerable; don't ever let them stray from adults.

BEARS

The most common predators in Washington are black bears—the population is 25,000-30,000, mostly found on the Olympic Peninsula and in the northeast corner of the state. Bear attacks are very rare: 14 have been reported over the past century, with one being fatal. If you encounter a bear in Washington, the odds are ten thousand to one that it's a black bear rather than a grizzly, even if its fur isn't black. There are only about two dozen grizzly bears in the entire state, all living in the North Cascades and the Selkirk Mountains.

If you're hiking in an area with a known bear population, take suitable precautions. Travel in a group. Make noise—talk, clap your hands, rattle a pan—and if possible walk with a breeze to your back; if bears know you're coming they'll avoid you.

When camping in the backcountry, store all food, soap, garbage, and clothes worn while cooking in a sack hung from a tree branch at least 10 feet up and four feet out from the tree trunk. In an established campground, keep such items in your car trunk. Don't sleep where you cooked dinner, and keep sleeping bags and gear away from cooking odors.

If you do encounter a bear, slowly detour out of its path and stay upwind so the bear will know you're there. Don't make abrupt noises or movements. While retreating, look for a tree to climb—one in which you can get at least 12 feet up and stay there until you're certain that the bear has left the area. If no tree is close, your best bet is to back slowly away.

Don't try to outrun the bear. Sometimes dropping an item such as a hat or jacket will distract the bear, and talking also seems to have some value in convincing bears that you're a human. If the bear sniffs the air or stands on its hind legs it is probably trying to identify you. When it does, it will usually run away. If a bear woofs and postures, don't imitate it, as this is seen as a challenge. Keep retreating. Most bear charges are bluffs; the bear will often stop short and amble off. If you're attacked by a black bear, fight back with whatever weapons are at hand; large rocks and branches can be effective deterrents, as can yelling and shouting.

In the rare event of a night attack in your tent, defend yourself *very* aggressively. Never play dead under such circumstances, since the bear probably views you as prey, and may give up if you fight. Before you go to bed, try to plan escape routes should you be attacked in the night, and be sure to have a flashlight handy. Keeping your sleeping bag partly unzipped also allows the chance to escape should a bear attempt to drag you away. If someone is attacked in a tent near you, yelling and throwing rocks or sticks may drive the bear away.

As an extra precaution you may want to carry a can of pepper spray, sold as "bear spray" in outdoor equipment stores. Note, however, that these sprays are effective only at close range and in non-windy conditions.

Resources

Suggested Reading

Egan, Timothy. *The Good Rain*. Vintage Books, 1990. A series of meditations on life in the Pacific Northwest by a *New York Times* columnist and Seattle native. It's been around for a while, but it's aged well.

Frye Bass, Sophie, and Florenz Clark. *Pig-Tail Days in Old Seattle*. Binford & Mort Publishing, 1973. A fascinating account of Seattle's early days as told by the granddaughter of Seattle founder Arthur A. Denny, with stories about some of the city's famous streets.

Halliday, Jan, and Gail Chehak. *Native Peoples of the Northwest*. Sasquatch Books, 2002. A good introduction to contemporary Northwest native cultures.

Kirk, Ruth, and Alexander, Carmela. *Exploring Washington's Past*. University of Washington Press, 2001. A different kind of travel guide that details the history of Washington's every nook and cranny.

Klingle, Matthew. *Emerald City: An Environmental History of Seattle*. Yale University Press, 2007. This book goes deep into the sometimes tenuous relationship between Seattle and its natural environment.

Mapes, Lynda. *Elwha: A River Reborn*. Mountaineers Books, 2013. An examination of one of the largest dam removal projects in the world, and the efforts to save the Northwest ecosystem.

McNulty, Tim. *Olympic National Park: A Natural History*. University of Washington Press, 2009. A look at the heart of the Olympic Peninsula's ecosystems, wildlife, and recent archaeological discoveries.

Morgan, Murray. *Skid Road: An Informal Portrait of Seattle*. University of Washington Press, 1951. Still in print after more than half a century, this thorough but conversational history of the founding of Seattle has been a sacred text for generations of locals.

Raban, Jonathan. *Driving Home: An American Journey*. Sasquatch Books, 2010. This wide-ranging collection of essays by a Brit expat includes numerous travel pieces that look at the Pacific Northwest with wry grace.

Internet Resources

TOURISM

Olympic Peninsula Visitor Bureau
www.olympicpeninsula.org
A regional organization that offers a synopsis of local destinations, things to do, and transportation information. The bureau is also considered the primary contact for travel writers, film scouts, and tour operators.

Seattle B&B Association
www.lodginginseattle.com
A member-based organization that provides a directory of local bed-and-breakfast venues.

Washington Lodging Association
www.stayinwashington.com
A complete listing of member hotels, motels, lodges, and B&Bs.

Washington Tourism Alliance
www.experiencewa.com
Run by a group of industry professionals, the state's official tourism website is rich with everything Washington. It's invaluable when planning a trip.

OUTDOOR RECREATION

The Mountaineers
www.mountaineers.org
A Seattle-based nonprofit organization that helps people explore, conserve, and learn about the lands and waters of the Pacific Northwest through sponsored excursions, events, and publications.

National Park Service
www.nps.gov
Detailed information, including fees, hours, trails, fishing regulations, and more.

Recreation.gov
www.recreation.gov
National parks and forests campground information, with options to reserve campsites.

U.S. Forest Service—
Pacific Northwest Region
www.fs.usda.gov/r6
Information on Oregon and Washington national forests, with external links and resources.

Washington Department
of Fish & Wildlife
http://wdfw.wa.gov
A complete online guide to fishing and hunting regulations, including seasonal and permit information.

Washington State Parks
& Recreation Commission
http://parks.state.wa.us
Information about Washington's diverse parks, including campground information and reservations.

Washington Trails Association
www.wta.org
A thorough guide to hundreds of trails throughout the state, with helpful reader comments about current conditions.

Index

XYZ

List of Maps

Acknowledgments

It's because of my wife, Nichole Byrne Lau, that I live in and love Washington. Throughout my work she's been my travel companion, my sounding board, and my support system. My greatest hope is that this book manages to capture some of her infectious enthusiasm for the state.

I never could have explored so much of Washington without the help of the state's unfailingly friendly local tourism reps. Special thanks to Dave Blandford in Seattle; Mary Brelsford, Martha Massey, and Allegra Pomeroy on the Olympic Peninsula; Ron Williams and Justin Yax in Walla Walla; Barbara Marrett and Shannon Borg on the San Juan Islands; Annette Bagley in Bellingham; Annette Pitts in the North Cascades; Kate Hudson in Spokane; Sherrye Wyatt on Whidbey Island; Lissy Andros in Forks; Casey Roeder in Skamania County; Heather Decker in Yakima; and Amy Hunter in Hood River.

At Avalon Travel I'm grateful to my editor, Kristi Mitsuda, for the patience and care she took with the guide. Thanks also to Albert Angulo for creating the maps, and to Lucie Ericksen for graphics and production.

Photo Credits

MOON NATIONAL PARKS

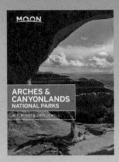

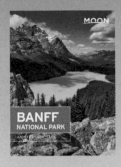

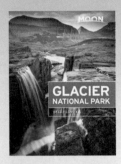

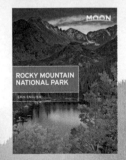

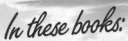

In these books:

- Full coverage of gateway cities and towns
- Itineraries from one day to multiple weeks
- Advice on where to stay (or camp) in and around the parks

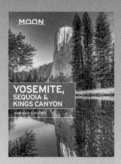

MOON ROAD TRIP GUIDES

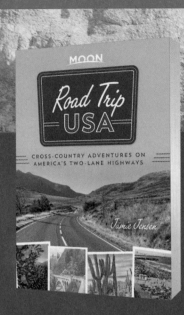

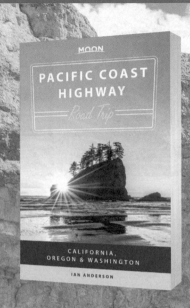

Road Trip USA

Criss-cross the country on America's classic two-lane highways with the newest edition of *Road Trip USA!*

Packed with over 125 detailed driving maps (covering more than 35,000 miles), colorful photos and illustrations of America both then and now, and mile-by-mile highlights

Advice on where to sleep, eat, and explore

Detailed driving directions including mileage and drive times

Itineraries for a range of timelines

Moon Travel Guides are available from your favorite bookseller.

Join our travel community!
Share your adventures using **#travelwithmoon**

MOON.COM
@MOONGUIDES

States & Provinces

WASHINGTON
MATTHEW LOMBARDI

OREGON
JUDY JEWELL & W.C. McRAE

BRITISH COLUMBIA
ANDREW HEMPSTEAD

Regions & Getaways

OLYMPIC PENINSULA
JEFF BIRLINGHAM

COASTAL OREGON
W.C. McRAE & JUDY JEWELL

VICTORIA & VANCOUVER ISLAND
ANDREW HEMPSTEAD

Cities

COLOR FOLDOUT MAP

SEATTLE
ALLISON WILLIAMS

Portland
PORTLAND

VANCOUVER
Including Victoria, Vancouver Island, and Whistler
CAROLYN B. HELLER

Road Trips & Outdoors

75 GREAT HIKES SEATTLE
MELISSA OZBEK

OREGON CAMPING
The Complete Guide to Tent and RV Camping
TOM STIENSTRA

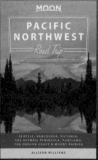

PACIFIC NORTHWEST *Road Trip*
SEATTLE, VANCOUVER, VICTORIA, THE OLYMPIC PENINSULA, PORTLAND, THE OREGON COAST & MOUNT RAINIER
ALLISON WILLIAMS

We've got you covered, PNW!

MAP SYMBOLS

═══ Expressway	○ City/Town	✈ Airport	⚑ Golf Course
─── Primary Road	◉ State Capital	✈ Airfield	P Parking Area
─── Secondary Road	⊛ National Capital	▲ Mountain	⬟ Archaeological Site
┈┈ Unpaved Road	★ Point of Interest	✦ Unique Natural Feature	⛪ Church
─── Feature Trail	• Accommodation		⛽ Gas Station
─── Other Trail	▼ Restaurant/Bar	⟅ Waterfall	∞ Glacier
┈┈┈ Ferry	■ Other Location	⚑ Park	▨ Mangrove
═══ Pedestrian Walkway	▲ Campground	⬚ Trailhead	⬚ Reef
▥▥▥ Stairs		✗ Skiing Area	⬚ Swamp

CONVERSION TABLES

°C = (°F - 32) / 1.8
°F = (°C x 1.8) + 32
1 inch = 2.54 centimeters (cm)
1 foot = 0.304 meters (m)
1 yard = 0.914 meters
1 mile = 1.6093 kilometers (km)
1 km = 0.6214 miles
1 fathom = 1.8288 m
1 chain = 20.1168 m
1 furlong = 201.168 m
1 acre = 0.4047 hectares
1 sq km = 100 hectares
1 sq mile = 2.59 square km
1 ounce = 28.35 grams
1 pound = 0.4536 kilograms
1 short ton = 0.90718 metric ton
1 short ton = 2,000 pounds
1 long ton = 1.016 metric tons
1 long ton = 2,240 pounds
1 metric ton = 1,000 kilograms
1 quart = 0.94635 liters
1 US gallon = 3.7854 liters
1 Imperial gallon = 4.5459 liters
1 nautical mile = 1.852 km

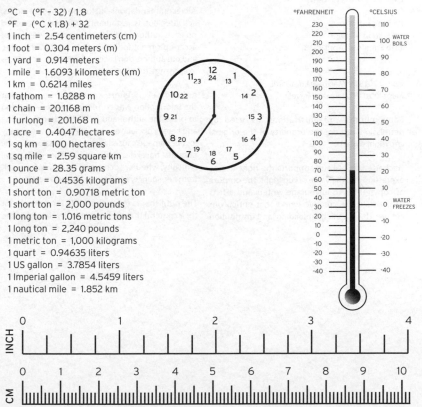

MOON WASHINGTON

Avalon Travel
Hachette Book Group
1700 Fourth Street
Berkeley, CA 94710, USA
www.moon.com

Editor: Kristi Mitsuda
Series Manager: Kathryn Ettinger
Copy Editor: Brett Keener
Graphics and Production Coordinator:
  Lucie Ericksen
Cover Design: Faceout Studios, Charles Brock
Interior Design: Domini Dragoone
Moon Logo: Tim McGrath
Map Editor: Albert Angulo
Cartographers: Larissa Gatt, Brian Shotwell
Indexer: Greg Jewett

ISBN-13: 9781631218910

Printing History
1st Edition — 1989
11th Edition — April 2018
5 4 3 2 1

Front cover photo: larch trees in the Enchantment Lakes Wilderness © Inge Johnsson / Alamy Stock Photo
Back cover photo: Cape Flattery, Olympic Peninsula © Fallsview | Dreamstime.com

Printed in China by RR Donnelley